Hong Kong Between 'One Country' and 'Two Systems':

Essays from the Year that Transformed the Hong Kong Special Administrative Region
(June 2019 – June 2020)

I0118956

Hong Kong
Between 'One Country' and 'Two Systems':
Essays from the Year that Transformed the Hong Kong Special Administrative Region (June 2019 – June 2020)
Larry Catá Backer (白 轲)

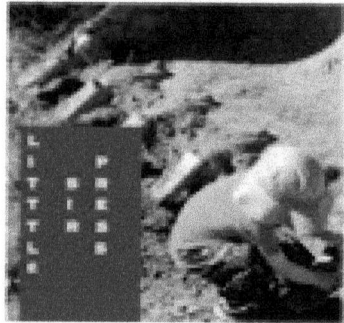

Little Sir Press (State College, Pennsylvania, USA)

First published 2021
by Little Sir Press, State College PA, USA 16803

Contact us at LittleSirPress@gmail.com.

Please cite this publication as:

Backer, Larry Catá (2020) *Hong Kong Between 'One Country' and 'Two Systems': Essays from the Year that Transformed the Hong Kong Special Administrative Region (June 2019 – June 2020)*, State College, PA: Little Sir Press.

Cataloguing-in-Publication Data

Name: Backer, Larry Catá, author.
Title: *Hong Kong Between 'One Country' and 'Two Systems': Essays from the Year that Transformed the Hong Kong Special Administrative Region (June 2019 – June 2020)*/ Larry Catá Backer.
Description: Paperback edition | State College, PA: Little Sir Press, 2020 | Includes bibliographic references and glossary.
Identifiers: LCCN --- ISBN 978-1-949943-03-0 (ebk); 978-1-949943-05-4 (paperback)
Subjects: LSCH: Political Science--Marxism—Hong Kong--China
LC record available

ISBN: 978-1-949943-03-0 (ebk) ; 978-1-949943-05-4 (paperback)

Typeset in Cambria

Dedication

This work is dedicated to Donna Marie, you know why.

———

The essays are offered to the people of Hong Kong who have served many as the subjects of several profound contemporary experiments in governance.

Contents

Part III: The Hardening of Positions Now More Fully Developed

Preface and Acknowledgements

"言有尽而意无穷" [Words and meanings are endless].

It will be hard to forget the late afternoon of 9 June 2019. People had been whispering for days about what was coming—some worried and others looked forward to whatever was to come with a sense of excited anticipation. Only three days before, as I was arriving in Hong Kong, there has been a rare protest against the proposed extradition bill[1] by Hong Kong's lawyers. People were angry; they believed this extradition bill might be the beginning of the end of Hong Kong's autonomy. Some people in Hong Kong suggested that this return of the extradition bill was meant as a means of reaching into Hong Kong to rectify[2] critics of the central authorities. And they did not want to see it gone—whatever the formal political relationship with the Mainland.

I did not pay much attention; my attention had been almost entirely diverted by a series of meetings. In any case, I

---

[1] The Fugitive Offenders and Mutual Legal Assistance in Criminal Matters Legislation (Amendment) Bill 2019 (2019 年逃犯及刑事事宜相互法律協助法例（修訂）條例草案)).

[2] Mao Zedong, "Speech at the Meeting of the Supreme Soviet of the USSR in Celebration of the 40th Anniversary of the Great October Socialist Revolution" (6 November 1957); available [https://www.marxists.org/reference/archive/mao/works/red-book/ch03.htm]. ("It is a movement for carrying out a nation-wide debate which is both guided and free, a debate in the city and the countryside on such questions as the socialist road versus the capitalist road, the basic system of the state and its major policies, the working style of Party and government functionaries, and the question of the welfare of the people, a debate which is conducted by setting forth facts and reasoning things out, so as correctly to resolve those actual contradictions among the people which demand immediate solution. This is a socialist movement for the self-education and self-remolding of the people"). For a sense of the way in which this term is used, see, e.g., Frederick C. Teiwes, "The Origins of Rectification: Inner Party Purges and education Before Liberation," *The China Quarterly* 65:15-53 (1976.)

thought, this protest might be just the start of an Umbrella Movement version 2.0 updated from its 2014 version1.0. I had been told that protests were scheduled that day against the Extradition Law that had been the subject of intense discussion among many people in Hong Kong. It was not clear what the central authorities in Beijing had planned or what the local government would do in the face of mounting disquiet on the street and, surprisingly, among Hong Kong's business leaders. Everybody had an opinion, of course. Few thought that the protests would amount to much in the long term. This was a city now used to mass manifestations of opinion, and as well, a city seemingly now beyond the large scale protests of the 2014 Umbrella Movement.

I was not prepared for the scale of the manifestations, even the very small glimpse of which I could see standing on the pedestrian bridges crossing Hennessey Road near the Wai Chai station. I stood for a long time looking at the faces of the individuals and then blurring them to see the aggregated face of the crowd. I assumed exuberance, but there was a funereal air to the manifestation of public sentiment, one that seemed to mix hope, fear, and a determination to push forward, whatever the cost. At the time many felt the cost would be small. They looked back on the apparent consequences of the Umbrella Movement and thought that this would produce something of a repetition from the authorities.

The year that followed was one of tremendous change. These changes, however, could not have been readily foreseen by the hundreds of thousands marching on 9 June 2019, the local officials who viewed this with some trepidation but with little deep concern, or the central authorities who expected quick and resolute response to avoid the embarrassments of the upheavals of 2014 and the Umbrella Movement. Few could have predicted that the protests would transform their objectives from resistance to the Extradition Law, permitting people from Hong Kong to be extradited to the Mainland, into a push for a substantially deeper and more permanent understanding of the "Two Systems" principle in the "One Country-Two Systems arrangement that served as Hong Kong's political model.

No one could have predicted the sustained support of the people for the protesters, the Five Demands as an organizing principle of local protest political action, of the violence that would follow the initial protests, of the detachment of the principles of democratic governance of Hong Kong from the Sino-British Joint Declaration, [3] and of the strong support by the international community for the protest movement. Likewise no one could have foreseen an equally strong transformation of the position of the central authorities, which moved from a more or less patient toleration and plan for gradual Sinification of Hong Kong to be completed by the end of the term of the Sino-British Joint Declaration to a strong move to incorporation of Hong Kong into its regional development plans. No one could have foreseen the way that the "One Country" principle would be developed and eventually manifested in the National Security Law for Hong Kong and associated regulations that would effectively reconceive the nature and practice of political autonomy in Hong Kong. And no one could have seen how a global pandemic might play a critical role in the great shifting of local power dynamics that made it possible to eventually crush the protest movement, successfully counter international support for the protesters at relatively little cost to the central authorities in Beijing, and reset the China-Hong Kong political model.

People, and especially elite chroniclers of events, prefer to travel into the future with their eyes firmly focused on the past. Society is organized, and tends to see itself—under the guidance of vanguards who have captured authority for this task one way or another—in a classically dysfunctional way, that is in a way that defies a normality. Society's present is only understood in relation to its past. The future cannot be unlocked, nor the present understood, in the absence of a well interpreted understanding of the past. That project of *intentionally* understanding the past provides the basis for orthodox society for reading, understanding, and evaluating the condition of its present, and for identifying the actions necessary to recast the past that vindicates its future.

---

3 Joint Declaration of the Government of the United Kingdom of Great Britain and Northern Ireland and the Government of the People's Republic of China on the Question of Hong Kong (19 December 1984); available [https://www.cmab.gov.hk/en/issues/jd2.htm].

To that end history becomes an obsession—to preserve the past, to mimic it, to liberate oneself from the past. But it is through the lens of the past that the present is understood and the future can be conceived. And thus the dysfunction: the past is never merely a collection of facts, but a chronicle of the societal present wrestling with its current self. One understands the past, then, only as a function of its use to the present; one understands the present only as its own reflection of the past. The dysfunctional, then, is the definition of the normal and becomes functional, that is it serves as the basis for recognizing the normal, the real, the "fact" or the proper interpretation of things.

In a sense, all history is bound up in "history issues"—and are centered on socio-cultural projects that are directed toward preserving the past into the present, of constituting the past as an indictment of present, or of understanding the past as an incomplete movement toward an idealized future. This changes very little whether the underlying premise of history is cyclical or progressive. The present mimics the past and that mimicry calls out either for rejection to break the pattern of repetition (and the failures of progress in historical development) or as evidence that the present might give way to a distinctive future. In any case, one has one's eyes firmly focused on the past. The history of the United States before 1865 provides a case in point. Reading the past— the journey from union in 1789, to secession, in 1861—has been the subject of varying interpretation and emphasis, depending for example, on whether the "present" national project involved nation building (1865 – 1937) or whether that contemporary project centered on slavery and race. The not much shorter history of Hong Kong also suggested a long period of distinctive "presets" making use of the past to manage its self-understanding and pointing societal objectives toward a managed future.

So it was that one might have been excused, given these baseline socio-cultural reflexes, of assuming that the great protests that started 9 June 2019 would somehow mimic the events of 2014 and its Umbrella Movement. There would be protests, international attention, much handwringing and blustery statements, and little but perhaps crucial compromise. But of course that backwards looking was far too narrow. It focused only on a reading within Hong Kong. It did not take into account that other key actors might read (backwards) their own histories, and their own interpretations of the Umbrella Movement in the (re)construction of their present moving forward. It failed, certainly to note that China itself was now a quite different political space in 2019 than it had been in 2014. It failed to recognize that the UK's present was molded by a rereading of its own history that might reconceive its role in the world and the forms and objectives to be emphasized. And it failed to read the way the United States had plunged into its own contemporary crisis of self-identity as it engaged in a tremendous battle over the meaning and implications of its own past (projected inwards to its domestic reconstitution and outwards toward its external relations).

From 9 June 2019, every major actor—and the 'priestly castes' of elite interpreters who were to chronicle the events that then transpired—all of them miscalculated. All of them were blind to the compulsions of others. All of them were so focused on themselves that the present came undone in the chaotic interplay of changing views of narrowly drawn pasts projected onto the present. Of course, a year later, one can at last see what the ultimate consequences of the events set in motion, at least symbolically, by those protests that started on 9 June and extend to the present. The protests appeared to mark a turning point, and the start of an end game, around the issue of the character and prerogatives of the Hong Kong Special Administrative Region (SAR) within China and in the world. An end game because one could trace the origins of this discussion back to the negotiations between the United Kingdom (perhaps as proxy for the international community) and the People's Republic of China for the return of land leased to the Hong Kong Crown Colony at the turn of the 19th century, and the ceding (back) of sovereignty over the smaller territory ceded to the United Kingdom by the last imperial dynasty in the 19th century.

The compromise reached to make possible those transfers became known as the "One Country, Two Systems" model. That model reconstituted the Crown Colony, both those lands ceded to Britain by the Imperial Chinese Government and those portions of the Colony situated on lands leased from China, as a single

Chinese Special Administrative Region ("SAR"). Within that SAR the Chinese government agreed to preserve certain features of its political-economic model, features that were incompatible with the Marxist-Leninist political-economic model of the rest of China. This arrangement was memorialized in an *international agreement* between China and the United Kingdom But the essence of that agreement conceded that Hong Kong was an *integral part of the People's Republic of China* and thus that its constitutional ordering would be related to and subsumed within the Chinese political order. And thus a fundamental contradiction was built into the arrangement from the very outset—a piece of national territory, but one subject to international constraints on the authority of the national government with respect to its governance. Still, it was the ambiguities within that contradiction that made the arrangement possible. It served as a space within which each side could indulge its own beliefs as to the fundamental character of the arrangement, the intentions and objectives of its provisions, and the relationship between the three parties to the arrangement—China, the U.K (and after to some extent the international community) and the people of Hong Kong. How those ambiguities would be exploited and then manifested in the governance of Hong Kong remained open.

The history of the SAR has shown the ways that the ambiguities in the arrangement could be used to the advantage of the parties, and how it chronicled the changing power relations between the two great power parties. One Country, Two Systems started life with a heavy emphasis on the "Two Systems" portion of the model. China was still at the start of what would be the wildly successful project of "socialist modernization." The emblem of that future was marked by the establishment of Shenzhen, just across the border from the Hong Kong SAR. And indeed, from the 1980s, one might even measure the relative position of Chinese economic development by noting the growth of Shenzhen as part of what became the great Pearl River delta manufacturing hub for transactions at first negotiated mostly in Hong Kong but then gradually migrating across the SAR border.

As Chinese economic power grew and along with it, China's political confidence and the elaboration of its political theory, the status of Hong Kong became increasingly focused, on the Chinese side, on the cultivation of the "One Country" part of the formula, and the stricter management of the "Two Systems" elements of the arrangement. This impulse grew even as Hong Kong developed its own unique political culture, and its sense of the SAR's relationship with the rest of the nation. As central authorities increasingly thought of integration and domestication, Hong Kong people (intellectuals, workers, and others mostly) increasingly cultivated the unique political culture of Hong Kong as an international city, one that had absorbed substantial elements of international political sensibilities. For them, "Two Systems" served as an internationally guaranteed right to develop autonomously, and as a constraint on the power of the Chinese central authorities of "misuse" of the One Country principles to absorb Hong Kong into the Chinese political-economic model. Hong Kong was part of China, to be sure, but a separable part, and one whose uniqueness would be guaranteed not by the Chinese state but by the international community.

That difference of view proved to be increasingly explosive after the end of the 20th century. That was a period marked by increased political differentiation—especially respecting the cultivation of civil and political rights—even as an increasingly frustrated China sought to more tightly align the Hong Kong SAR to its national goals and cultures, under the leadership of the vanguard. There were explosions almost from the start of the 21st century. Efforts viewed by the masses as threatening Hong Kong political "liberties" especially as against the central authorities, were the subject of political agitation. Many of these campaigns were successful enough to limit substantial threats to the central elements of Hong Kong's political self-conception.

But all this changed after 2014 and the Umbrella Movement. What started out as an effort of the central authorities to aid in the reform of Hong Kong's government, its forms of representation, and the relationship with national organs, became a mass response against threats to the democratic governance (such as it was and as it was understood within the broader constraints of the original One Country Two Systems deal) in Hong Kong. What was particularly notable was both the leadership of young people, mostly students, and their alliance with elements of the working class. Also notable was the way that the international foundations of the One Country Two Systems deal appeared to permit the internationalization of the Umbrella Movement. I suspect that 2014 marked a sort of moment of clarity for the Chinese central authorities—one in which they realized the extent to which the One Country Two Systems arrangement might pose a threat to their overall authority over Hong Kong. That threat was made more immediate given what appeared to be the emergence of policy that sought to align all of the cities of the Pearl River delta into a sort of aggregated whole. That planning also required a greater control over the entire region, and perhaps also likely, a greater emphasis on the One Country portion of the deal. As well, one enters here a time of increasing government suspicion of the projection of international arrangements, special procedures and the like into Chinese territory. Notions of foreign interference, especially as global discourse became increasingly critical of the Chinese political-economic model, began to loom larger. And suspicions only grew in the aftermath of the Umbrella Movement.

By 2019, then, the stage appeared to be set for explosion. On the one side was the alliance of Hong Kong elements, along with significant portions of the international community, who saw Hong Kong as an international city, one whose foundation was built on international law and treaty that constrained national power to reshape its political-economic model. This was the Hong Kong of Two Systems—pluralist, centering political and civil rights, transnational constitutionalist, and aligned with the sensibilities of global society. On the other side were the Chinese central authority and Hong Kong nationalists, who saw Hong Kong as an integral part of China, who were worried about separatist tendencies, and who sought greater integration with the rest of the nation. This was the Hong Kong of One Country—nationalist, focused on security and economic, social, and cultural rights, and seeking greater alignment with the rest of the nation (subject to protection of peculiarities that would over the generations perhaps disappear).

Still, as 2019 began, this contradiction and its explosive potential were viewed by many through the lens of past events—it was the natural order of things. There were expectations of realignment between One Country and Two Systems, but no one expected a challenge, and especially a successful challenge to the fundamental principles or their application. That is, no one expected the need or desire to resolve the fundamental contradiction of Hong Kong as an international city within China. But then, little notice appeared to be taken of what was going on beneath the polished surface of conferences, press events, and the routine of politics and bureaucracy in a city focused on prosperity. Hardly anyone, then, was prepared for the spiraling of events that was triggered by yet another point of friction (like so many before) between Hong Kong internationalists and nationalists—the Fugitive Offenders and Mutual Legal Assistance in Criminal Matters Legislation (Amendment) Bill 2019 (2019 年逃犯及刑事事宜相互法律協助法例（修訂）條例草案)(the "Extradition Law").[4]

Over the year that began in June 2019, Hong Kong became a nexus point of global conflict. What started as dislike of the Extradition Law, became part of a larger struggle on several levels. On one level the struggle pushed both internationalists and nationalists to more extreme positions and to give them the space to push for change that would have been unpalatable even a year earlier. Hong Kong also became a battleground in the conflict between the United States and China over the shape of the international trade order. And lastly, Hong Kong became an even more important battleground over the legitimacy of the internationalization of politics and constitutionalism. At the end of the process, Hong Kong was no longer faced with the adoption of an Extradition Law. Instead, a year later Hong Kong adopted a National Anthem Law and was forced to accept adoption of a National Security Law for Hong Kong (one which it had successfully avoided for decades).

At the same time Hong Kong internationalism appeared to collapse, or at least to evidence its weakness in the face of a resurgent Chinese national government. By the end of June 2020 it was becoming clear that there would be a fundamental shift from Two Systems to One Country; more importantly there would

---

[4] Fugitive Offenders and Mutual Legal Assistance in Criminal Matters Legislation (Amendment) Bill 2019; SBCR 1/2716/19; available [https://www.legco.gov.hk/yr18-19/english/bills/brief/b201903291_brf.pdf].

be a shift from the management of that arrangement from the international community to Chinese national authorities. It will take years to understand the magnitude of the changes and to see their effects in Hong Kong, and their effects on Chinese efforts to move to the center of shaping international affairs. As important, by the end of June 2020, Chinese political ideology had also evolved—the deepening of New Era theory, and its expression as policy, was decisive in shaping the increasingly muscular approach of the Chinese authorities toward both the nationalization of the Hong Kong issue and the significant refocus of the governing principle from Two Systems to One Country. To understand this shift one must understand Chinese Marxist-Leninism in its transition to the New Era, a transition that assumed its current trajectories after 2012 which continues to the present. One must also understand the rise of a self-conception of Hong Kong as a permanently autonomous political apparatus apart from the Mainland, a *political sovereignty* grounded in international norms but one that acknowledges China's claims of *territorial* sovereignty. Lastly, one must understand the changed international situation that made reliance on the international community, and the UK as the representative of that traditional global internationalism, a very great gamble.

These essays were written as the events unfolded. They are meant to retain the freshness of the moment. The essays are presented in the form of a diary that marks an intellectual progression that matches the march of events. The original drafts were written at the time the events analyzed were happening (each essay is dated to the time of its initial writing) and lightly edited for the book. The object is to capture not just the strategic and normative developments that produced the new order for Hong Kong in June 2020, but also to give a sense of the uncertainties and anticipations as the events themselves transpired during the course of the year. The process of ideological genesis from June 2019 to June 2020 is most immediately captured from a state of anticipation without the benefit of foresight. It is that immediacy that adds a layer of analysis to the usual post facto accountings and examination of events. That layering, anyway, is the aim. The essays, then, do not look back on events after the fact, but speculate, discover, and captures moments that from June 2020 look inevitable but which from the perspective of June 2019 appeared far less so. They are meant to retain the freshness of the moment.

Much like the protest and democracy movement itself, as well as the responses of local and central authorities and the international community, these events occurred in fits and starts from the initial mass protests to the adoption and enforcement of the Hong Kong National Security Law and the Allegiance Law to more quickly fold Hong Kong into a borough of the Pearl River Mega City planned for the region by the central authorities, an embedding occurring well before the anticipated 2047 end of the international agreement's term. The first half of 2020 marked the decisive move by the central authorities to resolve brought on by the protests. What followed was a period of substantial clean up.

By 2021, the transformation of Hong Kong was effective complete. While the National Security Law and the Allegiance Law laid the foundation for advancing patriotic elements and punishing others, the changes to the Hong Kong election law of 2021 effectively made it impossible for Hong Kong's internationalist camp, and those involved in the protests of 2019-2020, to effectively participate government. The arrest of over fifty pro-democracy campaigners, forty-seven of which were indicted in a single count,[5] on the eve of the announcement of the plans for moving forward with the reform of Hong Kong's election law in the National People's Congress in Beijing[6] signaled the end of the protest era and the finalization of the transformation of Hong Kong's two systems principle into an expression of a closely managed variation of the One Country principle, one that necessarily rejected civil and political internationalism in order to

---

[5] Jessie Pang, James Pomfret, Dozens of leading Hong Kong pro-democracy campaigners charged with subversion, *Reuters* (27 February 2021); available [https://www.reuters.com/article/us-hongkong-politics/dozens-of-leading-hong-kong-pro-democracy-campaigners-charged-with-subversion-idUSKCN2AS00J].
[6] 关于《全国人民代表大会关于完善香港特别行政区选举制度的决定（草案）》的说明 ——2021 年 3 月 5 日在第十三届全国人民代表大会第四次会议上 [Notes on the "Decision of the National People's Congress on Improving the Hong Kong Special Administrative Region's Electoral System (Draft)" at the Fourth Session of the Thirteenth National People's Congress on March 5, 2021]; available [http://www.xinhuanet.com/politics/2021lh/2021-03/05/c_1127172464.htm].

align with the basic principles of the political-economic system of the nation under the leadership of its vanguard.

> The central government is taking decisive action to develop a democratic election system that conforms to the conditions of Hong Kong and reflects the overall interests of society, to ensure that patriots govern Hong Kong and kick out the disruptors from Hong Kong. This will push Hong Kong's democracy toward a healthy, orderly and higher-quality level.[7]

The short road from June 2019, the last year of the initial phase (1997-2019) of Hong Kong's return to China, to 2020 and the start of Hong Kong's "New Era" is observed and considered in the essays that follow. In 2019 those who initially wrapped themselves in what they thought was the protective shielding of the Sino-British Joint, or even more audaciously, in the protections of international law and principles, found that these have provided little more than the shroud used to bury their aspirations in 2020. Now outcast and outsiders, they must adjust their aspirations to the new realities of Hong Kong or face rectification; fleeing has become dangerous. [8] "In Western democracies, they have been welcomed as refugees escaping Beijing's tightening grip over Hong Kong. In China, they have been denounced as violent criminals escaping punishment for their seditious activities."[9]

> The essays are offered in the spirit of the old saying--core of 当局者迷，旁观者清 [Insiders are blind to what bystanders

---

[7] Shen Du, "Improving Hong Kong's electoral system important for developing high-quality democracy," *China Today* (7 March 2021); available [http://www.chinatoday.com.cn/ctenglish/2018/zdtj/202103/t20210307_80 0238930.html].

[8] Natalie Lung and Kari Lindberg, " China Jails 10 Hong Kong Activists Over Attempt to Flee by Boat," *Bloomberg* (30 December 2020); available [https://www.msn.com/en-us/news/world/china-jails-10-hong-kong-activists-over-attempt-to-flee-by-boat/ar-BB1ckMSi]

[9] Austin Ramzy and Maria Abi-Habib, "As China Clamps Down, Activists Flee Hong Kong for Refuge in the West: China calls them "violent criminals." Asylum seekers from Hong Kong are the latest catalyst for deteriorating relations between Beijing and Western countries," *The New York Times* (24 October 2020); available [https://www.nytimes.com/2020/10/24/world/asia/hong-kong-asylum-seekers.html].

can see]--yet sensitive to the realities that insiders also know what bystanders cannot see. The essays are originated as and retain the flavor of a contemporaneous engagement with historical events as they unfolded. The essays, as well, are presented as the story of a rapidly changing analytical framework within which events occurred and through which they could be interpreted. The essays, then, are both a journal of events, and a journey. For its readers it may serve as a record of the way that the way of thinking about the situation of Hong Kong changed radically over such a short period of time. It is also, in part, a chronicle of the way in which larger events—the US-China trade war, and the COVID19 pandemic—can have a substantial effect on what would otherwise be a localized affair.

It is as important to underline that there is no great moral or political agenda to the essays. They take the world as the parties represent it, and then hold each to their respective representation. Do not expect this to be the work of a public intellectual with a (not so) hidden agenda. It is not meant as polemic, nor as apology. But it does relish recounting the idiosyncrasies of the protagonists, each bound within the constraints of their driving ideologies which drive them relentlessly through a series of events that for at least some of the actors became a deeply personal tragedy, even as for others it represented a triumph perhaps unimaginable when the protests began in June 2019.

The focus on discourse. The essays examine the events as they happened from the perspective of the rhetoric of the parties--their statements, their gestures, their performances on the streets, and ultimately their memorialization of these discourses in binding instruments most acutely expressed in the two of the three germinal laws of the new Hong Kong after June 2020--the National Anthem Law and the National Security Law. To some extent this discursive focus owes a debt to and might be comfortably embedded within analytic traditions that owe much to the insights of Guiguzi （鬼谷子）and its rhetoric,[10] which makes its appearance throughout the essays and perhaps binds

---

[10] Guiguzi （鬼谷子）, *Guiguzi: China's First Treatise on Rhetoric; A Critical Translation and Commentary* (Hui Wu (trans.); Carbondale: Southern Illinois University Press, 2016 (before 220 A.D.))

them together into something more coherent. These insights frame some of the analysis, as do the insights of critical thinkers from the Western tradition.

The essays are organized chronologically into six parts. They are critical essays in the sense that they try to make sense of events as they are occurring. Part I (Epilogue as Introduction) starts at the end of the story. It uses a fairly rare statement endorsed by a substantial majority of the representatives of United Nations Human Rights special procedures calling for the development of decisive measures to protect human rights in the face of the enactment by Chinese authorities of a National Security Law for Hong Kong to situate the end of the story that began with exuberant protests on 9 June 2019 and ended with the imposition of a legal order that effectively reshaped the character of the Hong Kong political order. It does this from the perspective of one of the international community--perhaps among the actors most adversely affected by the story that is Hong Kong between June 2019 and July 2020.

Part II consists of eleven chapter essays. These essays take the reader from the beginning of the protests in June 2019 to the end of August 2019. The essays serve as an analytical witness to the development of the initial phase of the Hong Kong protests. Step by step, as it occurred, it considered the escalations of ambitions and tactics of the protesters, the growing intransigence of local officials, and the start of what would become an elaborate and largely effective counter position of the Chinese central authorities. Much of what is developed in these early weeks provides the foundation for everything that develop thereafter. Positions that have their start, sometimes quite tentatively, in these early weeks, later emerge as powerful strategies in the months that follow.

Part III consists of seven essays. The essays critically chronical what then appeared to be the critical events taking place from the beginning of September to the end of November 2019. These take the reader through the next phase of development, one in which initial positions are fully developed and hardened. Here one sees fully developed the ideological position of the central authorities that in retrospect were faithfully memorialized in the

National Anthem Law, the National Security Law, and most recently in the amendments to the Election rules in the Hong Kong Basic Law in March 2021. At the same time, one encounters here the maturing of an aligned position of the various groups of protesters that sought to deepen the internationalization of its movement and preserve its efforts to permanently protect a measure of liberal democratic order in Hong Kong. Lastly the manifestation of international response, grounded first in the narrow strictures of the Sino-British Joint Declaration and thereafter in general fundamental principles of self-determination and the international civil and political rights of coherent political communities, is also well developed in this period.

Part IV then considers the relatively short period of stalemate between December 2019 and April 2020 in three essays that cover the apex of protester power in December 2019 and January 2020, and then the stalemate pause imposed by the realities of the worldwide COVID-19 pandemic. One moves here from the unabated storm of protest to the opportunity that pandemic provides local and national authorities to break that stalemate in their favor. It was during this period that the stakes around the proper conceptualization of the One Country Two Systems principle became clear. On the one side were the central authorities who now had fully developed the construct of the principle as a means of permitting autonomy within the discretionary authority of the state. On the other were the protesters and the international community who now saw in One Country Two Systems a principle of divided sovereignty in which the political choices of the Hong Kong community could be protected against encroachment by the central authorities, one based on international liberal democratic and human rights principles.

Part V then chronicles the end of the protest movement and the emergence of a "new era" Hong Kong between May and July 2020. Its seven essays critically chronicle the way that the central authorities drove events from May 2020, in a way that paralleled the way that protesters drove events in June through September 2019. This starts with the announcement of an intention to impose a National Security Law, through the imposition of first a National Anthem Law and then ending with the adoption of the National Security Law itself. It considers the critical importance of the development of the mechanics of a patriotic front as a means of dividing and managing the people of Hong Kong, and the relatively little opposition that the central authorities faced in successfully realizing its objectives.

The single essay that makes up Part VI serves as the afterword of the story that was told in chapters two through thirty. This is not just the end of the story of the protests in Hong Kong but also the beginning of the story of Hong Kong as a more integrated part of the Pearl River area of China. No longer an international city in the sense of internationally recognized and protected legal autonomy from its territorial sovereign, Hong Kong now rejoins the nation as a Chinese city with substantial international connections. Beyond that, Hong Kong's future is now far more closely aligned with that of the Chinese heartland and with the vision of China's central authorities for the nation as a whole.

The essays have been only lightly edited and footnoted to retain their connection with the time in which they were written; very little was done to update the essays or the writing except where necessary to add context. It was the journey from protests to National Security Law rather than its conclusion that is rich with insight about all of the principal participants in these events. My hope is that these essays may provide some perspective, not just on the events in Hong Kong as they unfolded, but on the evolution of Chinese and international political ideology in this crucial period of history. The object of these essays is not so much the accumulation of facts as t is to reveal the meanings that were constructed from out of responses to perceptions of threat and the undertaking of responsibility, where such action invited not just contradiction but conflict. Again it is worth emphasizing that the essays are meant to provide a record of thinking at the time the events were occurring, full of the presumptions, prejudices and perspectives of the times. Each one of them, then, is offered as a sort of temporally contingent witness statement, both of the times and of the thinking as events occurred, without benefit of foreknowledge of what was to come. And that, I hope, may be their ultimate value to those who read the essays in the years to come.

Thanks

As is common in undertakings of this sort, it took many people to make this book possible. Keren Wang, Flora Sapio, Gao Shan, Miaoqiang Dai, and Matthew McQuilla provided endless hours of patient listening and even more fruitful exchanges as the situation in Hong Kong that developed from the start of the June 2019 protests. The Coalition for Peace & Ethics provided substantial support for working through ideas and the space in which I could wrestle with what emerged as these essays. Many friends and colleagues patiently listened and sometimes argued or informed over the course of these events. I learned so much from those exchanges with colleagues all over the world. You know who you are. Lastly great thanks is owed to the Little Sir Press, whose patience and help in bringing this to publication cannot be overstated. .

Larry Catá Backer (白 轲)
State College
31 May 2021

Hong Kong
Between "One Country" and "Two Systems":

**Essays from the Year that Transformed the Hong Kong Special Administrative Region
(June 2019 – June 2020)**

Chapter 1

Saturday, 27 June 2020
An Epilogue as Introduction: "UN Experts Call for Decisive Measures to Protect Fundamental Freedoms in China" [联合国专家呼吁采取果断措施保护中国境内的基本自由] and Homesickness in International Human Rights Law

One generally comes to appreciate a way of life, and a way of understanding the fundamental taboos around which a society creates it operative ideal--*one appreciates these things*--only after they have gone. Appreciation is the expression of loss, and like idealization, *can only be fully realized as an act of nostalgia*. It is a form of reactionary expression among societal actors, especially elites, who--too late--come to realize that what they had, their way of life and the structures around which they policed the meaning of "right and wrong" has disappeared except in the empty rituals of its now hollowed out expression in the decaying fora of old orders. The pathos of this nostalgia, its suffering and pitiable condition, becomes more intense where actors remain oblivious to the passing of an age and the dawn of another.

One begins to see the full flowering of this nostalgia for a receding golden age, and its pathos, in the situation in Hong Kong. *What was won on the streets of Hong Kong from June to December 2019, the public and physical manifestation of an internationalist and liberal democratic narrative of self-determination, civil and political rights was lost by June 2020 in the power of the normative narrative developed and projected out by the Chinese central authorities, a narrative backed by a cage of legality against which there appeared to be little effective normative resistance.* Nature did not help those who held the streets; the COVID-19 pandemic made it easier to disperse the crowds and make it easier to substitute the narratives of Marxist Leninist norms for the civic engagement of the streets. And the international community, at the end, offered little more than rhetorical projections of a narrative that was increasingly detached from the changes experienced on the ground.

That expression of nostalgia, then, is especially poignant when it comes from outside; from an international order which may see in the situation in Hong Kong the reflection of the passing of its own golden age and the dawn of something else. Its pathos comes from the strength of its discourse, still redolent with the power of a narrative that once seemed poised for a deeper embedding in the global order. Perhaps it augurs the start of a silver age; or perhaps it is a sign of the dawn of an age of bamboo. And one can capture that longing which is nostalgia in the 26 June

Statement[11] issued in the name of virtually all representatives[12] of the UN Human Rights Special Procedures.[13]

---

[11] Agnès Callamard et al., "UN Experts Call for Decisive Measures to Protect Fundamental Freedoms in China" (26 June 2020); available [https://www.ohchr.org/EN/NewsEvents/Pages/DisplayNews.aspx?NewsID= 26006] (hereafter the "Special Procedures Statement"). The Statement was made available in English and Chinese. Chinese version, 联合国专家呼吁采取果 断 措 施 保 护 中 国 境 内 的 基 本 自 由 , available [https://www.ohchr.org/CH/NewsEvents/Pages/DisplayNews.aspx?NewsID= 26006&LangID=C] (Hereafter "Special Procedures Statement").

[12] The experts: Ms. Agnès Callamard, Special Rapporteur on extrajudicial, summary or arbitrary executions; Mr. David Kaye, Special Rapporteur on the promotion and protection of the right to freedom of expression; Ms. Mary Lawlor, Special Rapporteur on the situation of human rights defenders; Ms. Fionnuala D. Ní Aoláin, Special Rapporteur on the promotion and protection of human rights and fundamental freedoms while countering terrorism; Mr. Ahmed Shaheed, Special Rapporteur on freedom of religion or belief; Mr. Fernand de Varennes, Special Rapporteur on minority issues; Mr. Clément Nyaletsossi Voule,Special Rapporteur on the rights of peaceful assembly and association; Surya Deva, Elżbieta Karska, Githu Muigai (Chair), Dante Pesce, Anita Ramasastry (Vice-chair), Working Group on Business and Human Rights; Ms. E. Tendayi Achiume, Special Rapporteur on Contemporary Forms of Racism; Mr. Balakrishnan Rajagopal, Special Rapporteur on adequate housing as a component of the right to an adequate standard of living, and on the right to non-discrimination in this context; Ms. Leigh Toomey (Chair-Rapporteur), Ms. Elina Steinerte (Vice-Chair), Mr. José Guevara Bermúdez, Mr. Seong-Phil Hong, Mr. Sètondji Adjovi, Working Group on Arbitrary Detention; Mr. Diego García-Sayán, Special Rapporteur on the Independence of Judges and Lawyers; Mr. Michael Lynk, Special Rapporteur on the situation of human rights in the Palestinian Territory occupied since 1967; Mr. Michael Fakhri, Special Rapporteur on the right to food; Mr. Tomoya Obokata, Special Rapporteur on contemporary forms of slavery, including its causes and consequences; Mr. Nils Melzer, Special Rapporteur on torture and other cruel, inhuman or degrading treatment or punishment; Mr. Baskut Tuncak, Special Rapporteur on the implications for human rights of the environmentally sound management and disposal of hazardous substances and wastes;Mr. Léo Heller, Special Rapporteur on the human rights to water and sanitation; Mr. Livingstone Sewanyana, Independent Expert on the promotion of a democratic and equitable international order, Ms. Karima Bennoune, Special Rapporteur in the field of cultural rights; Ms. Kombou Boly Barry, Special Rapporteur on the right to education; Ms. Claudia Mahler, Independent Expert on the enjoyment of all human rights by older persons; Ms. Maria Grazia Giammarinaro, Special Rapporteur on trafficking in persons especially women and children; Mr. Dainius Pūras, Special Rapporteur on the right to physical and mental health; Members of the Working Group on Enforced or Involuntary Disappearances: Mr. Luciano Hazan (Chair), Mr. Tae-Ung Baik (Vice Chair), Mr. Bernard Duhaime, Ms. Houria Es-Slami, and Mr. Henrikas Mickevičius; Ms. Mama Fatima Singhateh, Special Rapporteur on sale and sexual exploitation of children; The Working Group on

The Statement is an excellent example of the classical style of these sorts of writings. It is divided into eleven short paragraph-statement. Paragraphs One and Two describes the two principal issues to which the Special Procedures Statement is directed. The first is a reminder of the communication of alarm by Special Procedures "regarding the repression of fundamental freedoms in China." The second focuses more specifically on the content of those communications directed toward the actions of Chinese authorities in Hong Kong, Tibet, and Xinjian.

Paragraph Three then declares that the National Security Law for Hong Kong violate China's international law obligations (a reference to the 1984 Sino-British Joint Declaration[14] identified

---

the use of mercenaries as a means of violating human rights and impeding the exercise of the right of peoples to self-determination: Mr. Chris Kwaja (Chair), Ms. Jelena Aparac, Ms. Lilian Bobea, Ms. Sorcha MacLeod and Mr. Saeed Mokbil; Mr. Olivier De Schutter, Special Rapporteur on extreme poverty and human rights; The Working Group on discrimination against women and girls: Ms. Elizabeth Broderick (Chair),Ms. Alda Facio, Ms. Meskerem Geset Techane, Ms. Ivana Radačić, andMs. Melissa Upreti (Vice Chair); Mr. Joe Cannataci, Special Rapporteur on the right to privacy.

[13] "The special procedures of the Human Rights Council are independent human rights experts with mandates to report and advise on human rights from a thematic or country-specific perspective. They are non-paid and elected for 3-year mandates that can be reconducted for another three years. As of September 2020, there are 44 thematic and 11 country mandates." United Nations, "Special Procedures of the Human Rights Council, About Special Procedures" (accessed 10 December 2020); available [https://www.ohchr.org/EN/HRBodies/SP/Pages/Welcomepage.aspx]. UN Special Procedures are an important mechanism of the UN Human Rights Council in their efforts to monitor and construct a coordinated and coherent international approaches to the international system of human rights and humanitarian law and norms. "In 2019, mandate holders issued 182 reports: 136 were submitted to the Human Rights Council, including 62 country visit reports, and 46 to the General Assembly." UN High Commissioner for Human Rights, Report of the Secretariat 2019 A/HRC/43/64 (20 April 2020); available [https://undocs.org/en/A/HRC/43/64]. See generally, e.g., Ingrid Nifosi, The UN Special Procedures in the Field of Human Rights (Antwerp: Intersentia, 2005) ("even though such mechanisms were created to accomplish mere theoretical studies, they have become true tools of human rights protection and monitoring" Ibid., p. 1)).

[14] Joint Declaration of the Government of the United Kingdom of Great Britain and Northern Ireland and the Government of the People's Republic of China on

in paragraph four by name) and in any case constitute the imposition of severe restrictions on civil and political rights.

Paragraph Four then makes the case for something like autonomous self-determination because of the distinctive history, culture, linguistic and legal traditions of Hong Kong which was at the heart of the guarantees of the 1984 Joint Declaration.

Paragraph Five then urges that China abide by the provisions of the 1984 Joint Declaration (as the Special Procedures understand them) and Chinese obligations under the International Covenant on Civil and Political Rights (ICCPR), a set of obligations that have not been affirmatively embraced by China. This "abiding can be demonstrated by withdrawing the National Security Law for Hong Kong.

Paragraph Six then uses this opportunity to broaden the need for engagement of human rights and humanitarian law and norms monitoring in China in light of the actions deemed alarming by the Special Procedures in Hong Kong, Xinjiang, and Tibet.

Paragraph Seven then acknowledges that all efforts at such engagement have been effectively dismissed by Chinese officials, noting that "the Government of China has responded to the communications of UN independent experts, if almost always to reject criticism."

By adopting this "rejectionist" posture, the Special Procedures Statement declares, in Paragraph Eight, that China has become an outlier in the community of nations. That aberrational character is demonstrated by the refusal of the Chinese state to permit all but five visits of Special Procedures.

Paragraph Nine then suggests that the international community bring China to heel—that is the international community join together to ensure China "respects human rights and abides by its international obligations."

---

the Question of Hong Kong (19 December 1984); available [https://www.cmab.gov.hk/en/issues/jd2.htm].

Paragraph Ten then urges China to correct its own behavior, presumably before the weight of this collective action might be felt, and to open its doors to the entry of Special Procedures.

Lastly paragraph eleven requests urgent action by the Human Rights Council to evaluate the list of charges against China made in the Special Procedures Statement, to establish another Special Procedure to monitor China, and to urge all member states to pressure China to better conform to expected human rights behaviors.

Make no mistake--the Special Procedures Statement is an excellent example of its kind. From the perspectives of its authors and the apparatus of the United Nations in Geneva, the Special Procedures Statement represents a clear ululation of what they believe remains the core of internationalist universalism to which all states within the United Nations system must adhere.

Keeping in mind China's obligations under international human rights law, and the obligation to adhere to the ICCPR with respect to the Hong Kong SAR, and in view of the UN Human Rights Council's prevention mandate to act on the root causes of crises which may lead to human rights emergencies or undermine peace and security, the UN experts call on the international community to act collectively and decisively to ensure China respects human rights and abides by its international obligations.

And yet, like so many other classical statements of this kind, it served more as an abandonment of an ideal than the expression of power. For, as might be expected, neither China nor the Human Rights Council, did much more than perhaps read the Special Procedures Statements before filing it appropriately.

The Special Procedures Statement, then, speaks to a nostalgia of a quite specific kind—of the longing for a return to internationalism for Hong Kong. The Special Procedures Statement was quite specific. First it affirmed the superiority of international law and norms over the domestic legal order's ambitions and objectives. It then insisted that these obligations be subject to the oversight of the international community. Note the language in a key part of the Statement:

> The independent experts urge the Government of China to abide by its international legal obligations, including under the International Covenant on Civil and Political Rights (ICCPR) and the Sino-British Joint Declaration, and withdraw the draft national security law for Hong Kong. The UN independent experts believe it is time for renewed attention on the human rights situation in the country, particularly in light of the moves against the people of the Hong Kong SAR, minorities of the Xinjiang Autonomous Region, the Tibet Autonomous Region, and human rights defenders across the country. The independent experts acknowledge that the Government of China has responded to the communications of UN independent experts, if almost always to reject criticism. [独立专家们敦促中国政府遵守其国际法律义务，包括《公民及政治权利国际公约》和《中英联合声明》规定的义务，撤回香港《国家安全法（草案）》。联合国独立专家们认为，现在应该再度关注中国的人权状况，特别是考虑到中国针对香港特区民众、新疆自治区和西藏自治区的少数民族，及全国各地人权维护者所采取的行动。独立专家们承认，中国政府虽然几乎总是拒绝接受批评，但是对联合国独立专家发出的信函作出了回应。][15]

The Special Procedures Statement provides an excellent mapping of the terrain of the golden age of rights, and of the potential of state-based global representative collective union based on states what was to be one of the great fruits of the (now fashionably despised) foundation of integration through economic globalization. That golden age of rights--overseen by a collective international vanguard embedded within the UN system, would provide increasingly mandatory guidance over the

---

[15] Special Procedures Statement, supra.

meaning of the framework of human rights which was to serve as the fundamental basis for the constitutive ordering (and disciplining) of states. It was a Leninist ideal that itself has now floundered in the face of a challenge from the largest non-international Leninist organ in the globe.

Yet the Special Procedures Statement, both in its gravity (virtually all of the Special Procedures signed onto the document) and its thrust, took on more of the quality of a dirge than of a demand. It grieves more than it pleads. It, indeed, resembles what one might expect of a mourners at a classical Irish wake or of the Jewish custom of leaving a burial chamber unsealed for three days—both to mark a passing and to exercise caution in the vent the passing was at least in some respects premature.[16] What is to be mourned is that the system itself—constructed as universal, appears unable to penetrate the increasingly robust internal order of a Chinese state perfectly content to participate in the crafting of international structures, but only on its own terms for the advancement of its own objectives "They further urge the UN Human Rights Council (HRC) to act with a sense of urgency to take all appropriate measures to monitor Chinese human rights practices."

To be sure, the Statement serves as a powerful expression. Yet its power is founded on its own conceptual baselines, a foundational way of conceptualizing the world and its ordering that is quickly receding . In the end, the Statement is most effectively heard as a keening (from Irish *caoinim* "I weep, wail, lament" usually for the dead), rather than what it purports to be: a robust expression of an authority of legitimating values and approaches to "the right" and "the good" grounded in the present. However, this lamentation for the dead, which is the Statement of the Special Procedures, is not for China, the purported object of the keening. Instead it turns on itself; it is more powerfully a mourning for themselves and their own authority in the face of a strategic indifference from a powerful state actor. It is to this that

---

[16] Dara Kelly, "Irish wake songs, pranks, and the history of Irish funerals" IrishCentral (20 January 2016); available [https://www.irishcentral.com/roots/the-truth-about-the-irish-wake-lewd-songs-pranks-were-part-of-the-tradition-174087771-237533321].

the Special Procedures are reduced, they can produce only the lament that "unlike over 120 States, the Government of China has not issued a standing invitation to UN independent experts to conduct official visits.").

The Special Procedures Statement provides an end note to a process of transformation that began in the 1980s that produced both the transfer of sovereignty of Hong Kong to China and the creation of "One Country, Two Systems" as the fig leaf meant to cover the eventual ramifications of that action. The statement serves as the epilogue (in the form of a reactionary prologue) to the inevitable transformation embedded within the actions that produced the current situation in Hong Kong, the quality of which (*then and now*) remain stubbornly beyond the reckoning of those propelling its inevitability. It is now left to their successors to offer an elegy, a *poetic song of lamentation*, in the form of the Special Procedures Statement.
It is worth then to briefly reflect on *nostalgia* and the project of international human rights law in the context of the situation in Hong Kong.

To that end one might consider the centrality of *homesickness in international human rights law.* Nostalgia is understood in its English sense as *homesickness*--the return not just to a place but to a time that is now irretrievably gone. What is meant to be recaptured is not lost. Quite the opposite, it is very much in evidence, but return is impossible because the conditions that gave it effect have changed irremediably.

The act of recapturing itself produces the lens through which one can see developed the ideal of a golden age. Golden ages can only be seen through the rear-view mirror of history as it recedes from the present. It is a homesickness that is expressed as a keening as the way that individuals express their longing for was and can never be again. But with the added sting that one was not aware of the thing lost until recovery was impossible.

The etymology of nostalgia in its current form reminds us that this term--and its performance--is a wholly modern construct (though its pre-modern expressions remind us that collective longing for a society gone with the wind, is an ancient reflex of collective transformations--at least among its reactionary elements).

> Modern Latin, coined 1688 in a dissertation on the topic at the University of Basel by scholar Johannes Hofer (1669-1752) as a rendering of German heimweh "homesickness" (for which see home + woe). From Greek algos "pain, grief, distress" (see -algia) + nostos "homecoming," from neomai "to reach some place, escape, return, get home," from PIE *nes- "to return safely home" (cognate with Old Norse nest "food for a journey," Sanskrit nasate "approaches, joins," German genesen "to recover," Gothic ganisan "to heal," Old English genesen "to recover"). French nostalgie is in French army medical manuals by 1754.Originally in reference to the Swiss and said to be peculiar to them and often fatal, whether by its own action or in combination with wounds or disease. By 1830s the word was used of any intense homesickness: that of sailors, convicts, African slaves.[17]

Nostalgia, like much in modern Western culture, has moved from the moral to the therapeutic sphere. What was once understood as sin is now refashioned as pathology. Both reflect the same impulse to identify and protect against deviations from collective orthodoxy. The sinner was punished and cured through acts of confession, contrition and reform; she was exorcised of her immorality. The deviant was treated and reformed; she is medicated or conditioned to internalize the collective conception of its own collective taboos and expectations and to make them her own. In both cases nostalgia produces pain--the pain for what has been lost, for what has been cut off.

This pain can be felt by collectives (and their institutions) as well as by individuals. It is the pain that is felt by a vanguard, for example, a homesickness of great intensity upon the realization that what had once been expected and natural is now

---

[17] Etymology Online, "Nostalgia" available at https://www.etymonline.com/word/nostalgia].

no longer so. It produces a keening that both embodies the pain of detachment from the ideal of itself that is receding, and that seeks through intense keening to reach across time and retrieve what is lost.

And that brings us to the lamentations of the Special Procedures, one directed to China, respecting the condition of Hong Kong (as well as other issues long festering). And silent but present, is the unspoken China's response--of rejection of silence and of the advice to enjoy the warmth of the new source of human rights centering in the international order. It reads much like another powerful lamentation--that found at the end of Wagner's libretto for Das Rheingold[18]--the first of four operas depicting aspects of the *Nibelungenlied.*[19] As Das Rheingold ends, the Rhein maidens from whose care the Rhein gold has been stolen and then cursed, cry for the return of their lost gold to Wotan and the other gods as they enter Valhalla. Their pleas are dismissed as it is suggested that they instead bask in the golden splendor of the god's new home.[20]

> **Rhine Daughters** *(in the valley, unseen)* Rhine-gold! Rhine-gold! guileless gold! how brightly and clear shimmered thy beams on us!
> * * *
> **Loge** *(calling down toward the valley)* You there in the water; why have you come crying to us? Hear what Wotan grants you! If the [Rhine] gold no longer gleams for you. Then from now on bask instead in the new splendor of the gods *(The gods laugh and cross the bridge during the following.)*
> **Rhine Daughters** Rhine-gold! Rhine-gold! guileless gold! O would that thy treasure were glittering yet in the deep! Tender and true 'tis but in the waters: false and base are

---

[18] Richard Wagner, Das Rheingold WWV 86A (1869).

[19] See, Arthur Thomas Hatto, *The Nibelungenlied* (Oxford: Penguin Classics, 1964).

[20] This relationship is explored as well from the perspective of the internal political community of Hong Kong in the shadow of the National Security Law passed in 2020, and to the same passage in essay Chapter 25, infra.

all who revel above! *(As the gods cross the bridge to the castle, the curtain falls.)*[21]

And thus, the start of the Special Procedures Statement, and the opening of its keening: "UN independent experts have repeatedly communicated with the Government of the People's Republic of China their alarm regarding the repression of fundamental freedoms in China." In translation to the more literary language form which it draws: 'we have called to you; we have called to you. . .and you have not answered.' The unanswered calls strike at the heart of the global human rights project as it seeks to project itself within China only to be repelled at its borders. The list is long but also a comprehensive assessment of the great gulf that separates the *weltanschauung* of the global human rights project from the human rights framework of Chinese Marxist-Leninism.

What is the essence of the keening? *The principal one is that of authority.* It is not just the "repression of fundamental freedoms", but rather the repression of those freedoms as their meaning has been constructed by the international community within which they serve as the vanguard. That suggests, almost immediately a conflict of authority (especially one understood in Leninist terms). The Special Procedures--and the apparatus of the international community has constituted itself the leading force, the Leninist vanguard, of human rights. Their guidance is both necessary and a condition precedent, to the authentication of the legitimacy of the actions of states and other actors within their constitutive orders.

It is not so much the violations of human rights that is at issue here, as it is the authority of the international human rights vanguard to exercise leadership and authoritative guidance with respect to its meaning and application within states. It is to their leadership that states must open their doors; it is to them that

---

[21] "Das Rheingold" by Richard Wagner libretto (English Swap German); available
[http://www.murashev.com/opera/Das_Rheingold_libretto_English_German].

states must account. They represent, in Leninist terms, the leading elements of global society with the authority to guide states toward the fulfillment of their fundamental obligations--in this case NOT to establish a communist society (the traditional expression of MARXIST-Leninism)--but to organize themselves within the taboos of international human rights law, principles and sensibilities under the leadership of the Special Procedures and the administrative organs of public international organizations.

China's rejection of those principles constitute a reactionary error. It is an error that must be corrected. That correction. in turn, requires China to "return home"--to accept the authority of the leading elements of global society and conform to their leadership in matters of global human rights, constituted as the basic premises of legitimate institutional organization in the world. But China has inverted this forma. And in a sense that is the ultimate irony of the keening. China acknowledges the fundamental power of the principle of Leninist organization and the right of the leading social forces to guide society toward the fundamental normative goals that are from their point of view inevitable. It is just that the Chinese Communist Party sees itself in the role of fundamental vanguards--and it sees its own normative order, as the supreme basis for ordering political. social, and economic reality. In inversion the possibility of effective interaction reduces itself to a very small space.

The secondary element of the keening is that of meaning. It is not enough to seize for one's collective self the mantle of vanguard leadership. One must also attach a moral order to that leadership. For the Chinese Communist Party those are expressed in Marxist principles as an evolving iterative process within the state .[22] For the UN apparatus (and generally within the leading elements in power in the West) the anchor of the moral-political order lies within international human rights law and norms expressed through the actions of duly constituted public international bodies allied with representative elements of states, civil society and other institutions (religious, economic, etc.). But

---

[22] Discussed in essay Chapter 30, infra.

that is not enough. It is in the authority of the vanguard to apply the moral order that the system is constructed. China has ruptured that system--and ruptured it thoroughly--by interposing the moral superiority of its own vanguard, and their authority to interpret and apply their own moral-political order, over that of the international human rights vanguard and the recognition and application of the global human rights moral-political order.

It is those oppositions that lie at the heart of the Special Procedures Statement. The key is the combination of the authority of the international order, and its authoritativeness sin identifying and interpreting (that is in giving meaning to) the basic moral-political elements with which the state must align their own (subordinate) constitutive orders. Here, China has made clear (like the United States), that it draws from but is not bound to the construction of the ordering premises of the international human rights order in operating its own moral-political order. Likewise, it does not recognize the supremacy of the international vanguard as the interpreter of those international norms from which it draws.

Understood in that way, and only in that way, does the Special Procedures Statement derive its power. And, indeed, if one accepts the core structural premises around which the Statement was built, its projection of discursive power and authority, as a performance of the vision of a world order it represents, is then both direct, clear, and well crafted. But the Chinese do not believe, and they cannot accept these core structural premises without betraying the fundamental principles on which their own political order is built. And that provides the great tension in the Statement's focus on Hong Kong.

China has rejected the primary authority of globally aligned political and civil rights--and has instead embraced a model of human rights in which security, economic, social, and cultural rights are centered. The liberal democratic camp takes the opposite view. China has adopted a relationship between the state and international organs as one requiring strict compliance with the international obligations of states, but like the American states that would eventually form the Confederate States of

America, they also believe that it is for the state to determine the meaning of that strict compliance. They reject other approaches as bullying and interference in domestic affairs, when undertaken by international bodies (but not of course when between states these are used to protect and perhaps project national interests). And they have firmly rejected the idea that public international law, including treaties, may penetrate the borders of states to constrain the ability of the state to organize its internal affairs to suit its political-economic model.

These are the *rejections that are so deeply lamented* in the Special Procedures Statement: *China rejects* the obligation to embed itself deeply within the leadership and guidance structures of international organs. *China rejects* the supremacy in its internal governance. *China rejects* the global human rights approach to the meaning of religious and civil liberties and to its authority to fashion its citizens according to its own moral-political principles, especially where that involves coercive elements. *China rejects* the authority of international instruments to constrain its internal political arrangements. *China rejects* any effort to reconstitute Hong Kong in language that suggests its distinctiveness sufficient to support even a limited amount of self-determination. *China rejects* the duty to conform to the behavior standards followed by other (even a vast majority of other) states. *China rejects* the idea that it must open its door to foreigners, especially foreign elements representing a vanguard bent on challenging its own internal leadership. And *China rejects* the principle that it is under any obligation to account to foreigners with respect to the application of its own political-moral order within the territory over which it claims sovereignty.

Turned around, these are the rejections around which the Special Procedures Statement is written. And in that writing, the Statement describes a world that is likely no longer attainable.

It is a world which recognizes the authority of a global community of actors to develop, by consensus and within representative international institutions, the basic principles within which all states and other actors would be bound to conform their behavior.

It is a world in which international law and international norms in whatever form crafted, would be respected by non-state actors, and embedded into the constitutive orders of all states.

It is a world in which the basic operation system of politics, law, economics, and morals, would be driven by, and interpreted through, the lens of human rights. *It is a world* in which the United Nations organs would constitute the common meeting place within which the global community would meet to bind themselves, hold each other to account, and enforce communal norms.

It is a world grounded in individual, rather than collective, human dignity. It is a world in which civil and political rights serve as the means of preserving authority as a sovereign element of the masses.

It is a world in which borders became permeable, porous, and retained to the extent it serves as a means of more efficiently enforcing global norms.

It is a world grounded in the basic operation principles of prevention, mitigation, and remediation of human rights. It is a world in which meaning is made collectively at the global level but implementation (supervised and subject to accountability measures) is undertaken locally.

This is the world of the golden age of global international human rights that emerged after 1945 and took on its definitive shape from the 1980s. Yet it is also a world whose ordering premises no longer appear to represent the forward movement of a united normative vanguard.

This is the world, however, that made aspiration of Hong Kong self-determination within China under the protection of principles of international law possible--at least conceptually. Only in this world, and during the golden age of human rights global internationalism, could Hong Kong be constituted as a creature of international law. Hong Kong is understood as having developed a distinctive "personality" that must be protected against interference by central authorities. Hong Kong is understood to fall squarely within the realization of civil and political rights as these have emerged in international organs, one that constrains the state from exercising authority to preserve order or interfere with individual activity except as developing international practice approves. And these are all the conceptions of Hong Kong now publicly and decisively rejected by China. And in the face of that rejection, the best the old order can do is to muster its most vulnerable elements--the Special Procedures with a mandate and little authority--rather than the community of states themselves--that appear to be able to muster the courage to do their duty by the system that generations have sacrificed to build. In the end, then, the Statement is as much a lamentation about the power of China to transform the global collective to something more to its liking, as it is a lamentation of the system itself to preserve its integrity to, exercise collective leadership.

Lastly, it should not bear repeating, but in this age perhaps everything bears repeating, that the system within which the Special Procedures are embedded is hardly necessarily doomed to the trash heap of history. The lamentation can be as much for change as it is for endings. Indeed, it is likely that one can see in the Special Procedures Statement the start of the Silver Age of global human rights internationalism, one in which states recede from the center, and the staffs of international organizations move to the forefront. Nor is it necessarily inevitable that as the old forms of global human rights internationalism and defenses of self-determination recede that Chinese Marxist Leninism will triumph as the basis of the post global international order rather than something else. Nor, again, is the passing of the old order golden age either a good or necessary objective, the wisps of the passing of which are embalmed in the Special Procedures Statement and so embalmed now transformed into an object of (reactionary) aspiration. It is not necessary to believe in the value of either, or even to believe in the necessary permanence of particular political-moral orders at the domestic or international level to understand the insights that the Special Procedure Statement provides as discourse, and as evidence of the current historical era and its self-conceptions, hopes, fears, and habits.

However, the convergence of those forces at this stage of historical development, and their conflict, cast an important light on the way that one historical epoch is indeed giving ground to another--the characteristics of which remain to be revealed.

For global human rights internationalists, Hong Kong represents tragedy and a challenge to the political-moral order that emerged after 1945 and continues to develop. For China, Hong Kong represents the tragedy of the dead hand--of the conflation of historical colonialism with contemporary international human rights regimes. Both actors embrace nostalgia here--for quite incompatible visions. Both seek to journey back home--to a time and place that is not the present. The intensity of that nostalgia is palpable in the Special Procedure Statement, but in equal measure in the Chinese insistence on pressing forward with the domestication of Hong Kong and the subordination of international obligations to domestic imperatives.

In either sense, this tragedy is one that has been in the making from the 1980s. It is a tragedy that embodies a central contradiction of the current global order, one that produced the entrapment of Hong Kong between two increasingly combative and incompatible ideological foundations of political-moral systems. Hong has been situated since the 1980s between the international community now come into its own and states now fully ready to seize an out-sized sovereignty decades after that became unfashionable among developed states. And Hong Kong serves as the space in which the continuing and unresolved issue of the indivisibility of human rights continue to play out against the backdrop of the division of those rights since the 1970s, as a matter of international law, between civil and political rights, and economic, social and political rights.

$$* \quad * \quad *$$

Chapter 2

Saturday 15 June 2019
The Clash of Empires? Playing With Fire in the Shadow of the Umbrella Movement

There is a great sense of expectation on the streets now. What had started out as a mass outpouring of protest against the extradition law,[23] now appears to have taken on a life of its own. People see in this movement forward a trajectory similar to that of the Umbrella Movement of five years earlier. They do not believe the central authorities in Beijing will act decisively against them—they dare the Central authorities to respond. For the protesters, the Umbrella Movement set the template for mass engagement and protests within One Country Two Systems; they may assume some of compromise and relatedly weak reprisals as an end game. Officials may believe that reprisals will energize the international community to threaten Chinese interests in ways that they could not ignore. Hong Kong may be Chinese, I am told,

---

[23] The Fugitive Offenders and Mutual Legal Assistance in Criminal Matters Legislation (Amendment) Bill 2019 (2019 年逃犯及刑事事宜相互法律協助法例（修訂）條例草案)); available [https://www.hklii.hk/eng/hk/legis/ord/503/index.html] Chinese version available [https://www.hklii.hk/chi/hk/legis/ord/503/]. It had been introduced 29 March 2019 and had its first reading 3 April 209. Its most controversial provisions would allow criminal suspects to be sent to Mainland China for trial and the great fear was that the amendments would provide Mainland authorities with a power to reach into Hong Kong to punish its critics. The view from the Mainland was very different, increasingly frustrated by the ability, for example, of Mainland Chinese, to use Hong Kong as a place to escape investigation and punishment for corruption. The idea that Chinese authorities could not reach into every inch of the national territory to advance its core objectives was becoming increasingly intolerable. Between 2014 and 2017 there was increasingly little middle ground on which to fashion face saving compromises. This became clearer in retrospect. See David Lague, James Pomfret and Greg Torode Fil, "Special Report: How murder, kidnappings and miscalculation set off Hong Kong's revolt," *Reuters* (20 Dec. 2019); available [https://www.reuters.com/investigates/special-report/hongkong-protests-extradition-narrative/]. In the end, tough, it was not the Extradition Bill but the New National Security Law that would set the stage for realizing the greatest fears of those seeking to maintain Hong Kong's status quo.

but it is an international city as well.[24] It is the ultimate special political zone, suspended between a vigorous international community and a rising Chinese state power.

Among the people themselves one senses the cultivation and now explosion of a powerful and powerfully pure sense of being wronged by officials who are exceeding their authority and abusing their discretion. At least as manifested on the streets, those who participate in these manifestations of the will of masses believe, perhaps naively that a showing of sincerity of the sort projected worldwide on the 9th might cause the central authorities to reconsider and to forebear, at least for a little while longer. For the central authorities, the protests present an ideological conundrum. On the one hand they might treat it as the opening expression of action under the mass line the response to which can then be guided by the vanguard under the principle of from the people to the people. In this sense the protests present a golden opportunity to demonstrate the way that Leninist ideology is flexible enough to be practiced even under conditions of autonomy. This evolves from Mao Zedong's notion of the "mass line" as "The Marxist theory of knowledge."[25] However, there is a fear, already present, that the alternative path may prove more alluring to central authorities--one that views the protests not

---

[24] See, Roda Mushkat, *One Country, Two International Legal Personalities: The Case of Hong Kong* (Hong Kong University Press, 1997).

[25] Mao Zedong, "Some Questions Concerning Methods of Leadership" (1 June 1943),Marxists.com   website;   available [https://www.marxists.org/reference/archive/mao/selected-works/volume-3/mswv3_13.htm], ¶4.

> In all the practical work of our Party, all correct leadership is necessarily "from the masses, to the masses". This means: take the ideas of the masses (scattered and unsystematic ideas) and concentrate them (through study turn them into concentrated and systematic ideas), then go to the masses and propagate and explain these ideas until the masses embrace them as their own, hold fast to them and translate them into action, and test the correctness of these ideas in such action. Then once again concentrate ideas from the masses and once again go to the masses so that the ideas are persevered in and carried through. And so on, over and over again in an endless spiral, with the ideas becoming more correct, more vital and richer each time. Such is the Marxist theory of knowledge.

merely as a threat to local authorities but as an infection that may challenge the authority of the vanguard itself.

My optimism about the potential presented here, even for the central authorities, is necessarily dampened with a strong dose of worry. Chinese authorities do not respond positively to perceived threats; and sometimes the authorities tend to err on the side of treating expressions as a threat and not an opportunity, even when what appears as a threat might eb managed through the application of the vanguards' leadership and working style. More importantly, the Chinese central authorities had shown a remarkable ability to exercise patience. They had shown a talent for retribution from the flanks. And they had been clearly signaling a substantial movement toward a reinvigoration of Leninism that points to the inevitability of change in the relationship between the central authorities in Beijing and those of the Hong Kong SAR.

More than that, the central authorities have been showing increasing frustration that is tied to an inability to reach into Hong Kong to more comprehensively implement core political objectives both within the Mainland and in the Special Administrative Areas--especially Hong Kong. All of this has been brewing, and is well known to be brewing, in the shadow of the Umbrella Movement of 2014. [26] It is unlikely that the central authorities have forgotten or perhaps even forgiven, what they might have viewed as failures and challenges which have largely gone unmet. While to the West the Umbrella Movement might by some appear to be destined for the back pages of the history of the periphery, it might well remain on the central authorities" list of unfinished business.

All of this appears lost to or dismissed by the so-called foreign friends of those who were marching. I fear that the

---

[26] And, of course, the Umbrella Movement was merely a more pronounced eruption of mass passion that had manifested itself before 2014 as well. See Tim Nicholas Rühlig, "Expressing my attitude and doing something impossible to make it happen ..."– Listening to the Voices of Hong Kong's Umbrella Movement Protesters," *Contemporary Chinese Political Economy and Strategic Relations: An International Journal* 3(2):747-818 (2017).

academics, politicians, civil society elements and governments, many comfortably based abroad, and all so very adept at manufacturing words, sentiments, and the simulacra of support from a safe distance, will eventually sacrifice what they have advanced as their internationalist positions respecting the SAR if only to ensure their own interests. Those thoughts augment my pessimism. I have every confidence that foreigners will continue to be brilliant at lending ideological support, but will not (perhaps cannot--a view held by some elements of the central authorities) really lend any support which imposed substantial costs or risks on them. That suggests that all it will take for the eventual suppression of these protests is a well targeted and calculated augmentation in the costs to foreign defenders of Hong Kong's protestors.

My greatest fear is grounded in false hope. My worry is that the idealism which appears to be so much a part of these manifestations that started on and have since intensified since 9 June 2019 have no anchor in the pragmatic realities of the Hong Kong's situation in the world. Indeed, these events at this time might well be the moment that the central authorities in Beijing might finish the clean-up they started after the end of the active phase of the Umbrella Movement. But why stop there; the protests also might provide the central authorities with the necessary excuse to transform the One Country - Two Systems principle. It is possible that even the most well intentioned and patriotic demonstrators are misreading the aspirations (and the ability) of the international community, starting with the United Kingdom, to protect them. I suspect that the West, despite its bleating about international law, would do little to protect contemporary civil and political life in Hong Kong in the face of force.

At the same time, the realities of the end game for Hong Kong are quite clear. The SAR is integral part of the People's Republic; the SAR is necessarily a political unit is subordinate to the central authorities. This is a reality that can only be postponed to 2047 by the international community. Nonetheless, the protests are fueled, it seems, by an underlying belief that even within the constraints of formal territorial sovereignty they might still achieve a measure of self-determination that extends even beyond 2047[27] and one that does not rely on the legalities of the Sino-UK Joint Declaration.[28]

In any case, it is not clear at this point that the international community has offered more, or even that it has started working through the implications of taking Hong Kong's situation out of the constraining framework of the Sino-British Joint Declaration of 1984[29] ration and basing protection of its autonomy, at least with respect to the development of its political culture, on an international law basis of some other sort. That would require the development of notions of shared sovereignty likely repugnant to the Chinese and other states as well. At the other extreme, independence was and is out of the question especially given the state of world politics in the summer of 2019. Political demonstrations are a risky way of inducing the central authorities to exercise a discretion in favor of continued political autonomy for the SAR of the sort it had enjoyed for twenty years or so. This holds true even though and perhaps because liberal democratic states tend to be quite fond of this technique especially when it manifests itself in other countries whose governmental systems are incompatible with the ideologies of their own.

My fears grow with the growing intensity of the protests. What started out as a huge demonstration of Hong Kong poplar will on 9 June has begun to become more violent, and the stakes appear to be growing higher even as the respective positions of

---

[27] Ibid., (my interview quotations reveal their relevance and demonstrate that we better understand them as part of a broader agenda for self-determination which plays out in four dimensions: democratic self-determination and the reform of the Chief Executive elections; social and economic self-determination; self-determination in terms of Hong Kong's unique identity; and institutional and political self-determination aiming at a far-reaching autonomy of the city if not independence. Ibid., 751).

[28] Joint Declaration of the Government of the United Kingdom of Great Britain and Northern Ireland and the Government of the People's Republic of China on the Question of Hong Kong (19 December 1984); available [https://www.cmab.gov.hk/en/issues/jd2.htm] (hereafter the Sino-UK Joint Declaration).

[29] Sino-UK Joint Declaration, supra.

Hong Kong Between "One Country" and "Two Systems"
2. The Clash of Empires?

24

the parties appear to harden. The use of rubber bullets on protestors, the closing of government offices on the 12th do not augur well for the future. And the decision today by Ms. Lam to indefinitely delay the Extradition Law has satisfied no one.[30] It seems that the parties are coming very close to a point of no return. That is what I fear most. Once that point is reached, once the central authorities decide that Hong Kong is irretrievably out of control, they are likely to step in. I have no illusions about the value of foreign friendships at that point; even more diminished are any illusions about the willingness of foreign states to intervene. The foreign friends of the protestors might at that point reflect on the value of intervention and pull back. One wonders the extent to which the central authorities are already banking on that eventuality. It is certainly a gamble, but is it one on which state policy responses can be built?

In the end the best they can hope for is the preservation of an ambiguous autonomy grounded in international agreements that stipulate that the area is part of Chinese territory. Pragmatically, at this point, it seems likely that, in any case, China officially will have a fully free hand within that territory by the end of the term of the Sino-British Joint Declaration of 1984.[31] And yet, there may be value n even limited intervention--not necessarily for the direct benefit of the Hong Kong protestors and their objectives, but in the competition among great states for the authority to drive the narrative and determine the value (good or bad) of state conduct. China might well achieve its objectives but at a perhaps substantial cost to its international ambitions.

My Western friends think this line of reasoning is implausible. My American friends are convinced that the United States, if not the U.K., will act vigorously in defense of Hong Kong

---

[30] "Hong Kong extradition law: government may pause passage of fugitive bill" *South China Morning Post* (14 June 2019); available [https://www.scmp.com/yp/discover/news/hong-kong/article/3055366/hong-kong-extradition-law-government-may-pause-passage] ("SCMP has learned that the Hong Kong government will hit the pause button on passing the controversial extradition bill as early as Saturday afternoon, after Beijing officials in charge of the city's affairs held meetings in Shenzhen to map a viable way out of the impasse.")
[31] Sino-UK Joint Declaration, supra.

and its liberties. But Americans have become better at talking about these things than of following through. Their elites are bitterly divided. And they are making a blood sport of their own politics. China is too powerful within the institutional structures of the United Nations system for there to be effective countermeasures taken in international organizations. But China can lose face—and face is important as it is embarking on an ambitious project to build from out of its well managed global production chains what appears to be a new form of hierarchical, hub and spoke model post global empire. It can set back Chinese efforts to internationalize the yuan. It might cost China valuable time and effort in the campaign to have a more influential place in international organizations. These are calculations, of course, all being made behind closed doors, and among people whose own agendas, loyalties, weaknesses and strengths remain obscure.

There may then be a sense of the inevitable, a tragic inevitable from the perspective of the people in the streets, to these protests, whether that inevitable occurs now or manages to be avoided until 2047 when it can no longer be put off. The Chinese central authorities *will* have their way; one just does not know when. The unknown is the price the central authorities might be willing to pay, as measured by the damage done to their internal and their external political and economic objectives, .

Let us consider that briefly in an ideological context. More specifically, I want to consider the possible shape of China's eventual end game and the timing of its responses in light to a very useful essay written by one of China's most prominent intellectuals. Jiang Shigong (强世功). Ironically, the essay was published on the eve of the June protests and I read a crude English translation on my flight to Hong Kong on the eve of the start of the protests—it is entitled " The Inner Logic of Super Large Political Entities: "Empire" and World Order" [超大型政治实体的内在逻辑："帝国"与世界秩序].[32] I read this in light of Jiang's earlier and more famous book, *China's Hong Kong : a political and*

---

[32] 强世功：超大型政治实体的内在逻辑："帝国"与世界秩序 [Jiang Shigong, "the internal logic of super-large political entities: "empire" and world order"] (4 June 2019); available [http://www.aisixiang.com/data/115799.html].

Hong Kong Between "One Country" and "Two Systems"
2. The Clash of Empires?

26

cultural perspective,[33] from which important elements of the idea of empire emerged.[34] These works align with my own thinking from twenty years before,[35] though Jiang's is deeply embedded in the ideologies of Marxist-Leninism and mine in the core logic of the post-1945 international order.

My sense is that if Jiang reflects the evolving thinking about China's place in the world, then the actions in Hong Kong will prove intolerable—and quickly. At some point, it seems likely, that China will react, and when it does, it is also likely that the experiment in One Country, Two Systems will be reshaped substantially. But in any case, the imperatives of a more clearly emerging imperial re-ordering, one that both Jiang and I see, though from different perspectives,[36] suggests that a rising post-global imperial power cannot tolerate internal weakness at its core. That intolerance is magnified in systems grounded in highly centralized administrative ideologies, like Chinese New Era Marxist-Leninism. The level of tolerance shrinks even more then internationalism is re-cast as the expression of empire whose order is fundamentally incompatible with that of China[37] and the need to maintain both sovereignty and sovereign order.[38] If the "core of the political system was to adjust policies to local conditions while preserving the centralized system in defense of the sovereignty of the empire," [39] then local conditions that threatened the sovereignty of the empire would have to be

---

[33] Jiang Shigong, *China's Hong Kong : A Political and Cultural Perspective* (Singapore: Springer, 2017).

[34] Ibid., 43-56.

[35] Larry Catá Backer, "Economic Globalization Ascendant: Four Perspectives on the Emerging Ideology of the State in the New Global Order," *Berkeley La Raza Law Journal* 17(1):141 (2006).

[36] For the work undertaken as part of the Coalition for Peace & Ethics Working Group on Empire, see the essays available at the Law at the End of the Day website; available [https://lcbackerblog.blogspot.com/search/label/CPE%20EmpireSeries].

[37] Jiang Shigong, *China's Hong Kong : a political and cultural perspective* (Singapore: Springer, 217), pp. 85-92 ("Hong Kong, the frontline of the clash between Chinese and Western civilizations" (Ibid. p. 85) "might become a base for Western to subvert China and incite civil unrest" (ibid., p. 90).

[38] Ibid., p. 90 (with reference to the historical origins of One Country Two Systems in the early efforts to solidify sovereignty over Tibet).

[39] Ibid., p. 94.

suppressed—sooner or later, And that is the potential tragedy of Hong Kong. More importantly, it did not matter as the forms of 19th century Empire would inevitably give way to 21st century Marxist-Leninist Empire (perhaps with their Western analogue in the US and Europe).[40] It bears stating that it is hardly tolerable within liberal democratic empire, like that of the United States, except that the tolerances and responses will more closely conform to the logic of that political-economic model.

Jiang, correctly I believe, starts by suggesting that the current narrative of sovereignty can effectively be understood as a mirage. "An important problem facing current political thought is the huge gap between the 'expression' of the theory of sovereign states in the mainstream discourse and the 'practice' of imperial politics in general.[41] It is a necessary mirage, of course, one at the heart of the post-1945 settlement that was institutionalized after the 1940s in the UN system and that ushered in the structures of globalization a generation later. Sovereignty and the premise of the formal equality of nations was constructed for two purposes. The first was to develop an ideology through which to transition from traditional territorially based empire to new structures of dependence could be undertaken with little dislocation.[42] The second was to ensure substantial flexibility in the new forms of dominance and dependence that made room for additional changes.[43]

---

[40] "However, watching the television footage of Thatcher's stumbling on the last step out of the Great Hall of the People after meeting Deng Xiao Ping, the superstitious Hong Kongers seemed to realize that Britain had lost to China on the issue of Hong Kong." Ibid., p. 117.

[41] In the original: "当前政治思想面临的一个重要问题就是主流话语中关于主权国家理论的"表达"与普遍的帝国政治"实践"之间的巨大鸿沟。" 强世功：超大型政治实体的内在逻辑："帝国"与世界秩序 [Jiang Shigong, "the internal logic of super-large political entities: "empire" and world order"] (4 June 2019).

[42] Larry Catá Backer, "God(s) Over Constitutions: International and Religious Transnational Constitutionalism in the 21st Century," *Mississippi College Law Review* 27:11-65 (2007).

[43] Larry Catá Backer, "Economic Globalization Ascendant: Four Perspectives on the Emerging Ideology of the State in the New Global Order," *Berkeley La Raza Law Journal* 17(1):141 (2006), pp. 145-153.

Jiang proposes to change the analytical lens, and in so doing to better reformulate the concept of "empire" for the modern age.

> Different from the concept of 'empire' in traditional ideological discourse, the 'empire' mentioned [in his articulation of the concept] is a descriptive social science concept used to describe a super-large political entity that exists in history [as well as] a philosophical and political effort in pursuit of universalism, that is, constantly universalizing its own form into a wider space and time.[44]

Empire, then, is a term that can be stripped of its most recent historical context—as useful as that has been in the negotiation between subaltern regions and their fading imperial masters while situating themselves within new systems of dominance and dependence. Jiang reduces the concept to a descriptor of the realities of power hierarchies that are manifested in different ways in different historical periods and that use a variety of tools as centering elements depending on the historical epoch. He describes the current epoch of empire as one of the "development and evolution of the 'Empire of the World' [from out of which] can we transcend the ideology of the sovereign state, understand the role of China today in the historical evolution of world empires, and contribute to China's future development."[45]

---

[44] 强世功：超大型政治实体的内在逻辑："帝国"与世界秩序 [Jiang Shigong, "the internal logic of super-large political entities: "empire" and world order"] (4 June 2019) ("不同于传统意识形态话语中的"帝国"概念，本文所说的"帝国"乃是一种描述性的社会科学概念，用来描述一种普遍存在于历史中的超大型政治实体，它既是一种包含内在复杂多样性的稳定秩序，也是一种追求普遍主义 (universalism) 的哲学思想和政治努力，即不断将自身形态普遍化到更广阔的时空之中。").

[45] In the original: "当前，人类历史正处在"世界帝国"（the Empire of the World）发展和演变的重要历史时刻。唯有从帝国的视角出发，理解帝国在历史演变中形成的不同形态，我们才能超越主权国家这一意识形态，理解今天中国在世界帝国的历史演进中所扮演的角色，并为中国未来的发展指明方向。" 强世功：超大型政治实体的内在逻辑："帝国"与世界秩序 [Jiang Shigong, "the internal logic of super-large political entities: "empire" and world order"] (4 June 2019).

Hong Kong Between "One Country" and "Two Systems"
2. The Clash of Empires?

29

Jiang spends much the essay in a useful analysis of the realities of sovereignty within the framework of the imperial structures he sees. His discussion is worth deep study, especially the notion of sovereignty, and its degrees, as mere expression of degrees of autonomy within imperial orders.[46] Much of it reflects a quite specifically manifested focus by Chinese elites on the Americans, their imperial ordering, and their inability to assert enough political will to keep it either their system or their imperial ordering intact. That sense of inability, that judgment about the weakening of strength of political character, then, in the minds of elements of the Chinese elite, reveals a fundamental ideological weakness that begs for a substitution by a system whose ideological convictions are stronger.

This is a set of political views and judgments that has been a generation or more in the making. The discussion of the formation of reginal civilization empires (区域性文明帝国的形成) is also useful as a perspective that is not embedded within millennia old western narratives but instead in equally ancient narratives from a different core power center. The discussion of the differences between and competition among oceanic and continental empires (大陆帝国与海洋帝国的全球竞争) also adds an important dimension, especially in the suggestion of the techniques of each and their quite distinct approaches to the apparatus of dominion as they (inevitably?) compete. The development nicely situates theory within a Marxist-Leninist context of progression through and the constraints of the realities of emerging, dominating, and fading historical eras—*sic transit gloria mundi.*

---

[46] Ibid., Where he noted: "It can be said that the sovereign state order is a special imperial form; without thinking about imperial competition and the construction of a new imperial order, we cannot even understand the concept of a sovereign state. Therefore, we must reorganize history from the perspective of empire and rethink the construction of sovereign states from the perspective of the construction of imperial order." [而且，主权国家的政治活动往往是以帝国秩序为担保的，可以说主权国家秩序乃是一种特殊的帝国形态；离开了对帝国竞争与建构新型帝国秩序的思考，我们甚至连主权国家这个概念都无法理解。因此，我们必须从帝国的视角来重新梳理历史，从帝国秩序建构的角度来重新思考主权国家的建构。].

I agree with Jiang's views about the centering of empire, especially after 1945. But I am less sure than Jiang about the existence of a stable and singular 'Empire of the World.'[47] My sense was that empire had never coalesced around a unipolar imperial power—that narrative was merely the expression of the propaganda (and quite useful in its time) of those seeking the development of multipolarity in empire making. Instead what Jiang sees as a single 'Empire of the World' I tend to understand as the idealized end object of empire in the current historical era, but that there are at least three quite distinct roads that are being travelled by the large power-hub states to get there.

> Perhaps less well understood is the way in which major views of globalization all tend to posit the end conceptions of globalization. More interesting still is that even the great anti-globalization perspectives do little to defend the traditional state system. Whatever the form of opposition, each essentially posits a global system in which the state plays a subordinate role. [48]

---

[47] Ibid., ("冷战结束后，美国抛开联合国乃至国际条约的单边主义，恰恰表明美国主导的"世界帝国"建构已经完成；今天无论是中国还是俄罗斯，都处在美国主导的"世界帝国"体系中。" [After the end of the Cold War, the United States put aside the unilateralism of the United Nations and even international treaties, which just showed that the United States-led "world empire" construction has been completed; today, both China and Russia are in the US-led "world empire" system. (]) Jiang's view that China and the Russian Federation are currently within the US-led 'world empire' system, may be overstating the case. First it overstates and may not completely well characterize the way that the old globalization model was constructed and operated (though it does reflect the hopes for certain members of the American ruling elites during the Clinton Administration in the euphoria of the fall of the Soviet Union). This is indeed alluded to with the reference to the "end of history" narrative popular among elites before the start of the 21st century. Second, it understates the extent of Chinese imperial autonomy more clearly visible since the start of the leadership of Xi Jinping—an autonomy the object of which had never been hidden by Chinese vanguard elements, just ignored by their counterparts in the West.
[48] Larry Catá Backer, "Economic Globalization Ascendant: Four Perspectives on the Emerging Ideology of the State in the New Global Order," *Berkeley La Raza Law Journal* 17(1):141 (2006), p. 142.

I posited three major approaches to empire in the current era. Only the first is considered by Jiang—the so-called Washington consensus of markets driven multilateral internationally institutionalized economic and political relations grounded in liberal democratic values. But there are two others—including theories of Empire that Jiang himself had earlier noted in the building of Chinese Marxist Leninist imperial structures.[49] The first is a state centered globalization, one in which the great imperial powers form the hubs of great systems of dependence fashioned together through the bounds of the organization of production and systems of mutual security. The second is a developing state centered system of globalization that produces a set of hollowed out states the wealth of which is owned by and operated through others, leaving to the state itself nothing more than to serve as the jailer for its labor resources.[50] Thus, China is no passive piece within another's new era empire, but a hub-power state seizing the moment of this stage of its historical development to (re)assert its own imperial dominion, but compatible with the characteristics of the times.

Jiang has made clear that the process of political control—be it Marxist-Leninist vanguard politics or the mass politics of liberal democracies—are all aspects of the extension and protection of imperial dependence around the metropolitan hub of empire.[51] In this case the Marxist Leninist Empire of China and the liberal democratic empire of the United States.[52] The former

---

[49] Jiang Shigong, *China's Hong Kong : a political and cultural perspective* (Singapore: Springer, 217).

[50] Larry Catá Backer, "Economic Globalization Ascendant: Four Perspectives on the Emerging Ideology of the State in the New Global Order," *Berkeley La Raza Law Journal* 17(1):141 (2006), p. 154-.162

[51] "The pushing of the democratic system around the world [and in Hong Kong] by Britain and America was often in the hope of using the ballot box to establish democracies for elites and even oligarchs who were actually dependent on British and American strength." Jiang Shigong, , *China's Hong Kong : a political and cultural perspective* , supra., p. 165.

[52] See Larry Catá Backer, "Economic Globalization Ascendant: Four Perspectives on the Emerging Ideology of the State in the New Global Order," *Berkeley La Raza Law Journal* 17(1):141 (2006) ("State Power Convergence and the Crisis of the State" Ibid., pp. 154-158). I noted that "globalization will usher in a new world order of caricatured states in which adherence to the forms of the traditional

Hong Kong Between "One Country" and "Two Systems"
2. The Clash of Empires?

32

building its empire around the Belt and Road Initiative, the latter having built its empire within the universalist retentions of economic globalization.[53] The empire might tolerate the small demonstration; it might tolerate a boisterous press, to a point anyway. It might also tolerate criticism, but it is unlikely to tolerate anything that is interpreted to signal a pulling away from the authority of the central authority to set and enforce the grounds rules through which Hong Kong's special relationship is managed and operated.

Jiang's perspective, then, is important for understanding what may well come from the insubordination of a territory, not at the periphery of China's emerging imperial structures, but at its very center. It speaks to a larger perspective of a powerful actor whose views tend to be sidelined.[54] At the same time, Hong Kong becomes extremely sensitive precisely because it serves as a constant reminder of the humiliations of the forms of empire that were effectively swept away with the end of the Second World War. The Chinese imperial apparatus remains unfinished as long as either the intrusion of a faded empire (the UK) remains pointed like a dagger aimed at the heart of China. That, however, has an end date—2047—if the Chinese are willing to be patient. But events since 2012 have suggested a substantially growing impatience.

More importantly, the determination that the UK's empire, of little account, has been inherited, transformed and is now

---

state system will serve as a cover for a global system operated by a corrupted aristocracy. . . of super states and associated non-state actors. Ibid., p. 156.

[53] Lee Jaehyon , "China Is Recreating the American 'Hub-and-Spoke' System in Asia," *The Diplomat* (11 September 2015); available [https://thediplomat.com/2015/09/china-is-recreating-the-american-hub-and-spoke-system-in-asia/] ("Chinese Chairman Xi has described this hub-and-spoke as system that the U.S. serves as the hub while Asian nations with military ties to it form the spokes. . . As China's Marching Westward policy starts to gain momentum, Asia's political, security, and economic systems are being reshuffled and a Chinese-style hub-and-spoke system is emerging. ").

[54] Jiang Shigong. *China's Hong Kong : A Political and Cultural Perspective* (Singapore: Springer, 2017) "The mainstream approach about Hong Kong or China is either from the western viewpoint or Hong Kong's own perspective on Hong Kong, or Hong Kong's perspective on China. Seldom do we see a narrative that is from China's perspective on Hong Kong." Ibid., p. 211).

operated through the US and its globalization empire apparatus raises the stakes. One need not worry so much about the meowing of a decrepit empire. But one might worry more where a more vigorous power has come into possession of something (Hong Kong) that could cause one injury. That worry becomes evident in Jiang's treatment of the transformation of his notion of a singular 'World Empire' from the British to the Americans.[55] From that perspective, and thinking in terms of traditional Chinese imperial characteristics, "A new imperialism model in which the United States inherited the "imperialism" developed in the late British Empire, but replaced the pound sterling with the U.S. dollar, while Japan and Western Europe are similar to the "autonomous territories" of the British Empire for the United States."[56] And underlying this is the notion that if the 'World Empire' is to be preserved, it must be undertaken by China, or the world runs the risk of a takeover by yet a very different empire, that which Jiang describes as one constructed by Islamic fundamentalists.[57]

And if Jiang's views reflect those of the Chinese leadership core（领导核心）—and there is no reason that they are inconsistent with Chinese "New Era" ideology or the Basic Line of the Chinese Communist Party—then any sign of instability within the heartland of an imperial model requires immediate attention to protect the integrity of the system. In this case, it might also provide that imperial system with the excuse necessary to (re) absorb the territory without regard to the political niceties of the Sino-British Arrangement. In the process two things will likely emerge: The first is the recognition of the final passage of the old

---

[55] 强世功：超大型政治实体的内在逻辑：“帝国”与世界秩序 [Jiang Shigong, "the internal logic of super-large political entities: "empire" and world order"] (4 June 2019) ("World Empire" First Edition: From Britain to America [“世界帝国”第一版：从英国到美国”]).

[56] Ibid., (“一种是美国继承了大英帝国晚期发展起来的“帝国主义”的新帝国模式，只不过用美元取代了英镑，而日本、西欧对于美国而言就类似于大英帝国的“自治领地””)

[57] Ibid. (“因此，未来的世界只能在此基础上进一步向前并加以重构，而无法彻底将此加以颠覆，除非整个世界退回到伊斯兰原教旨主义者所建构的世界帝国。” ["Therefore, the future world can only move forward and reconstruct on this basis, and cannot completely subvert this unless the entire world retreats to the world empire constructed by Islamic fundamentalists."])

imperial regimes of the 19th century and any shred of a fig leaf of UK authority or influence (other than as a subaltern power within either the EU or American imperial structures, whatever the outcomes of Brexit). The second is the clearer unveiling of the forms of the New Era Chinese imperial apparatus.

None of this, of course, is of significant interest to the millions in Hong Kong. While the leadership core of the Central authorities may have the Americans squarely in their sights, and empire on their plate, Hong Kong sees yellow. It sees the Umbrella Movement. It adheres to a way of thinking about their place in the world, and within the constellation that is China in ways that they might have thought benign but which may well have the opposite effect. The central authorities likely see yellow as well; they see the Umbrella Movement, but they are likely to draw quite different conclusions. They might see in the Umbrella Movement the fruit of the subversive seed planted by the retreating British to foment a situation that might lead to a viable movement of independence for Hong Kong. [58] But this may not suggest independence in the classical sense—rather might potentially open a different door, one to independence as a means of detaching Hong Kong from the Chinese and attaching it to the American imperial order,[59] something that the Chinese central

---

[58] Tim Nicholas Rühlig, "Expressing my attitude and doing something impossible to make it happen," supra, pp. 762-778 (aiming at self-determination).

[59] Here again, Jiang is quite explicit. See Jiang Shigong, *China's Hong Kong : a political and cultural perspective* (Singapore: Springer, 217) He notes with respect to the actions of the last U-K. administrator of the Crown Colony: "Patten's political reform plans aimed to strengthen the independence of Hong Kong by creating a political force to confront that of the central government." Ibid., p. 169. And with respect to democratization itself he explains that "democratization of Hong Kong as also the core issue in the state-building. At present, Hong Kong is like a " British colony without the British actual rule, " because the scars on the soul of the Chinese people (including Hong Kong people) caused by Patten 's political reform package rendered political identification in the country is nation-building very sensitive and fragile. . . If the democratization of Hong Kong comes in conflict with the authority of the Basic Law and the sovereign authority of the central government, the central government is bound to use its sovereign authority to curb radical democratic development in Hong Kong." Ibid., p. 200). That is precisely the way that first the Umbrella Movement, and now potentially this current round of protests against the extradition law may be viewed. See also ibid., p. 122.

Hong Kong Between "One Country" and "Two Systems"
2. The Clash of Empires?

35

authorities will not let happen. The shadow of the Umbrella Movement is local in Hong Kong, but it touches a quite sensitive imperial nerve in Beijing. And that might be a problem that will cause both sides to (mis)calculate.

To some extent, the grievances and fears expressed by people in Hong Kong are local. They have always tended to be local even when they implicate core issues of politics and international affairs. For a long time, theirs was a closed and insular world. But Shenzhen sits at their order. And Guangzhou is just down the road. And the Pearl River is an important element of China's maritime Belt and Road System. And there, again, the clash of empire peaks out. Hong Kong may be seeking are local solutions, yet also solutions buttressed by what I suspect will be the false hope of the crumbled UK empire or the transforming American one (mired as it is in civil war among its elites around the body of Mr. Trump). The greater the provocation, I fear, the more likely both the abandonment and the willingness to unveil Chinese power. The forms that these expressions of power will take remain to be seen—outright military intervention is unlikely. A police action may be more appealing, especially if it can be undertaken by people wearing the Hong Kong forces uniforms. More likely, it will be expressed by some form of use of the mechanics of law against those who have advanced the rule of law project worldwide more likely.

Nonetheless, the thrust of Jiang's analysis should be very much on the minds of those who are either engaged in this great debate within Hong Kong, or those outside of Hong Kong who see in these events an opportunity. In a context in which the Chinese leadership core may style itself as in the running to replace the Americans at the center of the global empire (in the way that the Americans displaced the British after 1945) or of displacing it with their own,[60] Hong Kong becomes a great symbol of those

---

60 强世功：超大型政治实体的内在逻辑："帝国"与世界秩序 [Jiang Shigong, "the internal logic of super-large political entities: "empire" and world order"] (4 June 2019) ("目前，美国在维持世界帝国上面临着巨大的压力，尤其是来自俄罗斯的抵抗和中国的竞争。但我们必须认识到，这种竞争是在世界帝国体系内展开的竞争，是"世界帝国"形成之后争夺帝国经济和政治主导权的斗争，实际上也可以理解为争夺世界帝国首都中心的斗争。" ["At present, the United

struggles and that transition. What to Hong Kong people may seem like an intensely felt but localized set of grievances, may in the eyes of those who manage the great imperial centers, be far ore. And the consequences will be borne by Hong Kong.

The greater pity, then, is that in the deliberate blindness caused by a horror of the recognition or discussion of the imperial form, makes a sounder approach to the issues that constitute the "situation" in Hong Kong. Hong Kong is about empire, and it is about the imperial machinations of the great hub states. That is not how this will be played by their elites, of course. Nor will be it aired this way by a servile and complicit press all too willing to advance what they are served by those engaged in these great transformative contests. Yet to ignore the realities that Hong Kong appears to be a convenient, if potentially tragic, piece of a series of long-term projects, may cause the sort of miscalculations that will produce the worst of all results for Hong Kong itself.

For China, the parameters within which that cost can be calculated is fairly straightforward. It must value the of action against Hong Kong, against the effects that this domestication of Hong Kong may have on its ability to extend authority within its peripheries. Here "One Country Two Systems" takes on quite a different aspect--one core and many systems revolving around but connected to and serving the core. For the core, international law must be rejected as a threat to sovereign integrity (unless of course it is merely the internationalization of domestic law or norms).

For the peripheries, international law must be embraced as the means through which networks of dependencies may be authenticated and domestic power projected outward. To the extent this thinking, this new post global imperialism, guides the Chinese central authorities (and perhaps those of other rising new imperial centers), then Hong Kong itself becomes a critical test of

---

States is facing tremendous pressure to maintain its world empire, especially resistance from Russia and competition from China. But we must realize that this kind of competition is a competition within the world empire system. It is a struggle for the economic and political dominance of the empire after the formation of the "world empire""]).

Hong Kong Between "One Country" and "Two Systems"
2. The Clash of Empires?

37

the model at the periphery of the core or as the core of a well-managed periphery.

✳ ✳ ✳

Chapter 3

Monday 29 July 2019
Mend-Break (Di Xi 抵巇): The Chinese Position on the Situation in Hong Kong; Statement of the Hong Kong and Macau Affairs Office of the State Council [国务院港澳办新闻发言人介绍对香港当前局势的立场和看法]

> A xi (巇 crevice/break) develops into a xia (罅 rift), the xia (罅) to a jian (澗 ravine), and the jian to an abyss. Before a fracture begins, it shows some sign (zhen 朕). It can be filled in to mend; it can be withheld to mend; it can be stopped to mend; it can be concealed to mend; it can be replaced to mend. These are the principles of Mend-Break (di xi 抵巇).[61]

The situation in Hong Kong has become increasingly complicated since the popular reaction against the extradition law erupted into mass street manifestations of popular power during the middle of June. Since then, the situation has become more fluid. The Hong Kong government has at least temporarily withdrawn the extradition law (which triggered these events) and its officials say they will listen better and take popular sentiment into account. [62] But protests have continued and demands

---

[61] Guiguzi (鬼谷子), *Guiguzi: China's First Treatise on Rhetoric; A Critical Translation and Commentary* (Hui Wu (trans.); Carbondale: Southern Illinois University Press, 2016 (before 220 A.D.)); Book I.4.1, pp. 53-54. Guiguzi also serves as a useful framing of strategic and rhetorical choices in other important respects considered in the essays, infra, at Chapters 8 (Assessing (Quan 權)), Chapter 12 (Resist-Reconcile (忤合 Wuhe)), Chapter 20 ((Open-Shut (Bai He 稗閤)), and Chapter 30 (Fundamental Principles (Fu Yan符言)).

[62] "Hong Kong Protestors Seize Government Headquarters, Clash With Police," CBS News (1 July 2019); Available [https://www.cbsnews.com/news/hong-kong-protests-renewed-demonstrations-turn-violent-today-2019-07-01/]. The article quoted Carrie Lam's speech at the commemoration of the transfer of Hong Kong to China: "This has made me fully realize that I, as a politician, have to

Hong Kong Between "One Country" and "Two Systems"
3. Mend-Break (Di Xi 抵巇): The Chinese Position on the Situation in Hong Kong

30

broadened to cover a generalized fear of how the "One Country Two Systems" will actually develop with what is perceived as more vigorous interventions by the central authorities in Beijing.

There has been violence on both sides as is the frustration at a situation that appears both rigidly unending and in that state stubbornly stable. The worst of this included the occupation of a Hong Kong Government building by protestors,[63] and the beating of people at a Hong Kong metro station ostensibly by bandit elements (but rumored to have been in the service of elements of the state apparatus),[64] which then provoked further protests to which police responded with rubber bullets and tear gas.[65] The

---

remind myself all the time of the need to grasp public sentiments accurately, . . . [and that she] will learn the lesson and ensure that the government's future work will be closer and more responsive to the aspirations, sentiments and opinions of the community." Ibid.

[63] James Griffiths, Julia Hollingsworth, Ben Westcott and Eliza Mackintosh, "Hong Kong's Carrie Lam responds to protester takeover of government building," CNN (1 July 2019); available [https://www.cnn.com/2019/07/01/asia/hong-kong-july-1-protest-extradition-intl-hnk/index.html].

[64] Helen Regan, "Fears of thugs-for-hire in Hong Kong after mob attack," *CNN* (23 July 2019); available [https://www.cnn.com/2019/07/23/asia/hong-kong-triad-arrests-intl-hnk/index.html] ("Six men have been arrested in Hong Kong in connection with a seemingly unprovoked and indiscriminate mob attack that injured 45 people at a metro station on Sunday night. . . . Tens of thousands had taken to the streets Sunday for the seventh consecutive weekend, amid an ongoing political crisis over a now-suspended extradition bill. Many of those caught up in the violence were returning home after taking part in mass demonstrations in the city, leading to accusations that the gangs had been paid to stoke unrest and target protesters." Ibid.)

[65] "Hong Kong protests: Police fire tear gas at Yuen Long rally," *BBC News* (27 July 2019); available [https://www.bbc.com/news/world-asia-china-49123445] ("Hong Kong police have fired tear gas at an unauthorised protest held by tens of thousands of people to condemn an attack by armed masked men last week. As a small group of protesters refused to disperse in the northern district of Yuen Long, police fired rubber bullets." Ibid.). Tear gas use by police had also hardened feelings among protestors and engendered some public sympathy early in the protests when it was use by police during the 12 June 2019 protests in front of the legislative building after debate on the Extradition Law was postponed. Damien Gayle, Kate Lyons, and Verna Yu, " Hong Kong protest: police fire teargas at demonstrators – as it happened," *The Guardian* (12 June 2019); available [https://www.theguardian.com/world/live/2019/jun/12/hong-kong-protest-demonstrators-and-police-face-off-over-extradition-bill-live].

frustration at increasingly aggressive methods by police appears only to have added to counteractions by local Hong Kong people.[66]

The fight for the "hearts and minds of both locals and the international community has intensified since the start of July. That much has become clear as both sides seek to strengthen their positions respecting not just the Extradition Law but likely as well a set of grievances, objectives and counter objectives that have been festering since the Umbrella Movement went silent as a public mass protest after December 2014.[67] Many of these are local, but key elements of many grievances touch on issues that are sensitive to Beijing's central authorities, especially as its core leadership moves the ideological focus from the historical era of "Reform and Opening Up" that gave the One Country-Two Systems" its internationalist flavor at the end of the 20th century, to the "New Era" of historical development under the core leadership of Xi Jinping, one that puts the party at the center and the core objectives of the central government above those of its autonomous regions.[68]

---

[66] Austin Ramzy, "Hong Kong Protest: Clashes With Police Turn Downtown Into Tear Gas-Filled Battlefield," *The New York Times* (28 July 2019); available [https://www.nytimes.com/2019/07/28/world/asia/hong-kong-police-protest.html] ("This was the third straight weekend that violent clashes had broken out since the demonstrations began nearly two months ago over an unpopular bill, . . . Since then, the demonstrations have grown into almost daily public displays of vitriol against the police, Hong Kong's leaders and the government in Beijing, throwing Hong Kong into its worst political crisis since it was returned to Chinese rule in 1997.).

[67] Adam Connors, "Hong Kong's Umbrella Movement: A Timeline of Key Events One Year On," ABC News Australia (updated 15 June 2019); available [https://www.abc.net.au/news/2015-09-28/timeline-hong-kong-umbrella-movement-one-year-on/6802388?nw=0]. For one analytical view, Tyler Headley and Cole Tanigawa-Lau, "Why Did Hong Kong's Umbrella Movement Fail?: The key to a successful protest in Hong Kong: economic pressure," The Diplomat (6 April 216); available [https://thediplomat.com/2016/04/why-did-hong-kongs-umbrella-movement-fail/].

[68] See, Larry Catá Backer, " Chinese Constitutionalism in the New Era: The Emerging Idea and Practice of Constitution in the 19th CPC Congress Report (November 7, 2017)," Working Papers Coalition for Peace & Ethics, No. 11/1 (November 2017); available [https://ssrn.com/abstract=3066974] or [http://dx.doi.org/10.2139/ssrn.3066974].

Hong Kong Between "One Country" and "Two Systems"
3. Mend-Break (Di Xi 抵巇): The Chinese Position on the Situation in Hong Kong

32

It makes sense, then, to pay special attention when functionaries from the Chinese State Council speak. Here it is especially worth considering (in the original Chinese and a crude English translation) the language used by the spokespersons of the Hong Kong and Macao Affairs Office of the State Council, Mr. Yang Guang and Ms. Xu Luying for cues about the way that the policy responses of the Chinese central authorities are being developed. The statements were well curated and presented in the form of an interview of these officials with Deputy Director of the State Council Information Office by Yan Yanchun (袭艳春).[69]

The reporting and reactions were not unexpected. The *South China Morning Post*—the usual gateway to outsiders in a local English language paper with global reach—noted the importance of the HKMAO Statement as reflecting the first articulation of a position by the central authorities in Beijing and provided a curated transcript framed in the following way:

The controversy over the shelved extradition bill has plunged Hong Kong into its biggest political crisis since its 1997 return to Chinese rule. The city continues to be rocked by mass protests with demonstrators demanding a full withdrawal of the bill. As protests have escalated and taken an increasingly violent turn in recent weeks, Hong Kong's police have struggled to restore order while facing a massive public backlash over their handling of demonstrators. The turmoil has not only worried Beijing's leaders but also put Hong Kong under the international spotlight as investors wonder if the financial hub has stumbled. The press conference on Monday by the Hong Kong and Macau Affairs Office under the State Council, the first by Beijing's top policy office on Hong Kong since the handover, suggested top

---

[69] 国务院港澳办新闻发言人介绍对香港当前局势的立场和看法 来源： 国务院新闻办公室网站 ； 发布时间 (2019-07-29) ["The spokesperson of the Hong Kong and Macau Affairs Office of the State Council introduces his position and views on the current situation in Hong Kong," State Council Information Office website (released 29 July 2019)]; available [http://www.locpg.gov.cn/jsdt/2019-07/29/c_1210220181.htm] (hereafter HKMAO Statement).

Hong Kong Between "One Country" and "Two Systems"
3. Mend-Break (Di Xi 抵巇): The Chinese Position on the Situation in Hong Kong

33

leaders had arrived at a view and formulated a response to the deadlock.[70]

And the student protester response:

> Hong Kong commuters could face traffic chaos on Tuesday morning, with protesters angry at Beijing's response to the extradition bill crisis planning a non-cooperative campaign at a major railway station and blockades of major roads. On social media on Monday night, the protesters also discussed organising another sit-in at the airport, hours after the Hong Kong and Macau Affairs Office under China's State Council expressed "resolute support" for the Hong Kong government over its handling of the saga.[71]

Protest leaders appear more than ever committed to a quite public campaign of pressure against the local authorities, and by implication against the central authorities in Beijing. They appear to mean to rely heavily on international pressure, and the fear for China, of the thwarting of its international ambitions, should their demands not be met, at least n some part. Can the count on the international community to act in line with their now easy discursive support? That is the question, and the calculation being made by the principal parties. It is reflected as well in the careful remarks of the HKMAO in this interview—one that sought to shed light on the trajectory of official thinking in Beijing but with a substantial amount of leeway in the details, enough anyway to permit shifting to meet the changing situation.

---

[70] "As it happened: how Beijing expressed 'resolute support' for Hong Kong's government," *South China Morning Post* (29 July 2019); available [https://www.scmp.com/news/hong-kong/politics/article/3020466/hong-kong-and-macau-affairs-office-speak-extradition-bill].

[71] Rachel Yeo , Michelle Wong , Phila Siu and Ng Kang-chung, "Hong Kong facing rush hour chaos as anti-government protesters plan major disruption to city's rail and road networks," *South China Moring Post* (30 July 2019); available [https://www.scmp.com/news/hong-kong/transport/article/3020553/hong-kong-facing-rush-hour-chaos-anti-government].

Hong Kong Between "One Country" and "Two Systems"
3. Mend-Break (Di Xi 抵巇): The Chinese Position on the Situation in Hong Kong

34

And, indeed, the HKMAO Statement was meant to be a very high profile expression of the basic outlines of the developing Chinese official positions. It also likely included a number of hints of thinking directed both to Hong Kong stakeholders, and the international community. Reading them reminded me of Guiguzi's the principles of Mend-Break (*di xi* 抵巇) with which this reflection starts.[72] It is at once both a vigorous announcement of developing Chinese official policy, but at the same time, one undertaken strategically with the "mend-break" principle in mind. One sees that clearly on a close examination of the text of the curated statement and the reporter questions and answers chosen for inclusion.

It will be useful, then, to read these carefully to understand the current thinking, as well as the extent to which China has begun to develop "red lines" which if crossed decisively may provoke equally or greater countermeasures. It also evidences the mend-break (*di xi* 抵巇) style: to mend relations with Hong Kong, to break relations with outsiders, to break agitators, to mend the fabric of prosperity and stability that contributes to the objectives of the central authority. In any case, a careful read suggests the contours of the "One Country Two Systems" principle in the "New Era" under the core leadership of Xi Jinping. It ought to be with great interest that the emerging application of the Chinese Communist Party Basic Line with respect to the autonomous regions in the New Era ought to be observed and studied, especially for its utility in thinking through reunification with Taiwan, and relations with Belt and Road states.

In addition to the larger points, there are a number of interesting positions that the HKMAO sought to underline: (1) the misunderstanding cultivated by some people in Hong Kong; (2) the possible pernicious effects of outside influences provoking an unjustified panic; (3) the framing of the issues as just touching on the extradition law; (4) the concern over alarmism and the rupture of appropriate engagement through official channels as

---

[72] Guiguzi (鬼谷子), *Guiguzi: China's First Treatise on Rhetoric; A Critical Translation and Commentary* (Hui Wu (trans.); Carbondale: Southern Illinois University Press, 2016 (before 220 A.D.)); Book I.4.1, pp. 53-54.

Hong Kong Between "One Country" and "Two Systems"
3. Mend-Break (Di Xi 抵巇): The Chinese Position on the Situation in Hong Kong

35

potentially threatening; (5) the warnings about the consequences of continued violence by what were characterized as radical and fringe elements themselves lawbreakers (extremist protestors (激进示威)); (6) the willingness of China to protect its constitutional order by all appropriate means when and as it chooses, in accordance with its interpretation of its rights and obligations under the one state two systems framework; (7) the different conceptual starting points for rule of law discourse between the Hong Kong protagonists and its conception and deployment within the political discourse of China; and (8) the willingness for the moment to continue to work through the local government, though with the warning that in China's view, the violence "has also seriously touched (触碰) the bottom line of the principle of "One Country, Two Systems."[73]

The interview statements were meant to announce—better put, to underline—the emerging position of the Chinese central authorities to the situation in Hong Kong.[74] The position was built around two related factors, each of which appeared to make it impossible for the central authorities to ignore what might otherwise have been dismissed as marginal local protests over peculiar local conditions. The first was that the continuing protests were violent (without reference to the sources of the violence of course). The second was that the protests had aroused both international and domestic attention. The reference to domestic interest is particularly telling. It suggests that the situation in Hong Kong cannot be contained and its narrative treated as a story of the quirks of a peripheral region. Rather the fear appears to be growing that the success of the protests might now affect the critically important domestic project of moving China toward its "New Era" Basic Line. That cannot be tolerated consist with the core principles of the New Era. Likewise, the

---

[73] HKMAO Statement, supra., passim.

[74] "杨光：近期，在香港围绕特区政府修订《逃犯条例》和《刑事事宜相互法律协助条例》，发生了一系列游行示威活动和暴力事件，引起国际国内广泛关注。[Yang Guang: Recently, a series of demonstrations and violent incidents occurred in Hong Kong surrounding the SAR government's amendments to the Fugitive Offenders Ordinance and the Mutual Legal Assistance in Criminal Matters Ordinance, which aroused widespread international and domestic attention.];" HKMAO Statement, supra., at 2019-07-29 15:02:01.

Hong Kong Between "One Country" and "Two Systems"
3. Mend-Break (Di Xi 抵巇): The Chinese Position on the Situation in Hong Kong

36

extent to which the international elements of Hong Kong's status provides a wedge into and the ability to affect those issues makes it likely that the Chinese central authorities will also try to detach Hong Kong from its international moorings.

At the same time, the HKMAO adopted what is a fairly standard approach—to minimize and narrow the scope of intervention in light of an example or two of a scandalous precipitating event, and an intimation that any intervention would be narrowly tailored. [75] Any doubt was cast as gratuitously alarmist and dismissed as an effort to cause social unrest unnecessarily.[76] The responsibility for the resulting social unrest was placed entirely on these rumormongers, [77] who were disrupting social harmony. As a consequence, Yang Guang explained, "since June 12, some radical demonstrators have deliberately created violent incidents, and their actions have completely exceeded the scope of peaceful demonstrations." [78] The consequences cannot be ignored by the central authorities, in part because it challenges not just their own authority but potentially the peace and stability of the state.

---

[75] "杨光:特区政府修订上述两个条例起因于一桩普通刑事案件。[Yan Guang: The amendment of the above two regulations by the SAR government resulted from an ordinary criminal case]." HKMAO Statement, supra., at 2019-07-29 15:02:16

[76] "杨光:．．．一些别有用心的人和媒体趁机散播各种危言耸听的言论，制造社会恐慌，阻挠法案在立法会审议通过。[Yang Guang: Some people with ulterior motives and the media took the opportunity to spread all kinds of alarmist remarks, create social panic, and obstruct the passage of the bill in the Legislative Council.]". HKMAO Statement, supra., at 2019-07-29 15:03:52.

[77] The central authorities have traditionally managed social discourse through application of criminal penalties for rumor mongering. In 2008, for example, "in Tibet in March, police have cracked 48 cases of "rumor-mongering" and detained 59 people, the Chinatibetnews.com website said, citing Xin Yuanming, deputy chief of police in Tibet's capital Lhasa. "A number of people with ulterior motives deliberately spread rumors and fanned ethnic sentiment," he was quoted as saying, adding that the alleged rumor-mongers had been urged on by people close to the Dalai Lama." "China detains 59 over spreading 'subversive rumors' in Tibet," Agence France Presse (26 December 2008); available [https://www.taiwannews.com.tw/en/news/822376].

[78] "杨光:但是，6月12日以来，一些激进示威者蓄意制造暴力事件，其行动完全超出了和平游行示威的范畴。" KMAO Statement, supra., at 2019-07-29 15:04:05.

Hong Kong Between "One Country" and "Two Systems"
3. Mend-Break (Di Xi 抵巇): The Chinese Position on the Situation in Hong Kong

37

The demonstrations and violent attacks in Hong Kong have been going on for more than a month. They have had a serious impact on Hong Kong's rule of law, social order, economy, people's livelihood, and international image. It makes all those who care about and cherish Hong Kong feel very sad.[79]

The consequences were crystalized in three points. The first was that violent demonstrations undermined the One Country Two Systems principle and could not be tolerated. Second, the core value of rule of law for Hong Kong is a function of and related to the maintenance of Hong Kong's prosperity and stability, and the preservation of both against unscrupulous people must be defended by the central authorities. And third, stability and prosperity cannot be achieved in the face of political discord; only through continuous development can the real problems of Hong Kong be solved. Freedom, for Hong Kong, then, must be measured against the development of Hong Kong's productive forces which can only be undermined by vigorous political discord—either in the legislature or on the streets.[80]

---

[79] "杨光：发生在香港的游行示威和暴力冲击活动已经持续了一个多月，对香港的法治、社会秩序、经济民生和国际形象造成了严重影响，令所有关心香港、珍爱香港的人倍感痛心。" HKMAO Statement, supra., at 2019-07-29 15:06:50.

[80] "杨光：香港回归以来，"一国两制"实践取得了举世公认的成就。"一国两制"、"港人治港"、高度自治方针得到切实贯彻落实。香港保持繁荣稳定，被公认为全球最自由的经济体，营商环境和国际竞争力得到国际社会的广泛认可。香港居民享有前所未有的民主权利和全世界范围内少见的广泛自由。香港的法治指数在全世界名列前茅。" ["Yang Guang: Since the return of Hong Kong, the practice of "one country, two systems" has achieved universally recognized achievements. The principles of "One Country, Two Systems", "Hong Kong People Administering Hong Kong", and a high degree of autonomy have been practically implemented. Hong Kong remains prosperous and stable. It is recognized as the freest economy in the world. Its business environment and international competitiveness have been widely recognized by the international community. Hong Kong residents enjoy unprecedented democratic rights and broad freedoms that are rare in the world. Hong Kong's rule of law index ranks among the best in the world."]." HKMAO Statement, supra., at 2019-07-29 15:08:20.

Hong Kong Between "One Country" and "Two Systems"
3. Mend-Break (Di Xi 抵巇): The Chinese Position on the Situation in Hong Kong

38

Yuang Guang's statement then ended with a strong support for Carrie Lam's government, to the ends of ensuring Hong Kong's stability and prosperity. "Practice has fully proved that "one country, two systems" is the best institutional arrangement for maintaining Hong Kong's long-term prosperity and stability. "[81] That is the essence of the core principle in One Country Two Systems, one read against the three bottom lines of central authority interpretation of its essence.[82] Left unsaid, of course, was what actions, or aggregation of actions, would be sufficient to cross these lines. What was unnecessary to state, however, was that it would be the central authorities in Beijing that would decide this, and they would do so without any consultation with or in deference to the international community or any international accord. It is becoming clear that "One Country" is acquiring a very specific meaning for the Chinese central authorities. That meaning is likely incompatible with the meaning taken for granted elsewhere—including in Hong Kong and among its intellectuals.

The well managed question and answer session that followed[83] also yielded additional clues about the future—none of them good from the perspective of the driving forces of the protests and their sympathetic audiences elsewhere. The most interesting part of the question and answer session was that not all questions and not every answer survived to find its way to the transcript posted on line. That suggests both a sensitivity to the

---

[81] "杨光：实践充分证明，"一国两制"是保持香港长期繁荣稳定的最佳制度安排。" HKMAO Statement, supra., at 2019-07-29 15:08:20 .

[82] This was underscored and expanded in Yang Guang's answer (Ibid., at 2019-07-29 15:30:36at) to a question posed by a Singapore Lianhe Zaobao reporter in which Yang described the triple bottom line of the One Country Two Systems principle: "These "three bottom lines" are: absolutely must not allow any harm to national sovereignty and security, and must never allow challenges to the central power and the Hong Kong Special Administrative Region Basic Law Authoritative and absolutely cannot allow the use of Hong Kong to carry out infiltration and sabotage activities on the Mainland." ["绝对不能允许任何危害国家主权安全、绝对不能允许挑战中央权力和香港特别行政区基本法权威、绝对不能允许利用香港对内地进行渗透破坏的活动。"] . HKMAO Statement, supra, at 2019-07-29 15:30:36. Note though the time gap between the time the question was asked Ibid., at (2019-07-29 15:17:14) and the start of the answer at 15:30:36.

[83] HKMAO Statement, starting at 2019-07-29 15:09:35.

Hong Kong Between "One Country" and "Two Systems"
3. Mend-Break (Di Xi 抵隙): The Chinese Position on the Situation in Hong Kong

39

issues and a determination that the issues required careful grooming before they could be in a state that would present the appropriate picture of things to outsiders. That is itself, quite useful, as a means of evaluating precisely what sort of picture the central authorities meant to paint, and as a means of decoding whatever messages were meant to be conveyed indirectly.

In this case the message was very, very clear:

First, the forms of One Country, Two Systems principle would continue to serve as the template within which the extent of autonomy permitted Hong Kong would be developed.

Second, any further development or application of the principle of One Country Two Systems would be directed under the guidance of the central authorities in Beijing.

Third, the international community would have little to say in the matter, precisely because of the way in which sovereignty would be interpreted by the central authorities over Hong Kong—that is international involvement ended with the handover in 1997, and any further use of international instruments would be considered form the Chinese side as interference in their internal affairs.[84]

---

[84] This is a point underlined in answer to a question posed by a Xinhua News Agency reporter (HKMAO Statement, supra., at 2019-07-29 16:14:53) by Yang Guang.

   The second point I would like to say is that Hong Kong is China's Hong Kong, and Hong Kong affairs are China's internal affairs, which cannot tolerate any external forces' interference. State Councilor Wang Yi and the spokesperson of the Ministry of Foreign Affairs have made statements on this attitude and position. This is our unwavering position. During this period of time, some politicians in Western countries have frequently made irresponsible remarks, arguing and even supporting some people. Their intentions are nothing but to mess up Hong Kong and turn Hong Kong into a trouble for China, and then contain or constrain China's development. This conspiracy will not succeed. [第二点我想讲，香港是中国的香港，香港事务是中国的内政，容不得任何外部势力横加干涉，这个态度、这个立场，国务委员王毅和外交部发言人已经多次做过表态，这是我们坚定不移的立场。西方国家的一些政客频频在这一段时间里说三道四，品头论足，甚至给一些人撑腰打气，他们的用心说穿了无

Hong Kong Between "One Country" and "Two Systems"
3. Mend-Break (Di Xi 抵巇): The Chinese Position on the Situation in Hong Kong

40

Fourth, the whole point of One Country Two Systems, and the measure of the value and characteristics of Hong Kong autonomy, would be based on the objectives of prosperity and stability.[85] Nothing else mattered, and the exercise of "peculiar" political rights would be strictly limited as a function of both prosperity and stability. Yang Guang emphasized the point in response to a question posed by a Hong Kong TVB reporter: "In our view, the most dangerous thing about the current situation in Hong Kong is that violent crimes have not been effectively stopped. The most important task for Hong Kong is to resolutely punish violent crimes in accordance with the law, restore social stability as soon as possible, and maintain the good rule of law in Hong Kong.[86]

Fifth, political agitation (other than that taken under the guidance of the Communist Party of course) would be considered destabilizing and a threat to prosperity.[87]

非是想把香港搞乱，把香港变成中国的一个麻烦，进而牵制或者遏制中国的发展。这个图谋是无法得逞的。谢谢。].

[85] Again this was made clear by Xu Luying of the HKMAO in response to a question by a reporter for the *South China Morning Post* referencing the significant drop in approval ratings for Carrie Lam. "The central government will continue to firmly support the Chief Executive Carrie Lam and the SAR government in governing in accordance with the law, unite and lead all sectors of Hong Kong to jointly maintain the prosperity and stability of Hong Kong's political situation." HKMAO Statement, supra., at 2019-07-29 15:34:18.

[86] HKMAO Statement, supra., at 2019-07-29 16:06:12 ("在我们看来，当前香港局势最危险的是暴力犯罪行为还没有得到有效制止，香港当前最重要的任务是坚决依法惩治暴力犯罪行为，尽快恢复社会安定，维护香港的良好法治。").

[87] One is reminded here of a key phrase in Mao Zedong, "On the People's Democratic Dictatorship" (30 June 1949) in commemoration of the 28th anniversary of the CPC; available [https://www.marxists.org/reference/archive/mao/selected-works/volume-4/mswv4_65.htm]: ""You are dictatorial." My dear sirs, you are right, that is just what we are. All the experience the Chinese people have accumulated through several decades teaches us to enforce the people's democratic dictatorship, that is, to deprive the reactionaries of the right to speak and let the people alone have that right."

Hong Kong Between "One Country" and "Two Systems"
3. Mend-Break (Di Xi 抵巇): The Chinese Position on the Situation in Hong Kong

41

Sixth, the police power may then be used lawfully to excise these threats to the stability and prosperity of Hong Kong.[88]

Seventh, political rights may not be used to threaten Chinese sovereignty over the Hong Kong SAR, nor to be incompatible with the core premises of the national political order and the national aspirations and objectives of its vanguard.

The question and answer sessions then appeared to provide an opportunity to flesh out some additional points. Xu Luying of the HKMAO underlined the importance of Hong Kong's financial stability as a key measure against which responses would be developed.

> The decline in business confidence will naturally increase the external risks faced by the financial industry. Therefore, we also believe that Hong Kong's top priority is to punish violent violations in accordance with the law, restore social order as soon as possible, and maintain a

---

[88] Again two quite important reflections from Mao Zedong's "On the People's Democratic Dictatorship," Supra. The first: "When anyone among the people breaks the law, he too should be punished, imprisoned or even sentenced to death; but this is a matter of a few individual cases, and it differs in principle from the dictatorship exercised over the reactionaries as a class." And second, the more structurally potent insight for Hong Kong:

> Who are the people? At the present stage in China, they are the working class, the peasantry, the urban petty bourgeoisie and the national bourgeoisie. These classes, led by the working class and the Communist Party, unite to form their own state and elect their own government; they enforce their dictatorship over the running dogs of imperialism -- the landlord class and bureaucrat-bourgeoisie, as well as the representatives of those classes, the Kuomintang reactionaries and their accomplices -- suppress them, allow them only to behave themselves and not to be unruly in word or deed. If they speak or act in an unruly way, they will be promptly stopped and punished. Democracy is practiced within the ranks of the people, who enjoy the rights of freedom of speech, assembly, association and so on. The right to vote belongs only to the people, not to the reactionaries. The combination of these two aspects, democracy for the people and dictatorship over the reactionaries, is the people's democratic dictatorship.

Hong Kong Between "One Country" and "Two Systems"
3. Mend-Break (Di Xi 抵巇): The Chinese Position on the Situation in Hong Kong

42

good business environment. This is of the highest importance.[89]

In response to a question from a Hong Kong TVB reporter,[90] Yang Guang deflected questions about the incident at the Yuen Long metro station. He dismissed statements that deviated from official accounts as "rumors and baseless slanders"—a suggestion that any such speculation would, in ordinary course on the Mainland constitute serious criminal activity in its own right. Instead he defended the Hong Kong police and suggested that considering the magnitude of social and political disruption they maintained restraint and professionalism. This is not good news for those driving the protests, and suggests that any inclination on the part of the local authorities to relent would not be viewed as a positive development by the central authorities in Beijing. He expressed the belief, "I believe that with the efforts of the Chief Executive Carrie Lam and the SAR government, the strict enforcement of the Hong Kong police force, and the joint efforts of patriots and Hong Kong people, Hong Kong society will be able to stop all kinds of violent crimes as soon as possible and make Hong Kong society back to normal track."[91] Interesting as well was the willingness of the HKMAO officials to deflect the question about the interventions of the People's Liberation Army and the collusion of foreigners in the protests.[92]

But perhaps the most interesting additional response came at the very end of the question and answer session. It was a mention in passing as Xu Luying answered a question posed by a Hong Kong reporter that touched on the scope of grievances of local Hong Kong people. Xu noted that the central authorities do not necessarily think of Hong Kong as an isolated region, but

---

[89] "如果营商环境、营商信心有所下降，自然会加大金融业所面临的外部风险，所以我们也认为香港的当务之急是要依法惩治暴力违法行为，尽快恢复社会秩序，维护好良好的营商环境，这是最重要的." HKMAO Statement, supra., at 2019-07-29 15:36:13.

[90] HKMAO Statement, supra, at 2019-07-29 15:36:58; answer ibid., at 16:06:12.

[91] Ibid., at 16:06:12 ("我相信，在林郑月娥行政长官和特区政府的努力下，在香港警队的严格执法下，在广大爱国爱港人士的共同努力下，香港社会一定能够尽快制止各种暴力犯罪行为，使香港社会重新回到正常的轨道上。").

[92] HKMAO Statement, supra., at 2019-07-29 16:21:22 - 2019-07-29 16:21:45.

Hong Kong Between "One Country" and "Two Systems"
3. *Mend-Break (Di Xi 抵巇): The Chinese Position on the Situation in Hong Kong*

43

rather as one to be more closely integrated with the rising Mainland cities of Guangzhou and Shenzhen, as well as Macao.

> The relevant central authorities will also continue to introduce a series of policies and measures to facilitate the development of Hong Kong residents in the Mainland, especially in the construction of the Guangdong-Hong Kong-Macao Greater Bay Area. In the process, it will consider expanding new space and adding new impetus to Hong Kong's development, so that Hong Kong residents, especially Hong Kong young people, will have more development opportunities. However, development must have a harmonious and stable social environment.[93]

As such, it may be that in the calculus of prosperity and political stability (including the control of popular violence) the central authorities may be as much concerned about the "Hong Kong Effect" within the greater Pearl River region as much as it is with the local issues of a key part of that larger region.

The central authorities, then, have made their position clear. Yet they have also made clearer their intention to apply (*di xi* 抵巇) strategies to overcome what they see as the challenges (for them) of the situation in Hong Kong. The West is likely unprepared either for the elaboration of this strategy or its implementation; their counter--limited to dialogue, and gesture--will likely also be a target of (*di xi* 抵巇). Perhaps the Sino-UK Joint Declaration would be broken, and a new relationship with the international community, with the central authorities standing between them and Hong Kong, will emerge. But it is too early to tell.

But more importantly, the people of Hong Kong driving events may have little notion of the potency of the strategies adopted. Even when translated into Western terms—not merely to heal rifts but to do so by widening rifts elsewhere, that is to mend and break, that is a strategy that will be interesting to see

---

[93] HKMAO Statement, supra., 2019-07-29 16:25:13.

Hong Kong Between "One Country" and "Two Systems"
3. Mend-Break (Di Xi 抵牾): The Chinese Position on the Situation in Hong Kong

44

play out. The central authorities have been quite clear. They will use the rift between the Hong Kong government and protestors to mend the break caused in the middle of the 19th century between what became Hong Kong and the rest of the Pearl River basin. They will mend the ideological connections between the Mainland and Hong Kong by widening the ideological rift between Hong Kong and the old empire (UK) the new (the US) and the contemporary international order (public and private). How this will ultimately translate into action remains unclear. But it is clear that some action is likely to be taken—in months or years, and as a function of advantageous circumstances as they might arise.

$$* \quad * \quad *$$

Chapter 4

Sunday 4 August 2019
Official and Unofficial Statements of the Political Authorities

The political situation in Hong Kong has remained fluid since the protests erupted in early June [94] over the SAR government's handling of a proposed Fugitive Offenders Ordinance. [95] Yet the Fugitive Offenders' Ordinance is symptomatic of a wider and longer term set of fears around the perhaps inevitable erosion of the characteristics of Hong Kong's autonomy as time marches toward 2047. For Hong Kong people, and their supporters outside China, the starting point for analysis is always the autonomous part of the relationship with the Mainland, and to downplay the part about Chinese sovereignty over the territories that comprise the SAR, along with their authority over its people. The 1984 Sino-British Joint Declaration [96] appears to have been reconstructed as an increasingly impermeable wall that provides international legal protection for the habits, customs, and traditions of Hong Kong against the sovereign ambitions of the Chinese central authorities.[97]

---

[94] Fion Li and Carol Zhong, "Why Hong Kong is Protesting (and May Do so Again)," *Bloomberg* (Quite Take 11 June 2019); available [https://www.bloomberg.com/news/articles/2019-06-11/the-extradition-law-that-s-got-hong-kong-protesting-quicktake].

[95] Kate Mayberry, "Hong Kong's controversial extradition bill explained," *Aljazeera* (11 June 2019); available [https://www.aljazeera.com/news/2019/6/11/hong-kongs-controversial-extradition-bill-explained]. The fear of undermining the autonomy and liberties of Hong Kong spring not only from the terms of extradition itself, but also from "proposed amendments to mutual legal assistance, which would allow outside investigators to request assistance from Hong Kong for criminal cases including search and seizure, and confiscation and restraint orders." Ibid.

[96] Joint Declaration of the Government of the United Kingdom of Great Britain and Northern Ireland and the Government of the People's Republic of China on the Question of Hong Kong (19 December 1984); available [https://www.cmab.gov.hk/en/issues/jd2.htm].

[97] Thus, for example, it is common in contemporaneous reporting to describe the relationship between China and Hong Kong in these terms:

Nonetheless, the political missteps, the clumsiness of the administration and its impatience with the complexities and pace of local politics, made a situation that could merely have been bad, worse. That the Extradition Law was so clumsily put forward was a pity, and an indication that even from the perspective of Chinese Marxist-Leninism, that the SAR government has failed fundamentally to practice the Mass Line,[98] even within the quite *sui generis* context of SAR governance. Indeed, Carrie Lam alluded to this in her own roundabout way during the now notorious and

---

1. Isn't Hong Kong part of China? Yes, but it's a semi-autonomous region. The city was an outpost of the British Empire for 156 years, during which time it developed into a global business hub. In a 1984 joint declaration, the British agreed to give the city back in 1997 -- at the end of a 99-year lease on much of the land -- and China promised to allow a "high degree of autonomy" for 50 years, including guarantees of free speech, capitalist markets and English common law under a "one country, two systems" arrangement.
Fion Li and Carol Zhong, "Why Hong Kong is Protesting (and May Do so Again),"
[98] The Mass Line is a core element of the Chinese Communist Party Basic Line. See Constitution of the Chinese Communist Party, "General Program;" available [https://fas.org/irp/world/china/docs/const.html]. It perhaps is best understood in the context of Hong Kong by reference to an early iteration in the writings of Mao Zedong:

To link oneself with the masses, one must act in accordance with the needs and wishes of the masses. All work done for the masses must start from their needs and not from the desire of any individual, however well-intentioned. It often happens that objectively the masses need a certain change, but subjectively they are not yet conscious of the need, not yet willing or determined to make the change. In such cases, we should wait patiently. We should not make the change until, through our work, most of the masses have become conscious of the need and are willing and determined to carry it out. Otherwise we shall isolate ourselves from the masses. Unless they are conscious and willing, any kind of work that requires their participation will turn out to be a mere formality and will fail... There are two principles here: one is the actual needs of the masses rather than what we fancy they need, and the other is the wishes of the masses, who must make up their own minds instead of our making up their minds for them.

Mao Zedong, "The United Front in Cultural Work" (30 October 1944); *in Selected Works* III:236-237; available [https://www.marxists.org/reference/archive/mao/selected-works/volume-3/mswv3_21.htm].

notably marred celebrations of the Hong Kong handover to China held in July.[99]

Recent actions on all sides continues to inflame a situation that remains dynamic. Ultimately social peace and good government must be restored, sensitive to the special conditions of Hong Kong as well as of the fundamental relationship between the Hong Kong SAR and the central authorities. Decision making will have to take into account not just the situation within the Hong Kong SAR, but, because the People's Republic of China is now an international global role model, the effects of the actions of governmental authorities on the standing and reputation of China in the world. That may require the avoidance of provocative statements.

There have been substantial provocations. The Chinese central authorities have sought to steer attention from local protestors to the machinations of other states. By recharacterizing the protests as foreign in form, method or sensibility, as not Chinese, it might it easier to apply decisive measures to excise this foreign "infection."[100] The Chinese Foreign

---

[99] The key portions of the speech were widely reported:

> In her speech, where she acknowledged the unhappiness of the protesters over a controversial extradition Bill, she promised to "actively reach out to young people of different backgrounds through various channels to listen to their thoughts"... "This has made me fully realise that I, as a politician, have to remind myself all the time of the need to grasp public sentiments accurately," she said in tones reminiscent of the two public apologies she has made since the protests began. "I am also fully aware that while we have good intentions, we still need to be open and accommodating. While the government has to ensure administrative efficiency, it still needs to listen patiently," she said.

Claire Huang, "Hong Kong's Carrie Lam promises to listen to young people in speech marking handover anniversary," *Straits Times* (1 July 2019); available [https://www.straitstimes.com/asia/east-asia/carrie-lam-promises-to-listen-to-young-people-in-speech-marking-handover-anniversary].

[100] See, e.g., "China Says Hong Kong Protest Violence 'Is Creation of U.S.'," *Bloomberg* (30 July 2019); available [https://www.bloomberg.com/news/articles/2019-07-30/china-says-hong-kong-protest-violence-is-creation-of-u-s] ("China said recent violence in Hong Kong protests was the "creation of the U.S.," for the first time laying direct blame

Ministry Spokesperson, then, could indulge in a bit a clever word play: "'It's clear that Mr. Pompeo has put himself in the wrong position and still regards himself as the head of the CIA,' Hua said, referring to Pompeo's previous role at the intelligence agency. 'He might think that violent activities in Hong Kong are reasonable because after all, this is the creation of the U.S.'" [101] This augmented the initial position statement of the Chinese authorities, issued in the form of a statement and interview style questions and answers of the Hong Kong and Macao Affairs Office of the State Council of 29 July 2019.[102]

The European Parliament, on the other side, adopted a resolution that called for the withdrawal by the Hong Kong Authorities of the Fugitive Offenders Ordinance.[103] Signed by 85 members of the AU Parliament, the document has no legal effect but provoked the officials of the Chinese Hong Kong and Macao Affairs Office to question whether the European legislators understood either concepts of sovereignty or of the rule of law.[104] And, of course, American elites cannot resist the temptation of seeking a space in which to drive public opinion. They expose an attitude that is likely commonly shared, positing the basic character of Chinese officials as bullies. This attitude also posits a fundamental disconnect between Chinese political principles and methods and respect for international law, norms, and human

---

on Washington as their dispute over the unrest escalates. Chinese Foreign Ministry spokeswoman Hua Chunying made the remark at a news briefing Tuesday" Ibid.).

[101] Ibid.

[102] 国务院港澳办新闻发言人介绍对香港当前局势的立场和看法 来源: 国务院新闻办公室网站 ; 发布时间 (2019-07-29) ["The spokesperson of the Hong Kong and Macau Affairs Office of the State Council introduces his position and views on the current situation in Hong Kong," State Council Information Office website (released 29 July 2019)]; available [http://www.locpg.gov.cn/jsdt/2019-07/29/c_1210220181.htm]

[103] Teddy Ng and Stuart Lau, "European Parliament approves motion on Hong Kong, as Beijing calls it full of 'ignorance and prejudice'," South China Morning Post (18 July 2019); available [https://www.scmp.com/news/china/diplomacy/article/3019177/beijing-says-hong-kong-motion-tabled-members-european]. The HKMAO Statement was discussed in some detail at Chapter 3, supra.

[104] Ibid.

rights (as conventionally constructed, understood, and applied by international organizations).[105] "The United States also has an interest in defending American values and its example. The world is watching to see whether the U.S. stands up for the right to free speech and peaceful political protest, rights that are enshrined in Hong Kong's Basic Law. . . [T]here will be significant and lasting costs if the United States abandons support for peaceful demonstrators."[106]

Within this stew pot of provocation and discursive "stance-creation," the situation continues to develop. The protestors have adopted a quite flexible approach to disruption that is hard to anticipate and prevent.[107] On the side of the protestors, there have been statements and strategies deployed to strike at the heart of the core operating principles announced by the local and central authorities as the key elements and objectives of One Country, Two States framework. The strikes are well targeted in this respect to undermine or threaten (with the object of inducing negotiation) around which the governance objectives of the Hong Kong and Mainland governments are built.

"A general strike aimed at bringing the city to a halt is planned for Monday. Many flight departures were shown as being cancelled on Monday and a source and media reports said this was due to aviation workers planning

---

[105] See, e.g., Ryan Haas and Susan A. Thornton, "On Hong Kong, the U.S. Must Find Its Own Voice," *Brookings* (30 July 2019); available [https://www.brookings.edu/blog/order-from-chaos/2019/07/30/on-hong-kong-the-us-must-find-its-voice/].

[106] Ibid. Curiously, the conventional position of American elites adopts some of the same language as that used as cover justification by Chinese central authorities—a focus on stability and prosperity and the need to manage protests and avoid violence, but of course to different ends. More importantly is the urging that the United States determine a means to publicly scold and then effectively sanction Chinese moves that cross some sort of undefined "red line." But in that too, US influence drivers mimic the Chinese "three red line" stance". Discussed in Chapter 3, supra.

[107] Tommy Monroe and Claire Jim, "Hong Kong government: protests are pushing city to 'extremely dangerous edge'," *Reuters* (3 August 2019); available [https://www.reuters.com/article/us-hongkong-protests-arrests/hong-kong-government-protests-are-pushing-city-to-extremely-dangerous-edge-idUSKCN1UU00X].

to strike. Late on Sunday, hundreds of masked protesters blocked major roads, spray painted traffic lights, started fires and prevented transport from entering the Cross-Harbour Tunnel linking Hong Kong island and the Kowloon peninsula."[108]

These are meant to apply well-worn revolutionary principles in China, and even more well-worn (but distinctly derived) notions of popular exercise of civil and political rights in liberal democratic systems. That in itself is a provocation of an ultimately superior power.[109]

At the same time the response from the local authorities has either continued to encourage complicity by non-state actors, or to have created a policy of coordination with them. [110] Statements from the commander of the Chinese military garrison just augmented the number of voices speaking from quite opposed positions, especially in the wake of mass arrests of

---

[108] Tommy Monroe and Claire Jim, "Hong Kong government: protests are pushing city to 'extremely dangerous edge'," *Reuters* (3 August 2019), supra; ("During the night, protesters split into several different directions to disrupt transport networks. Police said they were "seriously paralysing traffic and affecting emergency services" and warned them to stop immediately. The leaderless nature of the protests has seen participants adopt a strategy called "be water", inspired by a maxim of the city's home-grown martial arts legend, Bruce Lee, that encourages them to be flexible or formless.").

[109] Read through a Maoist lens the provocation becomes more fundamental
Revolutionary dictatorship and counter-revolutionary dictatorship are by nature opposites, but the former was learned from the latter. Such learning is very important. If the revolutionary people do not master this method of ruling over the counter-revolutionary classes, they will not be able to maintain their state power, domestic and foreign reaction will overthrow that power and restore its own rule over China, and disaster will befall the revolutionary people.
Mao Zedong, "On the People's Democratic Dictatorship" (30 June 1949) in commemoration of the 28th anniversary of the CPC; available [https://www.marxists.org/reference/archive/mao/selected-works/volume-4/mswv4_65.htm].

[110] "Attackers beat Hong Kong autonomy protesters in subway," *Deutsche Welle* (22 July 2019); available [https://www.dw.com/en/attackers-beat-hong-kong-autonomy-protesters-in-subway/a-49677354].

protestors charged with violent protests in the SAR.[111] "The garrison marked the anniversary with the release of a video showing PLA soldiers storming a Hong Kong-style street, complete with traditional Chinese characters and a Hong Kong taxi." Indeed, this intimation of violence to quell violence appeared to further the "mend-break" (di xi 抵巇): strategy of the central authorities.[112]

Additional parties have sought some level of intervention, both within and outside of the SAR. The so-called hacker collective Anonymous has been an element of Hong Kong protesting since the time of the Umbrella Movement.[113] There was an echo of this in the anarchist collective active in Hong Kong from the start of the 2019 protests.[114]. Likewise, transnational civil society elements also sought to project themselves into the

---

[111] Ben Westcott, "Hong Kong protests: Head of China's military garrison condemns violence," *CNN* (1 Aug. 2019); available [https://www.cnn.com/2019/08/01/asia/hong-kong-china-pla-intl-hnk/index.html].

[112] Discussed in Chapter 3, supra.

[113] In 2014, for example, Anonymous announced its support for the Umbrella Movement:

It has come to our attention that recent tactics used against peaceful protesters here in the United States have found their way to Hong Kong," a mechanical-sounding voice in the video says. "To the protesters in Hong Kong, we have heard your plea for help. Take heart and take to your streets. You are not alone in this fight. Anonymous members all over the world stand with you, and will help in your fight for democracy.

Justin Wm. Moyer, "Report: Hacker collective Anonymous joins Hong Kong's Occupy Central," *The Washington Post* (2 October 2014); available [https://www.washingtonpost.com/news/morning-mix/wp/2014/10/02/report-anonymous-hacker-collective-joins-hong-kongs-occupy-central/].

[114] "Hong Kong: Anarchists in the Resistance to the Extradition Bill: An Interview," Crimethinc (22 June 2019); available [https://crimethinc.com/2019/06/22/hong-kong-anarchists-in-the-resistance-to-the-extradition-bill-an-interview] . Later, by September, the position of the Hong Kong Anarchist Collective became clear, as well as its goals. See "Three Months of Insurrection: An Anarchist Collective in Hong Kong Appraises the Achievements and Limits of the Revolt," CrimethInc. (20 September 2019); available [https://crimethinc.com/2019/09/20/three-months-of-insurrection-an-anarchist-collective-in-hong-kong-appraises-the-achievements-and-limits-of-the-revolt].

protests in Hong Kong, and connect those protests to civil and political rights projects with a global dimension.[115]

Similarly, elements of the security forces are allowing themselves to fall into the stratagem trap of labeling all foreigners as "agents."[116] It was reported that

> Images showing foreign workers at the site of protests are being circulated, sometimes alongside speculative text questioning why they are there. Some images have been circulated so widely that one foreign worker and long-term Hong Kong resident said he was now recognised in the street, including by police. "I now sometimes have to pose for CIA selfies with protesters," he said, referring to a post which asked if he was a member of US intelligence."[117]

It is a trap in the sense that once embraced it substantially limits flexibility in dealing with the internationalist camp, but it is alluring precisely because it echoes discursive tropes that have been at the heart of the working style of the vanguard during its revolutionary period.[118] This appears to reflect emerging policy

---

[115] See, e.g., "Against extradition: Hong Kong Justice and Peace invokes solidarity of Catholics worldwide and the G20," *Asia News* (27 June 2019); available [http://www.asianews.it/news-en/Against-extradition:-Hong-Kong-Justice-and-Peace-invokes-solidarity-of-Catholics-worldwide-and-the-G20-47391.html].

[116] See, Laurel Chor, "'A cop said I was famous': China accuses foreigners in Hong Kong of being 'agents'," *The Guardian* (31 July 2019); available [https://www.theguardian.com/world/2019/jul/31/a-cop-said-i-was-famous-china-accuses-foreigners-in-hong-kong-of-being-agents].

[117] Ibid.

[118] Even from the beginning Mao Zedong adopted a particular and precise posture with respect to the foreigners and China:

> We often say: 'The Chinese Government is the counting-house of our foreign masters' . Perhaps there are some who don't believe this. We also say: 'The false show of friendship by foreigners (especially Englishmen and Americans) is merely a pretense of "amity" in order that they may squeeze out more of the fat and blood of the Chinese people'. Perhaps there are some who don't believe this either. Ever since the prohibition against the export of cotton was repealed owing to the opposition of the foreigners, it has been impossible not to

among certain elements of the central authorities and certainly of the foreign policy apparatus. The government has begun to insinuate that local protests are to well-coordinated and managed to be entirely local.[119] If they are not local then the local people are merely the dupes of foreign powers—whether they represent foreign states or international civil collectives remains unexpressed. But that doesn't matter when one is engaging in rumor mongering as a stratagem against one's enemies, or as Xi Jinping might phrase it, to "seize the ground of new media."[120] This was better expressed in an official editorial sanctioned by the central authorities.

> What is happening in Hong Kong is no longer the airing of real or imagined grievances. It is of the same hue as the color revolutions that were instigated in the Middle East and North Africa - local anti-government elements colluding with external forces to topple governments utilizing modern communication technology to spread rumors, distrust and fear. What is different here is that the central government as well as the majority of Hong Kong residents will stand firmly behind the SAR government and the police to foil their schemes.[121]

The "this is a foreign bacillus" strategy is potently tempting. It permits the central authorities the ability to separate

---

believe what we have just said to some extent. (Mao Zedong, "The Chinese Government and the Foreigners" (29 August 1923); available [https://www.marxists.org/reference/archive/mao/selected-works/volume-6/mswv6_08.htm].

[119] Opinion: "Outside meddling has colored protests: China Daily editorial," *China Daily* (28 July 2019); available [http://www.chinadaily.com.cn/a/201907/28/WS5d3d9ebda310d830564016 21.html] ("judging from the preparation, targeting strategies, riot tactics and abundance of supplies, it takes naivety akin to simplemindedness to truly believe these activities are not being carefully orchestrated.").

[120] Cary Huang and Keith Zhai, "Xi Jinping rallies party for propaganda war on internet," *South China Morning Post* (4 September 2013); available [https://www.scmp.com/news/china/article/1302857/xi-jinping-rallies-party-propaganda-war-internet].

[121] Opinion: "Outside meddling has colored protests: China Daily editorial," , *supra*.

good from bad, Chinese for outside, clean from dirty, pure from impure. And classified in this way, officials and other authorities are better positioned discursively at least to attack that which is despised as something that is apart, foreign, imported, not Chinese and certainly not compatible with local culture, values, traditions, and hopes, especially when they are understood through the lens of Chinese Marxist-Leninism. [122] More importantly, it permits strong action against the element—individuals, ideology, political agendas, and agitation—which is thus defined as outside the body of China. In this way China is not dealing with protests that reflect internal faults and contradictions. Rather, the definitional classification—the discursive divisions and the creation of this "foreign" body in the heart of the popular agitation—permits a further rhetorical strategy: it further mends the connection between the "true" people of Hong Kong and breaks the connection between Hong Kong-China and the agitators who are by definition not part of the successfully implemented ideology of the true body politic.

---

[122] The power of this discursive tactic was noted begrudgingly by the anarchist collectives involved in the protests. A portion of the interview is worth noting:

it's hilarious that tankies share the exact same opinion as our formal head of state. It's an open secret that various pro-democracy NGOs, parties, and thinktanks receive American funding. It's not some kind of occult conspiracy theory that only tankies know about. But these tankies are suggesting that the platform that coordinates the marches—a broad alliance of political parties, NGOs, and the like—is also the ideological spearhead and architect of the "movement," which is simply a colossal misunderstanding. That platform has been widely denounced, discredited, and mocked by the "direct action" tendencies that are forming all around us, and it is only recently that, as we said above, there are slightly begrudging threads on the Internet offering them indirect praise for being able to coordinate marches that actually achieve something. If only tankies would stop treating everybody like mindless neo-colonial sheep acting at the cryptic behest of Western imperialist intelligence.

"Hong Kong: Anarchists in the Resistance to the Extradition Bill: An Interview," CrimethInc (22 June 2019, supra. A "tankie" is a mocking term applied to Marxist-Leninists employing fascist tactics to suppress popular revolution. See Mike Harman, "Everything you ever wanted to know about tankies, but were afraid to ask," Libcom.org (8 March 2018); available [https://libcom.org/blog/everything-you-ever-wanted-know-about-tankies-were-afraid-ask-08032018]. Here it is a reference to Hong Kong and central authorities.

This is a very old approach, and one with significant Maoist roots in the principle of people's democratic dictatorship.[123] As a Maoist concept before the 1970s, the division was based on the central contradiction[124] of class struggle. Class struggle analysis could produce a definition of people that included some and excluded others, based on class distinctions.[125] But contradiction analysis remains a core part of the dialectical foundation of Chinese Marxism, one that, as Mao Zedong

---

[123] See, Mao Zedong, "On the People's Democratic Dictatorship" (30 June 1949) in commemoration of the 28th anniversary of the CPC; available [https://www.marxists.org/reference/archive/mao/selected-works/volume-4/mswv4_65.htm].

[124] Mao Zedong, "On Contradiction" (August 1937 and thereafter revised); available [https://www.marxists.org/reference/archive/mao/selected-works/volume-1/mswv1_17.htm] ("The universality or absoluteness of contradiction has a twofold meaning. One is that contradiction exists in the process of development of all things, and the other is that in the process of development of each thing a movement of opposites exists from beginning to end."). Mao Zedong noted the central element of contradiction analysis—the determination of the essence of the contradiction, its polarities, and then determine the method for meeting that contradiction and resolving it.

> For instance, the contradiction between the proletariat and the bourgeoisie is resolved by the method of socialist revolution; the contradiction between the great masses of the people and the feudal system is resolved by the method of democratic revolution; the contradiction between the colonies and imperialism is resolved by the method of national revolutionary war; the contradiction between the working class and the peasant class in socialist society is resolved by the method of collectivization and mechanization in agriculture; contradiction within the Communist Party is resolved by the method of criticism and self-criticism; the contradiction between society and nature is resolved by the method of developing the productive forces.

Ibid.

[125] Mao Zedong, "On the People's Democratic Dictatorship," supra. ("You are not benevolent!" Quite so. We definitely do not apply a policy of benevolence to the reactionaries and towards the reactionary activities of the reactionary classes. Our policy of benevolence is applied only within the ranks of the people, not beyond them to the reactionaries or to the reactionary activities of reactionary classes. . . Here, the method we employ is democratic, the method of persuasion, not of compulsion. When anyone among the people breaks the law, he too should be punished, imprisoned or even sentenced to death; but this is a matter of a few individual cases, and it differs in principle from the dictatorship exercised over the reactionaries as a class.").

suggested, is inherent in the march of history and in the necessary movements of opposite to push forward development.

The resolution of contradiction in one era serves merely to expose the contradiction inherent in the next.[126] "In order to reveal the particularity of the contradictions in any process in the development of a thing, in their totality or interconnections, that is, in order to reveal the essence of the process, it is necessary to reveal the particularity of the two aspects of each of the contradictions in that process; otherwise it will be impossible to discover the essence of the process. This likewise requires the utmost attention in our study."[127] Here Mao Zedong offers the utility of contradiction analysis in the context of revolutionary and counterrevolutionary activity in a form that suggests the strategies of the central authorities in classifying the struggle in Hong Kong not as domestic (the particularity of contradiction) but as international (the universal in contradiction).

> When a revolutionary civil war develops to the point of threatening the very existence of imperialism and its running dogs, the domestic reactionaries, imperialism often adopts other methods in order to maintain its rule; it either tries to split the revolutionary front from within or sends armed forces to help the domestic reactionaries directly. At such a time, foreign imperialism and domestic reaction stand quite openly at one pole while the masses of the people stand at the other pole, thus forming the principal contradiction which determines or

---

[126] Thus, for example, the General Program of the Chinese Communist Party Constitution describes the movement from the principal contradiction of class struggle during the Mao Zedong era, to the principal contradiction of socialist modernization during the Deng Xiaoping era, to the current contradiction of "between the ever-growing needs of the people for a better life and unbalanced and inadequate development. Constitution of the Chinese Communist Party, "General Program," available [http://www.xinhuanet.com//english/download/Constitution_of_the_Communist_Party_of_China.pdf]. See Mao Zedong, "On Contradiction," supra. ("Processes change, old processes and old contradictions disappear, new processes and new contradictions emerge, and the methods of resolving contradictions differ accordingly.").

[127] See Mao Zedong, "On Contradiction," supra.

influences the development of the other contradictions. The assistance given by various capitalist countries to the Russian reactionaries after the October Revolution is an example of armed intervention. Chiang Kai-shek's betrayal in 1927 is an example of splitting the revolutionary front.[128]

By drawing on the discourse of revolutionary civil war, it is possible to treat different classes of people in Hong Kong differently—and in the process to use Mend-Break (di xi 抵巇) strategy effectively.

It is to the elaboration of this di xi 抵巇 strategy, perhaps, that the authorities continue to contemplate their future responses. That contemplation has produced a new batch *of statements that ought to be taken seriously.* These statements, which follow in English, [129] each press home the narrative that the central authorities started to construct in the weeks after the protests began in early June.

First is the emphasis on the disrespect of the protestors for the symbols of the state and of the sovereign.[130] The references to the desecration of the national flag and national symbols were

---

128 Ibid.

129 Hong Kong SAR Government Police Press Release: "Strongly condemn the destruction of the national flag and violent conduct, (香港特区政府、警方：强烈谴责破坏国旗及暴力行为，)*People's Daily Today* ([August 4, 2019] ; available [https://mp.weixin.qq.com/s/AoNDSVsBKrrJKCJVyRvGrA]; Hong Kong Liaison Office's Statement, "This kind of lawlessness must be severely punished according to the law," (香港中联办发声：对这种无法无天的恶行，必须依法严惩), *People's Daily Today* (August 4, 2019)]; available [https://mp.weixin.qq.com/s/kaHJ8-Jef4Q-EGKCLEtE_A]; and The Hong Kong and Macao Affairs Office of the State Council Press Release: "The HKMAO severely condemns the insult to the flag: strict punishment according to law, without leniency," *People's Daily Today* (August 4, 2019); available [https://mp.weixin.qq.com/s/MIM2mN6Zo-qG3EE81xGCwQ]; With thanks to Flora Sapio for translations.

130 A national flag and national emblem law was included in Annex III to the Hong Kong Basic Law of 1 July 1997. It was applied to the SAR through the enactment of the National Flag and National Emblem Ordinance (Cap. 614); available [https://www.elegislation.gov.hk/hk/A401].

meant to paint the protestors as seeking to rebel against the sovereign. This, then, is no ordinary local protest but a rebellion. It is the act of breaking apart that then puts them outside of the protections accorded to the people. They begin to become enemies of the state—and of the society which nourished them. The performance of that rebellion is measured against the disrespect of national symbols—this is rebellion by analogy.

Second, the violence of the protestors also represents a breaking apart. The protestors have fallen outside the law by breaking those rules meant to preserve the core of what brings all of China together beyond the lawful respect for national symbols—the joint efforts to maintain stability and produce ever greater prosperity. This breaking of the fundamental fabric of society places them beyond law, beyond community, and makes them a danger to the community. But also suggests the only way toward mending--to fall back into law and lawfulness--and that is possible only within the legal fabric supplied by the central authorities through its One Country Two Systems principle of managed autonomy.

Third, it is to the police that the great task of mending will be assigned. To preserve society it is necessary to mend the rip in the rule of law, in the fabric of national sovereignty, and in the communal joint efforts to foster stability and enhance prosperity. The police, then, are the needle necessary to sew back together the social fabric. But needles are sharp—and they pierce. That pain must be endured to make the fabric whole again. And in the process, those portions of the social fabric that have become tattered must be cut off and cast away. That is the function of the police and that is the object of law. It is in this sense that the punishment must be severe and the law strictly observed.

香港特区政府、警方：强烈谴责破坏国旗及暴力行为
131

---

[131] Hong Kong SAR Government Police Press Release: "Strongly condemn the destruction of the national flag and violent conduct, (香港特区政府、警方：强烈谴责破坏国旗及暴力行为,)*People's Daily Today* ([August 4, 2019] ; available

人民日报 Today

部分人士 3 日在香港油尖旺区举行游行，期间，一些极端分子做出破坏国旗、冲击警署等行为。香港特区政府发言人 4 日凌晨对此表示强烈谴责。香港警方也对暴力行为予以最严厉谴责。警方公布，在驱散示威者的行动中拘捕超过 20 人。

特区政府发言人表示，示威活动期间，部分激进示威者有暴力冲击警署、破坏汽车、多处纵火等行为。同时，怀疑有示威者刻意破坏国旗，触犯香港特别行政区《国旗及国徽条例》。政府对于激进示威者目无法纪、蓄意破坏社会安宁，甚至挑战国家主权，予以强烈谴责。警方会严正执法，而使用暴力的违法示威者亦应受到法律制裁。

香港警方表示，对激进示威者的暴力行为予以最严厉谴责，并强调会对所有非法及暴力行为严正执法。警方有能力及决心维护社会安宁，绝不姑息任何暴力行为。

香港警方介绍，3 日晚至 4 日凌晨期间，示威者以围栏等杂物堵塞红磡海底隧道收费广场两边行车线，导致两边隧道封闭、交通严重受阻；部分激进示威者围堵尖沙咀警署，大肆毁坏警署外设施并在多处纵火；部分激进示威者包围黄大仙纪律部队宿舍，向宿舍投掷爆竹及大量杂物，严重威胁居民的人身安全。

香港警方介绍，在驱散示威者的行动中，拘捕涉嫌非法集结及袭击等行为的示威者超过 20 人。

[https://mp.weixin.qq.com/s/AoNDSVsBKrrJKCJVyRvGrA] (emphasis added in part in translation).

Hong Kong SAR Government Police: strongly condemn the destruction of the national flag and violent conduct
People's Daily Today [August 4, 2019]

On [August] 3 while some persons held a march in Yau Tsim Mong District, Hong Kong some extremists kept conducts such as destroying the national flag and attacking the police station. *In the early morning of [August] 4, strong condemnation was expressed by a spokesperson of the Hong Kong SAR government. Violence was also sternly condemned by the Hong Kong Police. The Police announced that more than 20 people were arrested during the operations held to disperse the demonstrators.*

A spokesperson of the SAR government stated that during the demonstrations, some of extremist demonstrators had violently attacked the police station, destroying vehicles, and committing arson in several places. At the same time, it is suspected that demonstrators deliberately destroyed the national flag, violating the National Flag and National Emblem Ordinance of the Hong Kong Special Administrative Region. The government strongly condemned extremist demonstrators' disregard for law and discipline [目无法纪], deliberate undermining of social peace to the point of challenging national sovereignty. The police will strictly enforce the law, and unlawful demonstrators who commit violence will also be subject to legal sanctions.

The Hong Kong Police said that they severely condemn the violence of extremist demonstrators and stressed that law will be strictly enforced [to punish] all illegal and violent acts. *The police have the ability and determination to maintain social peace and do not tolerate any violence.*

The Hong Kong Police said that from the evening of the [August] 3 to the early morning of [August] 4, demonstrators blocked the traffic lanes on both sides of the toll plaza of the Hung Hom Cross Harbour Tunnel using fences and various objects. As a result, the two sides of the tunnel were closed and the traffic was seriously obstructed. Some extremist demonstrators blockaded the Tsim Sha Tsui Police Station. The facilities outside the police station were destroyed and arson was committed in several places. Some extremists demonstrators surrounded the Wong Tai Sin Disciplined Services Quarters throwing firecrackers and a large number of objects into the dormitory, which seriously threatened the residents' personal safety.

The Hong Kong Police said that during the operation [held] to disperse the demonstrators, more than 20 demonstrators were arrested such conduct as for illegal assembly and attacks.

香港中联办发声：对这种无法无天的恶行，必须依法严[132]

人民日报 Today

　　中央政府驻香港特别行政区联络办公室负责人4日发表声明，严厉谴责香港极端激进分子侮辱国旗、挑战国家主权的违法行径。

　　该负责人表示，8 月 3 日下午，香港有丧心病狂的极端激进分子在尖沙咀扯下某建筑前悬挂的中华人民共和国国旗并扔入海中，这是继 7 月 21 日激进示威者围攻中联办、污损国徽后对国家尊严的又一次公开挑衅。该负责人强调，国家主权和尊严不容挑战，"一国

---

[132] Hong Kong Liaison Office's Statement, "This kind of lawlessness must be severely punished according to the law," (香港中联办发声：对这种无法无天的恶行，必须依法严惩), *People's Daily Today* (August 4, 2019)]; available [https://mp.weixin.qq.com/s/kaHJ8-Jef4Q-EGKCLEtE_A] (emphasis added in part in translation).

两制"原则底线不容触碰，包括广大香港同胞在内的全体中国人的爱国情感不容肆意伤害。对这种无法无天的 恶 行 必 须 依 法 严 惩 。

该负责人重申，坚定支持特区政府和香港警方严正执法，依法惩治暴力犯罪分子，维护香港法治和社会 稳 定 。

Hong Kong Liaison Office's statement: This kind of lawlessness must be severely punished according to the law
People's Daily Today [August 4, 2019]

On [August] 4, the head of the Liaison Office of the Central Government in the Hong Kong Special Administrative Region issued a statement *sternly condemning the illegal acts of Hong Kong extremists insulting the national flag and challenging national sovereignty.*

The person in charge said that on the afternoon of August 3, a deranged extremist [有丧心病狂的极端激进分子] in Hong Kong pulled down the flag of the People's Republic of China hanging in front of a building in Tsim Sha Tsui and threw it into the sea. This followed the July 21 siege of the Liaison Office by extremist protesters, [who] after defacing the national emblem, once again publicly challenged the dignity of the country. The person in charge stressed national sovereignty and dignity cannot be challenged. The bottom line of the principle of "One Country, Two Systems" cannot be touched. The patriotic sentiments of all Chinese, including the vast majority of Hong Kong compatriots cannot be hurt. *This kind of lawlessness must be severely punished according to the law.*

The responsible person reiterated that he firmly supports the SAR Government and the Hong Kong Police in law enforcement, punishment of violent criminals in accordance with the law, and upholding of the rule of law and social stability in Hong Kong.

————————

国务院港澳办严厉谴责侮辱国旗行径：依法严厉惩处，绝不手软 133
人民日报 Today

国务院港澳事务办公室发言人4日就香港8月3日晚数名极端激进示威者扯下某建筑物前悬挂的中华人民共和国国旗并扔入海中一事发表谈话，对有关恶劣行径予以严厉谴责。

该发言人表示，8月3日晚，数名蒙面黑衣示威者在香港尖沙咀扯下某建筑物前悬挂的中华人民共和国国旗，扔入海中。这一行径严重触犯了《中华人民共和国国旗法》和香港特别行政区《国旗与国徽条例》，公然冒犯国家、民族尊严，肆意践踏"一国两制"原则底线，极大地伤害了包括香港同胞在内的全中国人民的感情。我们对此表示强烈愤慨。我们坚决支持香港特别行政区警队和司法机构果断执法、严正司法，尽快将违法犯罪分子绳之以法。

该发言人表示，极少数极端激进分子侮辱国旗的丑陋行径再一次表明，他们的所作所为已经远远超出了自由表达意见的范畴，滑进犯罪的深渊。对此必须依法严厉惩处，绝不手软。

The Hong Kong and Macao Affairs Office of the State Council severely condemns the insult to the flag: strict punishment according to law, without leniency

————————————————

133 Hong Kong and Macao Affairs Office of the State Council Press Release: "The HKMAO severely condemns the insult to the flag: strict punishment according to law, without leniency" (), *People's Daily Today* (August 4, 2019); available [https://mp.weixin.qq.com/s/MIM2mN6Zo-qG3EE81xGCwQ] (emphasis added in part in translation).

People's Daily Today [August 4, 2019]

A spokesman for the Hong Kong and Macao Affairs Office of the State Council issued a statement on [August] 4, on several extremist demonstrators who on August 3 pulled off the national flag of the People's Republic of China hanging in front of a building and threw it into the sea, *expressing a severe condemnation of such a vile conduct.*

The spokesman said that in the evening of August 3, a number of masked protesters clad in black pulled off a flag of the People's Republic of China hanging in front of a building in Tsim Sha Tsui, Hong Kong and threw it into the sea. This act seriously violated the "*Law of the People's Republic of China on the National Flag*" and the "*Ordinance to provide for the use and protection of the national flag and national emblem in the Hong Kong Special Administrative Region and for incidental matters*". It flagrantly offended the dignity of the nation, the dignity of the ethnicity [民族尊严] and arbitrarily trampled on the "One Country, Two Systems" principle, greatly hurting the feelings of the entire Chinese People including Hong Kong compatriots. *We strongly support the Hong Kong Special Administrative Region Police Force and the judiciary's decisive enforcement strict justice, and their bringing criminals to justice as soon as possible.*

The spokesperson said that the vile acts of a very small number of extremists who insulted the national flag have once again shown that their actions have gone far beyond the scope of free expression and slipped into the abyss of crime. *This must be severely punished in accordance with the law, without leniency.*

The three Press Release Statements were coordinated to amplify the narrative and perspective that is becoming the more well-developed line of the local and national authorities in the face of the continuing violence and quickly changing objectives of the protestors, and the protestor factions. The statements were meant to echo each other, but to do so in a way that emphasized a united front among the leadership cores of the state administrative apparatus—from the police, to the SAR government, to the representatives of the central authorities. The focus on patriotism—the flag desecration issue—touches on the notion of foreign intervention and manipulation, and breaks the tie between the protestors and the "real" people of Hong Kong. Foreigners have no business projecting their agendas into the territories over which China is sovereign. At the same time that broken allegiance of the protestors triggers the responsibility of the police authorities to protect the state and law against them and their foreign managers. And the violence is conformation that to mend the Hong Kong SAR, it will be necessary to break the protestors—strictly and severely.

The failure of foreigners and the protestors to understand this developing perspective and its discursive power; the inability of either to appreciate its intimate connection with deep roots in Chinese Marxist-Leninist ideology and practice; the dismissal of the importance of these core areas and the red lines they represent, will likely produce a miscalculation that in terms of the power imbalance between the protagonists will not turn out well for the local people of Hong Kong now on the streets.

✳ ✳ ✳

Chapter 5

Monday 5 August 2019
Further Statement from the Authorities on the Situation in Hong Kong: 坚决支持香港警方严正执法制止暴力 ["Strongly Support the Hong Kong Police to Strictly Enforce the Law and Stop Violence"]

The situation in Hong Kong continues to be dynamic. Opinion polls[134] have been circulating about the mood of the population. The mood of the public in Hong Kong continues to run strongly counter to the narrative being created by the apparatus of local and central government authorities.

結語。調查於 7 月 24 至 26 日進行。由於事態發展迅速，調查結果發布時民意可能已有所改變，但仍有助各界掌握民意。近七成市民反對逃犯條例修訂，而反對者於各組群中均大幅超過支持者。特首、警隊和中央政府被認為是造成現時管治危機的最重要因素，而「外部勢力」在各組群中均被認為是不重要的因素。六成市民不滿警隊處理事件的整體表現。對於示威者表現屬於克制抑或有過度使用武力則意見紛紜，但較多市民認為示威者過度使用武力。反修例運動的各大訴求均有一定民意支持，當中又以設立獨立調查委員會和全面撤回條例修訂草案獲得的支持最多。年輕組群的意見明顯有異於其他人士，他們的不滿主要建基於對政府和制度的不信任，和對民主自由的追求。只針對房屋問題下功夫或專注發展經濟均並非對症下藥，不能解決當前困局。[Conclusion. The survey was

134 鍾庭耀, 修訂逃犯條例」民意調查結果簡報 (Zhong Tingyao, "Briefing on the Results of the Public Opinion Survey on the Amendment to the Fugitive Offenders Ordinance"), Hong Kong Public Opinion Research Institute (2 August 2019); available [https://static1.squarespace.com/static/5cfd1ba6a7117c000170d7aa/t/5d43f 2fa3b50bf0001af5d0c/1564734205477/pcf_anti_extradition_ppt_v2_pori.pdf] .

conducted from July 24 to 26. Due to the rapid development of the situation, public opinion may have changed when the survey results are released, but it still helps people from all walks of life grasp public opinion. Nearly 70% of citizens opposed the amendment to the Fugitive Offenders Ordinance, and the opponents significantly exceeded the supporters in all groups. The chief executive, the police force and the central government are considered to be the most important factors causing the current governance crisis, while "external forces" are considered unimportant factors in all groups. 60% of the public are dissatisfied with the overall performance of the police in handling the incident. There are divergent opinions on whether the demonstrators are restrained or have excessive use of force, but more people believe that the demonstrators have used excessive force. The major demands of the anti-regulation movement have a certain degree of public support. Among them, the establishment of an independent investigation committee and the complete withdrawal of the draft amendments have received the most support. The opinions of the young group are obviously different from those of others. Their dissatisfaction is mainly based on their distrust of the government and the system, and the pursuit of democracy and freedom. Efforts only to address the housing problem or focus on economic development are not the right medicine and cannot solve the current dilemma.][135]

In line with those results the unrest on the streets continues. And on the other side, the central authorities appear to encourage rumors of countermeasures preparations, especially by intimations of the trajectories of activity in Shenzhen recorded in long deleted tweets.

Its ripples now are extending beyond the small space that is the territory of the Hong Kong SAR outward along China's

---

[135] Ibid., PowerPoint slide 17.

maritime and overland silk roads.[136] It is understood, for example, that the Italian diplomatic corps have been tweeting about events and insinuating the possibility of effects of the HK situation on approaching China's Belt and Road Initiative, even as influential bloggers in Italy have taken the line of the Chinese central authorities, ridiculing the Hong Kong Protestors and suggesting that they are instruments of foreign civil and public forces.[137] Chinese exiles, on the other hand, seek to press a different perspective, one that ties the fate of Hong Kong. An opinion piece authored by Ai Weiwei and circulated by the New York Times asserted in part:

> Young people in Hong Kong are aware, too, that theirs is not just a local struggle. They know that Hong Kong, with its habits of civil freedoms inherited from British rule on one side and its confrontation with China's dictatorship on the other, is a laboratory for the world. Will — can? — a free populace that wishes to remain free be annexed by an authoritarian machine? That precedent would be a nightmare for the world. And perhaps a turning point.[138]

---

[136] "The Belt and Road Initiative is a hallmark economic strategy proposed by Chinese President Xi Jinping, seeking to link China to Europe and Africa through a land 'belt' and a maritime 'Silk Road'." And it remains controversial. Hog Wrong, "HSBC tweet backfires spectacularly after asking followers for views on China's 'Belt and Road' plan," Hong Kong Free Press (21 May 219); available [https://hongkongfp.com/2019/05/21/hsbc-tweet-backfires-spectacularly-asking-followers-views-chinas-belt-road-plan/].

[137] "Il caso di Hong Kong e i tentativi di destabilizzazione," Il Blog di Beppe Grillo ()15 June 2019); available [https://www.beppegrillo.it/il-caso-di-hong-kong-e-i-tentativi-di-destabilizzazione/].

[138] Ai Weiwei, "Can Hong Kong's Resistance Win?: A loss to Chinese authoritarianism would set a frightening precedent for the world," The New York Times (Perry Link (trans) 12 July 2019); available [https://www.nytimes.com/2019/07/12/opinion/hong-kong-china-protests.html]. Ai also raised the point of collusion between Chinese authorities and those foreigners within China's global economic orbit:

> China is not alone in wanting to avoid "trouble" in Hong Kong. Many people in Western government and business circles who profit from the Chinese system of oppression concur. Hong Kong is a hub of this system, and both sides stand to lose if Hong Kong's role is damaged or lost.

Ibid.

There are also fears that Hong Kong will be abandoned as a global financial center as it appears to merge with the Mainland.[139] The central authorities, it seems, are now applying the same strategy to foreigners as it is applying to local Hong Kong people—distinguishing between allies and enemies, seeking to come closer to allies and excising enemies as foreigners and law breakers.[140]

It is in the context of these fast-moving events that the publication today, in all local news outlets of a short headline article--坚决支持香港警方严正执法制止暴力 ["Strongly Support the Hong Kong Police to Strictly Enforce the Law and Stop Violence"]--issued by the "People's Daily Commentator" provides a valuable insight into the thinking and mood of the authorities in the current situation. It appears as an Upper A1 version [141]and a lower A2 version.[142]

Both parts of the article (Upper A1 and Lower A2)) appear below in the original Chinese and with a crude English translation. The English version includes added emphasis on those portions of the statements that may be worth additional focus.

A2 Version

---

[139] This issue raised here initially within months of the start of the protests became more important as events continued to unfold. This produced the start of academic debate on the global ramifications for the protests for Hong Kong. Some, interestingly enough aligned with the stability and prosperity narrative cultivated by local and central authorities since early in the protests. See, e.g., David R. Meyer, "The Hong Kong protests will not undermine it as a leading global financial centre," *Area Development and Policy* 5(3):256-268 (2020)

[140] Postscript: It will be useful to compare the evolution of this position with that of the protestors and internationalists, discussed infra Chapter 15.

[141] 坚决支持香港警方 严正执法制止暴力 (["Strongly Support the Hong Kong Police to Strictly Enforce the Law and Stop Violence"); *People's Daily Commentator* (5 August 2019); available [http://njrb.njdaily.cn/njrb/html/2019-08/05/content_544029.htm?div=-1].

[142] 坚决支持香港警方严正执法制止暴力 (["Strongly Support the Hong Kong Police to Strictly Enforce the Law and Stop Violence"); *People's Daily Commentator* (5 Augst 2019); available [http://njrb.njdaily.cn/njrb/html/2019-08/05/content_544039.htm?div=-1].

坚决支持香港警方严正执法制止暴力

人民日报评论员

从围攻立法会、香港中联办，到围攻警署、制造爆炸品等暴力武器，香港近期暴力行为不断升级，已令所有关爱香港的人痛心不已。香港当务之急是坚决支持香港警方严正执法制止暴力，尽快恢复社会安定，维护香港良好法治。

一个多月来，香港反对派和激进暴力分子蓄意制造暴力事件，已经完全超出了和平示威的范畴，脱离了诉求轨道、扭曲了事件本身。众所周知，事情起因于修订《逃犯条例》，但特区政府早就宣布暂缓修例，相应的立法工作也随之完全停止。然而，激进暴力分子不但没有止步，还变本加厉。他们围堵香港中联办、污损国徽、围攻警署、殴打警察、污辱国旗，甚至在非法游行集会中喊出"港独"的口号，不仅践踏香港法治，更触碰"一国两制"原则底线。种种迹象显示，激进暴力分子根本不是为了反修例诉求，根本就在于搞乱香港、搞衰香港，摧毁"一国两制"。

任何文明和法治社会都不会容忍暴力横行。我们看到，整个事件蔓延过程中，作为社会秩序的守护者，香港警方承受了巨大的压力。针对香港社会的和平游行集会，特区警方一直依法批准并提供必要的协助。然而，激进暴力分子以和平游行作掩护，每每突破法治底线，用砖头、铁枝甚至汽油弹攻击警察，使用有毒有害液体、粉末袭击警察，甚至咬断警察手指，其行径之残忍令人发指。（下转 A2 版）

Resolutely support the Hong Kong police to strictly enforce the law to stop the violence [Emphasis added]

People's Daily Commentator

From the siege of the Legislative Council, the Hong Kong Liaison Office, to the siege of police stations, the manufacture of explosives and other violent weapons, *the recent escalation of violence in Hong Kong has made people who love Hong Kong feel distressed.* Hong Kong's top priority is to resolutely support the Hong Kong police in strictly implementing law enforcement to stop the violence, restore social stability as soon as possible, and safeguard Hong Kong's good rule of law.

For more than a month, the Hong Kong opposition and radical violent deliberate violent incidents have completely exceeded the scope of peaceful demonstrations, separated from the track of appeals and distorted the incident itself. As we all know, the incident was caused by the revision of the Fugitive Offenders Ordinance. However, the SAR Government has long announced that the suspension of the amendments will be suspended and the corresponding legislative work will be completely stopped. *However, the radical violent elements have not only stopped, but have also intensified. They blocked the Hong Kong Liaison Office, defiled the national emblem, besieged the police station, beaten the police, insulted the national flag, and even shouted the slogan of "Hong Kong independence" in illegal meeting and assembly. They not only trampled on the rule of law in Hong Kong, but also touched the "one country, two systems" principle.* There are indications that radical violent elements are not aimed at anti-reforms. They simply confuse Hong Kong, ruin Hong Kong, and destroy "one country, two systems."

No civilization or rule of law society will tolerate rampant violence. *We have seen that the Hong Kong police have been under tremendous pressure as the guardian of social order throughout the spread of the incident.* The SAR police have always approved and provided necessary assistance in accordance with the peaceful procession rally in Hong Kong. *However, the radical violent elements used the peaceful march as a cover.* Every time they broke through the bottom line of the rule of law, they attacked the police with bricks, iron bars and even petrol bombs. They used poisonous and harmful liquids, powders to attack the police, and even bit the police fingers. The cruelty of their actions was horrendous. (Lower A2 version)

———

Upper A1 Version

坚决支持香港警方严正执法制止暴力

（上接 A1 版）他们还煽动仇警情绪，人肉搜索警察家人，恶毒咒骂警察子女。在个人与家庭都饱受身心困扰的情况下，香港警队仍坚守岗位、恪尽职守、无惧无畏、忍辱负重，令人敬佩，其专业精神值得香港市民的赞许。

暴力冲击行为已严重威胁香港公众安全，对香港法治、社会秩序、经济民生和国际形象都造成严重影响。零售业首当其冲受到冲击，一个多月来，营业额大幅下跌。人们忧心的是，如果暴力行为再持续，法治基础、营商环境、社会秩序等香港经济立足的根基势必遭到破坏。从目前态势看，要有效制止暴力，不能仅靠香港警方孤军奋战。香港各界都要充分行动起来，旗帜鲜明反对暴力、抵制暴力。

希望广大香港市民清醒地认识到当前事态的严重性，对激进暴力分子坚定说"不"，对企图摧毁"一国两制"、搞乱香港、搞衰香港的势力坚定说"不"，坚决阻止他们祸害香港的行径，坚决支持香港警方严正执法制止暴力。

香港是中国的香港。香港的繁荣稳定，事关 700 多万香港市民的福祉，事关国家的主权、安全，事关"一国两制"的前途命运。中央政府坚定地支持香港警方、有

关部门和司法机构依法惩治暴力违法行为，追究暴力
犯罪者的刑事责任。

载 8 月 5 日人民日报
新华社北京 8 月 4 日电

*Resolutely support the Hong Kong police
Strict law enforcement to stop violence* [Emphasis added]

(Upper A1 version) They also incited the hatred of the police, they crowdsourced information about the families of the police, viciously cursing the police children. In the case of both personal and family suffering, the Hong Kong Police Force still adheres to its duties, dedication, fearlessness and humiliation. It is admirable and its professionalism deserves the approval of the people of Hong Kong.

Violent shocks have seriously threatened the public safety of Hong Kong and have a serious impact on the rule of law, social order, economic livelihood and international image. The retail industry was the first to suffer, and its turnover fell sharply for more than a month. What people are worried about is that if the violence continues, the foundation of the rule of law, business environment, social order and other Hong Kong's economic base will be destroyed. From the current situation, to effectively stop the violence, *we cannot rely solely on the Hong Kong police to fight alone.* All walks of life in Hong Kong must take full action and have a clear-cut attitude against violence and resistance to violence.

I hope that the people of Hong Kong will clearly understand the seriousness of the current state of affairs, firmly say "no" to the radical violent elements, and firmly say "no" to the forces that attempt to destroy "one country, two systems", mess up Hong Kong, and ruin Hong Kong, and resolutely stop their scourge. Hong Kong's actions strongly support the Hong Kong police in strictly implementing law enforcement to stop the violence.

Hong Kong is China's Hong Kong. The prosperity and stability of Hong Kong is related to the well-being of more than 7 million Hong Kong citizens. *It is related to the sovereignty and security of the country and is related to the future and destiny of "one country, two systems."* The central government firmly supports the Hong Kong police, relevant departments and the judiciary in punishing violent violations and prosecuting the criminal responsibility of violent offenders.

On August 5, the People's Daily
Xinhua News Agency, Beijing, August 4th

———

Consider the recurring key phrases. The first touches on the *escalation of violence.* In the A2 Version it touches on the consequences for the "real" people of Hong Kong (as distinguished from the rebellious protestors: "*the recent escalation of violence in Hong Kong has made people who love Hong Kong feel distressed.*" Here one focused on the internal effects on good citizens in Hong Kong. In the A1 Version, on the other hand, the initial reference to the escalation of violence touches on more abstract bodies and on the body politic of China itself: the violence "*seriously threatened the public safety of Hong Kong and have a serious impact on the rule of law, social order, economic livelihood and international image.*"

The second touches on the aggressive overreaching of the protestors in contrast to the reactive restraint of the authorities. In the A2 Version one notes: "*the radical violent elements have not only stopped, but have also intensified,*" that the "*radical violent elements used the peaceful march as a cover,*" and that "*the Hong Kong police have been under tremendous pressure as the guardian of social order throughout the spread of the incident.* Here one is focused on the demonization of the protestors and their detachment form the body politic—the instrument for the earlier creation of distress. In the AI Version, the focus is on the coming together of the community with the police to repress the protesters. It declares: *"we cannot rely solely on the Hong Kong police to fight alone.* All walks of life in Hong Kong must take full action and have a clear-cut attitude against violence and resistance to violence."

The third touches on the effects to the body politic, and its internal and external integrity. In the A2 Version, the police are depicted as the instruments of popular vigilance against unruly forces. *"We have seen that the Hong Kong police have been under tremendous pressure as the guardian of social order throughout the spread of the incident."* The unruliness threatened to overturn the settled and stable order and was marked by signs of the real intent of the protestors—disrespect for the nation and a striving for Hong Kong independence. In the A2 version, *"It is related to the sovereignty and security of the country and is related to the future and destiny of "one country, two systems."* The protesters are criminals: the authorities patient and long suffering.

The contrast brings to mind the distinctions in the *I Ching* between the protestors and the local and central authorities. The former is embedded withing the notion of the "taming power of the small.[143] The allusion is to the consequences for the protestors of persisting in causing effects on law abiding individuals). The

---

[143] Here a reference to I Ching Hexagram 9, Hsiao Ch'u / The Taming Power of the Small. The interpretation from Richard Wilhelm, *I Ching or the Book of Changes* (3rd ed. (Cary F. Barnes (trans), NY Penguin Books, 1995) is useful:

The bottom line marked means: Return to the way. How could there be blame in this? Good fortune.

The 2nd line marked means: He allows himself to be drawn into returning. Good fortune.

The 3rd line marked means: The spokes burst out of the wagon wheel. Man and wife roll their eyes.

The 4th line marked means: If you are sincere, blood vanishes and fear gives way. No blame.

The 5th line marked means: If you are sincere and loyally attached, You are rich in your neighbor.

The top line marked means: The rain comes, there is rest. This is due to the lasting effect of character. Perseverance brings the woman into danger. The moon is nearly full. If the superior man persists, Misfortune comes.

latter is bound up in the "taming power of the great,"[144] those external relations and the bodies politic affected and the ultimate victory of those who assert power carefully. Indeed. Reading the two versions' discussion about violence becomes clearer in light of the *I Ching* Hexagrams and what it suggests for response. From a discursive perspective, it seems, even the heavens (traditionally understood) will ultimately vindicate the state. In the face of this rhetorical power, it is certainly necessary for the protestors to develop a discursive counter equally or more powerful. Yet this is precisely marks the greatest responsive failure of the protesters. The taming power of the small suggests a great need to reframe the great into the small. The protesters miss the opportunity, for example, to recast disrespect for the emblems of state to signs of allegiance to greater ideals that have been corrupted by those in power. They fail to turn the argument of lawlessness against the local authorities. They have only begun to turn the police repones against itself.

Those are the discursive strengths of the small. It will be interesting to see whether the protesters are able to undermine in this way the power of the great. I am not hopeful. The central authorities are sure of their objectives and comfortable in their ideology. The protesters may not be. In the process the protesters may miss the opportunity suggested by the opinion poll research

---

[144] Here a reference to Hexagram 26 of the I Ching, Ta Ch'u / The Taming Power of the Great. The interpretation from Richard Wilhelm, *I Ching or the Book of Changes* supra is again useful:

> The bottom line marked means: Danger is at hand. It furthers one to desist.
> The 2nd line marked means: The axletrees are taken from the wagon.
> The 3rd line marked means: A good horse that follows others; Awareness of danger, With perseverance, furthers. Practice chariot driving and armed defense daily. It furthers one to have somewhere to go.
> The 4th line marked means: The headboard of a young bull. Great good fortune.
> The 5th line marked means: The tusk of a gelded boar. Good fortune.
> The top line marked means: One attains the way of heaven. Success.

of Zhong Tingyao.[145] To the extent that in rare news conferences, [146] all that is offered are variations of distillations of liberal democratic rhetoric,[147] it is likely that this will not resonate as powerfully. They are prepared to be like water if the People's Liberation Army steps in,[148] and offered information (useful) and apologies.[149]

Nonetheless, the protesters do appear to have made a very small start to germinate a counter discourse to that already being generated by the central authorities. This is done self-consciously. They declared, for example, that "'This platform aims to act as a counterweight to the government's monopoly on the political discourse on this issue,' they said, adding they were not affiliated with any political party or group."[150] a political theory that would detach their demands from the confines of the Sino-British Joint Declaration[151] and its 2047 end date when they declare: "'The pursuit of democracy, liberty and equality is an inalienable right of every citizen. We therefore call on the government to refrain

---

[145] 鍾庭耀, 修訂逃犯條例」民意調查結果簡報 (Zhong Tingyao, "Briefing on the Results of the Public Opinion Survey on the Amendment to the Fugitive Offenders Ordinance"),

[146] "Protesters in Hong Kong decry government's 'empty rhetoric' amid warning from China," CBC (6 August 2019); available [https://www.cbc.ca/news/world/hong-kong-protests-news-conferences-1.5237036] ("Hong Kong protesters held an inaugural "People's Press Conference" on Tuesday to condemn what they called the government's "empty rhetoric" and instances of alleged police abuse.").

[147] "Masked Hong Kong protesters hold rare press conference ," CNA (6 August 2019(; available [https://www.channelnewsasia.com/news/asia/masked-hong-kong-protesters-hold-rare-press-conference-11785254] "'We call on the government to return the power back to the people and to address the demands of Hong Kong citizens,' they said as they read out their statements in both English and Cantonese."

[148]"Protesters in Hong Kong decry government's 'empty rhetoric' amid warning from China," supra.

[149] Ibid. ("At the protesters' news conference, they apologized for the inconveniences brought on by a general strike Monday that paralyzed regular workday operations in the city.").

[150] "Masked Hong Kong protesters hold rare press conference ," supra.

[151] Joint Declaration of the Government of the United Kingdom of Great Britain and Northern Ireland and the Government of the People's Republic of China on the Question of Hong Kong (19 December 1984); available [https://www.cmab.gov.hk/en/issues/jd2.htm].

from exterminating our right to pursue these universal values,' they said..." [152] There is a hint of the discursive upending of rhetoric of lawlessness; "They criticised the city's police force which they accused of showing a "total loss of self-discipline ... and their incompetence in carrying out their lawful duties." [153] The effectiveness of these beginnings has yet to be determined. But it will require that the discourse of the protesters, rather than their bodies, be more like water if it is to drown the already quite pervasive deployment of the rhetoric of the central authorities.

Still, there is a marked contrast between the discursive emphasis of the central authorities and those of the protester groups. While the central authorities have appeared to have already invested much in the development of a narrative discourse that is meant to shape the conversion about events in Hong Kong, the protester groups appear to continue to emphasize a physical discourse. The essence of that discourse are the physical bodies on the streets, those who seek to engage in the only way they may believe that is now open to them, through disruption of the normal flows of social and economic relations. The object of the performance of that discourse on the streets of Hong Kong appear to be meant to underline the unreasonableness of the central authorities, and the violence of the local authorities. The focus appears, though to remain on the event that sparked the protests at the beginning of June--the Extradition Law.

The protesters seek to make meaning with their bodies; the central authorities with their words; the local authorities through their police powers. Each is quite confident that their meaning making can be projected outward. It remains to be seem which actually prevails. The power of the small indeed!

✳ ✳ ✳

[152] "Masked Hong Kong protesters hold rare press conference ," supra.
[153] Ibid.

Chapter 6

Tuesday 6 August 2019
Thoughts on Albert Chen Hung-yee 陳弘毅 (Hong Kong U.): 理性溝通的困境 ["The Dilemma of Rational Communication"]

Beyond the great stakeholders in the turmoil within which Hong Kong has found itself, there are a few voices that seek to take a necessary and more Olympian view. These voices also have at their heart the long-term welfare of Hong Kong within its national context. They are witnesses to the tragic context in which they find themselves, completely aware of the compulsions that drive the great protagonists to an inevitable contradiction and its tragic (in the Greek sense) conclusions. And like the chorus in a Greek tragedy, [154] they serve as the principal witnesses and commentators of the action around them. They form part of the production of the tragedy but stand apart from the tragedy itself.

> Brecht describes the effect of watching Chinese actors: 'The efforts in question were directed to playing in such a way that the audience was hindered from simply identifying itself with the characters in the play. Acceptance or rejection of their actions and utterances was meant to take place on the conscious plane . . . Western techniques of alienation. . . are dependent less on acting style the method on which Chinese alienation is based, than on production methods, such as interrupting the action with 'irrelevant' songs, dances, and sermons.[155]

That distance between the central dramatic elements around which the tragic elements coalesce and the detachment of the

---

[154] Albert Weiner, "The Function of the Tragic Greek Chorus," *Theater Journal* 32(2):205-212 (1980) ("We therefore know what the chorus did: it danced and sang" Ibid., 205)

[155] Ibid., pp. 210-211, quoting, in part, *Brecht on Theater* (John Willett (ed. And Trans., NY: Hill and Wang, 1964) at p. 91.

Hong Kong Between "One Country" and "Two Systems"
6. Thoughts on Albert Chen's "The Dilemma of Rational Communication"

92

chorus as a production element—*as a part* and also *apart* from the drama about which they hover, as a stately interruption about but not within the action—nicely describes the perhaps awful position of academics in the context of the situation in Hong Kong

One of the most profound is that of Albert Chen Hung-yee 陳弘毅, a professor at the University of Hong Kong Department of Law.[156] Professor Chen served as a member of the Law Reform Commission of Hong Kong in 2002-08, a member of the Committee on Review of Post-Service Outside Work for Directorate Civil Servants in 2008-09, and a member of the Commission for Strategic Development of the Hong Kong Government in 2005-2012. He is currently a member of the Committee for the Basic Law of the Hong Kong Special Administrative Region under the Standing Committee of the National People's Congress of the People's Republic of China, a Justice of the Peace, and an honorary professor at the Renmin University of China, Tsinghua University, Peking University, Zhongshan University, Macau University, and the Institute of Advanced Studies in Social Sciences of Fudan University.

His essay, 理性溝通的困境[157] ["The Dilemma of Rational Communication"] first appeared on 2 August in the Ming Newspaper supplements [發表於《明報》副刊] is the first part of a promised two-part intervention. It is worth reading, especially for a sense of alternative paths toward a common goal. Its object is straightforward—to serve as a choral to move the course of events from the subconscious to the conscious plane to a particular end. The abstract makes that clear enough:

---

[156] Professor Chen's professional biography may be found on the website of the University of Hong Kong as of the date of the writing of this chapter; available [https://www.law.hku.hk/academic_staff/professor-albert-chen-hung-yee/].

[157] 陳弘毅/理性溝通的困境 ，發表於《明報》副刊 2019 年 8 月 2 日星期五; available https://news.mingpao.com/ pns/ 作 家 專 欄 /article/20190802/s00018/1564684946720/理性溝通的困境]. Post Script: Professor Chen's collection of selected works as it developed over his academic career, from 1984 to the present on issues of Hong Kong and Mainland China, will be published as *The Changing Legal Orders in Hong Kong and Mainland China: Essays on 'One Country, Two Systems'* (City University of Hong Kong Press, 2021)

香港正瀕臨動亂邊緣，不少社會人士（包括我在內）都呼籲大家向暴力說不，而通過和平理性的方式表達意見和對話，嘗試解決問題。[Hong Kong is on the verge of turmoil. Many people in the community (including me) are calling on everyone to say no to violence, and to express opinions and dialogue in a peaceful and rational way to try to solve the problem].[158]

In many ways it is an exquisite and beautifully written elegy to a historical era that some fear may be passing. But it at its heart it is an intervention that is as much about the production methods of discourse within Hong Kong, and between local people and the authorities, an elegant dance around the tragic figures who are at the core of the drama being played out on the stage of the SAR.

The essence of the intervention is in its opening: "香港正瀕臨動亂邊緣，不少社會人士（包括我在內）都呼籲大家向暴力說不，而通過和平理性的方式表達意見和進行對話，嘗試解決問題。[Hong Kong is on the verge of turmoil. Many people in the community (including me) have called on everyone to say no to violence, and to express their views and dialogue through peaceful and rational methods and try to solve problems].[159] There is a necessary understatement embedded in this opening—Hong Kong was already long into a turmoil that had acquired its contemporary dimensions in 2014, pausing only briefly (as time is counted within empires that last multiple millennia). The call for nonviolence was more sensitive. Having become the grand totem of the discursive position of the central authorities, as well as of local officials, the invocation of non-violence here could as easily signal a coming to terms with the rising transformation of authority in Hong Kong as it signaled a dispassionate effort to aid those with grievances to maximize the chances that they might be effectively heard.

---

[158] 發表於《明報》副刊 2019 年 8 月 2 日星期五, supra, available at the website address cited above.
[159] 陳弘毅/理性溝通的困境, supra.

Hong Kong Between "One Country" and "Two Systems"
6. Thoughts on Albert Chen's "The Dilemma of Rational Communication"

94

But then there is an interesting turn, an academic turn, that pivots the appeal from moorings in the local to that of high-level academic discourse. This is a pivot that takes the appeal well above the toxic street fighting of the protagonists and into the realms of theory—but theory developed by high level thinkers in post 1945 Germany whose influence has been decisive among elite academics and officials in the West, and especially within a liberal democratic tradition.

> 我以前曾經寫文章介紹哈貝馬斯的溝通理性理論，他堅信，在公民社會的"公共領域"，人們可以通過理性溝通，盡量達成共識，法律也應是在這種理性溝通的過程中產生的。 [I have written an article about Habermas's theory of communication rationality. He firmly believes that in the "public sphere" of civil society, people can reach consensus through rational communication, and the law should be produced in the process of rational communication.].[160]

Perhaps this suggests a subtle messaging; first as a means of providing a high-level distancing from the discursive no violence thrust of the central authorities (and thus suggest sympathy for the protestors) and second as a means of aligning sympathies with the internationalist part of the One Country Two Systems principles, all within the strict confines of the approved "no violence" line. But this is speculative. Still, the insertion of Habermas and Habermasian principles at this point as a constraint on violence in political communication cannot but induce an alignment between that insertion of communicative theory, and the insertion of the 1984 Sino-British Declaration as a constraint on the reading of One Country/Two Systems principles in measuring the legitimacy of the responses of the central (and local) authorities.

The scourge against which Professor Chen writes, then, is neither the grievances of the protestors nor the desires of the local and central authorities, but what he calls "populism."

---

[160] Ibid.

但是，這些年來，無論在香港或世界其他地方，民粹主義興起，理性溝通變得越來越不可能；社會撕裂，不同政見者意見十分對立，似乎沒有任何共同基礎，以進行理性溝通。[However, over the years, whether in Hong Kong or elsewhere in the world, populism has arisen, rational communication has become increasingly impossible; social tears, dissidents are very opposed, and there seems to be no common ground for rational communication].[161]

That is in line, of course, with the writings of global academic elites and their aligned communicative organs in the form of the elite press in the West, all of which have, since the election of Donald Trump to the US Presidency in 2016, taking a fairly coordinated position on the evils of what they have now described in the negative as "populism." [162] This is a populism that threatens

---

[161] Ibid.

[162] See, Fareed Zacharia, "Populism on the March: Why the West is in Trouble," *Foreign Affairs* (95(6):9-15 (Nov/Dec 2016); Laurent Bernhard ORCID Icon & Hanspeter Kriesi , "Populism in election times: a comparative analysis of 11 countries in Western Europe," *West European Politics* 42(6):1188-1208 (May 2019); Koen Abts and Stefan Rummens, "Populism versus Democracy," *Political Studies* 55(2):405-424 (2007); Tjitske Akkerman, "Populism and Democracy: Challenge or Pathology?," *Acta Politica* 38:147-159 (2003) .

This became much more concentrated and apparent after the defeat of Mr. Trump in the 2020 election, something that was not possible to anticipate at the time of the writing of this essay. See, e.g., Shaun Walker, Tom Philips, and Jon Henley, "End of Trump era deals heavy blow to rightwing populist leaders worldwide," *The Guardian* (11 November 2020); available [https://www.theguardian.com/us-news/2020/nov/11/end-trump-era-blow-rightwing-populist-leaders-worldwide-biden-victory-brazil-hungary] ("The end of the Trump presidency may not mean the beginning of their demise, but it certainly strips them of a powerful motivational factor, and also alters the global political atmosphere, which in recent years had seemed to be slowly tilting in their favour, at least until the onset of coronavirus."); Rob Schmitz, "After Trump, Europe's Populist Leaders Will Have 'Lost One Of Their Cheerleaders'," NPR (1 December 2020); available [https://www.npr.org/2020/12/01/938613764/after-trump-europes-populist-leaders-will-have-lost-one-of-their-cheerleaders] ("Voters in Hungary, led by Prime Minister Viktor Orban, and in Poland elected their populist leaders, but many have grown increasingly wary of their crackdowns on democratic

Hong Kong Between "One Country" and "Two Systems"
6. Thoughts on Albert Chen's "The Dilemma of Rational Communication"

96

democratic society (and might by implication threaten Marxist-Leninist societies as well). It is the antithesis of the communication that Professor Chen urges. It is a creature against which both protestors and the authorities might form a "united front."

And it is at this point that Professor Chen describes the heart of the dilemma for Hong Kong. That dilemma centers on what Professor Chen sees as the great, and perhaps growing distance between his ideal of Habermasian [163] rational communication [164] and the political and social reality of Hong Kong. "When the most basic values and opinions that people hold are very different, rational communication cannot be undertaken."[165]

But it is here as well that the real audience for this essay is better revealed. The essay is not written for the central authorities—though they are surely quite interested in what a prominent member of the Hong Kong academic establishment has to say—and to exact consequences if it displeases them in politically significant ways. No, the real object of this essay are the protestors themselves. Unlike the local and central authorities,

---

institutions. So, too, has the European Union. It has launched an investigation into both countries that could result in removal of their EU voting rights".

[163] See, e.g., Jürgen Habermas, *The Theory of Communicative Action: Reason and the Rationalization of Society* (Thomas McCarthy trans., New York: Polity Press, 194). Discussed in Eveline T. Feteris, *Fundamentals of Legal Argumentation* (Dordrecht: Springer (1999) pp. 62-72 (Chapter 6, "Habermas' Theory of Communicative Rationality").

[164] 陳弘毅／理性溝通的困境, supra. There he explains:
　　本來理性溝通的理想，在於參與者在自由平等的基礎上，誠意聆聽對方的意見，不堅持己見，如果對方的意見更有道理，便開放地予以接受，或至少作出妥協，求同存異，嘗試至少在某些方面達成共識，以解決紛爭。 [The ideal of rational communication lies in the fact that participants are willing to listen to each other's opinions on the basis of freedom and equality, and do not insist on their own opinions. If the other party's opinions are more reasonable, they will openly accept them, or at least make compromises, seek common ground while reserving differences, and try at least Some aspects reached a consensus to resolve disputes.].

[165] Ibid. ("當人們所相信的最基本的價值信念有很大的分歧，理性溝通便無從說起。").

Hong Kong Between "One Country" and "Two Systems"
6. Thoughts on Albert Chen's "The Dilemma of Rational Communication"

97

the protestors have not developed a united front. Instead, the factional fighting within the protest movement has both weakened their collective efforts, and pose a potentially fatal danger to their ability to exact concessions from the authorities.

It is to them that this essay reserves its strongest pleas:

目前香港建制派及其支持者與非建制派及其支持者的基本價值信念的分歧，便是如此嚴重。前者基本上支持和信任中央政府和特區政府；後者中較激進者則基本上不接受中央政府的權威及其正當性，也不認為特區政府的管治有其正當性。這樣的情況下，"一國兩制"中兩制的矛盾越來越深，"一國兩制"的路好像走得越來越窄，悲觀的人士甚至有窮途末路的感覺。[The current disagreement between the Hong Kong institutionalists and their supporters and the non-established factions and their supporters is so serious. The former basically supports and trusts the central government and the SAR government; the more radicals in the latter basically do not accept the authority of the central government and its legitimacy, nor do they believe that the governance of the SAR government has its legitimacy. Under such circumstances, the contradiction between the two systems in "one country, two systems" is getting deeper and deeper. The road of "one country, two systems" seems to be getting narrower and narrower, and pessimistic people even have the feeling that this is system is dead.][166]

One comes face to face here, then, with what might be an untimely meditation.[167] But its principal role of this expression, and of this counselling of the protesters, remains aligned with the fundamental task of the Greek Chorus in tragedy—to distract and

---

[166] 陳弘毅/理性溝通的困境, supra.

[167] Friedrich Nietzsche, *Untimely Meditations* (R.J. Hollinsdale (trans), 2nd ed., Cambridge University Press 1977) (esp. "Schopenhauer as Educator," ibid, pp. 125-194; the philosopher's task to be lawgivers as to the measure, stamp, and weight of things (ibid., 144) and to provide a new picture of life for their contemporaries, ibid., 141)..

Hong Kong Between "One Country" and "Two Systems"
6. *Thoughts on Albert Chen's "The Dilemma of Rational Communication"*

98

by distracting to aid the audience in the production of conscious action and response to circumstances. But who is being distracted here? In this case the principal audience are the protestors themselves, who would be rationalized into oblivion. But perhaps equally significant key audiences are the local and central authorities, to whom this discourse of the chorus signals allegiance. Lastly at the outer reaches of the theatre but still a critical audience for the theatre piece that is Hong Kong at the moment: the global community of elite academics and policymakers who might. These are addressed form the sidelines, to be sure. And the discursive tropes also mean to signal to them as well loyalty to core sensibilities (though certainly not to objectives). Here there is a cautioning as well for that anticipated time when that international elite will actually be required to put their values into action. In this context, it may well be that action will be generated by local and central officials--and the international elite will continue to generate the only real object they are capable of deploying--word. That las insight may well be the critical caution made to a stage full of actors who will hear but are unlikely to listen.

$$* \quad * \quad *$$

Chapter 7

Wednesday 7 August 2019
"Stop the Storm and Restore Order!" ["止暴制乱、恢复秩序"！]: A Warning About Criminal Elements, the Black Hand ("黑手"), and the Corruption of the Patriotic Education of the Young

Additional Statement by the Hong Kong and Macau Affairs Office of the State Council Official Views of Current State of Affairs in Hong Kong [国务院港澳办新闻发言人介绍对当前香港事态的看法]

> The Central Committee will never let a few people drag Hong Kong into dangerous situations with their own violent actions. Therefore, we propose that the most urgent and important task that Hong Kong is overwhelming at the moment is to "stop the storm and restore order." [168]

The Chinese State Council's representatives for the Hong Kong and Macau Affairs Office (HKMAO) have recently held a press conference in which they again expressed, this time in a pointed way, the official views of the Central Government, on the situation in Hong Kong.[169] Its central element continues to build on prior interventions by the HKMAO—local violence and the accusation of foreign interference driving or supporting that protests (including those that are violent).

The stakes, however, are higher. The central authorities are now carefully developing a powerful narrative through which to re-frame the protests that began on 9 June 2019 from one focusing

---

168 新闻办就香港当前事态的立场和看法举行吹风会, 2019-08-06 16:55 来源: 中国网 [The Information Office holds a briefing on the current situation and views of Hong Kong, 2019-08-06 16:55 Source: China Net]; available [http://www.gov.cn/xinwen/2019-08/06/content_5419266.htm] (hereafter HKMAO 6 August Statement at 15:12 (by Yang Guang).
169 HKMAO 6 August Statement, supra. ,

on a number of local issues that touch, to be sure, policy objectives of the central authorities, to one of lawless rebellion with respect to which public restraint is less necessary. The imagery and power of that discursive assault must be carefully considered and analyzed for what it may tell us about the way that the central authorities may, at any minute respond.

> If we speak with facts, the facts tell us two truths, or two basic truths: First, the current state of affairs in Hong Kong has evolved from a peaceful procession rally to a crime committed by a few people. Second, it has evolved from a peaceful expression of opinion to a challenge to the bottom line of the "one country, two systems" principle.[170]

Yet what is even more interesting are the hints provided about central authority thinking respecting the role of the educational system in Hong Kong in inciting the protests and what may likely be in store for Hong Kong academics in the future.[171] One does not speak here solely to the corruption of liberal democratic values and techniques but of the consequences of the failure to inculcate a necessary patriotism in youth.

Thus the current governmental intervention raises three key issues that will serve as the central authorities *leitmotif* going forward:[172] the first is the theme of lawlessness; the second is the

---

[170] Ibid. at 15:12 (by Yang Guang) (如果我们用事实来说话，事实告诉我们两条真理，或者说两个基本的真相：第一，现在的香港事态已经从和平游行集会演变为少数人肆意妄为的犯罪行径。第二，已经由和平的表达意见演变为对"一国两制"原则底线的挑战。).

[171] Ibid., at 15:23 (Xu Luying), discussed infra.

[172] Leitmotif, originally a musical term referring to a short and recurring musical phrase identified with a particular idea, person, event, emotion, objective and the like. Leitmotif is the way that complex ideas and principles can be condensed and made more immediate and impactful when projected onto an audience. It has become an important element in political discourse as well--not just sloganeering, it most primitive form, but also to express complex ideas and political narrative. See, e.g., Horst Köhler, "Global Partnership: Thoughts on a new leitmotif for international politics," *Development* 56:299-307 (2013); Tenson Muyambo, "The Fast Track Land Reform Programme in Post-Colonial Zimbabwe: A Sloganeering Gimmick?," in *The End of an Era? Robert Mugabe and*

theme of foreign interference; and the third is the theme of corruption of values especially by an educational establishment with no loyalty to the nation. The idea of leitmotif is important for events as they are propelled by their leading forces and vanguards for the consumption of the press, of internal and of external audiences. To the extent the central authorities can reduce their position to a few powerful short expressions that embody deeply held values--lawfulness, stability, corruption, violence--it may well win the war with the great mass of Hong Kong protesters without having to deploy a single person themselves.

The HKMAO 6 August Statement requires little commentary but much reflection. It is regrettable that the authorities have chosen to continue to emphasize the interfering foreign elements line.[173] But the foreign interference principle appears now to have become an global phenomenon in the New Era. At the same time it recalls older eras—European eras—when, for example, in the 1920 the Europeans were convulsed by rumors of 5th columns undermining their states and cultures,[174] and states worried about the "hidden hand" of enemy control of local elements.[175] It has been tinged with racism.[176] It appears now revived as well in the New Era of historical development of Europe and the United States in the later 20th and now in the early 21st century especially tied to the interjecting of foreign Black

---

a Conflicting Legacy (Munyaradzi Mawere, Marongwe Ngonidzashe, Fidelis Peter and Thomas Duri (eds); Bamenda, Cameroons: Langaa Research & Publishing (2018), pp. 323-351.

[173] Encountered and discussed in some of its aspects in essays at Chapters 2 and 3, supra.

[174] Robert K. Murray, *Red Scare: A Study in National Hysteria 1919-1920* (Minneapolis: University of Minnesota Press, 1955); Robert Loeffel, *The Fifth Column in World War II: Suspected Subversives in the Pacific War and Australia* (NY: Palgrave Macmillan, 2015).

[175] See, e.g., Panikos Panayi, "'The Hidden Hand': British Myths About German Control of Britain During the First World War," *Immigrants & Minorities: Historical Studies in Ethnicity, Migration, and Diaspora* 7(3):253-272 (2010).

[176] See, e.g., Brendan Fay, "The Nazi Conspiracy Theory: German Fantasies and Jewish Power in the Third Reich," *Library and Information History* 35(2):75-97 (2019); Ann Gomer Sunahara, *The Politics of Racism: The Uprooting of Japanese Canadians During the Second World War* (2nd Ed., Vancouver: Nikkei National Museum and Cultural Center).).

Hand ("黑手") in universities[177] and other sensitive areas.[178] A particularly virulent strain has infected the American left and right orthodox political factions, which have for quite different reasons also become alarmed about external interference in its internal affairs (Communist International and Russian interference, etc.).[179] The problem from all sides has intensified as technology has broadened the scope within which it is possible to conceive of the projection of foreign elements into domestic life.[180]

Today, it seems, China also joins in the general tenor of the times and seeks to construct a meaning[181] around the character of its domestic challenges as the manifestation of injudicious importation of foreigners and foreign ideas, as well as in the projection into China of foreign public and private power. It ought not surprise, though it might disappoint, that China also looks

---

[177] See, e.g., Edward J. Graham, "Confucius Institutes Threaten Academic Freedom," Academe (Association of American University Professors (AAUP) (Washington, D.C., 2014); available [https://www.aaup.org/comment/8073#.X-0gli1h0ll];
Luwei Rose Luqiu & John D. McCarthy, "Confucius Institutes: The Successful Stealth "Soft Power" Penetration of American Universities," *The Journal of Higher Education* 90(4):620-643 (2019).

[178] Jonas Parello-Plesner and Belinda Li, "The Chinese Communist Party's Foreign Interference Operations: How the U.S. and Other Democracies Should Respond," Hudson Institute (June 2018); available [https://s3.amazonaws.com/media.hudson.org/files/publications/JonasFINAL.pdf].

[179] Paul Baines & Nigel Jones, "Influence and Interference in Foreign Elections: The Evolution of its Practice," *RUSI Journal* 163(1):12-19 (2018). Generally Catherine Lotrionte, "Countering State-Sponsored Cyber Economic Espionage Under International Law," *North Carolina Journal of International Law* 40:443-541 (2015).

[180] Ministry of Foreign Affairs of Denmark, "Strengthened safeguards against foreign influence on Danish elections and democracy," available [https://um.dk/en/news/newsdisplaypage/?newsid=1df5adbb-d1df-402b-b9ac-57fd4485ffa4] ("Certain countries use influence campaigns targeting the domestic political environments in Western countries as a tool to reach their own foreign policy goals."); Daniel Mack, "An Era of Foreign Political Interference: Impulsive, Overcompensation of Australia, and a Comparison of Legislative Schemes with the United States," Emory International Law Review 34:367 (2020).

[181] Generally, Jan M. Broekman and Larry Catá Backer, *Lawyers Making Meaning: The Semiotics of Law in Legal Education II* (Dordrecht: Springer, 2013)

abroad and appears to embrace the idea that foreign elements play a part in a situation that is now extremely sensitive.[182]

Those states at the wrong end of these accusations— principally the old Center Empire (the United Kingdom) and the new one (the United States)—have reacted vigorously. The U.K. "summoned the Chinese ambassador over what it said were "unacceptable and inaccurate" comments made by Beijing regarding the UK's role in ongoing Hong Kong protests."[183] The UK authorities used the provocation to underline the international character of the status of Hong Kong as well as the nature of the international guarantees specified in the 1984 Sino-British Joint Declaration.[184] Jeremy Hunt, the British Foreign Secretary was quoted as stating:

> "there will be serious consequences if that internationally binding legal agreement were not to be honored." . . . "The UK signed an internationally binding legal agreement in 1984 that enshrines the 'one country, two systems rule,' enshrines the basic freedoms of the people of Hong Kong and we stand four square behind that agreement, four square behind the people of Hong Kong,"[185]

---

[182] In the context of Hong Kong this discursive trope intensified with the start of the demonstrations. "UPDATE 1-China tells U.S. to remove 'black hands' from Hong Kong," *Reuters* (23 July 20189); available [https://news.yahoo.com/1-china-tells-u-remove-100231943.html] ("We can see that U.S. officials are even behind such incidents," said Chinese Foreign Ministry spokeswoman Hua Chunying at a regular press briefing on Tuesday.).

[183] James Griffiths, "Diplomatic spat between UK and China after Beijing slams London's 'colonial' attitude to Hong Kong," *CNN World News* (4 July 2019); available [https://www.cnn.com/2019/07/04/asia/china-uk-hong-kong-intl-hnk/index.html].

[184] Joint Declaration of the Government of the United Kingdom of Great Britain and Northern Ireland and the Government of the People's Republic of China on the Question of Hong Kong (19 December 1984); available [https://www.cmab.gov.hk/en/issues/jd2.htm].

[185] James Griffiths, "Diplomatic spat," *supra.*

This elicited the expected counter by Chinese authorities who have more strongly suggested that the Joint Declaration is dead letter once sovereignty was transferred. In the process Chinese authorities taunted the U.K. with references to the passing of its imperium as well as its now unacceptable character. "Beijing has made a formal complaint about Mr Hunt, accusing the Conservative leadership contender of 'colonial-era delusions'. . . [UK Ambassador] Mr Liu said he was "disappointed" by the UK's response. He said . . . there would be further "problems" if the UK did not recognise China's sovereignty over Hong Kong, its 'territorial integrity and principle of non-interference in domestic affairs'."[186]

Chinese officials have also claimed that the protests were "the work" of the U.S.[187] The U.S. Secretary of State Mike Pompeo responded that the Foreign Ministry's spokesperson's comments were ludicrous.[188] At the same time the U.S. noted with sympathy the aspirations of the Hong Kong protestors and called for restraint and the avoidance of violence.[189] Alluding as well to the

---

[186] "Hong Kong protests: China tells UK not to interfere in 'domestic affairs'," BBC News (3 July 2019); available [https://www.bbc.com/news/uk-politics-48855643].

[187] "China accuses U.S. of being behind Hong Kong protests," Kyodo News (30 July 2019); available [https://english.kyodonews.net/news/2019/07/739b8c951b92-china-accuses-us-of-being-behind-hong-kong-protests.html] (Quoting Chinese Foreign Ministry spokesperson Hua Chunying "'There have been many American faces in the violent parade in Hong Kong, and even some American flags,' Hua added. In urging the United States to 'let go' of the Hong Kong issue, Hua warned, 'Those who play with fire only get themselves burned.'" Ibid.). See also Erin Hale, "China Accuses US of Interference Over Controversial Hong Kong Extradition Bill," Voice of America Cambodia (12 June 2019); available [https://www.voacambodia.com/a/china-accuses-us-of-interference-over-controversial-hong-kong-extradition-bill/4954879.html].

[188] Keegan Elmer, "Mike Pompeo rebukes China's 'ludicrous' claim US is behind Hong Kong protests: Protests are coming solely from the people of Hong Kong, who are asking their government to listen, Pompeo says," South China Morning Post (31 July 2019); available [https://www.scmp.com/news/china/diplomacy/article/3020749/mike-pompeo-rebukes-chinas-ludicrous-claim-us-behind-hong-kong].

[189] For the US response here: 美国务院反驳幕后黑手指控　市民示威反映自治权受侵蚀的不满, RFA (24 July 2019); available [https://www.rfa.org/cantonese/news/us-statement-07242019095419.html].

international framework within which One Country/Two Systems principal was understood, the "U.S.'s former Consul General to Hong Kong and Macau Kurt Tong also denied China's "foreign forces" accusation. . . He said the recent demonstrations reflect the deeper concerns of the Hong Kong people about losing their autonomy to Beijing through excessive interference despite their "one country, two systems" model."[190]

And yet the foreign interference discursive thrust must be taken quite seriously for both its external and internal components. In that respect, the HKMAO 6 August Statement references to 黑手 [black hand] [191] provide a conveniently ambiguous means of erecting a stronger wall between Hong Kong

---

美國國務院就中國外交部發言人在周二（23日）的記者會上，指控美國為香港亂局的幕後黑手提出反駁，指中方的指控無稽（ridiculous）。美國國務院較早前敦促各方保持克制，避免暴力。香港政府也必須尊重《基本法》所保障的言論和集會自由。當各種政治觀點得到尊重並可以自由表達時，社會就會得到穩定。美國國務院重申，香港正在進行的示威活動，反映了香港人的情緒，以及對香港自治權受到侵蝕的關注。[The US Department of State rebutted the accusation that the United States was behind the chaos in Hong Kong at a press conference held by the spokesperson of the Chinese Ministry of Foreign Affairs on Tuesday (23), saying that the Chinese accusations were ridiculous. The US State Department earlier urged all parties to exercise restraint and avoid violence. The Hong Kong government must also respect the freedom of speech and assembly guaranteed by the Basic Law. When various political opinions are respected and can be expressed freely, society will be stabilized. The US State Department reiterated that the ongoing demonstrations in Hong Kong reflect the sentiments of Hong Kong people and their concerns about the erosion of Hong Kong's autonomy.]. Ibid.

[190] Kitty Wang, "Pompeo Refutes Chinese Claims of US Involvement in HK Protests as 'Ludicrous'," NTD (2 August 2019); available [https://www.ntd.com/pompeo-refutes-chinese-claims-of-us-involvement-in-hk-protests-as-ludicrous_364786.html].

[191] "我们还要向那些肆无忌惮的极少数暴力犯罪分子和他们背后的黑手发出警告；中国一直称有外部的"黑手"卷入香港当前的事态；这次政治风暴幕后黑手是--些敌视中国发展的势力" [We also want to warn those unscrupulous violent criminals and the black hands behind them; China has always said that there are external "black hands" involved in the current state of affairs in Hong Kong; The black hand behind the political storm is something that is hostile to China's development] HKMAO 6 August Statement, supra.

and the international community, more broadly understood. Yet foreign elements need no longer be tied to states; and there are certainly many civil society groups with global networks with an interest in the developments in Hong Kong. It could as easily refer to involved Chinese citizens with dual nationality (Hong Kong and other states). These individuals and their organizations, together with their formal and informal links elsewhere, may be viewed as serving as a link from the SAR to whatever foreign elements the central authorities deem a useful object for discursive focus. In the case of the HKMAO 6 August Statement, that remains the great (and convenient) antagonist, the United States. That connection, in turn, nicely aligns with the thrust of more global Chinese interests in advancing their internationalist aspirations even as they lock the door to internationalism projected inward to the Hong Kong SAR.

The HKMAO 6 August Statement in large measure refines all of the elements already present in the earlier HKMAO Statement [192] The intertwining of the themes of violence as counterrevolutionary agitation, the imagery of the protestor as out-law and out-sider, the suggestion of the violence of the retribution that will come in order to vindicate law and the social order, and the suggestion that the protestors are tools of foreigners who are seeking to undermine the homeland and who are using the protestors to advance their own national interests by now is well worn. But the tone of these themes has been heightened; the language is more heated; the suggestion of the immense of repercussion made to appear more imminent. It has also provided a great cover for the undermining of the notion of Hong Kong's autonomy as attached in any way to its international status. That key connection between Chinese sovereignty over Hong Kong, the resulting incompatibility of international legal intrusions in the form of the 1984 Sino-British Joint Declaration[193] once the handover was completed in 1997, and the resulting characterization of the use of the international constraints on central authority exercises of power over Hong Kong as

---

[192] Discussed supra at Chapter 3.
[193] Citation supra note 15.

interference in the domestic affairs of China is amplified in these statements.

For the protestors, of course, the result is that they do become pieces in a much larger game and no longer the masters of their own (local) fates. In this context, the protests become a means through which the process of the Sinification of Hong Kong might be accelerated from so that it ends now rather than in 20147. The key step in that process is the detachment of Hong Kong from its international status, and the violence provides the necessary cover for taking the practical steps necessary to make that a reality on the ground. The irony will be lost on the protestors who believe that every act of defiance advances their position. It appears, at least plausibly in the calculations of the central authorities, that every such action will have the opposite (and for the central authorities felicitous) effect.

These discursive and objectives-based thrusts are all made clearer in the text of the HKMAO 6 August Statement itself, the English translation of which follows below. Special attention ought to be paid to the emphasis added to certain text that suggests the development of the themes described here. There is a repetition of key words and phrases that are used to underline certain positions and to warn people about the consequences that lie ahead. These are words with a specific resonance in China that may be less well comprehensible by outsiders. Discursively they weave a coherent statement that at once weaves together the people of Hong Kong into the fabric of all of the people of China, excludes the protestors as corrupted foreign agents, violent lawbreakers and revolutionary gangs bent on destroying the integrity of the Chinese state and the state of its constitutional law, and all foreign interventions as well as the attempted use of international law and norms as a threat to national sovereignty and national dignity.

Consider the following key terms that appear often in the transcript, the English language translation of which follows. The HKMAO 6 August Statement itself focused on several key words, phrases and concepts: "violent illegal activities",[194] "small group of radical demonstrators," [195] "extreme violent elements," [196] "radical violent elements" causing "chaos", [197] "radical demonstrations" having bad effects,[198] "guarding the homeland" by "Hong Kong compatriots" against the "chaos,"[199] "unscrupulous violent criminals,"[200] the majesty and dignity of law which must be severely applied, [201] and the distinction between criminal elements and "Hong Kong compatriots." [202] In the question and answer session that followed the delivery of the HKMAO 6 August Statement, additional key words and phrases appeared: the consequences for Hong Kong of its "dangerous situation," [203] "shocking violent crimes,"[204] "criminal activities,"[205] the fallacies

---

[194] HKMAO 6 August Statement, supra (" But we also see that violent illegal activities have continued for more than a week.").

[195] Ibid. ("A small group of radical demonstrators targeted the police, using tools ranging from bricks and irons to deadly weapons such as smoke bombs, petrol bombs, bows and arrows, and arson").

[196] Ibid. ("Extreme violent elements threw incendiary bombs at the police station and set fire to them in various places").

[197] Ibid. ("It must be clearly pointed out that in the current chaos in Hong Kong, some of the radical violent elements are standing at the forefront, and some are well-informed and misguided, but the supporters of the radical violent elements are inside and outside Hong Kong").

[198] Ibid. ("The iron-clad facts show that the radical demonstrations that have lasted for nearly two months are very serious and have a very bad impact").

[199] Ibid. ("It is now a crucial moment to stand firm and guard the beautiful homeland. . . I ask the Hong Kong compatriots to calmly think about a question: Once the chaos is out of control, who will eventually suffer? Who will benefit?").

[200] Ibid. ("We also warn the unscrupulous violent criminals and the black hands behind them: the fire will self-immolate, and the punishment will come!).

[201] Ibid. ("Violence against violence must not be soft. If the law is not punished, the law will be without dignity; if the law is not majestic, the rule of law will be gone).

[202] Ibid. ("In the final analysis, the fate of Hong Kong is in the hands of all Chinese people, including Hong Kong compatriots!).

[203] Ibid., ("She pointed out that Hong Kong is currently slipping into a dangerous situation").

[204] Ibid. ("have listed the shocking violent crimes that have taken place in Hong Kong in the past two months"). A variant is the expression of extreme violent crime, ibid. ("the so-called "uncooperative movement" and the so-called "three strikes" by the opposition are not normal expressions of appeals, but extreme violent crimes, crimes that seriously undermine public order and public interests").

[205] Ibid. ("in the face of such shocking violent criminal activities").

Hong Kong Between "One Country" and "Two Systems"
7. A Warning "Stop the Storm and Restore Order!"

109

of efforts to "recover" Hong Kong. [206] In addition, the emphasis on the legal space occupied by the protestors was emphasized by such repeating terms as "violence is violence" and it is illegal to violate the law."[207] Woven into the fabric of this discourse is the terminology of the "black hand" (" 黑手 ") that serves to both exclude the protestors from the body of the Chinese people and to separate what is Chinese (and internal) form what is external (and foreign). Foreigners "make irresponsible remarks,"[208] foreigners "meet and support" the protestors,[209] and through the protestors foreigners intervene in Hong Kong affairs.[210] These interventions must be identified and condemned.[211] The nature of the Black Hand interventions are both dangerous for China and put forward with evil intent.[212] Chinese dupes are advised to wake up and understand how they are being used and to join the mass of the

---

[206] Ibid. ("the Chief Executive Carrie Lam also mentioned a slogan issued by some people, called "Recovering Hong Kong, the revolution of the times". I also want to ask these people. Where is Hong Kong? Hong Kong is a special administrative region of the People's Republic of China. In a place like Hong Kong, what do you want to "recover"? Where do you want to "recover" Hong Kong? Therefore, they can be seen from their slogans. Their political motives are clear at a glance. Everyone knows that they are at the root of the "one country" in "one country, two systems", that is, to challenge this fundamental principle.").

[207] Ibid. ("No matter who it is or what kind of banner he is playing, it is illegal to violate the law, and violence is violence. As long as it is illegal, it should be resolutely stopped.").

[208] Ibid. ("Since the start of the revision of the Fugitive Offenders Regulations in February, some Western politicians and the Taiwan authorities have publicly stood at the forefront and made many remarks about reversing black and white and irresponsible remarks").

[209] Ibid. ("For example, in late March, the United States highly invited some of the opposition's leading figures to visit the United States, and arranged for the Vice President and the Secretary of State to meet and support them. Less than two months later, senior US officials met with the so-called "anti-extradition amendments and the United States and Canada" led by the opposition figures").

[210] Ibid. ("I think that these remarks have a common feature, that is, to support the demonstrators to support their strengths and encourage their efforts, and give advice to and intervene in the affairs of Hong Kong").

[211] Ibid. ("all condemned Western forces for interfering in Hong Kong affairs").

[212] Ibid. ("the black hand behind this political storm is hostile to China's development. The fundamental purpose of the forces is to make Hong Kong a battleground for the international game and to make Hong Kong a base against the Central Committee as a pawn to contain China").

Chinese people in the great task of nation building.[213] And lastly, the idea that as Hong Kong goes, so goes the nation—it becomes a point of national honor to ensure that Hong Kong not only remain where it is but that it continues on the path toward all around consolidation with the nation.[214]

It is against these well-developed discursive tropes; it is against this elaborate strategy of separating the local from the foreign of viewing the foreign as inherently suspicious and subversive and of concluding that any embrace of the foreign—its rhetoric, discourse , principles, or values—is an act of betrayal of the nation and its values, that the local protestors in Hong Kong and their allies within global civil society and among states sympathetic to their project must develop their own discourse. For the moment, though, all they appear to have to offer are the rhetorical tropes of abstract liberal democratic theory. That may not be enough. In the course of the question-and-answer session, the HKMAO was asked about the spokesmen for Hong Kong. This appeared to provide an opening to make what was a startling and long statement about the state of education and academics in Hong Kong.

Xu Luying of the HKMAO first suggested that "some recent violent clashes in Hong Kong have been said to be caused by some chaotic elements and hidden elements. They are not thinking about the health of young people. . . Young people became pawns and cannon fodder for their political plots.[215] Hong Kong youth may be the objective of this activity, but the fault lies with educators--"many teachers encouraged young students to go on

---

[213] Ibid. ("We advise those politicians who speak beautiful words and who are actually sowing the seeds of social hatred and opposition. They are more serious and awake, and your tricks are impossible. Or, as I said earlier, the future and destiny of Hong Kong are in the hands of the entire Chinese people, including the Hong Kong compatriots").

[214] Ibid. ("the Central Government and the people of the whole country Hong Kong's prosperous and stable support is real. The central government will never allow the offense of the "one country, two systems" principle to be unpunished, and will never let Hong Kong emerge from the turmoil that the SAR government cannot control and endanger national unity or security").

[215] HKMAO August Statement at 15:23 (by Xu Luying).

the streets and even participate in violent conflicts, when many children took to the streets."[216] This provides the foundation for the intimation that the Hong Kong education system must change.

> Therefore, I feel that school education and family education must have a correct guidance. We must strengthen the patriotism education and national education of Hong Kong youth, and let them understand their country and themselves comprehensively, deeply and objectively from an early age.[217]

Improper education makes foreigners of Hong Kong youth-- susceptible to outside corruption and disloyal to the nation in the service of powers that may not have China's best interests at heart. Patriotic education, and the inculcation of civic virtues, are seen as the cure, as a means of making Hong Kong people Chinese again. Faculty play the role of agents provocateurs.

Note the two-level criticism. First, of course, is the suggestion that teachers, corrupted by liberal democratic or other foreign, are a contributing factor to the state of instability in Hong Kong.[218] This is connected as well to the emerging line of the central authorities that the situation in Hong Kong is a consequence of the corruption of and interference of the "black hand" ("黑手") of the West. Second, is that the curriculum is both deficient (the passive failure) and that it teachers incorrect values (the active failure).[219] The rectification necessary to make this

---

[216] Ibid.

[217] Ibid.

[218] Postscript: By the end of 2020, the move to discipline teachers had generated support for private efforts to those ends. See, e.g., "China wields patriotic education to tame Hong Kong's rebellious youth," Straits Times (27 November 220); available [https://www.straitstimes.com/asia/east-asia/china-wields-patriotic-education-to-tame-hong-kongs-rebellious-youth] ("Interviews with Hong Kong political figures, teachers and school principals, and mainland Chinese officials, as well as a review of new educational materials, reveal that the school curriculum, teaching staff, exams and extra-curricular activities are all in Beijing's crosshairs.").

[219] Postscript: See, Selina Wang and Rebecca Wright, CNN, "Hong Kong's new rules have created confusion in the classroom. Some parents are pulling their children out," CNN (18 November 2020); available

right will require both a new set of parameters for the disciplining of teachers and for the control of the curriculum.

Neither of these issues have been a central element in the development of education policy in Hong Kong, which prides itself as a bastion of global vanguard trends in education, curriculum, and educational values. But it does suggest the decision by the central authorities that education policy being developed for Mainland China—tied to the inculcation of appropriate values and related working styles in education delivery [220] —will also be applied in some measure to Hong Kong. Again, the pattern is clear—detach Hong Kong from its centering in the international and bring it back closer to and within the national.[221]

[https://www.cnn.com/2020/11/17/asia/hong-kong-education-security-law-intl-dst-hnk/index.html] ("The Education Bureau has ordered schools to remove books and teaching materials that could violate the law. Administrators can call the police if someone insults the Chinese anthem, which must be played in schools on certain holidays. In September, a student who displayed a photo with the slogan "Free Hong Kong, Revolution Now" during class was suspended for a week.").

[220] Postscript Note: The shape of this patriotic education was refined toward the end of 2019. See, "China unveils outline for strengthening patriotic education," Xinhua (13 November 2019); available [http://www.china.org.cn/china/2019-11/13/content_75402721.htm] ("Patriotic education in the new era should be guided by Marxism-Leninism, Mao Zedong Thought, Deng Xiaoping Theory, the Theory of Three Represents, the Scientific Outlook on Development and Xi Jinping Thought on Socialism with Chinese Characteristics for a New Era, it said. The education, on the theme of realizing the Chinese Dream of national rejuvenation, should ensure that the love for the Party, the country and socialism go hand in hand, said" Ibid.).

[221] Postscript Note: By the end of 2020 these implications became clearer.
> The Education Bureau will focus on bolstering national security education and monitoring the quality of the city's teachers, while e-learning funding is set to be boosted, Chief Executive Carrie Lam announced during Wednesday's policy address. Schools should implement educational activities on the importance of national security and One Country Two Systems in order to instill "a sense of identity, belonging and responsibility towards the nation, the Chinese race and our society," Lam said.

Rhoda Kwan, "Policy Address 2020: Hong Kong education to instill Chinese belonging and identity; quality of teachers to be 'enhanced,' Hong Kong Free Press (26 November 2020); available [https://hongkongfp.com/2020/11/26/policy-address-2020-hong-kong-

None of this bodes well for Hong Kong academics, especially those who have become public figures. This is especially true where, as is becoming evident, the central authorities have targeted the academic establishment as a substantial culprit in the corruption of Hong Kong youth and as an underlying cause of the protest movements. And where, as here, the education establishment is also targeted in part for cultivating that very liberal democratic discourse, then it becomes dangerous. The danger lies not just for the protestors, but for the entire intelligentsia of Hong Kong .

Taken together, the three great strands of the HKMAO August Statement continues the process of the consolidation of the central authorities approach to the situation in Hong Kong. First excise the protestors out of the legitimate body politic. Second, associate that out-law element as unpatriotic and the tool of foreign powers bent on harming China. Third, blame the educational establishment for corrupting the children of Hong Kong to reject their own culture, values, and nation. To the extent this discursive strategy can be made to work, it provides a powerful challenge to the coherence and success of the protestors.

The translation of the full text of the HKMAO August Statement and curated Question and Answer Session follow. *Italics* has been added to emphasize language highlighted in the discussion above.

---

education-to-instil-chinese-belonging-and-identity-quality-of-teachers-to-be-enhanced/].

Spokesperson for the Hong Kong and Macau Affairs Office of the State Council shares views on the current state of affairs in Hong Kong
Published: 2019-08-06 Source: State Council Information Office website[222]

Yan Yanchun
Ladies and gentlemen, good afternoon everyone! Everyone is welcome to attend the briefing of the State Council Information Office. Last week, the State Council Information Office held a press conference and invited the spokesperson of the Hong Kong and Macao Affairs Office of the State Council to meet with you to introduce the position and views on the current state of affairs in Hong Kong. As Mr. Yang Guang said at the end of the last press conference, there will be more opportunities to communicate with you in the future. Today, we once again invited two speakers, Mr. Yang Guang and Ms. Xu Luying, to further communicate with you. First of all, please introduce Mr. Yang Guang.

Yang Guang
Dear friends from the press, good afternoon! We are holding a media briefing here today. Before the media briefing begins, I would like to borrow the lens of everyone to say hello to the people of Hong Kong.

Last week, we held a press conference to show our position and views on the current state of affairs in Hong Kong. The Hong Kong society and the international community are highly concerned about this. The people of the Mainland have also responded enthusiastically. We feel the strong positive energy of resolutely safeguarding the "one country, two systems" policy and the Basic Law, resolutely defending the rule of law in

---

[222] Original, citation at note 1, supra. Footnotes added with language from the original Chinese transcript.

Hong Kong, and resolutely supporting the Chief Executive and the SAR Government in their administration of the law and firmly supporting the Hong Kong Police Force in law enforcement.

But we also see that violent illegal activities have continued for more than a week. [223] On August 5, the opposition launched another strike aimed at smashing Hong Kong. Faced with this grim situation, more and more people realize that Hong Kong can no longer be chaotic! Today, I want to talk about how to do things about what happened in Hong Kong and what to do next.

It is well known that in the past two months, the demonstrations in Hong Kong have completely exceeded the scope of freedom of assembly, procession and demonstration. They have evolved into extreme violence, and the means are constantly being refurbished, the intensity is constantly escalating, and the destructiveness is intensifying. It's shocking. *A small group of radical demonstrators targeted the police, using tools ranging from bricks and irons to deadly weapons such as smoke bombs, petrol bombs, bows and arrows, and arson.* [224] Others on the Internet publicly advocated the use of deadly methods to attack the police. These acts have caused serious harm to the lives and property of Hong Kong police officers and the general public. 461 people have been injured in violent clashes, including 139 police officers. What is even more indignant and highly vigilant is that some radicals have torn up Hong Kong's Basic Law and defiled the National Emblem. On the evening of August 3, several shameless people dropped the flag of the People's Republic of China hanging in front of a building in Tsim Sha Tsui and threw it into the sea. This act seriously violated the law,

---

223 但我们同时也看到，过去一个多星期，暴力违法活动仍在持续.

224 一小部分激进示威者以警察为袭击目标，使用的工具从砖头、铁枝发展到烟雾弹、汽油弹、弓箭等致命武器，并实施纵火，还有人在网上公然鼓吹使用致命手法袭击警察。

blatantly offended the dignity of the country and challenged the bottom line of the "one country, two systems" principle. On August 5, the opposition launched a strike, which caused about 250 flights to be cancelled. Eight subway lines, such as Kwun Tong, stopped serving for more than five hours. The Hung Hom Tunnel and several traffic trunks were blocked. *Extreme violent elements* threw incendiary bombs at the police station and set fire to them in various places.[225] At 7 o'clock that night, the extreme militants once again pulled the flag down to Tsim Sha Tsui and threw it into the sea. These thugs are arrogant and aggressive. Waiting for them in the future will be a blow from the sword of law, a sharp on that column of arrogance that cannot be undone.

The demonstrations that have lasted for nearly two months, especially the violent attacks, have also had a serious impact on Hong Kong's economy and people's livelihood. According to the statistics of the SAR Government, the economic indicators of Hong Kong in the first six months of this year have fallen across the board except for a few industries. Hong Kong's GDP in the second quarter increased by only 0.6% in real terms over the same period last year, and the economy is facing significant downward pressure. 18 countries and regions have issued travel safety reminders to Hong Kong due to the current situation. Retail and tourism are the first to bear the brunt, and merchant sales and hotel occupancy rates have fallen sharply. What is more serious is that the current state of affairs in Hong Kong has seriously hit the confidence of international investors. They have publicly expressed their deep concern about the business environment in Hong Kong. Some international agencies have issued early warnings. The ongoing demonstrations and violent incidents have prevented Hong Kong's economic activities from proceeding properly. Hong Kong's rating may be affected.

---

[225] 极端暴力分子向警署投掷燃烧弹，在多处纵火。

It must be clearly pointed out that in the current chaos in Hong Kong, some of the radical violent elements are standing at the forefront, and some are well-informed and misguided, but the supporters of the radical violent elements are inside and outside Hong Kong.[226] In the chaotic port of China. These forces blatantly encourage the boldness of the radical violent elements, and coordinate, direct and fund their secret goals. They confuse right and wrong, reverse black and white, and try their best to advocate the so-called "civil disobedience" or even "violence can solve the problem" of the fallacies, beautification, and radical violence. They encouraged militants to engage in the so-called "non-cooperative movement" and implement "extreme pressure" in an attempt to force all Hong Kong citizens to become involved in political disputes and intensify social conflicts.

The iron-clad facts show that the *radical demonstrations that have lasted for nearly two months are very serious and have a very bad impact.*[227] They have already had a serious impact on Hong Kong's prosperity and stability and are dragging Hong Kong into a dangerous abyss!

So what should I do next? This is a major issue that everyone who cares about Hong Kong is thinking about. The situation in Hong Kong has developed to this grim step today. The urgent task before all Hong Kong citizens is very clear. It is a sentence: "stop the storm and restore order!"[228]

---

226 必须明确指出，在香港当前乱局中，站在前台的是部分激进暴力分子，居中的是部分被误导、被裹挟的善良市民，但幕后怂恿、支持激进暴力分子的则是香港内外的 "反中乱港" 势力。

227 铁一般的事实显示，这场持续了近两个月的激进示威活动性质十分严重、影响十分恶劣，

228 那么，下一步怎么办？这是每一个关心香港的人都在思考的重大问题。香港局势发展到今天这个严峻地步，摆在所有香港市民面前的急迫任务十分明确，就是一句话，"止暴制乱、恢复秩序"！

We must first appeal to the general public in Hong Kong: *It is now a crucial moment to stand firm and guard the beautiful homeland. To reject ignorance, paranoia, and abuse, like the white-haired old man who insisted on rejecting the demonstrator's flyer at the airport.*[229] Like the wage earners who rushed to work, they screamed at the saboteurs who were holding the subway doors and stopping the train. Like the loving grannies, take your own children who are full of inexplicable anger and take them home, and count down with distress. You have seen the big men who motivated young people to engage in violent assaulting police every day. Are their children doing the same? *I ask the Hong Kong compatriots to calmly think about a question: Once the chaos is out of control, who will eventually suffer? Who will benefit?*[230]

We must appeal to the SAR Government, the Judiciary and the police: At an important moment concerning the destiny of Hong Kong, all departments and agencies must take responsibility for the rule of law, perform their duties, strictly enforce the law, and exercise justice. *Violence against violence must not be soft. If the law is not punished, the law will be without dignity; if the law is not majestic, the rule of law will be gone.*[231] Here, I must make it very clear that the Central Committee's support for the Chief Executive Carrie Lam is unwavering and unwavering. The opposition's attempt to force Carrie Lam's resignation as Chief Executive is doomed to fail! I would like to once again express my sincere respect for the decisive law enforcement and strict law enforcement of the Hong Kong Police Force. The people of the whole country are your strong backing. We hope that people

---

[229] 现在已经到了坚定站出来守护美好家园的关键时刻。要像那位在机场坚决拒收示威者传单的白发老者那样，

[230] 请广大香港同胞们冷静地思考一个问题：一旦乱局不可收拾，谁终将受害？谁终将受益？

[231] 对暴力违法绝不能手软。违法不被惩处，法律就没有威严；法律没有威严，法治就荡然无存。

from all walks of life in Hong Kong will recognize the current state of affairs and firmly support the Chief Executive of the Legislative Council to lead the SAR Government in its administration of the law, firmly support the Hong Kong Police in its law enforcement, and firmly support the relevant departments of the Hong Kong SAR Government and the Judiciary in punishing violent criminals.

We also warn the unscrupulous violent criminals and the black hands behind them: the fire will self-immolate, and the punishment will come![232] All those involved in violent criminal activities, regardless of who they are, must be held accountable for their legal responsibilities, including the legal responsibility of the behind-the-scenes planners, organizers, and commanders! I must warn all criminals not to misjudge the situation, not to misjudge the exercise restraint as weakness, to underestimate the powerful and just power of Hong Kong society to uphold the rule of law and maintain stability, and to underestimate the central government and the people of the whole country to safeguard Hong Kong's prosperity and stability and safeguard the fundamental interests of the country. Strong determination and great strength! *In the final analysis, the fate of Hong Kong is in the hands of all Chinese people, including Hong Kong compatriots!*[233]

Thank you all.

08-06 15:09
Yan Yanchun
Thank you Mr. Yang Guang for his introduction. Enter the question and answer session below, and give the first question to the media in Hong Kong today.

---

232 我们还要向那些肆无忌惮的极少数暴力犯罪分子和他们背后的黑手发出警告：玩火者必自焚，该来的惩罚终将到来！
233 归根到底，香港的命运掌握在包括香港同胞在内的全体中国人民手中！

08-06 15:11
Hong Kong Cable Reporter
The Chief Executive, Mrs Lam, said yesterday that the anti-revision claims have deteriorated. She said that some people want to engage in revolution and challenge national sovereignty. Some commentators believe that the Chief Executive has labeled the five major demands of the people as "Hong Kong independence". Does the Central Government agree with the Chief Executive? ? Also, are people in Hong Kong going to the streets to engage in revolution? What does the central government think? If the anti-reforms continue, for example, before October 1st, will the central government sit still and ignore the dispatch of the garrison? The second question is that the Hong Kong and Macau Affairs Office has paid tribute to the Hong Kong Police Force at the first press conference. The spokesman for Yang Guang has once again paid tribute to the Hong Kong Police Force. This remark is that the police are even more arrogant and even aggressive. It is to strengthen the abuse of violence to arrest the public. What is the opinion of the Hong Kong and Macau Affairs Office? Should the Police Force review some of his enforcement methods and even apologize to the public for the recent increase in police conflict? Thank you.

08-06 15:12
Yang Guang
Thank you for your question. Although it raises two questions, there are actually two questions. I heard it, the clues of the two centers, and one of my opinions on the statement of the Chief Executive Carrie Lam at the press conference yesterday. The other is what the Hong Kong police are doing now.

I will answer the first question first. We also noticed that the Chief Executive of the Legislative Council Carrie Lam held a press conference yesterday. *She pointed out that*

Hong Kong is currently slipping into a dangerous situation.[234] She also said that she will not resign. She is more sure that the rule of law. It is the only way to solve the violence. To her speech, I deeply agree that I am deeply appreciative of the spirit of her performance. I think that in my speech just now, I have listed the *shocking violent crimes that have taken place in Hong Kong in the past two months.* [235] I also see that the momentum of such violent crimes has not been effectively curbed. If we speak with facts, the facts tell us two truths, or two basic truths: First, the current state of affairs in Hong Kong has evolved from a peaceful procession rally to a crime committed by a few people. Second, it has evolved from a peaceful expression of opinion to a challenge to the bottom line of the "one country, two systems" principle.

I noticed that at the press conference, *the Chief Executive Carrie Lam also mentioned a slogan issued by some people, called "Recovering Hong Kong, the revolution of the times". I also want to ask these people. Where is Hong Kong? Hong Kong is a special administrative region of the People's Republic of China. In a place like Hong Kong, what do you want to "recover"? Where do you want to "recover" Hong Kong? Therefore, they can be seen from their slogans. Their political motives are clear at a glance. Everyone knows that they are at the root of the "one country" in "one country, two systems", that is, to challenge this fundamental principle.*[236] Therefore, in the face of such

---

[234] 她指出，香港目前正在滑向一个危险的境地.

[235] 我想，我刚才的讲话当中，已经列举了近两个多月来香港所发生的触目惊心的暴力犯罪活动，

[236] 我注意到，在记者会上，林郑月娥行政长官也提到了一些人打出的一个口号，叫做"光复香港，时代革命"，我也很想问一问这些人，香港是什么地方？香港是中华人民共和国的一个特别行政区，在香港这样一个地方，你们想"光复"什么呢？你们想把香港"光复"到哪去呢？所以，从他们的口号就可以看得出来，他们的政治动机一目了然，路人皆知，就是冲着"一国两制"中的"一国"这个根本来的，就是要挑战这个根本。

shocking violent criminal activities [237] and serious challenges to the bottom line of the "one country, two systems" principle, is it still impossible to see that the current state of affairs has deteriorated? The Central Committee will never let a few people drag Hong Kong into dangerous situations with their own violent actions. Therefore, we propose that the most urgent and important task that Hong Kong is overwhelming at the moment is to "stop the storm and restore order." The Central Government unswervingly supports the Chief Executive of the Legislative Council to lead the SAR Government in its administration of the law and unswervingly support the Hong Kong Police Force in its law enforcement.

The second question is the comments of the police. As you said earlier, the Hong Kong Police Force has been strictly law enforcement and decisive enforcement in the recent period. I think that I am deeply appreciative of the professionalism demonstrated by the Hong Kong Police Force in acting in accordance with the law. I am thinking about a problem. Isn't it supposed to be like this? Of course it should be like this. Hong Kong is known as a society ruled by law. All Hong Kong people regard the rule of law as the core value they are proud of. What is the rule of law? The rule of law means that there are laws that must be followed. So what should the police do? That is, when crimes occur and when illegal activities occur, decisively and rigorously enforce the law, restore social order, and ensure social stability. *No matter who it is or what kind of banner he is playing, it is illegal to violate the law, and violence is violence. As long as it is illegal, it should be resolutely stopped. This is the specific manifestation of the police's due diligence. Only in this way*

---

[237] 这种触目惊心的暴力犯罪活动和对.

can the rule of law in Hong Kong be effectively defended.[238]

I want to reiterate that we express our sincere respect for the Hong Kong Police Force's fearless pressure and danger and strict law enforcement! Thank you!

08-06 15:20
CCTV reporter from CCTV
During the demonstrations in Hong Kong, a large number of young people rushed ahead, and there was no shortage of radical violence. What do you think of the spokesman for the young people in Hong Kong? Thank you.

08-06 15:23
Xu Luying
Thank you for the reporter's question. We have noticed that there are indeed some young faces in a series of demonstrations and violent clashes, and some people have blatantly violated the law. We are very saddened by these phenomena. Anyone with a discerning eye can see that some recent violent clashes in Hong Kong have been said to be caused by some chaotic elements and hidden elements. They are not thinking about the health of young people. They also push them to the evil roads. Young people became pawns and cannon fodder for their political plots. I think that with the increasingly conspicuous plots of the chaotic Hong Kong, the nuisance of the Hong Kong people, the self-respect of the young people, and the prosperity, stability and self-respect of Hong Kong, the face of "one country, two systems" is increasingly exposed, and more and more young people will see them. The face will be lost. In the process, in the course of the increasingly serious situation in Hong Kong,

---

238 也不管他打着什么样的旗号，违法就是违法，暴力就是暴力，只要是违法行为，就应该被坚决制止，这正是警方恪尽职守的具体表现，也唯有如此，香港的法治才能得到有效的捍卫。

we also deeply felt that there is indeed a problem in the national education of Hong Kong youth. Youth is an important period in the formation of outlook on life and values. In this period, loving the country and loving the motherland should be the first lesson of their school. But in many schools in Hong Kong, this class is very regrettable in many classrooms in Hong Kong. When many teachers encouraged young students to go on the streets and even participate in violent conflicts, when many children took to the streets and their parents did not stop, can we blame these young people alone?

Therefore, I feel that school education and family education must have a correct guidance. We must strengthen the patriotism education and national education of Hong Kong youth, and let them understand their country and themselves comprehensively, deeply and objectively from an early age. The nation, understand its own history and culture. The whole society should care about the healthy growth of young people and create a good, harmonious, stable and rule of law environment for the healthy growth of young people. The youth of Hong Kong are also young people of China. The youth of Hong Kong is the future of Hong Kong and the future of the country. The Central Government is always paying attention to the growth of young people in Hong Kong. We also know that young people in Hong Kong have indeed encountered many difficulties in their growth and face many confusions. We are all very clear and very empathetic. But these problems cannot be solved by violence or by illegality. I think if young people from Hong Kong come out and come to the mainland to look at it and look at the world, they will feel that our country is in a critical period of prosperity. Our country is in the process of realizing the great rejuvenation of the Chinese nation. In the critical period, if they closely link their future and destiny with the prosperity and development of the motherland, their future is very bright, and their path is very broad. Therefore, here, I also advise those young friends who have participated in demonstrations and even some violent conflicts, lost their way, and will return to the rule of law and order, to maintain Hong Kong's prosperity and stability, and not to The path of evil and the path of danger continue to move forward. thank you all![239]

08-06 15:25
Singapore Straits Times reporter
China has always said that there is an external "black hand"[240] involved in the current state of affairs in Hong Kong, but has not specifically stated what evidence to prove this. Does China have any evidence? In addition, which protesters are protesters supported by external forces? Ready to deal with them? Thank you.

08-06 15:31
Yang Guang

Thank you, you have raised a big question. Prior to this, the spokesperson of the Ministry of Foreign Affairs has repeatedly commented on this issue. Since you have asked, I would also like to answer this question.

We can look for evidence or clues about what they are saying from public reports. *Since the start of the revision*

---

239 所以，我感觉到，学校教育、家庭教育都要有一个正确的引导，要加强香港青少年的爱国主义教育、国民教育，要让他们从小就全面地、深入地、客观地了解自己的国家、自己的民族，了解自己的历史和文化。全社会都应该关心青年的健康成长，同时为青年的健康成长创造良好的、和谐的、安定的、法治的环境。香港的青年也是中国的青年，香港的青年是香港的未来，也是国家的未来，中央时时刻刻都在关注着香港青年人的成长。我们也知道，香港青年在成长过程中的确遇到了很多困难，也面临很多困惑，这些我们都非常清楚，也非常感同身受。但是这些问题是不能用暴力、用违法来解决的。我想，如果香港青年人走出来，多到祖国内地来看一看，多放眼世界，他们会感到，我们的国家正处在兴旺发达的关键时期，我们的国家正处在实现中华民族伟大复兴的关键时期，如果他们把自己的前途和命运与祖国的繁荣发展紧紧地联系在一起，他们的前途是非常光明的，他们的道路是非常宽广的。所以，在这里，我也奉劝那些已经参加了示威游行甚至一些暴力冲突的年轻朋友们，迷途知返，悬崖勒马，回到法治、秩序的正途来，维护好香港的繁荣稳定，而不要再向邪路和危险的道路上继续迈进一步。谢谢大家！
240 "黑手".

of the Fugitive Offenders Regulations in February, some Western politicians and the Taiwan authorities have publicly stood at the forefront and made many remarks about reversing black and white and irresponsible remarks.[241] Let's briefly review, for example, on March 21, the US State Department issued the "2019 US-Hong Kong Policy Law Report," which is much earlier than in previous years. It uses the word "regression" to describe Hong Kong's high degree of autonomy and has issued many statements. The rumors have threatened the rule of law in Hong Kong and eroded "one country, two systems." *For example, in late March, the United States highly invited some of the opposition's leading figures to visit the United States, and arranged for the Vice President and the Secretary of State to meet and support them. Less than two months later, senior US officials met with the so-called "anti-extradition amendments and the United States and Canada" led by the opposition figures.* [242] On June 13, some US lawmakers revisited the so-called "Hong Kong Bill of Rights on Human Rights and Democracy", arguing that they should regularly review or adjust their policies on Hong Kong and impose sanctions on relevant officials. In June, Pelosi said a famous saying, "The demonstrations in Hong Kong are a beautiful scenery." On June 25th, the former British Foreign Secretary Hunter asked Hong Kong to investigate the June 12 conflict. On July 8, the US Vice President and Secretary of State met with Li Zhiying respectively, openly discussing the issue of Hong Kong's amendments and Hong Kong's autonomy under "One Country, Two Systems." Wait a minute, there are still many, I will not go to read one by one, do not delay everyone's time. *I think that these remarks have a common feature, that is, to support the demonstrators to*

---

[241] 从 2 月份《逃犯条例》修订工作启动以来，一些西方政客和台湾当局就公然站在前台指手画脚，发表了很多颠倒黑白、不负责任的言论。

[242] 再比如 3 月下旬，美国很高调地邀请了一些反对派的头面人物访美，并且安排了副总统和国务卿会见，为其撑腰打气。随后不到两个月，美国高官又分别会见了反对派头面人物所带领的所谓的"反对引渡修例美加团".

support their strengths and encourage their efforts, and give advice to and intervene in the affairs of Hong Kong.[243] The situation in Hong Kong has deteriorated to the point where it is today. Some violent militants dare to unscrupulously carry out illegal activities and dare to openly challenge the bottom line of the principle of "one country, two systems." I think this is inconsistent with the irresponsible remarks of some Western politicians and their ignorance. Open, their "contributions" to the chaos in Hong Kong are also very impressive.

Recently, Yang Jiechi, director of the Office of the Central Foreign Affairs Working Committee, State Councilor and Foreign Minister Wang Yi have *all condemned Western forces for interfering in Hong Kong affairs.*[244] Mr. Tung Chee-hwa, vice chairman of the National Committee of the Chinese People's Political Consultative Conference, also pointed out that *the black hand behind this political storm is hostile to China's development. The fundamental purpose of the forces is to make Hong Kong a battleground for the international game and to make Hong Kong a base against the Central Committee as a pawn to contain China.* This voice is righteous and stern, and explains their bad intentions.[245]

Here, I want to emphasize that our principled position is that Hong Kong is China's Hong Kong and Hong Kong affairs will never allow any foreign countries to intervene. *We advise those politicians who speak beautiful words and who are actually sowing the seeds of social hatred and opposition. They are more serious and awake, and your tricks are impossible. Or, as I said earlier, the future and destiny of Hong Kong are in the hands of*

---

243 我想，这些言论都有一个共同的特点，就是为示威者撑腰打气、擂鼓助威，对香港的事务指指点点、横加干涉。
244 都斥责西方势力对香港事务的干涉.
245 这次政治风暴幕后黑手是一些敌视中国发展的势力，其根本目的就是要令香港变成国际博弈的战场，令香港变成反抗中央的基地，作为牵制中国的棋子。这个声音义正辞严，一语道破了他们的不良居心。

the entire Chinese people, including the Hong Kong compatriots.[246] You should not do the ridiculous thing of the "worm shaking the tree". Thank you.

08-06 15:35
Hong Kong Economic Times reporter
The revision storm has lasted for nearly two months, and the way people express their demands has also escalated. The biggest strikes, strikes, strikes and "non-cooperative movements" since the outbreak of the storm occurred yesterday, requiring the government to respond to the five major demands of the people. . May I ask the central government about this attitude. Thank you.

08-06 15:43
Xu Luying
Thank you for your question. The Hong Kong opposition forces encouraged the public to participate in the so-called strikes, strikes and strikes on August 5. We pay close attention to the progress of this matter. So far, let's see what they have done. In the early morning and morning, they blocked the main traffic, prevented the MTR from running, refused to perform flight missions, damaged traffic lights, set up roadblocks, and even cut wires, forcibly traffic, causing serious obstruction of many subway lines and important sections. The area was blocked and a large number of flights at the Hong Kong International Airport were grounded. According to incomplete statistics, at least 235 flights were forced to cancel, and a large number of shops were forced to close down. Many citizens could not go to work normally. It can be said that their behavior has seriously affected the normal life of the people and shocked the normal order of Hong Kong society. In the afternoon, some militants

---

[246] 我们奉劝那些说着漂亮话，实质上却干着播撒社会仇恨和对立种子的政客们，自重一点，也清醒一点，你们的伎俩不可能得逞。还是我刚才说的那句话，香港的前途和命运是掌握在包括香港同胞在内的全中国人民手中的，

continued to reapply, surrounded the police station, attacked the police, and carried out a series of violent attacks such as arson. In the evening, very few extreme militants threw the flag into the sea again. From the early hours of yesterday morning to less than 30 hours, this series of behaviors proved two more points:

First, the so-called "uncooperative movement" and the so-called "three strikes" by the opposition are not normal expressions of appeals, but extreme violent crimes, crimes that seriously undermine public order and public interests.[247] Behavior is a criminal act that challenges the bottom line of the principle of "one country, two systems" and violates the dignity of the country. Their purpose is to mess up Hong Kong, harm Hong Kong and ruin Hong Kong.

Second, their actions are completely unpopular and completely fail. I think that the organizers of this so-called "uncooperative movement" have a very ridiculous logic. Their so-called "strike" is to block traffic by a large area, so that everyone can't go to work normally, and many shops can't open, thus forming in disguise. The phenomenon of strikes, what is the strike caused by this strike? This is a joke in the world, it is a cover-up, self-deception. In fact, responding to them is embarrassing.

However, we have seen another scene. Many people went out early, did not affect the normal work, and the general public took the initiative to dismantle the roadblocks they set and pushed the black people who were blocking the subway. The vast number of Hong Kong citizens, as well as many political groups and associations that love Hong Kong and patriotism, have all condemned their actions. The patriotic Hong Kong people raised the five-star red flag again at 11 o'clock

---

247 第一，反对派搞的这场所谓的"不合作运动"、所谓的"三罢"，根本不是什么正常的诉求表达，而是极端的暴力犯罪行为，是严重破坏公共秩序和公共利益的犯罪行为.

last night. I don't know if you noticed it. Within a little hour after the flag was removed and thrown into the sea for the second time, there was a saying in the mainland media that "1.4 billion Chinese people are flag-bearers". I think that the majority of patriotic people who love Hong Kong are not alone. Behind us, our 1.4 billion Chinese people are united with them and share the same sympathy. Under such circumstances, the conspiracy of those who are chaotic and harboring Hong Kong is unpopular and will not succeed. We strongly condemn this kind of misfortune, port and port destruction at the expense of the stable life of Hong Kong's more than 7 million people and the prosperity and stability of Hong Kong. The central government will never allow these people to drag Hong Kong into danger. abyss. We strongly support the strict enforcement of the Chief Executive and the Special Administrative Region Government and the Hong Kong Police Force to quickly bring the perpetrators and criminals to justice. Thank you.

08-06 15:46
British Times reporter
Regarding the use of the military, I would like to ask a few more specific questions. As I mentioned earlier, the first task is to stop the riots and then restore order. The current situation is that the signs are not particularly good. I have several specific problems. The first question, has the Hong Kong Government asked Beijing to provide assistance to the troops stationed in Hong Kong? It's like what Mr. Yang said last week. The second question is whether the Standing Committee of the National People's Congress has now considered declaring a state of emergency under the Basic Law. Have you considered sending a PLA or a mainland police to assist the Hong Kong government? The third question, last week, the commander of the Hong Kong Regiment, Chen Daoxiang, said that the extreme violence was absolutely intolerable. The propaganda film of the troops stationed in Hong Kong also appeared last week. Recently, the Shenzhen

police also had drills for riot police. I want to know. What does the central government want to signal through these actions? Thank you.

08-06 15:48
Yang Guang
Thank you, you asked a lot of very specific questions, and finally asked a sentence, what kind of important signals. I also noticed the speech of Commander Chen Daoxiang. I want to say three sentences. *First, the glorious course of the People's Liberation Army in the past 92 years has proved that the Chinese People's Liberation Army is extremely reliable and incomparable in safeguarding the security of every inch of the sacred territory of the motherland. strong power. Second, the Chinese People's Liberation Army is both a mighty teacher and a civilized teacher. The People's Liberation Army listens to the party's command and the People's Liberation Army acts in accordance with the law. When talking about garrison, the garrison also acts in accordance with the law and acts in accordance with the relevant provisions of the Basic Law and the Garrison Law. Thirdly, we believe that with the unwavering support of the Central Government and the strong support of the people of the whole country including the Hong Kong compatriots, the Hong Kong SAR Government and the Hong Kong Police Force are fully capable of punishing violent crimes, restoring social order and restoring Social stability.*[248] Thank you.

08-06 15:50
Phoenix TV reporter

---

[248] 第一，中国人民解放军建军 92 年来的辉煌历程证明了一条，中国人民解放军是维护祖国每一寸神圣领土安全的无比可靠、无比强大的力量。第二，中国人民解放军既是威武之师，也是文明之师，人民解放军听党指挥，人民解放军依法办事。谈到驻军，驻军同样依法办事，依照《基本法》和《驻军法》的相关规定行事。第三，我们相信，有中央政府坚定不移的大力支持，有包括广大香港同胞在内的全国人民的大力支持，香港特区政府和香港警队完全有能力依法惩治暴力犯罪，恢复社会秩序，恢复社会安定.

We are also concerned that Carrie Lam's press conference held in Hong Kong yesterday just mentioned that Hong Kong is slipping into a dangerous situation recently, but she said that she will not resign. What does the spokesman think of her? Will the Central Committee ask Carrie Lam to resign? Thank you.

08-06 15:52
Yang Guang
I have already talked about this issue. In fact, I have talked about it more than once. Since you have asked, I will repeat it. The Central Government unswervingly and unwaveringly supports the Chief Executive of the Legislative Council, and the opposition's attempt to force the Chief Executive Carrie Lam to resign will not succeed. Thank you.

08-06 15:54
Yan Yanchun
The last question.

08-06 15:55
NBC Reporter
Do you mean that it is completely impossible for the Chinese military to intervene? Because you just said that the Hong Kong government and the police are fully confident in the current situation, so is it impossible for the military to intervene? Or is military intervention an option?

08-06 15:56
Yang Guang
Thank you, I have already answered this question. I forgot to add a sentence. The three points I have mentioned are a complete system. If I have to say one more sentence, I would like to say that *the Central Government and the people of the whole country Hong Kong's prosperous and stable support is real. The central government will never allow the offense of the "one country, two systems" principle to be unpunished, and will*

never let Hong Kong emerge from the turmoil that the SAR government cannot control and endanger national unity or security.[249] Thank you.

08-06 15:57
Yan Yanchun
Thanks again to the two speakers, thank you all. Today's briefing is over, thank you.

08-06 16:00

✳ ✳ ✳

[249] 中央政府和全国人民对香港繁荣稳定的支持是实实在在的，中央绝不允许对"一国两制"原则底线的冒犯不受惩处，也绝不会放任香港出现特区政府不能控制的危及国家统一或者安全的动乱。

Chapter 8

Thursday 8 August 2019
Assessing (Quan 權) the "Black Hand" (黑手) of Foreign Interference and the Justification for Intervention

One of the most interesting elements of the developing situation in Hong Kong is the move, now several weeks old, by the Central Government authorities to build a very strong case that at the root of the conflicts in Hong Kong are agents provocateurs representing foreign powers. But not just any old foreign power-- but the one foreign power with which China is currently engaged on multiple fronts in a fight for the redefinition of the relations between them. Of course I mean the United States.

In some respects Hong Kong offers a crisis form which China may well be tempted to seek advantage. One cannot blame them--the potential benefits are substantial. It provides a basis for legitimacy in intervention, it shifts focus form domestic conflict to foreign manipulation, and it may strengthen China's hand in both its current conflict with the United States over trade and in China's efforts to reshape the tenor and foundation of global international discourse (and China's place in the management of that narrative).[250]

All of this is fair game, one can suppose, within the rules of international engagement that have become the "new normal" after the rise of the current holders of positions of national leadership since 2014. A new historical era demands conformity to the rules (the "truths" of that era) that are manifested in the historical conditions within which states find themselves (the "facts" form which truth is derived). The Americans have themselves refined this technique for its own new era through the

---

[250] Ben Westcott, "China is Blaming the US for the Hong Kong Protests; Can that Really be True?" CNN (31 July 2019); available [https://www.cnn.com/2019/07/31/asia/us-china-hong-kong-interference-intl-hnk/index.html].

politics of "Russian interference" that has played a dominant role in the politics of discrediting the Trump administration. This is a tool that anyone, then, can use, to their own strategic ends.

In his Treatise on Rhetoric, Guiguzi speaks to the strategy of 'assessing' (quan 權).[251] Assessing is understood as a constellation of approaches centered on strategies of correct or authoritative power-authority (quanli 權力); of weighing or judging (quanheng 權衡); and of entitlement (quanli 權利). All speak to strategies of grounded in assessing, of taking stock (to use the Western merchant's form of the term, which at the same time highlights the strong cultural differences in term origin). Guiguzi speaks to the strategies of those who use speech to- persuade others. That, in turn, requires a conscious effort to mold speech that resonates with the character, nature, position, or desires of the listener.[252]

> Speakers who talk in equilibrium (jing yan zhe 靜言者) appease the opposition for the purpose of winning. Eloquence catering to someone's wish based on the prior knowledge of his mindset is called fawning talk (chan 諂). Eloquence of frequent citations in sophisticated words is called erudite talk (bo 博). Eloquence purporting to affect policies and plans is called power talk (quan 權). Eloquence of doubtless determination is called resolute talk (jue 決). Eloquence of poor quality that aims to stop the opposing side through attacks is called adverse talk (fan 反).[253]

---

[251] Guiguzi (鬼谷子), *Guiguzi: China's First Treatise on Rhetoric; A Critical Translation and Commentary* (Hui Wu (trans.); Carbondale: Southern Illinois University Press, 2016 (before 220 A.D.)); Book II.9.1. Guiguzi also serves as a useful framing of strategic and rhetorical choices in other important respects considered in the essays, supra, at Chapter 3 (Mend-Break (Di Xi 抵巇)), and supra Chapter 12 (Resist-Reconcile (忤合 Wuhe)), Chapter 20 (Open-Shut (Bai He 稗闔)), and Chapter 30 Fundamental Principles (Fu Yan 符言).

[252] Ibid., II.9.4, pp. 73-74.

[253] Ibid., II.9.1, p. 71.

The use of 'assessing' (quan 權) strategies appear to mark the form of approaches to the object of persuading internal and external listeners, listeners very differently situated, that the great source of the problem in Hong Kong is entirely due to the machinations of external forces externalizing the negative and threatening aspect of the situation in Hong Kong. That object of externalization is focused on appeasing the opposition through notions of a return to equilibrium, of fawning talk , of a measure of erudition, but mostly of 'power talk' (quan 權), 'resolute talk" (jue 決), and especially adverse talk' (fan 反).

This is the time for assessing in the context of Hong Kong's situation--of the way that what started as quite pointed controversy over a specific piece of legislation has now become something far more substantial--and the stakes that much greater. Each of these techniques appeals to a different and necessary audience; each forms part of a complex argument built on three relatively simple elements. Together, these appear to build a rhetorical framework for the articulation of the strategy of "assessing" that may point to the development by Chinese authorities of a coherent strategy to re-frame the situation in Hong Kong from one of domestic disturbance to one of foreign interference requiring the intervention of central authorities.

To that end, then, it is first necessary to identify a plausible foreign adversary. Here one deploys 'resolute talk' (jue 決). This is talk meant to suggest the resoluteness of the opposition through the process of rationalized exposure. It is pointed and meant to develop a rhetoric of resolute opposition to exposed bad" conduct by others. Second, it is necessary to weaken the character and cast doubt on the intentions of the identified adversary. That objective is furthered by attacking from the side, that is through attacks that develop an inference of bad motives through curated development of past actions elsewhere. This is the essence of 'adverse talk' (fan 反). This is talk meant to stop the opposing side through attacks, to force them to move from offense to defense. Third, it is essential to marshal evidence from which local interference might be surmised. Here one uses 'power talk' (quan 權). This is talk that is meant to adversely affect these "black hand" machinations by hobbling the ability of local forces to draw on these foreign resources, and thus to change policy. In the process policy is changed to favor the party successfully deploying power talk.

1. Resolute Talk (jue 决): Identify a plausible foreign adversary.

A prior chapter [254] considered the quite deliberate reference by Yang Guang (杨光) to the "black hand" (黑手) of foreign interference The use of the reference was made in this context:

> We also want to warn those unscrupulous violent criminals and the black hands behind them; China has always said that there are external "black hands" involved in the current state of affairs in Hong Kong; The black hand behind the political storm is something that is hostile to China's development."[255]

But the references in the HKMAO 6 August Statement was also used to point to the role of the United States, and to a lesser extent, the United Kingdom, as instigators.[256] In an extended statement,

---

[254] See Chapter 7, supra. The evolution of this position was considered in Chapters 3-5.

[255] 新闻办就香港当前事态的立场和看法举行吹风会， 2019-08-06 16:55 来源：中国网 [The Information Office holds a briefing on the current situation and views of Hong Kong, 2019-08-06 16:55 Source: China Net]; available [http://www.gov.cn/xinwen/2019-08/06/content_5419266.htm] (hereafter HKMAO 6 August 2019 Statement, *supra* ("我们还要向那些肆无忌惮的极少数暴力犯罪分子和他们背后的黑手发出警告； 中国一直称有外部的 "黑手" 卷入香港当前的事态；这次政治风暴幕后黑手是--些敌视中国发展的势力")

[256] HKMAO 6 August 2019 Statement, *supra* ("We can look for evidence or clues about what they are saying from public reports. Since the start of the revision of the Fugitive Offenders Regulations in February, some Western politicians and the Taiwan authorities have publicly stood at the forefront and made many remarks about reversing black and white and irresponsible remarks." [我们可以从公开的报道中去寻找你所说的他们干预的证据或者线索。从 2 月份《逃犯条例》修订工作启动以来， 一些西方政客和台湾当局就公然站在前台指手画脚，发表了很多颠倒黑白、不负责任的言论]).

he put forward evidence that he believed was decisive. Some of these revolve around intimations in the 2019 US-Hong Kong Policy Law Report.[257] The objection there was to the use "of the word "regression" to describe Hong Kong's high degree of autonomy." [258] In addition, interference was inferred from meeting between U.S. diplomatic and senior elected official with "opposition leading figures." [259] Also noted [260] was the revival, within days of the start of the protests in early June, of the of the "Hong Kong Human Rights and Democracy Act." [261] The encouragement of U.S. Canadian and U.K. officials and groups

---

[257] "2019 Hong Kong Policy Act Report," U.S. Department of State (21 March 2019); available [https://www.state.gov/2019-hong-kong-policy-act-report/](Key Finding: "implemented or instigated a number of actions that appeared inconsistent with China's commitments in the Basic Law, and in the Sino-British Joint Declaration of 1984, to allow Hong Kong to exercise a high degree of autonomy").

[258] HKMAO 6 August 2019 Statement, *supra.* (["以"倒退"这两个字来形容香港的高度自治，并多次发表声明，妄言修例威胁了香港的法治，侵蚀了"一国两制"。])

[259] HKMAO 6 August 2019 Statement ("For example, in late March, the United States highly invited some of the opposition's leading figures to visit the United States, and arranged for the Vice President and the Secretary of State to meet and support them. Less than two months later, senior US officials met with the so-called "U.S.-Canada group against the -extradition amendment" led by leading opposition figures". [再比如 3 月下旬，美国很高调地邀请了一些反对派的头面人物访美，并且安排了副总统和国务卿会见，为其撑腰打气。随后不到两个月，美国高官又分别会见了反对派头面人物所带领的所谓的"反对引渡修例美加团"。] and "On July 8, the US Vice President and Secretary of State met with Li Zhiying [founder of Next Media Group] respectively, openly discussing the issue of Hong Kong's amendments and Hong Kong's autonomy under "One Country, Two Systems."" [7 月 8 日，美国副总统、国务卿分别会见了黎智英，公然议论香港修例问题，以及香港在"一国两制"下的自治地位。]).

[260] HKMAO 6 August 2019 Statement, *supra* ("On June 13, some US lawmakers revisited the so-called "Hong Kong Bill of Rights on Human Rights and Democracy", arguing that they should regularly review or adjust their policies on Hong Kong and impose sanctions on relevant officials" [6 月 13 日，美国一些议员重提所谓"香港人权与民主法案"，妄称要定期检讨或调整对港政策，对相关官员实施制裁。]).

[261] H.R.3289 (related Bill S.1838) - Hong Kong Human Rights and Democracy Act of 2019; available [https://www.congress.gov/bill/116th-congress/house-bill/3289]. The Act includes a provision permitting the President to "impose property and visa-blocking sanctions on foreign persons responsible for gross human rights violations in Hong Kong."

were also noted, especially when they expressed praise for the protestors.[262] Yang Guang (杨光) made his point quite explicitly: "I think that these remarks have a common feature, that is, to support the demonstrators to support their strengths and encourage their efforts, and to point and intervene in the affairs of Hong Kong."[263] He laid the responsibility for the violence in Hong Kong, and its lawlessness, at the feet of U.S. and U.K. officials who cheered such activities outside of their own borders.[264]

Mr. Yang then drove home the point of the existence and objectives of this "black hand" strategy on the part of Western officials.   First he noted that his statements mirrored the accusations already leveled by senior central authority officials.[265] And then he proffered an explanation for its significance, one that went right to the heart of the sovereignty protecting stance that the central authorities were developing: "Mr. Tung Chee-hwa, vice chairman of the National Committee of the Chinese People's Political Consultative Conference, also pointed out that the black hand behind this political storm are forces hostile to China's development, its fundamental purpose is to make Hong Kong a battleground for the international game and to build Hong Kong as a base against the Central Government as a pawn to contain China."[266]

---

[262] HKMAO 6 August 2019 Statement, *supra* ("In June, Pelosi said a famous saying, "The demonstrations in Hong Kong are a beautiful scenery." On June 25th, the former British Foreign Secretary Hunter asked Hong Kong to investigate the June 12 conflict." [6 月，佩洛西说了一句著名的话， "香港发生的游行示威是一道美丽的风景线"。6 月 25 日，英国前外交大臣亨特要求香港就 6 月 12 日冲突进行调查。]).

[263] HKMAO 6 August 2019 Statement, *supra*.

[264] Ibid., ("the irresponsible remarks of some Western politicians and their ignorance. Open, their "contributions" to the chaos in Hong Kong").

[265] Ibid. ("Recently, both Yang Jiechi, director of the Office of the Central Foreign Affairs Working Committee, State Councilor and Foreign Minister Wang Yi have also denounced Western forces for their interfering in Hong Kong affairs." ["近期，中央外事工作委员会办公室主任杨洁篪，国务委员、外交部长王毅都斥责西方势力对香港事务的干涉，"]).

[266] Ibid. ("全国政协副主席董建华先生也一针见血地指出，这次政治风暴幕后黑手是一些敌视中国发展的势力，其根本目的就是要令香港变成国际博弈的战场，令香港变成反抗中央的基地，作为牵制中国的棋子。")

But this was hardly the first time the Black Hand metaphor was used to identify the United States as a prime instigator of the conflict in Hong Kong. On 24 July 2019, Time Magazine's online version reported from a Bloomberg source the use of the Black Hand trope by a Chinese Foreign Ministry official:

> There are "signs of foreign forces behind the protests," Chinese Foreign Ministry spokeswoman Hua Chunying told reporters Tuesday in Beijing. "I wonder if these U.S. officials can truthfully answer to the world the role the U.S. has played in recent events in Hong Kong." Her comments came after the U.S. State Department on Monday said attacks on protesters and other bystanders by criminal gangs was "particularly disturbing," according to a Voice of America report. Chinese Foreign Minister Wang Yi had blamed the "black hand" of Western forces for stirring up trouble in Hong Kong last month, without singling out the U.S.[267]

Pointedly, perhaps, the *South China Morning Post* circulated a story of the American Secretary of State denying the allegation.[268] On 31 July CNN distributed an article that also considered the issue, but that also suggested a coordination of accusation with China's allies.

---

[267] "China Urges U.S. to Remove 'Black Hand' From Hong Kong Protests," *Time* (via Bloomberg) (24 July 2019); available [https://time.com/5633383/china-hong-kong-u-s-foreign-forces/]. See also "China tells U.S. to remove 'black hands' from Hong Kong," Reuters (23 July 2019); available [https://www.reuters.com/article/us-hongkong-extradition-usa/china-tells-u-s-to-remove-black-hands-from-hong-kong-idUSKCN1UI0QJ]. For the referenced Voice of America report, see, Nike, Ching, "Hong Kong Anger Grows After Attack on Protesters," *Voice of America* (22 July 2019); available [https://www.voanews.com/east-asia-pacific/hong-kong-anger-grows-after-attack-protesters].

[268] Keegan Elmer, "Mike Pompeo rebukes China's 'ludicrous' claim US is behind Hong Kong protests," *South China Morning Post* 31 July 2019; available [https://www.scmp.com/news/china/diplomacy/article/3020749/mike-pompeo-rebukes-chinas-ludicrous-claim-us-behind-hong-kong] ("US Secretary of State Mike Pompeo has said it is "ludicrous" for China to claim the United States is behind the escalating protests in Hong Kong.")).

Chinese state media has run multiple editorials blaming the US for the chaos. The state-run tabloid Global Times alleged Monday that there had been "unprecedented levels of contact" between Hong Kong pro-democracy leaders and Western governments. "It is an open secret in Hong Kong that the forces protesting the extradition bill have been sponsored by the US," the paper said. North Korea has also leveled such claims at the US. In an editorial on Friday, state-run media Rodong Sinmun claimed the protests were the "outcome of a plot hatched by the US and other Western countries."[269]

On the other hand, members of the US Congress, and elements of American civil society (sometimes in coordination with other Western civil society communities) have expressed views of support either for the protests or their objectives. Arkansas Senator Tom Cotton released a statement linking the protests in Hong Kong to those at Tiananmen Square decades earlier: "The Tiananmen Square Massacre highlighted the Chinese Communist Party's brutality and treachery, which they have employed for thirty years to steal our jobs and threaten our security. If Beijing cracks down on Hong Kong, the United States ought not make the same mistake again."[270]" And earlier Senator Cotton had joined a group of elected officials to praise the courage and resistance spirit of the Hong Kong protestors against the state and its officials.[271] Speaker of the House Pelosi also issued a statement on

---

[269] Ben Westcott, "China is Blaming the US for the Hong Kong Protests; Can that Really be True?" *CNN* (31 July 2019); available [https://www.cnn.com/2019/07/31/asia/us-china-hong-kong-interference-intl-hnk/index.html], citing "Traitors seek to separate Hong Kong and fuel street violence," *Global Times* (29 July 2019); available [https://www.globaltimes.cn/content/1159595.shtml].

[270] Press Release, Office of Senator Tom Cotton, "Cotton Warns Chinese Communists Against Intervening in Hong Kong Protests," 6 August 2019; available [https://www.cotton.senate.gov/news/press-releases/cotton-warns-chinese-communists-against-intervening-in-hong-kong-protests].

[271] Press Release, "" 12 June 2019; available [https://www.romney.senate.gov/romney-cotton-colleagues-support-hong-kong-protesters]:

The people of Hong Kong are assembling in the streets to resist this threat to their freedom and send a message to the Chinese

6 August. In it she praised the "extraordinary outpouring of courage from the people of Hong Kong stands in stark contrast to a cowardly government that refuses to respect the rule of law or live up to the 'one country, two systems' framework which was guaranteed more than two decades ago. The people of Hong Kong deserve the true autonomy that was promised, with the full rights guaranteed by the Hong Kong Basic Law and international agreements."[272]

These statements have irritated the Chinese central authorities. Yet, transformed into evidence of intervention, they have proven useful in identifying a credibly large foreign power whose machinations can be used to explain the instability in Hong Kong. The irritation grows when that support appears to suggest some sort of transnational solidarity and when it reminds people of the international character of Hong Kong's current status, even as a part of China. Some of these officials have chosen to lump these unremarkable expressions of opinions by foreign officials and civil society elements as interference as well. "China's Foreign Ministry had strong words this week for members of the U.S. Congress weighing in on the Hong Kong protests: "Any attempt to interfere in Hong Kong affairs and China's internal affairs is doomed to fail.""[273]

Communist Party. "Hong Kong demonstrators know what happened in Tiananmen Square in 1989, unlike so many Chinese on the mainland. They know the risk they run by defying the Chinese Communist Party. The demonstrators' courage in the face of threats, police batons, and tear gas is an example for the world to follow. We support these demonstrators as they fight for freedom and call on Hong Kong and Chinese authorities to respect their right to peacefully protest."

[272] Press Release, "Pelosi Statement in Support of Hong Kong Protestors" (6 August 2019); available [https://pelosi.house.gov/news/press-releases/pelosi-statement-in-support-of-hong-kong-protestors].

[273] Shannon Tiezzi, "US Lawmakers Are Watching Hong Kong, and China Isn't Happy About That: After a series of statements from Congress members supporting the protesters, China's Foreign Ministry claps back," The Diplomat (8 August 2019); available [https://thediplomat.com/2019/08/us-lawmakers-are-watching-hong-kong-and-china-isnt-happy-about-that/].

At a regular press conference on August 7, Foreign Ministry spokesperson Hua Chunying was asked about U.S. Senators Tom Cotton (R-Arkansas) and Mitt Romney (R-Utah) expressing concern about the repression of protests in Hong Kong. Hua responded:

> The recent protests and demonstrations in Hong Kong have turned into radical violent behaviors that seriously violate the law, undermine security and social order in Hong Kong, and endanger local people's safety, property and normal life. No responsible government will turn a blind eye to such serious violent crimes. I want to ask these US senators, do you still remember how the American police dealt with the "Occupy Wall Street" movement in 2011? If Hong Kong's radical, violent and illegal activities happened in the US, what would the American police do? [Instead, in reacting to events in Hong Kong US officials and press] said that what was black was white [and what is white it called black] and talked nothing about the serious consequences of the radical, violent and illegal behaviors. Instead, you smeared the just actions taken by the Hong Kong police who have all along been professional, highly restrained and committed to safeguarding rule of law and social order. What are you really up to? What is your true intention behind the Hong Kong issue?[274]

The same line was taken in both identifying and responding to the remarks of Representative Pelosi. In response to a question, Foreign Ministry Spokesperson Hua Chunying declared:

> Nancy Pelosi and some other US politicians have been calling what is white black time and again, bolstering violent radical criminals and even justifying and

---

[274] "Foreign Ministry Spokesperson Hua Chunying's Remarks on August 7, 2019," Ministry of Foreign Affairs of the People's Republic of China; available [https://www.fmprc.gov.cn/mfa_eng/xwfw_665399/s2510_665401/2511_665 403/t1686991.shtml].

whitewashing their behaviors. They've also wantonly smeared and vilified the just move of the SAR government and police to uphold the rule of law and order. This is no different from covering up, conniving at and supporting illegal criminal behaviors, which again reveals their malicious intention of anti-China and messing up Hong Kong.[275]

But the response of the U.S. President works against their efforts to suggest American interference. In response to questions, the President stated: "Well, something is probably happening with Hong Kong because when you look at, you know, what's going on, they've had riots for a long period of time." The President then expressed national sovereignty principles that appeared sympathetic to the concerns of he central authorities: "And I don't know what China's attitude is. Somebody said that at some point they're going to want to stop that. But that's between Hong Kong and that's between China, because Hong Kong is a part of China."[276]

Still, American politics provide a rich field to mine for Chinese advantage. And that advantage—to cast the U.S. as the great instigator, could be exploited as well by the possibility of the enactment of a "Hong Kong Human Rights and Democracy Act"[277] Much more useful from the perspective of the "interference" narrative is the work of the Congressional-Executive Commission on China (CECC), which has been quite aggressive in the

---

[275] "Foreign Ministry Spokesperson Hua Chunying's Remarks on US House Speaker Nancy Pelosi's Erroneous Remarks on Hong Kong," Ministry of the People's Republic of China (7 August 2019), available [https://www.fmprc.gov.cn/mfa_eng/xwfw_665399/s2510_665401/2511_665403/t1686638.shtml].

[276] "Remarks by President Trump Before Marine One Departure" (1 August 2019); ("They'll have to deal with that themselves. They don't need advice.") available [https://www.whitehouse.gov/briefings-statements/remarks-president-trump-marine-one-departure-56/].

[277] H.R.3289 (related Bill S.1838) - Hong Kong Human Rights and Democracy Act of 2019; available [https://www.congress.gov/bill/116th-congress/house-bill/3289].

exposition of the U.S. position on Hong Kong.[278] Signals of support, however limited, may have indirect effect--by signally to local elements—the changing political consequences for China abroad of contemplated responses within China.

More importantly, one meets in the actions of the US Congress and the CECC potentially effective counter tactics in the form of a mirror strategy of constructing the central authorities themselves as the foreigner whose black hand is the case of the instability in Hong Kong. It is a strategy that suggests that similar political acts have also been in China's foreign relations toolkit, and they have been used in response to foreign decisions, especially when it is deemed to affect political or strategic interests of the Central Government. Those actions, of course, have Chinese characteristics, and have raised the countercharge of "bullying,"[279] Against these, resolute talk (jue 決) provides the rhetorical thrust of choice.

That choice then relies on the possibilities within this ambiguous space that are international relations among states— between direct projection of foreign power within another state, and the reaction of a state (and the determination of its own response) to what goes on in another—to resolutely apply and exploit the narrative of interference. But it can backfire as well. Sanctions against the apartheid regime in South Africa might be understood as interreference, though in that case it was one that eventually acquired substantial global support. At the same time the interference was indirect, it merely imposed rules of self-control by states on their own interactions with the target state. Nonetheless, China persists in expanding its rhetoric on

---

[278] Press Release, "Hong Kong: Chairs Urge Administration to "Strongly Condemn" Threat to Deploy PLA," (24 July 2019); available [https://www.cecc.gov/media-center/press-releases/hong-kong-chairs-urge-administration-to-condemn-PLA-deployment].

[279] See, e.g., "Australia to tackle foreign interference at universities," BBC (28 August 2019); available [https://www.bbc.com/news/world-australia-49492206]; Cf., Jimmy Quinn, "China Bullies Foreign Companies into Espousing Its Worldview," *The National Review* (7 June 2018); available [https://www.nationalreview.com/2018/06/china-bullies-foreign-companies-into-espousing-its-worldview/].

interference. And within that rhetorical choice is the advancement of a greater objective—the realignment of consensus within an interpretation of the One Country Two Systems principle. The black hand theory works well against foreigners if one can accept 'one country' as the central element of the principle. For China's adversaries, however, the same strategies can be used to portray China as the foreigner by emphasizing the 'two systems' elements of the principle. One sees here the elaboration of China's complex strategic gamble. But it should be borne in mind that others are also deploying rhetorical stratagems that mirror of those of the Chinese central authorities.

It follows, then, that the objective here is not truth but persuasion. The strategy is deliberate—to transform the ordinary into something that is menacing, and to detach the local from its sources and to re-attach it to a foreign, and therefore illegitimate, body. To that end the strategy of resolute talk (jue 決) can be deployed—and in quite interesting ways, by the central authorities. One sees here a pattern of efforts to clarify truth and untruth through 'jia '(假), citations that may unearth truth or untruth, through 'resolute talk' (jue 決). That strategy avoids the more pedantic rhetorical style of 'erudite talk' (bo 博) reserved for scholars and expert technical groups.[280] To identify the adversary is the key step in the rhetorical strategy of detaching the enemy from inside the local and transforming an internal adversary into a foreign threat.

2. Adverse talk (fan 反): Find character evidence that suggests that this adversary has already engaged in such conduct elsewhere

Identification of the enemy is merely the first step in the complex rhetorical strategy that is 'assessing' (quan 權). It is then also necessary to invest the adversary with evil qualities. The success of this objective requires a different sort of rhetorical approach.

---

[280] Guiguzi (鬼谷子), *Guiguzi: China's First Treatise on Rhetoric; A Critical Translation and Commentary, supra,* Book II.9.1, p. 70-71.

The essence of 'adverse talk' (fan 反) relies on the foundation of the rhetorical strategy of 'assessing' (quan 權) to persuade. "Polished persuaders use citations. Those who cite quotations must know how much and how little to borrow."[281] Citation suggests a borrowing, though in modern Chinese the term also suggests falsehood, or at least a misleading.[282] Lawyers, certainly understand the ability to use persuasive rhetoric to build stories that suggest a necessary conclusion by "verifying signs" (符驗).[283] The alignment of facts into a rationalized story is the essence of persuasion. In this case that essence is an arrow meant to strike at the character and trustworthiness of the foreigner now recast as meddling adversary.

This one is fairly easily accomplished—especially when one is dealing with a global power. First China can point to the US Global Magnitsky Act[284] projects as inherently designed to project US power (and thus interference) abroad.[285] And one can

---

[281] Guiguzi (鬼谷子), *Guiguzi: China's First Treatise on Rhetoric; A Critical Translation and Commentary, supra,* Book II.9.1, p. 70.

[282] Ibid., p. 70, n. 82.

[283] Ibid., p. 70.

[284] The Global Magnitsky Human Rights Accountability Act(Global Magnitsky Act, Title XII, Subtitle F of P.L. 114-328; 22 U.S.C. §2656 note), authorized the U.S. President to sanction persons and deny them entry into the United States where they are identified as engaging in human rights abuses, including corruption. See, "The Global Magnitsky Human Rights Accountability Act," Congressional Research Service (updated 20 October 20220); available [https://crsreports.congress.gov/product/pdf/IF/IF10576].

[285] Postscript Note: There were calls for use of Global Magnitsky sanctions a few days after this essay was first written. See, "Police brutality and political prosecution together are a toxic combination, says new Hong Kong Watch report," Hong Kong Watch (16 August 2019); available [https://www.hongkongwatch.org/all-posts/2019/8/16/police-brutality-and-political-prosecution-together-are-a-toxic-combination-says-new-hong-kong-watch-report] ("Consider using Magnitsky legislation to hold perpetrators of abuses to account."); see "Briefing: Police Brutality and Political Prosecution in Hong Kong Extradition Bill Protests," Hong Kong Watch (August 2019); available [https://static1.squarespace.com/static/58ecfa82e3df284d3a13dd41/t/5d56 8ca4d513b80001ad247f/1565953208103/Police+brutality+briefing.pdf]. That call by Hong Kong Watch became more definitive in September 2019; "MPs and Hong Kong Student Leaders call for UK to extend visa rights and to consider

recast the actions of the adversary as not just pointed against specific enemies but designed to hurt the welfare of the masses in target nations, with China positioned to play the role of protector and the agent for the restoration of prosperity and stability.[286] The terms used "restore normality"[287] echoes the key terms, stability and prosperity, that are transposed onto the heart of the Hong Kong debates.[288]

The most useful vessel for this effort is Venezuela. "Sweeping sanctions imposed by U.S. President Donald Trump on Venezuela are an act of "gross interference" and violate the norms of international relations, China said."[289] Here China can build on an old rhetoric of condemnation of blockages and comprehensive sanctions that have been developed by Cuban authorities since the 1960s.[290] The strategy, though, is to use Venezuela, for example, as evidence of the uncontrolled tendency—the evil character—of the United States and its insatiable drive to interfere in the affairs of other states. "'China urges the United States to face up to the essence of the Venezuelan issue, return to

---

Magnitsky sanctions of Hong Kong officials at Parliamentary event," Hong Kong Watch (9 September 2019); available [https://www.hongkongwatch.org/all-posts/2019/9/9/mps-and-hong-kong-student-leaders-call-for-uk-to-extend-visa-rights-and-to-consider-magnitsky-sanctions-of-hong-kong-officials-at-parliamentary-event]. The Chinese position became clearer in 2020 in response to European efforts to adopt their own version of the Global Magnitsky Act. "Chinese experts were concerned the legislation may be politicized and used as a tool to woo allies under the disguise of human rights in a so-called free and democratic world to contain and attack China." Liu Xin, "Chinese experts warn EU's Magnitsky laws could 'target certain country," Global Times (12 September 2020); available [https://www.globaltimes.cn/content/1209506.shtml].

[286] See, e.g., "Chinese Foreign Ministry Condemns US Blockade Against Venezuela," *TeleSur* (7 August 2019); available [https://www.telesurenglish.net/news/Chinese-Foreign-Ministry-Condemns-US-Blockade-Against-Venezuela-20190807-0028.html].

[287] Ibid.

[288] Considered in Chapter 9, infra.

[289] Darryl Coote, "China Condemns U.S. 'Interference' in Venezuela," UPI (8 August 2019); available [https://www.upi.com/Top_News/World-News/2019/08/08/China-condemns-US-interference-in-Venezuela/6961565247926/].

[290] See, e.g., Fidel Castro Ruz, *Obama and the Empire* (Ocean Press, 2011); Fidel Castro Ruz, *Reflexiones: Una selección de los comentarios de Fidel Castro (2007-2009)* (Colección Fidel Castro) (Spanish Edition; Ocean Sur Press, 2010).

the right path of respecting the international law and support the dialogue process of the Venezuelan government and the opposition,'" she said."[291] This adds credibility to its rhetoric of character assassination, which is essential toward the activation of the strategies of 'black hand' in Hong Kong.

Interference claims, however, go much deeper in China. They tie into old fears of the revival of US encirclement policies, which fueled Chinese opposition to the Trans Pacific Partnership (TPP).[292] And it underlies Chinese sensitivities with respect to US-Taiwan relationships.[293] "For almost two decades, Chinese strategists have worried about what they regard as the geopolitical encirclement of China. At various times, they have attributed that encirclement to the United States, then India, and most recently Japan."[294] The fear has guided Chinese thinking in 2018 opposing portions of the North American trade deal.[295] Here the notion is to paint the United States as an actor interfering in the duty of states to meet their international commitments and

---

[291] "Chinese Foreign Ministry Condemns US Blockade Against Venezuela," supra, (quoting Foreign Ministry spokesperson Hua Chunying; "The United States should let the Venezuelan people decide their future and immediately stop the bullying behavior of wantonly suppressing other countries." Ibid.).

[292] Discussed in Larry Catá Backer, "The Trans-Pacific Partnership: Japan, China, the U.S., and the Emerging Shape of a New World Trade Regulatory Order," *Washington University Global Studies Law Review* 13:49 (2014).

[293] David Brennan, "Chinese State Media Slams U.S. 'Flagrant Interference' with Huge Taiwanese Weapons Deal," Newsweek (12 July 2019); available [https://www.newsweek.com/chinese-state-media-slams-u-s-flagrant-interference-huge-taiwan-weapons-deal-1448891]. ("The People's Daily editorial suggested that the Taiwan weapons deal was just one element of American efforts to 'contain China.' It added that the 'irresponsible practice of the U.S.' will raise tensions, and warned that American leaders 'should not take chances and keep walking on the wrong pat.'").

[294] Felix K. Chang, "China's Encirclement Concerns" Foreign Policy Research Institute (24 June 2016); available [https://www.fpri.org/2016/06/chinas-encirclement-concerns/].

[295] Zhou Xin, "Chinese embassy in Canada condemns 'US veto' clause in North America trade deal," South China Morning Post (8 October 2018); available [https://www.scmp.com/economy/china-economy/article/2167395/chinese-embassy-canada-condemns-us-veto-clause-north-america].

responsibilities through fabrications of concepts meant to harm China.[296] This is 'adverse talk' (fan 反).

The essence of 'adverse talk' (fan 反) is eloquence of poor quality—direct sharp, brutal. That is now being delivered quite consciously. Taking a cue from Western discourse, Chinese diplomatic statements have become more pointed in a way recognizable to Western audiences. China's diplomats have become increasingly vocal and outspoken. This month, China's ambassador to London, Liu Xiaoming, gave a rare televised statement accusing the British government of meddling in Hong Kong, the scene of mass protests against Beijing's rule. Earlier this year, China's envoy to Canada publicly accused his hosts of "white supremacy," while the country's chief envoy in South Africa said President Donald Trump's policies were making the U.S. "the enemy of the whole world." [297] Crude, direct, and given the listeners, potentially effective.

The structural components become visible in this wider context. Like a good lawyer seeking to draw an inference of a likelihood that an accused acted in a particular way by pointing to a pattern of similar conduct in the past, the Central Government is seeking to make plausible its claims of interference by making a case that US foreign action is itself undeniably driven by an impulse to interfere. This pays additional dividends. First it advances Chinese efforts to develop its own model of internationalism based on principles of non-interference (for which an antipode in the form of the US is required). Second, it makes the case for a greater room to maneuver in Hong Kong. Third, it can be useful in managing its trade dispute with the US. And fourth, it may aid in advancing Belt and Road initiatives. Whatever happens in Hong Kong, this initiative likely has staying power.

---

[296] Ibid.

[297] Iain Marlow and Dandan Li, "You Are a Racist Disgrace.' Former National Security Advisor Susan Rice Chides 'Ignorant' Diplomat on Twitter," *Time* (15 July 2019); available [https://time.com/5626551/susan-rice-twitter-chinese-diplomat/].

3. Power Talk (quan 權): Marshal evidence from which local interference might be surmised.

The essence of 'power talk' (quan 權) is to affect policies and plans. It ties the bow on the rhetoric of resolute and adverse talk by signaling consequences and steps forward. This, too has been done, though the deliberately crude style of 'adverse talk' (fan 反) sometimes appears. This is talk not to an equal, but to the masses and through them to the leaders whose action one wants to influence.

One can start with tweeting—a habit that has now become popular as a primary means of popular communication in the wake of its effective use by President Trump. On 8 August 2019, for example, the *People's Daily* tweeted "'Occupy' protestor Joshua Wong admits meeting with US consulate -general staff in #HongKong after photo surfaces showing protestors with political unit chief. Wong said the meeting was about how the US can help and discourage local police, Ta Kung Pao reports."[298] Prominently on display was both the picture of the meeting and close ups of the US official identified.

To be sure, Chinese officials and their allies have continually pointed to meetings between Hong Kong individuals identified as part of the protest movement and U.S. officials. The Tweet distributed 8 August through the People's Daily is one example. Indeed, the meeting that was pictured in that Tweet also sparked an official response from the Central Government on 8 August 2019 in which the foreign ministry office in Hong Kong "issued a formal protest over a reported meeting between U.S. consular officials in the city and opposition figures, including prominent activist Joshua Wong. The statement demanded the U.S. explain the purpose of the meeting and "immediately cease interfering in Hong Kong affairs."[299]

---

[298] People's Daily, China, "Tweet," 1.30 am 8 August 2019; available [https://twitter.com/PDChina/status/1159335932014866432]
[299] Ben Westcott, "China is Blaming the US for the Hong Kong Protests," *supra n. 1.*

A news outlet, *China Times Post*, reporting for *Bloomberg*, provided more detail: "China's foreign ministry, which has previously said Hong Kong's ongoing unrest was "the creation of the U.S.," urged American diplomats in a statement to "draw a clear line with all anti-Chinese rioters, stop sending wrong signals to illegal violators, stop meddling in Hong Kong affairs, and stop going further down the wrong path.""[300] The meeting with Wong and other protestors was highlighted in a press organ of the central authorities (Wen Wei Po), which serves as a news outlet for the government.[301]

The Twitter feed of Dragon Wong 黄龙[302] amplified the official line with a tweet that was meant to accomplish two objectives. The first was to create an identity between the Umbrella Movement of 2014 and 2019 Extradition Law protests. The second was to identify the protestor leaders and their connections with the 'black hand' of the American government in Hong Kong. [303] And not just the American government, but international civil society. "What is not only omitted — but actively denied — is the fact that the HK opposition's core leaders, parties, organizations, and media ops are all tied directly to National Endowment for Democracy (NED) and Open Society Foundation (OSF)."[304] And then the point of all of this—the 'power

---

[300] Iain Marlow and Dandan Li, "China warns U.S. after diplomat meets with prominent protesters," *China Times Post* (10 July 2019); available [https://www.ctpost.com/news/article/China-warns-U-S-after-diplomat-meets-with-14290165.php].

[301] 文匯報, owned by Ta Kung Wen Wei Media Group, which is controlled by the liaison office of the Chinese government in Hong Kong. The Liaison Office of the Central People's Government I the Hong Kong Special Administrative Region (LOCPG) is an organ of the Chinese State Council and "also owns other media outlets, including Wen Wei Po, Ta Kung Pao, Hong Kong Commercial Daily and Orange News, a newly-setup online news site." Betsy Tse, "Basic Law Violations Seen in LOCPG Tightens Grip on HK Publishers," *Ejinsight* (9 April 2015); available [https://www.ejinsight.com/eji/article/id/1025075/20150409-basic-law-violation-seen-as-locpg-tightens-grip-on-hk-publishers

[302] Dragon Wong 黄; available [龙https://twitter.com/dragonwong2024/media].

[303] @DragnWong2024 (8 August 2019); available at [https://twitter.com/DragonWong2024/status/1159387459488059392].

[304] Ibid.

talk' (quan 權), emerges: the triumph of China's style of international relations. [305] Additional individuals have been identified in tweets that are circulating. [306] These suggest the possibility that officials are already building cases for prosecutions against identified individuals that may in part be strengthened by the development of the "Black Hand" theory now circulated by Chinese officials and their affiliates.

The response from Mr. Wong and U.S. officials was one of studied indifference. "Representatives of the United States Government meet regularly with a wide cross section of people across Hong Kong and Macau," said consulate spokesman Harvey Sernovitz" who noted further by example that "the day of this particular meeting, our diplomats also met with both pro-establishment and pan-democratic camp legislators, as well as members of the American business community and the consular corps. "[307] Wong emphasized that the object of the discussions centered on U.S. legislative responses to what the protestors have tried to convince the world are human rights violations by the police organs of Hong Kong, including the progress of the consideration of the Hong Kong Human Rights and Democracy Act. [308] There was, in his view, nothing special about the meetings. [309] Still, the battle lines have been drawn. And the consultation on the Hong Kong Human Rights and Democracy Act can only add fuel to the Central Government's fire seeking to connect the dots between local protestors and the U.S.

---

[305] Ibid., taken from the tweet of an account deleted from Facebook and Twitter; available
[https://twitter.com/DragonWong2024/status/1159387596478226432].

[306] Xu Keyue, "Chinese consulate in Australia praises patriotic students for counter-protest against separatists," Global Times (25 July 2019); available [https://www.globaltimes.cn/content/1159212.shtml].

[307] Iain Marlow and Dandan Li, "China warns U.S. after diplomat meets with prominent protesters," supra.

[308] Ibid.

[309] Ibid. ("In a Facebook statement on Wednesday, Wong acknowledged that he had met with a U.S. diplomat but shrugged off allegations that the meeting was proof of foreign interference. . . . . "This meeting is nothing special."")

But the essence of 'power talk' (quan 權) is to affect policies and plans. And that is precisely what is sought to be achieved here. The object is disruption—the coherence and persuasive strength of the protestors, as well as the discrediting of the Hong Kong Human Rights and Democracy Act. But by persuading the listener that there is a policy and planning being developed—by the United States through the Hong Kong protestors—the ultimate rhetorical aim is achieved—'assessing' (quan 權) the situation and recasting it to one's favor. And that strategy is neither interested in the fine points of the differences between engagement and interference by states, or in the contradictory actions taken by the party that invokes 'assessing' (quan 權). Here one is reminded of the way that the Chinese Foreign Ministry has continuously shrugged off Australian and New Zealand allegations of interference for its meetings, consultations, and statements directed toward Australian education.[310]

✳ ✳ ✳

---

[310] See, Damien Cave, "Chinese Nationalists Bring Threat of Violence to Australia Universities: A clash with Hong Kong supporters at a student protest could be a dark omen of what's to come," *The New York Times* (30 July 2019); available [https://www.nytimes.com/2019/07/30/world/australia/hong-kong-china-queensland-protests.html]; "Hong Kong, mainland Chinese students clash at New Zealand university over extradition bill," *South China Morning Post* (30 July 2019); available [https://www.scmp.com/news/asia/australasia/article/3020639/chinese-students-clash-new-zealand-university-over-hong-kong]; Xu Keyue, "Chinese consulate in Australia praises patriotic students for counter-protest against separatists," *supra*; "Queensland university students protest 'China-funded education,'" SBS News (updated 31 July 2019); available [https://www.sbs.com.au/news/queensland-university-students-protest-china-funded-education].

Chapter 9

Friday 9 August 2019
Thoughts on Violent Popular (Mob?) Action Against the Solid Virtues of Prosperity and Stability; Considering Albert Chen Hung-yee 陳弘毅 Essay on the Situation in Hong Kong Part 2: 一國兩制的博弈 ["The Game of One Country Two Systems"]

Last week Albert Chen Hung-yee (陳弘毅) posted the first of a two part essay, 理性溝通的困境 ["The Dilemma of Rational Communication"], which first appeared on 2 August in the Ming Newspaper supplements [發表於《明報》副刊]. That essay was the subject of an earlier engagement.[311] Today, Professor Chen posted the second part of the essay, 一國兩制的博弈 ["The Game of One Country Two Systems"]. It also originally appeared in the Ming Newspaper on 9 August 2019.[312]

In the first essay Professor Chen assumed the voice of the classical Greek chorus delivering the *parados* or entry song, in this case an elegy to discourse, and to the tragedy that is working its way to climax in Hong Kong. In the Second essay, 一國兩制的博弈 ["The Game of One Country Two Systems"], the tone shifts. It retains its distance from the central characters in the drama, but now uses the mechanics of the modern oracle--game theory, and classical economic theory of behavior--to both make a prediction and to urge at least one side in the current situation in Hong Kong to reconsider the path some of its members have chosen to attain goals which only partly overlap with that of the government camp.

---

[311] See Chapter 6, supra (Thoughts on Albert Chen Hung-yee 陳弘毅 (Hong Kong U.): 理性溝通的困境 ["The Dilemma of Rational Communication"])

[312] Albert Chen Hung-yee 陳弘毅, 一國兩制的博弈 ["The Game of One Country Two Systems"]; 發表於《明報》副刊 （2019年8月9日） [published in the supplement of Ming Pao (August 9, 2019)].

Here one enters the realm of the role of the chorus[313] in Sophocles' *Antigone.* [314] That choral role is one that Professor Chen now appears to embrace. In that role, he introduces key thematic or emotional elements essential to the unfolding of the inevitable course of the tragedy. Here, as well, Professor Chen lays out the elements of the tragedy that principle begot in a context whose course was set in motion years ago and by others.

> Thou hast rushed forward to the utmost verge of daring; and against that throne where justice sits on high thou hast fallen, my daughter, with a grievous fall. But in this ordeal thou art paying, haply, for thy father's sin. . . Reverent action claims a certain praise for reverence; but an offense against power cannot be brooked by him who hath power in his keeping. Thy self-willed temper hath wrought thy ruin. [315]

For these and other reasons, apparent to those who study it, Professor Chen's essay, 一國兩制的博弈 ["The Game of One Country Two Systems"], is worth reading.

Again, Professor Chen grounds his analysis in core discursive tropes of the liberal democratic and markets driven West. In language pregnant with ambiguity, Professor Chen frames his argument on the principle of economic rationality and rational choices constructs based on an insatiable drive to maximize *personal* welfare. [316] And yet rational choice is a

---

[313] G. M. Kirkwood, "The Dramatic Role of the Chorus in Sophocles," *Phoenix* 8(1):1-22 (1954) ("the chorus should take an active part not only in the dramatic action but also in the playwright's contest against his rivals in the dramatic competition" Ibid., n. 3).

[314] Sophocles, *Antigone* (R.C. Jebb, trans., MIT Classics Online (orig. 422 B.C.) ; available [http://classics.mit.edu/Sophocles/antigone.html]

[315] Sophocles, *Antigone, supra.,* (Chorus; strophe 3; antistrophe 3.

[316] Chen, supra. （"經濟學假定個人在選擇如何行動時是理性的，就是說他知道什麼結果對他有利或其目標是什麼，他會在不同選項中選擇一項，務求最大程度上實現其目標或取得最佳回報" ["Economics assumes that an individual is rational in choosing how to act, that is, that he understands what results are good for him or what his goals are. He will choose one among the different options in order to maximize his or her goals or achieve the best return."]).

symptomatic principal—it merely reveals the connection between choices and the (self) understanding of interest valued in relation to competing (personal) interests and (external) constraints.

This breezy positing that individuals—much less collective organs— "understand what choices are good for them" assumes much. It assumes that individual and collective choices align, that understanding is an autonomous process, and that it can somehow be distilled (or judged) as authentic or good. And yet those foregrounding ambiguities are precisely what appear in play in Hong Kong at the moment. Rational choice is an elegant rationalization of the past. But it provides virtually no value, other than as a n ex ante rationalization framework that then serves as justification for authenticating post hoc choices, by those in a position to judge and exact consequences. That is a profoundly Western approach to the resolution of a problem the trajectories of which one already has a final destination in mind.

Yet Professor Chen does have a point in starting the analysis in what might appear to some as in mid-field: such rational choices are hardly ever the elegantly detached processes of pure analytics that might be presumed from its expositions. And, indeed, sometimes these rational choices (already pre-rationalized for consumption) have already been made. In that context—in which decisions have been structured for the decision makers to make a particular conclusion inevitable given the rules of valuation and objectives that have been preset, the process of decision might seem to an outsider as little more than one of enlightening those for whom there is very little "rationality" to choices offered them, to embrace the choice as rational. That, certainly is the way one understands politics and political discourse, in the West.

Nonetheless, it is also a useful way of understanding the choice available within Marxist-Leninist systems. It is when they rub together that "choices" become both more pointed and more rational—but also where the underlying conflicts of valuations of these alternatives are exposed. These are the forms of the choices that appear to be "on offer" for the people of Hong Kong in the context of the current political disagreements and the choices made by all sides in expressing their options (election of action grounded in choices of objectives). This, then, is the context as well in which Professor Chen offers a "cost-effective calculation" approach.[317]

This, then, frames and constrains the strategies of game theory. This ought not to be surprising: every game has its rules. One cannot play basketball by reference to the rules of tennis. And therefore all games tightly constrain the choice universe offered to its players. This poses the difficulty of games in societal organization—for conflict sometimes occurs when the object of the conflict is about the game, that is the strategic interaction, to be played out (and the rules to be observed) rather than about the way that either side is conforming to the rules of a game they both believe they are playing. [318] Professor Chen assumes all stakeholders are in the same game. The central authorities insist that must be so (and like central authorities everywhere they point to the authority, legitimacy and power of the applicable rule book). But that is precisely the problem in Hong Kong: One Country Two Systems can to some suggest two sets of rules. The scene, then, is set for the performance of Antigone, and for the

---

[317] Thus, Professor Chen explains:

In the face of different options, I will consider the cost and benefit of each option, in order to get the maximum benefit at the lowest cost. Another application of rational hypothesis is game theory, which deals with the interaction of two or more parties. Each party's behavior may affect the behavior of the other party. When each party chooses how to act, that party must use the information it has (for example, about Information on how the other party will act), in order to maximize the interests of the parties in the process of interaction or to achieve their goals to the greatest extent possible. ["如果不同選項，我會考慮每選項的成本和效益，務求以最低成本獲取最大效益。理性假設的另一個應用便是博弈論，其處理的是兩方或多方互動的情況，每方的行為都可能影響對方的行為，每方選擇如何行動時，必須運用其掌握的資訊（例如關於對方會怎樣行動的資訊），務求在互動過程中實現己方利益的最大化或最大程度上實現自己的目標。"]

Ibid.
[318] Duncan Snidal, "The Game Theory of International Politics," *World Politics* 38(1):25-57 (1985).

conflict between Creon and Antigone over which the Chorus can only fret—and in this case perhaps declare allegiance to a specific set of applicable rules.[319]

And so to the "game" that is to be played in the field one calls Hong Kong. Referencing discursive tropes that derive from centering the "rational" in liberal democratic and Marxist-Leninist systems, he explain: "The concepts of "zero-sum game", "win-win" and "double lose" come from game theory."[320] And that is what Professor Chen offers as a basis for rationalizing the choices inherent in One Country-Two Systems in terms of value based outcomes for the parties. "We can consider the interests of all parties or the goals they wish to achieve, as well as the options for their actions."[321]

To that end Professor Chen focuses on the principal interests and goals of the Hong Kong officials and those of the central authorities—prosperity and stability.[322]

> For example, the central government and the SAR government's goal is to maintain Hong Kong's prosperity and stability while safeguarding the interests of "one country." Those in the pro-government camp all basically agree with this goal. . . However, the non-government camp members also hope that Hong Kong can maintain prosperity and stability.[323]

---

[319] It may be best to leave to the reader to consider who then plays the role of Tiresias, the seer whose prophesies are heard and dismissed until it is too late for either side, "a corpse for corpses." Sophocles, *Antigone, supra.*

[320] Ibid. ("零和遊戲"、"雙贏"、"雙輸" 等概念都來自博弈論。").

[321] Ibid. ("我們可考慮各方的利益或其所希望達到的目標，以及其行動的選項。").

[322] The centrality of these objectives and its high value to local and national officials have been quite clearly articulated almost from the start of the protests. Its initial presentation was considered supra, Chapters 4, 5, and 7.

[323] Ibid. ("例如，中央和特區政府的目標是在於在保障 "一國" 利益的前提下，維護香港的繁榮安定。建制派人士基本上認同此目標，. . . 但是，非建制派人士也希望香港能維持繁榮安定。")

Professor Chen, then, applies rational choice by assuming both the primary choice and its value to all of the parties. It follows, then, that additional values or choices, or now secondary objectives have lesser value. And, to the extent that the attainment of these objectives of secondary value exact a high price—including threats to the prosperity and stability of Hong Kong, then they must be abandoned, at least by anyone claiming any alignment with rationality. . . . and any allegiance to Hong Kong. And yet unmentioned is the fairly well-known frustration of ordinary Hong Kong people over the prior fifteen years who saw plenty of prosperity but much of it bypassing them;[324] this has been served up as a cause of the Umbrella Movement eruption and likely that of the current situation. One worries here about offering the word "prosperity" without offering its substance as well.

What is this secondary objective and what is the cost of strategic action directed toward its attainment? Professor Chen explains:

> The non-government camp hope that Hong Kong can achieve universal suffrage to protect the human rights and freedoms of Hong Kong people and encourage the government to hold Hong Kong people accountable through democratic elections. . . . Therefore, if they are rational, they should not agree to use violent resistance as a means to achieve their goals, because such resistance may endanger Hong Kong's ability to successfully achieve prosperity and stability.[325]

However, the issue is to merely the consequences of violence on the protection and elaboration of the goals of prosperity and stability. Rather, and decisively, it is the conclusion that the goals

---

[324] See, eg., Joseph Yu-shek Cheng, "The Emergence of Radical Politics in Hong Kong: Causes and Impact," *China Review* 14(1:199-232 (Spring 2014) (Special Issue: Urban and Regional Governance in China).

[325] Chen, supra. （ "而非建制派人士則希望香港能實現真普選，以保障港人的人權和自由和促使政府通過民主選舉向港人問責。. . . . 所以他們如果是理性的話，應該不會贊成以暴力抗爭為手段來實現其目標，因為這種抗爭可能會危害香港的繁榮安定，. . . . 。").

of the Hong Kong opposition are essentially unattainable: "而且成功達到其目標的機會相當渺茫" ["The chances of attaining its other goal are quite slim"]. [326] The conclusion, then, is also inevitable—in the face of the overwhelming likelihood of the failure of the "secondary" objective, and the cost of that effort on the achievement or protection of the objectives of prosperity and stability, "[t]herefore, it is irrational to choose violent protests in Hong Kong."[327]

Professor Chen heeds the voice of Creon, in Antigone: "disobedience is the worst of evils. This it is that ruins cities; this makes homes desolate; by this, the ranks of allies are broken into head-long rout; but, of the lives whose course is fair, the greater part owes safety to obedience. Therefore we must support the cause of order."[328] But now what was once poetry is reduced to the calculus of advantage. Perhaps that is necessary in the historical context in which it is written. But the result is the same. And the advice is sound.

Yet the soundness of that advice, and the integrity of the equations that now provide a rigid logic toward its anticipated end, depend in large measure on that thing unseen and abstract but nonetheless profoundly real, that is in the *value* of the thing to those who rely on that valuation to make their rational choices within their own logical frameworks. Professor Chen dismisses the value of the objectives of the protestors. That de-valuation is pragmatic—the goals have a slim chance of being realized. But to their proponents, the valuation is perhaps reversed—precisely because there is a slim chance of realization, the objective becomes more precious. And the preciousness of that value, even in defeat, even in the production of a city of martyrs, may for them make the costs to prosperity and stability all the more easy to bear. More importantly, that dismissal, in the context of the logical arrangement of costs and benefits, of objectives and impediments, suggests the fundamental difficulty of the logic. Where there is no agreement on valuation, and were the calculus of costs are a

---

[326] Ibid.
[327] Ibid. ("因此，在香港的情況選擇暴力抗爭，可說是非理性的").
[328] Sophocles, *Antigone*, supra.

function of the value of objectives, then it may well be impossible to deploy these logical relations except as post hoc rationalizations of a position that has already won.

That becomes evident, necessarily, in the way that popular violence is valued. He implies a tremendously high cost of violence—to prosperity and stability. Where those values are paramount, of course, any actions that might threaten them would necessarily produce a high (counter) valuation. That has been the view not just in Marxist Leninist systems but also in the West, from which Professor Chen draws the normative basis of analysis.[329] Non-violent protest has become the template for the West, as well as to a much lesser extent in Marxist-Leninist systems. The pieties around non-violent protests, however, hide what it exactly does—it shifts the risks and costs of violence to those who must maintain order—to the institutional apparatus charged with order and against which non-violent protests are directed. They are invited to lose control and by losing control create the martyrs that then enhance the likelihood of victory for the protestors (by moving mass opinion and the positions of outsiders with a stake in the contests).

More importantly, it privileges one way of giving meaning to the terms "stability and prosperity" over others. Already, since the start of the protests on 9 June that rift--now growing, has come into clearer focus--a focus that is papered over here. On the one hand one understands stability and prosperity from the perspective of the local and central authorities: conformity with law and norm, acceptance of the higher authority of officials and

---

[329] For an early example of the richness of the literature that was to come, see, e.g., Harrop A. Freeman, "The Right of Protest and Civil Disobedience," *Indiana Law Journal* 14(2):228-254; available [https://www.repository.law.indiana.edu/ilj/vol41/iss2/3]; John Morreall, The Justifiability of Violent Civil Disobedience," *Canadian Journal of Philosophy* 6(1):35-47 (1976). [Postscript: The notion has become embedded into the mythology of the American Republic, see, Anjannette Conner, "Six Times Civil Disobedience Changed the Course of U.S. History," Reference 9 July 2020]; available [https://www.reference.com/history/civil-disobedience-changed-course-us-history]]. The literature indeed is rich and the elaboration of theories applicable both to the peculiarities of the United States as well as to other states, especially developing states, has been the subject of much debate.

ultimately of the leading forces of society and politics, acceptance of the hierarchies of power and of the rules through which these hierarches--an interlinked chain of collective and leadership cores--operate, and of a very specific meaning of prosperity, or at least of the way it is measured. These are not merely expressions of Marxist Leninist meaning making, but also of that of the liberal democratic camp (though implemented in quite distinct ways). This is the voice of Cleon, of the 'establishment,[330]' of ordered engagement and of welfare that can be counted in things. It is a voice that distinguishes between elites and the people--between the core of leadership and the collective in terms of legitimacy, authority, and ultimately sovereignty. And it is the basis on which either popular error can be disciplined or corrupt elites can be removed. Thus it has no inherent ideological basis but has been as useful to Marxist Leninist vanguards,[331] as it has been to contemporary populists in liberal democratic orders.[332]

It is a powerful voice that is manifested in the law of 'establishing' order or overturning it. Indeed, the identity of stability and order can be strong. This is the voice of constitutionalism. It is against this voice that the bodies of the protesters on the street of Hong Kong speak. This is also an old voice, but the voice of transformation--of an explosive expression that is itself an expression of a dynamic stability and a more abstract prosperity. In American terms, if the voice of stability and prosperity, of Cleon, is that of the U.S. federal constitution, then the voice of the protesters, of Antigone, is that of the American Declaration of Independence.[333] One speaks to stability as order; the other speaks to stability as the process of political engagement itself and the protection of underlying normative

---

[330] Godfrey Hodgson, "The Establishment," *Foreign Policy* 10:3-40 (1973).

[331] Mao Zedong, "On the People's Democratic Dictatorship" (30 June 1949) in commemoration of the 28th anniversary of the CPC; available [https://www.marxists.org/reference/archive/mao/selected-works/volume-4/mswv4_65.htm]. g

[332] See Ruth Wodak, "The 'Establishment,' the 'Élites,' and the 'People'," *Journal of Language and Politics* 16(4):551-565 (2017).

[333] Discussed in Larry Catá Backer, Some Thoughts on The American Declaration of Independence and the Irish Easter Proclamation, 8 *Tulsa Journal of Comparative & International Law* 8:7 (2000).

principles that shape the character of a social-political order. Violence, then, on both sides, is a byproduct, or the expression of a fidelity to, notions of stability and prosperity that are fundamentally irreconcilable. Even at this point it becomes clear that the rationality of the choice ow open is misdirected--the choice is between quite distinct normative perspectives and the world of meaning and expectation each contains.

This may not then be a matter of rationality, as Professor Chen suggests, so much as it is a clear exposure of the distinctive rationalities that now divide the two camps. And that separation appears to be growing. That leaves little space for much of anything but lamentation. And it is with potentially great tragic irony that Tiresias' waring to Creon, much more than the elegance of quantitative analysis, that ought to counsel restraint on all of the actors: "For the altars of our city and of our hearths have been tainted, one and all, by birds and dogs, with carrion from the hapless corpse, the son of Oedipus: and therefore the gods no more accept prayer and sacrifice at our hands, or the flame of meat-offering; nor doth any bird give a clear sign by its shrill cry, for they have tasted the fatness of a slain man's blood."[334]

$$* \quad * \quad *$$

---

[334] Sophocles, *Antigone*, supra

Chapter 10

Tuesday 13 August 2019
Dividing the Baby, and Killing it, Too; Press Briefing Note from the United Nations High Commissioner for Human Rights [关于中国香港的新闻发布会 联合国人权事务高级专员发言人]

It has taken some time for the great and sometimes badly lubricated wheels of the United Nations Geneva apparatus to move in the direction of the situation in Hong Kong. That eventually some movement would occur was inevitable. Given the pace of events it is now unavoidable. But such a movement puts the UN Office of the High Commissioner in a delicate situation. The delicacy is made more complicated by the changing politics that increasingly divide a Chinese side of the political divide from that of a variable group of leading liberal democratic states.

The Chinese side would likely view any recognition of "trouble" in the SAR as both "sensitive" and as interference in the internal affairs of China. China, as a big power country, would tend to take umbrage—and has done so increasingly.[335] Of course that umbrage and sensitivity tends to work mostly in one direction; there is less worry about 'hurting the feelings of the people'[336] of

---

[335] Especially against the large global multinational enterprises. See, e.g., Chung Man, "Political sensitivity is key to doing business in China," *EJInsight* (26 January 2016); available [https://www.ejinsight.com/eji/article/id/1754335/20180126-Political-sensitivity-is-key-to-doing-business-in-China]. But it is also useful against foreigners who cross lines; Simon Lewis, "Swedish Activist Shown 'Confessing' on Chinese State Television," *Time* (19 January 2016); available [https://time.com/4186392/peter-dahlin-sweden-china-human-rights-confession-swede ("appearing to apologize for hurting "the feelings of the Chinese people" in his work with human-rights lawyers").

[336] Joshua Keating, "Who's hurt Chinese feelings the most?," *Foreign Policy* (11 December 2008); available [https://foreignpolicy.com/2008/12/11/whos-hurt-chinese-feelings-the-most/] ("the Chinese government criticized French President Nicolas Sarkozy for hurting "the feelings of the Chinese people" by meeting with the Dalai Lama" and listing countries in descending order of number of times that criticism had been made against them by Chinese officials).

Hong Kong Between "One Country" and "Two Systems"
10. *Press Briefing Note from the UN High Commissioner for Human Rights*

168

other states when it is in Chinese national interests.[337] though it should be noted that such umbrage appears much less in evidence when the interference is pointed elsewhere. On the other hand, many of the High Commissioner's other stakeholders have become increasingly vocal about the situation in Hong Kong and critical of the way it has been handled—using in many instances the language of international human rights. [338] International disquiet over the situation in Hong Kong preceded the start of the protests in June 2019.[339] These state and non-state actors also cannot be ignored.[340] This is true even as Hong Kong exposes rifts within Europe.[341]

---

[337] Consider for example, the controversy over the outward projection of China's United Front work; Mercy A Kuo, "China's United Front Work: Propaganda as Policy," The Diplomat (14 February 2018); available [https://thediplomat.com/2018/02/chinas-united-front-work-propaganda-as-policy/].:But it applies to more traditional areas, See, e.g., Joshua Meservey, "Report: The U.S. Should Call China's "Non-Interference" Policy in Africa What It Is—A Myth," The Heritage Foundation (6 July 2018); available [https://www.heritage.org/global-politics/report/the-us-should-call-chinas-non-interference-policy-africa-what-it-myth]. Also Rezaul H. Laskar, India again rejects China's interference in internal affairs," Hindustan Times (6 August 2020); available [https://www.hindustantimes.com/india-news/india-again-rejects-china-s-interference-in-internal-affairs/story-SfvaRBmV2WewBr8Kcx9OvI.html].

[338] The US response is discussed in Chapter 8, supra. See also,

[339] James Pomfret, "EU lodges formal diplomatic note against contentious Hong Kong extradition bill," Reuters (24 May 2019); available [https://www.reuters.com/article/us-hongkong-extradition-eu-idUSKCN1SU0OS] ("The EU Office in Hong Kong and Macau said in a brief statement in response to press inquiries that it had, together with diplomatic representatives from its member states, met with Hong Kong's leader Carrie Lam to 'carry out a demarche reiterating their concerns regarding the government's proposed amendments to Hong Kong's Fugitive Offenders Ordinance'").

[340] "Joint Statement by Canada and European Union on situation in Hong Kong," Government of Canada (17 August 2019); available [https://www.canada.ca/en/global-affairs/news/2019/08/joint-statement-by-canada-and-european-union-on-situation-in-hong-kong.html] (""Canada and the European Union recall their close relations with Hong Kong under the 'one country, two systems' principle and their strong stake in its continued stability and prosperity.").

[341] See, "EU's stance on Hong Kong must be same on Catalonia, says delegate in Brussels," Catalan News (6 October 2019); available [https://www.catalannews.com/politics/item/eu-s-stance-on-hong-kong-must-be-same-on-catalonia-says-delegate-in-brussels] (""We urge the EU to be consistent and what they declare for other conflicts, like Hong Kong, they apply

In contrast to the likely Chinese position on the contours of a "correct" statement from the OHCHR, these stakeholders would likely reject as "incorrect" any recognition of the trouble in Hong Kong that did not stress violations of human rights and did not include warnings against overt changes to the status of Hong Kong.[342] Failure to include both might be read as an unacceptable retreat from the broad principles of global human rights they have worked hard to embed--though it should be noted that this embedding appears to apply differently in a number of contexts.

In this context, then, it is clear that China likely would expect an expression of support for its restraint, a warning against foreign interference in its internal political order, and an acknowledgement of its right to act to protect what it views as the integrity of its system. Likewise, in that context it is clear that other state and non-state actors (mostly from the Western camp) would expect an expression of support for the protestors, of disapproval of the overreaction of police personnel and others, and an acknowledgement of the right of individuals to act to preserve the integrity of the global human rights system and its principles.

Given these constraints, it appears that the OHCHR has tried to give all parties what they desire—a statement, in the form of a "press briefing," that folds in on itself and sums to zero.[343] The trigger was the escalation of protests that targeted Hong Kong's international lifeline—the airport. [344] It was well done and

---

it also inside Europe. And for the Catalan issue, they have to work for a peaceful and democratic solution, which puts an end to repression against the pro-independence ideology," says Serret.").

[342] This turned out to be verified immediately after the OHCHR Statement was released, see, "Joint Statement by Canada and European Union on situation in Hong Kong,"supra.

[343] "Press briefing note on Hong Kong, China," United Nations (13 August 2019); available [https://www.ohchr.org/EN/NewsEvents/Pages/DisplayNews.aspx?NewsID= 24888&LangID=E] (Hereafter "Press Briefing").

[344] "'Act with restraint' UN human rights chief urges Hong Kong authorities and protestors, following airport disruption," UN News (13 August 2019); available [https://news.un.org/en/story/2019/08/1044141] (""After two consecutive

Hong Kong Between "One Country" and "Two Systems"
10. Press Briefing Note from the UN High Commissioner for Human Rights

170

elegantly expressed, but will it be read in the spirit in which it was delivered? Note the key words inserted at just the right time in support of both positions. It is easy, though to read into the words an unbalanced support for either side—depending on how the reader chooses to interpret the carefully worded text. It is now for the parties to sort through the contradictions, recast the statement in the best light possible for the furtherance of their respective goals, and perhaps respond in some way to the OHCHR itself in some to be determined way.

It is worth taking a moment, and only a moment, to sink into the semiotic ouroboros that is the High Commissioner's Press Briefing. The High Commissioner *first expresses concern.* The concern pulls in opposite directions, first toward "ongoing events" and then more specifically to "the escalation of violence that has taken place in recent days."[345] That, itself, was an odd imbalance of identification. "Ongoing events" can allude to actions and positions on both sides of the dispute within Hong Kong. But the reference to the violence might be taken as more pointedly directed toward the protestors, especially given the timing of the release of the Press Briefing.[346]

The High Commissioner *then condemns.* She condemns violence and the destruction of property—an important element of the position of Chinese central authorities. She notes the possibility of expressing views peacefully and is assured that the protesters will be heard—though hearing and influencing may be too quite distinct things in the absence of a calculation of power to inflict consequences.[347] To avoid that result—the role of peaceful expression as farce or theater, she "calls on the

---

days of chaos at Hong Kong International Airport, the UN High Commissioner for Human Rights (OHCHR) Michelle Bachelet expressed her concern and condemned "any form" of violence or destruction of property and urged the demonstrators to "express their views in a peaceful way").

[345] Press Briefing, supra.

[346] See quotation at n. 10, supra.

[347] Press Briefing, supra ("condemns any form of violence or destruction of property and urges everyone participating in the demonstrations to express their views in a peaceful way. She notes the Chief Executive's commitment to "engage as widely as possible" and to "listen to the grievances of the people of Hong Kong."").

authorities and the people of Hong Kong to engage in an open and inclusive dialogue aimed at resolving all issues peacefully."[348] And the carrot offered the Chinese central authorities—the greater probability of securing stability, and then prosperity for Hong Kong.[349]

The High Commissioner then nods in the direction of her European and liberal democratic stakeholders. This she does in the time-honored way by invoking the central rhetorical tenets of civil and political rights. But she does more than that, probably to the irritation of the Chinese camp: she ties that rhetoric of civil and political rights to the preservation of Hong Kong as the product of and subject to international agreement, and thus, as a space for the application of international law.[350]

Only then does the High Commissioner turn to the issue of police response to protester violence. But she was careful; where the protestor violence was treated as a conclusory matter worth less than a sentence, the matter of police violence was handled far more carefully, reviewing "credible evidence of law enforcement officials employing less-lethal weapons in ways that are prohibited by international norms and standards."[351] This was at least a little clever. It was both deferential to the Chinese side, and respectful, while at the same time underlining that it was not Chinese law but international norms and standards that applied to the judgment of police behavior in Hong Kong.

Yet imbalance returns. While the High Commissioner *condemns* protestor violence, she can only muster the will to *"urge* the Hong Kong SAR authorities to investigate these incidents

---

[348] Ibid.

[349] Ibid. ("This is the only sure way to achieve long-term political stability and public security by creating channels for people to participate in public affairs and decisions affecting their lives.").

[350] Press Briefing , supra ("The rights of freedom of expression and peaceful assembly and the right to participate in public affairs are expressly recognized in the Universal Declaration of Human Rights, as well as the International Covenant on Civil and Political Rights which is incorporated in the Basic Law of the Hong Kong SAR.").

[351] Press Briefing, supra.

Hong Kong Between "One Country" and "Two Systems"
10. Press Briefing Note from the UN High Commissioner for Human Rights

172

immediately" for conformity to international standards. [352] Likewise, she can only muster the will to urge official response to be undertaken with restraint and that violence be met only by proportionate counter-violence.[353]

And with the High Commissioner has done her duty to the international community. She has satisfied the desires of both sides, while at the same time assuring both that there is a substantially argue enough ambiguous space for to act to further their interests. To the internationalist liberal democratic West she gave an assurance of the central role of international standards for civil and political rights, and their direct applicability to Hong Kong. To Chinese officials she gave an unequivocal condemnation of non-state violence and the assurance that the state would have a freer hand were it to follow fair procedures and where the state could restrict itself to proportionate counter-violence, including, one imagines, detentions and criminal proceedings.

Chinese officials would have to pay a price—international oversight and the weakening of its stance of "non-interference" in its internal affairs. That may be too big and too bitter a pill to swallow. The sting of late Qing era imperial humiliations remains fresh in the discursive universe of Chinese political theory. The wounds are too fresh--at least as a discursive trope. Yet it represents the way, as well, in which something that is now normalized within the liberal democratic west—the interconnections between the domestic and international orders creating a permeable space for law and norms, is understood as

---

[352] Ibid. (", to ensure security personnel comply with the rules of engagement, and where necessary, amend the rules of engagement for law enforcement officials in response to protests where these may not conform with international standards.")

[353] Press Briefing, supra ("urges the Hong Kong SAR authorities to act with restraint, to ensure that the right of those who are expressing their views peacefully are respected and protected, while ensuring that the response by law enforcement officials to any violence that may take place is proportionate and in conformity with international standards on the use of force, including the principles of necessity and proportionality").

sovereignty threatening, indeed as incompatible with Leninist notions of sovereignty, in China.

This, then, should satisfy everyone, and no one.

✳ ✳ ✳

Hong Kong Between "One Country" and "Two Systems"
10. Press Briefing Note from the UN High Commissioner for Human Rights

174

Chapter 11

Friday 16 August 2019
Surya Deva on the International Human Rights Implications of the Situation in Hong Kong

The situation in Hong Kong continues to draw scant attention in the West. The continuing political agitation, however, has provided a very rich testing ground for many of the core principles of the Chinese and Western political models, especially in those small but important spaces where they intermingle. One of the more neglected areas in that context is the human rights effects of the dynamic situation in Hong Kong. There is good reason for that indifference. First, the application of a human rights lens is complicated by the substantial conceptual differences in the articulation of human rights within a Chinese Leninist framework, and the framework that has emerged under the guidance of the human rights apparatus in Geneva. Second, Hong Kong occupies a contingent space within that continuum of human rights--it is simultaneously deeply embedded within the Chinese Leninist system, and at the same time it remains an autonomous area whose contextually peculiar governance has been guaranteed pursuit to international treaty and in the constitutional organization of the People's Republic of China itself.

Yet, for those of us for whom these issues, at the nexus point of national and international organization, are understood to drive changes in conceptions of constitutional ordering in the coming decades, the human rights implications--whether under a Leninist or liberal democratic model--of the situation in Hong Kong serves as a bellwether for the way in which China and the rest of the world will come to order their relations. The implications, for example, for Belt and Road Initiative relations are worth considering.

It is in this context that Professor Surya Deva (School of Law of City University of Hong Kong), who currently serves as a member of the United Nations Working Group on the issue of human rights and transnational corporations and other business enterprises (UN Working Group),[354] has considered the human rights effects of one of the less well noticed aspects of the current dynamic situation in Hong Kong—the responsibilities of business enterprises in the context of Internationally recognized human rights responsibilities. Those obligations, endorsed by a unanimous Human Rights Council in 2011, including China, in the form of the UN Guiding Principles for Business and Human Rights (the UNGPs) now create a complex interplay of domestic law and international norms--mediated through the conduct of business enterprises straddling both, which to some extent may undercut the emerging position of the central authorities in distinguishing between its own sovereign authority and the interference of foreigners.

The UNGP distinguish between a *state duty to protect human rights*, and a corporate responsibility to respect human rights[355] The core duty of states with respect to human rights are embedded in their domestic constitutional orders and in their obligation to implement their international obligations--at least to the extent they bind. Around this core is a set of peripheries that are meant to eventually normalize the view out of the great human rights administrative centers, and deeply held along certain sectors of the global vanguard, that the state duty must be

---

[354] The UN Working Group was established by the Human Rights Council in 2011 by resolution 17/4. Among its principal functions is the promotion and dissemination of the *UN Guiding Principles for Business and Human Rights* (New York and Geneva: UN Press, 2011) (the UNGPs); available [https://www.ohchr.org/documents/publications/guidingprinciplesbusinessh r_en.pdf], endorsed by the Human Rights Council in 2011. The UN Working Group is also charged with capacity building functions, the promotion of good practices in the implementation of the UNGPs, to make recommendations for enhancing access to remedies, and to develop a regular dialogue and cooperation with governments and other actors. See the UN Working Group website; available [https://www.ohchr.org/EN/Issues/Business/Pages/WGHRandtransnationalc orporationsandotherbusiness.aspx].

[355] UNGP, supra; ¶¶1-24. See Larry Catá Backer, "Moving Forward the UN Guiding Principles for Business and Human Rights: Between Enterprise Social Norm, State Domestic Legal Orders, and the Treaty Law That Might Bind Them All," Fordham International Law Journal 38(2):457-542 (2015); available [https://ir.lawnet.fordham.edu/cgi/viewcontent.cgi?article=2382&context=ilj].

informed by and conform to international norms. These norms include that host of declarations, statements, principles, and other like that are not legally binding on states but are now effectively compulsory as the expression of the global political community (or at least of majority of them). This remains highly contested-- no more so than by the U.S. and the Chinese state organs.

Unlike the state duty to protect human rights, the *corporate responsibility to respect human rights* is centered both on systems of internal law and norms, and also on markets as drivers of behavior. Corporations are responsible to compliance with the International Bill of Human Rights as a baseline, plus of course the expectation that they will comply with applicable domestic law. Thus, unlike the state duty to protect human rights, which can vary dramatically from state to state, the corporate responsibility to protect is subject to the same core rules where ever they operate. They are market driven in the sense that markets are meant to provide the space within which enterprises are rewarded or punished for compliance. It is a system grounded in the quasi-legalization of business risk, which is not meant to vary across state boundaries, above and beyond localized legal risk which can vary along a production chain. Additionally, and again unlike the conception of the state duty to protect human rights, the corporate responsibility to respect is essentially compliance oriented, and grounded in the principle of prevent-mitigate-and remedy.

The differences between the state duty to protect and the corporate responsibility to respect human rights have important consequences. Differences between the emphasis and acceptability of international law or in the expectations built into different constitutional orders may result in different aggregations of rights available in different spaces along a global production chain. More importantly, it is possible that the international norm basis for the corporate responsibility to respect human rights may conflict with the extent and expression of rights within a domestic legal order. For example, while enterprises have responsibility for respecting both internal human rights covenants everywhere they operate, that may be difficult in jurisdictions that might be hostile to or marginalize or impose an interpretation to such rights which are inconsistent with global expectations. This becomes apparent, for example with respect to economic, social, and cultural rights in the United States, and civil and political rights in China.

The tensions inherent in these distinctive obligations are not merely abstract. The consequences of the Hong Kong protests for enterprises have now made this a live issue. The issue of the human rights responsibilities of enterprises, and the underlying state duty to protect human rights (that rests most acutely in this case on Hong Kong local and the Chinese central authorities) has been acutely felt as businesses find themselves torn between pressure from the protestors, the sympathies of their own employees and staff, and the desire for appropriate reaction by government authorities.

This has recently blown up in the context of the airport protests at Hong Kong, and the employees of Cathay Pacific Airlines. In mid-August 2019 Cathay Pacific terminated the employment of two ground staff over information leaks related to the protests and suspended a pilot following sanctions imposed by China's Civil Aviation Administration.[356] It was reported that

> The airline was caught in the political storm when one of its pilots was charged over a protest. Its chairman initially said that "we certainly wouldn't dream of telling [our staff] what they have to think about something". But China's aviation authority told the airline it would have to remove any staff involved in or supportive of protests from flights over its airspace. A state-owned bank rated

---

[356] Danny Lee, "Cathay Pacific sacks two ground staff over passenger information leak and says pilot charged over Hong Kong protests has been removed from flying duties ," *South China Morning Post* (10 August 2019); available [https://www.scmp.com/news/hong-kong/transport/article/3022263/cathay-pacific-tells-employees-expect-increased-security].

Cathay stock a strong sell and Chinese firms withdrew business.[357]

Those actions, in turn, produced additional protests by Hong Kong people, including many from the aviation sector, as businesses in Hong Kong are pressured by central government and Hong Kong authorities.[358]

Cathay Pacific was put precisely in the position of being torn between the exercise by the state of its duty to protect human rights (as they saw it) against the universal responsibility to respect the civil and political rights of their employees according to international standards. This echoes, in the context of business, the great chasm now opening between a statist national position being developed by the Chinese centra authorities that understands the "Two Systems" principle as inherent in and proceeds from the "One Country" paramount principle, against the position of international elites for whom the "One Country" principle as a residual element of the paramount "Two Systems" principles overseen by the international community which guarantees the eternal validity of one country.

In this case the contradictions directly touch on the development of the business and human rights framework which the Chinese centra authorities have already endorsed. Clearly, though, in this case they appear to have chosen, to put the best possible face on the actions, to interpret these two regimes of legalities[359] in their own way, and thus harmonize them to the "One Country" principle. On the one hand, the corporate responsibility to respect human rights of Cathay Pacific extended

---

[357] Tania Branigan and Erin Hale, "Cathay denounced for firing Hong Kong staff after pressure from China," *The Guardian* (updated 298 August 2019); available [https://www.theguardian.com/world/2019/aug/28/cathay-pacific-denounced-for-firing-hong-kong-staff-on-china-orders].

[358] Ibid. ("a retiree who gave her name as Miss Chan [said]. "They want to [persuade] the public that if you go on a demonstration you may be punished; even if you are not arrested, you might lose employment opportunities.").

[359] Generally on legalities in this context, see, Larry Catá Backer, And an Algorithm to Entangle them All? Social Credit, Data Driven Governance, and Legal Entanglement in Post-Law Legal Orders (October 2020); available SSRN [].

to the exercise of its employees civil and political rights. On the other hand, the state duty to protect human rights could view such exercises of civil and political rights as a threat to the human rights of stability and prosperity, and thus to undermine the hierarchy of rights which their political order mandates.

It is to these questions, to the way they ought to be resolved form the perspective of the vanguard elements of international human rights, that Professor Surya Deva recently examined the issue of the human rights consequences of business action, in the context of the responsibilities of Hong Kong's Cathay Pacific Airlines. Professor Deva teaches at the City University of Hong Kong Law Faculty, but has for several years also served as a member of the UN Working Group for Business and Human Rights, among the charges of which are the UNGP. His thoughts were widely circulated after publication in the *South China Morning Post*.[360] And are worth considering. They suggest that while much attention has been focused on the sovereignty centered controversies at the heart of the protests that erupted in their current form in early June, there are other, potentially equally important, frameworks of international law, public and private, that may also complicate the situation for all of the parties. In this case, the emerging and powerful frameworks within which states and other actors have acquired duties and responsibilities with respect to the human rights effects of their economic activities

Professor Deva first poses the contradiction and then offers a way forward--but a way that would invariably burden the enterprise to suit the needs of national and international governance actors. His conclusion--the airline must find a way to honor both the legitimate demands of the Chinese central authorities and its own international responsibilities. The alternatives are, quite frankly, largely unpalatable--for Cathay Pacific. That is the baseline from which Professor Deva proceeds through his examination. The baseline is augmented by the core

---

[360] Surya Deva, "China business or human rights? Hong Kong protests leave Cathay facing a tough balancing act," South China Morning Post (17 August 2019); available [https://www.scmp.com/comment/opinion/article/3022783/china-business-or-human-rights-hong-kong-protests-leave-cathay].

principle for aligning state duty and corporate responsibility: "The responsibility under the guiding principles is over and above any responsibility that companies may have under domestic laws. The UN Human Rights Council is also currently negotiating a treaty to add "legal teeth" to this responsibility."[361]

Deva notes that the web of international responsibilities within which Cathay Pacific's behaviors are bound are not limited to direct responsibility under the UNGP. The Organization for Economic Cooperation and Development (OECD) Guidelines for Multinational Enterprises (the "OECD Guidelines")[362] also applies because a key shareholder, Swire, a company incorporated in the UK, is a shareholder of Cathay Pacific. To act in conformity with these guidelines, Swire should "avoid causing or contributing to adverse human rights impacts and address such impacts when they occur". Moreover, breaches of the obligations in the OECD Guidelines could give rise to a specific instance action before a National Contact Point. Though these proceedings are neither binding nor legal in nature, they have had powerful effect.[363] In addition, Cathay Pacific's own private law might create a source either of legal or business risk. "Moreover, Cathay Pacific has a code of conduct which provides, among other aspects, that any "form of harassment or discrimination on the basis of ... political opinion will not be tolerated."[364] Notice here how the web of business and legal risk facing Cathay Pacific is far broader than mere duty to obey local law. And, indeed, notice that compliance with law or policy of a regulator of a part of its operational territory may indeed create contradictions in its responsibilities.

Those contradictions emerge with great force at the fault lines between governance systems whose basic goals and

361 Ibid.

362 OECD, Guidelines for Multinational Enterprises (Paris, OECD, 2011); available [http://mneguidelines.oecd.org/guidelines/].

363 See, Larry Catá Backer, Case Note: "Rights And Accountability In Development (Raid) V Das Air (21 July 2008) And Global Witness V Afrimex (28 August 2008); Small Steps Toward an Autonomous Transnational Legal System for the Regulation of Multinational Corporations," *Melbourne Journal of International Law* 10(1):258-307 (2009).

364 Surya Deva, "China business or human rights?," supra.

operationalization may in specific instances require irreconcilable responses. Those contradictions become manifested as quasi legal compliance issues for enterprises when such enterprises become entangled within the web of international norms and of private law, some of which attached to quasi-legal complaint like proceedings that may be brought against either the enterprise itself or its shareholders, especially those with controlling interests. [365] And here, then, is the conundrum of Hong Kong now reproduced in the context of the business activities of its enterprises. [366] This appears to be an analogue to the political issues One Country-Two Systems but now devolved from the political to the economic sphere.

It is in that context Professor Deva then assesses Cathay's discharge of its human rights responsibilities with international standards." [367] In Professor Deva's estimation Cathay Pacific comes up short. In the face of national reaction (and displeasure) with the conduct of its employees, Professor Deva notes, Cathay Pacific has done what it can to minimize its exposure to business and legal risk from China, but at a significant cost to its ability to meet its responsibilities under international standards.

> So far, Cathay has (i) sacked two of its airport employees for leaking information, (ii) terminated the employment of two pilots for their involvement in, or support for, protests, (iii) instructed that Cathay property should not be used to post non-work content or to make unauthorised public announcements, and (iv) advised its employees not to "express any radical opinions in social and open media" or "support or participate in illegal

---

[365] Guidelines for Multinational Enterprises (Paris: OECD, 2011); see also Larry Catá Backer, "Rights and Accountability in Development ("RAID") v DAS Air and Global Witness v Afrimex," supra.

[366] This is an issue long in the making the eruption of which has been avoided for the most part in significant form until now. See, Sonya Sceats and Shaun Breslin, "China and the International Human Rights System" (London: Chatham House, October 2012); available [http://dspace.jgu.edu.in:8080/jspui/bitstream/10739/173/1/NPHR8%20China%20%26%20Int%20HR.pdf].

[367] Surya Deva, "China business or human rights?," supra.

protests", or otherwise face disciplinary action, including termination of employment.[368]

What Cathay Pacific and its shareholder Swire can offer up, notes Professor Deva, are statements, which underline the alignment of the enterprise with the desires of state officials in connection with the protests.

> "We resolutely support the Hong Kong SAR government, the chief executive and the police in their efforts to restore law and order. We condemn all illegal activities and violent behaviour, which seriously undermine the fundamental principle of one country, two systems as enshrined in the Basic Law."[369]

And then Professor Deva judges compliance. With respect to information leaks, the company was justified in its actions and there were no human rights violations of worker rights. In effect, in such circumstances of political action, the worker bears the risk because they violate the law that is otherwise applied without collateral human rights consequences. As Professor Deva put it, is "as long as due process was followed and the disciplinary action was proportional to the alleged wrong conduct."[370]

Proportionality, process and context can work in the opposite direction. And, indeed, that they are factors significantly weakens an argument that human rights are always satisfied if workers are terminated "in accordance with law." Consider whether the judgment would be different had the leaked information gone to prevent human rights violations or to expose the complicity of the employer in huma rights violations. There, too, the answer might be the same. The employees might have

---

368 Ibid.; citing Danny Lee, "Cathay Pacific Sacks Two Ground Staff," supra; Danny Laee, Kinling Lo, and Louise Moon, "Cathay Pacific Threatens Staff With Sack After Beijing Draws Line on Hong Kong Protests," *South China Morning Post* (12 August 2019); available [https://www.scmp.com/news/china/politics/article/3022396/cathay-pacific-threatens-staff-sack-shares-plummet-after].

369 Surya Deva, "China business or human rights?," supra.

370 Ibid.

reported that to authorities--but to leak to on state actors remains problematic. And yet one expects that there is a line where even leaks, given the content of their information may serve human rights enhancing purposes that overcome the company's justification for termination because of the breach of law and enterprise rule. That, however, remains a hypothetical question in this specifically narrowly contextual instance. And yet the shadow of that hypothetical looms large here. And it might at some point prove useful to the protestors and their allies. Maybe. But the approach is one that challenges the dominant position of the central authorities with respect to these instances.

The application of international human rights standards to the matter of the pilots, however, may lead to a different result according to Professor Deva. But the grounds are narrow. First, the action is related to the exercise of civil and political rights. However, the dismissal was based on grounds of exceeding the protection of civil and political rights--that is on engagement in violent protesting--for rioting. Professor Deva notes that dismissal on those grounds might be justified except that in this case the pilots had not yet been convicted in a fair judicial proceeding and therefore the enterprise action was at best premature. Yet he also implies that even conviction in accordance with law may not be sufficient grounds for termination where, as here, the conviction was elated to the exercise of civil and political rights; that is "even if convicted, this should not be equated with a typical crime."[371]

The implication is clear enough--but also quite challenging for Cathay Pacific. Application of law that have human rights suppressing effects might not be blindly relied on to justify action against a worker--even if the state insists by putting economic pressure on the enterprise. The problem becomes more difficult were Cathay Pacific to be a state-owned enterprise and thus ordered by state officials to terminate employees after conviction on the basis of laws applied in a way that undermined civil and political rights (interpreted in accordance with international, NOT national, standards).

---

[371] Ibid.

Cathay Pacific is deeply embedded within webs of obligation to but not formally by the state. Still, one begins to see here that, from an international point of view, again, mere compliance with law is no protection or means of satisfying the international responsibility of enterprises to respect human rights. Indeed, the state duty to protect human rights under the UNGP might also include the duty to avoid using law or policy--or administrative determinations, in a way that harm human rights--from the perspective of international standards. Many states, China included reject this perspective, even as others embrace it. It does suggest, however, that enterprises like Cathay Pacific, especially in heavily regulated economic spheres, like transport, may implicate both state duty and corporate responsibility in ways that make both state and enterprise complicit in the violation of the duty or responsibility of the other. In this case, that difference, between state duty and enterprise responsibility, then poses a challenge to the emerging sovereignty-based position of the Chinese central authorities.

Professor Deva speaks to the corporate responsibility of Cathay Pacific in these circumstances but remains noticeably silent on the implications for the state duty to protect human rights--where the extent of that duty judged by international standards is incompatible with those under national standards. So focused, the analysis locates proportionality at its center.[372]

> The conduct of the other pilot hardly compromised passenger safety or harmed Cathay's reputation. The termination, which appears to have been done to please Beijing and discourage other staff from supporting protests, would run counter to Cathay's responsibility to respect the human rights of its employees.[373]

---

[372] This approach is deeply embedded in the UNGPs. UNGP ¶14 notes that the extent of the responsibility to respect may vary according to the scale and complexity of the means for meeting that responsibility "and with the severity of the enterprise's human rights impacts."

[373] Surya Deva, "China business or human rights?," supra.

Cathay Pacific, though, could have remained neutral. As it sought to do, or to distinguish its official position from that of its employees acting outside the scope of their employment. But the latter position is increasingly difficult--even at the heart of the West, where political positions evidenced on social media can lead to the loss of a job in ways that look unproblematic to those who find the exercise of political rights directed to specific objectives unpalatable or offensive.[374] And, indeed, Professor Deva offers the standard toolkit for enterprise neutrality as a fair basis for managing the "time, place, and manner" of the exercise of political and civil rights that do not make the enterprise complicit; directly complicit anyway. These include banning a variety of forms of politicking on company property.

Where the enterprise chooses not to be neutral--as when it injects itself into a political controversy, then the proportional balancing becomes more difficult. He offers the example of the condemnation of violence that threatens the Hong Kong Basic Law then they must apply that condemnation evenhandedly. That means that they can condemn protestor violence only against the violence also documented in the reaction or methods of the police and local officials for protecting state-based violence under cover of reaction or the protection of local law. by the Hong Kong protestors as an illustration. [375] And, indeed, Professor Deva suggests, Cathay Pacific ought to contribute to the fulfillment of its corporate responsibilities to respect human rights by making its facilities available to its employees to promote international human rights values--even against the state.

For Professor Deva, the last of Cathay Pacific's actions may raise the most profound problems. It is not uncommon for

---

[374] Julius Young, "Former Miss Michigan Kathy Zhu stripped of 2019 title says 'toxic' cancel culture to blame for ousting," *Fox News* (22 July 2019); available [https://www.foxnews.com/entertainment/former-miss-michigan-kathy-zhu-stripped-of-2019-title-says-toxic-cancel-culture-to-blame-for-ousting].

[375] Surya Deva, "China business or human rights?," supra. ("they should also condemn the Hong Kong SAR government, the chief executive and the police who are the root causes of these protests and have forgotten the "two systems" limb of the "one country, two systems" principle.").

enterprises to try to limit the expression of their employees. To some extent this derives from more ancient cultural assumptions that eliminated the autonomous agency of people who sell their labor to others. In those circumstances, it has not been uncommon to assume, without much thought, that these individuals "represent" their master and that their actions and activities whether or not work related must be understood as connected with or tied to their master. Though this suggests a remnant of the indica of servitude that one would have thought disappeared with the formal institutions of slavery, they have not. Indeed, the presumption that employees--as individuals--merge with their employer-aster remains deeply rooted in most societies, whatever they may officially say to the contrary. These are the premises that even the most advanced advocates of international human rights standards find hard to shake.

It is no surprise, then that Professor Deva here balances and is at his most pragmatic.[376] And rightly so of course given the cultural tastes of those who rule in all spheres of human activity. He acknowledges that implementation of the decision to forbid political speech outside of the work context poses problems--but those problems of focused on the human rights implications of the *methods used* to enforce the policy. "In effect, this could leave Cathay open to charges of being an agent of the Chinese government, rather than operating within the parameters of the Basic Law and the UNGPs."[377]

What options, then, for Cathay Pacific. Professor Surya suggests a balancing, the legitimacy and effects of which can only be known post hoc: Cathay's challenges can be "overcome only if

---

[376] He notes but doesn't judge the implications of the policy: a quite robust monitoring of employees and the development of a system of vales based judgments of the character of the activities monitored. Worse, he also acknowledges that the system would be anchored by and measured against the standards of local and national officials. Ibid.; citing Sum Lok-kei and Su Xinqi, "Some Hongkongers have phones checked for protest photos at mainland China border amid anti-government unrest," *South China Morning Post* (15 August 2019); available [https://www.scmp.com/news/hong-kong/politics/article/3022828/chinese-immigration-officials-inspect-hongkongers-phones].

[377] Surya Deva, "China business or human rights?," supra.

it explores ways to honour both the legitimate demands of Chinese authorities and its human rights responsibilities. "[378] That balancing in turn requires consultation--not just with local and national officials, but with all stakeholders. Professor Deva suggests that the choice is between profits and human rights. He notes that actions threatening its access to Chinese markets may not be viable, but he also suggests that forsaking the application of international human rights standards for those markets may also be untenable.[379]

Professor Deva admits the difficulty this task for the enterprise. Were Cathay to misbalance this juggling between legal compliance, business pressure, and legal effects, the consequences for the company will surely produce both legal and business risk. On the domestic level and from the Chinese side that misbalancing will be calculated by official assessment of company failure to center adherence to law as the core factor in any balancing. Cathay's flights might be cancelled and the company fined. On the international level and from the side of internal stakeholders that misbalancing follow from the failure to center international standards for the application of human rights laws and norms. That failure will also produce substantial business risk, and to some extent (especially in the context of human rights due diligence regimes) some possibility of compliance risk outside of China. Even though both misbalancing produce business risk, the immediate consequences of direct legal risk to Cathay Pacific at the moment is far greater from the Chinese side than from the international or internal side. On the other side, it is the potential for financial risk that might loom larger.

That calculation, more than any other, is likely to drive decision making at Cathay Pacific. Yet the UNGPs offer some means of approaching the contradiction that harmonizes to some extent the realities that enterprises face. Principle 24 acknowledges that all adverse human rights impacts may not be capable of simultaneous resolution. "In the absence of specific legal guidance, if prioritization is necessary business enterprises

---

[378] Ibid.
[379] Ibid. ("Cathay should not take lightly the "private power" of human rights").

should begin with those human rights impacts that would be most severe, recognizing that a delayed response may affect remendability."[380] One is thrown back then to tort--and to the core premise that enterprises may compensate for breaches where they cannot prevent or mitigate them. Tort creates a distinct set of problems--these center on the valuation of the harm, but there is much experience with respect to that in legislatures and courts.

Cathay Pacific may well have to bend to the legalities of Chinese requirements, but it may also have to be willing to compensate those whose human rights have been affected as a consequence. That, certainly, may be the position that Cathay Pacific will take to the outside world. For those who center human rights and prevention strategies, this will likely be troubling. Complicating this calculus is the growing expectation, especially among elements of the internationalist business and human rights community, that it is for business enterprises to serve as a vanguard force to confront and change the political and human rights approaches in China. As one influential commentator explained:

> I continue to believe that Western business is helping to unleash powerful forces of change in China. But when we look at the behavior of Western forms, it is clear that they are not doing their 'fair share' and there is much more they ca and should do. Foreign companies have settled into a complacent partnership with the Chinese government. This is not morally acceptable. Nor is it in the long term best interest of business.[381]

That may prove to be especially provocative in the contemporary context off Hong Kong. It will certainly feed the Black Hand (黑手) foreigner intervention discursive tropes that the central authorities are now cultivating.[382] That does not mean that the

---

380 UNGP ¶ 24 Commentary.
381 Michael A. Santoro, *China 2020: How Western Business Can--and Should-- Influence Social and Political Change in the Coming Decade* (Ithaca: Cornell University Press, 2015), p. x.
382 Discussed in essays Chapters 7-8, supra.

project of harmonization of business and human rights duties (of states) and responsibilities (of corporations)ought not to be harmonized across global production chains. It does mean, however, that the politics of this process appears now to have gotten a bit more complicated, and the costs and risks of accommodation, resistance and complicity have grown much larger.

$$* \quad * \quad *$$

Chapter 12

Monday 19 August 2019
Resist-Reconcile (忤合 Wuhe):"Opinions of the CPC Central Committee and the State Council on Supporting Shenzhen's Pioneering Demonstration Zone with Chinese Characteristics" [中共中央国务院关于支持深圳建设中国特色社会主义先行示范区的意见 （二〇一九年八月九日）]

> Compliance and cooperation, resistance and opposition call for suitable strategies of adjustment and reconciliation. Evolutions and conjunctures, cycles and junctures have their own forms and tendencies. Reverses and turnarounds respond to one another and regulate themselves.[383]

The connection between apparently autonomous but likely inter-connected threads of action by Chinese officials around the situation in Hong Kong has long been in the making. Yet it is only after the start of the protests of 9 June 2019, and thereafter of its intensifying passions, that that some of these threads have become more clearly visible, and their interconnections harder to resist. At the same time, the situation in Hong Kong also reveals what appears to be the strong connection, again, between the actions of officials and the ancient patterns of strategic impulses nicely examined in Guiguzi.

Earlier chapters have considered the value of Guiguzi in interpreting the strategic choices of officials around the issue of Hong Kong. [384]   A recent Opinion of the Chinese Central

---

[383] Guiguzi (鬼谷子), *Guiguzi: China's First Treatise on Rhetoric; A Critical Translation and Commentary* (Hui Wu (trans.); Carbondale: Southern Illinois University Press, 2016 (before 220 A.D.)); Book II.6.1, pp. 59-60.

[384] See, e.g., essays Chapters 3 (Mend-Break (Di Xi 抵巇)), 8 (Assessing (Quan 權)),

Committee [385] reveals, however, that these strategic choices appear t long predate the 2019 protests and even the 2014 Umbrella Movement, but that they might well have been set in motion around the time of the reversion of Hong Kong itself to China. What this chapter suggests is the importance of the rhetorical strategies of Resist-Reconcile (忤合 Wuhe) [386] in the long arc of central authority strategies for the re-incorporation of Hong Kong into the heart of the nation. Resist-Reconcile (忤合 Wuhe) strategies are most apparent generally in Deng Xiaoping's Reform and Opening Up strategies, and much more specifically illustrated in the ceding of autonomy for Hong Kong even as the central authorities began planning for the enveloping of that autonomy within a much greater integrated regional metropolis--one with Shenzhen at the center. One reconciled Hong Kong's autonomy even as one resists its pull out of the Chinese orbit, and one waits. Hardly noticed because of its pace, the protests in Hong Kong now appear to have made the movement more transparent and perhaps accelerated its progress.

---

[385] "Opinions of the CPC Central Committee and the State Council on Supporting Shenzhen's Pioneering Demonstration Zone with Chinese Characteristics (15 August 2019)" [中共中央国务院关于支持深圳建设中国特色社会主义先行示范区 的 意 见 （ 二 〇 一 九 年 八 月 九 日 ）]; available [http://politics.people.com.cn/n1/2019/0819/c1001-31301962.html] (hereafter Central Committee Opinion on Shenzhen"). A crude English language translation appears in Larry Catá Backer, The Situation in Hong Kong: "Opinions of the CPC Central Committee and the State Council on Supporting Shenzhen's Pioneering Demonstration Zone with Chinese Characteristics" [中共中央国务院关于支持深圳建设中国特色社会主义先行示范区的意见 （二〇一九年八月九日 ）]," Law at the End of the Day (19 August 2019); available [https://lcbackerblog.blogspot.com/2019/08/the-situation-in-hong-kong-opinions-of.html].

[386] *Guiguzi: China's First Treatise on Rhetoric, supra;* Book II.6.1-II.6.3, pp. 59-63 (Resist-Reconcile (忤合 Wuhe)). Cf., Joachim Gentz, "Rhetoric as the Art of Listening: Concepts of Persuasion in the First Eleven Chapters of the Guiguzi," *Asiatische Studien / Études Asiatiques* 68: 1001-1019 (2014). Guiguzi also serves as a useful framing of strategic and rhetorical choices in other important respects considered in the essays, supra, at Chapter 3 (Mend-Break (Di Xi 抵巇)), and Chapters 8 (Assessing (Quan 權)), and infra at Chapter 20 (Open-Shut (Bai He 稗閤)), and Chapter 30 (Fundamental Principles (Fu Yan符言)).

This strategy, to some extent, is also at the heart of One Country-Two Systems: to resist one must reconcile, to reconcile one must resist. Those are the positions across which the great stakeholders in the current developing relationship between protesting factions and the central authorities understand and react to each other. Both increasingly see their relationship as one that requires both resistance and a reconciliation, but each in accordance with the fundamental perspectives each wishes to dominate the way that their realities are understood and operationalized.

However, in this context, grounded in the generation long process of the enveloping of Hong Kong within China through the slow application of the Resist-Reconcile strategy embedded within the One Country-Two Systems principle that encounters the value of its ming-ming (明名 intelligent naming) form.[387] One Country-Two Systems rationalizes the oppositions of Hong Kong and the rest of the nation; it acknowledges resistance within Hong Kong even as it builds around it a pattern of reconciliation, from out of two systems, one country. That strategy is best realized on the ground--not through the deployment of rhetorical forms, but rather through the construction of One Country around two systems, enveloping and then digesting the two systems within one country. To these ends, Shenzhen, and the greater Pearl River Basin area is essential.[388]

Shenzhen, in its contemporary form, was born, in part, to demonstrate that a sound Socialist (that is a Chinese Marxist-Leninist) version of Hong Kong was not only possible, but

---

[387] Ibid., Book II.6.1. Here the text speaks to the strategy of intelligent naming that creates a space for reconciling and resisting. See ibid., at notes 25-26. One understands 名(naming) in its semiotic sense--to draw distinctions between objects (resist) and to align them (reconcile), or bian (辨) (arguments grounded in the drawing of distinctions) but in a way that rationalizes (明) the distinctions drawn .

[388] Cf. Chun Yang, "The Pearl River Delta and Hong Kong: an evolving cross-boundary region under 'one country, two systems'," *Habitat International* 30(1):61-86 (2006).

ultimately the better model for both cities.[389] Yet it was much more than that. Shenzhen was also designed to be the modern, built from the ground up, foundation, around which a "Pearl River" megacity could be built, into which the former UK and Portuguese colonies could be absorbed (in every sense of that term) along with their neighboring older cities (once known for their unruliness).[390]

That mega-city could serve as the incarnation of the China Dream (中国梦)[391] and suggest the ways in which the historically receding basis for social, political and economic organization (reflected in Hong Kong) could be recast and redirected for the new era.[392] That recasting, then, might also serve as a model which might find value all along the land and maritime Silk Roads of the Belt and Road Initiative.[393] Read at its broadest, the movement toward the consolidation of spaces through ties of economics, politics, culture, or any combination of these, might be transposable to those contexts where the consolidated spaces that are separated by (great) distances.

To some extent, the central authorities, under the leadership of the Communist Party of China (CPC), has been

---

[389] Cf. Juan Du, *The Shenzhen Experient: The Story of China's Instant City* (Cambridge: Harvard University Press, 2020); Weiwen Huang, "The Tripartite Origins of Shenzhen: Beijing, Hong Kong, and Bao'an," in Mary Ann O'Donnell, Winnie Wong, and Jonathan Bach, eds. *Learning From Shenzhen: China's Post-Mao Experiment From Special Zone to Model City* (Chicago: University of Chicago Press, 2017), pp. 65-85.

[390] Zhigang Li, Jiang Xu, Anthony G O Yeh, "State Rescaling and the Making of City-Regions in the Pearl River Delta, China," *Environment and Planning C: Politics and Space* 32(1):129-143 (2014).

[391] William A. Callahan, "The China Dream and the American Dream," *Economic and Political Studies* 2(1): 143-160; Shi, Yuzhi"中国梦区别于美国梦的七大特征" [Seven reasons why the Chinese Dream is different from the American Dream], *Qiushi* (20 May 2013).

[392] Jiangbo Bie, Martin de Jong, and Ben Derudder, "Greater Pearl River Deta: Historical Evolution Towards a Global City-Region," *Journal of Urban Technology* 22(2):103-123 (2015).

[393] Peter Ferdinand, "Westward Ho--The China Dream and 'One Belt, One Road': Chinese Foreign Policy Under Xi Jinping," *International Affairs* 92(4):941-957 (2016).

successful in achieving its first goal. Shenzhen is now an industrial powerhouse with a large and growing population sitting just beyond the old colonial border with Hong Kong. Yet the success has been molded as well by distributive realities--finance has been shifted to Shanghai in some respects--another variation of the absorption and transformation of a semi-colonial enclave in China, whose successful model, it might be hoped, could be projected outward.

But the ongoing situation in Hong Kong has, to some extent changed the character and pacing of these medium and longer term plans. The disturbances in Hong Kong have been treated by Chinese government and CPC authorities as directly challenging not so much their authority, but rather the authority of their guiding ideology. That is a challenge that cannot be ignored, even if Hong Kong is allowed to tolerate popular demonstrations over a longer term. Though much of those changes remain shrouded in secrecy, the State Council under the leadership of the CPC has, from time to time, suggested its content and direction.

In the response of officials, however, one can see the strategic rationalization embedded in the Resist-Reconcile (忤合 Wuhe) strategy. One develops reconciliation that carries with it the possibility of resistance, and one resists to reconcile. Hong Kong represents both the realities of reconciliation in the 1990s, built on a foundation that permits resistance to the form of initial reconciliation, provides the space for movement within it to resist, break and then forge new patterns of (now national) reconciliation.

Outwardly, the central authorities have sought to cauterize the ideological threat by recasting it as foreign. To that end the central authorities have expended much effort in their Black Hand campaign.[394] There the strategy applied was one of was Assessing (Quan 權). Beyond its utility in the ongoing trade negotiations with the United States and the protection of its Belt

---

[394] See essay Chapter 8, supra.

and Road Initiative (both understandable), recasting the Hong Kong narrative as foreign proves useful as discrediting it as contextually irrelevant, and its leaders as tools of a foreign power. This plays into now ancient and powerful Chinese discursive tropes about foreigners, unequal relationships, and threat.

Assessing (Quan 權) strategies, however, are a means, and not an ends in itself. It is not enough to recast the narrative in Hong Kong as foreign (and therefore not authentically Chinese) (resist 忤 Wu). It is also necessary to substantially strengthen and put forward the preferred (and native) alternative (reconcile 合 he). It is here that the Shenzhen model city ideal, and the historical imperative of the Pearl River mega-city, become important. Now the State Council and CCP Central Committee have put forward a counter-narrative that seeks to contrast the instability and decline of Hong Kong with the stability and progress of Shenzhen. To that end on 18 August 2019, via Xinhua News Agency, the authorities circulated "Opinions of the CPC Central Committee and the State Council on Supporting Shenzhen's Pioneering Demonstration Zone with Chinese Characteristics" [中共中央国务院关于支持深圳建设中国特色社会主义先行示范区的意见 （二〇一九年八月九日）] (the "Central Committee Opinion on Shenzhen).[395] It's strategic utility at this moment and in that place is unmistakable:

> At present, socialism with Chinese characteristics has entered a new era, supporting Shenzhen to hold high the banner of reform and opening up in the new era and building a demonstration zone for socialism with Chinese characteristics, which is conducive to promoting reform and opening up at a higher starting point, higher level, and higher goals, and forming a comprehensive deepening of Reform and comprehensively expand the new opening pattern; help to better implement the strategy of Guangdong, Hong Kong and Macao Dawan District, enrich the new practice of "one country, two systems"; help to take the lead in exploring the new path

---

[395] See Central Committee Opinion on Shenzhen, note 2, supra.

of building a socialist modernization and strengthening the country, and provide strong support for the realization of the great rejuvenation of the China Dream.[396]

The strategic intent could not be clearer. The protests in Hong Kong now assume an altogether different framing perspective, as does the importance of the prosperity and stability principle at the heart of the response of central and local authorities. If Hong Kong is slowly to sink into the larger metropolis which is the Pearl River Basin, and if it is to be, perhaps, a second order entity within that metropolis (following Shenzhen), then the protests both interfere with that slow process and present an opportunity to more expeditiously reconcile the autonomy of Hong Kong with the realities of its place within the metropolitan center of the southern region of China.

Any calculation of the future of Hong Kong ought to bear in mind this important declaration of policy. To that end, the document should be of special interest to those on either side of the political battles within Hong Kong. The Central Committee Opinion on Shenzhen includes an introduction and seven thematic sections. Each coils around the other to produce an intertwined web of reciprocal protocols, objectives, and iterations of relationship which, when summed, leave very little space for the sort of Hong Kong autonomy that foreigners and perhaps some of the protestors have in mind. A consideration of key points drives this home.

First, the opening section the Central Committee Opinion on Shenzhen makes clear that regional integration is also closely tied to its evolving interpretation of the One Country Two Systems principle. Both were the products of Deng Xiaoping's

---

[396] Ibid. ("当前，中国特色社会主义进入新时代，支持深圳高举新时代改革开放旗帜、建设中国特色社会主义先行示范区，有利于在更高起点、更高层次、更高目标上推进改革开放，形成全面深化改革、全面扩大开放新格局；有利于更好实施粤港澳大湾区战略，丰富"一国两制"事业发展新实践；有利于率先探索全面建设社会主义现代化强国新路径，为实现中华民族伟大复兴的中国梦提供有力支撑。").

strategy of Reform and Opening Up and each must be understood as deeply tied to the other. It also suggests the dynamic character of both regional integration (reconciliation) and the character of the autonomy at the heart of that effort through the One Country Two Systems principle (resistance). That dynamic character also suggests that the role of resistance and of reconciliation changes over time--that is it flips so that the resistance to full reconciliation in Two Systems in the 1990ss becomes the vehicle to reconciliation through One Country principles incarnated through the process of regional integration.

Second, the initial section on "overall requirements" of the Central Committee Opinion on Shenzhen emphasizes the emerging hierarchies of Chinese Marxist-Leninism in the New Era. These hierarchies are central to the document as a whole and color interpretations of all of its granular pronouncements. To ignore this is to misinterpret the document in the most fundamental way. This is a statement of fundamental reconciliation of the major actors that together will form an integrated Pearl River regional center. There is no space here for peculiarities in Hong Kong that contradict or interfere with this regional integration and coordination of economic planning, and the creation of a "model of socialist modernization and power."[397]

To that end, Shenzhen is to be understood as the vanguard model for the region. It is here that the central authorities will seek to create the model city, the model environment, the model workers and Communist Party cadres, the model culture, all contributing to prosperity and stability under the guidance of the vanguard leadership core of the state. That includes Hong Kong. Shenzhen will lead precisely because its growth will be cultivated for both a window into China and a window onto the world-- effectively displacing Hong Kong whose importance in that regard in the 1990s created the necessity for One Country Two Systems and permitted its (temporary) autonomy. By 2035, Shenzhen "should become a national model, and the city's comprehensive economic competitiveness should lead the world. . . . By the middle of this century, Shenzhen should become a global

---

[397] Ibid. ¶1.

benchmark city with competitiveness, innovation and influence."[398]

Third, the section of the Central Committee Opinion on Shenzhen on high quality development means to shift the leadership role of the region to Shenzhen. To that end, the intent appears to be to have Shenzhen serve as the driver of cooperation and integration of economic and technology related activity for the region.[399] It also , suggests the central role to be played by Shenzhen in the transformation of the prior era strategies for reform and opening up within a spatial and cultural context. To that end, Shenzhen is to be supported in becoming the regional center for both inbound and outbound relations.[400] The regional centering is directly expressed with Shenzhen slated for positioning as the hub of the new metropolitan region in which Macao, Hong Kong and Guangzhou will provide the spokes. In a sense, this applies the current pattern of economic, social and cultural institutional development--one that is built from out of a core (a leadership core, a national core, a regional core, etc.) and then expands outward through its key spokes. That is the pattern of the Belt and Road Initiative; it is the essence of New Era democratic centralism. It appears to be planned for Hong Kong as well. The shock, of course, for Hong Kong people, so used to thinking themselves as the core of the region, is the way that central authorities are already making clear that its position will change, and likely dramatically.[401]

Fourth, the discussion of democracy and rule of law in the Central Committee Opinion on Shenzhen, and especially its emphasis and on the shaping of modern urban civilization poses a greater challenge both for Hong Kong protestors and the character of the autonomy of Hong Kong.[402] Shenzhen is to be a

---

[398] Ibid., ¶3.
[399] Ibid., ¶¶4-5.
[400] Ibid., ¶ 6 (e.g., "Promote more international organizations and institutions to settle in Shenzhen. Support Shenzhen to hold international large-scale sports events and cultural exchange activities, build a national team training base, and undertake major home-based diplomatic activities")
[401] Ibid., ¶7.
[402] Ibid., ¶¶8-12

model of people's deliberate democracy--a key element of New Era political constitutionalism under the leadership of the Chinese Communist Party. [403] There are five key elements. The first, already mentioned, is the construction of Shenzhen as the ideal expression of Marxist Leninist governance under the principles of the New Era.[404] That ideal can then be used as a template for others and as the baseline against which other city governance (including that of Hong Kong) can be assessed. Second, Shenzhen is to serve as a model social credit system site.[405] The focus is on business and economic activity. [406] For Hong Kong business interests, this might well as serve as a warning of the development of another assessment baseline, especially for Hong Kong companies with substantial connections to the mainland. If Paragraph 8 targeted the development of an ideal model for public governance, and Paragraph 9 focused on the ideal structure for business conduct, then Paraph 10 focuses on the development of the ideal social environment for the forward progress of stability and prosperity.[407] And again, social credit is at the center of a system that incorporates Hong Kong.[408] Paragraphs 11 and 12 then emphasize the creation of model culture around and from out of Shenzhen as the core of such development.[409]

---

[403] Ibid., ¶8. Discussed in Larry Catá Backer and Miaoqiang Dai, "Socialist Constitutional Democracy in the Age of Accountability" (问责时代的社会主义宪制民主) (October 23, 2018). Available [https://ssrn.com/abstract=3271731].

[404] Central Committee Opinion on Shenzhen, supra, ¶8.

[405] Ibid., ¶9

[406] Ibid. ("implement credit supervision reform, and promote the law-abiding integrity management of various market entities").

[407] Ibid., ¶10.

[408] Ibid., ("Strengthen the construction of the social credit system and take the lead in building a unified social credit platform. Accelerate the construction of smart cities and support Shenzhen to build a large data center in Guangdong, Hong Kong and Macau."). For discussion, see, e.g., Larry Catá Backer, "Next Generation Law: Data Driven Governance and Accountability Based Regulatory Systems in the West, and Social Credit Regimes in China," *USC Interdisciplinary Law Journal* 28(1):123-172 (2018).

[409] Central Committee Opinion on Shenzhen, supra, ¶¶11-12. Thus for example ¶ 11 speaks to promoting "the innovation and development of public cultural services, and take the lead in building an inclusive, high-quality, sustainable urban public cultural service system." Paragraph 12 describes the need to center Shenzhen at the center of the development of a "digital cultural industry and

Fifth, the section of the Central Committee Opinion on Shenzhen on common prosperity also drives home the use of Shenzhen as a point of reconciling the approaches and life of the cities now forming a rim around Shenzhen.[410] In that context, the focus on reforming the education system[411] might pose a problem for the autonomous cultural basis of Hong Kong academic circles--especially for institutions and faculty that have taken their cue from their western counterparts in liberal democratic states. The implication, of course, is that the liberal democratic public intellectual[412] sitting comfortably protected within an academic institution may not survive the reconciliation of the Shenzhen with its regional spokes. And to some extent students will serve as the disciplinary assault forces. "We will enjoy "civil treatment" for the people and students living in Hong Kong and Macao who work and live in Shenzhen." [413] The development of "urban disaster prevention capabilities and strengthen emergency management cooperation in Guangdong, Hong Kong and Macau."[414] For Hong Kong people, this might seem like the way that one breaks resistance by programs of reconciliation, especially where the definition of disasters and emergencies might be determined by regional authorities.

Sixth, what may be viewed as implied in the first sixteen paragraphs of the Central Committee Opinion on Shenzhen is driven home by its concluding paragraphs. These focus on the strengthening of the Communist Party's leadership and Party building in the region. "We will implement the party's organizational line in the new era and encourage the SAR cadres

---

creative culture industry, and strengthen cooperation between Guangdong, Hong Kong and Macao digital creative industries."

[410] Central Committee Opinion on Shenzhen, supra, ¶¶13-14.

[411] Ibid., ¶13.

[412] For a sense of this cultural phenomenon in the liberal democratic west, see, e.g., Pierre Bourdieu, "The Corporatism of the Universal: The Role of the Intellectuals in the Modern World," Carolyn Betensky (trans) *Telos* 81:99-110 (1989).

[413] Central Committee Opinion on Shenzhen, supra, ¶14.

[414] Ibid., ¶16.

to take a new role in the new era."[415] It also points to a more vigorous role by national legislative and oversight organs in the governance of the regions with Shenzhen at its center.[416] And most importantly, the regionalization under the leadership "leadership of the Guangdong, Hong Kong, Macao and Dawan District Construction Leading Group"[417] is brought home at the conclusion of the Central Committee Opinion on Shenzhen. The pressure on autonomy for Hong Kong, for Hong Kong going its own way or moving towards a more international city model is quite direct. It is the regional group that serves as the leading group that will shape the extent of the autonomy afforded Hong Kong with the Shenzhen model at the center. Its object is to "strengthen guidance and coordination, and timely study and solve major problems encountered in the advancement of Shenzhen's pioneering socialist demonstration zone with Chinese characteristics."[418] The objects are unmistakable.

And thus the essence of Resist-Reconcile (忤合 Wuhe) applied to the situation in Hong Kong through the instrument of Shenzhen: "Those in antiquity who excelled in applying the method of turning back (Bei 背) and forth (Xiang 向) were able to exercise their authority (Xie) across the border and accommodate lords and nobles; they could create space to practice resist-reconcile and reshape it or turn it around for the purpose of reconciliation and unity."[419] That is the essence of the strategy of Shenzhen for Hong Kong. The future of Hong Kong is Shenzhen.

✻ ✻ ✻

---

[415] Ibid., ¶17.
[416] Ibid., ¶18.
[417] Ibid., ¶19.
[418] Ibid.
[419] *Guiguzi: China's First Treatise on Rhetoric, supra;* Book II.6.3, p. 62.

Chapter 13

Thursday 22 August 2019
Reflections on Zheng Yongnian: "The Capital of Protests" Who Controls Hong Kong?" [郑永年：“抗议之都” 谁主香港？]

"'I bought them in Shenzhen,' a smiling Wong, known affectionately as grandma, told Reuters of the flags, referring to the southern Chinese city across the border where she now lives. 'I had to ask secretly because they only showed the Chinese flag. So I asked them if they had the British flag and they take it out to show me. If you don't ask, they don't show.'"[420]

Now in its New Era of historical development, China has emerged as a great driving force for law and politics across a broad front of issues at the core of law, governance, politics and economics. The theoretical development centers on the re-orientation of the political-economic model around the current principal contradiction of Chinese Marxist-Leninism in the contemporary stage of Chinese development: "the contradiction between unbalanced and inadequate development and the people's ever growing needs for a better life."[421] This current

---

[420] Reuters, "Flag-waving 63-year-old gives Hong Kong protesters lesson in endurance" *NY Post* (3 July 2019); available [https://nypost.com/2019/07/03/flag-waving-63-year-old-gives-hong-kong-protesters-lesson-in-endurance/] ("Among the hundreds of thousands of protesters who have clogged the streets of Hong Kong in recent weeks, silver-haired, bespectacled "Grandma Wong," usually seen waving a large British flag, stands out.").

[421] Xi Jinping, "Secure a Decisive Victory in Building a Moderately Prosperous Society in All Respects and Strive for the Great Success of Socialism with Chinese Characteristics for a New Era (18 October 2017); available [http://www.xinhuanet.com/english/download/Xi_Jinping's_report_at_19th_CPC_National_Congress.pdf], p. 9-10. See, Xinghua Wei, "The principal contradiction and its evolution in the new era of the socialism society with Chinese characteristics: From the perspective of the Marxist political economy methodology" *China Political Economy* 1(1):2-12 (2018). It also makes sense to recall that Leninism is as well the "theory and tactics of dictatorship of the

contradiction follows the initial contradiction of class struggle, and the contradiction that followed from the start of the leadership of Deng Xiaoping--the contradiction of socialist modernization and the development of productive forces. Each of these contradiction were overcome to the extent necessary for the development of the nation, and each led to the success of that confrontation with contradiction led to the emergence of the next succeeding contradiction. The recognition and confrontation of the current contradiction serves as a entering element in the way that the central authorities understand the world and the framework through which they approach the challenges with which they are confronted.

In its outward expressions, the current contradiction centers around the re-construction of "international socialism," [422] of theories of imperialism devoid of its Western baggage of racism, occupation, and Western versions of cultural ethno-centrism.[423] It finds expression in the projection of Chinese theory in international forums, [424] and through its Belt and Road Initiative. [425] And for some, it might be understood as the

---

proletariat in particular." Joseph Stalin, The Foundations of Leninism (Beijing: Foreign Language Press, 1970), p. 2.

[422] Xi Jinping, "Secure a Decisive Victory," supra., p. 11.

[423] See Larry Catá Backer, "CPE Working Group on Empire: A Critical Gloss on Xi Jinping, 〈齐心开创共建"一带一路"美好未来〉 ["Working Together to Deliver a Brighter Future For Belt and Road Cooperation"] In the Shadow of the U.S.-China Trade Talks," Law at the End of the Day (13 May 2019); available [https://lcbackerblog.blogspot.com/2019/05/cpe-working-group-on-empire-critical.html#more]. See generally, Coalition for Peace & Ethics Working Group on Empire series, distributed through the blogsite Law at the end of the day, "CPE Empire Serie;" (from April 2019); available [https://lcbackerblog.blogspot.com/search/label/CPE%20EmpireSeries].

[424] Larry Catá Backer, "China," in *Tipping Points in International Law: Commitment and Critique* (Jean d'Aspremont and John Haskell, eds.; Cambridge University Press (forthcoming 2021)) (focus is on the emergence of an increasingly sophisticated and well-structured challenge by China to the current framework for international human rights law and norms, both in conception and application).

[425] Rafiq Dossani, "The Driving Force Behind China's Ambitious 'Belt and Road Initiative.' The Rand Blog (30 May 2017); available [https://www.rand.org/blog/2017/05/the-driving-force-behind-chinas-ambitious-belt-and.html].

structures of "informal" empire. [426] At its heart, however, it represents a movement of purification--of absorbing and refining the learning of the prior era and transforming it into something uniquely driven by and through the guiding ideology of the vanguard.

The practical development centers on the construction and operation of a centerpiece of Chinese extra-national constitutional theory—the One Country Two Systems principle,[427] and from there its extension to bilateral relations (contextually shaped) between China and its Belt and Road Initiative partners.[428] And it ought to apply the consequences of the shift toward a new primary contradiction to China's autonomous regions, including Hong Kong. Indeed, these trajectories have now appeared to converge around the emerging situation in Hong Kong. It is in that context that many have been following the shifting positions of governmental actors and other stakeholders in response to the social protests that have occurred in Hong Kong since June 2019.

Xi Jinping underlined the focus of this trajectory in his Report to the 19th CPC Congress.

> We will remain committed to the policy for the Hong Kong people to govern Hong Kong and the Macao people to govern Macao, *with patriots playing the principal role.*

---

[426] Matthew Craven, "What Happened to Unequal Treaties? The Continuities of Informal Empire," *Nordic Journal of International Law* 74(3-4):335-382 (2005).

[427] See, Roda Mushkat, *One Country, Two International Legal Personalities: The Case of Hong Kong* (Hong Kong University Press, 1997). This principle itself has been described as a dynamic mechanism to contain what are perceived to be an inevitable evolutionary process toward re-integration; Jiang Shigong, *China's Hong Kong : a political and cultural perspective* (Singapore: Springer, 2017). Alvin Y. So, ""One Country, Two Systems" and Hong Kong-China National Integration: A Crisis-Transformation Perspective," *Journal of Contemporary Asia* 41(1):99-116 (2011);

[428] Heng Wang, "China's Approach to the Belt and Road Initiative," *Journal of International Economic Law* 22(1):29-55 (2019); Larry Catá Backer, "Toward New Era Thought: Reflections on Xi Jinping, Speech at the Meeting Celebrating the 40th Anniversary of Reform and Opening Up," *Emancipating the Mind in the New Era: Bulletin of the Coalition for Peace & Ethics* 15(1):121-144 (2020).

We will develop and strengthen the ranks of patriots who love both our country and their regions, and *foster greater patriotism and a stronger sense of national identity among the people in Hong Kong and Macao*. With this, our compatriots in Hong Kong and Macao will share both the historic responsibility of national rejuvenation and the pride of a strong and prosperous China.[429]

Here there is a whiff of Mao Zedong's "On the People's Democratic Dictatorship."[430] The current contradiction at the heart of the present state Chinese Marxist-Leninist development gives rise to the need for a refocus on prosperity that is more generally available. Confronting the current contradiction in this time of the leadership of Xi Jinping appears also to be a function of strengthening national identity. That, in turn, produces an impulse to further patriotic education. That, in turn, is tied to the idea of the need to separate those who ae patriotic, that is who form part of the people around which the Two Systems elements may be constructed, from others. Only for the patriotic are the benefits of Hong Kong autonomy, its Two Systems principle, available. For the rest, the protesters, there is only the rigor of One Country and the obligation to conform or be punished. They are the contemporary versions, to paraphrase Mao Zedong's "On People's Democratic Dictatorship quoted above, of the running dogs of imperialism--and for them there is no Two Systems, there

---

[429] Xi Jinping, "Secure a Decisive Victory," supra., p. 50 (emphasis supplied).
[430] Mao Zedong, "On the People's Democratic Dictatorship" (30 June 1949); available   [https://www.marxists.org/reference/archive/mao/selected-works/volume-4/mswv4_65.htm].In the critical passage Mao explains:

> Who are the people? At the present stage in China, they are the working class, the peasantry, the urban petty bourgeoisie and the national bourgeoisie. These classes, led by the working class and the Communist Party, unite to form their own state and elect their own government; they enforce their dictatorship over the running dogs of imperialism . . . If they speak or act in an unruly way, they will be promptly stopped and punished. Democracy is practiced within the ranks of the people, who enjoy the rights of freedom of speech, assembly, association and so on. The right to vote belongs only to the people, not to the reactionaries. The combination of these two aspects, democracy for the people and dictatorship over the reactionaries, is the people's democratic dictatorship.

is only identification and punishment unless they behave themselves and are not unruly--but they have been quite unruly.

To be clear, then, there is a strong connection between the articulation of the current contradiction as a framing principle and the way that central authorities must interpret both the One Country Two Systems principles and the threat posed by the protesters. The current contradiction requires confronting the issues of uneven distribution of national wealth. That, in turn, impels a policy focused on advancing the principles of prosperity and stability without which it would be impossible to effectively overcome the current contradiction and pave the way to the next era of development. Instability threatens prosperity. Autonomy that encourages or permits instability, that threatens prosperity, is incompatible with a core principle on which the Chinese political-economic system is grounded and a threat to successful confrontation of the current contradiction. To bring alignment, it is necessary to ensure popular embrace of core principles. And to ensure that, the vanguard increasingly understands that this requires both patriotic education (of the young) whose corruption contributed to the threat, and a strong rectification of those who have placed themselves outside of the political community.

That combination, then, of current contradiction, and the notion of the people--as excluding those who do not share the national vision under the guidance of the vanguard--colors all readings of the One Country Two Systems principle. It suggests what may be coming and the great rift between the world view of those driving the protests in Hong Kong--internationalists grounded in the discursive tropes of liberal democratic societies, and those of Chinese Leninists. The protestors see the gross failures to address the primary contradiction and they seek accountability directly, in the international style of asserting political rights and extracting a cost to officials who fail in their duty. The failures of that conversation have produced the frustrations that exploded in the Umbrella Movement and now in the protests since June 2019. [431] For Chinese Leninists, the protests are a clear example of the instability and regime threat of permitting societal elements to "misbehave." Their protests detach them from solidarity with the people; they are no longer part of the patriotic masses, and for them the logic of Mao Zedong's democratic dictatorship would apply--punishment and a reward to patriots fostering stability and prosperity.[432]

This developing theory and its practice implications are among the most interesting advances in political, economic and cultural relations since the construction of the contemporary global system under the leadership of the United States and its allies. It is especially interesting both for the way it signals a quite dynamic building of an organic political philosophy of Chinese Marxist-Leninism, and for the way this political philosophy is projected outward to drive re-conceptualization of law and politics on a global level.

Less noticed but perhaps ultimately more important, has been the high-level discourse among elite intellectual circles with relations to the major actors in these processes of development. On occasion, these elite conversations among high status intellectuals are circulated. They provide sometimes brilliant insight into the forms and approaches that are likely to emerge in popular economic and political circles among the major actors. They are each worthy of careful reading in their own right, but are especially useful for a study of the emergence.

One of the more interesting conversations among the many is that between Albert Chen (陳弘毅), of the University of Hong Kong,[433] and Zheng Yongnian (郑永年), a professor and director of the East Asian Institute of the National University of

---

[431] Joseph Yu-shek Cheng, "The Emergence of Radical Politics in Hong Kong: Causes and Impact," *China Review* 14(1:199-232 (Spring 2014) (Special Issue: Urban and Regional Governance in China).

[432] Considered in Chapter 9, supra.

[433] Some of whose thoughts were the subjects of Chapters 6 and 9, supra.

Singapore.[434] Professor Zheng, like Professor Chen, is a public intellectual.[435] He has been at the forefront of intellectual movements and among the relevant academic community.[436] The interest, especially in the context of the current situation in Hong Kong, arises from the intuition that they each give to emerging positions on the key theoretical and practical developments of Chinese theories of imperialism in the New Era context in which Hong Kong has become a critical practical incubator—the site from which truth may be developed from facts.

Zheng Yongnian's recent essay, "The Capital of Protests" Who Controls Hong Kong? [郑永年：“抗议之都” 谁主香港?][437] appears to respond to the earlier essays of Albert Chen and for that reason alone is worth considering in the context of the development of academic and intellectual positions among the different parties in Hong Kong. It is also worthy of deep study both in its own right and for the way it reflects changing thinking about both Socialist New Era imperialist theory, and its global context (e.g., starting, it seems, with Singapore).

---

[434] Postscript Note: Professor Zheng has since May 2020 and director moved on to take up a position as head of global and contemporary China studies at the Chinese University of Hong Kong (CUHK) in Shenzhen .

[435] A current biography notes that "he has been a columnist for Xinbao (Hong Kong) and Zaobao (Singapore) for many years, writing numerous commentaries on China's domestic and international affairs." Zheng Yongnian, Bio, World Economic Forum; available [https://www.weforum.org/people/yongnian-zheng].

[436] See, e.g., Larry Catá Backer, Brief Thoughts on Zheng Yongnian: Is Marxism Really Revived in China? [郑永年：马克思主义在中国真的复兴了吗？],” Law at the End of the Day (24 June 2019); available [https://lcbackerblog.blogspot.com/2019/06/brief-thoughts-on-zheng-yongnian-is.html].

[437] 郑永年 [Zheng Yongnian], 抗议之都” 谁主香港？ [“'The Capital of Protests' Who Controls Hong Kong?"], 联合早报 [Lianhe Zaobao] (20 August 2019) (hereafter Zheng, "The Capital of Protests"); available [https://www.zaobao.com.sg/zopinions/views/story20190820-982364] original in Chinese. I will use my own crude translation. The full English translation may be found at Law at the End of the Day; available [https://lcbackerblog.blogspot.com/2019/08/reflections-on-zheng-yongnian-capital_22.html].

Professor Zheng sets the tone with the title. It suggests an oblique reference to popular control, the centering of the fundamental Maoist question of the identification of the people and the punishment of reactionaries. It is a question that suggests an answer deeply embedded in the New Era principle of patriotism as the foundation for meeting the challenge of the current contradiction. With it, it also carries with it the answer to its own question: that patriotic elements under the guidance of the vanguard take a leading role in the governance of Hong Kong and that those who misbehave, who are unruly, who cause instability, ought to be punished. That is the bridge that connects Mao Zedong's "On People's Democratic Dictatorship" to Xi Jinping's Report to the 19th CPC Congress and then to the situation in Hong Kong and from there to the re-centering of the One Country-Two Systems principle.

Professor Zheng's essay then starts, as it must, by positioning the situation in Hong Kong within a quite specific narrative context, a narrative context essential for the elaboration of Professor Zheng's complex and sophisticated argument. Indeed, the opening paragraphs (and to some extent the entire essay) may be reduced to a singular image with substantial text and subtext:

鼎 (Dǐng)

(an ancient three legged bronze cauldron; the throne or leadership "core"; or more broadly the state apparatus).

Hong Kong is not the cauldron itself, or figuratively the throne (as itself a symbol of the authority given to the leadership "core" by the mandate of heaven), but rather an element of its content. It is, however, an element of the cauldron that itself has upset the harmony that the cauldron represents; it has upset the order of things by its own fundamental disorder. An overturned cauldron spills its contents; to overturn the cauldron is to invite disorder and destroy prosperity.

"To put it bluntly, there is only one fundamental problem in Hong Kong, that is: Who is Hong Kong?"[438] That question suggests two key elements for the analysis that follows. The first is the cauldron itself. If China represents the cauldron right side up, then Hong Kong illustrates the consequences when the cauldron is turned upside down. Underlying this is a sense not just of imbalance in the natural order of things, of fundamental harmony, but of inversion. The cauldron turned upside down contains nothing, it spills its contents. The second references the contents of the cauldron--the core of leadership that shapes the cauldron itself. Here the cauldron upside carries a different connotation--that which ought to be at the periphery appears to become the core and the core is emptied of content. A cauldron that is upside down, a cauldron with an empty core of leadership, cannot be sustained.

To understand Hong Kong, then, within the stabilizing context of 鼎 "ding" one must understand the root of its instability, its disorder. To do that, one must first unearth the reason why disorder is the fundamental order of Hong Kong--and one must do that from the perspective of the "core" and from the foundational principles of harmony and prosperity which is itself the evidence of good order.

But that is not now Hong Kong. Professor Zheng presumes Hong Kong as the capital of protests, whose protests "have never been interrupted."[439] This is not just disorder but the essence of disorder as a structural ordering pattern: "Such frequent social protests in a city are rare in world history." The result is a social shackling whose product is inevitable--violence. Social harmony, the cauldron again, provides thick walls that protect harmony, bring order and prosperity under the ordering responsibility of a "core;" direction directly by popular collectives produces the opposite, an inverted social order--social disruption, cultures of protests, a threat to prosperity that shackles society and normalizes violence. This is the cauldron overturned--a powerful discursive trope with a wealth of underlying meaning in history,

---

[438] Zheng, "The Capital of Protests," supra.
[439] Ibid.

culture, politics, etc. That disorders produces the usual warnings that have been a constant theme of the pronouncement of central authorities, one that Professor Zheng underlines: "And it is not difficult to understand that any social protest, if the parties do not compromise, must end with violence. There are too many historical experiences to prove this inevitable result."[440]

Professor Zheng, then, brings us from the narrative positioning of the situation in Hong Kong to his own role in its elaboration--to investigate its causes and suggest a way to bring Hong Kong back to order and Harmony. To do that the intellectual must probe deeply into the contradictions that have produced disharmony, identify the "sickness" that is embedded in that disorder, and excise it. The process, as Professor Zheng will show, is made infinitely easier where the "sickness" is equated with the foreign (the way that viruses and bacterial are foreign to the human body), and thus identified, can be opposed to bring the body back to health. Again, in Professor Zheng's words: "To put it bluntly, there is only one fundamental problem in Hong Kong, that is: Who is Hong Kong?"[441]

To that end, Professor Zheng constructs a set of fundamental oppositions, one that mirrors the position of the emerging position of the central authorities. One is constructed as *endogenous* (and benign)--China and its elaboration of a system of sovereignty over territory to which the authority to rule has been delegated. He notes, for example, "China enjoys less and less actual sovereignty, manifested in a limited area of diplomacy, and enjoys only "honorary sovereignty" in most areas. Even the garrison has only symbolic meaning." And, indeed, the maintenance of One Country Two Systems has been costly to China to the advantage of those profiting from disorder in Hong Kong. Professor Zheng writes: "The actual situation is that in order to maintain "one country, two systems", the mainland has delivered a large number of benefits to Hong Kong in order to maintain its prosperity, at least economically.

---

440 Ibid.
441 Ibid.

The other is constructed as *exogenous*--the colonialist imperialism of the United Kingdom (principally though the shadow of the United States can be discerned at the edges). Here in the face of China's critical role in economic stands the unmoving wall that is the colonial legacy of the United Kingdom in the form of a legal architecture that itself ensures disorder. He concludes: "As far as governance is concerned, the most substantive legal system is not within China's sovereignty."[442]

Thus framed in the comfortable style of an oppositional binary, Professor Zheng is able to take the blunter discourse of the Black Hand [黑 手] [443] and elaborate a quite sophisticated theoretics of rule with substantial implications for the construction of an imperial order built around (like the rings of Beijing once expressed as walls with gates and now as motorways with exits) an ever widening circle of relationship between sovereignty and rule that extends outward from the center to the farthest peripheral regions. But to do that Professor Zheng must put Hong Kong in perspective and in order.

These fundamental oppositions--of harmony and chaos, of leadership core and popular chaos, of social peace and violence-- is then elaborated through the lens of four distinct lenses to themes. These themes include (1) the authority of the Hong Kong Chief Executive (the absence of a leadership core); (2) the persistence of foreign forces (the black hand as a structural element); (3) the contrast to Singapore (the model imperial partner); and (4) the fundamental contradiction of disorder and social harmony (the impossibility of social harmony in the face of an embedded foreign element)). Let us consider each in turn.

The Hong Kong Chief Executive:

Professor Zheng here subtly raises a point well made by Jiang Shigong and other Chinese scholars--that the transposition of forms of governance also transposes with it the underlying

---

[442] Ibid.
[443] An object of discussion in Chapters 7 and 8, supra.

ideology from which that form of governance derived.[444] In this case Professor Zheng pointedly directs attention of the Western structural element in the organization of the Hong Kong government: separation of powers and an autonomous judiciary singled out for special mention. These together strip the leadership core of its authority. And the singular lack of that authority contributes to disharmony--to a leaderless collective that then, in seeking to govern, becomes ungovernable. But for Zheng it does much more than that--it suggests the heart of his first theme about the structural embedding of instability and disharmony on Hong Kong--*that de-colonization has never, in fact, been successful, and that as a consequence of the constraints placed on China by the 1997 agreement* [445] *(and the one country two systems principle, Hong Kong remains effectively a dependency of the United Kingdom.* "The entire judicial system is still almost in the hands of the 'Hong Kong British authorities' who are 'reclusive'. Even the administrative system, except for the chief executive, is still receiving the 'whole' from the British Hong Kong authorities."[446]

With one bold brush stroke, Professor Zheng is able to transform a sector of the indigenous population and in the process to blot them out from the Chinese polity. There are marvelous echoes of a similar effort to recast, and thus dismiss, sectors of the Chinese population in the early period of Mao Zedong's leadership, though perhaps to different ends.

> You are dictatorial." My dear sirs, what you say is correct. That is just what we are. All the experiences of the Chinese people, accumulated in the course of successive decades, tell us to carry out a people's democratic dictatorship. This means that the reactionaries must be

---

[444] Larry Catá Backer, "Between the Judge and the Law: Judicial Independence and Authority With Chinese Characteristics," *Connecticut Journal of International Law* 33(1):1-41 (2017)).

[445] Joint Declaration of the Government of the United Kingdom of Great Britain and Northern Ireland and the Government of the People's Republic of China on the Question of Hong Kong (19 December 1984); available [https://www.cmab.gov.hk/en/issues/jd2.htm].

[446] Zheng, "The Capital of Protests," *supra.*

deprived of the right to voice their opinions; only the people have that right. Who are the "people"? At the present stage in China, they are the working class, the peasantry, the petty bourgeoisie and the national bourgeoisie. [who enforce] their dictatorship over the henchmen of imperialism . . . The people's government will suppress such persons. . . . The democratic system is to be carried out within the ranks of the people, giving them freedom of speech, assembly and association. The right to vote is given only to the people, not to the reactionaries. These two things, democracy for the people and dictatorship for the reactionaries, when combined, constitute the people's democratic dictatorship.[447]

This is an essential underlying trope--but now undertaken not in the context of class struggle but in the service of a new transformational anti-colonialism that is at the same time imperial in the sense of its approach to a hierarchical arrangement of political relations with China at the center.[448] It posits this new form of so-called socialist internationalism against the antique variations of imperial ordering represented by the United Kingdom. One can then repudiate the leadership of the old imperial orders in the construction of the 1997 agreement (an internationalized Hong Kong producing a state of constant disorder in the service of the anti-colonial socialist internationalism built around a national core). The object is to connect legal dependency on a foreign ideology with instability in a territory that is formally a Chinese dependency but in fact is beholden to another sovereign (or at least that sovereign's ghost).

To that end, Professor Zheng spends time in the essay suggest that the Chief Executive is structurally impeded from exercising authority. The impediment is a system that Professor Zheng suggests transforms the civil service into a political party

---

[447] Mao Zedong, "On the People's Democratic Dictatorship," supra.
[448] 强世功：超大型政治实体的内在逻辑： "帝国" 与世界秩序 [Jiang Shigong, "the internal logic of super-large political entities: "empire" and world order"] (4 June 2019); available [http://www.aisixiang.com/data/115799.html].

and a source of opposition to the Chief Executive. As a consequence, he argues, it has been difficult for the Hong Kong government to "make a difference." But he does this in a curious way--by measuring the *number* of "effective laws and policies. . . passed by the SAR government." [449] This is a curious measure indeed, and perhaps misleading for two reasons. One it is offered without attaching it to the satisfaction of a need. It might well be that large numbers of laws were unnecessary (but Professor Zheng has a different purpose in mind here--the need for lots of law to eliminate vestiges of the UK legal system for which numbers might matter more). The other is that quantity is usually not a satisfactory measure of quality. Professor Zheng does offer some examples of what he believes were good initiatives that were not adopted.

More interesting is Professor Zheng's notion that, if the Chief Executive is bereft of power then the power had to go somewhere (other than it seems to the civil service (itself an odd leap)). That power, however is unlikely to find its way to the collective. First, he is dismissive of the efforts at double universal suffrage.[450] Second, he sees in the devolution of power downward as the very definition of instability and disorder.

> First, "it is difficult to adjust", and no compromise can be reached. People have produced a "one step in place" political reform fantasy. In the process of winning, the protesters did not have the opportunity to fulfill their demands, but because there was no compromise, all opportunities were lost. Second, the protests turned into violence and developed into a devastating social movement "protest against protests" or a sporty society.

One moves back here to the cauldron upended. And it requires the machinery of government--and its core leaders, to set it right.

---

[449] Zheng, "The Capital of Protests," supra.
[450] See the state of debate in "Universal Suffrage in Hong Kong," *South China Morning Post*; available [https://www.scmp.com/topics/universal-suffrage-hong-kong].

The Black Hand [黑手] as a Structural Element that is Sourced in the Colonial Experience.

This gets Professor Zheng to a major insight in his marvelous essay--that the cause of disharmony in Hong Kong can be traced to the continued infection of foreign elements that have neither been absorbed properly or eliminated. One encounters here a variation of the "black hand" [黑手] discourse developed by the central authorities in the Hong Kong context[451] in a much more interesting context.

To get there, though, Professor Zheng notes that a straightforward national analysis grounded in the well-worm theories of simple de-colonization won't work because of Hong Kong's unique position as a global commercial center. To overcome that challenge Professor Zheng first posits the character of Hong Kong as an "international city." It follows from this internationalism that the recognition and tolerance of foreign forces is necessary. But it must necessarily also be controlled. And that is the missing element here. "This is reality, whether people like it or not. What needs to be addressed is whether the SAR Government has the ability to curb the negative effects of these foreign forces."[452] And thus the foreign element discursive trope is fully formed; here one finds a much more sophisticated encounter with the Black Hand.

Effectively, then, the picture painted is this: the ghosts of 19th century colonialism[453] (a colonialism whose ghosts haunt the People's Republic from the time of the Opium Wars "big bang" effect)[454] plague Hong Kong. These specters do more than haunt; they have *possessed* the international city. While the ghosts cannot be chased away (they are good for business) they must be

---

[451] See chapters 5 and 7 supra.
[452] Zheng, "The Capital of Protests," supra.
[453] E.g., Dong Wang, *China's Unequal Treaties: Narrating National History* (Lexington Books, 2008).
[454] e.g., W. Travis Hanes III and Frank Sanello, The Opium Wars: The Addiction of One Empire and the Corruption of Another (Sourcebooks, Inc., 2002);

used (exploited) but tightly controlled. The failure to assert that control threatens stability and prosperity, that is it threatens to overturn the cauldron. Here one finds a convergence with Chinese trade policies (and its echoes in the similar line of the U.S. Trump Administration). At the same time, one wonders whether the obsession with these now ancient tropes perversely do much to carry their effects forward to the present and to magnify their effects. In this sense this version of the Black Hand might both serve as a self-fulfilling prophesy or worse, serve as the catalyst for its construction in the first place. But that is a bridge now crossed.

The spectral character of this argument, it antiquarian turn, is nicely evidenced with its focus on the United Kingdom. But it is also crucial to the argument that the 1997 agreement[455] locked Hong Kong into a state of perpetual colonial status dependent on the United Kingdom but maintained by the People's Republic.

> As far as the impact of Britain on Hong Kong is concerned, to a large extent, after the return of 1997, Hong Kong has only changed from a British "direct colony" to a British "indirect colony." Except for some text changes and literal articles (even including the Basic Law), at the time of the return of Hong Kong in 1997, the authorities did not change anything. After the reunification, no major changes (especially institutional changes) have occurred to reflect Hong Kong people's autonomy or Chinese sovereignty. What the parties have endeavored is only the "rule of law" in Hong Kong.[456]

Yet the conflation of legal forms to contradiction in political system is to some extent a fairly thin reed onto which to hand this argument. It is at its most powerful as a formalist argument at the level of macro-analysis. Yet one wonders how well it holds up at the micro level.

---

[455] See Joint Declaration, supra.
[456] Zheng, "The Capital of Protests," supra.

Ironically, perhaps, that precisely is the problem; what makes Hong Kong so difficult for systems grounded in a fundamental ordering principle of leadership cores is the extent to which a space is available that may be managed but not controlled. It is here that the contradiction between systems becomes acute. But that is not a function of colonialism so much as an indigenous emerging political culture. And that is what poses the greatest challenge for Hong Kong's ultimate sovereign, one still in search of a resolution.

For this reason, Professor Zheng's discussion of the contribution of what he might term colonial rule of law sensibilities, focuses on what he perceives as its political effects. Here one moves from the abstract colonialism of legal systems, to the more concrete colonialism of entrenched power. It does so in two respects. First rule of law is the manifestation of the law as the mechanism of direct colonialization. Second, it also serves as the mechanics of an *indirect colonialism* to the extent law protects the interests of foreigners in Hong Kong's international cityscape through its discourse of rights to person and property.

> But this "rule of law" system has become the most effective tool for maintaining vested interests, especially for the UK. Not only that, because it is an "indirect colony", the British or other foreign forces, they only take advantage . . . without any responsibility. . . . It is the most effective "supervisor" of the SAR government and the most effective resistance to changes in Hong Kong.[457]

What makes this more striking is the quite profound way in which Professor Zheng is able to translate the central authorities' Black Hand campaign by refocusing it from the crude efforts of the United States to influence the protestors to a much more powerful indictment of the 1997 Agreement and the underlying basis of One Country Two Systems doctrine.

---

[457] Ibid.

That translation is not likely to entirely please the central authorities who remain committed to the principle--committed enough to threaten occupation of Hong Kong to preserve the system. Now does not appear to be the time to question One Country Two Systems fundamental premises. But the indictment is still potent in the way it resonates and its power is augmented by its elegant simplicity: that the Black Hand that undermines Hong Kong is not the Americans encouraging protest, but rather the Black hand is embedded into the core legal framework of Hong Kong, into its political culture, and into the values it encourages. Ironically this argument appears to come straight from a Western playbook--most successful deployed today by Western feminists and critical legal scholars but now nicely deployed to post-colonial decolonization.

Professor Zheng's notion of indirect colonialism is particularly interesting. There is something to the idea of shades of colonialism. But that also suffers a flaw--it conflates vertically ordered power relations which may be necessary and benign (for example the relationship between China and Singapore, or those between China and its Belt and Road Initiative partners) and colonialism. That is, colonialism and imperialism are conflated. However, it is possible to believe that this conflation is itself subject to interrogation, that it is no more than a vestige of a passing era, and that the two systems of power relationships are not necessarily identical.

Professor Zheng does have a sense of this in his nicely nuanced discussion of legal decolonization in the paragraphs that follow. None of these provide a satisfactory guide, with one possible exception--Singapore. That is the example Professor Zheng offers to Hong Kong. After independence, according to Professor Zheng, "the original colonial heritage was effectively decolonized, and while retaining a positive legacy, its negative aspects were removed leaving a rule of law that promotes social harmony." [458] Professor Zheng assures us that this "is in stark contrast to the 'rule of law' in Hong Kong. To a large extent, Hong Kong's 'rule of law' can effectively protect the interests of the

---

[458] Ibid.

original colonists, but it is difficult to enhance Hong Kong's own interests."[459] It is here, at last, that Professor Zheng can fuse his layering of contradictions to point to the core problem of Hong Kong--its imbalance.

The fundamental contradiction of disorder and social harmony.

That brings Professor Zheng to the consequences of disharmony and the inversion of the social order. That comes in two distinct but related forms. The first is tied to the paradox of a bottom-up governance in which power is not actually held by the "bottom." Here one has a variation of the ruling class control through the facade of democratic governance that is at the heart of much of the Leninist critique of Western liberal democracy. Professor Zheng refines these and applies them to the situation in Hong Kong to some effect. First, bottom-up power serves the vested interests of the "ruling elite" in Hong Kong. Second, the principal value of this relationships that the ruling elite is able to enjoy the benefits of protection without the bother of assuming any responsibility for the result. Instead, they have constructed a paper tiger Executive to misdirect popular anger to a convenient target. It is here that Hong Kong's western indirect colonial leash serves it purpose:

> The "rule of law" has the same logic for vested interests, that is, "the rule of law" is the most effective weapon to protect their interests from losses. Considering that Hong Kong's deep-rooted vested interests are now growing up during the British Hong Kong authorities, this logic is not difficult to understand.[460]

Here, again, Professor Zheng develops an indirect attack on the foundations of the One Country Two Systems policy. That policy now serves as the great obstacle to returning Hong Kong to a state of social harmony and its system to a natural stability. "But realistically, because it is the implementation of "one country, two systems", it is difficult for mainland China to change the colonial

---

[459] Ibid.
[460] Zheng, "The Capital of Protests," supra.

heritage of Hong Kong in the past. Only Hong Kong itself has this ability."[461]

Professor Zheng, however, argues that the current situation in Hong Kong makes clear Hong Kong's unwillingness or inability to change. That inability is also institutional and deeply embedded in Hong Kong's political, economic, legal, and social cultures. *He takes aim at Hong Kong's educational system, in ways that echo what appears to be the criticism of the central government, about the critical role of Hong Kong's education elite sin perpetuating ideologies of disharmony--of deliberately cultivating the upending of the cauldron of state.* Here, echoing the developing line of central authorities declared within weeks of the start of the protests in 2019,[462] Professor Zheng focuses on the role of education--especially on the lack of patriotic education:

> On the practical level, after the reunification, the colonial education has not only changed, but has intensified. The former democratic movement still had some "anti-British" flavors, but now it has turned to the mainland of the motherland. National identity has completely gone to the opposite side. It is necessary to clearly understand that the main body of the protesters over the years has been the younger generation who grew up after the reunification of 1997. They are also the mainstay of the "Hong Kong independence" power. [463]

This is a powerful indictment. We will be curious to see what, if any, response, Hong Kong's educational elite has to this charge.

Professor Zheng offers a way out, though--a greater emphasis on building programs that aim to *stress the one country part of the doctrine* and to give the two systems elements a more marginal

---

[461] Ibid.

[462] 新闻办就香港当前事态的立场和看法举行吹风会，2019-08-06 16:55 来源：中国网 [The Information Office holds a briefing on the current situation and views of Hong Kong, 2019-08-06 16:55 Source: China Net]; available [http://www.gov.cn/xinwen/2019-08/06/content_5419266.htm] (hereafter HKMAO 6 August Statement. Discussed supra at Chapter 7.

[463] Zheng, "The Capital of Protests," supra.

role. To solve the problem of One Country Two systems, then, one country must prevail over two systems. And to prevail, the foreign elements of two systems must first be identified and eliminated.

To that end, Professor Zheng proposes an approach that is likely to have some influence. He argues that the 1997 transfer was effectively both flawed and incomplete. It has produced the disharmony that has led directly to the current situation and has exposed what he terms the great contradictions of the return of Hong Kong to Chinese sovereignty. In effect, he suggests, there was no return, just the forms of return. What is necessary he suggest, is the actual return of Hong Kong to China in form and effect. To that end he proposes a second return of Hong Kong to China. That will be a matter for China--and not for Hong Kong. But it will involve a radical transformation of both one country two systems and of the legal, political, social and economic order in Hong Kong. Whatever one thinks of this approach, one must agree with Professor Zheng that "Things have already happened and Hong Kong cannot return to its original point."[464]

$$* * *$$

---

[464] Ibid.

Chapter 14

Monday 2 September 2019
'Two Systems' Internationalism Against 'One Country' Nationalism--Reflections on the G7 Declaration and the (Re)Construction of New Era Governance Systems

As the protests in Hong Kong entered its 13th week, a public dialogue that runs parallel to the protest has been taking place between and among state actors. The dialogue has been taking place on different occasions, the most notable one being the 2019 Summit of the Group of Seven (G7)[465] As it has become customary, at the end of the Summit, the countries of the Group of Seven (Italy, France, the United States, Germany, Canada, Japan and the United Kingdom), released a Leaders' Declaration.[466] The Declaration is a "one-page document summarizing the main decisions made on global crises."[467] Of its 259 words, the relevant portion of the Statement read in full as follows:

> The G7 reaffirms the existence and importance of the Sino-British Joint Declaration of 1984 on Hong Kong and calls for violence to be avoided.

This appears to be a robust statement in support of the notion of the "Two Systems" side of the One Country-Two Systems principle

---

[465] "G7 stands for the Group of 7. The seven G7 countries are Canada, France, Germany, Italy, Japan, the United Kingdom and the United States [which] represent 40% of global GDP and 10% of the world's population... The only rule is that the Presidency is held each year by one of the seven States in turn, which provides the necessary resources for the group's work and sets out its priorities." G7 France (2019); Who are the G7?; available [https://www.elysee.fr/en/g7/2019/01/01/what-is-the-g7]. The Group of 7 met in August 2019 in Biarritz France under the Presidency of the French Republic.

[466] Its Leaders' Declaration issued 26 August 2019 available [https://www.elysee.fr/en/g7/2019/08/26/g7-leaders-declaration].

[467] "G7 Leaders' Declaration,; available [https://www.elysee.fr/g7/2019/08/26/g7-leaders-declaration.en].

as grounded in internationalism, even as its One Country side might be founded in nationalism. The intimation, of course, is that while Hong Kong may be "Chinese" in its nationality, its governance is international.

The People's Republic of China is not part of the G7, perhaps in part because it might not be deemed to approach the G7's "foundation of shared values: democracy, respect for human rights and fundamental freedoms, free markets, and respect for international law in the same way. That means the members can discuss all subjects, even when they disagree."[468] Nonetheless, the G7's interest, and certainly its statement, appeared to challenge the cultivation of the Chinese approach to One Country-Two Systems.

The Chinese response was equally short and direct.

"We express our strong dissatisfaction and resolute opposition to the statement made by the leaders of the G7 Summit on Hong Kong affairs," Chinese Foreign Ministry spokesman Geng Shuang said at a press briefing in Beijing on Tuesday. "We have repeatedly stressed that Hong Kong's affairs are purely China's internal affairs and that no foreign government, organization, or individual has the right to intervene," he added.[469]

The Foreign Ministry also issued other related statements to the same effect. The Foreign Ministry did not reject the role of the Sino-British Joint Declaration of 1984 [470] so much as it marginalized its importance as a constitutional source for the

---

[468] G7 France; Who are the G/?, supra.
[469] "China 'resolutely opposes' G7 statement on Hong Kong" Press TV (27 August 2019); available [https://www.presstv.com/Detail/2019/08/27/604602/China-Hong-Kong-G7-statement].
[470] Joint Declaration of the Government of the United Kingdom of Great Britain and Northern Ireland and the Government of the People's Republic of China on the Question of Hong Kong (19 December 1984); available [https://www.cmab.gov.hk/en/issues/jd2.htm] (hereafter Sino-British Joint Declaration).

governance of Hong Kong and the protection of the rights of its residents.[471]

> With respect to the Sino-British Joint Declaration, I would like to reiterate that its ultimate purpose and core content is to affirm China's recovering of Hong Kong and resumption of exercise of sovereignty over it. With the return of Hong Kong to the motherland, the Chinese government exercises jurisdiction over it in accordance with the Constitution and the Basic Law. Under international law and basic norms governing international relations, no country or organization has any right to use the declaration as a pretext to meddle in Hong Kong affairs.[472]

These conflicting positions do much to crystalize the character of the normative divide that separates the understanding of the standing of Hong Kong and the sources of its governance. That divides also parallels the great conceptual chasm that separates Hong Kong's protesters--internationalists relying on the guarantees of the agreements through which Hong Kong was returned to China, and Chinese officials who viewed the international agreement for the handover to have been fully performed and of no further interest once the territory was repatriated.[473]

---

[471] August 27, 2019 statement of the spokesperson of the PRC Ministry of Foreign Affairs ("We deplore and firmly oppose such wanton comment in the G7 joint statement").

[472] Ibid.

[473] This is a position that has long been taken by the Chinese government. See, "China says Sino-British Joint Declaration on Hong Kong no longer has meaning," *Reuters* (30 June 2017); available [https://www.reuters.com/article/us-hongkong-anniversary-china/china-says-sino-british-joint-declaration-on-hong-kong-no-longer-has-meaning-idUSKBN19L1J1] ("Now Hong Kong has returned to the motherland's embrace for 20 years, the Sino-British Joint Declaration, as a historical document, no longer has any practical significance, and it is not at all binding for the central government's management over Hong Kong. The UK has no sovereignty, no power to rule and no power to supervise Hong Kong after the handover," Lu said." Ibid., quoting Foreign Ministry spokesman Lu Kang).

Part of it relates back to the way in which China has chosen to understand its history. That choice, of course, follows naturally from the ideological foundations of the nation, which provide the lens through which events acquire definitive meaning. The facts of a historical narrative, then, acquire significance only when they are imbued not just with meaning in themselves, but where that meaning provides the networks for interconnection (interpretive channels that appear natural and logical within the structures of the ideological framework through which they are encountered) that then can be used to weave a history.[474]

That history, invested with meaning in this way, accepts as valid the territorial expansion of the Chinese Empire as against others, eve when that expansion was forced through unequal treaties. On the other hand, such actions, when the empire was placed on the wrong end of inequality produced a situation-- especially respecting the ceding of territory, that must be understood as illegitimate and temporary. One gets a flavor of this in the rendering of history (for foreigners) distributed by instrumentalities of the Chinese authorities.[475] It is in that context, especially, and following that view of history, that the continued application of international arrangements over territory eternally claimed for the empire (in whatever form that empire takes as a function of China's progress through its historical stages of development) must also be suspect (pragmatically necessary but suspect all the same given dynamic power imbalances) and always temporary as the empire moves to reclaim its territory.

As such, the interest and relevance of the document and the response does not lie as much on the effects it can *directly* produce on the situation Hong Kong, but on what it may tell us about the way in which China and the G7 are coming to reconceive

---

[474] There is much here that resonates with Michel Foucault, *The Archeology of Knowledge and the Discourse on Language* ((A.M. Sheridan Smith, trans.; New York: Pantheon Books, 1972).

[475] Ministry of Foreign Affairs, Peoples' Republic of China, "The Chinese government resumed exercise of sovereignty over Hong Kong," (n.d.); available [https://www.fmprc.gov.cn/mfa_eng/ziliao_665539/3602_665543/3604_665 547/t18032.shtml] ("China does not recognize the three unequal treaties imposed on it by imperialism.").

the institutionalization of post-global empire along two quite distinct lines. For the G7, the language is grounded in the principles of the collective *imperium* built around the United Nations system and its community of states lead by a vanguard group of powerful states. From the G7's perspective, the imperium is built on the control of the violence of states within and outside of a sphere's of dominion. For China, the responsive language is built on the principle of an *imperium* built along the lines of productive power--it speaks the language of the imperium of the production chain centered in the leadership of a national collective. For China, the imperium produces aligned system of control and dependency that is interior to the national leadership core; it is built on the control of violence within its dependencies projected inward from abroad.

The G7 Leaders' Declaration on Hong Kong can be considered a political and rhetorical - and yet legitimate - move. It is meant to advance the discourse of internationalism which serves as the foundation for the way that liberal democratic states understand the status of Hong Kong *within* China. The Declaration is worth discussing, because it can reveal several of the global dynamics that surround and provide the rationalization of the Hong Kong protests through the mechanics of law and an internationalist understanding of sovereignty. Beyond popular theorizations about "Empire,"[476] the new sovereignty regimes we are witnessing are *composite regimes.* Each regime of sovereignty is composed of internal (endogenous) and external (exogenous) parts. The relationship between these parts, and other regimes of sovereignty, is determined by the network of relations that occur between any one of the endogenous and exogenous components, summed to the relations between all of the existing regimes of sovereignty. They are not a threat to law but rather law's apotheosis as the regulatory element of systems or vertically and horizontally arranged entities. .

As the situation in Hong Kong has become more sensitive, and even more dynamic, since the start of protests over an

---

[476] Michael Hardt and Antonio Negri, *Empire* (Harvard University Press, 2000).

Extradition Bill that the Hong Kong Government put forward (and then withdrew) and that the Central Government (for its own reasons) desires whatever the costs, the international framework within which Hong Kong—once ceded to the U.K by the then legitimate government of China—was ceded again to China's current legitimate government. At the center of this formal transference of sovereignty was the Sino-British Joint Declaration of 1984.[477] It's provisions served as the international framework within which China constructed its internal One Country Two Systems constitutional order. The Sino-British Joint Declaration, then, had both external and internal dimensions. And it tied together the two states that had been in a dynamic relation about the sovereignty (and control) of portions of the Pearl River Delta since the first third of the 19th century.

The Sino-British Joint Declaration consisted of a short main section of eight articles, and three substantive annexes. It's formal international character as treaty was emphasized by the formalities of its construction and ultimately of its deposit into the authenticating vaults of the United Nations in New York. It promised many things, but the principal one perhaps was that all promises were to terminate half a century from its signing. In a sense, then, the Sino-British Joint Declaration promised immediate sovereignty and eventual control. It set the tone for what was to become the One Country Two Systems Principle through the notion of a "high degree of autonomy" for Hong Kong (through 2047) and specified in some details the structures within which that autonomy would be maintained. It also embedded an international element with a mechanism for Sino-UK consultation the greatest utility of which ended with the transfer of 1997. As we are now discovering in the face of the clash between China's New Era political-economic model (along with its Xi Jinping Theory of Socialist (Positive Values) Empire and popular demonstrations (with an audience of sympathetic international actors) grounded in the values of post 1945 international imperialism (the vanguard role of the international community under the core leadership of the victorious allies emerging after 1945) has both brought the ambiguities of the

---

[477] Sino British Joint Declaration, *supra*.

Sino-British Joint Declaration to light and suggested its contradictions in the face of crisis.

But in many ways the new era of relations between China, the international community, international legal structures, and more specifically the United Kingdom has changed dramatically. China has sought to dump the Sino-British Joint Declaration on the trash heap of history and to attempt to pry Hong Kong out from its status as an international protectorate. The United States (and less the UK) have sought to revivify its terms both in the service of classical international law and its post 1945 great principles, and at the same time further their respective national interests. This clash notoriously erupted in public during the 2017 commemoration of the ceding of sovereignty over Hong Kong from the UK to China.[478]

The US noted its own reading of the meaning of the One Country Two Systems Principle as one grounded in international law with respect to which the international community was entitled to monitor and engage in its legitimate enforcement. The UK through Boris Johnson praised the then current state of affairs but noted the need as well to move One Country Two systems toward a greater degree of democratic and accountable government in Hong Kong measured by international standards which were built into Hong Kong's constitutional model. In effect,

---

[478] "China's Xi talks tough on Hong Kong as thousands protest for democracy," NBC (1 July 2017); available [https://www.cnbc.com/2017/07/01/chinas-xi-talks-tough-on-hong-kong-as-thousands-protest-for-democracy.html] (Chinese President Xi Jinping swore in Hong Kong's new leader on Saturday with a stark warning that Beijing won't tolerate any challenge to its authority in the divided city as it marked the 20th Anniversary of its return from Britain to China. . . "Any attempt to endanger China's sovereignty and security, challenge the power of the central government ... or use Hong Kong to carry out infiltration and sabotage activities against the mainland is an act that crosses the red line and is absolutely impermissible," Xi said.). Contrast Richard C. Bush, "Hong Kong: Twenty Years After Reversion," Brookings (16 October 2017); available [https://www.brookings.edu/on-the-record/hong-kong-twenty-years-after-reversion/] (describing sovereignty constrained by international law which might eb applicable to the status of Hong Kong). For a discussion from the time of the beginning of the current arrangement, see William H. Overholt, "Hong Kong and the Crisis of Sovereignty," *Asian Survey* 24(4):471-484 (1984). .

both states, following traditional models of international law, viewed Hong Kong's status as one that touched both on China's sovereign prerogatives, and on China's ceding of some of the prerogatives of control in return for a ceding to it of sovereignty over territory. Sovereignty then could be disaggregated, like other forms of property--distinguishing between control and territory. In effect, what both the UK and US noted was the disconnection between sovereignty and control. In this case control was ceded willingly in exchange for territorial sovereignty--and the international community had the documents to prove it.

After the publication of remarks by the UK and US governments on the anniversary of the ceding of Hong Kong, China responded in perhaps too honest a way: "The Chinese Foreign Ministry has declared the Sino-British Joint Declaration, that laid the groundwork for Hong Kong's handover, a "historical document that no longer has any realistic meaning", after Britain and the United States spoke of the binding effect of the 1984 treaty on China and the city. [479] "The Foreign Ministry Statement was eventually "clarified." Yet the essence of the statement appeared to survive except in the rarified world of diplomatic nuance.

> "He [Lu Kang Foreign Ministry Spokesperson] said 'it no longer has realistic meaning'. This is understandable when we look at the issue against the background that some country was trying to use the joint declaration for pointing fingers," Xu said. "But we have never denied the fact that the joint declaration is a treaty." While acknowledging the document registered with the United Nations was "not without [legally] binding effect", he

---

[479] Joyce Ng, "Sino-British Joint Declaration on Hong Kong 'no longer has any realistic meaning', Chinese Foreign Ministry says," South China Morning Post (30 June 2017); available [https://www.scmp.com/news/hong-kong/politics/article/2100779/sino-british-joint-declaration-hong-kong-no-longer-has-any] ("'It also does not have any binding power on how the Chinese central government administers Hong Kong. Britain has no sovereignty, no governing power and no supervising power over Hong Kong. I hope relevant parties will take note of this reality.'" Ibid., quoting Lu Kang Foreign Ministry Spokesperson)).

pointed out that its main text only mentioned Britain would "restore" Hong Kong to China, but included no provision for its rights and responsibilities after the handover.[480]

This was made clear at the time of the 2017 commemoration, when Xi Jinping also sought to re-center the meaning of the Sino-British Joint Declaration from one that emphasized its international character (and the *sharing of sovereignty*) to one that emphasized its domestic character (and the *transfer sovereignty*).[481] Xi Jinping's emphasis was the same as that raised more bluntly by the Chinese foreign ministry but the message was the same—to the extent there was an international element within the relationship of the central authorities and Hong Kong it was to be understood as an internal matter of empire rather than as an external matter of international protectorate.

In his remarks Xi Jinping emphasized four critical points. First he inverted the relationship between the Sino-British Joint Declaration's structure of the relationship between Hong Kong and the central government. For him it was critical to understand that the Sino-British Joint Declaration must be read in the light of the One Country Two Systems principle rather than the other way around. As a central element of this position was the development of a "correct" understanding of One Country Two Systems as grounded in the relationship between the central government and its territories rather than the embedding of international expectation about the ordering of a dependency through the structures of international agreement. He thus sought to transform the international character of Hong Kong (through 2047 at least) into one of a domestic (imperial)order in which the central authorities reserved to themselves the power to organize

---

480 "Beijing: Hong Kong Handover Treaty Still Binding," China Digital Times (11 July 2017); available [https://chinadigitaltimes.net/2017/07/beijing-says-sino-british-treaty-hk-handover-still-binding/] (quoting Xu Hong, director general of the Chinese foreign ministry's treaty and law department)).

481 "Full text of President Xi Jinping's speech on 'one country, two systems' and how China rules Hong Kong," South China Morning Post (1 July 2017); available [https://www.scmp.com/news/hong-kong/politics/article/2100856/full-text-president-xi-jinpings-speech-one-country-two].

and order the relations between itself and its territories. Second, that ordering was to be implemented in accordance with the constitutional documents of the central authorities rather than by reference to international instruments. Third, that for the central authorities the animating objective of the "two systems" portion of the principle was to ensure development (a modified application of the socialist modernization which anchored the Hong Kong variant within the Pearl River amalgam). And fourth that this two system model could only survive as long as a "harmonious and stable social environment" was maintained.

At the time the war of words was more rhetorical and abstract than anything else—provided for the amusement of the ruling castes of all stakeholders as they sought to play to internal and external audiences to further their own interests, all of which were complex. But the fuss has taken on a much more important character with the evolving situation in Hong Kong. The central authorities have sought to transform the Sino-British Joint Declaration's international supervision into the allegation of black hand interference or colonialism with increasingly less persuasive allusions to the weakness of China by reference to its decrepit Manchu era government[482] The UK (and more potently the US) have sought to emphasize the international protectorate obligations in the Joint Declaration as a means of ensuring that the governmental framework it crafted remains undisturbed (at least until 2047).

Nonetheless let us consider the Sino-British Joint Declaration on the broader context of Empire.

1. To some extent, the central authorities are now implementing Xi Jinping's "New Era" vision of the One Country-Two Systems principle in relation to Hong Kong. What the situation in Hong Kong has done is to accelerate central authority planning for the eventual incorporation of Hong Kong within its political and economic model.

---

[482] See, Chapters 7 and 9, supra.

2. But formalities are still important. It will be for the authorities in Hong Kong to seek the aid of the central authorities. But Hong Kong authorities will also be expected under One Country Two Systems to petition the central authorities for help. That help need not come in the form of direct intervention by force, but will come from "support" for actions developed under the leadership of the central authorities (the arrests of leaders of the protests; the identification of foreign elements in Hong Kong government and culture, and the planning for the excision of both).

3. In this context, the Sino-British Joint Declaration will retain its formal authority as a treaty. In that sense it will continue to be respected as an obligation of the central authorities in international law. But those obligations are increasingly viewed as fulfilled. And once fulfilled, the binding hold on the treaty itself fades into history. It is for that reason, in part, that the central authorities view continued international interest in Hong Kong as an illegal interference since whatever obligation it might have had under the Sino-British Joint Declaration have passed. Western states, global civil society elements and others, of course, take the opposite view. And both tend to advance their views with increasing force.

4. The central authority's position on the Sino-British Joint Declaration suggest its view on the construction of a double imperialism theory. One is external and the other is internal. *Externally*, the construction of the post 1945 global order and its principles of international law is bound up in the power of the community of states led by its leadership core (one can quibble over membership in the core but not into its existence) represents a new stage in imperial organization. This emerging stage recasts imperialism as a positive force shedding the now historically obsolete and debilitating elements of pre-1945 internationalism that had been grounded primarily in military force, racism, ethno-centrism, and (at least overt) exploitation. But even this emerging new form global imperial system is thought to reflect the values and cultures of both liberal democracy and markets-based capitalism. To that extent, certainly, new counter imperial models must be created, including perhaps a socialist model. *Internally*, the construction of regional and ideological coherent sovereignty

and control-based relationships among sub-communities of states (and ethnicities) represents a new form of imperial organization that now seeks to development win-win structures of solidarity on the basis of mutual interest contextually based on power relations. That system, in turn, requires the acknowledgement of a core state (e.g., China or the U.S.) as a hub from out of which spokes can be developed that brings within the collective all states and other actors who converge around a singular vision of relations (in whole or in part) built on economics (Belt and Road Initiative; America First, etc.) or otherwise.

5. New Era imperial order has an internal and an external element. The periphery of the core (hub) of the New Era imperial system is built around autonomous regions each of which is accorded a distinct range of flexibility depending on context. These are ordered within the language of sovereignty and internal constitutionalism. Beyond the internal periphery of the core are the spoke relations with states with various degrees of dependence on the core. These are ordered within the language of extra-sovereign instruments—contract (Memoranda of understanding and other instruments; loan and economic exploitation agreements etc.); and are formally international legal instruments. The extent of dependency and control depends on the relationship of the dependency to the core. Hong Kong falls well within the periphery of the core and is thus adjudged as an internal matter for the system of sovereignty and control that is the new form of empire.

6. Given this conceptual framework, it is unlikely that the central authorities will deviate from its development of a notion that all foreign interventions must be opposed. More importantly it will accelerate a progress of de-culturalization in which Hong Kong will lose its hybrid character and increasingly adopt the custom and practices of a peripheral territory of the core. This is particularly true with respect to the Twelve Core Socialist Values and the relationship of the economic and political model of this core-periphery to the core itself. In this context, the situation in Hong Kong serves as affirmation of the dangers of internationalization on the two levels of foreign interference and cultural development. It is in this context that all protest can be

re-framed as the expression of the foreign, and all deviation increasingly as a bacillus that threatens the economic and political order of the core.

7. But, because the territory is still peripheral and a bridge to other spoke-hub empires, the way in which Hong Kong will be disciplined will be contextually distinct. This is not the Turkish periphery. Hong Kong's history will likely produce the foundation for its further incorporation.

8. It is worth remembering that 2047 is not too far off. And that the only thing of consequence that may survive this long and drawn out transformation are the conceptual theories of empire which it has helped produce. That, at least is one way of looking at the end of the formal term of the Sino-British Joint Declaration.

9. And yet, that is the ultimate twist to the internationalist position of empire. One Country-Two Systems can survive the Sino-British Joint Declaration. First as a matter of its own internal model, the central authorities could decide to perpetuate the system, but now backed solely by domestic law. That, in a sense is where Chinese authorities already suggest is the current state of "law" respecting Hong Kong. The difficulty, for those protesting now, is that such a system, and its characteristics, would be entirely dependent on central authorities. Here, in terms of empire, the central authorities could continue to treat Hong Kong as a primary or mediating dependency--a special trade zone through which international contact could be funneled in special ways. More intriguing is the view from the other side--the idea that the Sino-British Joint Declaration effectively created a permanent international city, one that guaranteed to the people of Hong Kong the right of self-government within China but accountable to the international community. Note the difference here gauged by degrees of sovereignty: the people of Hong Kong under this view have no right of self-determination; rather they have a right of self-government within China, the boundaries of which are to be determined by international rather than national constraints.

10. It is likely that this possibility, the aim to make the realities of an internationalized One Country- Two Systems permanent in the form memorialized in the Sino-British Joint Declaration, that causes the Chinese central authorities the greatest worry and poses to their own ideal of imperial order the greatest threat. The question is to what extent do the Hong Kong protestors think this possible, or think this at all; to what extent is the international community willing to make good on this promise with more than words uttered at fancy meetings of high stats people? The Chinese central authorities are banking on the likelihood that the protestors are incapable and the international community too timid, to make good on this. Are they right?

$$* \; * \; *$$

Chapter 15

Tuesday 18 September 2019
"Two Systems" Internationalism: Congressional-Executive Commission on China Hearings on "Hong Kong's Summer of Discontent and U.S. Policy Responses"

The Congressional-Executive Commission on China was created by the U.S. Congress in 2000 "with the legislative mandate[483] to monitor human rights and the development of the rule of law in China, and to submit an annual report to the President and the Congress. The Commission consists of nine Senators, nine Members of the House of Representatives, and five senior Administration officials appointed by the President." [484] The authorizing legislation mandates the CECC to monitor compliance with human rights and the development of rule of law, to prepare a victims list of human rights defenders, encourage bilateral cooperation, and develop contacts with non-governmental organizations.[485] They have developed positions on a number of issues but grounded in the sensibilities of Western liberal democratic internationalism.

The CECC recognizes that only the Chinese people can decide China's direction and future, and that the United

---

[483] Congressional-Executive Commission on the People's Republic Of China, Hr 4444 ¶¶ 301-309 (106th Cong., 2nd Sess (2000)) (To authorize extension of nondiscriminatory treatment (normal trade relations treatment) to the People's Republic of China, and to establish a framework for relations between the United... (Enrolled as Agreed to or Passed by Both House and Senate)); available [https://www.govinfo.gov/content/pkg/BILLS-106hr4444eh/pdf/BILLS-106hr4444eh.pdf].

[484] Congressional-Executive Commission on the People's Republic Of China, CECC About, available [https://www.cecc.gov/about]. The CECC website's "Frequently Asked Questions (FAQs) page provide useful information about the CECC. See Congressional-Executive Commission on the People's Republic Of China, Frequently Asked Questions; available [https://www.cecc.gov/about/frequently-asked-questions].

[485] Hr 4444, supra, ¶¶ 302.

States cannot impose its will on the 1.3 billion citizens of the PRC. The Universal Declaration of Human Rights, which both China and the United States took part in drafting, the International Covenant on Civil and Political Rights and the International Covenant on Economic, Social and Cultural Rights set high human rights standards for all nations. The CECC seeks to encourage the Chinese Government to respect the rights that China's own constitution and laws guarantee to the Chinese people, and to bring its governmental practices into conformity with the international human rights standards. The Commission does not seek to impose U.S. standards on China.[486]

These are the sensibilities that underlie both the international community's approach to the protests in Hong Kong and to its own perceptions about the status of Hong Kong. It is grounded in a normative internationalism memorialized in hard and soft law produced by and through the U.N. and regional systems of state collectives that present both collective normative authority and a set of constraints on national action.[487] That grounding is meant to produce the ideal toward which all states aspire and with respect to which all states have a duty to help one another attain. In some respects, it provides the mirror image of the Marxist internationalism emerging in its forms in the New Era of Chinese historical development under Xi Jinping (sometimes referenced as "socialist internationalism"[488] and more traditionally in Western

---

[486] Congressional-Executive Commission on the People's Republic Of China, Frequently Asked Questions (What right does the United States have to examine human rights practices in China?); available [https://www.cecc.gov/about/frequently-asked-questions].

[487] Discussed in the context of transnational constitutionalism in Larry Catá Backer, "God(s) Over Constitution: Transnational Constitutionalism in the 21st Century," *Mississippi College Law Review* 27:11 (2008).

[488] Not to be confused with the Socialist International, an organization of like-minded collectives dedicated to the establishment of democratic socialism in the states of their residence or activity. It was established as a successor to the Labor and Socialist International in 1951 in Germany. See the website of the Socialist International; available [https://www.socialistinternational.org/].

Marxist thought as proletarian internationalism). [489] For that reason it has produced--though very late given the transparency of this process, fear and caution on the part of vanguard elements of the liberal democratic camp.[490]

CECC tends to serve as an excellent barometer of the thinking of political and academic elites in the United States about issues touching on China and the official American line developed in connection with those issues. CECC becomes an even more important barometer of coherence and fracture in policy approaches as the discipline of activities between the political parties and the President and Legislature fractures in new and dynamic ways. As such it is an important source of information about the way official and academic sectors think about China. As one can imagine many of the positions of the CECC are critical of current Chinese policies and institutions. More importantly, CECC's cultivation of key actors, especially around the peripheries of Chinese political discourse, has provided a key connection between Chinese actors and the dialogues and perspectives of western liberal internationalism grounded in a specific reading of international human rights law and norms.

---

[489] Xi Jinping, "Secure a Decisive Victory in Building a Moderately Prosperous Society in All Respects and Strive for the Great Success of Socialism with Chinese Characteristics for a New Era (18 October 2017); available [http://www.xinhuanet.com/english/download/Xi_Jinping's_report_at_19th_C PC_National_Congress.pdf] ("Chinese socialism's entrance into a new era is, in the history of the development of the People's Republic of China and the history of the development of the Chinese nation, of tremendous importance. In the history of the development of international socialism and the history of the development of human society, It is of tremendous importance."). See also, Larry Catá Backer, "Toward New Era Thought: Reflections on Xi Jinping, Speech at the Meeting Celebrating the 40th Anniversary of Reform and Opening Up," *Emancipating the Mind in the New Era: Bulletin of the Coalition for Peace & Ethics* 15(1):121-144 (2020); available [https://www.thecpe.org/wp-content/uploads/2020/04/15-1_FINAL_Pt_C_5_Comment_XiJinping_Speech_Backer.pdf].

[490] Cf., Daniel Tobin, testimony submitted to the U.S.-China Economic and Security Review Commission's postponed hearing on "A 'China Model?' Beijing's Promotion of Alternative Global Norms and Standards" 13 March 2020; available [https://www.uscc.gov/sites/default/files/testimonies/SFR%20for%20USCC %20TobinD%2020200313.pdf].

The CECC has made its position clear with respect to the situation in Hong Kong, and of the yardstick by which it will seek to measure Chinese responses. U.S. Representative James McGovern (D-MA) and U.S. Senator Marco Rubio (R-FL), the Chair and Cochair respectively of the bipartisan and bicameral Congressional-Executive Commission on China (CECC), issued a joint statement urging action by President Trump at the 2019 G7 meetings to press what they believed to be U.S. and international community interests in Hong Kong's autonomy.

> "At the G-7 summit this weekend, President Trump should raise the ongoing threats to Hong Kong's autonomy, human rights, and fundamental freedoms in discussions with other world leaders. The President and the international community should make clear that Beijing is expected to fully abide by the terms and the spirit of the 1984 Sino-British Joint Declaration, a legally binding treaty, and that intervention by mainland Chinese authorities against peaceful protesters in Hong Kong would further damage China's bilateral and multilateral relationships. U.S. and global interests are at stake if Hong Kong's autonomy continues to erode. Chairman Xi Jinping should understand that his government's willingness to uphold its international commitments will have a direct bearing on whether any agreements with Beijing, especially on trade, can ever be trusted."[491]

In connection with these events, CECC organized a hearing on the situation in Hong Kong. Held on 17 September 2019, CECC brought to Washington some of the key actors representing the protestors and others. "This hearing will examine developments in Hong Kong and the future of U.S.-Hong Kong relations in light of the ongoing demonstrations and the escalating tensions caused by police violence and threats by the Chinese government against

---

[491] "Hong Kong: Joint Statement by the Chairs Before the G7 Meetings in France"

Hong Kong's autonomy."[492] They include Joshua Wong: Secretary-General of 香港眾志 (Demosistō)[493] and "Umbrella Movement" Leader; Denise Ho: Pro-democracy Activist and Cantopop Singer and Actress; and Sunny Cheung: Spokesperson, Hong Kong Higher Education International Affairs Delegation (HKIAD).

It is in hearings such as this that one can better understand the character of the ideological positions of those who, having started with the idea of protesting limited expressions of what they viewed as threatening interference in Hong Kong autonomy, now understand the contest for control of the meaning of sovereignty within the context of Hong Kong. For internationalists the position is becoming clearer as against that of Chinese officials. While Chinese officials view sovereignty as undivided and subject to revocable agreements grounded in short term pragmatic considerations, internationalists view the construction of Hong Kong as an important outpost for post-global polycentric sovereignty.[494]

For the internationalist community, China's unitary view of sovereignty reflects the great defects of the reactionary views of the state that does not take into account the transformations made possible and necessary) by the porosity of borders that mark the realities of post 1945 globalization. No state has complete sovereignty, in the sense of control of people, gods, capital, and the like. But like property, sovereignty can be infinitely divided shared and exercise simultaneously--wholly and partially, as it suits the tastes of the international community. And it has suited the tastes of the international community to

---

[492] CECC, Program: Hong Kong's Summer of Discontent and U.S. Policy Responses (17 September 2019); available [https://www.cecc.gov/events/hearings/hong-kongs-summer-of-discontent-and-us-policy-responses].

[493] Postscript: Demosistō was a pro-democracy political organization founded in 2016 by Nathan Law, Joshua Wong, and Agnes Chow which collapsed shortly after the passage of the Hong Kong National Security Law in June 2020. See Aiden Jonah, "US-backed HK political party, Demosistō, collapses as China takes firm steps to prevent second colonization," The Canada Files (4 July 2020); available [https://www.thecanadafiles.com/articles/hkdosis].

[494] This was considered form the Chinese perspective in the essay at Chapter 14, supra.

increasingly constrain that sovereignty within a cage of regulation. The Sino-British Joint Declaration provides a template of a very specific kind--the vesting of territorial sovereignty in one state while detaching governance power rom that grant of sovereignty. It is in this sense that Hong Kong is a part of China (One Country) but also that its organization and political system are the product of international agreement and founded on international and customary law and norms (Two Systems).

Here, at last, one can begin to tease out the ideological position of both the Hong Kong protestors and of the international community. The alignment of these two groups is critical; some in the Hong Kong protest community may reasonably believe that the support of the international community can better advance their cause, even against the Chinese central authorities. That support might be made more powerful through an alignment of ideological approaches to the construction of a legally legitimate position on Hong Kong autonomy. The way that aligned ideological and discursive position is an important development, especially where it is expressed by Hong Kong protest leaders and among their U.S. friends. The key question, then, is whether this developing position may be as effectively deployed as the opposing ideological position developed by the Chinese authorities in the weeks after the start of the protests in June 2019.[495] To that end it is worth untangling the statements of each of the participants in the 17 September 2019 CECC program.

The statements of the CECC co-chairs, Senator Marco Rubio and Representative James McGovern set the tone and describe the space within which the internationalist perspective emerges. Representative McGovern underlined the internationalist perspective of shared sovereignty: "The "one country, two systems" framework was enshrined in the 1984 Sino-British Declaration and Hong Kong's Basic Law. This is an international treaty, signed by the Chinese government, to allow Hong Kong a "high degree of autonomy" with the "ultimate aim" of electing its Chief Executive and Legislative Council members by

---

[495] Discussed in the essays at Chapters 3-5; 7-8, supra.

universal suffrage." [496] He noted that from the internationalist baseline, it has been Chinese interreference--and its increasingly aggressive efforts to substitute itself for the international consensus agreement on the rules for governing Hong Kong--that, rightfully, led its people to protest (acts protected under international law and norms enshrined in Hong Kong's governance system through the Sino-British Joint Declaration). [497]

McGovern then placed the protests in a much wider context: "While the protests were sparked by concerns about the extradition bill, the heart of the discontent is that Hong Kong's political leaders do not represent and are not accountable to the people." [498] It was then up to the international community to protect the internationally guaranteed rights represented by the Hong Kong people who have taken to the streets. [499] Like the Chinese central authorities, Representative McGovern tied the two systems element of Hong Kong governance to the overall principles of stability and prosperity.[500] The emphasis here is that Hong Kong's prosperity is grounded in its international normative connections; interference will damage that without a viable substitute.[501]

---

[496] Statement of Rep. James P. McGovern, Chairman of the Congressional-Executive Commission on China (CECC) CECC Hearing on "Hong Kong's Summer of Discontent and U.S. Policy" (17 September 17, 2019); available [https://www.cecc.gov/sites/chinacommission.house.gov/files/documents/Hong%20Kong%20Sept%20Hearing%20Opening%20Statement%209-16-19_0.pdf].

[497] Ibid. ("The 2014 "Umbrella Movement" protests were sparked by the Chinese government reneging on its commitments to make Hong Kong more democratic").

[498] Ibid.

[499] Ibid. ("In light of the continuing erosion of Hong Kong's autonomy and the recent violence against peaceful protesters, I believe it is time for the United States to reconsider its policies toward Hong Kong.").

[500] Ibid. (I hope the Chinese government would understand that stability and prosperity can be achieved if Hong Kong's autonomy is respected).

[501] Ibid. ("Over the years, Hong Kong has prospered and become the financial center of Asia because of its strong commitment to the rule of law, good governance, human rights, and open economic system.").

Marco Rubio amplified these points in his own statement.[502] He emphasized the disproportionate responses of the local authorities against the protestors.[503] The object was similar to that employed by the Chinese authorities; Senator Rubio sought to paint the authorities as lawless and criminal.[504] So characterized, their political objectives might be painted with the same brush.[505] This is analogous to the Chinese efforts to do the same with the protestors.[506] Not only are the central authorities wrong on the legal basis for their actions but they appear ready to employ criminal methods to push forward their objectives. That delegitimization effort then extends to the effort to shift the debate from Two Systems to One Country.

> The actions of the government and of the people demonstrate that there are two Hong Kongs. The Hong Kong of the government, totally leveraged by the Chinese government, has proven that it's not committed to a free and autonomous future for Hong Kong, nor is it one of rule of law or of justice. The other Hong Kong, the real one, is the one of its people: the students, and youth activists, artists, journalists, doctors and nurses, lawyers, accountants, business people —from every walk of life. . . It is clear that these two very different Hong Kongs are colliding, and therefore the city is at a crossroads. . . Hong Kong's status as an international trade and

---

[502] Statement of Senator Marco Rubio, Chairman of the Congressional-Executive Commission on China (CECC) CECC Hearing on "Hong Kong's Summer of Discontent and U.S. Policy" (17 September 17, 2019); available [https://www.cecc.gov/sites/chinacommission.house.gov/files/documents/Ru bio%20Hearing%20Statement-- Hong%20Kong%27s%20Summer%20of%20Discontent.pdf].

[503] Ibid. ("there have been very credible reports that have emerged of the police's brutal treatment of demonstrators while in their custody. This weekend for example we saw images of the police holding down a protester whose head was bleeding and spraying into the wound on the head, pepper spray, which is an act of total cruelty.").

[504] Contrast the official Chinese position discussed at Chapter 5, supra.

[505] Ibid. ("he government's violent response to the demonstrations demands accountability. And yet, Lam and the Hong Kong government refuses to press for any accountability for the violence by Hong Kong's security forces that was committed and continues to be committed against peaceful protesters.").

[506] Discussed in essays Chapters 3-5, supra.

investment hub are just as threatened as long as the long-cherished freedoms of the Hong Kong people are being threatened. Threatened, by the way, not by us, but by the Communist Party of China.

And there it is. Like Representative McGovern, Senator Rubio is pressing for a US legislative response, in the form of the Hong Kong Human Rights and Democracy Act.[507] And as a perfect book end to the Chinese position, Senator Rubio declares: "Hong Kong is not a Chinese internal affair and the world has a responsibility to help the people of Hong Kong move towards a future that protects their individual freedoms and provides for civic well-being."[508]

Joshua Wong's statement nicely evidenced the transnational intertwining that give the internationalist position its theoretical authority, but that at the same time exposes its weaknesses in the face of the traditional advantages of sovereignty over territory.[509] Mr. Wong is no stranger to the CECC. He appeared before the CECC in 2017 in connection with hearings about the effects of Chinese interference in the internal affairs of Hong Kong in ways that threatened its international commitments and the internationally framed status of Hong Kong.[510] Here again one ought to be sensitive to the way in which the same concepts and tactics form mirror images of each other. Since well before the 2019 protests, the international community has sought to preserve the Two systems portion of the framework for the autonomy of Hong Kong against the interreference of China. China, in turn, has sought to advance the One Country portion of

---

507 Ibid.
508 Ibid.
509 Testimony of Joshua Wong, CECC Hearing on "Hong Kong's Summer of Discontent and U.S. Policy" (17 September 17, 2019); available [https://www.cecc.gov/sites/chinacommission.house.gov/files/documents/Joshua%20Wong%20C.E.C.C.%20Testimony%20-%20Sept.%2017%202019.pdf].
510 See Karen Cheung, "Hong Kong's 'One Country, Two Systems' agreement 'increasingly uncertain' in long-term, says US Congress Commission," Hong Kong Free Press (6 October 20187); available [https://hongkongfp.com/2017/10/06/hong-kongs-one-country-two-systems-agreement-increasingly-uncertain-long-term-says-us-congress-commission/].

the framework by arguing with increasing vigor against international interference.

He began by recalling his time before the Committee in 2017 when he warned the international minders of Hong Kong's autonomy of the potential challenges gathering force.[511] He then made his critical point--it was impossible for the central authorities to honor a system essentially incompatible with their own. [512] A limited tolerance might have been necessary on pragmatic grounds when it served to smooth the return of Hong Kong. But that done, only pragmatic calculation was left to determine when and under what circumstances those pragmatic necessities could be abandoned. In the context the central authorities might accomplish two things--first the return of sovereign control of Hong Kong; and second the investing of international law with Chinese characteristics. He spoke to the power of demonstration--to the exercise of civil and political rights as those are understood in liberal democratic states: "And then the unthinkable happened: Knowing that Beijing controlled enough votes in the Legislative Council, protesters surrounded the complex early in the morning, successfully preventing lawmakers from convening." [513] There are fine lines here--and drawing them can be difficult. Chinese officials and local Hong Kong officials complained about the lawlessness of the tactics. Liberal democratic factions tend to draw the line at violence, sometimes as law breaking (but that is impossible in light of the hagiographies of the US civil rights movement from the 1950s on). That was not, however, something to trouble oneself over very much in this case and in this room. And in this case there was a difference underlined by Joshua Wong as well as Senator Rubio-the disproportionate lawlessness of the authorities and their purported hirelings.

---

[511] Testimony of Joshua Wong, *supra* ("At the time, I warned about the probable disqualification of my friend Nathan Law, who had been Asia's youngest democratically-elected legislator and who is in the audience this morning. I also warned about massive political prosecution.").

[512] Ibid. ("The present state of affairs reveals Beijing's utter inability to understand, let alone govern, a free society").

[513] Ibid.

The movement reached a turning point on July 21. That night, thugs with suspected ties to organized crime gathered in the Yuen Long train station and indiscriminately attacked not just protesters returning home, reporters on the scene, but even passersby. The police refused to show up despite repeated emergency calls, plunging Hong Kong into a state of anarchy and mob violence.[514]

This is a critical passage. It resonates with the central authorities' core discursive point--that the protests are threatening the prosperity and stability of Hong Kong. Here, Joshua Wong turns that around and suggests that indeed Hong Kong's stability and prosperity are threatened, but by the actions of the local authorities and their agents. It is the lawlessness of the authorities that drive the protests.[515] Wong then points to the complicity of liberal democratic states--and certainly the craven disregard of human rights by enterprises enjoying all of the advantages of the systems that protect its liberties on global markets.[516]

"American companies mustn't profit from the violent crackdown of freedom-loving Hong Kongers."[517] But that is the Achilles heel--the critical point of weakness--of the globalization-based internationalist position. While international law and norms may bind, the logics of markets and production chains can as easily underline *de facto* what the systems and institutions it has built *de jure*. This is not just a problem for Hong Kong, but generally where there are misalignments between the realities of economic activity across borders--and the political control of markets--and the architecture and normative substance of

---

[514] Ibid.

[515] Ibid. ("On August 5 alone, the day Hong Kongers participated in a general strike, the police shot 800 canisters of tear gas to disperse the masses. Compare that to only 87 fired in the entire Umbrella Movement five years ago, and the police's excessive force today is clear").

[516] Ibid. ("Their increasingly liberal use of pepper spray, pepper balls, rubber bullets, sponge bullets, bean bag rounds, and water cannons — almost all of which are imported from Western democracies — are no less troubling").

[517] Ibid.

international principles. Indeed, Wong noted other misalignments as well, misalignments also made powerful within the logic of markets-based globalization, and the essence of its own current contradiction: "Beijing shouldn't have it both ways, reaping all the economic benefits of Hong Kong's standing in the world while eradicating our sociopolitical identity."[518]

Lastly, Wong noted the way that law itself can serve as its own subversion in the face of the actions of a faction of officials who appear intent on working against the rule of law through law itself. In this case, the arguments of illegality on which the local and central authorities base their construction of lawlessness against the protestors, and then use it to excise them from the authentic and patriotic body politic are produced by the very forces of the state itself: "Authorities have all but stopped issuing permits known as "letters of no objection," so virtually every demonstration is an 'illegal assembly.'"[519]

But arguments grounded in legality also have to face the inevitable legalities of the Sino-British Joint Declaration, and especially its 2047 end date. For that, he has nothing to say but this: "hat deadline is closer to us than it appears; there's no return."[520] Yet if there is no return, and there is only 2019 as a watershed, to what ends is the course of the future to be directed if not to One Country? The answer appears to be direct foreign intervention--the need for internationalists to protect their interests directly, grounded not so much in the text of the Sin-British Joint Declaration but in its spirit, and in the substantial potential negative effects on human rights of a move that would strip Hong Kong of its civil and political culture. And there it is--the Sino-British Joint Declaration has created a space protected by international law for the distinctive culture of Hong Kong to flourish. Once well established, interference with this distinctive culture might also be a gross violation of international human rights law and norms--even if the effects occur after 2047.

---

[518] Ibid.
[519] Ibid.
[520] Ibid.

It is this last point that was well underscored during the testimony of Denise Ho.[521] "This is a plea for universal human rights. This is a plea for democracy. This is a plea for the freedom to choose... This is a global fight for the universal values that we all cherish, and Hong Kong is in the very frontlines of this fight."[522] She notes the character of the One Country-Two Systems principle as carrying within it the contradictions of two opposing imperial systems: "If Hong Kong falls, it would easily become the springboard for the totalitarian regime of China to push its rules and priorities overseas, utilizing its economic powers to conform others to their communists values, just as they have done with Hong Kong in the past 22 years."[523]

Like Joshua Wong, Denise Ho is careful to tie the protests in Hong Kong to notions of mass democracy and popular expression one without the need for a vanguard party.[524] From a Chinese Marxist-Leninist perspective it is something of a slap. Another slap aimed in the direction of the central authorities--the intimation that Chinese authorities could not even get the "mass line" right. And like Joshua Wong, Denise Ho emphasized the lawlessness of the police action. The object, of course, is the same as that of the central authorities but with a different target: to challenge the authority and legitimacy of their actions and thus the cause those actions sought to further.[525] But more than that, the testimony sought to suggest intent--this was not passions out of control but a deliberate policy of strategic aggression--at least from the perspective of the normative practices of liberal

---

[521] Testimony of Denise Ho, CECC Hearing on "Hong Kong's Summer of Discontent and U.S. Policy" (17 September 17, 2019); available [https://www.cecc.gov/sites/chinacommission.house.gov/files/documents/Denise%20Ho_CECC%20179%20Testimony_Final.pdf].

[522] Ibid.

[523] Ibid.

[524] Ibid. ("It is a leaderless movement, with widespread participation from people of all walks of life.").

[525] Ibid. ("Since June, the Hong Kong police has shown excessive brutality in their use of force, arresting and beating up peaceful protesters heavily at uncountable occasions. More than 1400 people have been arrested up to date, with even more (including journalists, first aiders and social workers) severely injured by tear gas, rubber bullets, water cannons, and the police's indiscriminate use of batons.").

democratic states.[526] And it included an intent to subvert the rule of law: "On August 11th, police obstructed pro bono lawyers from providing legal assistance to arrested protesters in the Sun Uk Ling Holding Center, violating the legal rights of 54 persons."[527]

It remains only to reassert the point made earlier by Joshua Wong:

> But at the core, it has always been about fundamental conflicts between these two very different set of values : on one side, the China model, which has no respect over human rights and rule of law, and demands for their people's submission. And the other, a hybrid city that has enjoyed these freedoms for the most of its existence, with a deep attachment to these universal values that the United States and other western societies are also endeared to.[528]

That hybridity is then taken as the reason for the stability and prosperity of Hong Kong--an international hybrid city; Danzig on the South China Sea.[529]

To this, the testimony of Sunny Cheung added the fears of absorption into the greater Pearl River basin metropolitan area.[530] Again the issues of police brutality, of the development of the

---

[526] Ibid. ("From the early weeks, they have deliberately hidden their ID numbers, refused to show warrant cards even on request, therefore making it impossible for citizens to verify the legitimacy of plainclothes officers, nor to hold any police officer accountable for their violations.").

[527] Ibid.

[528] Ibid.

[529] Ibid. ("Hong Kong has become one of the most globally interconnected, financially important trading economies in the world, helping bring countries closer together through finance and today, the flow of data, goods, ideas, culture and people.").

[530] Testimony of Sunny Cheung, CECC Hearing on "Hong Kong's Summer of Discontent and U.S. Policy" (17 September 17, 2019); available [https://www.cecc.gov/sites/chinacommission.house.gov/files/documents/CECC%20Written%20Statement%20Sunny%20Cheung.pdf] ("Hong Kong is gradually become more and more like China. The grand plan and ambition of the Greater Bay Area project is to completely erase our identity as Hong Kongers").

unique and international character of the political culture of the city, and of the bad faith of the local government were stressed.[531] But also here a plea for protection--especially for protestors and a request that US legislative responses, especially in the form of the Hong Kong Human Rights and Responsibility Act would be put forward.[532] And lastly, the special status of Hong Kong as an international city--beyond the narrow legalities of the Sino-British Joint Declaration.[533] The last point is important, for it speaks to the possibility of the development of international cities whose autonomy can be guaranteed by the international community even if they exist formally as part of the sovereign territory of a state.[534]

Lastly, the testimony of Sharon Hom echoed much of came before. But in a more detailed way[535] But she takes a different approach--one that parallels that of the Chinese central authorities. One Country-Two Systems cannot work as a balance because its two poles are incompatible.[536] But where the Chinese central authorities then conclude on the basis of their territorial sovereignty that the inevitable result is One Country; Hom concludes that the inevitable result is Two Systems because China

---

[531] Ibid.

[532] Ibid.

[533] Ibid. ("Hong Kong is an international city, China has benefited from its special customs status, 70% foreign investment of China comes from Hong Kong. China utilizes Hong Kong to do illegal trading with North Korea and Iran and even purchases weapons from European countries which should have weapon embargo on China. Therefore, international powers also have a say in the city's future.").

[534] There are echoes here of another time and the conundrums of the international status of free cities, which was particularly relevant in the context of Danzig before 1939. See, e.g., Ian F.D. Morrow, "The International Status of the Free City of Danzig," *British Yearbook of International Law* 18:114 (1937).

[535] Testimony of Sharon Hom, CECC Hearing on "Hong Kong's Summer of Discontent and U.S. Policy" (17 September 17, 2019); available [https://www.cecc.gov/sites/chinacommission.house.gov/files/documents/H OM%20CECC%20Hearing%20Testimony%20Sep%2017_CORRECTED%20FIN AL.pdf].

[536] Ibid. ("the Hong Kong example proves that dictatorship and democracy cannot co-exist.").

ceded authority over Hong Kong's governance to the international community as the price of territorial sovereignty.[537]

This last point was also embedded in the more national security directed testimony of Daniel Garett.[538] "Xi Jinping's New Era 'One Country, Two Systems' model embracing political struggle, an enemy-friend binary, and foregrounding Chinese national security as the paramount lens for governing the Special Administrative Region and implementing 'One Country, Two Systems.'"[539] But he leaves the reader back at the initial problem--one that a few of the participants also could not get around--that all of this effort, staying true to the letter of the internationalism that secured Hong Kong's governance guarantees, dies with the Sino-British Joint Declaration in 2047.[540]

If that is the case, then one is merely gearing up for a delaying action. It is likely that there is hope that with this delay to 2047, anything can happen. What that "anything" is will likely be grounded in principles of self-determination--whether or not self-determination is tied to independence or the fracturing of sovereign authority over the SAR.[541] But it is a much weaker position than one built on the substantive right of Hong Kong to chart its own governance course under international law. And

---

[537] Ibid. ("more effective use of international normative statements and recommendations regarding Hong Kong").

[538] Testimony of Daniel Garrett, CECC Hearing on "Hong Kong's Summer of Discontent and U.S. Policy" (17 September 17, 2019); available [https://www.cecc.gov/sites/chinacommission.house.gov/files/documents/20 190917-GARRETT-Eroding%20OCTS%20HK%20Under%20NatSec-CECC%20Testimony-Sourced%20Version.pdf].

[539] Ibid.

[540] Ibid. ("Congress should pass a resolution – and encourage other nations to do the same – that unequivocally declares that implementation of "One Country, Two Systems" in Hong Kong is not the exclusive domain or the sovereign internal affairs of Communist China (until 2047) as the territory was part of the Free World and was only handed over by the United Kingdom with the understanding that the communist system would not be introduced for fifty-years.").

[541] Tim Nicholas Rühlig, "Expressing my attitude and doing something impossible to make it happen ...."– Listening to the Voices of Hong Kong's Umbrella Movement Protesters," *Contemporary Chinese Political Economy and Strategic Relations: An International Journal* 3(2):747-818 (2017) at 762-778.

there ultimately lies the great problem for the international camp-
-their inability to see past territorial sovereignty.

* * *

Chapter 16

Tuesday 17 September 2019
Black Hand [黑手]/ Red List [红名单]: China, Law and the Foreigner; Mutual Engagements on a Global Scale

The essay considers an issue that tends to be overlooked in the sometimes mad drive to become or remain an influence leader with impact, at least among public intellectuals.[542] Indeed, the mania, especially among academics and others who peddle ideas for a living, but who serve institutional masters increasingly obsessed with short term data driven "evidence" that "someone out there is listening (actually that someone out there "important" is listening at least as those things are understood through analysis of "correct" data bits). [543] The issue, of particular importance in the context of cross cultural, and cross political conversations among communities whose long term relationships have neither been entirely equal nor harmonious, *touches on the*

---

[542] Pierre Bourdieu, "The Corporation of the Universal: The Role of Intellectuals in the Modern World," *Telos* 81: 99-110 (1989); Paul A. Bové, *Intellectuals in Power: A Genealogy of Critical Humanism* (New York: Columbia Univ. Press, 1986).

[543] Impact measures make communication a second order activity. It is effectively merely the object that is the subject of a measure. The measure, rather than the content of the object, becomes the primary means for investing the object with both meaning and value. See, Abbie Brown, John Cowan, and Tim Green, "Faculty Productivity: Using Social Media and Measuring its Impact," Educause Review (2 May 2016); available [https://er.educause.edu/articles/2016/5/faculty-productivity-using-social-media-and-measuring-its-impact]; Heather Piwowar, "Altmetrics: Value All Research Products," Nature, vol. 493, no. 159 (2013); available [http://www.nature.com/nature/journal/v493/n7431/full/493159a.html?WT.ec_id=NATURE-20130110].

way communication is projected and received[544] and in the process shapes and is shaped by the source of the communication .[545]

China provides an excellent canvas against which these projections can be sharply observed. More importantly, its canvas is itself a complex and dynamic weave of history, culture, desire and the difficulties of communicating even when one assumes a common language. But mostly communication, as it has come to be used in the context of the Hong Kong protests specifically and between self-constituted communities (political, economic, cultural, religious) in general, is about the way in which *people* tend to serve as cultural projectiles, as well as the way that institutions develop the gloves with which these projectiles may be caught, examined and, if necessary discarded or remade for an entirely different game.[546] The objectification of ideology through the symbolic remaking of people as vessels for the projection of signs and meaning appears to mark the end of the great period of global convergence that reached its zenith between 1989 and 2013.

For those interested in the way in which communication translates into the strategies of politics, filtered through ideology, the focus state of communication in the context of the Hong Kong

---

[544] From a structural perspective, this invokes the mechanics and filtering of structural coupling. See, Niklas Luhmann, "Operational Closure and Structural Coupling: The Differentiation of the Legal System," *Cardozo Law Review* 13:1419-1441 (1991). This involves the process of communicating across systems in ways that informs the communication and is a function of its source. It involves a process of translation and incorporation of communication, the meaning and signification of which is made possible by its reconstitution into the framework of the receiving unit. "But without structural coupling there would be no perturbation and the system would lack any chance to learn and transform is structures." Ibid., 1433.

[545] This touches on a core issue of semiotics: "more like exploring a forest where cart trails or footprints do modify the explored landscape, so that the description the explorer gives of it must also take into account the ecological variations that he has produced." Umberto Eco, *A Theory of Semiotics* (Indiana University Press, 1976), p. 29.

[546] In this sense one can see illustrated Luhmann's insight that "Structural coupling presupposes and organizes decoupling." Niklas Luhmann, "Operational Closure and Structural Coupling: The Differentiation of the Legal System," supra., 1433.

suggests consequences for both Hong Kong and discourse across ideology. For students of language and communication, the tropes themselves provide fodder for an inquiry into transposition and context. And for students of politics, the essay provides a foundation for considering the modalities of communication among emerging new era empires and their imperial centers.

To that end, this essay considers the cultural and discursive tropes,[547] their political and social effects, that have marked the way in which comprehensible mutual engagement between China and foreigner have been constructed. These forms of engagement with the "foreign" has ancient discursive roots in China and among the states that traditionally projected their foreigners into China. It suggests the character of the mutual engagement between China and foreigners (especially foreigners viewed as representatives of equal or dangerous powers) as a form of cultural discourse that reflects an oscillation between caution and utility for which a set of definitive cultural tropes of the foreigner have been constructed with the participation of those foreigners who have embraced or at least utilized these discursive tropes. It suggests the forms of structural coupling that both shapes communication and manages its penetration within the Chinese system in ways that preserve the systems autonomy but which permits that system to absorb communication[548] and through that process adapt to changing environments--internal and external.[549]

After an Introduction, Part 2 examines the model through the lens of a 1911 essay authored by Edward Capen, an American

---

[547] Discourse here is understood as a site for power--and the organization of forms of discourse as shorthand for collections of presumptions. See, Daniel Punday, "Foucault's Body Tropes," *New Literary History* 31(3):509-523 (2000).

[548] See, Humberto R. Maturana and Francisco Varela, *El arbol del conocimiento: Las bases biológicas del entendimiento humano* (Santiago de Chile: Editorial Universitaria, 1994), pp. 49-63, 154-155.

[549] "In this way, structural coupling provides a continuous influx of disorder against which the system maintains or changes its structure." Niklas Luhmann, "Operational Closure and Structural Coupling: The Differentiation of the Legal System," supra, p. 1443.

protestant missionary. [550] Capen's report suggests the seven archetypes of the foreigner around which engagement is constructed: (1) the missionary; (2) the expert; (3) the sycophant; (4) the colonizer; (5) the expatriate; (6) the entrepreneur; and (7) the company person (or salaryman). These are mutually reinforcing archetypes. They reflect the views both of the exporting and importing culture. The difference, and of course, it is a great difference, is the way that such archetypes are identified.

For the recipient (Chinese) system, the foreigner archetypes may be divided into two broad categories within which Capon's seven types might be organized. The first is the useful foreigner. The useful foreigner may have the greatest value and the state may develop incentives to attract useful foreigners--and to construct them through a series of policies of rewards (and punishments for those who are not useful). The second is the dangerous foreigner. The dangerous foreigner is a threat to culture and the sovereignty of the state. This is the foreigner that cannot be managed by the recipient state because they are already an instrument of a foreign authority, either public (a competing state) or private (for example an international religious community).

The challenge for China, then, is to identify and encourage the useful foreigner, and to tightly control and suppress the dangerous foreigner. To those ends, the variations in the types of foreign inward projection makes a difference and requires distinctive approaches to management. More importantly, the character of the foreign may well determine the extent to which the foreign may be permitted in. Consider the missionary archetype, one that represents a potentially subversive agent within the Chinese body politic, but which may be useful for some of the knowledge they provide (especially of the way foreigners think and operate). They are devalued in China for their danger, but conversely, the exporting state values the missionary-- whether a religious missionary before 1945 or an ideological

---

[550] Edward Capen, "The Western Influence in China," *The Journal of Race and Development* 3(4): 412-437 (1913) (merged into *Foreign Affairs* in 1922)

missionary after the collapse of the Soviet Union--for precisely the reasons they may be devalued in China.[551]

Part 3 then suggests internal and external lessons that might be drawn. Internal lessons are first centered on the challenges for those designated to receive and transpose such knowledge—Chinese scholars who serve as the internal intermediaries for foreign knowledge. The second relates to the mechanics for managing acceptable and dangerous knowledge for intermediaries and for the masses.

The external lessons will be more difficult—these center on the consequences of replication of the patterns of Chinese engagement with foreigners when China itself becomes the foreigner in its outbound relations. The dangers of the inverse replication of these archetypes is already lurking in China's Belt and Road Initiative relations. But one might acquire a more definitive sense of those challenges in the context of the Chinese "Black Hand" campaign in Hong Kong in 2019.[552]

This chapter, then, speaks to the constructions of space established to make somewhat comprehensible mutual engagement between China and foreigner. The mutual engagement was constructed on a national scale during the last imperial dynasty. But its tropes have significant (and inverted) implications in this new era of Chinese power and influence. Where the traditional construct put China at the center of a national approach to engagement with the foreigner, those same tropes may now both constrain and challenge China as it emerges onto the world stage where it may well play the role of the foreigner. In effect. To understand the way that China and foreigners engage, to understand the black hand and the red list, is to understand the challenges and constraints that China may face in as it seeks to play the role of the foreigner in the imperial

---

[551] Well described in Han Liu, "Regime-Centered and Court-Centered Understandings: The Reception of American Constitutional Law in Contemporary China," *The American Journal of Comparative Law* 95-150 (2020).
[552] See discussion essays Chapters 5-7, supra.

courts of the global community in which it will necessarily be the foreigner.

1. The Black Hand, the Red List, and the Contextualization of the Foreigner.

One of the most interesting elements of the developing situation in Hong Kong is the move, now several weeks old, by the Central Government authorities to build a very strong case that at the root of the conflicts in Hong Kong are agents provocateurs representing foreign powers. [553] That strategic move was singularly focused not just on any old foreign power--but the one foreign power with which China is currently engaged on multiple fronts in a fight for the redefinition of the relations between them. Of course, one might understand this to mean the United States. Peripherally, it applies to second order foreign powers—the United Kingdom and the European Union and the G7. [554] Nonetheless, it may also apply to allies--it is the inward projection that counts.

In some respects, Hong Kong offers a crisis from which China may well be tempted to seek advantage. One cannot blame them--the potential benefits are substantial. It provides a basis for legitimacy in intervention, it shifts focus form domestic conflict to foreign manipulation, and it may strengthen China's hand in both its current conflict with the United States over trade and in China's efforts to reshape the tenor and foundation of global international

---

[553] Statements of the State Council's representatives for the Hong Kong and Macau Affairs Office the Current State of Affairs in Hong Kong [国务院港澳办新闻发言人介绍对当前香港事态的看法]; available [http://www.locpg.gov.cn/jsdt/2019-08/06/c_1210231451.htm].

[554] Teddy Ng, Kinling Lo, and Jun Mai, China protests over British Foreign Secretary Jeremy Hunt's warning on Hong Kong agreement, *South China Moring Post* (3 July 2019) < https://www.scmp.com/news/china/diplomacy/article/3017095/china-protests-britain-over-british-foreign-secretary-jeremy>; Press TV; China 'resolutely opposes' G7 statement on Hong Kong; available [https://www.presstv.com/Detail/2019/08/27/604602/China-Hong-Kong-G7-statement].

discourse (and China's place in the management of that narrative).[555]

All of this is fair game, one can suppose, within the rules of international engagement that have become the "new normal" since 2014 in the wake of the rise of transforming ideologies driven by the current holders of positions of national leadership in the most powerful states. A new historical era demands conformity to the rules (the "truths" of that era) that are manifested in the historical conditions within which states find themselves (the "facts" form which truth is derived).[556] The Americans have themselves refined this technique for its own new era through the politics of "Russian interference" that has played a dominant role in the politics of discrediting the Trump administration.[557] This is a tool that anyone, then, can use, to their own strategic ends.

This reframing of the character of the protests in Hong Kong that were ignited in 2019 by the efforts to consider an unpopular Extradition Bill from one of domestic disturbance to one of foreign interference requiring the intervention of central authorities has an ancient discursive form. To the ends of this sort of project it has been necessary to identify a plausible foreign adversary, to find character evidence that suggests that this adversary has already engaged in such conduct elsewhere; and lastly to marshal evidence from which local interference might be surmised. But what makes the engagement interesting is that this construction and utilization of the "black hand" must be

---

[555] See, e.g., John Harney and Kevin Hamlin, Trump Linking Trade to Hong Kong Risks Playing Into Xi's Hands, Bloomberg (14 Aug. 2019); available [https://www.bloomberg.com/news/articles/2019-08-14/trump-in-praising-xi-links-hong-kong-protests-to-trade-war].

[556] Xi Jinping, "Secure a Decisive Victory in Building a Moderately Prosperous Society in All Respects and Strive for the Great Success of Socialism with Chinese Characteristics for a New Era," Delivered at the 19th National Congress of the Communist Party of China (October 18, 2017); available [http://www.chinadaily.com.cn/china/19thcpcnationalcongress/2017-11/04/content_34115212.htm].

[557] Robert S. Mueller III, Report On The Investigation Into Russian Interference In The 2016 Presidential Election (Washington, DC: US Dept of Justice March 2019); available [https://www.justice.gov/storage/report.pdf].

undertaken in a way that does not reduce the utility of known foreigners whose identities may be included on "white (or red) lists."[558]

These forms of engagement with the "foreign" has ancient discursive roots in China. But they are at the same time roots that have been tenderly cultivated by those foreign elements that have sought to frame the terms of engagement with China. It suggests the character of the mutual engagement between China and foreigners (especially foreigners viewed as representatives of equal or dangerous powers) as a form of cultural discourse that reflects an oscillation between caution and utility for which a set of definitive cultural tropes of the foreigner have been constructed with the participation of those foreigners who have embraced or at least utilized these discursive tropes.

One is already beginning to see emerge in the rhetoric of the Hong Kong protests many of the traditional tropes of the foreigner, [559] as useful and dangerous, to both China and the international community. The missionary, the expert, the sycophant, the colonizer, the expatriate, the entrepreneur, and the company person all appear to be playing a role in the situation that is Hong Kong. All of these types carry with them both positive value and danger from the perspective of China. But that is a challenge of China's own making in the sense that, in the contemporary era, and certainly in its modern forms since the start of Reform and Opening Up, [560] China has sought both to create incentives for the receipt of foreign knowledge and at the

---

[558] "What China Experts Have to do to get on Beijing's visa "whitelist"," *The Washington Post* (5 September 2019); available [https://www.washingtonpost.com/opinions/2019/09/05/what-china-experts-have-do-get-beijings-visa-whitelist/].

[559] Edward Capen, "The Western Influence in China," *supra.*

[560] Yonglong Lu, Yueqing Zhang, Xianghui Cao, Chenchen Wang, Yichao Wan, Meng Zhang, "Forty Years of Reform and Opening Up: China's Progress Toward a Sustainable Path," *Science Advances* 5(8) eaau9413 (7 Aug. 2019); available [https://advances.sciencemag.org/content/5/8/eaau9413/tab-pdf]; Larry Catá Backer, "Toward New Era Thought: Reflections on Xi Jinping, Speech at the Meeting Celebrating the 40th Anniversary of Reform and Opening Up," *Emancipating the Mind: Bulletin of the Coalition for Peace & Ethics* 15(1):121-144

same time strictly control its influence within society, especially political society.

Even as the protests started one encountered an underlying contradiction in the way that the foreigner and foreign knowledge was received in China--especially Hong Kong. On the one hand technical knowledge directed to the state appeared to satisfy the need to aid in the state objectives of socialist modernization; on the other hand, to the extent that knowledge provider sought to engage directly with elements of the population--especially its academic and social elite, there was a sense that this constituted a potential subversion of the political, social, and economic order. Here one sees the missionary, the expert, and the colonizer tropes all competing for prominence in the way that specific actors and specific knowledge is conveyed. For the state this suggests the dangerous foreigner--the black hand. For the protesters this suggests the helping hand of self-actualization politically and socially.[561]

At the same time Chinese officials and elites might view this sort of knowledge as dangerous missionary interventions.[562] But it also raised substantially the nature of this engagement as a threat to the social and political order through the corruption of the young and the projection back into the state of Hong Kong people who have effectively been detached from the social and political fabric of the nation. [563] Knowledge in this case, the structural coupling of distinct systems, thus produces benefits but also generates danger--especially where knowledge can turn individuals against their own society. This is knowledge as betrayal which the Chinese system necessarily understands as a threat requiring excision. [564] For the protesters, of course, the opposite is true--this is the sort of knowledge that is liberating and contributes to an interconnected prosperity tied not to the state but to the international political order. It is the engagement with the expatriate, viewed as a positive by the protesters (and the

---

[561] See discussion essay Chapter 2, supra.
[562] See discussion essays Chapters 1 and 2, supra.
[563] See discussion essay Chapter 3, supra.
[564] See discussion essay Chapter 5, supra.

internationalized local elites that support them) and as a negative by the central authorities.[565] Indeed, for the foreigner, the role of the missionary has become as important now as it might have been in Capen's time, though now substituting the advancement of the normative ideals of the international order for that of the Christian faith.[566]

Indeed, the ambiguous role of the foreign and the character of its reception within China places the local intermediaries of that engagement--Chinese intellectuals and academics--in an awkward position.[567] Here they must carefully balance conflicting roles, and avoid a categorization as themselves the leading force of the projection of threatening foreign intervention. There is irony here when core foreign analytical notions are deployed for the purpose of resisting the translation of foreign normative values into a local context.[568] In that respect they play, for both sides, the role of expert translator and incorporator, of entrepreneur, and for some the role of salaryman.[569] Here the great danger for those in the middle is to avoid the role of sycophant--and to be wary of the foreigner coming into the Chinese context playing that role. The state, however, is already keen on seeing and interpreting the actions of local elites as conveyors and as instruments of the foreign--benign if sycophantic and threatening if more in the foam of the colonizer, entrepreneur or especially as the missionary[570] Indeed, Hong Kong since the start of the protests appears to have become the site of an intense debate about the way that foreign engagement is understood, and its meaning--and meaningfulness--is assessed as against Chinese needs.[571]

Indeed, the protests since 2019 has also appeared to sharpen the focus on the core principles--the ideological lenses-- through which popular engagement with the state can or must be

---

[565] See discussion essay Chapter 4, supra.
[566] See discussion essay Chapter 15, supra.
[567] See discussion essay Chapter 6, supra.
[568] See discussion essays Chapters 6 and 9, supra.
[569] See discussion essays Chapters 6-7, supra.
[570] See discussion essay Chapter 7, supra.
[571] See discussion essay Chapter 8, supra.

viewed. Fr example, the focus on the principles of prosperity and stability as the framing lens can serve as a way both to identify the character of the foreign, and its value (or threat) to the social order.[572] Indeed, the role of local elites as a mediating element for the inward projection of the foreign is becoming a central issue in the context of the protests and turmoil in Hong Kong. That presents a conundrum for those foreign elements that wish to continue to project their knowledge, values and the like into China (as the missionary, expert, entrepreneur and the like) but in a way that permits local officials to adjudge that projection as useful.[573] For others, however, the missionary role is paramount, as is the cultivation of colonizers and expatriates. The impulse applies not just to knowledge coming in but also local knowledge projecting out.[574]

Most importantly, the character of engagement informed by these archetypes appears to touch on the contest for control of the meaning and application of the One Country Two Systems principle itself.[575] From China's perspective, the very principle might itself be understood as a foreign insertion--and especially when it is read to position Two System self-determination over the unifying thrust (as they see it) of the One Country part of the principle. The same applies to foreign engagement who see the same issue but from their perspective the threat is the outward project of Chinese One Country approaches and the normative values that might represent, as the central authorities seek to extract from this engagement with the foreign those elements necessary for its implementation of the vanguard's Basic Line in the "new era."[576] The external lessons will be more difficult—

---

[572] See discussion essay Chapter 9, supra.

[573] See discussion essay Chapter 10, supra.

[574] See discussion essays Chapters 11 and 13, supra.

[575] See discussion essays Chapters 12, 14-15, supra.

[576] The Constitution of the Communist Party of China (revised and adopted at the 18th National Congress of the Communist Party 24 October 2017); available [http://www.xinhuanet.com//english/download/Constitution_of_the_Communist_Party_of_China.pdf] provides in relevant part:

> The basic line of the Communist Party of China in the primary stage of socialism is to lead all the people of China together in a self-reliant and pioneering effort, making economic development the central task, upholding the Four Cardinal Principles, and remaining committed to

these center on the consequences of replication of the patterns of Chinese engagement with foreigners when China itself becomes the foreigner.[577] The dangers of the inverse replication of these archetypes is already lurking in China's Belt and Road Initiative relations. But one might acquire a more definitive sense of those challenges in the Chinese "Black Hand" campaign in Hong Kong in 2019.

2. The Contemporary Emergence of the Foreigner—The Contemporary Archetypes

The template for the engagement between China and the "foreign" was well set by the end of Qing dynasty. It had deep roots in a pattern of engagement and detachment with the foreign that can certainly be traced back to long established dynastic oscillations. Long periods of imperial versions of "Reform and Opening Up"[578] were followed by equally long periods of closing borders.[579] Much of was of course bound up on perceptions of Chinese strategies to meet external threats or to absorb innovation for the betterment of its own internal development.

---

reform and opening up, so as to see China becomes a great modern socialist country that is prosperous, strong, democratic, culturally advanced, harmonious, and beautiful. (Ibid., General Program).

[577] Ibid. ("All Party Members must . . . strive to fulfill the three historic tasks of advancing modernization, achieving China's reunification, and safeguarding world peace and promoting common development, achieve the two centenary goals, and realize the Chinese Dream of national rejuvenation." Ibid.)

[578] E.g., during the Tong dynasty. See, e.g., Denis Twitchett, *The Writing of Official History Under the T'ang* (Cambridge: Cambridge University Press,1992) ,198-205; Marc Abramson, *Ethnic Identity in Tang China* (Philadelphia: University of Pennsylvania Press ,2008), pp.83-107. The relation with foreigners, though oscillated between the more open early years of the dynasty and the more suspicious later period, especially after the An Shi Rebellion and those that came after. Adam C. Fong, ""Together They Might Make Trouble": Cross-Cultural Interactions in Tang Dynasty Guangzhou, 618-907 C.E.," *Journal of World History* 25(4):475-492 (2014)

[579] E.g., during the Ming and early Qing dynasties. See, e.g., Lydia H. Liu, *The Clash of Empires: The Invention of China in Modern World Making* (Cambridge: Harvard University Press, 2006). See also, Wan Ming, "Formation and Changes of Overseas Policy in the Early Ming Dynasty," *Ming Qing Yanjiu* 11(1): 61-71 (2002); Dilip K. Basu, "Chinese Xenology and the Opium War: Reflections on Sinocentrsm," *The Journal of Asian Studies* 73(4):927-940 (2014).

Some of it was forced and though its benefits might serve development, the process was difficult culturally.[580]

This oscillating pattern has been repeated form the establishment of the Republic in 1911, accelerating perhaps after the establishment of the People's Republic in 1949. Engagement in the early Republic period might be understood in terms of mimicry of the foreign as the means of contextually relevant modernization.[581] After 1949 Chinese policy evidenced periods of opening up and closing off and the waxing and waning of the influence of foreign trained Chinese and foreign advisors.[582] The period 1949-1957might be understood as one of specific opening up to the Soviet Union and the Communist international.[583] A period of closing off began in 1957 which produced a purging of Soviet (direct) influence and efforts toward indemnification and rectification on a closed system model. The Great proletarian Cultural Revolution saw the first wave of indigenization produce both international transformation and an effort toward outward projection. Neither had lasting effect as policy though people argue about their indirect and subtextual effects.[584] The contemporary period is marked by the well-known and often studied principles of Reform and Opening Up, which itself has now been marked by its own reform under "New Era" principles.

It was in the context of this foreign driven engagement that Edward Capen wrote in the early part of the second decade of the 20th century as part of a special sociological and missionary

---

[580] E.g., the early Yuan and late Qing dynasties, as well as the Republican period, for example. See, e.g., Diana Preston, *The Boxer Rebellion: The Dramatic Story of China's War on Foreigners That Shook the World in the Summer of 1900* (NY: Walker & Co., 2001).

[581] E.g., the Six Codes of the Kuomintang modeled on European Codes undertaken with foreign trained Chinese drafting and Western legal scholars advising.

[582] Anne-Marie Brady, *Making the Foreign Serve China: Managing Foreigners in the People's Republic* (NY: Rowman & Littlefield, 2003).

[583] The influence of the Soviet Union in this early period is both well-known and not entirely harmonious. But all the same foreign (Soviet) influence was useful and managed to the extent then possible given contextual power relationships and strategic needs.

[584] Patricia Thornton, Peidon Sun and Chris Berry (eds.), *Red Shadows: Memories and Legacies of the Chinese Cultural Revolution* (Cambridge, 2017)

research project.[585] Capen speaks to the framework of Western influence in China. He describes four principle channels through which Western influence has reached China. [586] The first is through direct pressure by foreign governments that succeeded in forcing changes in the treatment of foreigners and the protection of their interests. Here one sees a manifestation of what will later be understood as the Black Hand. The second is through the penetration of China by foreign enterprises "as a result of which China was opened to Western influence as exerted by the trader and his agents."[587] The third channel was through a program of leading by example undertaken by exposing Chinese students and officials to the West and its practices. Already the problematic relationship was nicely framed here—between the need for Western experiences and the danger that posed to the Chinese government model. [588] The last channel was the missionary. In the 19th and early 20th century missionary work was religious—after 1989 it became far more ideological in line with the internationalization of the normative structures of globalization. But in both cases the work also focused on political and cultural transformation.[589] This was a lesson well learned by China as it set off on its own missionary work with its own version of global community in the form of the Belt and Road Initiative.[590]

It is possible to see in the organization of the question of foreign influence in China the template that, a century later, still

---

[585] Capen, supra, 412.

[586] Ibid., 412-13. Note here, form the first, the way these may be echoed in Chinese practices in international forums as well as in the construction of the Belt and Road Initiative.

[587] Ibid., 412.

[588] "The experiences of the Chinese who have settled in western lands, chiefly along the western shores of the American continent, and still more recently the introduction of western books and the publication in China of books and periodicals that give the facts about western life, thought and achievements, have spread the knowledge and influence of things western, especially among students and the progressive classes" Ibid., 413.

[589] Ibid., 413 (their "quiet and pervasive personal influence has had very much to do with laying the foundations for the new regime").

[590] But one might wonder the extent to which that effort might also carry with it the consequences of the version described by Capen, at least in terms of the responses and resistance of those onto whom this missionary work would be received of (economic) necessity.

influences Chinese inbound and outbound engagement. Indeed, it is possible to suggest that this template and its underlying ideological presumptions actually nicely into current patterns of relationships and what does it means going forward. Capen identified 4 key questions, which are both odd and of interest: (1) what Western influence has accomplished; (2) what in Chinese culture or practices Western influence should not destroy; (3) where China can learn from the West; (4) how the West can be most helpful?

The questions themselves are telling, especially from a perspective of national equal status. They reveal the way the relationship between the foreign and China was understood and structured. They effectively define the relationship between China and its engagement with the foreigners as one that must be effectively unequal in at least four related respects.

First, *the West is active; China is passive.* This is inherent in the form of the first question—to ask what Western influence has accomplished is to premise that China is in need of that influence toward certain ends the normative basis is itself to be supplied from abroad. This is an attitude that still pervades; and it is especially strong among legal and academic scholars, especially constitutional scholars who might be understood (since 1989) as the West's contemporary missionaries. Second, the *West projects out; China receives.* The foreigner is Yang; China is Ying. The West spreads its seed; the soil of China is a fertile ground into which that seed may be inserted, and thus inserted tended until it bears fruit. What China has to offer, then, is its fertility. But that fertility is to be used to enhance the work of those with the task of approximate political and cultural horticulture. Third, *China is the student; the west is teacher.* This is, in essence the foundation of Reform and Opening Up. But here one opens a site for resistance and eventually for the turning of the tables. To be a student is to hope one day to be the teacher. And who better to teach then one's former teacher. Here one sees the seed of Chinese internationalism in the new era as well as the blindness of the West to the ideological character of its own interventions. Fourth, *the West can modulate and is flexible; China is rigid, set in its ways, and predictable.* Several thousand years of history is a terribly deep crust to break through. But it also suggests that in the absence of revolutionary transformation rigidity causes paralysis. There is an echo here that found expression in the Cultural Revolution.

But it also produced some degree of caution revealed by Capen's second question. But even that recognition of value in indigenous cultural foundations is measured by its utility to the project of "modernization." Echoing contemporary tropes, Capen noted that survival is its own imprimatur. The foundations of that survival, in the face of an equally ancient rigidity, include practical ethics.[591] It also includes the power of the collective in Chinese social and institutional life—what Capen terms the ability to cooperate—along with deep cultures of scholarship and Chinese political genius (even a genius in need of modernization).[592] But these are all passive virtues—a static ability in need to direction. That, for Capen ought to be provided by the West; for the Chinese Communist Party, of course, direction ought to come from the vanguard. Common to both positions, though, is the passivity of the collective and their need for instruction. Again, this is a template very much still influential within and beyond China. It serves as the basis for the answer to Capen's third question— what China can learn from the West—its culture, industry, and social-political organization.[593]

Reading Capen's long report produces the detail made understandable by premises of the nature of engagement. He makes very clear the scope and importance of those contribution of the West into China: industry development, education, political system, everything from the development of a postal service to the steam train to the telegraph. All are understood to be products of the West and not indigenous; these innovation are imported into China. To the same effect the characterization of other innovations:

---

[591] Ibid., 428-30. This observation acquires some irony in the face of the movement toward a social credit system that was itself founded on the challenge of lack of integrity within Chinese society, culture and economic life. See, e.g., Larry Catá Backer, "China's Social Credit System: Data-Driven Governance for a 'New Era'," 118(809) *Current History* 209-2014 (September 2019).
[592] Ibid., 429-30.
[593] Ibid., 432-33.

the consumer market, and Western models of education. Most important of all Western politics, adopting western models of as a prerequisite for admitting China into the family of nations and therefore for undoing the nature of the treaty.

Underlying Capen's reading of the nature of engagement are a set of presumptions about the scope of behaviors that can now be better understood in the form of seven tropes.[594] The tropes themselves are built into the answer to the last question— how the West can be the most helpful.[595] These mark the useful limits of the scope within which Chinese engagement with the foreign continues to be managed. But these are also tropes that have been enthusiastically adopted by those foreigners who seek such engagement (either for themselves) or on behalf of institutions (public or private) whose interests they serve or seek to serve). As such it is useful to consider these tropes from a double perspective--each with its own and sometimes quite different meaning. Both the Chinese and the foreign embrace the model of the useful foreigner, for example. But "usefulness" is quite different when viewed from the perspective of the foreigners or from that of the Chinese. and through which foreigners assume. It follows that while the tropes are shared by home and host states, their value, and the understanding of what each means, ca vary substantially.

The Chinese response is framed against the archetypes described above. The Chinese official response varied and ranged from uncritical opening up to efforts to lock out foreign innovation. Uniformly cultivated was both suspicion of all foreign influence, and an interest in profiting from foreign innovation. In ways that mark much of 20th century development--what receiving states want is the trinkets and know how; they can do without the underling ideology and influence. Yet this response also rests on the construction of archetypes of the foreign--*variations of the trope of the useful and the dangerous foreigner.* This pattern of

---

[594] Listed above(1) the missionary; (2) the expert; (3) the sycophant; (4) the colonizer; (5) the expatriate; (6) the entrepreneur; and (7) the company person (or salaryman).
[595] Capen, supra., 433-37.

managing foreign interventions has modulated, but was relatively well established in the last century. Among the most important forms of response are patterns of invited influence and its tropes from the late Qing dynasty to the present. This is foreign intervention by invitation and for limited purpose. Beyond these forms of managed intervention are a range of responses. These include *adopting the ideal of the useful stranger.*[596] This is the foreigner who is meant to be useful to the state. But such useful foreigners can also be useful to factions seeking or protecting power. Alongside the ideal of the useful foreigner is that of *the ideal of the stranger as threat*. These are the strangers with respect to which the only possible relationship, one based on punishing the carriers of cultural-political contagion.

And thus there is a danger of turning foreign influence into political instruments. At this point the useful stranger becomes the threatening stranger, and the utility of foreign knowledge becomes the exposure to a foreign virus that may attack the balance and harmony of the political society that sought to use knowledge but discard its ideological threat. This instrumental use of foreigners for domestic politics arises especially in the early and late republic period. Useful stranger responses can also connect Chinese indigenous practice to globe practices and ideas. The stranger, however, exists as an autonomous being who whom the object of interaction is also serves personal and collective interest. Their interactions are also meant to prove useful to their own communities, institutions and patrons. Mediating between the useful stranger and the stranger as virus is a dynamic process that has not been elegantly applied. Resistance to the threatening stranger takes several forms. These include expulsions of foreigners, control of incoming ideas and persons, restriction on information and practice, and a mandatory indigenization of foreign ideas. Welcoming of the useful foreigner also takes a variety of forms, mostly falling along a spectrum of managed inbound activity. These can be used to block foreign influence or to transpose ideas into Chinese terms.

---

[596] Cf., Anne-Marie Brady, *Making the Foreign Serve China: Managing Foreigners in the People's Republic* (NY: Rwman & Littlefield, 2003).

Let us consider each of the tropes more carefully.

2.1. The Missionary. The missionary is the core template and an ancient collection of premises about the relationship between foreign and Chinese cultures. It is a modern expression of traditional approach and it is grounded in the notion of superiority. What motivates the foreigner who sees herself as a missionary?[597] First is the assumption that China is inefficient or undeveloped, and west or outside or foreigner has something that China lacks and that China cannot develop for herself.[598] This is the understanding of the template of this archetype. Whether it is true or not is debated all the time. But the presumption is central to the missionary who believes that her way is superior and that the recipient must change by becoming just like the missionary.[599]

This is among the most interesting aspects about Capen, the idea of changing: it is about changing the society, its politics and economics. But the missionary preserves some things. Capen speaks about keeping small things such as Confucius family solidarity, scholarship and community strength, but all of them have to ripped apart and rework on western terms.[600] This is missionary: it is the assumption of inferiority of indigenous and it is multidimensional traditionally as we have seen as missionary in 19th century with religious, the early republic period you have technicians comes in and societal and ultimately political as well, because the ground of all of these is to transform China into either a democratic monarchy European style or republic in some accepted form.   They know what's the best, they are still everywhere in academic, political circus. Today the missionary type is not limited to religious groups, but includes any person or group who seeks to convert China into embracing the culture, politics, economics, and the like that is brought to China by the missionary.

---

[597] The traditional forms of which were heavily criticized in the late Qing by some. See, Alexandre Michie, *Missionaries in China* (London: Edward Stanford, 1891).
[598] See, Jerome Ch'en, *China and the West: Society and Culture 1815-1937* (Routledge); Chapter 2.
[599] Michie, *Missionaries in China*, supra.
[600] Capen, supra., 433-37

2.2. The Expert. The next stereotype is the expert. She differs from the missionary in that the expert does not espouse a particular ideology, instead she advances a particular methodology. This is the archetype of the technocrat—of systems rather than of ideology. There is various type, for the law, the lawyers, judges and people like me, the academics. There are two focuses, the first is the technician, and the second is the system builder. The technician focuses on the details of the problem, building everyday law and legal institutions. They are the consultants for the corporations or labor codes, for example. The other is more sensitive because it brings technique and process to systems, including the political and administrative order. In that sense it also is a political project. The one for which expertise usually drawn is technician. Let's bring in French code, let's think about German procedure law and Japanese constitutionalism. But even then, the student could prove to be a fast earner and turn the tables on their teachers. [601] But what was once about legal structures and industrial modernization in the late Qing is now research and development and global competitiveness.[602] It has significant resonance in Hong Kong.[603]

What is more profound in 19th century and even today, although today these experts tend to work outside of China, is the system builder, those who would reorder China's constitutional and political order for the obvious reasons.[604] Here the technician and the missionary meet. The idea is that the current Chinese system is a transitional system, and that it must be changed to embrace some ideal from abroad. This argument has a long history. It was advanced in 1910, the 20s and again after 1949. It

---

[601] Yong Lam, "Policing the Imperial Nation: Sovereignty, International Law, and the Civilizing Mission in Late Qing China," *Comparative Studies in society and History* 52(4):881-908 (2010).

[602] Oliver Gassmann, "Motivations and Barriers of Foreign R&D Activities in China," *R&D Management* 34(4):423-437 (2004).

[603] Daniel R. Fung, "Constitutional Reform in China: The Case of Hong Kong," *Texas International Law Journal* 39:467 (2003).

[604]

remains important now.[605] And it had indigenous roots as well.[606] The argument ensures the need for outside expertise because it presumes that indigenous Chinese institutions are fragile and illegitimate and that foreign ideas are essential to facilitate a necessary change. But expertise has a sometimes short shelf-life. Capacity building evidences success when it is no longer required, and when the student can become the teacher.[607]

2.3. *The Sycophant.* These are the foreigners who will say whatever you what to hear. This Sycophant at first appears as the inverse of the missionary archetype. But they tend to serve as a brake on development. The sycophant is a paid echo, and that is not very helpful. They also tend to be an instrument. They tended to promote the position of those whose interests they seek to serve in factional politics. The danger with sycophant is that you are never sure who he serves. Once that service is understood the archetype loses value, though not entirely in an age where echoing of a position can be as useful as quality of a singular voice. One cannot trust the sycophant, but one can use her. Whether serve internal faction or a master abroad. One cannot trust the sycophant, but one can use her—still she can be more dangerous than the missionary or expert.

2.4. *The Colonizer.* The next archetype is the colonizer. This is the modern form of the missionary. But this archetype does not serve another state or a religion; it tends to serve a broader global order within which the state is subsumed. Here

---

[605] "Premier Li Keqiang reiterated on Tuesday (Feb 2) China's commitment to expand opening-up with stronger resolve, saying that the government will keep improving institutional mechanisms to attract more foreign talent and offer more convenience for expats in China." "China open to foreign experts, says Chinese premier Li," The Star (3 February 3¡2021); available [https://www.thestar.com.my/aseanplus/aseanplus-news/2021/02/03/china-open-to-foreign-experts-says-chinese-premier-li].

[606] Qianfan Zhang, "A Constitution Without Constitutionalism? The Paths of Constitutional Development in China," *International Journal of Constitutional Law* 8(4):950-976 (2010).

[607] Yan Wang, *Chinese Lega Reform: The Case of Foreign Investment Law* (Routledge, 2002); Peter Ferdinand, "Westward Ho--The China Dream and 'One Belt One Road': Chinese Foreign Policy Under Xi Jinping," *International Affairs* 92(4):941-957 (2016).

one encounters the class of global internationalists.[608] For the colonizer China should be treated like other states—but all states should be understood as subordinate to a superior order. The colonizer is made possible by and is the representative of the ideological framework of the current phase of globalization. Over the course of 15 or 20 years, there has arisen a global community and global orders which exist beyond the state. Classical historical study usually treats the foreigner as a representative of some specific foreign state, as Americans, Chinese, or British persons, for example.

That is no longer the case. Over the last 50 years the archetype of the colonizer has developed a loyalty to an ideology—ecological, sociological, religious, and the like, which owe no particular allegiance to any state. They exist on a different political level. Especially when dealing with the case of civil society, and global groups, these groups tend to break down the barrier of the state and represent global interest. These are foreigner who represent global norms—and they are particularly important in emerging global consensus and global norms over labor rights, human rights, information accessibility and the like. They are individuals and groups that are foreign but not bound by any foreign state but foreign. Their agenda is similar to the missionary in the sense that they view their own ideological framework as superior and one that must be embedded in all states. China is not singled out but it is not ignored. The colonizer seeks the same sorts of changes in the United States This is something very new. Most of states are still trying to understand the colonizer, but I assure you that global civil orders and regulatory community are now very real and influential and they do play the role of the foreigner to the same extent as individuals tied to the traditional ideologies of political states did a century ago.

2.5. *The Expatriate*. The Expatriate is an emerging archetype and one that is likely to become more important for

---

[608] Within the academic industry they serve as a manifestation of a global class that serves its own interests. See, e.g., Leslie Sklair, *The Transnational Capitalist Class* (Blackwell, 2001).

China in the coming decades. They are individuals who have emigrated from China—temporarily or permanently—and who now serve to bring foreign ideas back onto China. They provide a more trusted and immediate essential link between China and foreign ideas. There are two types. First is the Chinese who have emigrated on a permanent basis and are citizens of western states. The second, which has exploded in number after the 1980s, are Chinese sent aboard to study and who return to hold key positions within government, Party and state.

This is a critical archetype; it provides the state with an element of trust and to detach the element of modernization from its sources. And it detaches foreign knowledge from the interests of foreign states and their citizens. But it also raises new and complex questions. The Expatriate is an ambiguous foreigner. On the one hand she is not foreign at all, but a local person who has observed the foreign first hand and then returned. But it is not clear whether such an encounter with the foreign has left the Expatriate changed. He has two parts. The Chinese part and foreigner part. The idea is that one cannot be trust. There is a problem is that once they go out, one is never really quite sure about whether they are or remain loyal. To minimize this there have been reports of substantial efforts by officials to avoid corruption of the young studying abroad by absorbing sensitive foreign values. It gives anxiety and gives rise to the need for monitoring and checks.

2.6. *The Entrepreneur.* The Entrepreneur archetype is a variant of the Expert. These are the modern consultant. They sell foreignness; they are merchants of knowledge and know-how. China is an external market for the sort of expertise that might be sold at home as well. Of course when China buys foreign ideas through employees, they have the same problem as other consumers of goods or services: the problem is choosing among products offered for the best product, the best deal and for continuing service when knowledge does not prove to be useful. This is a particular problem in China but other countries as well. The entrepreneurs are indifferent to theory focusing only on advantage to their own agenda.[609] They tend to play legal systems against each other. That poses some risk to both the home and host states of entrepreneurs.

Of particular interest is the business of academic knowledge, especially knowledge with a social or political utility or effect. The Entrepreneur archetype is at its most refined in the form of the purveyor of intellectual goods—merchants of knowledge and know how—perhaps like those reading this essay. For them, China is an opportunity useful for external market advantage in academia and elsewhere. The Entrepreneur archetype is not necessarily interested in theory but rather in only advantage—advantage in home state prestige markets, in access and in the control of an orthodoxy of point of view that may then be pressed within China and in the home state as well. The Entrepreneur builds a business of influence from the knowledge purveyed. They are the builders of "schools of thought" that tickle the interest of the political or communications classes. This is a business built on a stakeholder mentality with repercussions in the global sphere where conflict among legal "products".

2.7. *The Salaryman.* People who serve a foreign organization serves someone other than themselves.[610] This is the foreigner who acts to further not their own interests (that is the Entrepreneur) but rather the interests and normative values of an

---

[609] This is sometimes more transparent during the Hong Kong protests. See essay in Chapter11, supra.

"Most firms in Hong Kong that engage in business with mainland China know that there is always a degree of political risk that needs to be navigated," Duncan Innes-Ker, regional director for Asia at The Economist Intelligence Unit, said Monday. "Companies may find that their employees' activism turns into a political risk in mainland China, if this campaigning becomes associated with the firm's brand." (Joel Gehrke, "China pressuring corporations to crack down on Hong Kong protesters," *Washington Examiner* (19 August 2019); available [https://www.washingtonexaminer.com/policy/defense-national-security/china-pressuring-corporations-to-crack-down-on-hong-kong-protesters])

[610] There are vague but useful overtones to the Japanese salaryman. See, e .g., Tatsuya Lida and Jonathan Morris, "Farewell to the salaryman? The changing roles and work of middle managers in Japan," *The International Journal of Human Resource Management* 19(6):1072 (2008).

organization other than the state—enterprises, financial and other markets, or civil society. When Walmart and KFC coming in, they provide expertise, who do they service, do they serve Americans in home country or their own production or value chains (the multinational corporation itself) with millions of employees in different locations with their own regulatory agenda. This archetype is the enterprise variant of the colonizer. In this case, the foreigner may not serve the state, but instead serves the multinational enterprise, its culture interest and objectives. That is, here as in global civil society, one encounters non-state actors who themselves are regulatory foreigners, who also produce expertise into a state that used to be reserved to state.

The hybridity of this archetype complicates its essence. These exercise expertise and fall into categories of missionary, expert or sycophant. The difficulty for China is distinguishing between states and non-state actors where the effects of both can be similar. More importantly, perhaps, is the difficulty of managing the intermediaries who are essential actor sin the translation of the knowledge produces into the state.

3. Lessons.

There are lessons that might be harvested from this consideration of the rhetorical and policy tropes through which engagement with the foreigner (and foreigner interventions in China) appear to be ordered. One set of lessons look inward. The other can be projected outward.

3.1. Inward Projections. An animal with four back legs cannot move forward. Applying old responses to the projection of foreign knowledge will not produce benefit to China. Modern times may require rethink about the response to the foreign the way which it is received, analyzed, and observed or discarded. I take a very famous paragraph from a very famous speech of Deng Xiaoping as one of the most sophisticated approaches to the issue. [611] Though it is often reduced to cliché it does suggest

---

[611] Deng Xiaoping, Emancipate the Mind, Seek Truth from Facts and Unite As One in Looking to the Future (Dec. 13, 1978)

lessons and cations which are usually overlooked as these insights are reduced to a recitable catechism. The central element of that insight is the difficult task of balancing the CPC's fundamental undertaking to draw from the foreign and the foreigner while at the same time producing reform that avoids both left and right error.[612] And going back to Mao Zedong, also of the risk of institutionalizing these relations with foreigners in a way that reduces their role to a well-managed system of rigidity and bureaucratism.[613]

Foreigners are essential element of reform. But this is a generalizable insight of no great merit. The problem is the way in which these foreign interventions might be made compatible with Chinese needs. Rigidity and bureaucratism—the tendency toward the left error of closing the mind and the borders—would tend to reduce the inflow of ideas to those pre-digested and approved by a bureaucracy. That produces a closed circuit of sycophancy that has sometimes bedeviled the project. At the same time reducing the project of useful foreigners to a game of technology transfer for indigenous practice and then blocking the foreign source produces a right-wing error that impedes China's international ambitions.[614]

But in this process of internal embedding one also needs to pay attention to three critical factors. The first revolves around

---

<https://dengxiaopingworks.wordpress.com/2013/02/25/emancipate-the-mind-seek-truth-from-facts-and-unite-as-one-in-looking-to-the-future/>.
When it comes to emancipating our minds, using our heads, seeking truth from facts and uniting as one in looking to the future, the primary task is to emancipate our minds. Only then can we, guided as we should be by Marxism-Leninism and Mao Zedong Thought, find correct solutions to the emerging as well as inherited problems, fruitfully reform those aspects of the relations of production and of the superstructure that do not correspond with the rapid development of our productive forces, and chart the specific course and formulate the specific policies, methods and measures needed to achieve the four modernizations under our actual conditions.

[612] Constitution of the Communist Party of China, supra, General Program.

[613] Famously critiqued by Deng Xiaoping. See Deng Xiaoping, "

[614] These are problems not unknown in the West. The west has a long history of a position of Inequality when look into each other's legal political system and browning it, that is an essential element of intercourse.

the issue of compatibility with global consensus approaches. It makes little sense to bring in a set of rules that grounded on a particular political ideology if the political ideology is complete incompatible with the home ideology, it has to be changed with some caution.[615] The ability to understand this, and to avoid using that knowledge as a basis for building a barrier to knowledge sharing poses one of the great difficulties for the new era ideology of engagement.

The second focuses on the issue of intelligibility. Foreign interventions must be understood on their own terms. But that requires the cultivation of deep cultural knowledge; it also requires an ability to translate from out of one set of cultural terms to another. For some bases of knowledge that may prove difficult. But the problem of transposition remains a real one. To receive knowledge while blocking any ability to understand and utilize its ideology (even where it is incompatible with the of the receiving state), is to hobble all efforts at engagement. Or at least it suggests that such engagement serves purposes other than either reform or opening up.

The third focuses on the issue of compatibility with China's internal normative order. It may not be enough to wall off the social and cultural from the technical and commercial. If, indeed, all expressions of behavior are ideologically centered, then there is no way to receive foreign innovation without understanding and adjusting to the ideological presumptions through which these modalities prove successful. This has proven to be a sensitive challenge. It is especially sensitive because it sits at the point of contact between the foreigner and those in China who must be relied on to interpret and apply with Chinese characteristics.

But the real issue of the archetypes in their inward projection is the challenge of the *allegiance of the indigenous intermediary*. If the object of engagement is to harvest knowledge,

---

[615] Larry Catá Backer, *Between the Judge and the Law—Judicial Independence and Authority with Chinese Characteristics,* 33(1) Connecticut Journal of International Law 1-41 (2017).

then it is necessary to assure the state and the institutions and cultures it has set itself to protect, that those charged with the acquisition of knowledge from the foreigner archetypes are themselves not subverted by the foreigner themselves. There is always the fear that "Opening Up" will produce not "Reform" but the sweeping away of the essence of China so that it becomes nothing more than the expression of foreign culture domestically (and imperfectly) applied. The result is not just "Opening Up" but also a counter tendency toward closing down. The saga of Unirule[616] is perhaps emblematic—though it too presents a far more complicated story.[617] But they also produce the reaction of the black hand (intermeddling beyond that managed by the state) and the red list (encouragement of knowledge providers that produce what the state deems useful and not sensitive) to maintain the environment in which knowledge and engagement can be carefully curated.

These, then, suggest cautions that in turn suggest the need to break past the archetypes. The first refocuses engagement from copying to a position of influence on current or desired objectives. The second requires a focus on capacity building rather than on renting knowledge. The third requires a move away from passivity in the receipt of knowledge to active engagement in its generation. The last is the most difficult—the development of sound ideological analysis that avoids internal political instrumentalism. All of these, in turn, return the issue to one of patterns of bureaucratism and bureaucratic rigidity. To solve the problem of the foreigner—that is to break past the ancient

---

[616] Lily Kuo, "Chinese liberal thinktank forced to close after being declared illegal," *The Guardian* (28 Aug. 2019); available [https://www.theguardian.com/world/2019/aug/28/chinese-liberal-thinktank-forced-to-close-after-being-declared-illegal].

[617] Consider Xu Zhangrun, "Our Current Fears and Expectations" (我们当下的恐惧与期待) appeared on the official website of the Unirule Institute of Economics (天则经济研究所), which caused considerable reaction globally but especially in China. See also, Backer, Larry Catá and Sapio, Flora, "To Seek the Future in the Past: Thoughts on Xu Zhangrun: 'Our Current Fears and Expectations' (评许章润:我们当下的恐惧与期待)" (August 19, 2018); available [https://ssrn.com/abstract=3234782].

discursive tropes and uses of the foreigner—one needs to break an even more ancient pattern of bureaucratism grounded in the construction of systems based on the exercise of substantial administrative discretion subject to personal oversight and otherwise unaccountable. But that is a tall order.[618] Developing a much sounder ideological analysis requires ideological analysis suited to Chinese conditions that can detach what is worth receiving from what has less relevance to local conditions understood through the lens of the domestic political-economic system. It also permits a greater clarity, on the part of the foreigner, in tempering and more consciously deploying these tropes effectively toward their own ends. Conflict is not ten avoided, but clarity and autonomy is enhanced in inter cultural conversation.

Going forward China faces additional external problems of dealing with the foreign. First the issue of the foreign has itself been recast by the structures of globalization. It is now much harder to identify the foreign in a reflexive environment in which

---

[618] Deng Xiaoping, "Emancipate the Mind, Seek Truth From Facts, and Unite as One in Looking to the Future" (13 December 1978), The Selected Works of Deng Xiaoping (online); available [https://dengxiaopingworks.wordpress.com/2013/02/25/emancipate-the-mind-seek-truth-from-facts-and-unite-as-one-in-looking-to-the-future/]. Deng distinguishes between the ossifying power of managerial bureaucratism ("it is essential to overcome the evils of bureaucracy. Our present economic management is marked by overstaffing, organizational overlapping, complicated procedures and extremely low efficiency. Everything is often drowned in empty political talk" Ibid.) and political bureaucratism ("This kind of bureaucratism often masquerades as "Party leadership", "Party directives", "Party interests" and "Party discipline", but actually it is designed to control people, hold them in check and oppress them" Ibid.). Both contribute to rigidity and rigidity is itself an anti-Socialist condition:

> People whose thinking has become rigid tend to veer with the wind. They are not guided by Party spirit and Party principles, but go along with whatever has the backing of the authorities and adjust their words and actions according to whichever way the wind is blowing. They think that they will thus avoid mistakes. In fact, however, veering with the wind is in itself a grave mistake, a contravention of the Party spirit which all Communists should cherish. It is true that people who think independently and dare to speak out and act can't avoid making mistakes, but their mistakes are out in the open and are therefore more easily rectified. Ibid.

the state is not always at the apex and its borders are increasingly permeable. The issue of the foreigner in China might well have been effectively superseded by the issue of the global in China and of China itself in the global. The foreign is no longer always an issue of state projecting foreign ideas; globalization has liberated both regulation and production of political ideas from the state and now vested in global civil society, and multinational commercial enterprises. It is hard to find the foreign in an organization or institution that has made itself indigenous to many places. That is the world in which countries like China and United States now operate. In this context, an adherence to the old tropes impedes rather than furthers reform and opening up and appears increasingly anachronistic.

It is for that reason, perhaps, that the Chinese Black Hand strategy in Hong Kong has failed to generate much reaction in a global community in which such issues are now internalized and managed. This environment requires a different and more sophisticated view of the foreign and a different sense about what the foreign means (and how it may be useful) as knowledge both coming in and coming out. Transnational law and transnational norms are the systems that make up this is reality that you all know. At the same time, it may well have informed the Chinese all around approach to its construction of its Socialist globalization model in its Belt and Road Initiative. China now plays host to the foreign--which remains tied to the old tropes of utility and danger, while projecting its own power through its own networks, in which Chinese people may find themselves falling within Capon's tropes.[619]

3.2. *Outward Projections.* The leaders of the Chinese Communist Party have made clear especially since the 16th party congress that moving forward under the leadership of the Communist Party it is necessary for the country to project Chinese

---

[619] For a taste, see, e.g., Jiaotao Li, Bin Liu, and Gongming Qian, "The belt and road initiative, cultural friction and ethnicity: Their effects on the export performance of SMEs in China," *Journal of World Business* 54(4):350-359 (2019); Tim Winter, "One Belt, One Road, One Heritage: Cultural Diplomacy and the Silk Road," *The Diplomat* (29 March 2016); available [https://thediplomat.com/2016/03/one-belt-one-road-one-heritage-cultural-diplomacy-and-the-silk-road/].

knowledge and interests into international discussion more vigorously. That is a work in progress. But the outward lesson for China is very clear. The old days are gone, China is now increasingly a foreigner in lands in which they can influence significantly. Its systems and ideologies are studied. China must develop its own ways of projecting its own value without making the same mistakes that China has criticized west for hundreds of years. That requires much more sophisticated understanding of the nature of that projection and much deeper study of China's policy as it moves out into Africa and as it moves through its state owned enterprise into a transnational space and international organization developing international norms and rules.

The old discursive patterns, now reversed, may well inhibit the ability of China to extend its influence as it constructs its own approach to world ordering through its Go Out policies, through its Belt and Road Initiative,[620] and through its efforts to refocus international law and norms.[621] If China falls into the

---

[620] See, e.g., National Development and Reform Commission, Ministry of Foreign Affairs, and Ministry of Commerce of the People's Republic of China, "Vision and Actions on Jointly Building Silk Road Economic Belt and 21st-Century Maritime Silk Road" (State Council authorized 23 March 2015); available [http://en.ndrc.gov.cn/newsrelease/201503/t20150330_669367.html].

> The Initiative is an ambitious economic vision of the opening-up of and cooperation among the countries along the Belt and Road. Countries should work in concert and move towards the objectives of mutual benefit and common security. To be specific, they need to improve the region's infrastructure, and put in place a secure and efficient network of land, sea and air passages, lifting their connectivity to a higher level; further enhance trade and investment facilitation, establish a network of free trade areas that meet high standards, maintain closer economic ties, and deepen political trust; enhance cultural exchanges; encourage different civilizations to learn from each other and flourish together; and promote mutual understanding, peace and friendship among people of all countries.

Ibid., Part III.

[621] See, e.g., Larry Catá Backer, "On the Internationalization of China's "New Era" Theory: Brief Thoughts on the UN Human Rights Council Resolution: "On promoting mutually beneficial cooperation in the field of human rights" (A/HRC/37/L.36)." Law at the End of the Day (24 March 2018); available [http://lcbackerblog.blogspot.com/2018/03/on-internationalization-of-

same traditional archetypes that we mentioned, they would end up like England and US with the same problem that west had in China. These are the problems and criticisms that China will have as well. One got a taste of these effects in the context of China's Belt and Road Initiative with the transfer of control of a Sri Lankan port to China.[622] The echoes of the ceding of Hong Kong to the UK a century or so earlier was unavoidable. And yet that analysis appeared unavailable to a Chinese bureaucracy that might have found that knowledge less useful. And yet, with it comes the sure knowledge of inversion. If China is now the foreigner, will these seven tropes now mark the pattern of its engagement with its own receiving political societies?

3.3. The lessons from Hong Kong 2019. Nowhere, perhaps, is this more apparent than in the Chinese Black Hand campaign against foreigners and foreign interventionism in Hong Kong during the 2019 protests. The use of the archetypal tropes were much in evidence in the campaign to point to a foreign adversary, to posit the character of that adversary as hostile, and to show the disruptive force of that interference. The consequence is also well understood—the use of the tropes to begin a cycle of again closing borders to the foreign now recast as hostile and not useful.

First, state authorities sought to identify a plausible foreign adversary.[623] State authorities made the quite deliberate reference (by Yang Guang (杨光)) to the 黑手 [black hand] of

---

chinas-new.html] (Coalition for Peace & Ethics Working Paper No. 1/3 (March 2018); available [http://lcbackerblog.blogspot.com/2018/03/on-internationalization-of-chinas-new.html].

[622] Kai Schultz, Sri Lanka, Struggling With Debt, Hands a Major Port to China, New York Times (12 Dec. 2017); available [https://www.nytimes.com/2017/12/12/world/asia/sri-lanka-china-port.html].

[623] Ben Westcott, "China is blaming the US for the Hong Kong protests. Can that really be true?," CNN World (31 July 2019); available [https://www.cnn.com/2019/07/31/asia/us-china-hong-kong-interference-intl-hnk/index.html].

foreign interference.[624] But the references was also used to point to the role of the United States as a principal instigator.

> *For example, in late March, the United States highly invited some of the opposition's leading figures to visit the United States, and arranged for the Vice President and the Secretary of State to meet and support them. Less than two months later, senior US officials met with the so-called "anti-extradition amendments and the United States and Canada" led by the opposition figures.* On June 13, some US lawmakers revisited the so-called "Hong Kong Bill of Rights on Human Rights and Democracy", arguing that they should regularly review or adjust their policies on Hong Kong and impose sanctions on relevant officials. . . . Wait a minute, there are still many, I will not go to read one by one, do not delay everyone's time. *I think that these remarks have a common feature, that is, to support the demonstrators to support their strengths and encourage their efforts, and to point and intervene in the affairs of Hong Kong. . . .* Recently, Yang Jiechi, director of the Office of the Central Foreign Affairs Working Committee, State Councilor and Foreign Minister Wang Yi have *all accused the Western forces of interfering in Hong Kong affairs.*[625]

But this was hardly the first time the Black Hand metaphor was used to identify the United States as a prime instigator of the conflict in Hong Kong. On 24 July 2019, Time Magazine's online version[626] reported from a Bloomberg source the use of the Black

---

[624] See discussion at Chapter 7, supra. The use of the reference was made in this context:"我们还要向那些肆无忌惮的极少数暴力犯罪分子和他们背后的黑手发出警告； 中国一直称有外部的"黑手"卷入香港当前的事态；这次政治风暴幕后黑手是--些敌视中国发展的势力 [We also want to warn those unscrupulous violent criminals and the black hands behind them; China has always said that there are external "black hands" involved in the current state of affairs in Hong Kong; The black hand behind the political storm is something that is hostile to China's development.]."

[625] Ibid.

[626] "China Urges U.S. to Remove 'Black Hand' From Hong Kong Protests," *Time;* available [https://time.com/5633383/china-hong-kong-u-s-foreign-forces/].

Hand trope by a Chinese Foreign Ministry official: "There are "signs of foreign forces behind the protests," Chinese Foreign Ministry spokeswoman Hua Chunying told reporters Tuesday in Beijing. "I wonder if these U.S. officials can truthfully answer to the world the role the U.S. has played in recent events in Hong Kong."[627] Her comments came after the U.S. State Department on Monday said attacks on protesters and other bystanders by criminal gangs was "particularly disturbing."[628] Chinese Foreign Minister Wang Yi had blamed the "black hand" of Western forces for stirring up trouble in Hong Kong last month, without singling out the U.S.[629] Pointedly, perhaps, the *South China Morning Post* circulated a story of the American Secretary of State denying the allegation.[630]

Yet the archetypes would suggest that there was plenty of fuel for this fire. Members of the US Congress, and elements of US civil society (sometimes in coordination with other Western civil society communities) have expressed views that have irritated the central authorities.[631] The central authority has tended to lump these unremarkable expressions of opinions by foreign officials and civil society elements as interference as well. "China's

---

[627] Ibid.

[628] Nike Ching, "Hong Kong Anger Grows After Attack," Voice of America (22 July 2019); available [https://www.voanews.com/east-asia-pacific/hong-kong-anger-grows-after-attack-protesters].

[629] Ibid.; see also "China Tells U.S. to Remove "Black Hands" From Hong Kong," Reuters (23 July 2019); available [https://www.reuters.com/article/us-hongkong-extradition-usa/china-tells-u-s-to-remove-black-hands-from-hong-kong-idUSKCN1UI0QJ].

[630] Keegan Elmer, "Mike Pompeo rebukes China's 'ludicrous' claim US is behind Hong Kong protests," *South China Morning Post* (31 July 2019); available [https://www.scmp.com/news/china/diplomacy/article/3020749/mike-pompeo-rebukes-chinas-ludicrous-claim-us-behind-hong-kong], accessed 5 Set. 2019 ("US Secretary of State Mike Pompeo has said it is "ludicrous" for China to claim the United States is behind the escalating protests in Hong Kong."), with reference to Clifford Lo , Ng Kang-chung , Zoe Low , Rachel Cheung and Phila Siu, "Hong Kong protesters injured in drive-by firework attack from private vehicle after clashes outside police stations," *South China Morning Post* (20 July 2019); available [https://www.scmp.com/news/hong-kong/law-and-crime/article/3020677/44-out-49-arrested-sundays-clashes-between-extradition].

[631] Discussed in essay Chapter 15, supra.

Foreign Ministry had strong words this week for members of the U.S. Congress weighing in on the Hong Kong protests: "Any attempt to interfere in Hong Kong affairs and China's internal affairs is doomed to fail.""[632]

The Chinese are likely especially irritated about the possibility of the enactment of a "*Hong Kong Human Rights and Democracy Act,*" [633] which US Speaker of the House of Representatives Pelsoi suggested was now on the table in the House, and which has been supported by influential U.S. elites. Yet such political acts in response to foreign decisions have been quite common for China, especially when it is deemed to affect political or strategic interests of the Central Government. Yet, it is hard to resist the perceived value of connecting these acts with the situation actually on the ground in Hong Kong. And to some extent, of course, such actions may have indirect effect--by signally to local elements the changing political consequences for China abroad of contemplated responses within China.

Second, foreigner tropes were deployed suggest that this adversary has already engaged in such conduct elsewhere. China could point to the US Global Magnitsky Act [634] projects as inherently designed to project US power (and thus interference) abroad. But recently China has sought to create the inference of the plausibility of Hong Kong interference by making claims about the tendency of the US to interfere in other places. Most recently that was noted by the high profile Central Government condemnation of what it termed US interference in Venezuela.[635]

---

[632] Shannon Tiezzi, "US Lawmakers Are Watching Hong Kong, and China Isn't Happy About That," The Diplomat (8 Aug. 2019); available [https://thediplomat.com/2019/08/us-lawmakers-are-watching-hong-kong-and-china-isnt-happy-about-that/*, Accessed 5 Sept. 2019.

[633] S.417 introduced in the Senate by Marco Rubio (R-FL) 115th Congress 2nd Sess.; available [https://www.congress.gov/bill/115th-congress/senate-bill/417/all-actions].

[634] Formally known as the Russia and Moldova Jackson–Vanik Repeal and Sergei Magnitsky Rule of Law Accountability Act of 2012, Pub.L. 112–208, Statutes at Large 126 Stat. 1496.

[635] Darryl Coote, "China condemns U.S. 'interference' in Venezuela," UPI (8 Aug. 2019); available [https://www.upi.com/Top_News/World-

But interference claims go much deeper in China. They tie into old fears of the revival of US encirclement policies, which fueled opposition to the Trans Pacific Partnership (TPP), also built on old tropes of foreign intentions.[636]. And it underlies Chinese sensitivities with respect to US-Taiwan relationships.[637] It has guided Chinese thinking in 2018 opposing portions of the North American trade deal.[638] Taking a cue from Western discourse, Chinese diplomatic statements have become more pointed in a way recognizable to Western audiences. China's diplomats have become increasingly vocal and outspoken. China's ambassador to London, Liu Xiaoming, gave a rare televised statement accusing the British government of meddling in Hong Kong, the scene of mass protests against Beijing's rule. Earlier this year, China's envoy to Canada publicly accused his hosts of "white supremacy," while the country's chief envoy in South Africa said President Donald Trump's policies were making the U.S. "the enemy of the whole world."[639]

News/2019/08/08/China-condemns-US-interference-in-Venezuela/6961565247926/], accessed 20 Aug. 2019).

[636] See . Larry Catá Backer, "The Trans-Pacific Partnership: Japan, China, the U.S., and the Emerging Shape of a New World Trade Regulatory Order," 13 *Wash. U. Global Stud. L. Rev.* 13:49 (2014); available [https://openscholarship.wustl.edu/law_globalstudies/vol13/iss1/6] (accessed 3 Sept. 2019).

[637] David Brennan, "Chinese State Media Slams U.S. 'Flagrant Interference' With Huge Taiwan Weapons Deal," Newsweek (12 July 2019); available [https://www.newsweek.com/chinese-state-media-slams-u-s-flagrant-interference-huge-taiwan-weapons-deal-1448891] ("The People's Daily editorial suggested that the Taiwan weapons deal was just one element of American efforts to "contain China." It added that the "irresponsible practice of the U.S." will raise tensions, and warned that American leaders "should not take chances and keep walking on the wrong path."").

[638] Zhou Xin, "Chinese embassy in Canada condemns 'US veto' clause in North America trade deal," *South China Morning Post* (8 October 2018); available [https://www.scmp.com/economy/china-economy/article/2167395/chinese-embassy-canada-condemns-us-veto-clause-north-america].

[639] Iain Marlow and Dandan Li, "'You Are a Racist Disgrace.' Former National Security Advisor Susan Rice Chides 'Ignorant' Diplomat on Twitter," *Time* (July 2019); available [https://time.com/5626551/susan-rice-twitter-chinese-diplomat/].

The structural components become visible in this wider context. Like a good lawyer seeking to draw an inference of a likelihood that an accused acted in a particular way by pointing to a pattern of similar conduct in the past, the Central Government is seeking to make plausible its claims of interference by making a case that US foreign action is itself undeniably driven by an impulse to interfere. This pays additional dividends. First it advances Chinese efforts to develop its own model of internationalism based on principles of non-interference (for which an antipode in the form of the US is required). Second, it makes the case for a greater room to maneuver in Hong Kong. Third, it can be useful in managing its trade dispute with the US. And fourth, it may aid in advancing Belt and Road initiatives. Whatever happens in Hong Kong, this initiative likely has staying power.

And third, the trope suggested the importance of marshalling evidence from which local interference might be surmised. China has continually pointed to meetings between Hong Kong individuals identified as part of the protest movement and U.S. officials. The Tweet distributed 8 August through the *People's Daily* is one example. Indeed, the meeting that was pictured in that Tweet also sparked an official response from the central authorities.[640]

The Western press (Bloomberg) reported more detail: "China's foreign ministry, which has previously said Hong Kong's ongoing unrest was 'the creation of the U.S.,' urged American diplomats in a statement to 'draw a clear line with all anti-Chinese rioters, stop sending wrong signals to illegal violators, stop meddling in Hong Kong affairs, and stop going further down the wrong path.'"[641] Additional individuals have been identified in

---

[640] "Also Thursday [8 August 2019], the Chinese foreign ministry's office in Hong Kong issued a formal protest over a reported meeting between U.S. consular officials in the city and opposition figures, including prominent activist Joshua Wong. The statement demanded the U.S. explain the purpose of the meeting and "immediately cease interfering in Hong Kong affairs." Ben Westcott, "China is blaming the US, supra.

[641] Iain Marlow and Dandan Li, "China warns U.S. after diplomat meets with prominent protesters," Bloomberg (8 Aug. 2019); available

tweets that are circulating.[642] These suggest the possibility that the central authorities or SAR authorities are already building cases for prosecutions against identified individuals that may in part be strengthened by the development of the "Black Hand" theory now circulated by the central authorities. One sees here the response to archetypes of the expatriate and the need to avoid the conversion of Chinese students into instruments of foreign colonization.

But the use of these archetypical tropes suggests as well that its deep penetration has also affected Chinese outward engagement. Just as the Chinese are quick to draw on the tropes in advancing their strategic interests in Hong Kong, they are also deploying them in the projection of their own interests abroad. One is reminded here of the way that the Chinese Foreign Ministry has continuously shrugged off Australian and New Zealand allegations of interference for its meetings, consultations, and statements directed toward Australian education. [643] There is something of an irony to see how on the one hand the tropes can be used defensively within China and offensively beyond. The foreigner trope thus becomes useful in many ways.

4. Conclusion.

[https://www.ctpost.com/news/article/China-warns-U-S-after-diplomat-meets-with-14290165.php] accessed 30 Aug. 2019).

[642] e.g., Xu Keyue, "Chinese consulate in Australia praises patriotic students for counter-protest against separatists," Global Times (27 July 2019); available [http://www.globaltimes.cn/content/1159212.shtml] accessed 30 Aug. 2019.

[643] see, e.g., Chinese Nationalists Bring Threat of Violence to Australian Universities, The New York Times (30 July 2019); available [https://www.nytimes.com/2019/07/30/world/australia/hong-kong-china-queensland-protests.html] accessed 5 Sept. 2019); "Hong Kong, mainland Chinese students clash at New Zealand university over extradition bill," *South China Morning Post* (30 July 2019); available [https://www.scmp.com/news/asia/australasia/article/3020639/chinese-students-clash-new-zealand-university-over-hong-kong] accessed 4 Sept. 2019; Xu Keyue, "Chinese consulate in Australia praises patriotic students for counter-protest against separatists," Global Times (27 July 2019); available [http://www.globaltimes.cn/content/1159212.shtml] accessed (30 Aug. 2019); "Queensland university students protest 'China-funded education'," SBS News (31 July 2019); available [https://www.sbs.com.au/news/queensland-university-students-protest-china-funded-education] accessed 30 Aug. 2019).

The relationship of China to the foreigner has been complicated since the end of the Qing. It is hard to avoid the 1913 approach of Edward Capen with which we began to understand the relationship of foreigner to China; but that is the trap for China in its engagement with law in the global sphere. One should ask: What Chinese influence has accomplished; What Chinese influence should not destroy; Where a state can learn from China; How China can be most helpful? But the greater insight suggests the cultural tropes necessary for the creation of structures within which knowledge engagement may be curated, and thus curated, controlled. The Great Firewall[644] in this sense is a small example of the implementation of a much broader and deeper cultural-political strategy that has acquired a life of its own.

These are the questions that Chinese actors must ask as they deepen Chinese footprints in Africa, Latin America and Asia. Can China avoid the traps and tropes of Western engagement with China from the last century? Can China avoid the traditional pattern of instrumentalism and suppression? How to avoid these traps will be the greatest Challenge for China as it pursues its go out policies and engages in national and international forums.

$$* \quad * \quad *$$

---

[644] See, e.g., The Great Firewall of China, Bloomberg (5 Nov. 2018); available [https://www.bloomberg.com/quicktake/great-firewall-of-china].

Chapter 17

Wednesday 25 September 2019
The "Five Demands," the Legitimacy of Force, and the Constitution of the "Two Systems" Principle

Since the start of the protests in June, the national and local officials have worked hard to develop a coherent and coordinated narrative of the situation in Hong Kong, the legitimacy of their interpretation of the 'One Country-Two Systems' principle, and as a consequence, the illegitimacy of foreign engagement and of the protests themselves. [645] The international community has also been busy, though perhaps less effective. While the usual organs of the international community have expressed what appears to be the usual and somewhat ambiguous responses, there has also been something of an effort to articulate a position on the international character of One Country-Two Systems and of the necessary role not just of the international community, but also of international law and norms as well in the construction of governance principles in Hong Kong.[646]

Central to the development of the internationalist position is the notion that sovereignty is not a unitary concept.[647] "Rather than being a binary concept, sovereignty can be understood more like a continuum, or a bundle of different kinds of functions and authority."[648] The idea here is that globalization and the post-war settlement made obsolete the notions, famously articulated in Hobbs, that the sovereign power may not be divided,[649] a principle central to the Chinese focus on the primacy of the 'One Country' part of the principle. Internationalists take the position--sadly

---

[645] Discussed in Chapters 3-5; 7-8, and 12, , supra.

[646] Discussed in Chapters 10-11, 14-15, supra.

[647] A good starting point for this sort of discussion in liberal democratic context are Carmen Pavel, *Divided Sovereignty: International Institutions and the Limits of State Authority* (Oxford, 2015); Stephen D. Krasner, *Sovereignty: Organized Hypocrisy* (Princeton University press, 1999); pp. 3-42

[648] Pavel, *Divided Sovereignty,* supra, p 20.

[649] Thomas Hobbs, Leviathan (Cambridge University Press, 1991) , pp. 213-214.

poorly articulated--that sovereignty can be divided. More specifically in the case of Hong Kong that sovereignty can be split between a territorial sovereignty (the sovereignty of 'One Country'), and governance sovereignty (the sovereignty of 'Two Systems').[650]

This core contest between world ordering perspectives in the political realm has become increasingly clear as what started out as a very narrow (through quite passionate) eruption of anger triggered by what had been perceived as political overreaching by the people of Hong Kong, has now metastasized into a contest over the legitimating ordering principles of state and international authority. [651] If sovereignty is inalienable, indivisible, and incapable of error within the organism of the state,[652] then official responses to threats to the sovereign themselves can be understood as harm free, if undertaken in accordance with law. If sovereignty is polycentric and capable of delegation or partition, then acts in defense of the portion of sovereign authority vested in a unit itself is defensible as against acts that represent a threat. Nothing is ever that simple, of course--except when it comes to the construction of narrative frameworks that are essential for the management of a consensus view of the meaning of the conflicts observed in Hong Kong.

One sees evidence of this ratcheting up of the stakes in the protests since June 2019. Where it leads is hard to say. But one thing is clear--that the authority for violence is at the center of the efforts. Tied to this authority (or legitimacy) of violence are quite conflicting notions of sovereignty and its defense. On the one side one encounters the legitimate use of violence by the police and the lawless violence of "rioters." On the other side one encounters the

---

[650] Discussed in Chapter 15, supra.

[651] The origins of this trajectory, of course, long preceded the protests of June 2019. See, e.g., Stephan Ortmann, "The lack of sovereignty, the Umbrella Movement, and democratisation in Hong Kong," *Asia Pacific Law Review* 24(2):108-122 (2016).

[652] "The Sovereign, merely by virtue of what it is, is always what it should be." Jean-Jacques Rousseau, "Social Contract," in 38 *Great Books of the Western World: Montesquieu; Rousseau* (C.G: Cole, trans., Chicago: Great Books, 1952), p. 387, 392.

legitimate use of violence in defense of the liberties of the people against the disproportionate use of force by a state whose illegitimacy is itself evidenced by the disproportion of its use of force.

Consider the evolution of protest objectives that moved from resistance to the extradition bill to the "Five Demands"[653] that have emerged as the central formal objectives of Hong Kong protestors. These "Five Demands" crystalize   the more comprehensive political strategy that has emerged among the Hong Kong protestors. The "Five Demands include: (1) full withdrawal of the extradition bill; (2) a commission of inquiry into alleged police brutality; (3) retracting the classification of protestors as 'rioters;' (4) amnesty for arrested protesters; and (5) dual universal suffrage, meaning for both the Legislative Council and the Chief Executive."[654] It is worth considering each in slightly more detail.

The withdrawal of the extradition bill suggests the loss of confidence in the government headed by Carrie Lam. Better put--the protesters no longer trust the government to either keep its word or to act in ways that reflect popular opinion. It "sees through" the strategic artifice of functionally halting work on the extradition bill but refusing to withdraw it.   That suggests a stalling tactic rather than a concession; it suggests bad faith on the part of officials. Yet to make this demand is to require local officials to lose face. And that may be practically impossible, especially if such a loss of face is interpreted (as it well might be) as a concession by central authorities, without whose approval it is unlikely that local authorities can do anything.

This demand was fairly easy to meet--if only because a formal withdrawal of the bill means nothing as it does not constrain a future government from re-introducing a new version

---

[653] Wong Tsui-kai, "Hong Kong protests: What are the 'five demands'? What do protesters   want?,"   Discover   News   (20   August   2019);   available [https://www.scmp.com/yp/discover/news/hong-kong/article/3065950/hong-kong-protests-what-are-five-demands-what-do].
[654] Ibid.

of the bill in altered local circumstances.[655]   And indeed on 4 September, Carrie Lam announced that the extradition bill would be withdrawn; it was a long process. [656] "With Wednesday's announcement, Lam has now conceded to one of five key demands of the demonstrators. However, the chief executive did not respond to protesters' other demands."[657] The idea, perhaps, was to concede to one and resist the other, far more consequential demands in the hopes that since the principal object of the protests erupting in June had been met, then the *raison d'etre* for them would disappear and the protests along with it.

The reason it appeared to take so long to make even this concession appears to be the reluctance of the central authorities to approve a strategy that conceded even this point.[658] The central

---

[655] Lily Kuo and Verna Yu, "Hong Kong's leader withdraws extradition bill that ignited mass protests," The Guardian (4 September 2019); available [https://www.theguardian.com/world/2019/sep/04/hong-kong-lam-to-withdraw-extradition-bill-say-reports] ("In a five-minute televised address on Wednesday, Lam said her government would formally withdraw the controversial bill to "fully allay public concerns" .... "She has to do something otherwise it's going to be ugly," said Michael Tien, one of the pro-Beijing lawmakers who attended a meeting with Lam before her announcement. "So she is making this gesture now, this concession. There is a month in between where she was hoping things would die down."").

[656] Chris Cheng, "Hong Kong Officially Withdraws Controversial Extradition Bill from Legislature," *Hong Kong Free Press* (23 October 2019); available [https://hongkongfp.com/2019/10/23/just-hong-kong-officially-withdraws-controversial-extradition-bill-legislature/] The reporting noted: "Chief Executive Carrie Lam announced the suspension of the bill on June 15, though the move failed to allay public anger. Two million people marched in protest the next day, according to organiser estimates. On July 9, Lam declared the bill "dead" but stopped short of announcing a full withdrawal. Responding to one of the core demands made by protesters, Lam finally said on September 4 that the bill would be formally withdrawn at the legislature." Ibid.

[657] Lily Kuo and Verna Yu, "Hong Kong's leader withdraws extradition bill," Supra.

[658] "Amid crisis, China rejected Hong Kong plan to withdraw extradition bill," *Korea Times* (30 August 2019); available [https://www.koreatimes.co.kr/www/world/2021/02/683_274872.html] ("Earlier this summer, Carrie Lam... submitted a report to Beijing that assessed protesters' five key demands and found that withdrawing a contentious extradition bill could help defuse the mounting political crisis in the territory. The Chinese central government rejected Lam's proposal to withdraw the extradition bill and ordered her not to yield to any of the protesters' other

authorities appear to have sought to make a point--that any concession would undermine their position on the centrality of the One Country principle reflected in their earlier public articulations of their position. They recognized the likelihood that any concession would undermine their position on the domestication of Hong Kong governance within China.[659]

By the time the central authorities were willing to concede even the small demand touching on withdrawal of the bill, events had moved far beyond this simple relational binary that aligned the protests solely to resistance to the extradition bill. "Social unrest in the city has since taken on broader anti-government sentiment as protesters push for greater democracy in Hong Kong."[660] A concession of the sort made belatedly on 4 September might have had the intended effect in July, is unlikely to produce anything other than a heightened sense of purpose. And the evidence for that is the Five Demands itself. The Five Demands start but do not end with the withdrawal of the Extradition bill. It is to the additional four demands that the protestors are now focused. And these significantly up the stakes. They serve as a direct contest over the legitimacy of the government's actions, of its authority, and of the legitimacy of the central authorities projection of power into Hong Kong. Indeed, to question the authority of the police, to insist on an amnesty that questions the legitimacy of the actions of the local officials, and to

---

demands at that time, three individuals with direct knowledge of the matter told Reuters.").

[659] James Pomfret and Greg Torode, "Exclusive: Amid crisis, China rejected Hong Kong plan to appease protesters - sources," Reuters (30 August 2019); Available [https://www.reuters.com/article/us-hongkong-protests-china-exclusive/exclusive-amid-crisis-china-rejected-hong-kong-plan-to-appease-protesters-sources-idUSKCN1VK0H6] ("'They said no' to all five demands, said the source. 'The situation is far more complicated than most people realize.' . . . The official confirmed that Beijing had rejected giving in to any of the protesters' demands and wanted Lam's administration to take more initiative." Ibid.)

[660] By the end of the year that sensibility, already evident in September when the essay was written, became more widely reported in the Western press. Vivian Kam, "Hong Kong unrest hits 6-month milestone, protesters' demands see little response from government," CNBC 8 December 2019); available [https://www.cnbc.com/2019/12/08/hong-kong-protests-5-demands-see-little-response-from-city-government.html]

demand the substantial reform of the constitution of the SAR all go to the re-invigoration of the internationalist aspects of the "two Systems" principle.

It does more than reinvigorate the internationalist foundations of the Two Systems principle. The Five Demands effectively seek to detach the Two Systems principle from its connection to the Sino-British Joint Declaration, one with a termination date of 2047, and seeks to find a way, in international legalities, to make the arrangement permanent. In this respect the last four of the Five Demands, then, seek to transform and make permanent the Two Systems principle and to anchor it firmly in liberal democratic principles based on international norms. This was certainly recognized by the Speaker of the US House of Representatives in her Statement issued on the day of the announcement of the withdrawal of the extradition bill:

> The long-overdue withdrawal of the dangerous extradition bill is welcome news, but much more must be done to fully realize the legitimate aspirations of the Hong Kong people, as guaranteed under 'One Country, Two Systems.' The people of Hong Kong deserve the future of justice, real autonomy and freedom from fear that they were promised, and for which they have long been courageously fighting. "The pro-Beijing leadership in Hong Kong must ensure a political system accountable to the people, including granting universal suffrage and investigating police violence. The escalating violence and use of force perpetrated by the Hong Kong authorities against their own people in recent weeks, which has led to tragic loss of life, must end now.[661]

The second and third demands, then, raise the stakes considerably and put into play the authority and legitimacy of the actions of local officials in response to the protests. The second, seeking a commission of inquiry into police response to the protests, effectively seeks to attack the legitimacy of the use of

---

[661] "Pelosi Statement on Withdrawal of Hong Kong Extradition Bill," (4 September 2019); available [https://www.speaker.gov/newsroom/9419].

state power in the context of the exercise by the protestors of their civil and political rights as those had come to be understood in the special conditions of Hong Kong.[662] The idea here is to reverse the polarities of violence to suggest that it is the police rather than the protestors who were acting unlawfully, and therefore without either authority or the protection of law.[663]

This effort does not appear to have gone unnoticed. Indeed, Lam was quite careful to limit the concessions of the local officials to the issue of the extradition bill. Lam insisted that the issue of police conduct was an internal matter to be handled, in the first instance, by the police themselves through its Complaints Against Police Office (CAPO) [664] and the Independent Police Complaints Council.[665] To move the question of police violence outside of the established methods of monitoring and response is to concede that the system itself cannot authoritatively address the issue. And it is that lack of authority that local officials would find impossible to concede. And yet for the protesters, the essence of their claims has moved beyond the extradition bill to the constitutional legitimacy of the local state apparatus as evidenced by its efforts to undermine the Hong Kong constitutional settlement through the use of police force.

---

[662] These notions became more crystalized in anti-government criticisms in the months that followed. Michael Chugani, for example wrote: "By now, our leaders should know violence won't end just because they demand it. They have lost all legitimacy, which makes their words meaningless. But they keep on condemning violence as if that alone would stop it. . . The moral high ground belongs to the protesters. They were forced into using violence after Lam ignored their peaceful voice." Michael Chugani, "Not just five demands, five lessons too for Carrie Lam," EjiInsight (24 October 2019); available [https://www.ejinsight.com/eji/article/id/2281638/20191024-not-just-five-demands-five-lessons-too-for-carrie-lam].

[663] Wong Tsui-kai, "Hong Kong protests: What are the 'five demands'?, supra ("On June 12, police dispersed protesters outside Legco with what protesters say is excessive force. They have criticized these actions ever since. Protesters also have little confidence in the current police watchdog, the Independent Police Complaints Council.").

[664] Complaints Against Police Office (投 訴 警 察 課); available [https://www.police.gov.hk/ppp_en/11_useful_info/cap.html].

[665] Independent Police Complaints Council (IPCC) ("獨立監察警方處理投訴委員會") Ordinance (Cap. 604, Laws of Hong Kong (1 July 2009)); available [https://www.ipcc.gov.hk/doc/en/download/IPCC_Bill.pdf].

Leading academics within Hong Kong recognized the transformative elements embedded within what appeared at face value to be a set of five fairly straightforward demands. [666] Especially interesting was the well-developed position of Hong Kong University Professor Albert Chen, [667] who had already positioned himself as an authoritative commentator of and public intellectual focused on the events from June 2019.[668] Reflecting ancient Western liberal governance principles, Chen first concedes that the state has or ought to be conceded something close to a near monopoly on violence. But that authority to violence can be legitimately exercised only under the constraints of law.[669] The question that then comes to the foreground is one

---

[666] Vivian Kam, "Hong Kong unrest hits 6-month milestone, supra ("Government opposition was fueled by anger with police conduct as well as how Lam's administration dealt with the protests, Ma Ngok, associate professor in the department of government and public administration at the Chinese University of Hong Kong, told CNBC. "The government hasn't actually responded, so a lot of people think they just cannot give up on the protest" Ma said.")

[667] Albert Chen Hung-yee (陳弘毅), --"Who Will Supervise the Police?" [誰來監督警察？] Mingpao（明報報料）(19 September 2019); available [https://news.mingpao.com/ins/文摘/article/20190919/s00022/156887687

4345/誰來監督警察-（文-陳弘毅）]. A crude English translation may be accessed online [https://lcbackerblog.blogspot.com/2019/09/the-situation-in-hing-kong-albert-chen.html].

[668] Considered in Chapters 6 and 9, supra.

[669] Albert Chen Hung-yee (陳弘毅), --"Who Will Supervise the Police?" [誰來監督警察？], supra:

在現代法治社會中，正如任何政府官員一樣，警察的權力是法律所賦予的，警察行使其權力時，不得超越其法律的授權。例如法律授權警方在拘捕被合理地懷疑犯法的市民時使用必要的武力，但如警察在法律並無授權其使用暴力的情況下，對市民使用暴力，例如予以毆打，這便構成刑事犯罪。在"佔中"期間發生的"七警案"和警司朱經緯案，便是典型的例子。(In a modern society ruled by law, as with any government official, the power of the police is conferred by law, and the police must not exceed the authority of their laws when exercising their powers. For example, the law authorizes the police to use the necessary force when arresting citizens who are reasonably suspected of breaking the law. However, if the police do not authorize the use of violence by law, the use of violence against the public, such as beatings, constitutes a criminal offence. The "seven police cases"

of monitoring the lawfulness of the exercise of police violence. "The issue of the issue of the police is important because it is related to whether the rule of law can be enforced, whether it can implement the principle of equality under the law, whether it is the protection of the rights and freedoms of citizens, and the prevention of a monopoly on the legal use of force. The right of the police violates the freedom and human rights of the people while exercising their powers."[670]

For Chen, then, there is a direct and proportional connection between adherence to core rule of law, human rights, and democracy principles and the attention it pays to the supervision of the police. To that end Chen draws not on the application of this Principe in China (One Country) but in the practices of Western liberal democratic states (Two Systems).[671] The intimation is subtle but telling--one cannot draw on governance and accountability principles from Hong Kong's territorial sovereign in order to gauge the lawfulness of police violence, but must instead (and naturally) draw on Hong Kong's governance sovereigns to engage in an appropriate legal-political analysis. This is a reality arising from the historical context of Hong Kong's development, and of the local conditions that exist because Hong Kong's culture was shaped within these external (and now international) approaches.[672]

And yet that also provides a basis for protecting the legitimacy of the current situation (One Country PLUS Two Systems). The system of police supervision is the expression of the approach to the legitimation of state power through law evolved in the liberal democratic traditions that have been internationalized and in that way deeply embedded in Hong Kong's culture. He noted that "The IPCC also hired five experts

---

and the police chief Zhu Jingwei, which occurred during the "Occupy" period, are typical examples.)
[670] Ibid. ("監警問題之所以重要，　一方面是因為它關係到法治是否得以伸張，是否能貫徹法律之下人人平等的原則，也關係到公民的權利和自由是否得以保障，防止對合法使用武力有壟斷權的警方在行使其權力時侵害到人民的自由和人權。").
[671] Ibid.
[672] Ibid.

with extensive experience in police affairs from the United Kingdom, Canada, Australia and New Zealand to assist in the above review and assessment." [673] It follows that its complaint procedures must be respected and protected as an expression of the Two Systems principle within the One Country framework of Hong Kong. This conclusion can then be used to two distinct ends. The first is to align support for the police with a legally framed constraint on their use of force--one that preserves the legitimacy of the police within the traditions of liberal democratic sensibilities. [674] The other is to detach the question of police misconduct from the larger questions of the character and future of the Two Systems model itself.[675] Chen in this way seeks to bring both sides closer to a middle point form which dialogue might be possible. And yet those efforts might by this point already be too subtle, too generous, and too late.

Related to this last point is the third demand, to retract the classification of protestors as rioters. The term has legal connotation in Hong Kong--rioting is a criminal offense with the possible imposition of a ten year prison term. [676] The local authorities were quite strategic in using the term--to create the narrative of the protestors as outlaws--as outside the law. [677] "It was no offense to kill an outlaw: indeed in the strictest sense of the law, it appears rather to have been the duty of every man to do so."[678] Thus on one side stands the state and its institutions as

---

[673] Ibid. ("監警會還特別聘請了五位來自英國、加拿大、澳洲和紐西蘭的在監警事務上有豐富經驗的專家，協助上述審視和評估工作。").

[674] Ibid. ("I think that the IPCC has tried its best to play its role and play the role of supervisor in handling the police's demonstrations of the campaign." 我認為監警會已經盡力發揮其功能，就警方對於這次運動的示威活動的處理，扮演監督者的角色。)

[675] Ibid. ("It is not a comprehensive investigation of the background and causes of the regulatory storm, but even if such a committee is established in the future, it is estimated that it cannot replace the functions of the IPCC." 它不是一個全面調查修例風波的背景和成因的調查委員會，)

[676] Wong Tsui-kai, "Hong Kong protests: What are the 'five demands'?, *supra*

[677] H. Erle Richards, "Is Outlawry Obsolete?" Law Quarterly Review 18:297-304 (1902) ("The effect of a judgment of outlawry was at first to put the outlawed person entirely beyond the protection of the law in every sense" Ibid., 298).

[678] Ibid., p. 298.

the cauldron of legality, and on the other, the protestor as an instrument of anarchy, rejecting and standing outside not just law but the lawfully constituted body politic.

It is in this sense that the contemporary cultural overtones of ancient and now obsolete legal principles served a useful purpose for local officials. Those overtones retain the idea that outlaws are not entitled to the protections of the state. Such a designation might then affect the analysis of the extent of force that might be reasonably applied to suppress this sort of outlawry. The protestors, though, seek again to reverse polarity--to indict the police as the real rioters in Hong Kong, and conversely of the protesters as lawfully resisting the unlawful actions of the police. As the outlaws, and therefore to suggest that the assertion by the local authorities of power reflected in their resistance to protest as illegitimate. At bottom, these reversals of legitimacy are founded on quite distinct notions of the locus of sovereign governance authority. Local authorities look to Beijing; protestors look to their internationally guaranteed rights. Each views the breach of the exercise of their sovereign prerogatives through the lens of the lawlessness of the other side. To secure consensus on the source of lawlessness, then, is to strengthen the claims that acting with right on their side.

That sensibility is made more apparent with the fourth and fifth of the five demands--amnesty and fundamental legislative reform. Though the Five Demands speak in terms of amnesty, the context suggests vindication rather than the exercise of sovereign grace.[679] The suggestion, in context, is that local officials exceed their authority, that the arrests were taken unlawfully and in conjunction with the supplemental unlawfulness of the police. Amnesty is then used as a means of recognizing the illegality of the act of arresting the protestors, and of recognizing the legality of the protests under the "Two Systems"

---

[679] Kris Cheng, " Explainer: Hong Kong's Five Demands – amnesty for all arrested protesters," *Hong Kong Free Press* (25 December 2019); available [https://hongkongfp.com/2019/12/25/explainer-hong-kongs-five-demands-amnesty-arrested-protesters/] ("Chief Executive Carrie Lam has maintained – for months – that offering any kind of amnesty would send the wrong signal and would be an affront to the rule of law.")

principle. The Five Demands then draw on a wider international discourse of amnesty as a means of confession by state authorities of their excesses (under cover of law) as much as it is the application of amnesty as the remedy by the state against the victims of its own lawlessness.[680]

A compromise position--not amnesty but pardon-- appears also to have been proposed.[681] Here the local officials could reaffirm the illegality of the actions of the protesters but at the same time use their authority as an act of clemency for the reconstruction of social solidarity. Note the difference between the two terms--an amnesty wipes clean the slate of offense, a pardon relieves the offender of the consequences of their offenses. One involves nullifying the offense, the other serves as an act of clemency but not of overcoming of the offense.[682]

At the same time, the act of amnesty could be turned around to further cement the One Country principle. Amnesty can be understood in its original sense of forgetting (from the Greek ἀμνηστία).[683] In this sense the forgetting may be undertaken only by that government that has the sovereign authority to remember (and punish). That itself can constitute the expression of power which, if exercised in an appropriate context, could be used to further cement the authority of the territorial sovereign over that of the international governance architecture left in place after the transfer. Yet it appears the central authorities cannot bring themselves to see ort use it that way. There may be good reason. If the sovereign shows a disposition to "forget" offenses through amnesty in Hong Kong, might it also be nudged to "forget" offenses in Shanghai, Wuhan, or Beijing? The problem with Two System

---

[680] Consider, for example, Milena Sterio, "Rethinking Amnesty," Denver Journal of International Law and Policy 34(3):373-400 (2006); Lisa J. LaPlante, "Outlawing Amnesty: The Return of Criminal Justice in Transitional Justice Schemes," *Virginia Journal of International Law* 49(4):915-984 (2009)

[681] Ibid. ("According to RTHK last month, the government has examined whether to offer pardons after the judicial process on a case-by-case basis. The mechanism could be carried out under Article 48 of the city's Basic Law,").

[682] Consider Harrop A. Freeman, "A Historical Justification and Legal Basis for Amnesty Today," *Law and the Social Order* 3:515-537 (1971).

[683] Consider Peter Krapp, "Amnesty: Between an Ethics of Forgiveness and the Politics of Forgetting, *German Law Journal* 6(1):185-196 (2005).

amnesty, in this case, may well be its potential repercussions in One Country.

The call for fundamental political change presents an even greater challenge. First, the reforms proposed would deepen the differences in political cultures between the SAR and the rest of the nation. That, in turn, would move Hong Kong farther from the trajectory of development of political culture under the leadership of the vanguard party. And that hard split in the direction of political development trajectories would then produce an impossible contradiction for central authorities. If the vanguard party is obligated (within the parameters and premises of its own guiding ideology) to move the nation toward the eventual establishment of a communist society throughout the territory of China, then the encouragement (or even toleration) of movement that appears to go in any other direction would appear to pose a great threat to the core mission of the vanguard party and to its responsibility to the nation. From the One Country perspective this is intolerable. From the Two Systems perspectives, of course, the vanguard conceded this point and accepted its possibility from the time it bound itself to One Country Two Systems in the Sino-British Joint Declaration. [684] Two Systems principles suggests, then, that if the vanguard seeks to align trajectories, it would have to do it through other means. In that context--forcing a shift in trajectory, and in the political culture of the SAR, is intolerable.

Local officials, of course, ignored the demands for legislative reform and amnesty; they were effectively dismissed as extra-legal. [685] And from the perspective of local and central

---

[684] Joint Declaration of the Government of the United Kingdom of Great Britain and Northern Ireland and the Government of the People's Republic of China on the Question of Hong Kong (19 December 1984); available [https://www.cmab.gov.hk/en/issues/jd2.htm] (hereafter Sino-British Joint Declaration).

[685] This was a position expressed through Carrie Lam's supporters. See Regina Ip, "Carrie Lam has Done all She Can to Meet the Five Demands; Protesters Must Know Their Limits," South China Morning Post (15 September 2019); available [https://www.scmp.com/comment/opinion/article/3026897/carrie-lam-has-done-all-she-can-meet-five-demands-protesters-must] ("Unfortunately, the chief executive does not have any power to grant a blanket amnesty or universal suffrage").

authorities, this would be expected. Yet that local and central authorities have been put in this position--that they now are faced with dealing with, responding, to the Five Demands before a global audience, suggest the ways in which a protest--once narrowly focused on a clumsy effort to impose an extradition law, has transformed the political landscape of Hong Kong. The resulting radicalization of the position of protesters and of the local and central authorities have now transformed the political contest in ways that make resolution far more difficult. And that is the point--the initial responses to the June protests have now managed to transform the response from a local matter to a matter touching on the fundamental nature of One Country and of Two Systems, one in which compromise may no longer be possible.

Perhaps Yok-sing (Jasper) Tsang, a member of the pro-Beijing camp, summed up the situation nicely in an interview given after this chapter was originally written but which reflects its spirit:

> When Carrie Lam announced the suspension, she still said that it had been the right thing to do, that the purpose of the bill was to suppress loopholes in our law that had to be suppressed. But the people didn't accept that, and the protesters put up their five demands. And it became a kind of political confrontation. . . Carrie said that a suspension was equivalent to a withdrawal. The protesters were saying: "Say the word!", while our side said: "Don't say it!" Finally, when she said it, the other side said: "we're not satisfied with that."
>
> Same thing with the other demands: a commission of inquiry. She doesn't want to do it because of objection from the police. But my colleagues said: "You said 'no', there is no need for such an inquiry; the IPCC is enough. Don't betray us again!" But we don't know, maybe in a

week or two, it will be set up... It seems the government is unwilling to do anything until it is too late.[686]

The Five Demands, then, point to the construction of a coherent and (from the perspective of the central authorities) radical and transformative agenda. They point to the primary principle of self-determination now applied *within* a sovereign. [687] The Five Demands suggest that international norms rather than national principles must ultimately frame that right, and protect it, even as a state may retain its sovereignty over a territory but not its power to impose a political economic model.[688] This is sure to meet substantial opposition not just from Chinese central authorities,[689] but perhaps from other states that themselves may be facing issues of autonomous regions looking for greater autonomy from the center.

And yet there is a failure here as well. The Five Demands begin to produce an ideological text that might challenge the narrative supremacy of the discourse that the Chinese central authorities have been developing almost since the start of the protests. At the same time the Five Demands fails to take full

---

[686] "Interview: Ex-Head of legislature Jasper Tsang says the gov't is weakest player of four in Hong Kong's struggle," Hong Kong Free Press (16 November 2019); available [https://hongkongfp.com/2019/11/16/interview-ex-head-legislature-jasper-tsang-says-govt-weakest-player-four-hong-kongs-struggle/] (interviewing Yok-sing (Jasper) Tsang is a veteran politician of the pro-Beijing camp.

[687] For a taste of this, see Clifford D. May, "Why Hong Kong has a right to self-Determination: Come to think of it, so does Greenland," *Washington Times* (27 August 2019); available [https://www.washingtontimes.com/news/2019/aug/27/why-hong-kong-has-right-self-determination/]

[688] This builds on notions that became more plausible in the wake of the Umbrella Movement, at least among leading elements of the protester movements. See, Kong Tsung-Gan, "City of broken promises: Is self-determination the only way left for Hong Kong?," *Hong Kong Free Press* (22 October 2017); available [https://hongkongfp.com/2017/10/22/city-broken-promises-self-determination-way-left-hong-kong/].

[689] Song Zhe, "Self-Determination in Hong Kong is a Non-Issue: Historically, legally and culturally, the city belongs to China. Better to focus on its advantages as part of one country," *Wall Street Journal* (18 October 2016); available [https://www.wsj.com/articles/self-determination-in-hong-kong-is-a-non-issue-1476807740].

advantage of its discursive potential. Perhaps that will come as the constellation of protest groups begin to coalesce around the implications of the Five Demand and better develop its ideology. Those normative and ideological implications are powerful within the liberal democratic and international communities. And they point to alternative notions of sovereignty-within-sovereignty that are already at the center of discussion in large European states. The challenge for the protest movements remains the same, however. That challenge centers on the alignment between the street politics that have proven effective since June and the development of an ideological framework and structure which can be sold to the masses and serve as a specific basis of support from allies.

✳ ✳ ✳

Chapter 18

Sunday 20 October 2019
Students at the Center and the University Response --CUHK Vice-Chancellor and President Professor Rocky S. Tuan's Open Letter 中大校長段崇智教授公開信

The situation in Hong Kong has evolved dramatically since it began its current phase in June 2019. What started out as a very large mass protests against the decisions of senior Hong Kong functionaries, undertaken with the knowledge of the central government, has now become mired in a complex and fluid expression of popular discontent that has spilled out along many fronts. That discontent has veered into violence and has been met by violence.[690] At the same time, both the central authorities and the various protest factions have sought to reach out for allies among a wide group of public and private international actors, or to blame the "black hand" (" 黑手 ") foreign interests in the situation of Hong Kong. [691] For one group these inward projections serve as the vindication and foundation of "Two Systems" principle; for the other they serve as the negation of "One Country" principle and a direct assault on national sovereignty. And in all of this one notes the relentless escalation, in discourse and objectives, of what had been, now in retrospect, a narrow confrontation that might have been judiciously contained in June 2019.

But several months of protests and the ramping up of rhetoric, along with the more entrenched ideologies they

---

[690] Billie Thomson, "Hong Kong police are blasted for 'tackling' a student during a school strike in support of anti-government movement," *Daily Mail* (3 September 2019); available [https://www.dailymail.co.uk/news/article-7423043/Hong-Kong-police-accused-tackling-student-school-strike.html] ("University students use umbrella to practice self-defense technique to prevent possible violent during clashes at Chinese University of Hong Kong in Sha Tin on Tuesday").

[691] Discussed in essays Chapters 7-8, supra.

Hong Kong Between "One Country" and "Two Systems"
18/19/20. Students and the University; Shenzhen and Hong Kong; Xi Jinping's Storm

316

represent have now upped the stakes, transforming a conflict primarily local into a great cleavage point between liberal democratic and Marxist-Leninist, and between nationalist and internationalist fault lines. Hong Kong protesters tactics have increasingly focused on the fundamental differences between the political cultures of Hong Kong, as it has been developing since 1997, and the rest of China. Their tactics have caught the attention of the press, certainly, but have also been designed to reduce the space within which dialogue or compromise is possible. On China's National Day (1 October 2019), for example, protesters marked the 70th anniversary with a self-styled national day of mourning; "'There is no National Day celebration, only a national tragedy,' demonstrators shouted – a new slogan coined specifically for October 1." [692] The clashes with police then provoked responses from both influential civil society organizations, [693] and the U.K. government. [694] This, in turn, produced more protests, this time fueled in part by the injuring of protestors in the 1 October demonstrations.[695] At least one of

---

[692] Holmes Chan, "'Day of mourning': Protests erupt around Hong Kong districts as China National Day marred by tear gas, clashes," *Hong Kong Free Press* (1 October 2019); available [https://hongkongfp.com/2019/10/01/day-mourning-protests-erupt-around-hong-kong-districts-china-national-day-marred-tear-gas-clashes/] ("crowds of black-clad protesters did not always follow the lead of the veteran pan-democrats, with some opting to chant the familiar slogans such as "Liberate Hong Kong, the revolution of our time."").

[693] "Hong Kong: Shooting of protester must be investigated amid alarming escalation of police use of force," Amnesty International (1 October 2019); available [https://www.amnesty.org/en/latest/news/2019/10/hong-kong-shooting-of-protester-must-be-investigated-amid-alarming-escalation-of-police-use-of-force/] (""The shooting of a protester marks an alarming development in the Hong Kong police's response to protests. The Hong Kong authorities must launch a prompt and effective investigation into the sequence of events that left a teenager fighting for his life in hospital. Police should only use lethal force in response to an imminent threat of death or serious injury and only as a last resort.")

[694] "UK Says Use of Live Ammunition in Hong Kong Is Disproportionate," *U.S. News and World Report* (1 October 2019); available [https://www.usnews.com/news/world/articles/2019-10-01/uk-says-use-of-live-ammunition-in-hong-kong-is-disproportionate] (""Whilst there is no excuse for violence, the use of live ammunition is disproportionate, and only risks inflaming the situation," Raab said in a statement.")

[695] Holmes Chan, "Hundreds March in Protest as Hong Kong Reels From Police Shooting of Student," *Hong Kong Free Press* (2 October 2019); available

these manifestations was also driven by students in solidarity with an injured classmate.[696]

The local authorities responses to what they view as provocations, and more importantly of increasingly effectively attacks on the legitimacy of their responses to the protests (and their failure to resolve the issues--one way or another) has fueled even more protests, and more international responses in support of an internationalist framework for approaching the issues and resolution of the situation in Hong Kong. The invocation of the colonial era (and since useful on occasion to suppress popular agitation) Emergency Regulatory Ordinance, [697] on 4 October 2019 by the Lam government to prohibit the wearing of face masks in public "on public danger grounds" provides an example.[698] Protests again erupted, this time in response to the

---

[https://hongkongfp.com/2019/10/02/hundreds-march-protest-hong-kong-reels-police-shooting-student/] ("Hundreds marched from Chater Garden in Central in protest, chanting slogans such as "Hong Kong police intentionally commit murder" and "disband the police force now."").

[696] Kimmy Chung and Chan Ho-him, "Schoolmates of Hong Kong teen shot by police hold sit-in as college faces pressure to condemn force," *South China Morning Post* (2 October 2019); available [https://www.scmp.com/news/hong-kong/politics/article/3031200/schoolmates-hong-kong-teen-shot-police-hold-sit-college].

[697] CAP 241 Emergency Regulations Ordinance (rev. 13 December 2018); available [https://www.hklii.hk/en/legis/ord/241/]. For a historical accounting of the Act, see Norman Miners, "The Use and Abuse of Emergency Powers by the Hong Kong Government," *Hong Kong Law Journal* 26:47-57 (1996).

[698] "Anti-mask law gazette," News Hong Kong Government (4 October 2019); available [https://www.news.gov.hk/eng/2019/10/20191004/20191004_181429_379.html]. The local officials supported their invocation of the POO this way:

> Since June 9, more than 400 public order events arising from the proposed amendments to the Fugitive Offenders Ordinance have been staged with a significant number of events ending up in outbreaks of violence, the Government said. It noted the acts of radical and masked protesters had seriously breached public peace and posed widespread and imminent danger to the community. The prohibition on facial covering is urgently needed for police investigation and collection of evidence, and for deterring violent and illegal behavior, it said.

Hong Kong Between "One Country" and "Two Systems"
18/19/20. Students and the University; Shenzhen and Hong Kong; Xi Jinping's Storm

318

anti-mask rules.⁶⁹⁹ The Western press tended to view the efforts as provocations.⁷⁰⁰ Protests continued throughout October

At the same time, lawfare strategies were also deployed--that is the use of the legal structures of Hong Kong against the policies and governance of Hong Kong by local officials. This served to underline both the extent to which the protests had become more focused on fundamental issues, and in its methodologies, the great differences between internationalist governance in Hong Kong and that possible within the rest of the nation. Those differences, in turn, might then further support the argument that Two Systems was not merely a matter of international agreement, but also tied to the fundamental human rights of Hong Kong people (and in this way detach the legitimacy of Hong Kong autonomy in its current forms from the four corners of the Sino-British Joint Declaration with its 2047 expiry date). Initially the Court of First Instance refused to grant an interim

---

699 "All MTR services suspended across Hong Kong as chaos erupts in multiple districts," *Hong Kong Free Press* (4 October 2019); available [https://hongkongfp.com/2019/10/04/breaking-mtr-services-suspended-across-hong-kong-chaos-erupts-multiple-districts/] ("Road occupations – as well as vandalism of state-owned or pro-Beijing shops and government facilities – were seen in almost two dozen separate locations in Hong Kong, from the financial heart of Central to Sheung Shui near the Chinese border"); see also 【禁蒙面法．示威】港九新界多區仍有人群聚集未散（不斷更新）(23:53). Ming Pao (in Chinese) (4 October 2019); available [https://m.mingpao.com/ins/港聞/article/20191004/s00001/157017233318 2/【禁蒙面法-示威】港九新界多區仍有人群聚集未散（不斷更新）].

700 James Pomfret and Greg Torode, "Explainer: Hong Kong's controversial anti-mask ban and emergency regulations," *Reuters* (4 October 2019); available [https://www.reuters.com/article/us-hongkong-protests-explainer/explainer-hong-kongs-controversial-anti-mask-ban-and-emergency-regulations-idUSKBN1WJ1FM] ("Early indications suggest that it may be counterproductive or even inflammatory, at least in the short term. Even before the bill was confirmed on Friday afternoon, thousands were gathering in the central business district and some shopping malls, with many sporting masks and chanting."); Jen Kirby, "The Hong Kong government tried to ban face masks. Protesters are already defying it," *Vox* (4 October 2019); available [https://www.vox.com/world/2019/10/4/20898568/hong-kong-protests-face-masks-ban-carrie-lam] ("But so far, the ban has only galvanized those opposed to Hong Kong's government.").

Hong Kong Between "One Country" and "Two Systems"
18/19/20. Students and the University; Shenzhen and Hong Kong; Xi Jinping's Storm

319

injunction.[701] But the court later rules that the granting of powers to Carrie Lam by the Executive Council under the Emergency Powers Act was unconstitutional, and also determined that the prohibition on mask wearing at unlawful assemblies was also inconsistent with the Hong Kong Basic Law.[702] The case was heavily criticized by the government and its supporters and some former jurists.[703] It is on appeal, but suggests the value of the use of the judiciary to advance objectives of more firmly drawing the autonomous character of the institutions of Hong Kong. One will expect a reaction from the central authorities at some point--as the extent of the autonomy of legalities of Hong Kong as against those of the People's Republic are tested. Here is where the disjunctions between One Country and Two Systems will likely be more formally pronounced; but not today.[704]

---

[701] "Judge explains reason for not allowing injunction," *RTHK News* (8 October 2019); available [https://web.archive.org/web/20191010054913/https://news.rthk.hk/rthk/en/component/k2/1485021-20191008.htm?archive_date=2019-10-08] ("In the written judgement handed down on Tuesday, Justice Godfrey Lam said it would be difficult and rash to form a considered view on the merits now, given the complexity of the matter").

[702] Kwok Wing Hang and others v. Chief Executive in Council and Another, [2019] HKCFI 2884; available [https://legalref.judiciary.hk/lrs/common/ju/ju_body.jsp?AH=&QS=&FN=&currpage=T&DIS=125574#p42].

[703] For later coverage, see Henry Litton, "Why challengers of Hong Kong's anti-mask law have no case" *South China Morning* Post (20 January 2020); available [https://www.scmp.com/comment/opinion/article/3046561/why-challengers-hong-kongs-anti-mask-law-have-no-case].

[704] Postscript: The case was eventually appealed to the Court of Final Appeal, Kwok Wing Hang and others v Chief Executive in Council; Chief Executive in Council and another v Kwok Wing Hang and others; Leung Kwok Hung v Secretary for Justice and another, (Argued 24-25 November 2020; Decided 21 December 2020) [2020] HKCFA 42: FACV 6/2020, FACV 7/2020, FACV 8/2020, FACV 9/2020; available [https://legalref.judiciary.hk/lrs/common/ju/ju_body.jsp?AH=&QS=&FN=&currpage=T&DIS=132498#]. The Court dismissed the appeal and affirmed the legality of the act and the anti-mask regulations. By then, of course, everything had changed. See discussion essay Chapter 29, infra.
It is helpful to understand the importance of the principle of stability and prosperity, as articulated by central and local government officials from the start of the protests in June as an important background element in the context of the balancing undertaken by the court.

Hong Kong Between "One Country" and "Two Systems"
18/19/20. Students and the University; Shenzhen and Hong Kong; Xi Jinping's Storm

320

The battle lines, then, are now drawn not just between the Hong Kong protesters and the local authorities, but between the central authorities and their more clearly defined vision of "One Country" against the international community also developing a more refined and permanent view of "Two Systems."[705] Some states have sought to change their own national positions with respect to Chinese relations on the basis of the way the situation in Hong Kong develops. This effort has been led by the United States with respect to which Hong Kong forms one layer of a complex puzzle that in the aggregate constitutes U.S.-China relations.[706] And it has brought into play international norms and

---

The situation on the streets and in other public places in Hong Kong had become dire. Members of the public were fearful of going out to certain places and significant inconvenience was caused to the public at large by the blockage of roads and closure of public transport facilities. There is a clear societal benefit in the PFCR when weighed against the limited extent of the encroachment on the protected rights in question. As Mr Benjamin Yu SC submitted, the PFCR affects a range of different people in Hong Kong. Although some people might wish to demonstrate in public but with a facial covering as a form of expression or for reasons of privacy, there were others who might wish to demonstrate peacefully but who were deterred from doing so because of the ongoing violence. The interests of that latter category should be given due weight in the balance. Similarly, due weight must be given to those persons who had sustained personal injury or property damage as a result of the actions of the violent protesters. And finally, the interests of Hong Kong as a whole should be taken into account since the rule of law itself was being undermined by the actions of masked lawbreakers who, with their identities concealed, were seemingly free to act with impunity. (Ibid., §146)

Gone here are any references to police violence and proportionality--it serves only a marginal role in the analysis, and has been confined to an internal matter to be handled by the appropriate governmental mechanism. As Foucault reminds us, the society must be defended. Michel Foucault, *'Society Must be Defended': Lectures at the College de France 1975-76* (David Macey, trans., Picador, 1997) ("And I think that at this point we are in a sort of bottleneck, that we cannot go on working like this forever; having recourse to sovereignty against discipline will not enable us to limit the effects of disciplinary power. Ibid., 39).

[705] See discussion in essay Chapter 10, supra.

[706] Kevin Breuninger, "Mike Pompeo says 'something like Tiananmen Square' in Hong Kong would make a US-China trade deal 'more difficult'," *CNBC* (20 August 2019(; available [https://www.cnbc.com/2019/08/20/pompeo-violence-in-

actors as well. [707] These also produced a response from the protesters in Hong Kong. [708] They have moved from the mere protection of rights under the Sino-UK Joint Declaration[709] (and with it the 2047 end date of those protections from outside), to the idea that the Sino-British Joint Declaration merely manifests the broader rights to political self-determination of Hong Kong within China.

The result has been a tremendously large spectacle amplified by the press and social media outlets, all of which has captured global attention. The recent actions by the National Basketball Association, the Chinese state, and a variety of famous people all of whom were simultaneously seeking to manage a narrative [710] suitable to their needs, and responding to the resulting acts of resistance by others,[711] suggest the significance of the reverberations of the protests in Hong Kong. The efforts of all this activity have played out in ways that have suggested the

---

hong-kong-would-make-china-trade-deal-more-difficult.html] ("Over the weekend, President Donald Trump said that a trade deal "would be very hard" to do "if they do violence. If it's another Tiananmen Square ... I think it's a very hard thing to do if there's violence."").

[707] Discussed in essays Chapters 11 and 14, supra.

[708] Jennifer Creery, "'Fight with Hong Kong': 130,000 gather to urge US to pass human rights act to monitor city's autonomy, organisers say," *Hong Kong Free Press* (15 October 2019); available [https://hongkongfp.com/2019/10/15/fight-hong-kong-130000-gather-urge-us-pass-human-rights-act-monitor-citys-autonomy-organisers-say/] ("Many held up printed signs of popular US patriotic symbol Uncle Sam with the phrase: "Fight for freedom, stand with Hong Kong." ... The event also saw speeches from Secretary-General of pro-democracy party Demosistō Joshua Wong, pro-democracy lawmaker Au Nok-hin, pro-independence leader Andy Chan, and Sunny Cheung – a student leader who led a group to lobby the US Congress last month, among others.").

[709] Joint Declaration of the Government of the United Kingdom of Great Britain and Northern Ireland and the Government of the People's Republic of China on the Question of Hong Kong (19 December 1984); available [https://www.cmab.gov.hk/en/issues/jd2.htm] (hereafter the Sino-UK Joint Declaration).

[710] Jeremy Sugarman, "Narrative Matters," *American Journal of Bioethics* 1(1):46 (2001). ("what becomes morally salient can be influenced by the manner in which we tell, read, and hear stories" Ibid., 46)

[711] On the role of counternarrative, Tal Kastner, "Policing Narrative," *SMU Law Review* 71:1117-1152 (2018).

intimate connection between local Hong Kong issues, global trade, and their alignment to apparently fundamentally irreconcilable political-economic models of national organization.[712] These then produced further protests in Hong Kong, as the connection between the local protests, global reaction, and then further reaction intensified.[713] That understanding, in turn, has played a role in the strategic calculations of the Chinese central authorities, as has been plain since June, but it has increasingly also played a role in the strategic calculation of U.S. political actors.[714]

All of this has been well covered by others in the official press and requires little commentary other than perhaps to notice its utter banality.[715] Far less noticed, and worthy of substantial analysis, is the role of the university, and university stakeholders (particularly administration and faculty stakeholders) in shaping and responding to the evolving situation in Hong Kong. It is not for nothing that the university remains a central actor. Many people drawn to the protesting groups are part of or have strong ties to the Hong Kong universities and their networks. Faculty has sought to engage in the situation in Hong Kong.[716]

---

[712] Arjun Kharpal, "Chinese state media and Tencent suspend broadcast of NBA preseason games in China," *CNBC* (8 October 2019); available [https://www.cnbc.com/2019/10/08/china-state-tv-suspends-nba-broadcasts-after-morey-hong-kong-tweet.html]; James Palmer, "The NBA is China's Willing Tool," Foreign Policy (7 October 2019); available [https://foreignpolicy.com/2019/10/07/us-businesses-like-the-nba-are-chinas-willing-tools/].

[713] "Protesters stand with Morey, down on Lebron," *RTHK News* (15 October 2019); available [https://web.archive.org/web/20191214110447/https://news.rthk.hk/rthk/en/component/k2/1486375-20191015.htm%3Farchive_date%3D2019-10-15] (""We do not need the money from China, we're not you, Lebron!" one masked fan told the crowd through a microphone. Others put up posters depicting the LA Lakers forward holding a giant 100 yuan note in his outstretched arms.").

[714] See, H.R.3289 - Hong Kong Human Rights and Democracy Act of 2019; available [https://www.congress.gov/bill/116th-congress/house-bill/3289].

[715] Peter Burdon, Gabrielle Appleby, Rebecca LaForgia, Joe McIntyret and Ngaire Naffine, "Reflecting on Hannah Arendt and Eichmann in Jerusalem: A Report on the Banality of Evil,'" *Adelaide Law Review* 35:427(2014).

[716] See discussion essays Chapters 13, and 17, supra.

But perhaps most important, the central authorities have made clear, almost from the beginning, that they lay the blame, at least in part, on the education system for the situation in Hong Kong. We have drawn attention to this in earlier commentary.[717]

> Therefore, I feel that school education and family education must have a correct guidance. We must strengthen the patriotism education and national education of Hong Kong youth, and let them understand their country and themselves comprehensively, deeply and objectively from an early age. The nation, understand its own history and culture. The whole society should care about the healthy growth of young people and create a good, harmonious, stable and rule of law environment for the healthy growth of young people. The youth of Hong Kong are also young people of China. The youth of Hong Kong is the future of Hong Kong and the future of the country. The Central Government is always paying attention to the growth of young people in Hong Kong.[718]

Indeed, for example, the connection between schools, their students, faculty, administration and other stakeholders, has not been hidden. Schools, for example, have been pressured to take a public stand to condemn police violence.[719] Pressure has also been applied to induce schools to support the local authorities, or as an alternative to induce these institutions to reduce their involvement in the political situation.[720]

---

[717] See discussion in essay Chapter 7.

[718] 新闻办就香港当前事态的立场和看法举行吹风会，2019-08-06 16:55 来源：中国网 [The Information Office holds a briefing on the current situation and views of Hong Kong, 2019-08-06 16:55 Source: China Net]; available [http://www.gov.cn/xinwen/2019-08/06/content_5419266.htm] (hereafter HKMAO 6 August Statement.

[719] Kimmy Chung and Chan Ho-him, "Schoolmates of Hong Kong teen shot by police hold sit-in," supra ("Hundreds of pupils and alumni joined in solidarity on Wednesday to show support for the 18-year-old shot by police on National Day, as managers at his Hong Kong school faced pressure to condemn the force.").

[720] "Hong Kong's school students and teachers are suffering from emotional problems over anti-government protests, survey finds," *South China Morning Post* (19 September 2019); available

University students and alumni have focused on the university as a front in the controversy. It was reported on 18 October that "Thousands of University of Hong Kong graduates have passed a resolution calling for Chief Executive Carrie Lam Cheng Yuet-ngor, an HKU alumna, to resign as varsity chancellor, saying she has – in her own words – "caused unforgivable havoc" to the city."[721] But it does remain a battle front: "A group of 45, made up of pro-Beijing figures and a former senior official, said the resolution violated HKU's statutes on the convocation and called for the "offending part" on Lam's responsibility for the crisis to be removed."[722]

University administrations have not remained silent. They have also responded, especially as the character of the interactions have become more violent and also less restrained on the part of officials and protestors. That response is well worth considering for the way in which it suggests the social and political role of the university, as well as the evolution of its sense of obligation to stakeholders and the ways in which it must manifest its mission. One gets a sense of the current state of that response, as well as its evolving nature, in the "Open Letter" circulated by Chinese University of Hong Kong Vice Chancellor and resident Professor Rocky S. Tuan 段崇智, to the CUHK community on 18 October 2019. [723] Whatever one thinks of this position and

---

[https://today.line.me/hk/v2/article/1R899v] ("Schools should provide a safe and secure environment for students to learn. Activities " such as the class boycotts and human chains " have impacted both students and teachers, he said. "We firmly oppose the idea of bringing political demands into campuses," he said." Ibid., quoting Wong Kam Leung, President of the Hong Kong Federation of Education Workers)

[721] Alvin Lum, "University of Hong Kong graduates vote by landslide in support of resolution calling on city leader Carrie Lam to resign as varsity chancellor," *South China Morning Post* (19 October 2019); available [https://www.scmp.com/news/hong-kong/politics/article/3033657/university-hong-kong-alumni-threaten-legal-action-over-vote].

[722] Ibid.

[723] 香港中文大學校長 段崇智 各位中大同學、同事、校友 (18 October 2019) [Rocky S. Tuan, Vice-Chancellor and President, The Chinese University of Hong

Hong Kong Between "One Country" and "Two Systems"
18/19/20. Students and the University; Shenzhen and Hong Kong; Xi Jinping's Storm

325

approach, one thing is quite clear: the way that universities view the scope of their mission to their students and as social actors, at least this one and at least in Hong Kong, appears to be changing. And that also be a consequence of the evolving situation in Hong Kong.

The Open Letter is noteworthy in several respects.

First, it asserts the responsibility of the university for the well-being of its students during the course of the protests. It does so without denying the Hong Kong Authorities' power to maintain order and civil peace ("*The University is expected to make best use of its status, standing, and influence to ensure a fair treatment of the related issues and the students affected*" "各方都期望大學憑藉其公信力、影響力，讓有關事件及受影響同學得到最公平的處理。").[724] Here is a manifestation of university autonomy that looks to global consensus but that run counter to expectations of universities from the perspective of the central authorities. The issue of autonomous authority. Of course, is also at the heart of the protests and of the cultural clashes in the view of the role of education, one that the central authorities have been criticizing almost from the beginning of the protests.

Second, in this sense, the University seeks to serve as a Western style *human rights defender* against violations by the state authorities of their own self-imposed legal constraints *("I cannot over-emphasize that, irrespective of why our students were arrested, the police should ensure that the rights of the arrested must not be infringed upon during arrest and detention"* "我在此嚴正指出，無論同學因何事被捕，警方必須確保在拘捕及扣留過程中，被捕人士應有的權利不被剝削。").[725] This position is

---

Kong Dear Students, Colleagues, and Alumni] (hereafter Tuan Letter); copy in original Chinese and translation on file with author.

[724] Ibid.

[725] Ibid. The Office of the High Commissioner for Human Rights defines a Human Rights Defender as "people who, individually or with others, act to promote or protect human rights in a peaceful manner. Special Rapporteur on Human Rights Defenders, "About Human Rights Defenders," Office of the High Commissioner for Human Rights,; available

Hong Kong Between "One Country" and "Two Systems"
18/19/20. Students and the University; Shenzhen and Hong Kong; Xi Jinping's Storm

326

particularly sensitive as it touches on a matter that has received substantial attention from the global human rights community[726] in ways that may not be entirely compatible with Socialist approaches to human rights or the responsibilities and protection of human rights defenders.[727] Again, this suggests an alignment of the self-conception of the university and its role with the internationalist position in Hong Kong. The effort to intimate the applicability of the (non-binding to be sure) UN Declaration on Human Rights Defenders [728] (even obliquely) signals very strongly the position of the university.

Third, the university has used its own networks to provide resources for students who seek to complain against disciplinary breeches by state (usually police) officials ("*To responsibly deal with the above cases, the University had promptly elicited help from volunteer alumni lawyers, especially those with experience in gender equality and human rights issues. We hope that with such legal assistance and consent of the students concerned, each case can be properly documented and submitted to the relevant authorities as a formal complaint and representation so as to facilitate prompt, fair and open investigations";* "為嚴肅處理以上同學的個案，大學即時聯繫了義務校友律師，特別是在處理性別平等及人權問題方面有豐富經驗的律師協助同學。我們希望在律師的協助下，每個個案的詳細情形都可以以書面陳述撰寫出來，在同學的同意下，讓大學可以協助將個案呈交相關機構作出正式申訴及陳述，並促請相關機構盡快作出公平、公開、

[https://www.ohchr.org/EN/Issues/SRHRDefenders/Pages/Defender.aspx] (last accessed 31 March 2021).

[726] See discussion essay Chapter 12, supra. The UN Working Group for Business and Human Rights has also advanced guidance to business for protecting human rights defenders. See Working Group for Business and Human Rights, "Informal Background Note: Human Rights Defenders and Civic Space--the Business and Human Rights Dimension" (5 December 2017); available [https://www.ohchr.org/Documents/Issues/Business/ForumSession6/UNWG _ProjectHRDsBackgroundNote12052017.pdf].

[727] See, e.g., Amnesty International, "Human Rights Defenders," website available [https://www.amnestyusa.org/campaigns/human-rights-defenders/] (last accessed 31 March 2021).

[728] United Nations Declaration on Human Rights Defenders, General Assembly Resolution A/RES/53/144 (1998); available [https://undocs.org/A/RES/53/144].

公正的調查。").[729] Here the university is taking a position that challenges the discursive posture of the central authorities which have suggested that there ought to be a presumption of lawful conduct by the police in the face of the unlawful actions of the protesters. The view of the central authorities is inherently Leninist;[730] the university takes a position more closely aligned to the sensibilities of liberal democracy.

Fourth, as an influential human rights defender and protector of its student stakeholders, the university has a duty to intervene directly with the highest level state authorities to ensure that the rule of law mechanisms that the state authorities have imposed on themselves are implemented. This lobbying and oversight responsibility is not merely technical but reflects the political responsibilities of the university in Hong Kong ("*In view of the gravity of the matter, I will write to the Chief Executive to exhort her to initiate independent investigation of the 20 or so cases involving CUHK students outside existing mechanisms. This will hopefully reaffirm the rule of law and restore public confidence*";" 基於事件的嚴重性，我會去信行政長官，希望行政長官考慮針對現時大學已掌握初步資料的約 20 宗個案，在現有機制以外作出嚴正跟進，讓法治精神得以彰顯，讓信心得以重建。").[731] Here one encounters the substantially distinct views of rule of law between its Socialist and liberal democratic versions.[732] Western internationalists are highly critical of the Chinese approach--and certainly they are right if only in the sense that the Socialist approach is grounded in principles incompatible with the fundamental normative structures of liberal democratic political economic orders.[733]

---

[729] Tuan Letter, supra.

[730] See discussion essays Chapters 7-8, supra.

[731] Tuan Letter, supra.

[732] State Council of China, White Paper: "The Socialist System of Laws with Chinese Characteristics" (October 2011); available [http://english.www.gov.cn/archive/white_paper/2014/09/09/content_2814 74986284659.htm].

[733] For a nice example, see Carl F. Minzer "China's Turn Against Law." *The American Journal of Comparative Law* 59(4):935-984 (2011).

Hong Kong Between "One Country" and "Two Systems"
18/19/20. Students and the University; Shenzhen and Hong Kong; Xi Jinping's Storm

328

Fifth, the university has an obligation to protect the territorial integrity of its learning and congregation spaces against state abuses. (*"At the meeting last week, concern over the unjustified presence of police discharging duties on campus was voiced time and again. Within the property boundary of our University campus, we will do everything we can to safeguard the legal rights of all our members."*; "在上星期的會面中，很多同學都向我表達對於警察進入校園的關注。在校園範圍內，大學會盡一切努力維護每一位成員的合法權益。一般情況下，如警察欲進入校園，保安處會先向警方查詢到校原因，了解警方是執行法庭搜查令，或是在涉案人士同意下作出調查，或有合理懷疑相信有涉嫌犯罪人士在某處所內").[734] The issue here is sensitive. The university effectively suggests that the university is a sanctuary and that it may control its own space for the protection of its students, even when they might be persons of interest to the police. More importantly, it suggests a rejection of the idea being developed now about the need to distinguish between patriotic individuals and those who might be viewed as instruments of foreign powers. The Black Hand issue is ignored here and in the process the university takes a risk in the eyes at least of conformity with the expectations of the central authorities.

Sixth, the university can serve as a space within which mass line politics can be ordered and effectively communicated to the authorities, but with the understanding that the authorities have a duty to both hear and respond fairly in order to preserve their own legitimacy, even within the context of the political-economic model of One Country Two Systems. But that also requires a shift back to the peaceful and more abstract expression of ideas and desires that remains in the realms of discussion. Such a shift back would serve as a means of avoiding the sort of violence that could be viewed as a threat to the state instead of an expression of or demand for dialogue.[735]

---

[734] Tuan Letter, supra.
[735] There is something of a nascent global academic dialogue along these lines. Cf. David Lyons, "Violence and Political Incivility," *Mercer Law Review* 63(3):835-844 (2012); Graham Glover, "University Protests, Specific Performance, and the Public/Private Law Divide," *The South African Law Journal* 134(3):466 (2017).

Hong Kong Between "One Country" and "Two Systems"
18/19/20. Students and the University; Shenzhen and Hong Kong; Xi Jinping's Storm

329

It is my belief and deep conviction that sincere, direct and honest dialogue will lead us out of the present impasse, but strong polarization will never bring compromise. Reconciliation of the schism can only be approached and reached with sincerity and honesty. The success of Hong Kong depends on the rule of law and Hong Kong people being united behind it. The negative sentiments in society have reached an alarmingly critical point. The escalating violence and acts of destruction must stop. The government must act fast to come up with feasible strategies to solve the problems in order to rekindle hope for the younger generations who are the future of Hong Kong. 香港的成功有賴香港人的團結及法治精神。現時社會上的負面情緒已達臨界點，不斷升級的暴力及破壞行為必須停止，政府必須盡快、盡力提出可行方案解決社會上各種問題，方可以為這一代的年青人——香港的未來，重燃希望。[736]

One is invited to read this passage in its liberal democratic sense. And certainly to those outside of Hong Kong to whom this was projected, it would read like a reasonable call to the sort of democratic dialogue that underlies the idealized premises of the liberal democratic system and its privileging of civil and political rights.[737]

Nonetheless, one can also see in this passage a more subtle gesture extended toward the Marxist Leninism of the central authorities--a suggestion that there is no fundamental dispute with the baseline principles of the nation's political-economic model. Read "correctly," the university may be reaching out to offer a Hong Kong version of the *mass line* suitable for the distinctive political model permitted it under the One Country Two Systems framework. [738] But Hong Kong's own leading

---

[736] Tuan Letter, supra.

[737] See, e.g., Toni Massaro, "Freedom of Speech, Liberal Democracy, and Emerging Evidence on Civility and Effective Democratic Engagement," *Arizona Law Review* 54(2):375-442 (2012

[738] For a similar approach, see Paul Saba, "Chairman Mao's Teachings on the Mass line: Combining Communist Leadership With the Masses," *The Call* 5(34) (1976;

academic forces have already expressed some reluctance to recast student activity in Marxist Leninist terms, much less to translate their action into something that might be considered a legitimate dialogue with officials.[739] Two Systems principles (at least as the university would like to see that principle understood) [740] suggests that if popular expression is to engage somewhere, it is someplace other than with the national central authorities. That dialogue has shifted outward to and through the international community as the essence of the Two Systems part of the One Country principle. Again the university evidences discursively a strong attachment to internationalism and indirectly aligns its sensibilities with those of the protesters.

Seventh, the university is seeking to play a role in managing the situation in Hong Kong. At the same time, that insertion is necessary because both its primary stakeholders and those governments which ultimately will decide on the role of the university within the evolving political-economic model in Hong Kong both insist. The university is attempting to steer a course between these two camps in ways that preserves to itself a set of core values that they hope will be preserved once the situation in Hong Kong is resolved. It is not clear that strategy will be successful. In this strategy the university appears to reflect the position of the Hong Kong academic establishment. Before 2019 the position would have been unremarkable. In the face of the protests it is not clear that the position can be maintained without a measure of risk.

But it is also clear that there is virtually no other path left to the university. And yet universities remain at the center of the protests--caught between their missions, their responsibilities, their duties, and their principles.[741] They serve as sanctuaries

---

available [https://www.marxists.org/history/erol/ncm-3/call-mass-line.htm]; Graham Young, "On the Mass Line," *Modern China* 6(2):225-240 (1980).

[739] See discussion essay Chapter 6, supa.

[740] Consider the discussion essays Chapters 6 and 9, supra.

[741] K.K. Rebecca Lai, "How Universities Became the New Battlegrounds in the Hong Kong Protests," *New York Times* (19 November 2019); available [https://www.nytimes.com/interactive/2019/11/18/world/asia/hong-kong-protest-universities.html].

even as they represent the order and stability incarnated in the apparatus of state. Universities serve as intellectual spaces within which the strategies and principles of the protests, and their political objectives can be developed and disseminated. But universities ae also physical spaces within which protestors may group, regroup, and confront the physical force of the disciplinary measures taken by local officials.[742] By November the conflation of both roles was quite evident: "Protesters moved *en masse* into five Hong Kong university campuses, turning them into fortresses and stockpiling gasoline bombs, catapults, bows and arrows, and even javelins. Most of the campuses were cleared by the weekend, with hundreds of protesters finally congregating at the Polytechnic University."[743] These also serve as a point of entry for internationals standard on the constraints imposed on local authorities. [744] Moreover, it underlines the position of central authorities that continue to urge the suppression of unrest and the use of force (by definition lawful in the face of provocation).[745]

---

[742] By November 2019, those two aspects of university involvement would erupt in sustained violence. See Ibid. Among the core universities at the vanguard of these movements are Hong Kong Polytechnic University, Hong Kong Baptist University, City University of Hong Kong, and the University of Hong Kong. Ibid.

[743] Tiffany Liang, Anna Kam, Casey Quackenbush, and Gerry Shih, "Small group of protesters holds out at Hong Kong university after mass arrests," *The Washington Post* (19 November 2019); available [https://www.washingtonpost.com/world/asia-pacific/china-admonishes-hong-kong-judiciary-after-mask-ruling-raising-pressure-on-citys-tenuous-freedoms/2019/11/18/3e3999de-0a51-11ea-8054-289aef6e38a3_story.html].

[744] Tiffany Liang, Anna Kam, Casey Quackenbush, and Gerry Shih, "Small group of protesters holds out at Hong Kong university after mass arrests," supra. The report noted the international response:

> U.N. human rights spokesman Rupert Colville, . . . expressed concern about increasing violence by young people "who are clearly very angry, with deep-seated grievances." But Colville, who speaks for the U.N. High Commissioner for Human Rights, also urged authorities to "address the humanitarian situation" of the remaining protesters holed up at the university. In Washington, the U.S. Senate, in a unanimous vote, passed . . . [the] Hong Kong Human Rights and Democracy Act [which] now goes to the House of Representatives, which earlier approved its own version of the measure.

[745] Ibid. ("'Tolerance cannot reform the rioters. Restraint cannot stop the crimes,' the Communist Party's official People's Daily newspaper said in a front-page editorial.)

To its students the university urges caution but embraces the role of protector and middle tier *parens patriae*. To the state, and both of its governments, it attempts to serve as a super ego (e.g., "we will hold you to your own rules to preserve the rule of law ideology central to your legitimacy"). To the international community it offers a discursive position that underlines the university's fidelity to core international values in hopes of a mutual expression of solidarity. Students may well reject the proffer as too little and too late (though they will accept the help as it comes). The central authorities may well have already made up their minds, and it is therefore only a matter of determining the sort of conduct that will prove useful in determining whether a university (and its faculty) will eventually find themselves on a blacklist or a red list. However, that is a story for another essay of a completely distinct character.[746] The international community may embrace the discursive stance of the university but offer little more than gestures of support and commiseration in the face of opposition. Stuck in the middle, the university has little choice; but like all actors in the middle of a contradiction it will likely not emerge from this conflict without perhaps substantial injury to itself or its stakeholders.

$$* \quad * \quad *$$

---

[746] See discussion essay Chapter 16, supra.

Chapter 19

Sunday 20 October 2019
Shirley Ze Yu on Hong Kong and the Construction of Post-Global Empire

It is rare to see analysis in conventional news sources that actually have something interesting to say (rather than being outlets for the opinion management directed by states, or other actors with the power to wield these media tools). That is especially the case in the context of the situation in Hong Kong. The ultimate tragedy that has been unfolding in its current form in Hong Kong since June 2019 is connected to larger trends that are becoming clearer now. This essay considers the nature of these changes, and Hong Kong's place within them from the perspective of a refreshingly honest, but likely overlooked, Opinion Essay recently published in the *South China Morning Post* by Shirley Ze Yu.[747] Dr. Shirley Ze Yu is senior visiting fellow at the London School of Economics, a fellow at Harvard Kennedy School and a former Chinese national television (CCTV) news anchor.

The Opinion Essay suggests the consequences and contemporary manifestations of the growing pains that accompany the current (great) transitions of political-economic models that started in earnest after the shock of events between 2001[748] and 2008[749] as these models emerge from the status quo

---

[747] Shirley Ze Yu, "China would rather see Hong Kong lose its role as a financial gateway than ever cede political control," *South China Morning Post* (15 October 2019); available [https://www.scmp.com/comment/opinion/article/3032733/china-would-rather-see-hong-kong-lose-its-role-financial-gateway].

[748] Even the academic intelligentsia at the time thought things were going to be different, though it is not clear that their loyalty to their own ideologies also clouded their vision of what lay ahead. See, e.g., "Theory and International Institutions: Conversation with Robert O. Keohane (9 March 2004); available [http://globetrotter.berkeley.edu/people4/Keohane/keohane-con5.html] (Globalization and 9/11).

[749] Jean-Yves Huwart and Loïc Verdier, *Economic Globalization: Origins and Consequences* (Organization for Economic Cooperation and Development (Paris: OECD Insights, 2013); available [https://www.oecd-

ante of the post 1945 settlement of the (more or less unitary) global order (finalized after 1989).[750] Neither the Hong Kong protests nor its ramifications are occurring in some space detached from the complexities of the dynamic movements of social, political, cultural and economic forces in constant development all around what might be mistaken as the eternal insularity of the physical and psychic space that is Hong Kong. These great transitions are as much a contributing cause of the character and trajectories of the conflicts in Hong Kong, manifested in forms "natural" to that context, as they will affect the course of Hong Kong's future within these larger movements. These larger movements are occurring both within China and in the international sphere. What these transitions produce remains to be seen, but its character is already being felt in the movement toward the post-global merchant empires of the Belt and Road Initiative and the America First model, and by whatever names they will style themselves in the near future.[751]

What these mean for the possibilities of creating and maintaining a distinctive international city state in the form of contemporary Hong Kong, within the Chinese nation-state, remains to be seen. Shirley Ze Yu reminds us that those possibilities may be dictated in large part both by geography and the course of development of the spaces around Hong Kong within

---

ilibrary.org/docserver/9789264111905-en.pdf?expires=1613252660&id=id&accname=guest&checksum=97BFAEC6F2DF0A09D1D44F66AC4D5DD7], "The 2008 Financial Crisis--A Crisis of Globalization?," pp. 127-145.

[750] For one version current among leading figures of the Western vanguard intelligentsia,, see Michael J. Mazarr, "The Real History of the Liberal Order," *Foreign Affairs* (7 August 2018); available [https://www.foreignaffairs.com/articles/2018-08-07/real-history-liberal-order].

[751] Considered in the essays in Emancipating the Mind in the Era of Globalization: Bulletin of the Coalition for Peace & Ethics 14(1):1-148 ("From Globalization to Empire: Essays From the Coalition for Peace & Ethics Working Group on Empire"); available [https://www.thecpe.org/little-sir-press-a-self-publishing-collective/emancipating-the-mind-bulletin-of-the-coalition-for-peace-and-ethics/issues-emancipating-the-mind-bulletin-of-the-coalition-for-peace-ethics/volume-14-no-1-june-2019/]. See also essays at Law at the End of the Day, CPE Empire Series; available [https://lcbackerblog.blogspot.com/search/label/CPE%20EmpireSeries].

which Hong Ong forms a part. To better understand where Hong Kong may be going, then, it may be necessary to better understand the realities of the development of the Pearl River Delta. And to better understand the development of the Pearl River Delta it may be necessary to understand its role in the development of Chinese engagement both within speres of global production and in the construction of a New Era Marxist Leninist society.

Within those broad macro change trajectories one encounters an almost endless series of micro points of explosions--the way that earthquakes evidence specific nodes of motion along much larger tectonic plates.[752] Each of these micro explosion points produce great disruption, but they are not self-contained. Each is a contribution to larger movements and changes along the fault lines in which they exist. The situation in Hong Kong is one of those micro explosions; the US-China trade realignments (and the inevitable decoupling that they represent)[753] is another.[754]

The tragedy of these micro explosions is that while they follow their own logic--in the case of Hong Kong, those of the emerging internationalist cultural expectations built into the rhetoric of protestors, against that of the central authorities--they are inevitably trapped within the confines of the tectonic plates of longer term trends against which the possibilities of local events are constrained. For Hong Kong that means, as it has since the 1840s, that the city-not-exactly-a-state remains trapped between imperial systems whose evolution both fuels the narrative of the actors, and constrains the scope of potential outcomes. More

---

[752] For another version of this approach, see, e.g., Michael Mann, "Globalization and September 11," *New Left Review* (Nov/Dec 2001); available [https://newleftreview.org/issues/ii12/articles/michael-mann-globalization-and-september-11].

[753] This continues, see, Michael A. Witt, "Prepare for the U.S. and China to Decouple," *Harvard Business Review* (26 June 2020); available [https://hbr.org/2020/06/prepare-for-the-u-s-and-china-to-decouple].

[754] "China's ambassador to Britain, Liu Xiaoming, faced off with BBC Newsnight a few hours after the face-mask ban was declared in Hong Kong. He repeated that Hong Kong's situation is "under control". And, contrary to the anarchy and chaos the rest of the world observes, he is correct." Shirley Ze Yu, "China would rather see Hong Kong lose its role as a financial gateway than ever cede political control," *supra*.

Hong Kong Between "One Country" and "Two Systems"
18/19/20. *Students and the University; Shenzhen and Hong Kong; Xi Jinping's Storm*

336

specifically, for Hong Kong's role in China's post-global imperial Leninist (again in the sense of the development of relationships grounded in hierarchy and vertically ordered sets of expectations of responsibility and obligation built around the management of global production controlled from a vanguard center) political-economic model it appears to mean a *transformation from jewel of the Pearl River Delta to a small part of the Pearl River Delta economic zone.* One got a taste of this in the context of the central authorities' plans for Shenzhen.[755] Now it comes much more to the foreground.[756]

China's post-global empire is being built around the Belt and Road Initiative. It is grounded on core political principles of interlocking and hierarchically arranged structures of leadership cores guiding collectives. That core-collective relationship then serves as the basic framework for organizing political and economic relations and also in the construction of institutions developed for its operation. The core-collective framework is both compatible with the emerging 'New Era' theory of Leninist political organization and is replicated as the fundamental building block of Chinese political and economic life, both within institutions and among them. For the Belt and Road Initiative, China serves as the core of a coordinated economic-political system around which are increasingly distant collectives that extend from near to far periphery.[757] These are the modern manifestation of tributary states, the relations with which produce the win-win solutions at the heart of Chinese foreign policy. But the emerging imperial system is also marked by the ability both to control its internal operations between core and collectives, and to defend itself against rival imperial projects,

---

[755] Discussed in the essay Chapter 12, supra.

[756] Shirley Ze Yu, "China would rather see Hong Kong lose its role as a financial gateway than ever cede political control," supra ("Hong Kong has been under China's control, territorially and administratively. In fact, Hong Kong has also increasingly fallen into China's economic orbit. It is only a matter of time before Hong Kong's political system follows.").

[757] Cf., Yiping Huang, "Understanding China's Belt & Road Initiative: Motivation, Framework, and Assessment," *China Economic Review* 40:314-321 (2016); Weidong Liu and Michael Dunford, "Inclusive Globalization: Unpacking China's Belt & Rad Initiative," Area Development and Policy 1(3):323-340 (2016).

principally those of the U.S. and its nascent (though remarkably contested) America First project. To that end, it is necessary to ensure the construction of an internationalized currency (the yuan), and to manage territory through which trade and production can be operated for the win-win strategy.[758]

Within this construction, Hong Kong has always served as a transitional outer territory of the imperial core. It was necessary as a convergence points of empires, in this case between the emerging new Chinese Leninist model, and the old discredited 19th century model (with its inherently now rejected core organizational notions of racism, ethnocentrism and direct territorial control). It served as a vital point in the Reform and Opening Up strategy [759] and, like it, represented a necessary transitional plan to move China from its post-Revolutionary to its "New Era" stage of historical development. Technology transfer, know how, intelligence, righting historical grievances and 19th century humiliations (though like all core empires without any sense of the humiliation core prerogatives might produce in peripheral regions) and the like were essential features of that arrangement. The One Country Two Systems, one with a sunset provision, appears to have been meant to drive home the point. The West, of course, was clueless as it read these movements from the perspectives of its own inter-cultural battles and its own historical contradictions. Thus distracted, they could only be themselves but with little by way of equally forward looking strategies acknowledging the inevitability of changes that even leaders in peripheral states saw fairly clearly.

---

[758] Cf., John Ross, "The Basis of China's 'Win-Win' Foreign Policy Concept," China.org.cn (30 March 2015); available [http://www.china.org.cn/opinion/2015-03/30/content_35194074.htm].

[759] Shirley Ze Yu, "China would rather see Hong Kong lose its role as a financial gateway than ever cede political control," supra ("The late Chinese leader Deng Xiaoping was one of the 20th century's most skilled statesmen. He employed pragmatic remedies in every policy domain in China for the deep wounds left by the Cultural Revolution. He was the chief architect of China's economic reform and opening up, and the maxim associated with his approach is "crossing the river by feeling the stones". The framework for Hong Kong's return was another of Deng's ingenuous experiments.")

But Hong Kong also served as a distraction for rising competing Empires, and a source of false reassurance for fading empires (among which there had been an almost successful effort to universalize their political-economic model now recast as grounded in markets, human rights, and multiple variations of exculpatory measures for the consequences of the now discredited effects of the old imperial model). It was certainly in that sense that Hong Kong served its highest purpose geopolitically as a way to buy time while China prepared for its "New Era" by successfully managing its transitional aspects of its long term political line through "Reform and Opening Up." That was sufficiently appealing for the fading European (now international) norms-making imperial model. It was partially satisfying to the merchant empire model of what would emerge as America First. The later model, of course, was only one of the two choices for a deeply divided American political-economic elite torn between the rupture from its earlier post 1945 model, and the more transitionally satisfying (and old model preserving) alternative that reached its most developed form under the Obama administration.[760]

But the central authorities appear always to have selected Hong Kong for absorption into a greater Pearl River Delta economic grouping.[761] China has made no secret of this, though one has to be sensitive to the meanings of words and actions to see it clearly. It was not for nothing that the Reform and Opening Up period has always focused in part on the old imperial borderland with the ancient imperial rival. Over the long term it could not have escaped notice that Shenzhen was built to dwarf and then absorb Hong Kong. But Hong Kong was also built as the space through which a critical element of Chinese imperial organization could take shape--the development and operation of an imperial currency that eventually could be used to solidify the

---

[760] Discussed in Larry Catá Backer, Conflating Economics and Politics, Security and Prosperity--President Obama Addresses the United Nations, Law at the End of the Day (23 September 2010); available [https://lcbackerblog.blogspot.com/2010/09/conflating-economics-and-politics.html].

[761] Discussed in the essay Chapter 12, supra.

coordinated operation of its collective arrangements within its land, maritime and space "roads."[762]

> A pragmatist and an authoritarian, Deng delivered market reform under communist rule; he fiercely put an end to the Tiananmen pro-democracy protests in 1989. Were he still alive, he would not have brooked the unrest in Hong Kong. He believed that "development is the only hard truth". Forty years ago, he knew Hong Kong's open market and liberal economy would be good for China's development. Without Hong Kong, there would not have been a prototype for China's market reform in the 1980s. China's first capitalist gateway was Hong Kong. The first few mainland Chinese to strike it rich, or become "10,000 yuan people", were all connected to trade in Hong Kong. But, in the years to come, Hong Kong is more likely to resemble a modern Chinese metropolis than a Western city.[763]

Hong Kong could serve in that respect the same function (pointed outward from empire) that Shenzhen served in the area of manufacturing and supply chain "roads" internally. Many of the lessons learned were then transferred to other cities within the core--notably Shanghai--or outward to internal periphery states, notably Singapore.[764] While it served that purpose, Hong Kong could continue to operate as a global "open city."

---

[762] Shirley Ze Yu, "China would rather see Hong Kong lose its role as a financial gateway than ever cede political control," supra ("In signing the Sino-British Joint Declaration in 1984, British prime minister Margaret Thatcher prophesied that economic change in China would eventually lead to political change. Events have proved her to be right in prediction, but wrong about the direction. Ominously, the "Iron Lady" tumbled down the steps of the Great Hall of the People during her visit to Beijing for talks with Deng. He might have been the wiser of the two.")

[763] Shirley Ze Yu, "China would rather see Hong Kong lose its role as a financial gateway than ever cede political control," supra.

[764] Shirley Ze Yu, "China would rather see Hong Kong lose its role as a financial gateway than ever cede political control," supra, ("In the development plan unveiled for China's Greater Bay Area, Hong Kong is not the centre, but one of four metropolitan centres. Not only is the Greater Bay Area envisioned as a competitor to Silicon Valley, it also integrates Hong Kong into China's economic network").

In any case, the Belt and Road system is now substantially framed and its operationalization is no longer risky. The Asia Infrastructure and Investment Bank has now reached a quick maturity as an imperial disciplinary financial force (the way that the old IFIs serve that role first for the post 1945 settlement order, and thereafter for emerging competitive imperial models). London is an alternative; there is potentially little room left to tolerate the political quirks of a place whose utility has been consumed by the metropolis as it builds its hub and spoke system.[765]

Indeed, it might be presumed that, increasingly, the inner periphery states now serve the core in a more disciplined manner, especially against the outer territories of competing imperial orders.[766] And as the old imperial orders sink into peripheral roles, there are better bases for situating the imperial financial machinery--China has been (with a delicious sense of irony and revenge) eyeing its old nemesis the UK, as the space from which it will operate its global financial machinery.

And what of Hong Kong then? Likely before June 2019, the idea was a planned slow decline and absorption into a Greater Pearl River Delta area, perhaps with the same status as Singapore within the political-economic model, adjusted for history and context.

---

[765] Shirley Ze Yu, "China would rather see Hong Kong lose its role as a financial gateway than ever cede political control," *supra.*, ("Hong Kong's shoes could perhaps be filled by London. The recent takeover bid for the London Stock Exchange Group was clearly an attempt to turn London into another financial hub for China.
If Hong Kong were to lose its special status in its trade with the United States, neither Tokyo, nor Singapore nor Sydney could replace it as a premiere financial marketplace. Only London could meet China's growing demand for a deep and wide offshore financial centre, as China continues to amass economic influence in Europe and the rest of the world.")
[766] Lt Gen H S Panag (retd), "It's time India stopped seeing China's border moves as 'salami slicing'" The Print (17 October 2019); available [https://theprint-in.cdn.ampproject.org/c/s/theprint.in/opinion/india-stopped-seeing-chinas-border-moves-as-salami-slicing/306828/amp/].

China is not likely to grant Hong Kong liberal democracy under its model of universal suffrage. Nor will China allow Hong Kong to break free, not under Xi Jinping's leadership nor anyone else's. To Xi, Hong Kong is indubitably under China's control; it is only a question of wielding hard power or soft power. . . *Slowly, Hong Kong's DNA will start to change. Beijing's soft power will firmly implant itself into Hong Kong.*[767]

Hong Kong's monied interests no doubt have been adjusting their positions--and hedging based on that--for years. Though of course that is conjecture. At the same time, China managed to realize the risk of this strategy--just as its plans for Hong Kong's evolution to a new historical stage were being carefully developed, Hong Kong's masses were inheriting some of the conceptual manifestations of the One Country Two Systems model, but in a global rather than a Chinese direction. That was the contradiction that erupted in June 2019. And that is the contradiction that will eventually be settled to the satisfaction of China's central authorities. . . eventually. But that is also a contradiction whose resolution will require payment of a price that might well benefit China's imperial rival.

That last point is key here to the calculations likely being made by all participants in this protest. By now it is clear that the stakes are far greater than the issue of the Extradition Law. The discourse on the streets of Hong Kong have sharpened not merely the ideological structures of the major players, but it has also more starkly drawn the differences between them. Those differences will likely mark the boundaries of the post global territories that appear to be emerging, which are manifested as much by the territories of production as they are by the relationships of sovereignty and economic ordering within states. The alignment s of One Country Two Systems, like the alignments between Shenzhen and Hong Kong, and between China and its BRI partners, each framed in contextually distinct bit aligned ways.

---

[767] Shirley Ze Yu, "China would rather see Hong Kong lose its role as a financial gateway than ever cede political control," supra, (emphasis added).

Hong Kong Between "One Country" and "Two Systems"
18/19/20. Students and the University; Shenzhen and Hong Kong; Xi Jinping's Storm

342

These are some of the ideas deeply embedded within the Opinion Essay published by Shirley Ze Yu. It ought to be taken seriously. It likely represents some strongly held views of elements of the central authorities. And it reinforces the notions that whatever the immediate resolution of the situation in Hong Kong, it is really only a prelude to, and another step in the construction of, at least part of the post global world order. This much, however, is clear:

> Whether Beijing decides to end the protests with boots on the ground has become a secondary determinant of the city's future. For all societies and civilizations, history has always moved towards progress, though not always in a linear fashion. In China's long history, the unrest in Hong Kong will be only a minor scar. The outcome will be against the wishes of many hoping for a free and democratic fragrant harbour. Hong Kong will no longer be the same.[768]

$$* \quad * \quad *$$

---

[768] Shirley Ze Yu, "China would rather see Hong Kong lose its role as a financial gateway than ever cede political control," supra.

Chapter 20

Monday 18 November 2019

Open-Shut (*Bai He* 稗闔) Strategies: 习近平;止暴制乱 恢复秩序是香港当前最紧迫的任务 [Xi Jinping; Stopping the storm and restoring order is Hong Kong's most urgent task at present]

The Open-Shut (*Bai He* 稗闐) strategy represents the ultimate Daoist law of transformation and different methods of persuasion (*Shui* 説)... Open means opening with speech (*Yan* 言). It is *yang*. Shut means closing in silence. It is *yin*... It is said that death and destruction, worry and anxiety, poverty and disadvantage, suffering and humiliation, abandonment and damage, loss, disappointment, harm, torment and punishment are yin, which is called ending.[769]

There has been much coverage of the latest round of activity by students and government responses around the current situation in Hong Kong.[770] Many governments, including that of the United States, will likely react in their own ways to the final resolution of the Hong Kong situation,[771] including legislative

---

[769] Guiguzi (鬼谷子), *Guiguzi: China's First Treatise on Rhetoric; A Critical Translation and Commentary* (Hui Wu (trans.); Carbondale: Southern Illinois University Press, 2016 (before 220 A.D.)); Book I.1.4 - I.1.5, pp. 41. Guiguzi also serves as a useful framing of strategic and rhetorical choices in other important respects considered in the essays, supra, at Chapter 3 (Mend-Break (Di Xi 抵巇)), Chapter 8 (Assessing (Quan 權)), and Chapter 12 (Resist-Reconcile (忤合 Wuhe)). Also infra at Chapter 30 (Fundamental Principles (Fu Yan 符言)).

[770] Some consideration in essay Chapter 19, supra.

[771] Ian Marlow and Daniel Flatley, "What Hong Kong Losing Its U.S. 'Special Status' Means," *Bloomberg* (2 October 2019); available [https://www.bloomberg.com/news/articles/2019-10-02/what-u-s-congress-is-and-isn-t-doing-about-hong-kong-quicktake]; Scott W. Harold, "U.S: Policy Options for Hong Kong," The Rand Blog (2 December 2019); available [https://www.rand.org/blog/2019/12/us-policy-options-for-hong-kong.html].

Hong Kong Between "One Country" and "Two Systems"
18/19/20. Students and the University; Shenzhen and Hong Kong; Xi Jinping's Storm

344

efforts.[772] The Chinese central authorities, as well, have not been remiss in developing their own position and ensuring that it is widely known.[773] In the process, something that started as the expression of a frustration directed toward the local government about specific legislative approaches, but also fueled by long simmering frustrations, has now boiled over into a long and sustained campaign that has solidified an oppositional position among Hong Kong protesters. That solidification has crystalized around a reinvigorated internationalist reading of the Two Systems principle that sees in Hong Kong a political and societal culture distinct enough from that of the rest of the People's Republic of China to require a permanent state of autonomy, one grounded in and supported by international principles and institutions.

This increasing disjunction between those holding tightly to the One Country principle (and inherent within it the notion of the Sinification of Hong Kong political culture), and those holding an increasingly coherent view of the Two Systems principle (and inherent within it the internationalization of a principle of Hog Kong autonomy detached from the Sino-British Joint Declaration and its 2047 end date). The positions are incompatible and have been tearing the unitary One Country-Two Systems principle into two, with each increasingly separated from the other.

Even as the One Country-Two Systems principle is being torn in two, there appears to be a dynamic stalemate on the ground. Each side has been moving its pieces on the chessboard that is Hong Kong without any sense of any decisive movement toward victory for either side. The recent legalization of that contest, in the form of the fight against the invocation of the

---

[772] Hong Kong Human Rights and Democracy Act of 2019 H.R.3289/S1838; Pub.L. 116-76; 113 Stat. 1161; 22 U.S.C. §§5725-5726 (2019) — 116th Congress (2019-2020). Among other things the Act The Department of State shall certify annually to Congress as to whether Hong Kong warrants its unique treatment under various treaties, agreements, and U.S. law. The analysis shall evaluate whether Hong Kong is upholding the rule of law and protecting rights enumerated in various documents, including (1) the Sino-British Joint Declaration regarding Hong Kong's return to China, and (2) the Universal Declaration of Human Rights.
[773] See, e.g., essays Chapters 3-5, 7-9, supra.

Emergency Powers Act to impose a "no-mask" rule provides a case in point.[774] The idea there is to invoke the authority of the state against its own leaders to develop an authoritative application of the unique culture of Hong Kong against efforts to more tightly embed it within the political cultures overseen directly by the central authorities.

Yet even as protesters and their allies are working with sympathizers in the global community, and are seeking to invoke and solidify the distinctive legal culture of Hong Kong, the core leadership of the People's Republic of China is also seeking to present their perspective to a global audience. These objects are easy enough to grasp: the first is to make the case for the evolving Chinese interpretation of the One Country Two Systems principle with "One Country" at the center. The second is to try to develop wedges in internal public sentiment (and reduce international community support) for the position of the protesters and their interpretation of the One Country Two Systems principle with "Two Systems" in the center.

To that end the Chinese core of leadership was presented with a near perfect opportunity to present its views to a potentially friendly audience when President Xi Jinping attended the eleventh meeting of the BRICS leaders in Brasilia[775] It was reported by the Chinese Foreign Ministry that at the BRICS Summit President Xi Jinping "made clear the Chinese government's solemn position on the current situation in Hong Kong."[776] The summary text of those remarks were made

---

[774] Considered briefly in essay Chapter 19, supra.

[775] Letícia Casado and Manuela Andreoni, "BRICS Turn 10: BRICS group pledges increased integration through New Development Bank loans at Brasilia Summit as doubts about sustainability linger," *Diálago Chino* (15 November 2019); available [https://dialogochino.net/en/infrastructure/31731-brics-turns-ten/] ("Leaders from Brazil, Russia, China, India, and South Africa met for the 11th BRICS summit in Brasilia this week to discuss the future of the bloc and identified loans supporting sustainable development from the New Development Bank (NDB) as a key element in strengthening integration").

[776] "Xi Jinping: The Most Urgent Task for Hong Kong at Present Is to End Violence and Chaos and Restore Order," Ministry of Foreign Affairs of the People's Republic of China (18 November 2019); available [https://www.fmprc.gov.cn/mfa_eng/zxxx_662805/t1716590.shtml].

available in the original Chinese,[777] as well as in English.[778] Both are brief but dense with meaning and all the more important for the effort to directly project out the emerging Chinese position to key allies and friendly governments.

---

[777] 习近平：止暴制乱 恢复秩序是香港当前最紧迫的任务 [Xi Jinping: Stopping the storm and restoring order is Hong Kong's most urgent task at present], Xinhuanet (14 November 2019); available [http://www.xinhuanet.com/politics/2019-11/14/c_1125233663.htm].

习近平：止暴制乱 恢复秩序是香港当前最紧迫的任务

新华社巴西利亚 11 月 14 日电 当地时间 11 月 14 日，国家主席习近平在巴西利亚出席金砖国家领导人第十一次会晤时，就当前香港局势表明中国政府严正立场。

习近平指出，香港持续发生的激进暴力犯罪行为，严重践踏法治和社会秩序，严重破坏香港繁荣稳定，严重挑战"一国两制"原则底线。止暴制乱、恢复秩序是香港当前最紧迫的任务。我们将继续坚定支持行政长官带领香港特别行政区政府依法施政，坚定支持香港警方严正执法，坚定支持香港司法机构依法惩治暴力犯罪分子。中国政府维护国家主权、安全、发展利益的决心坚定不移，贯彻"一国两制"方针的决心坚定不移，反对任何外部势力干涉香港事务的决心坚定不移。

[778] "Xi Jinping: The Most Urgent Task for Hong Kong at Present Is to End Violence and Chaos and Restore Order,", supra.

Xi Jinping: The Most Urgent Task for Hong Kong at Present Is to End Violence and Chaos and Restore Order
2019/11/18
On November 14, 2019 local time, President Xi Jinping made clear the Chinese government's solemn position on the current situation in Hong Kong when attending the 11th BRICS Summit in Brasilia, Brazil.

Xi Jinping noted, the continuous radical, violent and criminal activities in Hong Kong have severely trampled on the rule of law and social order, severely undermined Hong Kong's stability and prosperity, and challenged the bottom line of "one country, two systems" policy. The most urgent task for Hong Kong at present is to end violence and chaos and restore order. We will continue to firmly support Chief Executive in governing Hong Kong Special Administrative Region in accordance with law, and support the Hong Kong police in strictly enforcing law, and support the Hong Kong judicial organs in bringing violent criminals to justice according to law. The Chinese government is determined to safeguard national sovereignty, security and development interests, implement the "one country, two systems" policy, and opposes any foreign interference in Hong Kong affairs.

However, the difficulty with the official English translation is the way that it flattens out some of the language as it appears in the original Chinese--and thus, to some extent, also flattens the meaning and message meant to be conveyed in the original to Chinese speaking populations. A slightly different version follows for which it may be useful to consider in more detail. The original is indented in *italics*; commentary then follows

> *Xi Jinping: Stopping the storm and restoring order is Hong Kong's most urgent task at present.*

The language Xi Jinping uses references back to the statements delivered by the Hong Kong and Macao Affairs Office (HKMAO) during the course of a press conference on 6 August.[779] In both cases the words used were the same-- 止暴制乱 (Zhǐ bào zhì luàn). The term is usually translated as "stop the violence and chaos" but the allusion to the storm is washed out of that more literal translation.

Stop the storm suggests the character of the absence of control that can tear a society apart. But it also reflects the notion that storms, as destructive as they can be, are temporary things. Once the storm passes then things return to normal and people pick up where they left off. More pointedly, the idea here is that the strong itself may cause damage but will not affect the trajectory of forward movement under the leadership of the vanguard party exercised through the actions of the central and local authorities. The storm itself--the protesters, then are also an uncontrolled element, once that cases damage but that cause no lasing harm--a typhoon perhaps but nothing more hurling its energy against something that might be damaged but which cannot be overcome.

> *Xinhua News Agency, Brasilia, November 14th Local time on November 14, when President Xi Jinping attended the eleventh meeting of the BRICS leaders in Brasilia, the*

---

[779] The subject of the essay Chapter 7, supra.

current situation in Hong Kong shows the Chinese
government's solemn position.

The remarks were meant to be projected outward to friendly
states, and also reported for domestic consumption in the
Mainland (as well as read among Hong Kong elements and their
sympathizers abroad). Because it was given by President Xi, it was
assumed there would be global coverage--and certainly the
security and foreign ministry apparatus of other states would be
listening carefully. Here again, the notion of a solemn position is
meant to contrast the temporary power of the storm with the
solidity and authority of the wall against which it will spend its
strength.

Xi Jinping pointed out that the persistent violent criminal
acts in Hong Kong have seriously trampled on the rule of
law and social order, seriously undermined Hong Kong's
prosperity and stability, and seriously challenged the
bottom line of the "one country, two systems" principle.
Stopping the storm and restoring order is Hong Kong's
most urgent task at present.

This is the heart of the remarks and lays out in compact form, the
position of the central authorities as it has been developing over
the course of the last six months. Its rhetorical purpose is one of
drum beat. Every word is another blow to the drum which
produces the rhythm of the steady march from storm to triumph,
a march that leads away from the protestors and their struggle to
a greater incorporation of Hong Kong within China.

The key words, each a drum beat: (1) persistent violent
criminal acts; (2) seriously trampled the rule of law; (3) seriously
trampled social order (4) seriously undermined Hong Kong
prosperity; (5) seriously undermined Hong Kong stability; and (6)
seriously challenged the "One Country-Two Systems" principle.
Taken together, this persistence of serious challenge will itself
cause the end of One Country Two Systems as the social order will
seek to protect itself. That is the "storm", the violence and chaos
that must be stopped. Notice the unity of the six key phrases here
that are meant to paint a picture of authority and legitimacy--of

deliberation and probity, on the side of the authorities--and of chaos and destruction on the side of the protestors.

The *basso ostinato:*[780] (a) persistent (b) *violent* (3) **criminal** (4) ***acts***. Four beats pounded constantly. Boom, *boom*, **boom**, ***boom***. Persistence suggests intentionality; violence suggests harm to the innocent; criminal suggests that the persistent violence stands outside the law, that is that the persistence of the violence is not meant to further socially positive normative or political (lawful) objectives; and acts suggest a concrete manifestation that can be measured and that reveals the extent of violent criminality. The statement then carries with it its own set of judgments and presumptions which the audience is meant to embrace as presuppositions. To embrace this notion, this narrative of persistence, of violence, of criminality, and of action, is to strip the protesters of legitimacy, and of connection with the polity. It clears the field for the state and its apparatus as the only thing that stands between the destroyer and the stability and prosperity of the people.

Over this ostinato a melody that plays as a four part-fugue[781] built on variations tied to a core concept: seriously, *seriously*, ***seriously*** ***seriously***. One starts with the subject--*trample human rights*. Its answer repeats the subject in a different voice--*trampled the social order*. The countersubjects are developed--*undermine prosperity and undermine stability*. These are then developed freely over the ostinato (persistent, violent, criminal, acts). Together one hears (for the statement is best appreciated heard, like music) a complex interweaving of the ostinato--serious persistent violent criminal acts--under equally intertwining melodic themes: trampled human rights and social order; undermined prosperity and stability.

---

[780] In music--for this is what Xi's remarks are meant to be, music--a persistent motif or pattern repeated over and over

[781] Again in music, the essence of imitative counterpart in which each of in this case four themes are presented, developed against each other and counter expositions, before concluding.

And eventually this fugue over basso ostinato (for it is a hybrid form of music making) comes to its conclusion: the end of the One Country-Two Systems principle. That is the ending of the music should the storm persist. The storm is itself that basso ostinato--serious   persistent, violent, criminal, acts. And the melodies lead to the end of Hong Kong.

Interestingly, the Chinese leadership core miss the dissonance in that fugue and its basso ostinato. And it is simply this: the fugue need not necessarily threaten One Country Two Systems. Indeed, the melody might as easily have ended with a call to strengthen One Country Two Systems; to threaten its end is to suggest the power of persistent, violent, criminal, acts, of the success of a trampling of rule of law and the social order, and of the undermining of prosperity and stability. To insist that such a four part fugue threatens One Country Two Systems is to suggest the power of the protesters. And in the long run that might well be the wrong tune to sing.

We will continue to firmly support the Chief Executive to lead the Government of the Hong Kong Special Administrative Region in accordance with the law, firmly support the Hong Kong Police in law enforcement, and firmly support the Hong Kong Judiciary in punishing violent criminals.

And indeed, that tune gone wrong is then emphasized. If the One Country Two Systems principles is threatened, it is in the response of a large hegemon to the annoyance of flies. That could evidence weakness more than strength, And that is the great risk of the central authority's line supporting local officials--already well proven to have not handled their responsibilities well--nor of the police, who have proven at times (and for international consumption, more of a burden than a vindication. The Vanguard party had a choice--it could appear as the great intervenor bringing peace and a change of leadership in exchange for stability and the end of violence. It might have even negotiated the punishment of leaders. It might have better considered the value of Mend-Break (*Di Xi* 抵巇) [782] strategies--breaking the local authorities to mend Hong Kong. But the central authorities were already using the strategies of Mend-Break (*Di Xi* 抵巇) to advantage in August 2019, but with a different trajectory. The basso ostinato of Xi's remarks--criminality and violence must be punished in accordance with law--serve as the break; mending comes for the local authorities which serve as the instrument of breaking the protester movement and the foreign sympathizers who empower them.

> *The determination of the Chinese government to safeguard national sovereignty, security, and development interests is unshakable. The determination to implement the "one country, two systems" principle is unwavering, and the determination to oppose any outside forces' interference in Hong Kong affairs is unwavering.*

Here the strategies of Mend-Break (*Di Xi* 抵巇) make an opening to further an overarching strategy of Open-Shut (*Bai He* 稗閤).[783]

So Xi speaks to the small and limiting which must make way again for the virtuous--the local authorities. Xi starts from the small and dangerous and ends with the positive and lofty. He starts with the danger of protest and ends with the authority of the state. He starts with the drumbeats of disorder and ends with a call to the lofty ideals of sovereignty, security and development. These ideals he proffers to a community of states already deeply committed to sovereignty, security and development especially against internal and external threat. And against these ideals are the constant drum beats of disorder, of persistent violent criminal acts. This is Open-Shut (Bai He 稗閤).

Note the Chinese two thrust narrative strategy of Open-Shut (*Bai He* 稗閤) in this case. First is the use key words and

---

[782] Guiguzi (鬼谷子), *Guiguzi: China's First Treatise on Rhetoric; A Critical Translation and Commentary* , supra ,Book I.1.1. 4.1, pp. 53-54.
[783] Ibid., Book I.1.3, pp. 40 (""those who invite a shut strategy invite sincere response form others).

phrases that invoke the normative foundations of Hong Kong's global sympathizers to control the interpretation and implications of action in Hong Kong. Second is the elaboration of the foreigner intervention rhetoric that has been evolving since June 2019. None of this is new but might be usefully read in light of changing conditions on the ground. "All speeches (Yan 言) that employ yang are "beginning." This sort of speech (Yan 言) talks about positive things and is used to launch business. All speeches (Yan 言) that employ yin are "ending." This sort of speech (Yan 言) talks about negative things and is said to get a plan canceled." [784] This is precisely what Xi offers to the BRICS leaders in Brasilia. For the protesters, there is only the small--the way of the criminal, the storm that damages but does not destroy, that threatens but which must be resisted. But to his friends in the community of BRICS states he offers a solidarity grounded in the lofty values of sovereignty, security and development around which he wraps a Chinese One Country-Two Systems principle.

$$* \quad * \quad *$$

---

[784] Ibid., Book I.1.5.

Chapter 21

Monday 30 December 2019
Stalemate: The Storm Continues Unabated

> The man of superior virtue is not (conscious) of his virtue, hence he is virtuous.
>
> The man of inferior virtue (is intent on) not losing virtue, hence he is devoid of virtue.
>
> The man of superior virtue never acts, nor ever (does so) with an ulterior motive.
>
> The man of inferior virtue acts, and (does so) with an ulterior motive.
>
> The man of superior kindness acts, but (does so) without an ulterior motive.
>
> The man of superior justice acts, and (does so) with an ulterior motive.
>
> (But when) the man of superior *li* [禮] acts and finds no response; he rolls up his sleeves to force it on others. [785]

As this year grinds to its end, stalemate seems to be very much in the air. More than that, Hong Kong appears to have started to accustom itself to a constant state of action and reaction within a fairly constrained set of parameters. Despite the deployment of significantly ostentatious rhetorical strategies on both sides over the course of the last six months, there appears to be very little movement toward resolution. This is not to suggest that there hasn't been substantial amounts of activity, of the development of rhetorical strategies, and of alignments and

---

[785] Laotse, "The Book of Tao," in *The Wisdom of China and India* (Lin Yutang, ed., and trans.: New York, Modern Library 1955) "Degeneration, Book II.38; p. 583, 604). *Li* [禮] is a rich concept with origins in religious sacrifice but morphing to conclude a complex of notions around ideals and practices of ceremony, ritual, decorum, custom and the like to protect, enhance and project communal meanings and forms. Cf., Wong Yew Leong, "*Li* and Change," The Paideia Project (1998); available [http://www.bu.edu/wcp/Papers/Asia/AsiaWong.htm]. On the Confucian notion of *li* [禮] in its transnational context, see Keren Wang, *Atlas of Sacrifice: Legal and Rhetorical Foundations of Economic Globalization* (Routledge, 2019).

realignments of individuals and institutions in, through and outside of Hong Kong. Rather it is to suggest these actions-reactions have assumed a rhythm, or a cadence, whose repetitions can now be better discerned. In the process, Hong Kong's state of anarchy, and its resulting fragility, has produced a measure of stability, or at least of predictability, around which people can arrange their lives to pursue the ordinary necessities of living.

Within this dynamic stability, however, the last six months have produced significant changes that eventually may contribute to a resolution of the situation either toward a national One Country model or toward an internationalist Two Systems model. To those ends, one sees more clearly an ecology of actors that are the incarnation of Laotse's metaphors of superior and inferior virtue, of superior kindness and justice, but most importantly, of superior *li* [禮].

Keren Wang reminds us that ritual takings of things of human value, including ritual human sacrifice, has been continuously practiced for as long as human civilization itself has existed. Ample historical records suggest ritual sacrifices were performed as crisis management devices. Large scale human sacrifices in Shang dynasty China were organized as responses to severe food shortages. Ancient Greece devised the specialized sacrificial forms of total oblation and scapegoating as apotropaic responses to ward off catastrophes. The Aztec Empire introduced a highly institutionalized form of ritual warfare, known as the "Flower War," for the purpose of calendrical population control during periods of famine. Sacrificial rituals of the past should not be considered fundamentally divorced from the governmentality of twenty-first-century. The source distribution structure of late-capitalism, too, reproduces itself via the ritual inculcation of its core values and normative practices. The rhetoric of sacrifice are re-appropriated into the workings marketization politics, and are deployed in rendering dehumanizing measures of the prevailing political-economic system that make them appear palpable and inescapable.[786]

---

[786] Keren Wang: "Reexamining Ritual Sacrifice in Late-Capitalism;" Presentation at the 48th Annual Conference of the Society of Australasian Social Psychologists

Likewise those reflexes are much in evidence within Chinese Marxist-Leninism, as it too, seeks to re-appropriate the markers and symbols, the practices of prosperity and stability as inescapable and values maximizing. Ritual inculcation of Marxist-Leninist core values through the normalization of socialism with Chinese characteristics, with the normalities of socialist modernization, and with the values framework of the twelve core socialist values all contribute to systems of custom, of practice, of *li* [禮] every bit as powerfully reproducible--scalable and transposable, as the system of late capitalism against which it is sometimes measured and in opposition to which it re-constructs itself within its local context. In either case, when "the man of superior *li* [禮] acts and finds no response; he rolls up his sleeves to force it on others."[787]

Hong Kong presents us with many actors of superior the man of superior *li* [禮] who have been rolling up their sleeves in November and December. But one wonders where these individuals and institutions of superior *li* [禮] may also mark actors of inferior virtue and superior justice. Ulterior motive is not hidden by individuals of inferior virtue and superior justice--that is their respective essence. Yet it does provide the context within which such individuals, when exercising their superior *li* [禮], act without virtue or kindness, but with justice as the great ulterior motive with which li is infused.

The playing out of ulterior motives through the reproduction and emphasis of the forms of government, of custom, propriety, decorum and forms, that advance wither the Two Systems or One Country principle was very much in evidence in November. The key event, of course, was the late November local elections. Here the application of the internationalist Two Systems *li* [禮] produced a strong popular slap to the ambitions of local officials and indirectly to the ambitions of the central

---

(SASP) at the University of New South Wales, Sydney, Law at the End of the Day (29 April 2019); available [https://lcbackerblog.blogspot.com/2019/04/keren-wang-reexamining-ritual-sacrifice.html#more].

[787] Laotse, "The Book of Tao," supra, "Degeneration, Book II.38; p. 604).

authorities for political transition in Hong Kong. At the same time it highlighted the autonomy and difference between political cultures in Hong Kong and that of the rest of the nation.

> Hong Kong's voters have delivered an unprecedented landslide for pro-democracy candidates in local elections, in a powerful show of solidarity with the city's protest movement and rebuke to the government over its handling of the crisis. . . Carrie Lam had claimed the support of a "silent majority" for her hardline response and refusal to compromise. Sunday's vote, widely seen as a proxy referendum on the city's future, exposed that stance as a sham. People turned out in record numbers to eject pro-Beijing politicians [who] held on to little over 10 percent of the 452 openly contested seats.[788]

The response was quite different from local and state officials. Carrie Lam bent to the discursive power of the election in an internationalist style. She accepted the result, pledged to "listen humbly."[789] Of course she could take a more magnanimous view because the effect of the council elections would be limited-- especially on her exercise of power. At the same time the result could also be turned around to suit the needs of Lam's own motives: "'I would readily accept that, including deficiencies in governance, including unhappiness with the time taken to deal with the current unstable environment, and of course to end violence,' she said." [790] Part of that set of motives includes

---

[788] Emma Graham-Harrison and Verna Yu in Hong Kong, "Hong Kong voters deliver landslide victory for pro-democracy campaigners," The Guardian (25 November 2019); available [https://www.theguardian.com/world/2019/nov/24/hong-kong-residents-turn-up-for-local-elections-in-record-numbers] ("Pro-democracy candidates won a majority of seats on all 18 councils, although they will only control 17 because a large number of government appointees shifted the balance of power in the Islands district.").

[789] Ibid. ("Lam said on Monday her government would respect the election results and would "listen humbly" to the views of the public.").

[790] Kris Cheng, "Hong Kong District Council election: No concessions, but gov't will reflect and improve, says Chief Exec. Carrie Lam," Hong Kong Free Press (26 November 2019); available [https://hongkongfp.com/2019/11/26/hong-kong-

retaining control of the process. To that end she waits word from the central authorities[791] and proposed "an independent review committee to look at cause of social unrest, modelled on Britain's response to the 2011 Tottenham riots, but she did not give a timetable or further details."[792] Here, Lam was able to counter her electoral defeat to some extent by refusing to concede any but the first of the Five Demands.[793] In this she decisively aligned her position with that of the central authorities, a position that effectively gave her very little bargaining discretion.

The central authorities, however, used the occasion to advance their own superior *li* [禮] much more directly. "'Whatever happens, Hong Kong is always a part of China and any attempts to create chaos in Hong Kong or to jeopardise its prosperity and stability will not be successful,' said the Chinese foreign minister, Wang Yi, during a visit to Japan."[794] The implications are clear--a sense that Two System elections may eventually be incompatible with One Country consultative democracy.[795] One feels the individual of superior *li* [禮] roll up their sleeves and get to work.

Sleeve rolling was likely necessary because of the effects of the situation in Hong Kong on the state of the equally dynamic and tempestuous relations between the United States and China. Here, days after the Hong Kong elections U.S. President Donald Trump signed the Hong Kong Human Rights and Democracy Act.[796] Mr. Trump appears to have acted reluctantly. "In a

---

district-council-election-no-concessions-govt-will-reflect-improve-says-chief-exec-carrie-lam/].

[791] Ibid. ("Lam also said she had not received any instructions from Beijing following the election").

[792] Ibid.

[793] Discussed in essay Chapter 17.

[794] Emma Graham-Harrison and Verna Yu in Hong Kong, "Hong Kong voters deliver landslide victory for pro-democracy campaigners," *supra*.

[795] See, Larry Catá Backer and Miaoqiang Dai, "Socialist Constitutional Democracy in the Age of Accountability (问责时代的社会主义宪制民主)" (October 23, 2018). Available at SSRN: [https://ssrn.com/abstract=3271731] or [http://dx.doi.org/10.2139/ssrn.3271731].

[796] Hong Kong Human Rights and Democracy Act of 2019 (HKHRDA) (S. 1838; Pub.L. 116–76, 113 Stat. 1161 (2019) (imposes sanctions against China and Hong Kong officials considered responsible for human rights abuses in Hong Kong,

statement, Trump spoke of 'respect' for Chinese President Xi Jinping and said he hoped the 'leaders and representatives of China and Hong Kong will be able to amicably settle their differences'." [797] This appears to have provided potential encouragement for the formal response of the Chinese central authorities. The central authorities have warned that "it was ready to take unspecified 'firm countermeasures'. 'The nature of this is extremely abominable, and harbours absolutely sinister intentions,' the foreign ministry said in a statement."[798]

The battle of the independent commissions of inquiry exploded again in the beginning of December. The pro-democracy faction moved to impeach Carrie Lam. "Civic Party lawmaker Alvin Yeung moved the motion in the city's Legislative Council (LegCo), backed by 24 other pro-democracy lawmakers, which accuses Lam of "serious breach of law and/or dereliction of duty" and calls for an independent investigation into her conduct."[799] The core of the complaint centered on the character of Hong Kong's political system and the practices of democratic action.[800] The effort was rejected in a contest that continued to draw attention to the space that separates the pro-Beijing from the pro-democracy camp.[801]

---

requires the United States Department of State and other agencies to conduct an annual review to determine if changes in Hong Kong's political status justify changing the terms of the trade relations between the U.S. and Hong Kong).

[797] Su Xinqi and Sebastian Smith, "Furious China threatens retaliation over US law on Hong Kong," Hong Kong Free Press (28 November 2019); available [https://hongkongfp.com/2019/11/28/trump-signs-law-supporting-hong-kong-protesters/].

[798] Ibid.

[799] Man Hoi-tsan and Lu Xi, "Hong Kong Lawmakers in Impeachment Bid Against City's Leader Carrie Lam," Radio Free Asia (4 December 2019); available [https://www.rfa.org/english/news/china/impeachment-12042019110630.html].

[800] Ibid. ("Lam had shown "disregard of mainstream opposing views," and had "unrelentingly pushed through a highly controversial bill," according to the text of the motion."). The action originated in July bit was delayed until December.

[801] Kris Cheng, "Motion to impeach Hong Kong Chief Exec. Carrie Lam rejected at legislature by pro-Beijing camp," Hong Kong Free Press (5 December 2019); available [https://hongkongfp.com/2019/12/05/motion-impeach-hong-kong-chief-exec-carrie-lam-rejected-legislature-pro-beijing-camp/].

When proposing the motion, Civic Party lawmaker Alvin Yeung said the government wrongly thought the conflict could be resolved by handing out cash and provide more subsidised housing. "No one had too little freedom and dignity to lose in our society. Our compatriots took to the streets with the knowledge they might be subject to police brutality and they might be jailed for multiple years if convicted," he said.[802]

The pro-Beijing camp is not happy with Lam's government as well. But they come at their criticism from the other end of the spectrum.[803] In both cases superior *li* [禮] is very much at work. "He who handles the hatchet for the master carpenter seldom escapes injury to his hands.[804]

This more esoteric view may not make much difference to the usual discursive forms around which the situation in Hong Kong is parsed. But that is the point--whether one speaks to actors, or to those who seek to extract meaning from the situation, one speaks to individuals and institutions with ulterior motives. One speaks to individuals and institutions of inferior virtue, of limited kindness, but of much justice and superior *li* [禮]; one speaks here to ulterior motive framed around the construction and re-production of *li* [禮] itself. In the end the path of li chosen may produce of community of inferior virtue. "Patching up a great hatred is sure to leave some hatred behind. How can that be regarded as satisfactory? . . . The virtuous man is for patching up. The vicious for fixing guilt. But 'the way of Heaven is impartial, it sides only with the good man.'"[805]

---

802 Man Hoi-tsan and Lu Xi, "Hong Kong Lawmakers in Impeachment Bid Against City's Leader Carrie Lam," supra.

803 Kris Cheng, "Motion to impeach Hong Kong Chief Exec. Carrie Lam rejected at legislature by pro-Beijing camp," supra.

804 Laotse, "The Book of Tao," supra, Book I.64.

805 Ibid., Book I.79.

Chapter 22

Monday 30 March 2020
The COVID-19 Factor

Coronavirus appears to be having a substantial global effect. Within a matter of weeks, it has been transformed in the global consciousness from a flu like infection to a global *epidemic* with substantial enough mortalities (especially among the old and immunocompromised) to be declared a global *pandemic* by the World Health Organization on 11 March 2020.[806] Medical facilities are overwhelmed in Europe after China spent the greater part of a month in a virtual national lockdown as death tolls rose and health facilities were overwhelmed.

It is no surprise that this pandemic is beginning to have substantial spillover effects. It is even less surprising that those spillovers in Hong Kong are affecting in significant ways the power dynamics that have marked relations between protesters, local and national authorities, and the international community since the start of the protests in June 2019.

The high-water mark of protester power appears to have been reached in early December 2019 and early January 2020, when , in addition to electoral victories, protesters were able to mobilize hundreds of thousands of people. On 8 December 2019 " More than 800,000 people participated in the march, according to organizers the Civil Human Rights Front (CHRF), in what appeared to be a resounding show of support for the movement after six months of occasionally violent unrest. The police put the figure at 183,000."[807] A month later over a million people took to the streets was ended abruptly by police countermeasures, even

---

[806] Domenico Cucinotta, and Maurizio Vanelli, "WHO Declares COVID-19 a Pandemic," *Acta Biomed* 91(1):157-160 (19 March 2020).

[807] James Griffiths, "Hong Kong protesters keep up pressure with mass march," CNN (9 December 2019); available [https://edition.cnn.com/2019/12/08/asia/hong-kong-protest-march-intl-hnk/index.html].

as the police continues to insist on reporting numbers that were vastly lower than those reported by the protester groups.[808]

But by late January 2020 fears were already beginning to grow that the dynamic was changing. "For authorities in both Hong Kong and in Beijing, there must be, in some circles, something of a sense of relief. The pro-democracy protests that defined 2019 had become a deadly hydra that was exhausting the resources and credibility of both governments. The enforced shutdown as a result of the coronavirus pandemic looks to have solved a pressing political problem, at least in the immediate term."[809]

The protester movement, however, sees things differently. In some sense the youth of the protester core appears to have worked in their favor under conditions of pandemic and the enforced isolation (and denial of mass access to the streets). These forces have been able to access tactics and ideas from a global community to aid their objectives, for example with the turn to the so-called "Lennon Walls." [810] These groups were already comfortable with online community and communication. "'The effect on the movement itself [of Covid-19] is surprisingly low to me, perhaps because the 'brain' of the movement hasn't been on the ground for months already – people have already adapted to movement online. People who are planning things are still

---

[808] "Organisers say over 1mn took part, condemn police," RTHK.hk (1 January 2020); available [https://news.rthk.hk/rthk/en/component/k2/1500561-20200101.htm?archive_date=2020-01-01].

[809] J.J. Rose, "Coronavirus and the Hong Kong Protest Movement," *The Interpreter* (23 March 20220); available [https://www.lowyinstitute.org/the-interpreter/coronavirus-and-hong-kong-protest-movement].

[810] Jeff Hou, J (2020) "Lennon Walls' herald a sticky-note revolution in Hong Kong," *The Conversation* (18 January 2020); available [https://theconversation.com/lennon-walls-herald-a-sticky-note-revolution-in-hong-kong-129740] (""Lennon Walls," have sprung up on buildings, walkways, sky bridges, underpasses and storefronts and carry messages like "Hong Kongers love freedom," "garbage government" and "We demand real universal suffrage."").

planning things online.'"811 New tactics have now become more commonly used. "Since the pandemic protests have become smaller in scale, with sporadic gatherings in which protesters stage sit-ins during the lunch break or gather in shopping malls to chant slogans together."812

But the greater impetus for this shift may be tied to the way that the authorities have themselves sought to capitalize on the pandemic with respect to both the protests and also in the way in which they have sought to expand their authority in the wake of the challenge of disease containment. As such it might not be the disease but rather an intensification of police countermeasures against the protesters that generate responsive measures form the protester movement.813 A sort of economic solidarity has also developed, reported in the Western press, in which members of the protester community will patronize protester friendly establishments.814

However, especially among the core group of protesters, people who must work for a living and students, there also is a

---

811 J.J. Rose, "Coronavirus and the Hong Kong Protest Movement," supra (Quoting Andy "who helps coordinate communications for the Hong Kong protest movement").

812 Milan Ismangil and Maggy Lee, "Protests in Hong Kong during the Covid-19 pandemic," *Crime, Media, Culture: An International Journal* 17(1): 17-20 (2020) ("Since the pandemic protests have become smaller in scale, with sporadic gatherings in which protesters stage sit-ins during the lunch break or gather in shopping malls to chant slogans together."")

813 Ibid., ("With the government stepping up its efforts to 'stop violence and curb disorder' through police arrests and the restriction of public gatherings through disease control regulations, the protest movement has found new expression within everyday life").

814 "Yellow or Blue? In Hong Kong, Businesses Choose Political Sides," *The New York Times* (19 January 2020); available [https://www.nytimes.com/2020/01/19/world/asia/hong-kong-protests-yellow-blue.html] ("Hong Kong is color-coded — and bitterly divided. The yellow economy refers to the hue of umbrellas once used to defend demonstrators against pepper spray and streams of tear gas. That is in contrast to blue businesses, which support the police." Ibid.).

growing exhaustion. Quoting 36-year-old clerk Freesia,[815] one report explained:

> Like so many Hongkongers, he has spent much of the last seven months risking injury and prosecution by attending protests pushing for greater democracy and police accountability. But after 7,000 arrests and little sign of Beijing making any concessions, he wondered whether it was time for a change in tactics. "We have to think of another way to fight for democracy instead of purely relying on street protests," he told AFP, waving a flag with the slogan "Liberate Hong Kong, revolution of our times".[816]

Part of the difficulty centered on the viability of the Five Demands[817] as a baseline for negotiation; part appears to be a function of the need to change tactics as increasing numbers of core protester groups find themselves in jail. The change, however, does not seem to have changed public opinion or its intensity.[818]

But weeks later the focus of concern shifted from the possible successes of changes in police tactics to the possible effects of the coronavirus infections, especially given the way that the infection had produced drastic restrictions on movement in China. But the Coronavirus concerns also cut in another direction. It focused renewed criticism on local authorities for their failures to respond to the coronavirus epidemic in a more robust manner.[819] The contradictions of this position will be difficult to

---

[815] Jerome Taylor and Yan Zhao, "'A little break': Hong Kong protesters mull tactics as intensity fades," Hong Kong Free Press (23 January 2020); available [https://hongkongfp.com/2020/01/23/little-break-hong-kong-protesters-mull-tactics-intensity-fades/].

[816] Ibid.

[817] Discussed in essay Chapter 17, supra.

[818] Jerome Taylor and Su Xinqi, "'Not done yet': Virus delivers blow to Hong Kong protests but rage remains," Hong Kong Free Press (25 February 2020); available [https://hongkongfp.com/2020/02/25/not-done-yet-virus-delivers-blow-hong-kong-protests-rage-remains/].

[819] Jen Kirby, "How Hong Kong's protests are shaping the response to the coronavirus: Coronavirus fears are transcending politics in Hong Kong and transforming the protest movement," Vox (7 February 2020); available

overcome. But the instinct to protest remains strong. This was especially directed against the local government's decision to keep its borders open with Mainland China. "Thousands of newly unionized health care and hospital workers went on strike this week, stressing that Lam's inaction threatened to overwhelm the territory's health care system, especially if mainland Chinese visitors sought medical care in Hong Kong."[820] The effect appears to be to repurpose the protests from a focus on the Five Demands to one that adds pressure on local authorities to more effectively protect the health of the local population. Local officials responded, but this might well have been a poisoned chalice.

Yet again, here, the contradictions may well have a very negative effect on the power of the protesters to mobilize mass support. The tendency of states in confronting the epidemic, now globalized with the declaration of pandemic, has been to substantially restrict individual movement, public assembly, and to close borders. These approaches, perhaps valuable for purposes of minimizing health threats (only time will tell, though one has the Chinese experience suggesting that it may work), can also effectively shut down the protests. But even that is not clear as the spread and virulence of the coronavirus appears to have had limited impact so far, especially after the local authorities adopted comprehensive measures to control the spread of COVID-19.[821]

And yet the same reporting suggests that local authorities may see in coronavirus a ready-made means of more legitimately extending the police power in ways that, while directly targeting

---

[https://www.vox.com/2020/2/7/21124157/coronavirus-hong-kong-protests-china-carrie-lam] ("Lam has resisted completely sealing off Hong Kong's borders with mainland China, having closed all but three of Hong Kong's 14 crossings. Lam has said that the "almost unique" relationship between Hong Kong and mainland China would make a total shutdown too disruptive and discriminatory. The government has also instituted a 14-day quarantine on all visitors from mainland China.")

[820] Ibid.

[821] Helen Davidson, "Hong Kong: with coronavirus curbed, protests may return," *The Guardian* (15 March 2020); available [https://www.theguardian.com/world/2020/mar/15/hong-kong-with-coronavirus-curbed-protests-may-return].

health, indirectly weakens the protest movement itself by effectively making it impossible for protesters to organize mass demonstrations.[822] "For the Chinese government — and its unelected proxy leaders in Hong Kong — the end of the financial hub's huge rallies that engulfed the city for seven months straight has been a rare spot of good fortune in an otherwise grim start to the year."[823] At the same time, among the protesters is the continuing belief that "the unrest will simply reignite once the epidemic fades in a city still seething with popular anger and where neither its leader Carrie Lam nor Beijing have addressed the issues fueling years of rising resentment."[824]

The protesters, though, ought to be worried. The local authorities do appear to have succumbed (and quite rightly as a tactical matter from their perspective) to the temptation to use the pandemic to move aggressively forward on their use of the police power in ways that would have been unthinkable as late as mid-January. The most ominous sign is the resort to new regulatory measures. "A new Hong Kong regulation banning public gatherings of more than four people, enacted last week in an effort to combat the coronavirus pandemic, immediately stoked fears that it might be used to crack down on political dissent—and it appears to be happening already.[825]The regulation, Prevention and Control of Disease (Prohibition on Group Gathering),[826] commenced 19 March 2020 and is effective initially for three months.

---

[822] Ibid. (""I think the government is gaining confidence that it is getting better control over the situation and is gradually prodding to see how far it can go with its crackdown," says Kong Tsung-gan, a writer, educator and activist who participated in the Umbrella movement.").

[823] Jerome Taylor and Su Xinqi, "'Not done yet': Virus delivers blow to Hong Kong protests but rage remains," supra.

[824] Ibid.

[825] Mary Hui, "Hong Kong police are using coronavirus restrictions to clamp down on protesters," *Quartz* (1 April 2020); available [https://qz.com/1829892/hong-kong-police-use-coronavirus-rules-to-limit-protests/].

[826] Press Release, Prevention and Control of Disease (Prohibition on Group Gathering) Regulation, distributed 298 March 2020; available [https://www.info.gov.hk/gia/general/202003/28/P2020032800720.htm].

What makes the regulation most interesting are its exemptions. Taken together, it becomes clear that virtually the only assemblies that are prohibited are those that have proven so vexing to local and central authorities since June 2019. That cannot have gone unnoticed. Though the measure by its terms makes it even more difficult to apply the tactics of protest to protest the measure. Added to that, of course is the new calculus for protesters. Now they risk their health, and more importantly the health of their elderly relatives with whom they necessarily come in contact with, by choosing to protest.

Indeed reporting now suggests the way that the dynamic of police and protesters are now changing after the passage of the new measures.

> Yesterday, protesters gathered outside the Prince Edward subway station in Hong Kong to mark seven months since a major event in last year's protests, when riot police officers stormed into the station beating passengers indiscriminately. But the protesters were quickly dispersed, subdued, and detained, as police warned them to leave "to avoid the spread of the disease in society." Public trust in the local police force is at all-time lows, and unresolved police brutality continues to be an ongoing problem.[827]

Perhaps the result of these new pressures will be to require a change of tactics, one made more plausible by technology. There have been reports of the use of the now traditional practices of doxing and cyberbullying by all sides in the Hong Kong.[828] Indeed the use of surveillance, especially by the local authorities, has in part spurred the development of counter

---

[827] Mary Hui, "Hong Kong police are using coronavirus restrictions to clamp down on protesters," supra.

[828] Paul Mozur, "In Hong Kong Protests, Faces Become Weapons: A quest to identify protesters and police officers has people in both groups desperate to protect their anonymity. Some fear a turn toward China-style surveillance," *The New York Times* 26 July 2019); available [https://www.nytimes.com/2019/07/26/technology/hong-kong-protests-facial-recognition-surveillance.html].

measures (mask wearing to avoid facial recognition), and responses form the local authorities (efforts to enact measures prohibiting the use of masks). These fights, of course, have been upended by COVID-19. Masks are now mandatory (a reversal of the government's tactics) but other surveillance mechanisms certainly are available. While the local authorities have the capability of deploying platforms and data banks of activities among Hong Kong residents to feed analytics and then use them to develop systems of rewards and punishments--a sort of anti-protester social credit system[829]--they do not appear to have done so in any significant way yet. Likewise protester use of doxing strategies may be less effectively where COVID-19 restrictions make movement more difficult. And it is important to remember that these tactics have no specific ideology.[830]

$$* \quad * \quad *$$

---

[829] Discussed in Larry Catá Backer, Next Generation Law: Data-Driven Governance and Accountability-Based Regulatory Systems in the West, and Social Credit Regimes in China," *Southern California Interdisciplinary Law Journal* 28:123-172 (2018).

[830] "'Bulletproof' China-backed doxxing site attacks Hong Kong's democracy activists," *Hong Kong Free Press* (1 November 2019); available [https://hongkongfp.com/2019/11/01/bulletproof-china-backed-doxxing-site-attacks-hong-kongs-democracy-activists/].

Chapter 23

Sunday 19 April 2020
The COVID-19 Accelerator Effect: The Situation in Hong Kong and the Virtual Conflict Between the United States and China

More than a dozen leading pro-democracy activists and former lawmakers in Hong Kong were arrested on Saturday in connection with the protests that raged in the city last year, the biggest roundup of prominent opposition figures in recent memory. . . Fifteen activists between 24 and 81 years old were rounded up on suspicion of organizing, publicizing or taking part in several unauthorized assemblies between August and October and will face prosecution, the police said on Saturday without disclosing their names, following protocol.[831]

"Et puis la vengeance *se mange très-bien froide*, comme on dit vulgairement."[832] Indeed, It appears that the officials of the Hong Kong local government has decided to treat themselves to a delectable cold feast, consuming those who just a few weeks ago still appeared to pose a substantially untouchable threat to their authority, and to their ability to carry out the guidance of the central authorities. This is not a revenge feast served up by the central authorities, however. It is a feast prepared for local

---

[831] Elaine Yu and Austin Ramzy, "Amid Pandemic, Hong Kong Arrests Major Pro-Democracy Figures," The New York Times (18 April 2020); available [https://www.nytimes.com/2020/04/18/world/asia/hong-kong-arrests.html] ("Rarely have so many prominent pro-democracy figures — over a dozen — been arrested at once. The arrests signaled a broader crackdown on the antigovernment movement that roiled the semiautonomous city last year.").

[832] Eugène Sue; Jean Cavalier, et al. (1841) , "XVII, Révélations [XVII, Revelations]", in Mathilde: Mémoires d'une Jeune Femme [Mathilde: Memoirs of a Young Woman](in French), volume 3, third edition, Paris: Librairie de Charles Gosselin, page 53; available [https://books.google.com/books?id=tpZUAAAAcAAJ&pg=RA1-PA53#v=onepage&q&f=false] (in English: And so revenge is very well consumed cold, as the vulgar say").

authorities by an unexpected global pandemic whose effects have provided an unprecedented opportunity for the state to rid itself of an increasingly threatening challenge to its leadership.[833]

In one sense, the arrests were not unexpected. Nor, for that matter was the timing. The pattern was well set in the aftermath of the Umbrella Movement. In that case the local authorities waited years before striking, They were patient, bending enough to restore order, and then, once the population was distracted in the pursuit of prosperity, they struck. And, to underline the point, the date chosen was meant to be auspicious. "Just one day after Hong Kong's new leader was chosen by Beijing, police are planning to arrest student leaders and other prominent figures involved in the huge 'Umbrella Movement' pro-democracy protests."[834] And in a greater irony, given what was to come, those protesters were sentenced[835] on the eve of the 2019 protests, or thereafter freed.[836] Joshua Wong has been in and out of prison and the judicial apparatus since 2017. In this respect, at least, things appear to be normal, as that term has one to be understood in Hong Kong.

The COVID-19, however, has now clearly changed the dynamics of the protests in Hong Kong. The stalemate at the end of 2019, grounded in part on the ability of the protesters to mobilize hundred and sometimes hundreds of thousands of

---

[833] For the classic analysis, see, William H. McNeill, *Plagues and Peoples* (NY: Anchor Doubleday, 1977)

[834] "Police Arrest Umbrella Protesters One Day After Pro-Beijing Leader Elected in Hong Kong," *CTN News* (27 March 2017); available [https://www.chiangraitimes.com/thailand-national-news/world-news/police-arrest-umbrella-protesters-one-day-after-pro-beijing-leader-elected-in-hong-kong/].

[835] Matthew S. Schwartz, "'Umbrella' Protesters Sentenced For 2014 Hong Kong Pro-Democracy Demonstration ," *NPR* (24 April 2019); available [https://www.npr.org/2019/04/24/716628971/umbrella-protesters-sentenced-for-2014-hong-kong-pro-democracy-demonstration].

[836] "Hong Kong 'Umbrella' movement leader freed from prison: Chan Kin-man has no regrets for role in 2014 civil disobedience, says sacrifice needed to achieve universal suffrage," *Al Jazeera* (14 March 2020); available [https://www.aljazeera.com/news/2020/3/14/hong-kong-umbrella-movement-leader-freed-from-prison].

people to support them, appears to have now been broken by the COVID-19 global pandemic. Where the protesters had managed to acquire the sympathies of the people with their political program since June 2019, the needs of people to protect themselves and their families against potentially debilitating illness has now again shifted authority back to the state. And the state appears all too willing to use the expectations of the people to act to protect their health in ways that also permit them to act, and act decisively, against the leading elements of the protester factions in Hong Kong.

Like others, I recently noted [837] that the COVID-19 pandemic has provided a cover or a portal or an excuse, or a convenient nodal point (depending on thew perspective one chooses to view events) for the acceleration of transformations (but not their genesis), *the trajectories of which were already clear.*

> Plague accelerates even as it transforms. There is no magic to plague; it operates in the environment in which it appears, and is both constrained by that environment (technology, societal taboos, hygiene and the like) and provides it with the openings through which rising societal contradictions, or its discontents, might be resolved or the level of their intensity advanced. One sees both in the wake of COVID-19.[838]

For those starting from this premise, then, COVID-19 has not been used to make meaning; rather it has served as the prism through which that meaning acquires a more complex coloring.

---

[837] Larry Catá Backer, "The Metamorphosis of COVID-19: State, Society, Law, Analytics," *Emancipating the Mind: Bulletin of the Coalition for Peace & Ethics* 15(2): 261-352 (2020); available [https://www.thecpe.org/wp-content/uploads/2020/12/15-2_FINAL_Pt_C_5_Backer_COVIDEssay.pdf].
[838] Ibid., p. 264-265.

Nowhere is this made clearer than at the borderlands of emerging post-global Empires. [839] Those borderlands can be abstract (as in the territorialization of global production chains built on the hub-and-spoke-model of America First or China's Belt and Road Initiative). Or it can be evidenced in forays at the physical frontiers of Imperial domains. These are neither natural nor inevitable spaces (real or virtual; concrete or abstract). Rather they are point along a continuum chosen because they appear to signal a weak point in the construction of the protective boundaries that are being constructed to define and separate one Imperial system from another.

For all kinds of reasons, Hong Kong has appeared to serve such a purpose. More importantly, since the start of 2020, Hong Kong has also proven to be an important site from which one can observe the character of the *COVID-19 accelerator effect.* The convergence and the likely consequences of these post-global imperial system conflicts in Hong Kong (here understood as a physical territory and as an abstract space that itself stands for competing narratives of order and of historical progression), accelerated by pandemic, has moved to another stage in the wake of the April 2020 arrests of Hong Kong opposition figures by the authorities. [840]

In going back to the arrests of April 2020, one can appreciate its significance from another perspective. That is, these arrests represent not just the repetition of a pattern of revenge that has become deeply engrained in the working style of the police and prosecutorial apparatus of Chinese authorities, but something new as well. That "something new" suggests the power of COVID-19 to upend the stalemate of the last half a year and to open the possibility of a more accelerated and perhaps brutal movement toward the end of the protests to the satisfaction of the central authorities.

---

[839] The Coalition for Peace & Ethics Working Group on Empire, Empire Series," Law at the End of the Day; available [https://lcbackerblog.blogspot.com/search/label/CPE%20EmpireSeries].
[840] Elaine Yu and Austin Ramzy, "Amid Pandemic, Hong Kong Arrests Major Pro-Democracy Figures," supra.

More than a dozen leading pro-democracy activists and former lawmakers in Hong Kong were arrested on Saturday in connection with the protests that raged in the city last year, the biggest roundup of prominent opposition figures in recent memory. * * * The high-profile arrests were made as Hong Kong battled to contain the coronavirus outbreak, which has helped quiet down the huge street protests but fueled further distrust of the authorities. [841]

The authorities were able to strike just as it acquired a legitimate basis for ensuring that its actions would meet little effective opposition. By effective, of course, one means by massing people on the streets. It has become clear that in Hong Kong words (like the ones in this essay)--and rhetorical performances (like those of many foreign states)--can provide a narrative baseline for justifying action or rallying support. But power resides in those who can assert it against the bodies of their opponents without significant damaging consequence. And here, in this instance, COVID-19 has changed entirely the calculus by which those decisions are made. That calculus now appears to point quite strongly in favor of the authorities. People, fearful of the disease, will not fill out onto the street to protest actions they feel strongly about. The police may also fear, but they obey, and they can deploy to the streets at the will of the authorities. That changes everything.

The actions of the Hong Kong authorities are not unique; and the temptations of the virus for local authorities anxious to manage popular rage when it spills onto the streets appears to be as contagious as the COVID-19 virus itself. The result perhaps is an acceleration of the impulse to protect people against contagion in ways that also protect the state against the people.[842]

---

[841] Ibid.

[842] See, Alexandra Stevenson, Austin Ramzy and Tiffany May, "In Hong Kong, the Coronavirus Strikes a Wounded City," *The New York Times* (7 February 2020); available [https://www.nytimes.com/2020/02/07/business/hong-kong-coronavirus.html]. Discussed in essay Chapter 22, infra.

> In response to the COVID-19 pandemic, many countries rushed through legislation and policies that did not comply with international human rights law and standards. This included legislation creating a presumption in favour of the police when determining whether it is reasonable to use of lethal force. . . State of emergency laws further conferred unfettered powers on governments to take measures to respond to COVID-19... such measures disproportionately restricted the rights to freedom of peaceful assembly and freedom of expression. . . At the policy level, governments have defined approaches that enabled excessive use of police powers to suppress the rights to freedom of expression and peaceful assembly.[843]

Here one can think of the arrests as potentially the opening salvo of an campaign that will likely seek to resolve the dispute, and in a way that moves Hong Kong decisively from Two Systems to One Country. That this movement in the meaning of the principle can be viewed as plausible now may be the result of the way that COVID-19 appears to be creating the perfect conditions for such an acceleration. First it has substantially destroyed the ability of the Hong Kong population to mobilize in the streets. Second, it has substantially eliminated the ability of the international community, and those powerful protectors of Hong Kong's Two Systems model abroad, as Europe and North America face their own crises of pandemic. The resulting closures of borders provides the perfect setting for the performance of the reified nationalism that is embedded in the centrality of One Country over Two Systems.

In a sense, COVID-19 has been able to act as an accelerator precisely because it was so effective in changing this calculus of the cost of assertions of power--from ones that favored the

---

[843] *COVID-19 crackdowns: Police abuse and the global pandemic* (London: Amnesty International (17 December 2020); available [https://www.amnesty.org/download/Documents/ACT3034432020ENGLISH.PDF], pp. 8-9.

protestors to one that favored the state authorities. It revealed, in the process, the ultimate weakness of the Two Systems element of One Country-Two Systems, to the extent that Two Systems was inherently dependent on a strong connection between popular agitation on the streets in Hong Kong and strong support for those protests within the international community in a way that could damage the interests of the central authorities with respect to important policy objectives. The structural responses to pandemic were all it appears to take to bring that entire delicate house down on its foundations.

At the same time it produced conditions that made it possible for the central authorities to effectively counter what they have perceived all along as a core threat to their political economic model and to their conception of the proper role of international law and its relation to the assertion of sovereign authority by states. For central authorities, the notions of split or shred sovereignty was incomprehensible and threatening. Other states might view positively the forward march of globalization through the further abandonment of the restrictions of territorial borders in place of which a more uniform set of core principles, favorable to local exercise of political discretion conforming to emerging norms of international (mostly human rights and sustainability) principles. These notions have been developed as the heart of the ideal of globalized constitutionalism in which international norms would be placed at the center and national orders would be rebuilt around these standards overseen by a broad consensus among the community of states.[844] Hong Kong's Two Systems principles emerged after 2014 as a poster child of this progressive thinking among internationalist elements heavily represented within the UN system elites and among the core dominant political factions of developed liberal democratic states and their academic facilitators.

That emergence, at its core, and from a legal perspective, the situation in Hong Kong is fundamentally a challenge for and a

---

[844] Described in Larry Catá Backer, "God(s) Over Constitution: International and Religious Transnational Constitutionalism in the 21st Century," *Mississippi College Law Review* 27:11 (2008).

test of the complex political-economic model that China has constructed, one which distinguishes the application of that model among its territories. It was all the more so as Chinese elites might have begun to consider that Two Systems itself was changing in unacceptable ways that would make it possible for the principle to survive until the end of the end of the term of the Sino-British Declaration in 2047.[845] Indeed, that appears to be the sentiment that had been expressed more forcefully by protesters.

> Hong Kong was never British, despite being a British colony. It has never been Chinese either, despite being geographically and now politically linked to them. It's fundamentally always been just Hong Kong. It is its own place, with its own unique identity, and the people here would very much like to be able to keep that, preserve that and expand that – and to stop having the rules of their existence defined for them, and imposed upon them. Hong Kong people have their own voice, and want it heard."[846]

If, in fact, Two Systems had become a principle of international law, then China might necessarily view its genesis from treaty provision to general principle as a direct threat to its planning objectives, and as an effort to deprive it of the "benefit of its bargain" with the United Kingdom at the time of the agreement for the return of leased territories and the ceding of the territories what had been alienated lawfully in the 19th century.

For China, then, the challenge of Two systems has proven to be a delicate and sensitive matter requiring the balancing of a number of objectives around the core driving premises of its political-economic order.[847] By now it has become clear that One Country-Two Systems can no longer be understood as something creates a finely tuned balance among principles of equal dignity.

---

[845] E.g., Jiang Shigong, *China's Hong Kong : A Political and Cultural Perspective* (Singapore: Springer, 2017).

[846] Ben Hillier, "2019 Movement, Winter Coronavirus — Is Hong Kong's springtime coming?," *Europe Solidaire Sans Frontières* (20 February 2020); available [http://www.europe-solidaire.org/spip.php?article52124].

[847] Discussed in essay Chapter 2, supra.

Instead, more than six months into the protests it has become clear that the protests merely illuminate the efforts to resolve the contradiction inherent in One Country-Two Systems in favor of one principle or the other. I have been suggesting that this contest has produced quite remarkably well articulated defenses on either side. Neither side, however, had the strength to succeed in imposing its version of primacy (One Country or Two Systems at the center). COVID-19 now appears to be changing that.

The delicacy of that change is most apparent from the recent writing of leading Hong Kong academics. They appear to be the last among those with an interest in the preserving the statis quo and who, in the process continue to seek to protect the very delicate line that defines Hong Kong as a challenge for the integrity of internal governance of China, and as a site for its international dimensions.[848] And yet the efforts of those actions reveal better its futility than its success. It suggests that what the traditional Hong Kong academic elite have left is the inglorious task of maintaining a rearguard action as COVID-19 accelerates the inevitable contest which they continue to hope disappears.

And thus one encounters an almost surreal academic engagement with the protest movement as well as with the position of local and central authorities. This element of academic surrealism was better exposed in the wake of the arrests of prominent Hong Kong protest leaders. While they dance around the rhetorical performances of both sides that will eventually determine the fate of One Country-Two Systems, they expose their own strategic positioning and perhaps weakness, caught as they are between their global networks (and their expectations) and the expectations of officials. As such, it was not the arrests that was the center of interest here, rather it was the statements by the representative organs of the central authorities in Hong Kong made immediately before the arrests that captured the intellectual imagination. That initially produced intense local

---

[848] See, Chen Zimo and Willa Wu, "Experts confirm liaison office's role not limited by Article 22," *China Daily* 19 April 2020); available [https://www.chinadailyhk.com/article/128027].

coverage.[849] This, in turn, touched on the connection between the timing of the statement and the subsequent arrests that served as the initiation of this current situation "The arrests came just hours after China's liaison office asserted in a strongly-worded statement that it and the Hong Kong and Macau Affairs Office (HKMAO) – China's top bodies overseeing the city's affairs – are "authorised by the central authorities to handle Hong Kong affairs."[850] It was undertaken, analysts quite correctly noted, with an eye to upending what appears to central authorities as the possibility of reshaping Two Systems into a principle that could extend beyond 2047 in its current form. The pandemic provided the perfect opportunity in this respect. "The veteran China watcher, Johnny Lau, said Beijing is trying to hit hard at Hong Kong while the world is busy dealing with Covid-19. 'In Xi Jinping's eyes this is an opportunity to shuffle the cards and to assert its narrative," he said. "If the foreign countries turn a blind eye and fail to rein in [China's power], they would also suffer.'"[851]

Indeed, after six months of protests, the task facing Chinese central authorities, even with accelerator and disrupting opportunities presented in the form of the pandemic, remain formidable. They are formidable, in large measure, because six months of stalemate has permitted not just a refinement of the Chinese position on One Country, but also the refinement and expansion--within quite powerful global consensus principles of international law--of the local protestor and international position on Two Systems. As a consequence, Hong Kong, which might ordinarily not have served so usefully as a wedge point for

---

[849] Alvin Lum, "Leading legal adviser says Beijing offices right to criticise opposition lawmakers," *South China Morning Post* (19 April 2020) ; available [https://www.scmp.com/news/hong-kong/politics/article/3080564/leading-legal-adviser-says-beijing-offices-right-criticise] ("Beijing authorities were acting within their right to warn Hong Kong opposition lawmakers against paralysing proceedings in the legislature, which was a "scandalous" failure of governing that had already led to "significant malfunctioning" of the body's constitutional role, a leading legal expert said.")
[850] Verna Yu, "Police in Hong Kong arrest 15 activists amid autonomy warnings," *The Guardian* (18 April 2020); available [https://www.theguardian.com/world/2020/apr/18/police-in-hong-kong-arrest-14-activists-amid-autonomy-warnings] (
[851] Ibid.

inter-Imperial competition, has been transformed into a wedge point for two great contests. The first is between the international and nationalist camps. The second, deeply attached to the first, is the contest between two rising forms of post global imperial models.[852]

Hong Kong now provides the perfect site for engagement. Hong Kong is different--born of a series of international agreements, and bound up in its own history of territorial trading under the rules of 19th Century imperial constructions--it provides an almost ideal opportunity for competitor aggregations of power to test China's. And not just that; it produces substantial value-added for the project of internal meaning making as a means of advancing narratives of differences in the construction of imperial order (their respective constitutional-moral orders).

China, perhaps inadvertently, or because of the irresistible nature of the "in-between-ness" of the situation in Hong Kong, has effectively conceded this status--physically within China and abstractly occupying more than one "space." In defending the police action, China, as it has become accustomed to doing when irritated by others, blamed the *black hand of foreign interference-*[853]-as if its own people were entirely robotic and without a will that could be turned in any direction.

> China blamed Western forces and defended police conduct after Hong Kong endured another weekend of violent clashes between protesters and police. Some "irresponsible people" in the West have applied "strange logic" that made them sympathetic and tolerant to "violent crimes" but critical of the police force's "due diligence," a Chinese government spokesman said at a news briefing Monday. "At the end of the day, their intention is to create trouble in Hong Kong, make Hong

---

[852] "From the CPE Working Group on Empire: Ruminations 87-- Reflections on President Trump's July 4th Speech and the Convergence of the Rhetorics of Empire," Law at the End of the Day (6 July 2019); available [https://lcbackerblog.blogspot.com/2019/07/from-cpe-working-group-on-empire.html].

[853] Discussed essays Chapters 7-8, 13, supra.

Kong a problem to China, in order to contain China's development," said Yang Guang, spokesman for the Chinese Cabinet's Hong Kong and Macao Affairs Office, without mentioning any specific individuals or countries. He added that such attempts will come to nothing because Beijing will tolerate no outside interference in Hong Kong's affairs.[854]

But as we have suggested elsewhere,[855] the "black hand defense" comes with its own risks--especially risks to the ultimate Chinese premise of the condition of Hong Kong within the borders of Chinese political sovereignty. Before the pandemic, that risk, for example, could be seen in the need for a police official from Hong Kong having to travel to the United Nations in Geneva to defend its actions before an international public body[856] The greater irony is that this humiliation (from the perspective of the central authorities) occurs only weeks before the arrests are made. This can be seen both as a sign of weakness at the peripheries of imperial sovereign authority, and (from an outsider perspective) an admission of the special and international status of that territorial space which ought otherwise to be assumed to be well within the borders of Chinese sovereign authority.

What the internationalist community understood as the expression of political dissent and mass politics, and conformation of the political culture of Hong Kong that had to be protected in line with international standards, Chinese authorities might understand as a threat to its basic responsibility to maintain stability to produce local prosperity. From a Chinese perspective, then, the acceleration of its incorporation of Hong Kong--not just

---

[854] Yanan Wang and Katie Tam, "China defends Hong Kong police, blames Western forces," *Yahoo News* (29 July 2019); available [https://news.yahoo.com/china-says-western-politicians-stirring-090017793.html].

[855] Discussed in essay Chapter 16, supra.

[856] Chen Zimo, "HK police defend 'vilified' reputation in Geneva," *China Daily* (10 March 2020); available [https://www.chinadailyhk.com/article/123752] ("In a direct effort to clear the name of the much-maligned law enforcement agency, the deputy commissioner of the Hong Kong Police Force, Oscar Kwok Yam-shu, set out to establish the "truth" in Geneva of what has happened in Hong Kong over the past eight months").

within the national territory, but within the political-economic model (with a substantially smaller autonomy)--was made necessary by its core responsibility to maintain order inside its domain. One Country, in effect, was the answer to the chaos of Two Systems.

Disorder undoes everything; order is the foundation upon which the political-economic model can thrive. Inside a conceptual view that considers the mechanisms of the domestic legal-political order supreme over any international obligation (a view that in its own way it shares with many important actors in the United States) the disorder in Hong Kong made acceleration inevitable before COVID-19.[857] What COVID-19 provided was a context within which it was possible (even necessary given what might come after) to accelerate this policy trajectory. In effect, the arrests were necessary, and necessary now, because any delay would present authorities with the more difficult task of maintaining order in the absence of COVID-19 to impose a virus driven order. The Statement of the Hong Kong Government in that respect is telling, emphasizing the lawfulness of the arrests and the duty to maintain order.[858]

But it is precisely the acceleration of Chinese central authority in Hong Kong that also strengthens the response outside of China. That response is built on the notion that the assertion of direct sovereignty itself is an admission of its absence. That absence, in turn, can only be explained through the operation of those international arrangements under which an issue of contested sovereignty (at least with respect to a part of that territory) was resolved. Acceleration, in this context, then, is viewed both as an admission of incomplete internal sovereignty and of an intention to breach international promises. That, in turn,

---

[857] See discussion in essays Chapters 12, 19.

[858] "Arrests Based on Evidence," News.gov.Hong Kong (18 April 2020); available [https://www.news.gov.hk/eng/2020/04/20200418/20200418_173118_961. html?type=ticker] ("It emphasised that under the Police Force Ordinance, Police have the duty to take lawful measures for apprehending all persons whom it is lawful to apprehend and for whose apprehension sufficient grounds exist. The bureau noted that the relevant arrests were made based on evidence from investigations and strictly according to the laws in force.").

can then be generalized by competing imperial orders into the suggestion that China values its promises only to the extent that it suits. The conclusion--the narrative to be woven from this--China cannot be trusted, not just respecting Hong Kong, but more generally with respect to all of its promises.

> "The United States condemns the arrest of pro-democracy advocates in Hong Kong," US secretary of state Mike Pompeo said. "Beijing and its representatives in Hong Kong continue to take actions inconsistent with commitments made under the Sino-British Joint Declaration that include transparency, the rule of law, and guarantees that Hong Kong will continue to 'enjoy a high degree of autonomy'."[859]

The responses of the UK [860] and the International Bar Association[861] underlined this twin notion of distrust of China to abide by international standards, and the application of those principles to the governance of the SAR.

China's foreign affairs office in Hong Kong might be understood to have fallen into the trap thus created by falling back to the "Black Hand" defense: "The spokesperson said the US politicians were "condoning evil acts and making a travesty of the rule of law by ignoring facts, distorting the Sino-British Joint Declaration, and trying to exonerate anti-China troublemakers in

---

[859] "US and UK condemn arrest of Hong Kong democracy activists," *The Guardian* (19 April 2020; from Reuters); available [https://www.theguardian.com/world/2020/apr/19/us-and-uk-condemn-arrest-of-hong-kong-democracy-activists] (quoting US secretary of state Mike Pompeo).

[860] Ibid. ("In Britain, a Foreign Office representative said the government expected any arrests and court procedures to be "conducted in a fair and transparent manner". The Foreign Office also said the right to peaceful protest was "fundamental to Hong Kong's way of life" and authorities should avoid "actions that inflame tensions".).

[861] Ibid. ("The International Bar Association said Hong Kong authorities should not encroach on human rights and the legal system must guard against any abuses of power while the world was preoccupied with the coronavirus pandemic. The association condemned the arrests of Lee and Ng, who have been active human rights and rule of law campaigners during their careers.")

Hong Kong on the pretext of 'transparency', 'the rule of law' and 'a high degree of autonomy'."[862]

That defense, however, did nothing to counter the really important thrust of the condemnation--not one having to do with the SPECIFIC situation in Hong Kong (of some but not central importance to competing empires) but of the situation in Hong Kong as a MEANS of accelerating the construction of a narrative of difference, but one that requires a more robust decoupling. That becomes clearer not from the US foreign ministry (with its own limited vision and the need to focus in a particular way), but instead from a ministry closer to the heart of the organization of the competitor empire--the office of the US Attorney General:

> In a separate statement, U.S. Attorney General William Barr called the arrests "the latest assault on the rule of law and the liberty of the people of Hong Kong." "These events show how antithetical the values of the Chinese Communist Party are to those we share in Western liberal democracies," he added, saying the arrests and other actions "demonstrate once again that the Chinese Communist Party cannot be trusted."[863]

The implication, at least for imperial construction, become clear: if one cannot trust the Chinese, then for the instrumentalists of US economic activity the implications are clear--hedge in the operation of supply chains and be wary of market dependence either at the buying or selling end). For others, it serves to draw in starker terms the border between the two imperial organizations. Where both compete for territory (again not physical but conceptual, and with it the control of the factors of

---

862 Natalie Wong, "Beijing foreign affairs office in Hong Kong hits back at governments for criticising arrests of pro-democracy figures," *South China Morning Post* (19 April 2020); available [https://www.scmp.com/news/article/3080591/beijing-foreign-affairs-office-hong-kong-hits-back-governments-criticising].

863 "US and other foreign governments condemn Hong Kong arrests of democracy activists," *Reuters* (19 April 2020); available [https://www.cnbc.com/2020/04/19/us-condemns-arrests-of-hong-kong-democracy-activists.html].

production necessary for the design and operation of global production) then this border drawing can be effectively used.

Yet it is the COVID-19 accelerator that lends additional power to what otherwise might have been more lukewarm responses. One gets a hint of this from the statement issues by the Australian Foreign Minister Marise Payne: "'That this has happened in the midst of the global crisis stemming from COVID-19 is concerning. Actions that undermine stability are never acceptable, but to do so during a crisis of this magnitude erodes goodwill and trust," she said."[864] (At the same time, the Editorial Board of the US Wall Street Journal begins an editorial this way: "The world is learning some unpleasant truths about China's Communist Party amid the Covid-19 pandemic, and the latest example comes from Hong Kong. "[865]

For those without the necessary imagination to connect the dots and draw the intended picture, the West provides a substantial set of sources of appropriate explanation to drive home the point. One can only marvel at the coincidence that on the heels of the Hong Kong arrests, H. R. McMaster, a retired United States Army lieutenant general, is a former White House national security adviser publishes (incongruously enough) an essay in *The Atlantic*.[866] Its object was both to more clearly define the borders of the two empires, and to suggest that these conceptual borders have hard effect.

---

[864] Eryk Bagshaw, "Payne condemns Hong Kong arrests of democracy advocates amid coronavirus, *The Sydney Morning Herald* (19 April 2020) ; available [https://www.smh.com.au/world/asia/labor-joins-us-uk-in-condemning-hong-kong-arrests-of-democracy-advocates-20200419-p54l61.html].

[865] The Editorial Board, "China's Hong Kong Roundup: Beijing increases its hold on the territory with a spate of arrests," *The Wall Street Journal* (19 April 2020); available [https://www.wsj.com/amp/articles/chinas-hong-kong-roundup-11587310986]..

[866] H.R. McMaster, "How China Sees the World--And how we should see China," *The Atlantic* (May 2020); available [https://www.theatlantic.com/magazine/archive/2020/05/mcmaster-china-strategy/609088/?utm_source=facebook&utm_medium=social&utm_campaign =share].

China has become a threat because its leaders are promoting a closed, authoritarian model as an alternative to democratic governance and free-market economics. The Chinese Communist Party is not only strengthening an internal system that stifles human freedom and extends its authoritarian control; it is also exporting that model and leading the development of new rules and a new international order that would make the world less free and less safe... And, on balance, the Chinese Communist Party's goals run counter to American ideals and American interests.[867]

And the essay clearly suggest that a necessary consequence must be decoupling, with quite specific and conceptual border enhancing focus. The decoupling includes within the university-research complex, the industrial-technology complex, and telecommunications.[868] All of this reflects emerging consensus views within the American ruling factions. More interesting is the focus on a defense "against Chinese agencies that coordinate influence operations abroad—such as the Ministry of State Security, the United Front Work Department, and the Chinese Students and Scholars Association. At the same time, we should try to maximize positive interactions and experiences with the Chinese people. "[869]   Lastly, the decoupling suggested countermeasures, within which Hong Kong could easily fall. "The U.S. and other free nations should view expatriate communities as a strength. Chinese abroad—if protected from the meddling and espionage of their government—can provide a significant counter to Beijing's propaganda and disinformation."[870]

All of this, of course, is then underlined by the US line adopted in the wake of the Hong Kong arrests. One cannot understand the international position on Hong Kong without understanding the contradictions between internationalization for Hong Kong, and the re-nationalization of home state

---

[867] Ibid.
[868] Ibid.
[869] Ibid.
[870] Ibid.

communities by the very liberal democratic states advancing internationalist policies. The arrests of high profile protest leaders or influencers, the controversy over the projection of central authority opinions within the policy bailiwick of local officials and their characterization as "foreign" interference within the Two Systems principle, and the liberal democratic simultaneous policies of decoupling with China and engaging (within international parameters) in Hong Kong suggest a set of criss crossing vectors of actions and policies that inevitably weaken the approach of the internationalist camp. Here, then, is the advantage to the Chinese approach to One Country that is now likely to be pressed and intensified. Against this the internationalists can offer little resistance--only concepts.

It is in this context that one can usefully consider recent actions undertaken in Hong Kong, as well as the power of the international reactions it might produce. Those together will then be even more purposefully fitted together within the larger framework of the construction of the meaning of the global order from the narrative spinning of its Chinese and American makers. None of this is spectacular or new--what makes it interesting is the way that it might be used to understand and define the characteristics and modalities of the COVID-19 Accelerator Effect on inter-imperial systemic relations.

The accelerator works in two directions simultaneously. Internally, it changes the scope and character of the movement to the end of the special status for Hong Kong within Chinese sovereign space. Sovereignty merges with control. It is the traditional understanding that the relationship of a political collective (the state) to the territory under its control and the people (within that territory) is subject to its lawful authority. [871] That suggests an incompatibility between self-determination principles within a sovereign entity and the indivisible principle of sovereignty itself. Yet even under ideal notions of sovereign authority, there has always been a sense of constraint. Put differently, the limits against which Chinese

---

[871] Alexander Passerin D'Entrèves, *The Notion of the State: An Introduction to Political Theory* (Oxford University Press, 1967), pp. 1-11.

political theory in the international realm must both work within, and to the extent possible exploit, in the matter of Hong Kong, is subject to consensus notions that restrain a state in the exercise of unrestrained sovereign authority even with respect to its own people and territories.[872]

Externally, it accelerates the movement toward the decoupling of empire and the refinement of the conceptual territories of each. Sovereignty becomes fractured permitting a decoupling of formal territorial sovereignty from sovereign control.[873] Conceptual territories, more than physical space, mark the actual territorial limits of post-global empire as a function of control. [874] Formal territorial sovereignty serves to limit assertions of competing claims. Conceptual territories, territories grounded in effective control, serve now as the basis around the meaning of sovereignty might be attempted. Conceptual territorialization, of multi-level sovereignty, appears to be at the heart of emerging theories of post global empire, including those with Marxist Leninist foundations. That certainly is one way to read key theorists like Jiang Shigong.[875] The objectification of the systems around which contemporary empire is constructed, is the essential framework within which these systems can be incarnated, and thus incarnated and managed across what will become secondary borders (territory, ethnicity, religion, and the like).

In this case, Hong Kong provides an important point of development of the conceptual character of sovereignty within empires that can manage and absorb all sorts of territories with varying degrees of sovereign autonomy from the imperial center. For Chinese central authorities, Hong Kong is constructed as close to the core of the heartland. As such, its autonomy--understood as delegations of sovereign discretion--can be tolerated but only

---

[872] Consider in this context Stephen Krasner, *Sovereignty: Organized Hypocrisy* (Princeton University Press, 1999), pp. 1-41

[873] Carmen E. Pavel, *Divided Sovereignty: International Institutions and the Limits of State Authority* (Oxford University Press, 2015).

[874] Dan Sarooshi, *International Organizations and Their Exercise of Sovereign Powers,* "Oxford University Press 2005)

[875] Discussed in the essay Chapter 2, supra.

to a point. For internationalists, and its allies within the American political vanguard, autonomy suggests not connection (with delegation) but decoupling that builds protective barriers against assertions of certain forms of sovereign authority from an imperial center.

Chinese officials have been developing their conceptual basis for its relationships with territories like Hong Kong with increasing refinement and coordination since before the events of June 2019. That intense and coordinated development has not been matched by the Hong Kong protesters, their international allies or the Americans. The problem arises not just from the structural fracture of the protesters but also from the weakness of a liberal democratic camp whose own ideological factional fighting has made it far more difficult to embrace a consensus position on Hong Kong that offers protesters any sort of basis for protecting their autonomous, much less driving its provision.[876] Still it may be too early to and quite foolish to dismiss either approach.

$$* \quad * \quad *$$

---

[876] Consider Promise Li, "A Left Case for Hong Kong Self-Determination," *Spectre* (3 April 2020); available [https://spectrejournal.com/a-left-case-for-hong-kong-self-determination/].

Chapter 24

Saturday 23 May 2020

On Resolutely Resolving Contradiction 《全国人民代表大会关于建立健全香港特别行政区维护国家安全的法律制度和执行机制的决定（草案）》("Decision of the National People's Congress on Establishing and Improving the Hong Kong Special Administrative Region's Legal System and Implementation Mechanism for Maintaining National Security (Draft)")

In retrospect, one of the great ironies of the protests that started in Hong Kong in June 2019 might well have been that it signaled the start of the end of that 50 year period of autonomy to be enjoyed on the basis of the strict application of an international pact which runs its course in 2047.[877] A further irony that builds on the first also describes its converse: the official reactions to the protests led to almost a year of intense public demonstrations of the development of a distinctive and self-aware political culture in Hong Kong (with roots in the intensification of introspection after 1997) which demonstrators thought worth not just defending but expanding and achieving even at great cost.[878]

The protesters sought to first embed their objectives in the protection of the One Country-Two Systems project within the internationalism of the Sino-British Joint Declaration[879] and then

---

to detach that internationalism from the Sino-British Joint Declaration itself and embed it in general principles of international law and localized civil and political rights, especially in notions of self-determination within the formal sovereign authority of a state.[880] At the same time, the Chinese central authorities moved as aggressively in the opposite direction, detaching the status of Hong Kong from its international foundations, and stressing its rejection of any sort of recognition of divided sovereignty.[881] This has received halfhearted support from the foreign internationalist camp,[882] though the "idea" of Hong Kong as a stable space for shared sovereignty "might suggest that its relevance on the international level has not expired with the hand-over ceremony."[883] Nonetheless, within the Hong Kong context itself, the intelligentsia remains divided, though cautious in its subtle defense of the protesters and more vigorous outspoken in the service of the central authorities.[884]

What started out in June 2019 as a fight over the application of the "One Country-Two Systems" principle to what appeared to be the narrow issue of extradition and projection of central authority police actions in Hong Kong has produced had, by the end of 2019, produced a remarkable effect.

First the responses of both sides (and of the foreign community in their oversight role) effectively split the principle

---

the Question of Hong Kong (19 December 1984); available [https://www.cmab.gov.hk/en/issues/jd2.htm].

[880] See, e.g., Klaus Günther, "Divided Sovereignty, Nation, and Legal Community," *Journal of Common Market Studies* 55(2):213-222 (2017); Jiri Priban, "Multiple Sovereignty: On Europe's Self-Constitutionalization and Legal Self-Reference," *Ratio Juris* 23(1):41-64 (2010); Ruth Lapidoth, "Sovereignty in Transition," *Journal of International Affairs* 45(2):325-346 (1992).

[881] Discussed in essays Chapters 2-5, supra.

[882] See discussion essays Chapters 14-15, supra. Whatever the level of support, its theory remains substantially grounded in the legalities of the Sino-British Joint Declaration and a much more amorphous sense of the application of the superior principles of international law but only through the decisions and actions of states.

[883] Lorenz Langer, "Out of Joint?--Hong Kong's International Status from the Sino-British Joint Declaration to the Present," *Archiv des Völkerrechts* 46(3):309-344 (2008).

[884] See discussion essays Chapters 6, 9, 13, and 19, supra.

in two. The One Country Two Systems principle became a pair of interrelated principles--(1) One Country (recognizing the territorial integrity of China including Hong Kong), and (2) Two Systems (recognizing the political autonomy of the Hong Kong SAR in accordance with its developing customs and traditions, that development being under the control of local people). Second, the argument about One Country Two Systems, now two principles, was then transformed into a contest over their relationship. What the parties are fighting about now, what the discourse has become, is a critical contest over which--One Country OR Two Systems principle--would serve as the primary constitutional basis for ordering Hong Kong's political system.

Either way, what appeared lost was the initial and once critical factor in the analysis. That factor--the scope, character, and consequences of the 2047 term end of the Sino-British Joint Declaration--appears to have quietly become irrelevant in the calculus of every stakeholder. [885] Better put perhaps, what appeared to have occurred was that for the One Country side, the Sino-British Joint Declaration became dead letter once the territories were returned (or ceded) to China. For the Two System side, the Sino-British Joint Declaration became merely the starting point for the development of a local culture whose legitimacy would be a function of the international law of self-determination. *For both, then, the Sino-British Joint Declaration became a gateway.* For Hong Kong Democrats has become a gateway to autonomy guaranteed by international law (and the international community). For Chinese central authorities it was the pathway to the recognition by the international community of its sovereign rights to the former British Crown Colony (including those portions of it ceded by China or leased by Chinese authorities to the UK). And yet one might have considered, going into the protests starting in June, 2019, that this term end would have counselled patience on the part of the central authorities and

---

[885] Considered in Yunxin Tu, "The Question of 2047: Constitutional Fate of "One Country, Two Systems" in Hong Kong, *German Law Journal* 21:1481 (2020). (considering three possible interpretations: "Unchanged for 50 years" as international promise, "unchanged for 50 years" as political commitment, and "unchanged for 50 years" as constitutional obligation).

caution on the part of the protesters. Patience might well have been the core residual meaning of the Sino-British Joint Declaration is only because of the character of its 2047 term, with respect to which some meaning had to be developed. Lamentably, 2047 has produced neither patience nor caution.[886]

In the process, the protests of 2019 did much to shed light on the character of what had emerged as political culture--and the idealized aspirations of its fiercest adherents--of an autonomous Hong Kong under One Country Two Systems. This represents, in a way, the apotheosis of the "Two Systems" part of the international framework for the governance of Hong Kong. This part of the equation was, at least form the perspective of 1997, to have an international character, and to be based on the primacy of autonomous development subject to a limited embedding of the political cultures of the state asserting ultimate (but until 2047) not entirely exclusive sovereignty. Its principle character was to give great weight to the "Two Systems" part of the equation and to read the "One Country" part as residual and remote.

At the same time, the protests forced Chinese central authorities and their allies to confront the very same questions of the character of the political culture of Hong Kong, and its place within the greater Pearl River area and China generally from the idealized perspective of the Marxist-Leninist and national political-economic model of the Chinese state. That, in turn, represented the need to refine the "One Country" part of the equation in the context of a dynamically evolving New Era theory for the overall governance of the nation under the guidance of the Chinese Communist Party. This part of the equation, at least from the perspective of 2047, to have an overwhelmingly national character, and to be based on the primacy of the collective development of the state as a coherent and integrated whole, subject to a limited (and decreasing) toleration for differences in political cultures that must, in any case, not impede national goals and direction. This approach required the "Two Systems" part of the equation to be read within and under the primary structure of the "One Country" principle.

---

[886] See an initial consideration in essay Chapter 2, supra.

The two positions produced a contradiction that required resolution. This is contradiction (矛盾论) in the Maoist sense of the "law of the unity of opposites."[887] It is in its essence the resolution of binary oppositions that in turn produce additional or succeeding binaries. These binaries exist in multiple, sometimes relational, forms, and once understood within their ecologies could be rationalized along a continuum of importance. "There are many contradictions in the process of development of a complex thing, and one of them is necessarily the principal contradiction whose existence and development determine or influence the existence and development of the other contradictions."[888] Within Chinese Marxist-Leninist theory, the vanguard is tasked with identifying the principal contradiction for each era of Chinese historical development.[889] During the period of the leadership of Mao Zedong, the principal contradiction was class struggle. The development of productive forces assumed the role of principal contradiction from the leadership of Deng Xiaoping and his immediate successors. From the time of the leadership of Xi Jinping, the principal contradiction shifted to the balance between unbalanced and inadequate development and the people's need for a better life.[890]

Within the historical context of Hong Kong, though, since 1998, the principal contradiction has been the "One Country-Two Systems" principle itself. This contradiction required resolution. The formal answer provided by the international agreements

---

[887] Mao Zedong, "On Contradiction" (August 1937), reprinted Marxists.org; available [https://www.marxists.org/reference/archive/mao/selected-works/volume-1/mswv1_17.htm].

[888] Ibid.

[889] Constitution of the Communist Party of China (revised and adopted at the 19th National Congress of the Communist Party of China 24 October 2017); available [http://www.xinhuanet.com//english/download/Constitution_of_the_Communist_Party_of_China.pdf], General Program ¶¶ 4-7.

[890] Xi Jinping, "Secure a Decisive Victory in Building a Moderately Prosperous Society in All Respects and Strive for the Great Success of Socialism with Chinese Characteristics for a New Era, Report to the 19th CPC Congress 2017," China Daily 18 October 2017); available [http://www.chinadaily.com.cn/china/19thcpcnationalcongress/2017-11/04/content_34115212.htm].

around which transfer was effectuated signaled that time was to be the ultimate means of resolving the contradiction. Specifically, 2047 was to end the period of moving from U.K. colonialism to national integration, and potentially, the autonomous status of Hong Kong, but as a matter wholly within the discretion of national authorities.[891] But that position appears to have little appeal to any of the camps embedded within the contradiction of Hong Kong's internationalist autonomy within China's sovereignty.

This rejection of Sino-British Joint Declaration literalism produces a number of discursive tropes that have dominated the press coverage. The "One Country" camp would necessarily see in international engagement a foreign interference. The "black hand" perspective remains strong among the "One Country" camp.[892]

> A state-controlled news agency accused the city's pro-democracy opposition of having "schemed with external forces in attempts to create a 'colour revolution'". Beijing has repeatedly alleged that the pro-democracy camp was receiving support from the CIA in the United States, as well as other foreign governments.[893]

---

[891] The Sino-British Joint Declaration, supra, in a well-known section, provides: "The National People's Congress of the People's Republic of China shall enact and promulgate a Basic Law of the Hong Kong Special Administrative Region of the People's Republic of China (hereinafter referred to as the Basic Law) in accordance with the Constitution of the People's Republic of China, stipulating that after the establishment of the Hong Kong Special Administrative Region the socialist system and socialist policies shall not be practised in the Hong Kong Special Administrative Region and that Hong Kong's previous capitalist system and life-style shall remain unchanged for 50 years."

[892] Owen Churchill and Teddy Ng, "US' Hong Kong democracy act slanders China to a level close to madness, Foreign Minister Wang Yi says," *South China Morning Post* (21 November 2019); available [https://www.scmp.com/news/china/diplomacy/article/3038789/us-hong-kong-democracy-act-slanders-china-level-close-madness] ("Chinese Foreign Minister Wang Yi has described the passage through Congress of US legislation targeting China as "madness" that will damage the countries' relationship.").

[893] Matthew Doran, "Australia joins Canada and UK in condemning China's move to 'clearly undermine' Hong Kong's autonomy," *ABC News* (22 May 2020);

For the "Two Systems" camp, on the other hand, foreign interference (at least before 2047) is turned around. *Here the "black hand" of foreign interreference is that of China.* This trope has emerged in more recognizable for in the context of the announcement and proffered justification of a Chinese plan to promote a new security law for Hong Kong, [894] which was delivered by Wang Chen, Vice Chairman of the Standing Committee of the National People's Congress, which marks a decisive turning point in the contest between Hong Kong protesters and their internal allies, and the central authorities.[895] Already, from the Two Systems side, it has been described as the end of Hong Kong.[896]

The joint statement by Australia's Foreign Minister Marise Payne, British Foreign Secretary Dominic Raab and Canadian Foreign Minister Francois-Philippe Champagne make this clear.

---

available [https://www.abc.net.au/news/2020-05-23/australia-canada-uk-condemn-china-move-in-hong-kong/12279426] ("A Chinese official said the National Congress was exercising its "constitutional power" to set up a new legal framework and enforcement mechanism to ensure national security in Hong Kong").

[894] 《全国人民代表大会关于建立健全香港特别行政区维护国家安全的法律制度和执行机制的决定（草案）》 ("National People's Congress on the Establishment and Improvement of the Hong Kong Special Administrative Region to Maintain National Security"); available [https://news.sina.cn/gn/2020-05-22/detail-iirczymk2984337.d.html?from=wap].

[895] It is important to note that the actual explanation was distributed several days later as 关于《全国人民代表大会关于建立健全香港特别行政区维护国家安全的法律制度和执行机制的决定（草案）》的说明 (Explanation of the "Decision of the National People's Congress on Establishing and Improving the Hong Kong Special Administrative Region's Legal System and Implementation Mechanism for Maintaining National Security (Draft)") (28 May 2020); available [http://www.gov.cn/xinwen/2020-05/28/content_5515771.htm].

[896] Eliza McPhee, "Australia issues a joint statement with the UK and Canada condemning China's anti-protest laws in Hong Kong," Daily Mail (23 May 2020); available [https://www.dailymail.co.uk/news/article-8350153/Australia-issues-joint-statement-UK-Canada-condemning-Chinas-security-laws-Hong-Kong.html] ("Some pro-democracy lawmakers have denounced the plans as 'the end of Hong Kong'.").

The legally binding Joint Declaration, signed by China and the United Kingdom, sets out that Hong Kong will have a high degree of autonomy... It also provides that rights and freedoms, including those of the person, of the press, of assembly, of association and others, will be ensured by law in Hong Kong and that the provisions of the two United Nations covenants on human rights ... shall remain in force. . . Making such a law on Hong Kong's behalf, without the direct participation of its people, legislature or judiciary, would clearly undermine the principle of 'One Country, Two Systems', under which Hong Kong is guaranteed a high degree of autonomy."[897]

The issue of the foreign, then, becomes an ironic marker o the contradiction posed within the alignment of "One Country and Two Systems" within the parameters of the current strategic discourse.

The 2019 protests, though, brought out into the open what had been simmering under the surface--the realization by both the "Two Systems" and the "One Country" camps that the time was coming perilously close for political culture altering steps to be taken in anticipation of 2047. In this sense the protests represented, in some respects, the opening gambit of a series of final "negotiations" around which the post 2047 autonomy of Hong Kong would be crafted. The time chosen was serendipitous in the sense that it was not clear that in the mutual provocations of both camps from some years previous the Extradition Law would provide the signal to more aggressive negotiation through the power of mass mobilization. It was clear, though, that such a step would have to be taken during a time when the international character of the status of Hong Kong was still strong enough to induce foreign state stakeholders (and the international community) a space for participation in the negotiations. For the "Two State" camp, that required privileging the 1997 sensibility of Hong Kong as a n internationalized space (at least to some

---

[897] Quoted in Matthew Doran, "Australia joins Canada and UK in condemning China's move to 'clearly undermine' Hong Kong's autonomy," supra.

extent); for the "One Country" camp, that produced a necessary counter-thrust that would seek to both privilege and accelerate the conditions of national control anticipated in 2047.

The strategies, of course, augmented the contradictions inherent in the temporary status quo of Hong Kong. And it was meant to. On the one hand it provided a last chance to modify or reinterpret the international agreement before that possibility was foreclosed by the passage of time. It was meant to welcome, and indeed, create incentives for foreign intervention precisely because the international agreement provided a formal cover for such action in law (if interpreted "correctly"). On the other hand, it provided what appeared to be a challenge for the anticipated changes for 2047 and a potential extension of this sovereignty managing condition for Hong Kong that was made politically impossible in China. To counter that thrust, the only logical counter thrust would have to be to accelerate the arrival of 2047 by recasting the international instrument as legally insufficient (and thus the international interventions as foreign interference), and to unveil more quickly and transparently the planning for Hong Kong from the time its autonomous status would become a matter of grace.

The COVID-19 pandemic provided the space within which the relative positions of both camps were deeply affected. Pandemic effectively made mass mobilization dangerous in ways that could not be overcome by protest leaders. At the same time the quick triumph of Mainland authorities over the COVID-19, at least enough to start a return to full operation, gave the "One Country" camp its chance to move swiftly during this window provided by the virus. And so they have. Even so, the "One Country" camp appears to have been somewhat cautious. Its current proposal is bound up in a "Security Law" whose breadth might be theoretically elastic (and less so as one comes closer to 2047) but which might be initially drafted benignly enough to further erode the power base of the "Two Systems" camp both within and beyond Hong Kong.

Prudence might also be necessary because Hong Kong has become another battlefront in a much more important conflict between the two emerging global imperial systems--the United States and China.[898] That involves the re-ordering of global trade relations, the de-coupling and re-alignment of the two economies, and the contest between these post-global imperial systems to control international governance space (or divide it between them with the Europeans as the mediators). It also evidences substantial traps, for example in the form of projections of US global power (exercised through the instruments of economic activity control) respecting the Xinjiang Autonomous Region,[899] and in the projection of Chinese power through strategic investment and resource control (as well as in contests for control of the mechanisms for global finance) and a contested (in the West) instrumentalization of its going out policies in the education field.[900]

Within this analytical space, the likely actions of all participants become clearer. The constraints to action and counter action become clearer as well. In the process China will be required to more clearly develop the "One Country Two Systems" principles, but one already sees how that will involve at a minimum the primacy of "One Country" and the necessary role of

---

[898] For a taste of the discussion, usually framed in the context of control for driving globalization, see, Aaron Friedberg, "The United States Needs to Reshape Global Supply Chains," Foreign Policy (8 May 2020); available [https://foreignpolicy.com/2020/05/08/united-states-reshape-global-supply-chains-china-reglobalization/].

[899] See Congressional Executive Commission on China Staff Research Report, "Global Supply Chains, Forced Labor, and the Xinjiang Uyghur Autonomous Region" (March 2020); available [https://www.cecc.gov/sites/chinacommission.house.gov/files/documents/CECC%20Staff%20Report%20March%202020%20-%20Global%20Supply%20Chains%2C%20Forced%20Labor%2C%20and%20the%20Xinjiang%20Uyghur%20Autonomous%20Region.pdf].

[900] E.g., Racueal Legerwood, "As US Universities Close Confucius Institutes, What's Next?: US Defense Law Behind Closure of Chinese Government Cultural Centers," Human Rights Watch (27 January 2020); available [https://www.hrw.org/news/2020/01/27/us-universities-close-confucius-institutes-whats-next#US China control global production chains]; Gary Sands, "Are Confucius Institutes in the US Really Necessary?: The teaching of Chinese language and culture in the U.S. will remain important, but are Chinese government funded institutes the best option?," The Diplomat (20 February 2021); available [https://thediplomat.com/2021/02/are-confucius-institutes-in-the-us-really-necessary/].

the CPC in guiding the future course of the exercise of autonomy within its ideological framework, the context of which has been made quite clear over the last several years. For the "Two System" camps (both within Hong Kong and among international actors) it will require a reassessment of what may be possible to preserve within an overall framework in which the idealized autonomy of the 2019 protests will be unattainable. That, in turn, will require careful negotiation, but whether the negotiation will be undertaken on the streets or elsewhere remains to be seen. For other states, the international law wedge that the status of Hong Kong provided will likely shrink (for the Europeans) and grow wider (for the Americans and perhaps Australia[901]). Hong Kong, like the pandemic, and like the situation in the other autonomous regions (and along the Belt and Road) provides a critically important space within which the US can, like the Chinese, also define and defend their own ideology, their status as a first tier power, and the process of decoupling and reordering the global system of economy, society, and culture. But it will also put greater pressure on international actors to choose sides.

The long road to 2047 has just gotten shorter, even as the distance between ideologically ordered political-economic systems has widened. In the process of rationalizing both expect a substantial amount of collateral damage--to individuals, institutions, relations, and the way things are understood and valued. That is to a large extent inevitable, even if the pacing of events was not. In the end 2047 will come; if it has not already announced its imminent appearance. It is time now to see and understand, from the "One Country" position, how the "Two Systems" principle can be more rationally aligned with New Era ideology and the leadership of both state and CPC. But it is not yet 2047. *And it is not clear that when it comes it will mean anything.*

So one remains in a fractured interpretive stasis. Hong Kong remains firmly a creature of international agreement *within* China until 2047. Hong Kong may also have acquired a meaning

---

[901] Aoki Midori, "The Deepening Rift Between Australia and China," NKH World News (15 October 2020); available [https://www3.nhk.or.jp/nhkworld/en/news/backstories/1327/].

as an autonomous community beyond the limits of the narrow legalities of the Sino-British Joint Declaration. Or it may have already merged firmly into the body of the nation, indistinguishable and unreachable by the structures, responsibilities, authority, or command of international law. That debate may continue; it certainly must continue under the shadow of 2047 until then. Until 2047, then, the international community may push the central contradiction of "One Country Two Systems" toward resolution in accordance with its own dialectical vectors, now well revealed The revelation--to confront the contradiction from the internationalist side it is necessary (with great craft) to invert Chinese Marxist-Leninist principles to advance those of its own politics-economic model ("Two Systems" within "One Country" here perhaps in the form of an attempted extra-territorialization of the European Union model of "Unity in Diversity"). [902] Contradiction, in this context, is resolved by rejecting the legitimacy of a unitary and undivided sovereignty, central to the Chinese position and rejecting as well the applicability of that notion as the ordering element of the One Country Two Systems principle as applied to the political model of Hong Kong.

Whatever that development, one thing remains quite clear--at least through 2047 China will scrupulously adhere to its international obligations. And in the inevitable movement of time towards 2047, the central authorities will also seek to confront

---

[902] E.g., "Unity in Diversity," European Commission; available [https://cordis.europa.eu/article/id/27389-unity-in-diversity] (the phrase is also the motto of the European Union); CVCE, "The Motto of the European Union" (7 July 2016); available [https://www.cvce.eu/en/education/unit-content/-/unit/eeacde09-add1-4ba1-ba5b-dcd2597a81d0/fefea7bf-b49d-49db-b06e-a32a06ff1538/Resources#15a2404d-d959-41e0-80bd-cfabeb5e270e_en&overlay]. The EU has a strong ideological position in favor of the practice of extra territorialization as a substitute for more aggressive forms of projections of power abroad . It avoids the indelicacies of European colonial pasts while achieving some control or management objectives of the targets of extra territorialization. See, Bettina Bruns and Dorit Happ, "EU Extra-territorialization and Securitization: What Does It Mean for Ukraine and Belarus?," in Bettina Bruns, Dorit Happ, H. Zichner H. (eds) *European Neighbourhood Policy. New Geographies of Europe* (London: Palgrave Macmillan, London, 2016), pp. 139-159.

the central contradiction of One Country Two Systems by applying its own dialectical forces, those now well developed in its New Era thought.[903] But it will do it on its own terms; since at least 2017 Chinese officials have floated the proposition that the Sino-British Joint Declarations' terms are not effectively internalized within the constitutional system of the People's Republic of which Hong Kong is an indivisible part.[904]

> "Now Hong Kong has returned to the motherland's embrace for 20 years, the Sino-British Joint Declaration, as a historical document, no longer has any practical significance, and it is not at all binding for the central government's management over Hong Kong. The UK has no sovereignty, no power to rule and no power to supervise Hong Kong after the handover," Lu said.[905]

The contradiction, of course, is that this strict adherence will be interpreted as a fundamental breach by the international community.[906] The dispute was academic until the protests began

---

[903] This is well described in the work of Jiang Shigong on Hong Kong, discussed in the essay Chapter 2, supra.

[904] "China refutes UK, U.S. remarks on Hong Kong affairs," Xinhuanet (30 June 2017); available [http://www.xinhuanet.com/english/2017-06/30/c_136407724.htm].

[905] "China says Sino-British Joint Declaration on Hong Kong no longer has meaning," Reuters (30 June 2017); available [https://www.reuters.com/article/us-hongkong-anniversary-china-idUSKBN19L1J1] (quoting the statement of Foreign Ministry spokesman Lu Kang).At the time the reference was made there was some controversy over the exact translation of the statement (《中英联合声明》就中方恢复对香港行使主权和过渡期有关安排作了清晰划分. 现在香港已经祖国怀抱 20 年, 《中英联合声明》作为一个历史文件, 不具有任何现实意义, 对中国中央政府对香港特区的管理也不具备任何约束力). Discussed in Julian Ku, "Grammar Matters: Did China Really Declare that the Entire Sino-UK Joint Declaration is "Not At All Binding"? Maybe Not," Lawfare Blog (3 July 2017); available https://www.lawfareblog.com/grammar-matters-did-china-really-declare-entire-sino-uk-joint-declaration-not-all-binding-maybe-not

[906] Alistair Smout, Kylie MacLellan and Bella Barber, "Britain rejects Chinese view of Hong Kong declaration as 'historic document'" Reuters (rev. 2 July 2019); available [https://www.reuters.com/article/us-hongkong-extradition-britain-duncan/britain-rejects-chinese-view-of-hong-kong-declaration-as-historic-document-idUSKCN1TX1KL].

in 2019. Its use as the opening through which the contradiction between One Country and Two Systems can be resolved is the essence of 全国人民代表大会关于建立健全香港特别行政区维护国家安全的法律制度和执行机制的决定（草案）》("National People's Congress on the Establishment and Improvement of the Hong Kong Special Administrative Region to Maintain National Security")[907] and the anticipated actions of the National People's Congress Standing Committee to come.

The importance of this proposal cannot be underestimated. And it was not by the vanguard forces of the internationalist camp. The United States condemned the effort as a clear repudiation of the Sino-British Joint Declaration and an assault on the liberties of Hong Kong people. But it relied on the formalist internationalism built into the Sino-British Joint Declaration.

> The United States condemns the People's Republic of China (PRC) National People's Congress proposal to unilaterally and arbitrarily impose national security legislation on Hong Kong. The decision to bypass Hong Kong's well-established legislative processes and ignore the will of the people of Hong Kong would be a death knell for the high degree of autonomy Beijing promised for Hong Kong under the Sino-British Joint Declaration, a UN-filed agreement.[908]

The emphasis was a narrow one--on the formal binding legality of the Sino-British Joint Declaration.[909]

---

[907] 《全国人民代表大会关于建立健全香港特别行政区维护国家安全的法律制度和执行机制的决定（草案）》, supra.

[908] Mike Pompeo, Press Release, "P.R.C. Proposal to Impose National Security Legislation on Hong Kong," U.S. Department of State (22 May 2020); available [https://2017-2021.state.gov/prc-proposal-to-impose-national-security-legislation-on-hong-kong/index.html].

[909] Press release, "Joint Statement from the UK, Australia and Canada on Hong Kong" (22 May 2020); available [https://www.gov.uk/government/news/joint-statement-from-the-uk-australia-and-canada-on-hong-kong].

That China is marching at a faster pace toward 2047 and its vision for Hong Kong going forward does not mean the end of "One Country, Two Systems." What it does mean, at least form the actions of the NCP and the symbolic effect of the National Security Law for Hong Kong, is that the driver of the interpretation of that system, its principles and operation, will shift decisively from Hong Kong to Beijing, and it will become far more deeply embedded within the Chinese New Era Marxist Leninist dialectic. The NCP document makes this explicit--that is its great innovation: "One country" is the premise and basis for the implementation of "two systems." It follows that "two systems" autonomy is dependent on and subordinate to "one country" and unified within "one country." Autonomy is then possible only within the permitted scope defined by the fundamental political principles of "one country." What had been understood discretely within China and effectively ignored elsewhere, has now become an explicit statement of the fundamental contradiction of the 1997 transfer and its proposed resolution.

To that end, it is likely that from this point on it may be useful to think about the contradiction that is One Country Two Systems as a sub-part of the transitional dialectic from capitalist, through socialist, to communist society.[910] Hong Kong will be expected to proceed on that path at its own pace; but proceed it must. The "One Country Two Systems" model will develop new forms suitable to the New Era of Chinese development What the consequences of that necessary internal movement will be on the contradiction that is the fracturing of global governance between New Era liberal democratic and Marxists world views remains to be seen.

---

[910] E.g., Mao Zedong, "Dialectical Materialism" (April-June 1938), reproduced in Marxists.org from Selected Works of Mao Zedong vol. 6); available [https://www.marxists.org/reference/archive/mao/selected-works/volume-6/mswv6_30.htm], chapter 2 ¶6 ("The philosophies of all reactionary forces are theories of immobilism. Revolutionary classes and the popular masses have all perceived the principle of the development of the world, and consequently advocate transforming society and the world; their philosophy is dialectical materialism.").

The explanation of the Chinese National Security Law framework 关于《全国人民代表大会关于建立健全香港特别行政区维护国家安全的法律制度和执行机制的决定（草案）》的说明[911] provides both the justification for the coming action to be taken--decisively it appears--by the National People's Congress, as well as its justification. It represents a quite robust action that is likely meant to change the entire landscape of the current impasse between local authorities and Hong Kong protesters. Its author, Wang Chen, Vice Chairman of the Standing Committee of the National People's Congress, starts by making a case for the necessity and importance of a national security law for Hong Kong. [912] It is grounded on two objectives, both concrete expressions of the position of the central authorities since early on in the protests in July and August 2019. These are the objectives of improving the legal system and its enforcement mechanism. This he argues, falls well within the parameters of the "One Country-Two Systems" principle. That principle has been the basis for the growth in the prosperity of Hong Kong, which has been threatened by uncontrolled disruption since June 2019.

> Especially since the "Regulations Amendment Disturbance" occurred in Hong Kong in 2019, the anti-China forces against Hong Kong have openly advocated "Hong Kong independence", "self-determination", "referendum" and other propositions, engaged in activities that undermine national unity and split the country; openly insulted and defiled the national flag and the national emblem incited Hong Kong people to oppose China and the Communist Party, besieged the central government agencies in Hong Kong, discriminated against and crowded out mainland personnel in Hong Kong; deliberately disrupted Hong Kong's social order, violently opposed police

---

[911] (Explanation of the "Decision of the National People's Congress on Establishing and Improving the Hong Kong Special Administrative Region's Legal System and Implementation Mechanism for Maintaining National Security (Draft)") (28 May 2020), initial reference supra note 13.

[912] 关于《全国人民代表大会关于建立健全香港特别行政区维护国家安全的法律制度和执行机制的决定（草案）》, supra, ¶1.

enforcement, damaged public facilities and property, and paralyzed government governance and the operation of the Legislative Council.

The echo of the central authorities' line is clearly apparent here, now refined and repurposed as justification for the imposition of legal reform from the Chinese national apex sovereign. All of the tropes are here: the need to protect the supreme objectives of prosperity and stability,[913] the lawlessness of the protests, and the transformation of those protests from mere local grievances to efforts to destabilize the state.[914] Also present is the presence of "black hand" of foreign interference as justification for firm countermeasures. [915] Indeed, the initial paragraph provides a quite succinct crystallization of the evolution of the position of the central authorities from the time of the commencement of the protests. [916]

Wang Chen then reminds readers of the responsibility of officials written into Article 23 of the Hong Kong Basic Law that imposes a duty to protect against subversive activities and the like and forbids collusion with foreign elements.[917] The role of the universities and other educational establishments in the subversion does not go unremarked. [918] Lastly, the need for

---

[913] Ibid. ("Maintaining Hong Kong's long-term prosperity and stability and safeguarding national security are facing risks that cannot be ignored.").

[914] Discussed essays Chapters 7, 20, supra.

[915] Ibid. ("It should also be noted that in recent years, some foreign and foreign forces have openly interfered in Hong Kong affairs, intervened and disrupted through various means such as legislation, administration, and non-governmental organizations. They have joined forces with Hong Kong's anti-China and Hong Kong forces to fight against Hong Kong").

[916] Discussed in essays Chapter 20.

[917] 关于《全国人民代表大会关于建立健全香港特别行政区维护国家安全的法律制度和执行机制的决定（草案）》, supra, ¶1.

[918] 关于《全国人民代表大会关于建立健全香港特别行政区维护国家安全的法律制度和执行机制的决定（草案）》, supra ("The relevant law enforcement work needs to be strengthened; Hong Kong society needs to vigorously develop education on safeguarding national security, and generally strengthen the safeguarding of national security. awareness.").

national intervention is also explained as a function of the paralysis of local officials.[919]

Wang Chen then turns to the general requirements and basic principles for a Hong Kong national security law.[920] The basic principles all mirror the development of the central authorities' view of preeminence of the "One Country" principle in the "One Country-Two Systems" concept. That requires among other things, " to adhere to the guidance of Xi Jinping's Thought on Socialism with Chinese Characteristics for a New Era, and fully implement the 19th National Congress of the Communist Party of China and the Second 19th National Congress of the Communist Party of China."[921] The implications are clear, especially for those who suggested that Hong Kong's organic political development might be provided with the freedom to move in the other direction. This is confirmed by the integrationist principle, which was also highlighted, one that was already made apparent in the development of regional planning in the Pearl River Delta.[922]

To frame the appropriate approach, five principals were put forward--each interpreted within the overarching principles of Chinese sovereignty over Hong Kong and the guiding principles of its "New Era" theory expressed in the contemporary basic line of the Communist Party of China. These are safeguarding national security, improving the One Country-Two Systems principle, and adhering to the rule of law, opposing foreign interference, and protecting (only) the legitimate rights and interests of Hong Kong residents.[923] That suggests what is being targeted. These include the identification and suppression of illegitimate interests, a heightened obligation to observe and contain the foreign in Hong Kong, a move toward Socialist Rule of law and away from its liberal democratic expressions, a refocus of One Country-Two Systems to put One Country at the center, and a singular focus on

---

[919] Ibid.
[920] Ibid., ¶ 2.
[921] Ibid.
[922] Discussed in essay chapter 12.
[923] 关于《全国人民代表大会关于建立健全香港特别行政区维护国家安全的法律制度和执行机制的决定（草案）》, supra, ¶ 2.

the principles of prosperity and stability. Read broadly, of course, the national security law draft would effectively quash the Hong Kong protest movement's "Five Demands,"[924] and likely subject its authors to prosecution.

Section 3 of the explanation is then devoted to a summary of the contents of the draft national security law for Hong Kong. The seven principle sections of the draft national security law are then summarized in one paragraph.[925] The first would confirm both the One Country-Two Systems" principle and its embedding in the domestic legal order of China. The second, conversely, would prohibit foreign engagement with the One Country-Two Systems principle and develop countermeasures against any such efforts at interference. The third would impose on local authorities the responsibility for ensuring "the maintenance of national sovereignty, unity and territorial integrity." [926] Read broadly, it would effectively suppress any notion of an autonomous political culture or related notions of shared or split sovereignty. The fourth would establish appropriate local institutional organs for resolutely enforcing the obligations imposed under the national security law against all who would pose a danger. The fifth "clearly stipulates that the Chief Executive of the Hong Kong Special Administrative Region shall regularly submit reports to the Central People's Government on the Hong Kong Special Administrative Region's performance of its duties to maintain national security, conduct national security education, and lawfully prohibit acts and activities that endanger national security."[927] The sixth strongly domesticates the "One Country-Two Systems" principle. It moves the center of its development and administration from the international realm to the jurisdiction of the National People's Congress. It also declares the power of the national government to intervene directly in Hong

---

924 Discussed in essay at Chapter 17, supra.
925 关于《全国人民代表大会关于建立健全香港特别行政区维护国家安全的法律制度和执行机制的决定（草案）》, supra, ¶ 3.
926 Ibid.
927 Ibid.

Kong affairs under conditions of instability.[928] The last specifies an effective date for the legislation.

Taken together one can discern a revolution in the making. Better put, a long anticipated and quite direct effort to overcome the contradiction that was the One Country-Two Systems principle at the time of its genesis at the end of the 20th century. The action is a direct challenge not just to the protesters but also to the internationalist camp. If it is successful--and there is a strong suspicion that this project will succeed, it marks the end even of the pretensions of the internationalist community to have any authority in the construction of the global order. It challenges the development of notions of shared sovereignty and of transnational constitutionalism so painstaking built within the halls of otherwise influential international organizations. With the national security law for Hong Kong, the old contradiction at the heart of the post-World War Two global order--national diversity unified by the international order[929]--is overcome by a triumph of a socialist basis for internationalism. For the protesters, and especially for the objectives that they have cultivated since the beginning of June 2019, this cannot be good news.

新华社北京 5 月 28 日电[930]

---

[928] Ibid. ("clarify the task of the relevant laws of the Standing Committee of the National People's Congress to effectively prevent, stop and punish any serious harm that occurs in the Hong Kong Special Administrative Region such as secession of the country, subversion of state power, organization of terrorist activities, etc.").

[929] Discussed in Larry Catá Backer, "God(s) Over Constitutions: International and Religious Transnational Constitutionalism in the 21st Century," *Mississippi College Law Review* 27:11-65 (2008).

[930] Original available [http://www.gov.cn/xinwen/2020-05/28/content_5515771.htm].

关于《全国人民代表大会关于建立健全香港特别行政区维护国家安全的法律制度和执行机制的决定（草案）》的说明 ——2020 年 5 月 22 日在第十三届全国人民代表大会第三次会议上
全国人民代表大会常务委员会副委员长 王晨

各位代表：

我受全国人大常委会的委托，作关于《全国人民代表大会关于建立健全香港特别行政区维护国家安全的法律制度和执行机制的决定（草案）》的说明。

一、从国家层面建立健全香港特别行政区维护国家安全的法律制度和执行机制的必要性和重要性

香港回归以来，国家坚定贯彻"一国两制"、"港人治港"、高度自治的方针，"一国两制"实践在香港取得了前所未有的成功；同时，"一国两制"实践过程中也遇到了一些新情况新问题，面临着新的风险和挑战。当前，一个突出问题就是香港特别行政区国家安全风险日益凸显。特别是 2019 年香港发生"修例风波"以来，反中乱港势力公然鼓吹"港独"、"自决"、"公投"等主张，从事破坏国家统一、分裂国家的活动；公然侮辱、污损国旗国徽，煽动港人反中反共、围攻中央驻港机构、歧视和排挤内地在港人员；蓄意破坏香港社会秩序，暴力对抗警方执法，毁损公共设施和财物，瘫痪政府管治和立法会运作。还要看到，近年来，一些外国和境外势力公然干预香港事务，通过立法、行政、非政府组织等多种方式进行插手和捣乱，与香港反中乱港势力勾连合流、沆瀣一气，为香港反中乱港势力撑腰打气、提供保护伞，利用香港从事危害我国国家安全的活动。这些行为和活动，严重挑战"一国两制"原则底线，严重损害法治，严重危害国家主权、安全、发展利益，必须采取有力措施依法予以防范、制止和惩治。

香港基本法第 23 条规定："香港特别行政区应自行立法禁止任何叛国、分裂国家、煽动叛乱、颠覆中央人民政府及窃取国家机密的行为，禁止外国的政治性组织或团体在香港特别行政区进行政治活动，禁止香港特别行政区的政治性组织或团体与外

国的政治性组织或团体建立联系。"这一规定就是通常所说的
23 条立法。它既体现了国家对香港特别行政区的信任,也明确
了香港特别行政区负有维护国家安全的宪制责任和立法义务。
然而,香港回归 20 多年来,由于反中乱港势力和外部敌对势力
的极力阻挠、干扰,23 条立法一直没有完成。而且,自 2003 年
23 条立法受挫以来,这一立法在香港已被一些别有用心的人严
重污名化、妖魔化,香港特别行政区完成 23 条立法实际上已经
很困难。香港现行法律中一些源于回归之前、本来可以用于维
护国家安全的有关规定,长期处于"休眠"状态。除了法律制
度外,香港特别行政区在维护国家安全的机构设置、力量配备
和执法权力等方面存在明显缺失,有关执法工作需要加强;香
港社会需要大力开展维护国家安全的教育,普遍增强维护国家
安全的意识。总的看,香港基本法明确规定的 23 条立法有被长
期"搁置"的风险,香港特别行政区现行法律的有关规定难以
有效执行,维护国家安全的法律制度和执行机制都明显存在不
健全、不适应、不符合的"短板"问题,致使香港特别行政区
危害国家安全的各种活动愈演愈烈,保持香港长期繁荣稳定、
维护国家安全面临着不容忽视的风险。

党的十九届四中全会明确提出:"建立健全特别行政区维护国
家安全的法律制度和执行机制,支持特别行政区强化执法力
量。""绝不容忍任何挑战'一国两制'底线的行为,绝不容
忍任何分裂国家的行为。"贯彻落实党中央决策部署,在香港
目前形势下,必须从国家层面建立健全香港特别行政区维护国
家安全的法律制度和执行机制,改变香港特别行政区国家安全
领域长期"不设防"状况,在宪法和香港基本法的轨道上推进
维护国家安全制度建设,加强维护国家安全工作,确保香港
"一国两制"事业行稳致远。

根据宪法和香港基本法,结合多年来国家在特别行政区制度构
建和发展方面的实践,从国家层面建立健全香港特别行政区维
护国家安全的法律制度和执行机制,有多种可用方式,包括全
国人大及其常委会作出决定、制定法律、修改法律、解释法律、
将有关全国性法律列入香港基本法附件三和中央人民政府发出
指令等。中央和国家有关部门在对各种因素进行综合分析、评
估和研判的基础上,经认真研究并与有关方面沟通后提出了采

取"决定+立法"的方式,分两步予以推进。第一步,全国人民代表大会根据宪法和香港基本法的有关规定,作出关于建立健全香港特别行政区维护国家安全的法律制度和执行机制的决定,就相关问题作出若干基本规定,同时授权全国人大常委会就建立健全香港特别行政区维护国家安全的法律制度和执行机制制定相关法律;第二步,全国人大常委会根据宪法、香港基本法和全国人大有关决定的授权,结合香港特别行政区具体情况,制定相关法律并决定将相关法律列入香港基本法附件三,由香港特别行政区在当地公布实施。

2020 年 5 月 18 日,第十三届全国人民代表大会常务委员会第十八次会议听取和审议了《国务院关于香港特别行政区维护国家安全情况的报告》。会议认为,有必要从国家层面建立健全香港特别行政区维护国家安全的法律制度和执行机制,同意国务院有关报告提出的建议。根据宪法和香港基本法的有关规定,全国人大常委会法制工作委员会拟订了《全国人民代表大会关于建立健全香港特别行政区维护国家安全的法律制度和执行机制的决定(草案)》,经全国人大常委会会议审议后决定,由全国人大常委会提请十三届全国人大三次会议审议。

二、总体要求和基本原则

新形势下从国家层面建立健全香港特别行政区维护国家安全的法律制度和执行机制工作的总体要求是,坚持以习近平新时代中国特色社会主义思想为指导,全面贯彻党的十九大和十九届二中、三中、四中全会精神,深入贯彻总体国家安全观,坚持和完善"一国两制"制度体系,把维护中央对特别行政区全面管治权和保障特别行政区高度自治权有机结合起来,加强维护国家安全制度建设和执法工作,坚定维护国家主权、安全、发展利益,维护香港长期繁荣稳定,确保"一国两制"方针不会变、不动摇,确保"一国两制"实践不变形、不走样。

贯彻上述总体要求,必须遵循和把握好以下基本原则。

一是坚决维护国家安全。维护国家安全是保证国家长治久安、保持香港长期繁荣稳定的必然要求,是包括香港同胞在内的全中国人民的共同义务，是国家和香港特别行政区的共同责任。任何危害国家主权安全、挑战中央权力和香港基本法权威、利用香港对内地进行渗透破坏的活动，都是对底线的触碰，都是绝不能允许的。

二是坚持和完善"一国两制"制度体系。"一国"是实行"两制"的前提和基础，"两制"从属和派生于"一国"并统一于"一国"之内。必须坚定不移并全面准确贯彻"一国两制"、"港人治港"、高度自治的方针，准确把握"一国两制"正确方向，充分发挥"一国两制"制度优势，完善香港特别行政区同宪法和香港基本法实施相关的制度和机制。

三是坚持依法治港。宪法和香港基本法共同构成香港特别行政区的宪制基础。必须坚决维护宪法和香港基本法确定的香港特别行政区宪制秩序，严格依照宪法和香港基本法对香港特别行政区实行管治，支持香港特别行政区行政长官和政府依法施政，牢固树立并坚决维护法治权威，任何违反法律、破坏法治的行为都必须依法予以追究。

四是坚决反对外来干涉。香港特别行政区事务是中国的内政，不受任何外部势力干涉。必须坚决反对任何外国及其组织或者个人以任何方式干预香港事务，坚决防范和遏制外部势力干预香港事务和进行分裂、颠覆、渗透、破坏活动。对于任何外国制定、实施干预香港事务的有关立法、行政或者其他措施，国家将采取一切必要措施予以反制。

五是切实保障香港居民合法权益。维护国家安全同尊重保障人权，从根本上来说是一致的。依法有效防范、制止和惩治危害国家安全的极少数违法犯罪行为，是为了更好地保障香港绝大多数居民的生命财产安全，更好地保障基本权利和自由。任何维护国家安全的工作和执法，都必须严格依照法律规定、符合法定职权、遵循法定程序，不得侵犯香港居民、法人和其他组织的合法权益。

三、决定草案的主要内容

决定草案分为导语和正文两部分。导语部分扼要说明作出这一决定的起因、目的和依据。全国人民代表大会的相关决定，是根据宪法第三十一条和第六十二条第二项、第十四项、第十六项的规定以及香港基本法的有关规定，充分考虑维护国家安全的现实需要和香港特别行政区的具体情况，就建立健全香港特别行政区维护国家安全的法律制度和执行机制作出的制度安排。这一制度安排，符合宪法规定和宪法原则，与香港基本法的立法宗旨和确立的有关制度是一致的，将有效地维护香港特别行政区国家安全，有力地巩固和拓展"一国两制"的法治基础、政治基础和社会基础。

决定草案正文部分共有7条。第一条，阐明国家坚定不移并全面准确贯彻"一国两制"、"港人治港"、高度自治的方针；强调采取必要措施建立健全香港特别行政区维护国家安全的法律制度和执行机制，依法防范、制止和惩治危害国家安全的行为和活动。第二条，阐明国家坚决反对任何外国和境外势力以任何方式干预香港特别行政区事务，采取必要措施予以反制。第三条，明确规定维护国家主权、统一和领土完整是香港特别行政区的宪制责任；强调香港特别行政区应当尽早完成香港基本法规定的维护国家安全立法，香港特别行政区行政机关、立法机关、司法机关应当依据有关法律规定有效防范、制止和惩治危害国家安全的行为和活动。第四条，明确规定香港特别行政区应当建立健全维护国家安全的机构和执行机制；中央人民政府维护国家安全的有关机关根据需要在香港特别行政区设立机构，依法履行维护国家安全相关职责。第五条，明确规定香港特别行政区行政长官应当就香港特别行政区履行维护国家安全职责、开展国家安全教育、依法禁止危害国家安全的行为和活动等情况，定期向中央人民政府提交报告。第六条，明确全国人大常委会相关立法的宪制含义，包括三层含义：一是授权全国人大常委会就建立健全香港特别行政区维护国家安全的法律制度和执行机制制定相关法律，全国人大常委会将据此行使授权立法职权；二是明确全国人大常委会相关法律的任务是，切实防范、制止和惩治发生在香港特别行政区内的任何分裂国家、颠覆国家政权、组织实施恐怖活动等严重危害国家安全的行为和活动以及外国和境外势力干预香港特别行政区事务的活动；三是明确全国人大常委会相关法律在香港特别行政区实施的方式，即全国人大常委会决定将相关法律列入香港基本法附件三，由香港特别行政区在当地公布实施。第七条，明确本决定的施行时间，即自公布之日起施行。

全国人民代表大会根据新的形势和需要作出的上述制度安排，包括授权全国人大常委会就建立健全香港特别行政区维护国家安全的法律制度和执行机制制定相关法律，进一步贯彻落实了宪法和香港基本法的有关规定。香港特别行政区根据香港基本法第 23 条规定仍然负有维护国家安全的宪制责任和立法义务，应当尽早完成维护国家安全的有关立法。任何维护国家安全的立法及其实施都不得同本决定相抵触。

本决定作出后，全国人大常委会将会同有关方面及早制定香港特别行政区维护国家安全的相关法律，积极推动解决香港特别行政区在维护国家安全制度方面存在的突出问题，加强专门机构、执行机制和执法力量建设，确保相关法律在香港特别行政区有效实施。

《全国人民代表大会关于建立健全香港特别行政区维护国家安全的法律制度和执行机制的决定（草案）》和以上说明，请审议。

Xinhua News Agency, Beijing, May 28th, by wire

Explanation on the "Decision of the National People's Congress on Establishing and Improving the Hong Kong Special Administrative Region's Legal System and Implementation Mechanism for Maintaining National Security (Draft)"——At the Third Session of the Thirteenth National People's Congress on May 22, 2020

Wang Chen, Vice Chairman of the Standing Committee of the National People's Congress

Distinguished delegates:

I was entrusted by the Standing Committee of the National People's Congress to give an explanation on the "Decision of the National People's Congress on Establishing and Improving the Legal System and Implementation Mechanism for Maintaining National Security in the Hong Kong Special Administrative Region (Draft)."

1. The necessity and importance of establishing and improving the legal system and enforcement mechanism of the Hong Kong Special Administrative Region to safeguard national security at the national level

Since the return of Hong Kong, the country has firmly implemented the policy of "one country, two systems", "Hong Kong people ruling Hong Kong" and a high degree of autonomy. The practice of "one country, two systems" has achieved unprecedented success in Hong Kong. At the same time, some new situations and problems have also been encountered in the practice of "one country, two systems". , Facing new risks and challenges. At present, a prominent problem is that the national security risks of the Hong Kong Special Administrative Region have become increasingly prominent. Especially since the "Regulations Amendment Disturbance" occurred in Hong Kong in 2019, the anti-China forces against Hong Kong have openly advocated "Hong Kong independence", "self-determination", "referendum" and other propositions, engaged in activities that undermine national unity and split the country; openly insulted and defiled the national flag and the national emblem incited Hong Kong people to oppose China and the Communist Party, besieged the central government agencies in Hong Kong, discriminated against and crowded out mainland personnel in Hong Kong; deliberately disrupted Hong Kong's social order, violently opposed police enforcement, damaged public facilities and property, and paralyzed public governance and the operation of the Legislative Council. It should also be noted that in recent years, some foreign and foreign forces have openly interfered in Hong Kong affairs, intervened and disrupted through various means such as legislation, administration, and non-governmental organizations. They have joined forces with Hong Kong's anti-

China and Hong Kong forces to fight against Hong Kong. All together they have supported Hong Kong's anti-China and chaotic forces, provided a protective umbrella for them, and used Hong Kong to engage in activities that endanger our national security. These actions and activities seriously challenge the bottom line of the principle of "one country, two systems", seriously undermine the rule of law, and seriously endanger national sovereignty, security, and development interests. We must take effective measures to prevent, stop, and punish them in accordance with the law.

Article 23 of the Hong Kong Basic Law stipulates: "The Hong Kong Special Administrative Region shall enact laws on its own to prohibit any acts of treason, secession, sedition, subversion of the Central People's Government and theft of state secrets, and prohibit foreign political organizations or groups from conducting political activities in the Hong Kong Special Administrative Region. It also prohibits political organizations or groups in the Hong Kong Special Administrative Region from establishing ties with foreign political organizations or groups." This provision is commonly referred to as Article 23 of the legislation. It not only reflects the state's trust in the Hong Kong Special Administrative Region, but also makes it clear that the Hong Kong Special Administrative Region has the constitutional responsibility and legislative obligations to maintain national security. However, since the return of Hong Kong for more than 20 years, due to the strong obstruction and interference of anti-China forces and external hostile forces, Article 23 legislation has not been completed. Moreover, since the setback of Article 23 legislation in 2003, this legislation has been severely stigmatized and demonized by some people with ulterior motives in Hong Kong. It is actually very difficult for the Hong Kong Special Administrative Region to complete Article 23 legislation. Some relevant provisions in Hong Kong's current laws that originated before the return to China that could have been used to maintain national security have been in a "dormant" state for a long time. In addition to the legal system, the Hong Kong Special Administrative Region has obvious deficiencies in the establishment of institutions, allocation of strengths, and law enforcement powers for safeguarding national security. The relevant law enforcement work needs to be strengthened; Hong Kong society needs to vigorously develop education on safeguarding national security, and generally strengthen the safeguarding of national security. awareness. In general, the 23 legislation clearly stipulated in the Hong Kong Basic Law is at risk of being "shelved" for a long time. The relevant provisions of the current laws of the Hong Kong Special Administrative Region are difficult to effectively implement. The legal system and enforcement mechanism for safeguarding national security are obviously incomplete and incompatible. The "short-board" problem of non-compliance has caused the Hong Kong Special Administrative Region's various activities that endanger national security to intensify. Maintaining Hong Kong's long-term prosperity and stability and safeguarding national security are facing risks that cannot be ignored.

The Fourth Plenary Session of the 19th Central Committee of the Party clearly stated: "Establish and improve the legal system and enforcement mechanism for the special administrative region to maintain national security, and support the special administrative region to strengthen law enforcement." "We will never tolerate any behavior that challenges the bottom line of 'one country, two systems', and will never tolerate it. Any act of splitting the country." To implement the decision and deployment of the Party Central Committee, under the current situation in Hong Kong, it is necessary to establish and improve the legal system and enforcement mechanism of the Hong Kong Special Administrative Region to maintain national security at the national level, and to change the long-term "non-defense" in the national security field of the Hong Kong Special Administrative Region. "The situation is to promote the establishment of a national security system on the track of the Constitution and Hong Kong's Basic Law, strengthen the maintenance of national security, and ensure that the cause of "one country, two systems" in Hong Kong is stable and long-term.

According to the Constitution and the Hong Kong Basic Law, combined with the country's practice in the construction and development of the Special Administrative Region system over the years, the establishment and improvement of the Hong Kong Special Administrative Region's legal system and enforcement mechanism for safeguarding national security at the national level are available in a variety of ways, including the National People's Congress and its Standing Committee makes decisions, enacts laws, revises laws, interprets laws, includes relevant national laws in Annex III of the Hong Kong Basic Law, and issues instructions from the Central People's Government. On the basis of comprehensive analysis, evaluation, and judgment of various factors, the central and relevant state departments, after careful study and communication with relevant parties, proposed a "decision + legislation" approach and proceeded in two steps. In the first step, the National People's Congress, in accordance with the relevant provisions of the Constitution and the Hong Kong Basic Law, made a decision on establishing and improving the Hong Kong Special Administrative Region's legal system and enforcement mechanism for safeguarding national security, made certain basic provisions on related issues, and authorized the Standing Committee of the National People's Congress. To formulate relevant laws on the establishment and improvement of the Hong Kong Special Administrative Region's legal system and enforcement mechanisms for safeguarding national security; the second step, the National People's Congress Standing Committee, in accordance with the authorization of the Constitution, Hong Kong Basic Law and relevant decisions of the National People's Congress, and in light of the specific circumstances of the Hong Kong Special Administrative Region, formulate relevant laws It also decided to include relevant laws in Annex III of the Hong Kong Basic Law, and the Hong Kong Special Administrative Region will announce and implement them locally.

On May 18, 2020, the 18th meeting of the Standing Committee of the 13th National People's Congress heard and reviewed the "Report of the State Council on the Maintenance of National Security in the Hong Kong Special Administrative Region". The meeting believed that it is necessary to establish and improve the legal system and implementation mechanism of the Hong Kong Special Administrative Region to safeguard national security at the national level, and agree to the recommendations made in the relevant report of the State Council. In accordance with the relevant provisions of the Constitution and the Hong Kong Basic Law, the Legislative Affairs Committee of the Standing Committee of the National People's Congress drafted the "Decision of the

National People's Congress on Establishing and Improving the Legal System and Implementation Mechanism of the Hong Kong Special Administrative Region to Maintain National Security (Draft)", which was approved by the Standing Committee of the National People's Congress. After deliberation at the meeting, it was decided that the Standing Committee of the National People's Congress should submit it to the Third Session of the 13th National People's Congress for deliberation.

2. General requirements and basic principles

Under the new situation, the overall requirement for establishing and improving the legal system and implementation mechanism of the Hong Kong Special Administrative Region to maintain national security at the national level is to adhere to the guidance of Xi Jinping's Thought on Socialism with Chinese Characteristics for a New Era, and fully implement the 19th National Congress of the Communist Party of China and the Second 19th National Congress of the Communist Party of China. In the spirit of the Central, Third and Fourth Plenary Sessions, thoroughly implement the overall national security concept, adhere to and improve the "one country, two systems" system, and organically integrate the maintenance of the central government's overall governance of the special administrative region with the protection of a high degree of autonomy of the special administrative region, and strengthen the maintenance of the country Security system construction and law enforcement work firmly safeguard national sovereignty, security, and development interests, maintain Hong Kong's long-term prosperity and stability, ensure that the "one country, two systems" policy will not change or waver, and ensure that the practice of "one country, two systems" is not deformed or out of shape.

To implement the above-mentioned overall requirements, the following basic principles must be followed and grasped.

The first is to resolutely safeguard national security. Maintaining national security is an inevitable requirement for ensuring the long-term stability of the country and maintaining the long-term prosperity and stability of Hong Kong. It is the common obligation of all Chinese people, including Hong Kong compatriots, and the common responsibility of the state and the Hong Kong Special Administrative Region. Any activity that endangers the national sovereignty and security, challenges the central authority and the authority of the Hong Kong Basic Law, and uses Hong Kong to infiltrate and sabotage the mainland is a touch on the bottom line and must not be allowed.

The second is to uphold and improve the "one country, two systems" system. "One country" is the prerequisite and basis for the implementation of "two systems", which is subordinate to and derived from "one country" and unified within "one country". We must unswervingly and fully and accurately implement the principles of "one country, two systems", "Hong Kong people ruling Hong Kong", and a high degree of autonomy, accurately grasp the correct direction of "one country, two systems", give full play to the advantages of the "one country, two systems" system, and improve the Hong Kong Special Administrative Region in relation to the implementation of the Constitution and Hong Kong Basic Law Systems and mechanisms.

The third is to adhere to the rule of law in Hong Kong. The Constitution and the Hong Kong Basic Law jointly constitute the constitutional basis of the Hong Kong Special Administrative Region. It is necessary to resolutely maintain the constitutional order of the Hong Kong Special Administrative Region as determined by the Constitution and the Hong Kong Basic Law, govern the Hong Kong Special Administrative Region in strict accordance with the Constitution and the Hong Kong Basic Law, support the Chief Executive and the government of the Hong Kong Special Administrative Region in governing in accordance with the law, and firmly establish and resolutely maintain the authority of the rule of law. Violations of the law and undermining the rule of law must be investigated in accordance with the law.

The fourth is to resolutely oppose foreign interference. The affairs of the Hong Kong Special Administrative Region are China's internal affairs and are not subject to interference by any external forces. We must resolutely oppose any foreign countries and their organizations or individuals interfering in Hong Kong affairs in any way, and resolutely prevent and contain external forces from interfering in Hong Kong affairs and conducting split, subversion, infiltration, and sabotage activities. The state will take all necessary measures to counteract any legislative, administrative or other measures formulated and implemented by foreign countries that interfere with Hong Kong affairs.

The fifth is to effectively protect the legitimate rights and interests of Hong Kong residents. Maintaining national security is fundamentally the same as respecting and protecting human rights. Effectively preventing, stopping and punishing the very few illegal and criminal acts that endanger national security in accordance with the law is to better protect the lives and property of the vast majority of Hong Kong residents, and to better protect basic rights and freedoms. Any work to maintain national security and law enforcement must strictly follow the law, comply with statutory functions and powers, and follow statutory procedures, and must not infringe the lawful rights and interests of Hong Kong residents, legal persons and other organizations.

3. The main content of the draft decision

The draft decision is divided into two parts: the introduction and the body. The introductory part briefly explains the cause, purpose and basis of this decision. The relevant decisions of the National People's Congress are based on the provisions of Article 31 and Article 62 of the Constitution, Articles 2, 14, and 16, and the relevant provisions of the Hong Kong Basic Law, with full consideration of safeguarding national security. According to actual needs and the specific circumstances of the Hong Kong Special Administrative Region, institutional arrangements have been made for the establishment and improvement of the Hong Kong Special Administrative Region's legal system and implementation mechanism for safeguarding national security. This institutional arrangement complies with the constitutional provisions and principles, and is consistent with the legislative purpose of the Hong Kong Basic Law and the relevant systems established. It will effectively safeguard the national security of the Hong Kong Special Administrative Region and will effectively consolidate and expand the legal and political foundation of "One Country, Two Systems". Foundation and social foundation.

There are 7 articles in the main body of the draft decision. The first article states that the country will unswervingly and fully and accurately implement the policy of "one country, two systems", "Hong Kong people ruling Hong Kong", and a high degree of autonomy; emphasizing the adoption of necessary measures to establish and improve the Hong Kong Special Administrative Region's legal system and enforcement mechanism for safeguarding national security, and prevent, Stop and punish behaviors and activities that endanger national security. Article 2 states that the state resolutely opposes any foreign or foreign forces interfering in the affairs of the Hong Kong Special Administrative Region in any way and adopts necessary measures to counter it. Article 3 clearly stipulates that the maintenance of national sovereignty, unity and territorial integrity is the constitutional responsibility of the Hong Kong Special Administrative Region; it is emphasized that the Hong Kong Special Administrative Region should complete the national security protection legislation stipulated by the Hong Kong Basic Law as soon as possible. It is necessary for the administrative organs, legislative organs, and judicial organs of the Hong Kong Special Administrative Region to effectively prevent, stop and punish acts and activities that endanger national security in accordance with relevant laws and regulations. Article 4 clearly stipulates that the Hong Kong Special Administrative Region shall establish and complete institutions and enforcement mechanisms for safeguarding national security; the relevant agencies of the Central People's Government for safeguarding national security shall set up institutions in the Hong Kong Special Administrative Region as necessary to perform duties related to safeguarding national security in accordance with law. Article 5 clearly stipulates that the Chief Executive of the Hong Kong Special Administrative Region shall regularly submit reports to the Central People's Government on the Hong Kong Special Administrative Region's performance of its duties to maintain national security, conduct national security education, and lawfully prohibit acts and activities that endanger national security. Article 6 clarifies the constitutional meaning of the relevant legislation of the Standing Committee of the National People's Congress, including three meanings: First, the Standing Committee of the National People's Congress is authorized to formulate relevant laws on the establishment and improvement of the Hong Kong Special Administrative Region's legal system and enforcement mechanisms for safeguarding national security. The legislative authority will be exercised accordingly; the second is to clarify the task of the relevant laws of the Standing Committee of the National People's Congress to effectively prevent, stop and punish any serious harm that occurs in the Hong Kong Special Administrative Region such as secession of the country, subversion of state power, organization of terrorist activities, etc. National security behaviors and activities and activities of foreign and foreign forces interfering in the affairs of the Hong Kong Special Administrative Region; the third is to clarify the way in which relevant laws of the Standing Committee of the National People's Congress will be implemented in the Hong Kong Special Administrative Region, that is, the Standing Committee of the National People's Congress has decided to include relevant laws in the Annex to the Hong Kong Basic Law 3. The Hong Kong Special Administrative Region shall announce and implement it locally. Article 7: Specify the implementation time of this decision, that is, it will be implemented from the date of promulgation.

The National People's Congress has made the above-mentioned institutional arrangements in accordance with the new situation and needs, including authorizing the Standing Committee of the National People's Congress to formulate relevant laws on the establishment and improvement of the Hong Kong Special Administrative Region's legal system and enforcement mechanisms for safeguarding national security, and further implement the Constitution and the Hong Kong Basic Law. related terms. The Hong Kong Special Administrative Region still has the constitutional responsibility and legislative obligation to maintain national security in accordance with Article 23 of the Hong Kong Basic Law, and it should complete relevant legislation to maintain national security as soon as possible. Any legislation to safeguard national security and its implementation shall not conflict with this decision.

After this decision is made, the Standing Committee of the National People's Congress will work with relevant parties to formulate relevant laws on the maintenance of national security in the Hong Kong Special Administrative Region, actively promote the resolution of outstanding issues in the Hong Kong Special Administrative Region in maintaining the national security system, and strengthen specialized agencies, enforcement mechanisms and law enforcement. Strength building to ensure the effective implementation of relevant laws in the Hong Kong Special Administrative Region.

Please review the "Decision of the National People's Congress on Establishing and Improving the Hong Kong Special Administrative Region's Legal System and Implementation Mechanism for Maintaining National Security (Draft)" and the above explanations.

* * *

Chapter 25

Tuesday 26 May 2020
For Whom is Hong Kong Home? "One Country-Two Systems," the National Security Law and the Development of a Patriotic Front

> "You are too irritating." We are talking about how to deal with domestic and foreign reactionaries, the imperialists and their running dogs, not about how to deal with anyone else. With regard to such reactionaries, the question of irritating them or not does not arise. Irritated or not irritated, they will remain the same because they are reactionaries. Only if we draw a clear line between reactionaries and revolutionaries, expose the intrigues and plots of the reactionaries, arouse the vigilance and attention of the revolutionary ranks, heighten our will to fight and crush the enemy's arrogance can we isolate the reactionaries, vanquish them or supersede them. We must not show the slightest timidity before a wild beast.[931]

Over the course of the last year, I have been closely following some of the writing of Chen Hong-yee (陳弘毅), an eminent global academic and constitutional scholar as he has undertaken a difficult role, to publicly take a middle path guided almost entirely by the relevant principles and ideology expressed through law and exercised through political decisions.[932]

This Olympian view is both profound and distancing. And that reflects the contradiction of the political situation in Hong Kong now--the time for considered discourse, for considered stock taking guided by reason, may well be over. Professor Chen

---

[931] Mao Zedong, "On the People's Democratic Dictatorship" (30 June 1949); Selected Works Vol. 4, reprinted in Marxists.org; available [https://www.marxists.org/reference/archive/mao/selected-works/volume-4/mswv4_65.htm].

[932] Considered in the essays Chapters 6, 9, supra.

represents Nietzsche's Apollonian voice;[933] "[f]or Apollo wants to grant repose to individual beings precisely by drawing boundaries between them and by again and again calling these to mind as the most sacred laws of the world, with his demands for self-knowledge and measure."[934] He serves as an incarnation of the Aeschylean tragic chorus, and in that role, incarnates the voice and guidance of the gods (in this context the central authorities who remain off stage but deeply engaged)[935] spiced with a deep concern of the fate that he foresees for tragic hero. That role of the tragic hero, of the Dionysian element of the tragedy that is Hong Kong, is assumed by that amorphous but coherent group that constitutes the Hong Kong protesters.[936]

The current situation in Hong Kong has moved toward the culmination of its Dionysian phase.[937] That dialectic which is the opposition of the Apollonian and the Dionysian, [938] and the contradiction it embodies, might well have been inevitable under the circumstances of the production of the national security law draft and its dramatic intervention, unbalancing what had been a year of tense equipoise between competing local factions whose objectives played out against the much greater stakes of the

---

[933] Friedrich Nietzsche, "The Birth of Tragedy" (1886) in *The Birth of Tragedy and the Case of Wagner* (Walter Kaufmann (trans); NY: Vintage Book, 1967), pp. 30-144 ("For Apollo wants to grant repose to individual beings precisely by drawing boundaries between them and by again and again calling these to mind as the most sacred laws of the world" Ibid., §9, p. 72).

[934] Ibid., ¶9, p. 72.

[935] It is in fear and awe of the gods that the chorus seeks to intervene, to seek mercy from the gods and prudence from the tragic hero--in both cases, ultimately, to no avail.

[936] Ibid., ¶ 9 ("the high tide of the Dionysian destroyed from time to time all those little circles in which the one sidedly Apollonian 'will' had sought to confine the Hellenic spirit."; p. 72).

[937] Ibid. "In this sense the Dionysian man may be said to resemble Hamlet: both have for once seen into the true nature of things, —they have perceived, but they are loath to act; for their action cannot change the eternal nature of things; they regard it as shameful or ridiculous that one should require of them to set aright the time which is out of joint." Ibid., ¶ 7pp. 60)

[938] Ibid ¶ 12 "the discordant and incommensurable elements in the nature of Aeschylean tragedy. Let's recall our surprise at the *chorus* and the *tragic hero* of that tragedy. . . til we rediscovered this duality itself as the origin and essence of Greek tragedy, as the expression of two interwoven artistic impulses, the *Apollonian* and the *Dionysian*. Ibid ¶12, p. 81).

contest between Leninist nationalism (One Country) and sovereignty fracturing internationalism (Two Systems).[939] The rapture of the Dionysian state cannot last; once its passion is exhausted it is left to return to the realm of the gods--to the state of stability and prosperity and order, to an Olympian state now reenergized by the spent passion of the Dionysian element of its cultural (and in this case political) dialectic.

Perhaps it is in that role--as the chorus looking to pick up the pieces, to bury and preserve what can be preserved, of the spirit of the tragic hero under conditions of restoration, that Professor Chen has published his thoughts on the National Security Law for Hong Kong now being considered by the central authorities.[940] The essay is worth a careful reading as much for what it says as for the way it is said. Its most profound point is its orientation. That orientation is one that explicitly draws attention to the perspective of those who consider Hong Kong home--not matter what--from others resident in Hong Kong, particularly foreigners and residents who, when things don't go their way, may emigrate.

> 我們對於當前的局面，應如何思考呢？對於同一問題，當然可以有不同的觀點和角度。我寫這篇文章，就是想表達一種我相信是「以香港為家的我們」的觀點和角度，這很可能有別於正在準備移民的人的觀點和角度，也可能有別於在海外的華人或外國人的觀點和角度，當然也有別於中國內地居民的觀點和角度。[How should we think about the current situation? For the same problem, of course, there can be different views and angles. When I write this article, I want to express a point of view and angle that I believe is "we who use Hong Kong as our home". This may be different from the point of view of people who are preparing to emigrate,

---

[939] Discussed in the essay Chapter 24, supra.

[940] Chen Hongyi（陳弘毅）談國安法爭議：以香港為家的我們的心聲 [On the National Security Law Controversy: Views of those Who Consider Hong Kong Home] was published as part of the 215th issue of Hong Kong 01 Weekly News (May 25, 2020) "Disputes on National Security Law: Voices of Those Who Consider Hong Kong Home."

and may also be different from those overseas. The views and perspectives of Chinese or foreigners are of course different from those of mainland Chinese residents.]

It is the voices of those who will stay, rather than the others, that perhaps ought to be given greater weight by those with the power to make decisions about the issues. The voices of those that will stay ought to be reassured, they are told, by the marginal effect, the intended national security measures, will have on them. "A new national security law tailor-made for Hong Kong will only target "a small group of people" to plug a legal loophole exposed by violent anti-government protests in the city and will not affect the livelihood of ordinary citizens, Vice-Premier Han Zheng has assured local deputies to Beijing's top advisory body."[941]

And, indeed, the national security law draft fits nicely into the response developed by the central authorities since the start of the protests in June 2019, that sought to develop a taxonomy of Hong Kong people distinguishing between those who were committed to Hong Kong on its terms, and everyone else. National security offers a deeply developed taxonomic base founded on important notions of patriotism. And patriotism, in turn, could be managed in a way that welcomes patriots into the nation under the protection of the national security law, excludes others, and manages the rest as foreigners whose protection is dependent on the state of relations between state officials and their correspondents abroad. That "everyone else," then, could be marginalized, contained and appropriately managed, as "China has dismissed other countries' complaints about the proposed legislation as "meddling," saying the proposed laws will not harm Hong Kong autonomy or foreign investors."[942]

---

[941] Natalie Wong , Gary Cheung and Lilian Cheng, "Two Sessions 2020: Hong Kong national security law will only target 'small group of people', Vice-Premier Han Zheng says as Beijing hits back at critics," *South China Morning Post* 23 May 2020); available [https://www.scmp.com/news/hong-kong/politics/article/3085791/two-sessions-2020-hong-kong-national-security-law-will-only].

[942] Ed Flanagan and Justin Solomon, "Hong Kong police fire tear gas, water cannons at protest against proposed security law," NBC News (24 May 2020);

And the foreign, the Dionysian element, continued to exhaust its passion against the gods, despite the good counsel of the chorus, ever fearful of the divine retribution that now looms in ever more concrete form. In the face of the inevitable, the protests continued, now re-impassioned by the very mechanisms that will likely destroy them. "One who identified herself by her last name, Lang, said: 'There is nothing else we can do really. We have to do something that is helpful instead of just giving up.'"[943]

One cannot help by recall the address by former Hong Kong leader Tung Chee-hwa, another member of the Apollonian chorus of which Professor Chen is a part, but possibly to a different effect.

In a 24-minute speech broadcast to Hongkongers on Monday, Tung warned that the city had become a weak link in the security of the nation ... 'If you do not plan to engage in acts of secession, subversion, terrorism or conspiring with foreign influence in connection with Hong Kong affairs, you will have no reason to fear,' he said, a day after thousands took to the streets to oppose the impending law and radical protesters returned to violence and vandalism. * * * "What's more worrying is how some anti-China forces in the West have distorted the truth and openly supported anti-China radicals in Hong Kong ... We can no longer tolerate how foreign forces have conspired with radicals in Hong Kong to put at risk China's sovereignty, its authority and the legitimacy of the Hong Kong Basic Law."[944]

---

available [https://www.nbcnews.com/news/world/hong-kong-police-fire-tear-gas-water-cannons-protest-against-n1213951].

[943] Ibid.
'China wants to control us. We just want to be ourselves and live with our freedoms, so that's why we are here,' one protester told NBC News.

[944] Kimmy Chung and Ng Kang-chung, "Hong Kong needs national security law because it is 'easy target for hostile foreign opportunists': former leader Tung Chee-hwa" (26 May 2020); available [https://www.scmp.com/news/hong-kong/politics/article/3086015/hong-kong-needs-national-security-law-because-it-easy].

Those who call Hong Kong home fear the gods. And the gods have made clear that acts of hubris--that the passion of Dionysus unconstrained, will not be tolerated for long. The gods have now revealed the instrument of correction. And still the Dionysia in Hong Kong cannot be contained.

And yet, like Tung, that urge toward a construction of a taxonomy that modernized the great taxonomic impulse of Mao Zedong "On the People's Democratic Dictatorship," [945] with political consequences, weighs heavily in Professor Chen's essay. Not that this is wrong, in itself. And indeed, it is that commitment to Hong Kong that perhaps ought to weigh more for political discourse than that of those who may have a distinct commitment to Hong Kong, one measured by the likelihood that they might leave. The value of an opinion, then, might be weighed against the amount of risk one incurs in taking that opinion. Those with no exit (or who choose that option), then, take on a much greater risk than others. At the same time, it does suggest a hierarchy of perspective that aligns with that of the Central Authorities.

Here again, one encounters Nietzsche's Dionysian Hamlet. Yet for them, even among those who would call Hong Kong home, there appears value in the deceptions at the heart of 三十六计, the Thirty Six Stratagems. [946] The stratagem 打草驚蛇 / 打草惊蛇 (disturb the grass to scare the snake), [947] and once that is done 走為上計 / 走为上计 (if all else fails, retreat) [948] nicely embraces the passion and the ultimate outcome of the actions that have evolved since 2019. It also embraces the tragedy of that stratagem--for

---

[945] Mao Zedong, "On the People's Democratic Dictatorship (30 June 1949), supra. and quote at note 1, supra.

[946] Peter Taylor, *The Thirty-Six Stratagems: A Modern Interpretation Of A Strategy Classic* (Oxford: Infinite Ideas Limited, 2013).
Thirty-Six Stratagems: Bilingual Edition, English and Chinese: The Art of War Companion, Chinese Strategy Classic, Includes Pinyin Paperback – June 7, 2016 by Sun Tzu (Author), Zhuge Liang (Author), Sun Bin (Author), Dragon Reader (Editor)

[947] Ibid., Stratagems for attacking situations, No. 13, p. 56.

[948] Ibid., Stratagems foe desperate situations, No. 36, p. 129.

having scared the snake, the protesters are about to feel the poison in its bite--unless they can flee.

For Chen application of these stratagems produces a greater harm for those who call Hong Kong home, for those who will not (or cannot) flee. For him the stratagem 李代桃僵 (sacrifice the plum tree to preserve the peach)[949] appears the sounder strategy. For others, a field of only plum trees destroys the value of the orchard. Indeed, the stratagem of sacrificing the plum tree is sometimes understood as the stratagem for offering a sacrifice to appease the gods. In this case, the sacrifice is quite plain--the protesters, and the bulk of their position. And what does one preserve? That, indeed, will be put to the gods, though those offering up the sacrifice will surely hope that they--prudent and careful--will be among its beneficiaries. This stratagem of preservation is thus augmented by another, one with the promise of some reward. It is, perhaps then, best understood as propelled by the insights of the stratagem 順手牽羊 / 顺手牵羊 (take the opportunity to pilfer the goat)[950] of seeking whatever advantage on can, however small, from a position of disadvantage. This a strategy of long term reduced expectation, of a moderately prosperous society, and of seizing what is not carried off by the greater powers. It embodies the power of the small.

Professor Chen's conclusion provides the perfect foundation for considering its quite nuanced arguments:

在去年反修例運動高潮時，我曾感覺到，香港「一國兩制」的路正走得愈來愈窄，看不到任何希望。所謂山窮水盡疑無路，柳暗花明又一村，但願「國安法事件」的危機可以成為一個轉機，在看來瀕臨失敗邊緣的「一國兩制」事業崩潰之前，力挽狂瀾。更希望曾誤入歧途的青少年能回頭是岸，回歸尊重他人權利和遵守體現社會成員共同利益的法律的正路，我相信這是以香港為家的我們的衷心盼望。[At the climax of the Anti-Amendment Movement last year, I once felt that the

---

[949] Ibid., Stratagems for opportunistic situations, No. 11, p. 49.
[950] Ibid., No. 12, p. 52.

road of "one country, two systems" in Hong Kong is getting narrower and narrower, and I see no hope. The so-called mountains and rivers are full of doubts, and there is another village in the dark. I hope the crisis of the "national security law incident" can become a turning point. Before the collapse of the "one country, two systems" cause that seems to be on the verge of failure, it will turn the tide. I also hope that the young people who have gone astray can return to the shore and return to the right path of respecting the rights of others and complying with laws that reflect the common interests of members of society. I believe this is our sincere hope that Hong Kong is the home.]

And there it is. Not just an offering to the gods, but a chorus to remind us of the lessons that must be learned as one contemplates the body of the Dionysian tragic hero now brought low by the insatiable expression of heroic passion.

Beyond that, it might be argued that one is left with nothing--the Stratagem 無中生有.[951] Yet there is great substance within that space that appears ready to be filled with something. To those ends, there are nods to all key elements. *To the Central Authorities* there is an unswerving commitment to the fundamental principled vision of the vanguard: "我們同屬一個命運共同體 [We all belong to a community of shared destiny]" and the emphasis on peace, security and prosperity. As well, there is an echo of the key line of the Central Authorities--that the law is meant to target only a small number of unruly elements.[952]

To the pan-democrats there is the offer of the support for legalism, for a scrupulous attention to the forms and effects of the law thorough which the relationship between Hong Kong and the Central Government have been developed, and thus developed, applied: "In this regard, I hope that the drafters will be able to speak up and listen to the opinions of Hong Kong people. . . We

[951] Ibid., Stratagems for opportunistic situations, No. 7, p. 37.
[952] See, Natalie Wong , Gary Cheung and Lilian Cheng, "Two Sessions 2020: Hong Kong national security law will only target 'small group of people', supra.

also hope that this legislation can comply with the rule of law and the principle of non-retroactivity of criminal law."

And there is the warning in the form of a plea: "We hope that this National Security Law can reflect the spirit of "one country, two systems", respect the difference between the two systems, and will not directly apply the criminal regulations on national security in mainland China to Hong Kong, but take into account Hong Kong's common law system and the current The human rights standards applicable to Hong Kong seek to achieve an appropriate balance between safeguarding national security and individual rights and freedoms."[953]

> The coverage of subversion under the new law was much wider than what was proposed in the local Article 23 bill back in 2003, according to Basic Law Committee member Albert Chen Hung-yee, a University of Hong Kong law professor. . . Chen noted that the new law targeted subversive acts that were against the "state power", instead of only the "central government" as in the 2003 version. . . it covers many more administrations, including Hong Kong and other local authorities," he added."[954]

But in the end, it appears that "One country" is a legal basis for the relationship between Hong Kong and the Central Authorities, and "Two Systems" is the way that legal discretion is to be exercised "within a cage of regulation."[955] And yet that is not the ultimate object. For a West obsessed with human and political rights, that appears to be at the center of the current back and forth on the shaping of the One Country Two Systems

---

[953] 陳弘毅談國安法爭議, supra.

[954] Natalie Wong , Gary Cheung and Lilian Cheng, "Two Sessions 2020: Hong Kong national security law will only target 'small group of people', supra.

[955] An Baijie, "Xi Jinping vows 'power within cage of regulations' "*China Daily* (23 January 2013); available [http://www.chinadaily.com.cn/china/2013-01/23/content_16157933.htm] ("Quoting an example from the Qin Dynasty (221-206 BC), Xi said that officials should learn lessons from history. The Qin Dynasty was overthrown because the people rejected unpopular policies, including high taxes and extravagance at public expense.").

framework. Yet it is likely that this is not the case from the side of the central authorities. They have made it quite clear that human rights for the collective springs from a baseline of stability and prosperity. And that it is precisely the disturbance of both that constitute to their minds a fundamental violation of the (human) rights of the collective.[956]

In the spirit of Professor Chen's perspective-based analysis let me offer two other points of reference. First, that the binary structures behind the National Security law goes deeper than security, although that is the way it manifests in this case. That binary reflects ancient Marxist-Leninist roots at the foundation of Leninist vanguardism. The essence of that outlook posits, as it must, that there exists leading force in society moving forward, and that this leading force, when organized, has a duty to guide the rest of society on the right path forward. Those who accept guidance are cared for and brought within the community. Those who reject guidance reject membership in the community; they represent a threat to the social and political order. From the perspective of Marxist Leninist theory, currently applied, they are unpatriotic rejectionists, and represent a threat to the fundamental objectives and responsibilities of the vanguard as well as to the stability and prosperity of society.

A parable from Han Feizi (韓非子) drives home the point:

楚人有鬻盾與矛者，譽之曰：「吾盾之堅，物莫能陷之。」以譽其矛曰：「吾矛之利，於物無不陷也。」或曰：「以子之矛陷子之盾，何如？」其人弗能應也。夫不可陷之盾與無不陷之矛，不可同世而立。There was once a man in the state of Chu, who was selling shields and lances. He was praising them saying: "My shields are so firm, that there is nothing that can pierce them." He praised his lances saying: "My lances are so sharp, that there is nothing that they cannot pierce." Someone asked: "What if you used your lances to pierce your shields?" The man could not answer. A shield that

---

[956] Discussed in essays chapters 2-5, supra.

cannot be pierced and a lance that can pierce everything cannot exist in the same world.[957]

To understand the national security law draft one must understand the parable and study carefully Mao Zedong, both updated for the New Era. In that context, only action within the parameters permitted under the guidance of the vanguard's leadership core is to be encouraged. For the rest, one moves away from the community and the protection of the vanguard itself.

Second, and perhaps of more durable quality: it is not the differences in perspective among those who call Hong Kong home against others that supply the entirety of the core perspectives that may matter. There is another, one less concerned about legality and the formal status of Hong Kong and much more concerned about planning for the Pearl River region for the long term, a planning in which Hong Kong must necessarily be absorbed within a larger economic unit. And that absorption, in turn, requires the re-construction and instrumentalization of what makes Hong Kong different.

This is a perspective the physical manifestation of which is already well on its way to completion and given form in the construction of what I have called the Greater Pearl River City.[958] Indeed, it is economic planning in light of the imperatives of the CPC Basic Line socialist modernization and Socialist Market Economy objectives, that may be at center stage.[959] From this

---

[957] From Han Feizi (韓非子) reproduced in Fei Han (The Project Gutenberg eBook (released 27 December 2007); available [https://www.gutenberg.org/cache/epub/24049/pg24049-images.html]; translation credit 矛 盾 ; available [https://en.wiktionary.org/wiki/%E7%9F%9B%E7%9B%BE]; 《難一》4.

[958] Discussed in essays Chapters 12-13 and 19.

[959] 中共中央 国务院 关于新时代加快完善社会主义市场经济体制的意见 [Central Committee of the Communist Party of China Opinions on accelerating the improvement of the socialist market economic system in the new era] (11 May 2020); available [http://www.gov.cn/zhengce/2020-05/18/content_5512696.htm]. I noted elsewhere: "The changes rationalized in the Opinion, which are meant to decisively to bring the political-economic model within the core of the New Era ideological line, are animated by the concept of contradiction. The resolution of contradiction informs the specifics of the

perspective, the disciplining of Hong Kong assumes a collateral character, a necessary step in the process of creating this new coherent economic unit. The friction occurs precisely because the 2047 timeline does not match the Central Authority's timeline for the construction of this economic unit. Evidence of this might be gleaned from reporting published in the wake of the Security Law challenge .[960]

Beyond that, there is also a potential lesson for the central authorities as well, one first considered by Mao Zedong. It is a lesson that ends this essay in the way it is begun, with the central element of dividing the people among patriots and others, and of developing systems of rewards and punishments to suit their character, the times, and the overall objectives of the vanguard in its responsibilities for leading the entire nation toward the goals which even it cannot alter.

We have had much valuable experience. A well-disciplined Party armed with the theory of Marxism-Leninism, using the method of self-criticism and linked

---

Socialist Market Economy through which it acquires an important instrumental role in the progress from this new era to the next. But the resolution of contradiction applies as well at a micro-analytical level." Larry Catá Backer, "中共中央 国务院 关于新时代加快完善社会主义市场经济体制的意见 [Central Committee of the Communist Party of China Opinions on accelerating the improvement of the socialist market economic system in the new era]," Law at the End of the Day (21 May 2020); available [https://lcbackerblog.blogspot.com/2020/05/central-committee-of-communist-party-of.html]. The insight applies with even more force to the situation in Hong Kong.

[960] Timmy Shen, "China Development Bank Backs Greater Bay Area With $50 Billion Lending Pledge," *Caixin* (26 May 2020); available [https://www.caixinglobal.com/2020-05-26/china-development-bank-backs-greater-bay-area-with-50-billion-lending-pledge-101559243.html] ("China Development Bank (CDB), the country's top policy lender, has pledged financing of 360 billion yuan ($50.4 billion) this year to support the development of the Greater Bay Area (GBA), a cluster of cities in southern China that the government wants to transform into a financial, technology and innovation powerful. . . CDB said it aims to build its Hong Kong branch into an international syndicated loan center and bookkeeping center in a bid to better serve cross-border businesses related to national strategies such as the GBA and the Belt and Road Initiative.")).

with the masses of the people, an army under the leadership of such a Party; a united front of all revolutionary classes and all revolutionary groups under the leadership of such a Party -- these are the three main weapons with which we have defeated the enemy. . . Whenever we made serious mistakes on these three matters, the revolution suffered setbacks. Taught by mistakes and setbacks, we have become wiser and handle our affairs better. It is hard for any political party or person to avoid mistakes, but we should make as few as possible. Once a mistake is made, we should correct it, and the more quickly and thoroughly the better.[961]

It is sometimes appropriate for the chorus to have the last word over the body of the tragic hero undone by the flaws of passion that for a brief moment held the spark of a greatness that ultimately reached in the wrong direction. The protesters, indeed, invoked the gods--but the gods they invoked--now long resident in foreign lands, did not come.

The final image that captures this moment, and its tragedy, well: In the final scene of Richard Wagner's Das Rheingold,[962] the Rhein maidens, whose gold has been stolen and then cursed, and then ultimately used by the gods to pay the giants for their construction of their final home--their Valhalla--and the return of one of the goddess held hostage to secure payment, beg for the return of their gold. The (old) Gods, now intent on entering Valhalla across the rainbow bridge to await the end of their time, know that this is impossible. Through Loge, the fire spirt tamed by Wotan and quite self-aware of the tragedy of the current circumstances, the Gods reply to the supplication:

Ihr da im Wasser! was weint ihr herauf?
Hört, was Wotan euch wünscht!

---

[961] Mao Zedong, "On the People's Democratic Dictatorship (30 June 1949), supra.
[962] Richard Wagner, *Das Rheingold* WWV 86A (1869) ; [available [http://www.murashev.com/opera/Das_Rheingold_libretto_English_German]. This is the second time the imagery of the last scene of Das Rheingold has been used. It also served as an elegy image for the international community on essay Chapter 1, supra.

Glänzt nicht mehr euch Mädchen das Gold,
in der Götter neuem Glanze sonn't euch selig fortan!

You there in the water; why have you come crying to us?
Hear what Wotan grants you!
If the [Rhine] gold no longer gleams for you,
Then from now on bask instead in the new splendor of
the gods![963]

And thus the likely lesson embedded within the new national
security law for Hong Kong. For patriots, for those who call Hong
Kong home, there is the embrace of the heavens. For the others,
there is only to bask in the receding warmth of the departing gods.
This is an insight Mao Zedong understood all too well: "All the
experience the Chinese people have accumulated through several
decades teaches us to enforce the people's democratic
dictatorship, that is, to deprive the reactionaries of the right to
speak and let the people alone have that right."[964]

✳ ✳ ✳

---

[963] Ibid., scene 4.
[964] Mao Zedong, "On the People's Democratic Dictatorship (30 June 1949),
supra.

Chapter 26

Sunday 31 May 2020
The "Four Great Errors" and the Stratagems of Meaning Making

Friedrich Nietzsche quite famously spoke to the four great errors of causation: (1) The error of confusing cause and consequence; (2) The error of a false causality; (3) The error of imaginary causes; and (4) The error of free will.[965] These are the errors on which the entirety of a rationalized *weltanschauung* may be built.[966] Yet that is the point--the 'Four Great Errors' may be best understood as the Four Great Stratagems of collective organization. They reveal a sensibility rather different from that of the ancient stratagems well known in China.[967] They also have a quite distinct objective--to borrow under objectives to the constructions of means from which reality appears to acquire its solidity. The errors remind one that collective reality is based on shared meaning, and on the power to create and maintain that meaning. They also suggest a baseline error on which the other four are revealed: The greatest error, then may be an indulgence of a belief the objectivity of causality removed from the ideological process of collective meaning making.

The situation in Hong Kong suggests the relevance of the insights of the Four Great Errors, as both stratagem and as collective meaning making. But it is meaning making grounded in

---

[965] Friedrich Nietzsche, *Twilight of the Idols: Or How to Philosophize With a Hammer* (1888) (Antony Ludovici (trans) Gutenberg Project eBook No. 52263 (2016); available [https://www.gutenberg.org/files/52263/52263-h/52263-h.htm]; pp. 33-43.

[966] In the context of international law discussed in Larry Catá Backer, "The Fuhrer Principle of International Law: Individual Responsibility and Collective Punishment," Penn State International Law Review 21(3):509-567 (2003); available
[http://elibrary.law.psu.edu/psilr/vol21/iss3/5?utm_source=elibrary.law.psu.edu%2Fpsilr%2Fvol21%2Fiss3%2F5&utm_medium=PDF&utm_campaign=PDF CoverPages].

[967] Peter Taylor, *The Thirty-Six Stratagems: A Modern Interpretation Of A Strategy Classic* (Oxford: Infinite Ideas Limited, 2013).

the inversion at the heart of the Four Great Errors. It is a quite conscious understanding of the malleability of inference, and of the potential for well managed ordering of the binaries that appear at the heart of the errors that seem to drive action and discourse in and around Hong Kong since 2019. The irony of error is that error requires a referent. And the control of the referent-- the point of meaning from which error may be determined--has been at the heart of the contradiction that is Hong Kong. Nietzsche would free us of the (false) attachment to a referent that is itself the source of error.[968] And yet it is the error-referent nexus, the connection between a set of beliefs that present reality in a precise way, and the consequences that follow, that produces control from error. And that is ultimately the power of error--when it serves as an instrument of a consciously higher objective.[969] And that marks the power of error in Hong Kong where error is understood as a conscious imposition of direction on the causalities that are meant to produce specific consequences from consciously developed context. The referent, of course, around which error is manifested and curated, is the principle of 'One Country-Two Systems' itself.

It is only within the conceptual context of error (or in Leninist terms better put--contradiction) that one is left to ask oneself whether almost the entirety of the discursive element of this period has been an exercise in inversion to political, personal and institutional ends. Here Nietzsche's narrative ideal--in the form of 'One Country Two Systems' --serves as the (contested) ordering element around which the relevant questions of error

---

[968] Friedrich Nietzsche, *Twilight of the Idols*, supra (" No one is responsible for the fact that he exists at all, that he is constituted as he is, and that he happens to be in certain circumstances and in a particular environment. The fatality of his being cannot be divorced from the fatality of all that which has been and will be... One is necessary, one is a piece of fate, one belongs to the whole, one is in the whole,—there is nothing that could judge, measure, compare, and condemn our existence, for that would mean judging, measuring, comparing and condemning the whole. *But there is nothing outside the whole!*" Ibid., ¶ 8)

[969] Ibid. ("This is not the result of an individual intention, of a will, of an aim, there is no attempt at attaining to any "ideal man," or "ideal happiness" or "ideal morality" with him,—it is absurd to wish him to be careering towards some sort of purpose. We invented the concept "purpose"; in reality purpose is altogether lacking.").

can be framed. To what extent are the events driving decisions, or leader decisions driving events? Does ideology and principle inevitably lead to the actions taken or do the actions taken form ideology in action? Are leaders exercising will or are they prisoners of the meaning-making boxes in which they operate; that is are leaders trapped by the logic of the meaning systems in which they are embedded or by acting are they trapping meaning within their personal universe of desire for meaning? Are cause and effect little more than the ritualization of ancient tropes of seeing the world and each other, or are we by seeing each other now ritualizing causation for the same effect? These questions generally describe the phenomenon of cultivating, as ideology, the inability to see beyond the end of one's nose, especially where one's interests are at issue.[970]

These are the questions that tend to be avoided. They are inconvenient precisely because of the convenience (for politics) of the cultivation of error. In this sense, the four great errors underline Nietzsche's ironic sub textual point--that the greatest of the error is the disbelief in error. Put a different way, error is possible only in a context in which one believes that one is actually seeking truth rather than objective aligned to ideological frameworks. As Nietzsche suggested, these are the sorts of questions that expose the soul of a system, and that of those who drive them. And not just them. It exposes, as well, the view from below (the many below) the leadership core which appears to be the only collectives worth considering as animated abstractions with a collective will. And yet to do that ignores the agency (or its lack) in popular collectives from below. If only as an act of "criticism/self-criticism (itself redolent with error), the exercise of distilling discourse within these structures of error may provide an antidote to the managed reaction that is expected of

---

[970] "Not one looks backward, onward still he goes, Onward still he goes, Yet ne'er looks forward further than his nose." Alexander Pope, *An Essay on Man : Moral Essays and Satire* (London: Cassell & Co., 1891 (1734)); available [https://www.gutenberg.org/files/2428/2428-h/2428-h.htm]; Epistle IV

those subjected to a carefully guided interpretation of official text.[971]

More to the point here, the insights of these stratagems (and the battles over the ordering referent)[972] may be especially relevant to an understanding of the discourse and commentary surrounding the decisions, first by the Chinese central authorities to go forward with a National Security Law for Hong Kong,[973] and then, by the actions taken in response by other states, [974]

---

[971] Consider in this context, and from an institutional historical perspective, Lowell Dittmer, "The Structural Evolution of 'Criticism-Self-Criticism'," *The China Quarterly* 56: 708-729 (1973).

[972] Friedrich Nietzsche, *Twilight of the Idols*, supra ('The Improvers of Mankind; ¶5). Nietzsche, no friend of ideological orthodoxy noted in this respect:

"The morality of breeding and the morality of taming, in the means which they adopt in order to prevail, are quite worthy of each other: we may lay down as a leading principle that in order to create morality a man must have the absolute will to immorality. This is the great and strange problem with which I have so long been occupied: the psychology of the "Improvers" of mankind. . . . Neither Manu, nor Plato, nor Confucius, nor the teachers of Judaism and Christianity, have ever doubted their right to falsehood. They have never doubted their right to quite a number of other things To express oneself in a formula, one might say:—all means which have been used heretofore with the object of making man moral, were through and through immoral." (Ibid.).

[973] Decision of the People's National Congress on Establishing and Improving the Legal System and Enforcement Mechanisms for the Hong Kong Special Administrative Region to Safeguard National Security [全国人民代表大会关于建立健全香港特别行政区维护国家安全的法律制度和执行机制的决定] adopted by the third session of the thirteenth National People's Congress on 28 May 2020 authorizing the National People's Congress Standing Committee (NPCSC) to promulgate a national security law in Hong Kong; as published in the Gazette of the Standing Committee of the National People's Congress of the People's Republic of China (15 June 2020), pp. 284 et seq.; available [http://www.npc.gov.cn/wxzlhgb/gb2020/202008/158578c7025e4760b486b225a4a9a903/files/ed3147d4e88d434aa615c6dd3c1c9eca.pdf]. Postscript, the national Security Law was enacted in June 2020. See Associated Press, "China passes draft of controversial Hong Kong national security law," *Los Angeles Times* (18 June 2020); available [https://www.latimes.com/world-nation/story/2020-06-18/china-passes-draft-hong-kong-national-security-law].

[974] See, e.g., Council of the European Union, "Declaration by the High Representative, on behalf of the European Union, on the announcement by China's National People's Congress spokesperson regarding Hong Kong," (22

especially the United States,[975] with significant interests in Hong Kong's status. Lastly, it helps frame the inevitable form and content of the response by the central authorities[976] to the equally inevitable form and content of the foreign reaction to their initial decision on the national security law.

The Four Great Errors are not ideological in the sense of deviation from an all-around way of seeing the world as inevitably understandable in a singular and precise way. They are grounded in a certain perspective of morality and baseline principles that detaches them from 'truth' and attaches them much more closely to culture and collective meaning making.

May 2020); available [https://www.consilium.europa.eu/en/press/press-releases/2020/05/22/declaration-by-the-high-representative-on-behalf-of-the-european-union-on-the-announcement-by-china-s-national-people-s-congress-spokesperson-regarding-hong-kong/]; Press release Joint Statement from the UK, Australia and Canada on Hong Kong (22 May 2020); available [https://www.gov.uk/government/news/joint-statement-from-the-uk-australia-and-canada-on-hong-kong]; Japan summons Chinese envoy over HK security law (28 May 2020); available [https://news.rthk.hk/rthk/en/component/k2/1528928-20200528.htm?] ("'It is the long-standing policy of Japan to attach great importance to upholding a free and open system which Hong Kong has been enjoying and the democratic and stable development of Hong Kong under the 'One Country Two System' framework.'").

[975] Michael R. Pompeo, Press Statement: "P.R.C. National People's Congress Proposal on Hong Kong National Security Legislation," U.S. Department of State (27 May 2020); available [https://2017-2021.state.gov/prc-national-peoples-congress-proposal-on-hong-kong-national-security-legislation/index.html]. See also Tucker Higgins, "Pompeo declares that Hong Kong is no longer autonomous from China, threatening trade with U.S.," *CNBC* (27 May 2020); available [https://www.cnbc.com/2020/05/27/pompeo-declares-hong-kong-no-longer-autonomous-from-china.html] ("Trump's own intentions remain unclear, making it difficult to predict the administration's next steps. The president has expressed only limited interest in the Hong Kong protests, and has so far shown little appetite for actions that could jeopardize his nascent trade deal with Beijing. The White House did not immediately respond to a request for comment.").

[976] "China expresses firm opposition to foreign countries' joint statement on NPC decision on national security legislation for Hong Kong," *Xinhua* (30 May 2020); available [http://www.china.org.cn/china/Off_the_Wire/2020-05/30/content_76107595.htm].

That is why the moral judgment must never be taken quite literally: as such it is sheer nonsense. As a sign code, however, it is invaluable: *to him at least who knows, it reveals the most valuable facts concerning cultures and inner conditions, which did not know enough to "understand" themselves.* Morality is merely a sign-language, simply symptomatology: one must already know what it is all about in order to turn it to any use.[977]

Indeed, to understand the insight of the errors it is necessary to start at the opposite pole of ideology--that ideological frameworks produce the conditions for the construction of causal relations which are consistent with ideology, but incomprehensible outside of the rationalizing system of that ideology. That connection between the systematic interpretation of the world applying ordering principles and causality then suggest the contingency of ordering frameworks and the fragility of meaning.

At bottom, then, these errors are inherent in the failings of individuals and human society both of which are still captive to an obsession to rationalize everything around them. That obsession hides another--the obsession for control. To rationalize, to order events, objects, and signs--to invest each with a meaning within a rational order proceeding from a unified center of meaning making, is to maintain the illusion of control. Everything in its place and a place for everything. . . if everything is placed it can be abstracted and modeled. And if it can be abstracted and modeled it can be controlled. The essence of modern predictive analytics is an ancient as the human drive to organize reality within systems of religion, science, psychology, race, class, etc.

Rationalization, in turn, is bound up in fear--the fear of chaos. But chaos is now understood in a substantially precise

---

[977] Friedrich Nietzsche, *Twilight of the Idols*, supra, 'The Improvers of Mankind' ¶ 1 (emphasis added) ("Moral judgment, like the religious one, belongs to a stage of ignorance in which even the concept of reality, the distinction between real and imagined things, is still lacking: so that truth, at such a stage, is applied to a host of things which to-day we call "imaginary"; Ibid.)

way--not as the absence of order, but in the absence of an order (rationalization) system that can be controlled by those who would make meaning of the world around them and the people within it. In this sense its approaches its etymological origins in the Greek *khaos* "abyss, that which gapes wide open, that which is vast and empty." [978]   What cannot be perceived cannot be understood, what cannot be understood cannot be controlled, what cannot be controlled must be surrounded with the ritual elements of control--expiation, sacrifice, bargaining, sign reading and intermediation. It is the pursuit of the illusion of control that sometimes drives religion, ideology, and simulation. That leads one to another central insight--that the will to rationalization at the heart of Nietzsche's Four Great Errors, that the very rationalization, is an ironic, and perhaps conscious, *inversion*. Thus, one cannot separate error from its underlying foundation in the certain knowledge of the fragility of the foundations from which it is even possible to speak about error. Put differently, the four great errors do not point in specific directions.   Rather they suggest relations among antipodes of analysis and judgment the trajectories, vectors and conclusions of which are wholly dependent on the moral starting point, on the starting point from which individuals or collectives can be understood to be improved.[979]

---

[978]   Etymology   Online,   "Chaos;"   available [https://www.etymonline.com/word/chaos].   Also noted is the theological layering that enriched the meanings and meaning overtones of the word that speak to the use of the word in relation to a state of utter confusion. That theological layer is important in the emerging context of Hong Kong's 'One Country-Two Systems' principle. In both cases it is fair to understand chaos as the state of the universe before a divine imposition of order. Chaos here acquired the sense not merely of a cosmic emptiness before being filled by order, but also the sense of chaos as disorder--a disorder that could be contrasted to the ordered universe of *kosmos*. Ibid. With the national security law draft one understands the actions of the central authorities the way one could envision the act of ordering creation from out of the disorder and emptiness that Hong Kong had become (in their sense of the world) from the start of the protests in 2019. To that chaos and ordering, grounded in the great structures of prosperity and stability was required--at least as the sign of the ordering to come.

[979] Friedrich Nietzsche, *Twilight of the Idols*, supra, 'The Improvers of Mankind' ¶ 2 (In all ages there have been people who wished to "improve" mankind: this above all is what was called morality. But the most different tendencies are concealed beneath the same word. Both the taming of the beast man, and the

The first error inverts cause and consequence: "The newspaper reader says: such and such a party by committing such an error will meet its death. My superior politics say: a party that can make such mistakes, is in its last agony—it no longer possesses any certainty of instinct." [980] This is the error that extracts facts from truth. This is the territory of the simulation and of predictive analytics. This is also the territory of the black hand, of the fifth column and of foreign interference.[981] This is the error that produces both the US exit from WHO (Chinese interference) [982] and the Chinese National Security Law (US interference).[983] This first error--the deliberate inversion of cause and effect--has played a powerful role in shaping the situation in Hong Kong. And it is especially on display in the back and forth between the Chinese and US governments since the NCP meeting and the forward movement of the draft National Security Law. One can start with "Because China is one country, the National Security Law is necessary;" this can as easily be inverted to become, "the National Security Law is necessary precisely because China is not yet 'One Country' enough." Likewise, "Hong Kong is no longer autonomous from China because of the adoption of the national security law and therefore its favorable trade relationship with the U.S. must be revoked" can be inverted to become "because China determined that a favorable trade relationship with the world through Hong Kong was no longer

---

rearing of a particular type of man, have been called "improvement": these zoological termini, alone, represent real things." Ibid.).

[980] Ibid., 'The Four Great Errors, ¶ 1.

[981] Discussed in essay Chapter 16.

[982] Allan Smith and Elyse Perlmutter-Gumbiner, "Trump administration gives formal notice of withdrawal from WHO," NBC News (7 July 2020); available [https://www.nbcnews.com/politics/donald-trump/trump-administration-gives-formal-notice-withdrawal-who-n1233100] (Trump said at the White House in late May that the U.S. would be "terminating" its relationship with the WHO over its response to the COVID-19 pandemic... "The world needs answers from China on the virus. We must have transparency." Ibid.).

[983] Bethany Allen-Ebrahimian, "With new security law, China outlaws global activism," *Axios* (7 July 2020); available [https://www.axios.com/china-hong-kong-law-global-activism-ff1ea6d1-0589-4a71-a462-eda5bea3f78f.html] (""One of the main purposes of having the national security law is to quash the international front of the movement," said Nathan Law, a Hong Kong pro-democracy lawmaker, who spoke to Axios after he fled the city last week.").

necessary it was possible to begin the adoption of the national security law." Cause and effect, then, are anchored in the referent from which such a determination can be made.   That is the essence of the inversion of cause and consequence which is the basis for the justifications of the United States and China.

The second of the great errors compounds the first. The error of false causality is based on the belief that all causes proceed from the individual doing the perceiving. It is a self-reflexive exercise that conforms the individual at the center of her reality and then develops an experiential universe on that basis.

> "Man projected his three "inner facts of consciousness," the will, the spirit, and the ego in which he believed most firmly, outside himself. He first deduced the concept Being out of the concept Ego, he supposed "things" to exist as he did himself, according to his notion of the ego as cause. Was it to be wondered at that later on he always found in things only that which he had laid in them?— The thing itself, I repeat, the concept thing was merely a reflex of the belief in the ego as cause."[984]

This is the error of narcissistic causality, of the cult of the leader, and of the reflection of all things as a manifestation of a leader principle.[985] This is the space where the measure is the refection of that which measures; its signature in the West is that common law judge and her imposition of meaning on law. Here we center on the recent overt tendencies of both empires to feel themselves besieged and surrounded--and in return to strike out to surround their competitors. For the United States, its measures are taken because China's actions suggest that rather than Hong Kong

---

[984] Friedrich Nietzsche, *Twilight of the Idols*, supra, 'The Four Great Errors,' ¶ 2.
[985] Ibid. For Nietzsche, of course, this is the false causality of what Nietzsche identified as the priest--the vanguard or leader group to which is consigned the responsibility for making and operationalizing meaning. But that responsibility becomes measured at the same time by reference to that responsible group--it becomes the reflection of the group in a closed loop of meaning making by reference to the meaning maker.

changing China, China will change Hong Kong.[986] For China, its measures are taken because the actions of foreigners increase the risk that rather than China changing Hong Kong, Hong Kong will change itself, and indirectly China as well." [987] For the U.K., Australia, and Canada, the critically important false causality is the one that they have sought to construct between international law embedded within the vessel of the Sino-British Joint Declaration [988] and the limitations on the exercise of Chinese national sovereignty, one at the heart of the core referent of the internationalist camp[989] that they meant to represent. This is also the false causality around the anticipated migration from out of Hong Kong as a result of the actions of China, first, and then the United States. [990]

---

[986] Michael R. Pompeo, Press Statement: "P.R.C. National People's Congress Proposal on Hong Kong National Security Legislation," supra ("While the United States once hoped that free and prosperous Hong Kong would provide a model for authoritarian China, it is now clear that China is modeling Hong Kong after itself").

[987] "China expresses firm opposition to foreign countries' joint statement on NPC decision on national security legislation for Hong Kong," supra (Foreign Ministry spokesperson Zhao Lijian stated: "Not a single country in the world allows activities endangering national security including secessionist activities in its territory.")

[988] Joint Declaration of the Government of the United Kingdom of Great Britain and Northern Ireland and the Government of the People's Republic of China on the Question of Hong Kong (19 December 1984); available [https://www.cmab.gov.hk/en/issues/jd2.htm].

[989] Joint Statement from the UK, Australia and Canada on Hong Kong (22 May 2020), supra ("The legally binding Joint Declaration, signed by China and the UK, sets out that Hong Kong will have a high degree of autonomy. It also provides that rights and freedoms, including those of the person, of the press, of assembly, of association and others, will be ensured by law in Hong Kong, and that the provisions of the two UN covenants on human rights (the International Covenant on Civil and Political Rights and International Covenant on Economic, Social and Cultural Rights) shall remain in force").

[990] "China's security law sends Hong Kong residents dashing for exit," *The Japan Times* (31 May 2020); available [https://www.japantimes.co.jp/news/2020/05/31/asia-pacific/china-security-law-hong-kong-residents/] ("For many in Hong Kong who've long feared an erosion of their freedoms under Chinese rule, last week marked a tipping point. Spurred to action by Beijing's decision to impose controversial national security legislation on the former British colony, residents have been flooding migration consultants with questions on how to move their families overseas.").

The third, imaginary causes, is tied to the obsession with the comfort of the familiar. It is the means by which an ideology may be constructed to provide a perspective of meaning that reinforces itself in itself. "The banker thinks immediately of business, the Christian of "sin," and the girl of her love affair."[991] This is the semiotic error. It speaks to the error of accounting for things, of making meaning, based on a metrics of the self. And not just of the self, but it is the reconstruction of the present in the image of the memory of the past self--when the banker thinks immediately of business, he thinks of himself in the course of business in the form of the present understanding of the accumulation of past experience in those things and matters with which he has experience.

This, then, is the error that sees everything through the meaning constructed a priori. It is meaning derived from a re-imagined past. And it is the modality of error closest to the heart of the operation of political economic modeling. For what more powerful than the projection forward of the accumulated wisdom of the past constructed to serve the present for those charged with the leadership of the nation. It is the making of conscious imaginaries that provide the most powerful element in the construction and protection of the solidarity of the people-- connecting their past to their present, and using it as a launchpad for the future. It is a quintessentially Leninist error, but also one at the heart of the practice of the common law, and of liberal democratic attachment to the customs and traditions of its peoples. In that both China and the United States are twins and their twinning quite evident in their responses to the situation in Hong Kong, and its forward movement through the enactment of the national security law for Hong Kong. It is the basis that serves as the foundation of the approach of the European Union. Here the EU speaks quite boldly of itself in the construction of the causalities that are the relationship between China and its autonomous regions.[992]

---

[991] Friedrich Nietzsche, *Twilight of the Idols*, supra, 'The Four Great Errors,' ¶ 5.
[992] Council of the European Union, "Declaration by the High Representative, on behalf of the European Union, on the announcement by China's National People's

It is, as well, the realm of the algorithm and of the 'magic' of big data based analytic modelling. It is thus the error constructed through the filling of gaps, of the fantasy of interpolation and of the graph. It is the land of the chartists and those who acquire facts through extrapolation.[993] But it is also the land of well managed political speculation that can be as easily used as a diversion as it can be used as a means of finding cause. This is the land of the COVID-19 wet markets. Another imaginary cause, this one from Secretary Pompeo related to the changes in the status of Hong Kong:

> Pompeo, appearing on Fox News' "Sunday Morning Futures," said that China's leadership has broken its promise of preserving Hong Kong's autonomy by pursing tighter control over Hong Kong. . . "It is a different Chinese Communist Party today than it was 10 years ago," Pompeo said. The party is "intent upon the destruction of Western ideas, Western democracies, Western values."[994]

And yet it is possible to take the position that the Chinese Communist Party has not changed, nor has it broken any promise. What has changed is the willingness of the Americans to accept that the CPC is as it is. What has also changed is the willingness of the Americans (at least for the moment) to tolerate the inevitable

---

Congress, *supra* ("The European Union has a strong stake in the continued stability and prosperity of Hong Kong under the 'One Country Two Systems' principle. It attaches great importance to the preservation of Hong Kong's high degree of autonomy, in line with the Basic Law and with international commitments, as well as to the respect for this principle").

[993] Hans Dewachter, "Sign predictions of exchange rate changes: Charts as proxies for Bayesian inferences," *Weltwirtschaftliches Archiv* 133:39–55(1997); Christian D. Dock and Lukas Menkhoff, "Exchange rate expectations of chartists and fundamentalists," *Journal of Economic Dynamics and Control* 37(7):1362-1383 (2013).

[994] Yueqi Yang and Jordan Robertson, "U.S. Has No Basis to Give Hong Kong Special Treatment, Pompeo Says," *Bloomberg* (31 May 2020); available [https://www.bloomberg.com/news/articles/2020-05-31/pompeo-says-u-s-now-has-no-basis-to-treat-hong-kong-specially].

forward movement of the CPC (as and because it is what it is) as against its (the Americans') own interests.

The last, the falsity of free will tends to be the hardest. It is grounded on the rejection of individual purpose and views the construction of collective consciousness as the means by which any individual will is necessarily eradicated through the construction of communal will in the name of facilitating the will of the individual. Will in this sense can only be measured against something outside of the individual, and yet that very act of measuring or assessing destroys the viability of a will that is wholly individual. [995] Here one is deeply embedded in the willfulness of de-coupling. Where China sees mutually beneficial cooperation and win-win relations within the Hong Kong SAR irrespective of its internal governance,[996] the United States sees the exacerbation of unequal treaty relations that require correcting.[997] Between them, American (and other) enterprises will appear to have the free will to choose as they like; but there is no free will here, only the consequences of choosing sides--and for most that has already been done. [998] As Nietzsche noted: "Wherever men try to trace responsibility home to anyone, it is

---

[995] Friedrich Nietzsche, *Twilight of the Idols*, supra, 'The Four Great Errors,' ¶ 7.

[996] Newley Purnell, "U.S. Businesses Brace for Damage as Tensions Grow Over Hong Kong," *The Wall Street Journal* (31 May 2020); available [https://www.wsj.com/articles/u-s-businesses-brace-for-damage-as-tensions-over-hong-kong-grow-11590931298?emailToken=78b52389bca7a9ec4594a385a6aa5509bQ4JkPvuv uGTRn+mU660RXOHBTb8Hhw8aK0DPn7CyNXMIHbc4w4Vjf4+bQ8YBz0suRcG lD+vabO6WSYVcMPDoY1U8S5x22EOmzNBpXu4gNNUOTPQfxwBH5EDuTpRhP la&reflink=article_email_share] ("'We do not believe that sanctions or trade restrictions against Hong Kong are justified,' a Hong Kong government spokesman said Saturday. 'They will lead to a breakdown of the mutually beneficial Hong Kong-U.S. relationship built up over the years and only hurt local and U.S. businesses in Hong Kong and the people working for them.'" Ibid.).

[997] Donald J. Trump, "Remarks by President Trump on Actions Against China" (30 May 2020); available [https://trumpwhitehouse.archives.gov/briefings-statements/remarks-president-trump-actions-china/].

[998] Newley Purnell, "U.S. Businesses Brace for Damage as Tensions Grow Over Hong Kong," supra ("For many Americans in Hong Kong, "it's an emotional and fragile moment," said Ms. Joseph, whose chamber represents hundreds of American companies. "Many of us have worked and lived here for many years and we love Hong Kong.").

the instinct of punishment and of the desire to judge which is active."[999]

Of the Four Great Errors (Stratagems), in the context of the situation in Hong Kong, it is the last that is the most powerful. Neither of the two great Empires can proceed except as they have proceeded. Even a US under a democratic administration would come to a similar place (though by a quite different and likely more circuitous route). Both are prisoners of their ideology, and of their increasing commitment to the meaning of that ideology in the current era. Both leadership cores, as well, are deeply trapped within the logic of the administrative and ideological framework over which they appear to head. But here two things: First, to think that the leadership core by heading the apparatus of political and administrative power can impose their will on events misses the power of the first great error by inverting cause and effect. Both leadership cores[1000] lead because the institution over which they preside have permitted them to lead in these directions. They lead, in other words, by permission of those who are led, and the power of their leadership is closely aligned to the tolerance of the institutional collectives over which they have been given over lordship.[1001]

Second, it is only by inverting cause and effect that it is possible to construct the narrative of the leadership core itself as something autonomous and superior. Chinese Marxist Leninist theory makes that quite clear, though its practice has been cloudy of late. The same is true for the primary of liberal democracy, where the indulgence in the error of the great leader detached and

---

[999] Friedrich Nietzsche, *Twilight of the Idols*, supra, 'The Four Great Errors,' ¶ 7.
[1000] 领导核心 traditionally refers to the leadership core of the Chinese communist Party. See 领 导 核 心 Baidu; available [https://baike.baidu.com/item/领导核心/23151655]. But I use it here to reference all similar cores of leadership who are responsible for the guidance of their communities, in whatever way that guidance is manifested through the application of the political economic model through which this 领导核心 is constituted.
[1001] Discussed more fully in Larry Catá Backer, "The Fuhrer Principle of International Law: Individual Responsibility and Collective Punishment," supra.

above, has served the interests of the leaders' enemies more than the value of the construction of the leader cult to its object.

Third, the error of a false free will is compounded, especially in the text of the back and forth between the United States and China since the issue of the National Security Law arose, by the resort to strategic use of the other great errors (especially that of imaginary and false causes) as triggers for the exercise of discretion over which there was little discretionary space at all. Thus, Hong Kong was put in play not because of the exercise of the will of the leadership core, but the ideology that drove each of these empires made the situation in Hong Kong inevitable--and the textual ecology created around Hong Kong (from the handover documents through recent legislation) provided the ground on which such stratagems could be cultivated effectively.

The Four Great Errors are at their most useful as a structure of accountability; of stocktaking. Events, especially like those around the situation in Hong Kong, tend to acquire a life of their own. It is a life where officials and the public may feel swept along by events; where it is possible to spin out thrust and counter thrust on the basis of virtually anything but considered contextually based thought. These are the sorts of events in which reality becomes somewhat detached from the principles and objectives that themselves are reconstituted as "things"--with a life of their own whose satisfaction must be attained. And, of course, the events in Hong Kong can be telescoped from a granular examination of people in Hong Kong to the relationship of those events as interconnected with everything around which the Chinese and Americans now battle for the constitution of shared space. Hong Kong, then, becomes the center of a calculus of global finance (and dollar versus yuan internationalization); of the meaning and making of sovereignty in China even as it is remade elsewhere on quite different foundations; on trade and trade systems; and on the construction from out of a thousand places like Hong Kong of new imperial orders.

Yet to get to all of that one has to cultivate a deep appreciation for discourse, and for gesture. And one has to be sensitive to the way that discourse and gesture ultimately produce facts--only some of which can be well managed by those with the authority to unleash them. In the end, one ought to become more sensitive to issues of context--of the drive toward rationalization; of the power of ideology to shape a world constrict within which the exercise of will become constrained and directed; the tenuously of the great man theory of history; and so on. But in the end, and by whatever name to causal forces one decides best suits their frame of reference, what becomes clear is that the Hong King that emerges from pandemic in 2020 will be nothing like the Hong Kong on the eve of the demonstrations of June 2019. The route to the new era will be paved with stratagem, and the quite conscious cultivation of error.

$$* \quad * \quad *$$

Chapter 27

Monday 1 June 2020
Inaugurating the New Era for Hong Kong with the National Security Law and the Cancellation of the Tiananmen Vigil

> There is also a good side to mistakes, for they can educate the people and the Party. We have had a good many teachers by negative example, such as Japan, the United States, Chiang Kai-shek, Chen Tu-hsiu, Li Li-san, Wang Ming, Chang Kuo-tao and Kao Kang. We paid a very high price to learn from these teachers by negative example. In the past, Britain made war on us many times. Britain, the United States, Japan, France, Germany, Italy, tsarist Russia and Holland were all very interested in this land of ours. They were all our teachers by negative example and we were their pupils.[1002]

The COVID-19 accelerator [1003] continues to serve as an important instrument in the rectification of Hong Kong. It supplies the cover under which opposition forces can be split and the objectives of the central authorities more decisively advanced. On the eve of the enactment of the new national security measures for Hong Kong, this promises to herald the new Hong Kong, one that clearly exposes the weakness of the internationalist camp to do much more than incite a local population to assert positions and then leave them to their fates when national forces intervene. Here one comes face to face with the application of the insights, now updated for the "New Era" of Mao Zedong's insights about normative and political "paper tigers"--originally and incorrectly

---

[1002] Mao Zedong, "U.S. Imperialism is a Paper Tiger" (14 July 1956, From Selected Works of Mao Zedong, reproduced by Marxists.org; available [https://www.marxists.org/reference/archive/mao/selected-works/volume-5/mswv5_52.htm] (part of a talk with Latin-American leaders).
[1003] Discussed in essays Chapters 22-23, supra.

applied to the United States but more powerfully applied perhaps to the internationalist camp.[1004]

The symbolic marker of this passage nicely dressed for the occasion by the requisites pandemic responses is the shutdown of the traditional annual Tiananmen gatherings, [1005] a gathering increasingly irritating to the central authorities.[1006] To that end, Hong Kong police have officially banned the city's annual Tiananmen Square vigil for the first time in 30 years, citing

---

[1004] Mao Zedong, "U.S. Imperialism is a Paper Tiger," supra. Moa Zedong more relevant insight may be here nicely applied:

> Only when imperialism is eliminated can peace prevail. The day will come when the paper tigers will be wiped out. But they won't become extinct of their own accord, they need to be battered by the wind and the rain. When we say U.S. imperialism is a paper tiger, we are speaking in terms of strategy. Regarding it as a whole, we must despise it. But regarding each part, we must take it seriously. It has claws and fangs. We have to destroy it piecemeal. For instance, if it has ten fangs, knock off one the first time, and there will be nine left, knock off another, and there will be eight left. When all the fangs are gone, it will still have claws. If we deal with it step by step and in earnest, we will certainly succeed in the end.

[1005] To get a sense of the great gulf between Hong Kong before 2020, one need only consider the way that the South China Morning Post described the incidents at Tiananmen in 1989:

> China was gripped by a pro-democracy movement in 1989, triggered by the death of reformist ex-leader Hu Yaobang. Mass street protests, weeks-long sit-ins and hunger strikes at Tiananmen Square by students and residents became the order of the day as demonstrators complained about corruption and demanded greater democracy as well as government transparency. The social unrest culminated in a brutal military crackdown on June 4 ordered by Beijing that effectively ended the movement and continues to be the subject of great controversy to this day. "Tiananmen Square crackdown 30th anniversary," (6 June 2019); available [https://www.scmp.com/topics/tiananmen-square-crackdown-30th-anniversary] (a website still available for viewing in early 2021).

[1006] Kimmy Chung and Holly Chik, "Hong Kong police ban city's annual Tiananmen Square vigil for first time in 30 years, citing Covid-19 threat," *South China Morning Post* (1 June 2020); available [https://www.scmp.com/news/hong-kong/politics/article/3086982/hong-kong-police-cite-covid-19-threat-banning-annual].

ongoing social-distancing measures and health concerns amid the Covid-19 pandemic.[1007]

> The vigil's organiser, the Hong Kong Alliance in Support of Patriotic Democratic Movements of China, said alliance members would still enter Victoria Park to observe a moment of silence that night, and called on the public to light candles across the city and join an online gathering to commemorate the June 4, 1989, crackdown. * * * The vigil, where calls for an end to "one-party dictatorship" have been routinely heard, is under a fresh spotlight this year as Beijing moves forward with a tailor-made national security law for Hong Kong.[1008]

Hong Kong's pro-democracy camp "asked supporters in Hong Kong and around the world to light candles in their homes or other private places and post the images online."[1009]

This, it might be said, represents the new state of affairs in Hong Kong in the wake of the determination by Chinese central authorities to approve a National Security Law for the HKSAR, and the subsequent declaration of the United States that Hong Kong was no long autonomous of the rest of the nation, a view shared by the US's Anglo-Australian allies. [1010] Even as these states declared that the special status of Hong Kong was voided in violation of the Sino-British Joint Declaration specifically and international law generally, Chinese authorities declared that nothing of the kind happened, only on adjustment to the core conditions within which that special status could be managed. One side privileged the treaty under which the territory was returned to China in 1997; the other on the fundamental character of

---

[1007] Austin Ramzy, "Hong Kong Bans Tiananmen Vigil for 1st Time, in New Challenge to Protests," The New York Times (1 June 2020); available [https://www.nytimes.com/2020/06/01/world/asia/Hong-kong-Tiananmen-vigil-banned.html].

[1008] Kimmy Chung and Holly Chik, "Hong Kong police ban city's annual Tiananmen Square vigil for first time in 30 years, citing Covid-19 threat," supra.

[1009] Austin Ramzy, "Hong Kong Bans Tiananmen Vigil for 1st Time, in New Challenge to Protests," supra.

[1010] Discussed essay Chapter 26, supra.

sovereignty. And in that back and forth, over the course of the last year, both sides have decisively developed--and substantially extended the distance between--One Country ad Two systems. What had been one principle embodying a central contradiction in 1997 has now been resolved, but in two fundamentally distinct ways.[1011] COVID-19 here merely provided a cover for a quite conclusive move, one now manifested publicly in a most dramatic way.

The Sino-British Joint Declaration, signed 19 December 1984 between the United Kingdom and China,[1012] provided the formula through which both leased and ceded portions of the British Crown Colony would revert to Chinese sovereignty from July 1, 1997 but as a special administrative region subject to certain expectations about its administration specified in the document. These expectations, in the aggregate, have been commonly referenced as the principles of "One Country, Two Systems." China's obligations under the Treaty, and the UK (along with the generalized interest of the international community in the protection and integrity of treaties) were to "remain unchanged for 50 years" that is until 30 June 2047.[1013]

Yet nothing remains unchanged, not even the administration of a treaty, especially one that is intimately bound up with issues of sovereignty. In retrospect, the status of Hong Kong as a special administrative region of China will likely be seen as consisting of two phases. The dividing point might likely be May 2020 and the declaration by Chinese officials and institutional bodies to adopt for Hong Kong a National Security Law applicable to the SAR and the consequential international reaction.

Now may be a good time to look back to 1997 and forward to 2047 to consider the fundamental rupture in the concept of Hong Kong that occurred in 2020, and what that suggests both for

---

[1011] Discussed in essay Chapter 24, supra.

[1012] Joint Declaration of the Government of the United Kingdom of Great Britain and Northern Ireland and the Government of the People's Republic of China on the Question of Hong Kong (19 December 1984); available [https://www.cmab.gov.hk/en/issues/jd2.htm].

[1013] Ibid., §3(¶12).

the future of the Special Administrative Region, and the evolution of more flexible definitions of sovereignty within international orders. It suggests that a useful way of understanding the Declaration, and the evolving conception of "One Country, Two Systems" is to divide the period between 1997 and 2047 into an initial international phase for One Country Two Systems in Hong Kong (1997-2020), and now a national phase for One Country Two Systems (2020-2047).

Let one suppose it is the year 2120. From that vantage point it might be possible that our progeny will be taught the history of Hong Kong this way:

> For many centuries Hong Kong was an island of little significance to an Empire whose seat (and interests) usually lay elsewhere. It became strategically important in the wake of the first of the great wars that exposed the decadence of the Empire when the island was ceded to the British in 1842 after the First opium War, along with a sliver of coastal area (Kowloon) ceded in 1860. Those ceded territories were augmented by a larger territory leased by the Empire to Britain for 99 years in 1898. China was entitled to the return of the leased land in 1997. As that lease termination date approaches the successors to the Imperial State, now organized under the leadership of the Chinese Communist Party, insisted on the return of ceded territory. The nominal reason was based on a discrediting of the basis of both the lease and the original ceding of territory by what was then described as unequal treaties.

> That principle, in turn, had its genesis in a pretension of the late 20th century that treaties between states required sovereign equality to be legitimate, a notion that slipped into substantial disuse as both the Chinese and U.S. post global imperial machineries created hub and spoke bases

systems of treaty-based dependencies along the production chains they controlled. And indeed, much of the core territories of the great powers in the 22nd century must be understood as the product of many centuries of both conquest and of inequality in treaty relations among states.

Even assuming the legitimacy (or permanence) of the original 19th century territorial cessions by the Imperial government, without the leased territories, the remaining land was indefensible and of marginal strategic value. In the calculus of the British government then in power it was determined that as a matter of political calculation Britain ought to not merely return the leased territories but also to cede its own territory back to China to be effective at the time the term of the territorial leases expired. Such a strategy was not undertaken from a position of weakness, but rather suggested a bargaining stratagem the purpose of which was to seek to better embed China into the trajectories of emerging global political economic model of globalization. That, in turn, required adherence to notions of markets driving macro-economic planning, of free movement of goods, capital, investment (and to some extent) people, and of a system of international consensus serving as the source of normative political, economic, and societal development. Systems.

To that end, Britain was able to extract significant concessions from China to that end. Those were memorialized in the Sino-British Joint Declaration, signed 19 December 1984, and the establishment of the "One Country, Two Systems" policy. [1014] The Declaration was

---

[1014] Joint Declaration of the Government of the United Kingdom of Great Britain and Northern Ireland and the Government of the People's Republic of China on

supposed to extend from the handover of all territories in 1997 until 30 June 2047 and constituted an international obligation of China, though one with respect to which there was no authoritative interpretive mechanism. That was left to politics--and politics was a matter of power and global influence. As it turned out, the British calculation was only partially vindicated. China did decisively move (at least for a time) toward a markers Marxist markets model of organization.[1015]

Yet not even half way through the term of the handover agreement, two events happened that changed the carefully curated terms memorialized in the Sino-British Joint Declaration. The first was the evolution of a self-consciously autonomous view among certain factions within Hong Kong politics, with the sympathy of many people, that sought to embed Hong Kong's distinctive political model within the protections of international law and norms. The object was to ensure that Hong Kong's system could continue to evolve independently of that of the national development, and that this development would be protected past 2047. This was marked by the development of the position of the protesters from one against the imposition of Extradition Law to the Five Demands.[1016] The second was the strong rejection by Chinese central authorities of any the international framework for the governance of Hong Kong against the increasingly comprehensive imposition of its own political

---

the Question of Hong Kong (19 December 1984); available [https://www.cmab.gov.hk/en/issues/jd2.htm].

[1015] Larry Catá Backer, "Central Planning Versus Markets Marxism: Their Differences and Consequences for the International Ordering of State, Law, Politics, and Economy," *Connecticut Journal of International Law* 32(1):1-47 (2017).

[1016] Discussed in essay Chapter 17, supra.

economic model as a constraint on the exercise of Hong Kong political autonomy. This position advanced and defended the central authorities' own political economic model against encroachment by global (and fundamentally liberal democratic sensibilities. The position was characterized by an insistence on the imposition of its own construction of Hong Kong autonomy within which One Country principles constrained and defined the extent to which the Two Systems principles would be implemented under the guidance of the vanguard Communist Party of China.

This double consequence, and its fundamental fracture might best be understood as occurring within, and the history of the Sino-British Joint Declaration might be partitioned into, two distinct historical phases. These historical phases loosely mark the way that the critical stakeholders in this contest approached and sought to resolve the contradiction that was the One Country-Two Systems principle as presented in 1997.[1017]

The first phase might be eventually understood as the international phase of the Hong Kong transition. This was a phase in which much prominence was placed on the "Two Systems" portion of the basic principle of the SAR's organization and operation. It was in place from 1 July 1997 until May 2020. And it will be recalled as the period when Hong Kong was formally national (a part of China) but functionally international (a global city within which the international community had a formal stake pursuant to the Sino-British Declaration. It reflected the intention of the British (and global)

[1017] Discussed in essay Chapter 24, supra.

side of the declaration which at the time had the authority to make that interpretation authoritative. It was an interpretation that China tolerated (for its own strategic reasons) but did not embrace.

This international phase was a product of, and characterized by, an adherence to the loftiest aspirations of a transnational constitutional movement that saw its apogee between 1945 and 2016. It was marked by a core premise of sovereignty deeply embedded in international principles and subject, broadly, to the constraints of international law.[1018] It saw no difficulty in the concept of sovereignty as a porous concept which could be shared, constrained, detached, borrowed and limited by a higher law of the collective of states within the international order. More specifically the international phase might be understood as grounded in the development of a set of specific characteristics of autonomy around the principles of the *International Covenant on Civil and Political Rights*.[1019] It was an autonomy built on the development of the productive forces of law, courts and free civil expression, even if under the long shadow of sovereign authority exercised at the national level. That would have been the context in which the narrative of the decision to deny the vigil permit would have been understood. "COVID-19 must not be used as an excuse to stifle freedom of expression... 'With this ban, and a disastrous national security law

---

[1018] Larry Catá Backer, "God (s) Over Constitutions: International and Religious Transnational Constitutionalism in the 21st Century, *"Mississippi College Law Review* 27:11 (2008).
[1019] International Covenant Civil and Political Rights (16 December 1966, entered into force 23 March 1976) United Nations, Treaty Series, vol. 999, p. 171.

looming, it is not clear if Hong Kong's Tiananmen vigil will ever be allowed to take place again.'"[1020]

This was a phase in which Hong Kong was constructed as a special international city, one built on transnational institutions, law, and politics. Hong Kong was the expression of the ideal of political globalization, one deeply embedded in the emerging discourse of these ideals among the international intelligentsia. But it was an international city constructed out of the narrative of the progressive and liberal democratic international order--a city built on and managed through, the product of, international law and principles. Nominally tied to a domestic legal order, it was meant to serve as a model on which an international normative order could actually be constructed on the ground.

The operative result, and the narrative constructed in support of it, was that the Special Administrative Region was in a permanent phase of full integration with the international political and economic community. It represented the new era of internationalized sovereignty for China. But it was also a model for other places as the way "forward" toward an internationalized ideal, one protected in concert by the international community. But of course, that was the problem; such a state of affairs could last only as long as there was will in the international community to make good on its aspirations, especially in the face of national opposition.

[1020] "Hong Kong: People must be allowed to peacefully mark Tiananmen anniversary," *Amnesty International* (1 June 2020); available [https://www.amnesty.org/en/latest/news/2020/06/hong-kong-people-must-be-allowed-to-peacefully-mark-tiananmen-anniversary/](quoting Joshua Rosenzweig, Amnesty's deputy director for East and Southeast Asia.).

The second phase might eventually be remembered as the national phase of the Hong Kong transition. It began with the delayed session of the Chinese National People's Congress in May 2020 and could be marked (for those who find such markers of value) to have commenced formally from the day that the NCP formally directed the enactment by its Standing Committee of a National Security Law for Hong Kong.[1021] It will be recalled as the period during which Hong Kong transitioned from an international to a purely domestic space within China and more closely aligned with national aspirations and methods. During this period the international attachments of Hong Kong that separate it from the rest of Chinese sovereign territory will be reset--slowly at first, but at an increasing pace. This reflects the intention of the Chinese side of the declaration, which could only be realized once China had the power and standing to wrest effective control from the internationalists. It was and remains an interpretation that the international community tolerated when it had no effect, and then, after 2020, opposed with increasing vigor.

The national phase was a product of, and characterized by, an adherence to the loftiest aspirations of a post global sovereignty. It was marked by a conception of the international as inherently subordinate to, and transposable only within, the national context of a domestic constitutional order and subject to the vagaries of

---

[1021] Nectar Gan, "China approves controversial national security law for Hong Kong," CNN (28 May 2020); available [https://www.cnn.com/2020/05/28/asia/china-npc-hk-security-law-intl-hnk/index.html] ("China's Premier Li Keqiang said Thursday after the parliamentary meetings that the law was designed for the "steady implementation of 'one country, two systems'" -- a formula that guarantees Hong Kong its autonomy and freedoms -- and for "Hong Kong's long term prosperity and stability."").

its political-economic model. Sovereignty was an internal affair of state, as was the transposition of international obligations with respect to any portion of the national territory. It saw no problem with the notion of international law as a set of political obligations administered at the international level through the language and formalities of law, but still at its core no more than the political undertaking among states, valuable only to the extent that they remained mutually advantage and produced a win-win result.

More specifically the national phase might be understood as grounded in the development of a set of specific characteristics of autonomy around the principles of the national political-economic model as the expression of the principles in the *International Covenant on Economic, Social, and Cultural Rights*. It was an autonomy built on the nurturing of an institutional framework through which productive forces could be developed, security and stability (social order) could be maintained, and the integrity and coherence of the nation respected. It was useful as a middle space for the projection of domestic aspirations abroad organized through programs such as the Belt and Road Initiative. It was a special economic zone with extra waivers, waivers that were the temporary price necessary to be paid to ensure a peace transfer of sovereignty. Protection of the economic objective required, as a consequence, protection against the three evil forces of separatism, extremism, and terrorism.[1022]

[1022] Sam Dupont, "China's war on the 'Three Evil Forces'," Foreign Policy (25 July 2007); available [https://foreignpolicy.com/2007/07/25/chinas-war-on-the-three-evil-forces/] ("We can laugh about the language being used, but Chinese diplomacy is actually becoming pretty sophisticated. With the strong states of Central Asia, Beijing's message is about combating evil and crushing dissent.").

This was a phase in which Hong Kong was constructed as a special international city, but one built on the internationalization of economic activity. It was a city deeply embedded within the domestic legal order of the state which claimed sovereignty, but was the highest expression of a special trade zone. That, indeed, was how the SAR itself marketed its self-construction: "Hong Kong has positioned itself to become the world city of Asia. This positioning is designed to highlight Hong Kong's existing strengths in areas such as financial services, trade, tourism, transport, communications, and as a regional hub for international business and a major city in China." [1023] The object is to construct an "international city" the way that London and New York could claim that status. To that end, the state, not the international community, could provide the waivers necessary to meet this economic objective but in a way that preserved the core objectives of that political order--stability, security, and sovereignty. It was to be a brand, and an aid to marketing the SAR.[1024]

The operative result, and the narrative constructed in support of it, was that the Special Administrative Region was in a temporary transitional phase from foreign colony to integral (and integrated) part of the nation. That transition was to be used to strip away direct international connection to the extent they would not be useful for national objectives. What remained was tolerated only at the sufferance of the national authorities, though they were committed to strict compliance with Treaty obligation. The strictness

---

[1023] Government of Hong Kong, "Asia's World City" (last accessed 14 March 2021); available [https://www.info.gov.hk/info/sar5/easia.htm].
[1024] Ibid.

of that interpretation was to be undertaken wholly within the state apparatus and grounded in the core principles of Chinese Marxist-Leninism and the CPC Basic Line in the current stage of historical development.

At this point one can only guess how the second phase will end, and how the story of the transition of Hong Kong from colony to integrated part of the People's Republic of China, will be where constructed. What is certain is that the second phase will extend formally, at least, through 30 June 2047. At that time, depending on the stage of historical development of China, Hong Kong might be absorbed within the greater Pearl River Urban complex long in the making. The form of that absorption remains to be seen, yet it seems inevitable--made more so by decisions likely made at the time of the operationalization of the Reform and Opening Up Era under the leadership of Deng Xiaoping. It is likely that Hong Kong will retain a vestigial special status as a free trade or export zone; perhaps it will serve as a special space within the Pearl River area in which foreigners might operate under rules a little different than elsewhere in China. Or perhaps it will become a district of a larger urban space and useful for the tourist trade.

What will be beyond dispute, though, is that after 30 June 2047, Hong Kong will become an integral part of the vanguard responsibility of the Chinese Communist Party under whose leadership, and subject to its Basic Line, the Hong Kong administration will be expected (like the rest of China) to operate. All efforts to detach Hong Kong's autonomy from the Sino-British Joint Declaration, or add international constraints otherwise to the exercise of Chinese sovereignty over what had been the British Crown colony will end in failure. That failure will have substantial reverberations elsewhere and undermine the effort of international elites to fashion a robust theory of divisible political sovereignty. Instead, other measures with the same effect will likely be developed. These will likely follow production chains.

Like the Chinese vanguard, the international community is also speaking of a new era within the core of its authority.[1025]

From this vantage point it is easier to understand the discursive and operational stances taken by all of the principal actors around the situation in Hong Kong. The Chinese State and the United States and its allies held and continue to hold substantially incompatible views of the circumstances and meaning of the transfer. Each has much invested in their own narrative. For China it is an essential part of its own notion of sovereignty and national integrity. For the rest it is an essential part of what is left of that grand vision of transnational constitutionalism and multilateral mutuality within the logic of markets, of globalization, and of the core principles proceeding from civil and political rights-based cultures. For the people of Hong Kong who form part of the protest movement the result was from their perspective tragic. They sought the support of international law and the international community and found only words. China discovered the same thing--a globe full of paper tigers ow stripped of another of its pretensions.[1026] All the same, a divided society, from the elites down to the most humble working person, it appears that both sides will by 2047 experience the tragedies of shifting narratives and its quite personal effects for a long time to come. Indeed, and ironically from both sides, 2047 has already ceased to have any meaning--except for the rigid formalism of internationalist responses that seek the cloak of international legality to defend or contest the actions on all sides in the context of Hong Kong's political model and its future.

[1025] As the website of the UN Office of the High Commissioner for Human Rights notes: "Since the unanimous endorsement of the UN Guiding Principles on Business and Human Rights (UNGPs) by the UN Human Rights Council in 2011, a new era of socially responsible and sustainable business has taken shape and continues to build momentum." Office of the High Commissioner for Human Rights, "Mandatory human rights due diligence (mHRDD)," (last accessed 14 March 2021); available [https://www.ohchr.org/EN/Issues/Business/Pages/MandatoryHRDD.aspx] ("A wave of responsible business legal requirements is impacting markets across the world, with mandatory human rights due diligence (mHRDD) regimes already in place or in development across a growing number of jurisdictions, particularly in the EU context.").

[1026] Mao Zedong, "U.S. Imperialism is a Paper Tiger," *supra.*

Chapter 28

Thursday 4 June 2020
The SAR Government Passes the National Anthem Ordinance（國歌條例草案）Reinforcing the Architecture of Two Systems WITHIN One Country

> The spectacle grasped in its totality is both the result and the project of the existing mode of production. It is not a supplement to the real world, an additional decoration. It is the heart of the unrealism of the real society. In all its specific forms, as information or propaganda, as advertisement or direct entertainment consumption, the spectacle is the present model of socially dominant life. It is the omnipresent affirmation of the choice already made in production and its corollary consumption. The spectacle's form and content are identically the total justification of the existing system's conditions and goals. The spectacle is also the permanent presence of this justification, since it occupies the main part of the time lived outside of modern production.[1027]

The situation in Hong Kong is in part driven by gesture. It has provided one of the great spectacles of the first third of the 21st century. Gesture, in turn is not merely an act, but it is an act in time. The spectacle of gesture acquires its power by its timing. Two events of note may be understood for their importance both as gesture and as important elements of the nationalization of the Hong Kong SAR within the "One Country, Two Systems" principle. The first, highly symbolic, was the determination, under cover of COVID-19, to cancel the traditional vigil traditionally held on 4 June. [1028]

[1027] Guy Debord, *Society of the Spectacle* (Fredy Perlman and Jon Supak, trans., St. Petersburg, FL: Red & Black, 1977), chp. 1 ¶6; reprinted by Marxists.org; available [https://www.marxists.org/reference/archive/debord/society.htm].
[1028] Discussed essay Chapter 27, supra.

The second, and the object of this essay, was the approval on 3 June 2020 of the National Anthem Bill (國歌條例).[1029] "The law was passed with 41 votes for and one against. Those who were able to vote were largely from the pro-Beijing camp, as pro-democracy lawmakers were taking part in a noisy last-minute protest that meant they could not vote. "A murderous state stinks forever," they shouted."[1030]

The deliberations provided a cavalcade of spectacle and the performance of gesture for the ages. The stage was set around a heavily guarded legislative complex (with memories of prior protests starting in June 2019 still fresh in the minds of those orchestrating events within the building. One member of the DAB party (supportive of the position of the central authorities) declared during the course of deliberations that "If lawmakers oppose the national anthem bill, they are violating basic political ethics." [1031] This appeal to political ethics was countered by appeals to the likelihood of arbitrary arrest. "Democratic Party lawmaker Wu Chi-wai said ... "Are we going to see more and more draconian laws and harsher penalties?" he asked. "We used to have more tolerance and respect for the government."[1032]

But the central spectacle of passage was reserved for Eddie Chu and Ray Chan who charged towards Legislative Council (LegCo) President Andrew Leung

---

[1029] National Anthem Bill, Ordinance No. 2 of 2020; available [https://www.legco.gov.hk/yr18-19/english/bills/b201901111.pdf] (hereafter National Anthem Ordinance).

[1030] Verna Yu, "Hong Kong protesters hold banned Tiananmen vigil as anthem law is passed," *The Guardian* (4 June 2020); available [https://www.theguardian.com/world/2020/jun/04/hong-kong-tiananmen-vigil-ban-china-national-anthem-bill-protest] ("The voting took place hastily late on Thursday afternoon after a pause of four hours. An earlier session was suspended after pro-democracy lawmakers Eddie Chu and Ray Chan tried to cause the bill to be delayed by protesting and throwing pungent liquid on the floor" Ibid.).

[1031] Jennifer Cherry and Rachel Wong, "Hong Kong passes law to criminalise insult of Chinese national anthem," Hong Kong Free Press (4 June 2020); available [https://hongkongfp.com/2020/06/04/breaking-hong-kong-passes-law-to-criminalise-insult-of-chinese-national-anthem/] (quoting Elizabeth Quat).

[1032] Ibid.

holding protest placards reading "Murderous states stinks for eternity," and a container of foul-smelling liquid was dropped on the floor. The meeting was adjourned for several hours whilst police and fire service department personnel carried out an on-site investigation.
* * *Upon resumption in a separate room, Leung pressed on with the final vote without allowing remaining lawmakers to speak. Ted Hui from the Democratic Party subsequently marched forward and spilt liquid on the floor before being removed by security.[1033]

Together this theater of legislative action provided the appropriate backdrop to the longer term spectacle, the continuous gesture, that is the National Anthem Ordinance. For while the passage of the National Anthem Bill was itself spectacular, the resulting Ordinance is itself the constitution of a living and constant gesture--a gesture of reaffirmation, of the performance of the affirmation of allegiance to a territory and a political-economic order. It is a signal--it is the dynamic representation of the symbol of the state performed by those from which allegiance is required. It is the expression of belonging that augments the semiotics of allegiance represented by flags and banners. [1034] Indeed what can be noted about flags has equal applicability in the context of anthems:

What is needed is something far more direct and simple, an object that can serve as a sign, the shared meaning of which produces the incarnation-disembodiment-reconstitution at the heart of identity. A color field is needed that can incarnate the abstract and disembody the physical. A flag is needed through which the collective can become the individual and the individual

---

[1033] Ibid.

[1034] Larry Catá Backer, "Bannermen and Heralds: The Identity of Flags; the Ensigns of Identity," in *Flags, Identity, Memory: Critiquing the Public Narrative through Color,*
Anne Wagner and Sarah Marusek, eds. (Dordrecht: Springer 2020).

the collective. What is needed is a standard, a banner, a coded field of color and drawing, that makes the meaning of identity visible.[1035]

Its importance then, cannot be underestimated in the transformation of Hong Kong away from its internationalist to a more nationalist allegiance wrapped within the rituals of allegiance. The national anthem is understood as the incarnation of the state, "a symbol and sign of the People's Republic of China."[1036] The signification of that sign is expressed through the performance of rituals of respect, dignity and positive affirmance (in this case through playing and singing). [1037] This meaning making is then mandatory--the law of the rituals of the signification of the state must be structured through the coercive symbolism of law and the performance of the police power of the state.[1038] The ends of this meaning making are hardly esoteric or difficult to grasp--through the complex interplay of gesture and spectacle, which enriches, may sometimes serve as a veil of the obvious: the purpose for all of this spectacle is "to promote patriotism."[1039] That is a critical element, one that the central authorities have adopted an "all around" (comprehensive) approach.[1040]

It is in that context that it is worth considering the passage of the National Anthem Ordinance (the text of which follows below) in the context of the transformation of Hong Kong as an international City, and the premises around which "One Country, Two Systems" will be interpreted going forward well beyond the end of the term of its mandatory term in 2047 under the increasingly irrelevant (within China) terms of the Sino-British Joint Declaration.

[1035] Ibid.
[1036] National Anthem Ordinance, supra, Preamble (1).
[1037] Ibid., Preamble (2).
[1038] Ibid., Preamble (3) ("Ordinance is to be enacted to preserve the dignity of the national anthem, to regulate the playing and singing, the broadcast and the use of the national anthem, to enhance citizen awareness of the People's Republic of China").
[1039] Ibid.
[1040] See discussion essay Chapter 25, supra.

The National Anthem Ordinance runs 23 pages (and follows in full below). That itself is a telling gesture--the weight of the document suggests the weightiness of the matters it covers. Size, in this case, matters. The physical extent of the Ordinance serves as an objectification of its importance. It consists of 6 parts, a Preamble, and three schedules. Beyond its semiotics,[1041] the Preamble is simple and direct--the national anthem as a symbol of the singular state, gives rise to both positive and negative obligations. *The positive obligations* are to sing the national anthem at appropriate occasions as directed now by statute. *The negative obligations* are to avoid acts of disrespect against the symbol that will now be taken as disrespect for the state.

Part 1 provides basic definitions of key terms. Defined are concepts such as "national anthem" and "national flag."[1042] Both lyrics and score are set forth in Schedules that are quite precise. There is a history here that echoes the turbulence of the early era of the history of the People's Republic of China. The "March of the volunteers" was adopted in 1949 with the establishment of the current government and political system. However, it was suppressed during the Cultural Revolution, and, when restored in 1978, it reappeared with a new set of lyrics. The original lyrics were restored in 1982.[1043]

Part 2 focuses on the playing and singing of the national anthem. It provides an official recording for popular use and references the standard score.[1044] It details anthem etiquette, and specifies the occasions when it is to be played. Lastly it imposes a "principle of dignity" respecting both playing and singing.[1045] The question of the mechanics of offense to dignity (and the power

---

[1041] Text and notes 10-14, supra.

[1042] National Anthem Ordinance, supra, Part 1 §2(1).

[1043] Tim F. Liao, Gehui Zhang, and Libon Zhang, "Social Foundations of National Anthems: Theorizing for a Better Understanding of the Changing Fate of the National Anthem of China," *Journal for the Theory of Social Behavior* 42(1):106-127 (2012).

[1044] National Anthem Ordinance, supra, Part 2 §4.

[1045] Ibid., Part 2 §3 ("The national anthem must be played and sung in a way that is in keeping with its dignity")

relations it reinforces) remains to be developed and applied. More to the point, perhaps, to some extent, the "etiquette" rules [1046] provide a conduct baseline for judging dignity. The performance of resect, however, is the critical element of this regulation.

Part 3 specifies the offenses for breaching the responsibilities set out in Part 2. It prohibits citizens from using the national anthem in certain settings, such as for commercial purposes, at private funerals, or as background music.[1047] It also bans citizens from insulting the national anthem in any way, such as altering its lyrics or singing it in a distorted way. The National Anthem Ordinance makes it clear that it is for the state to control the spectacle of Anthem performance; there is very little space for popular "ownership of the National Anthem--the national anthem, then is a state function that calls for popular participation at the instance of officials.[1048]

Part 3 also signifies the baseline offense as a form of public counter-gesture. These are gestures that take on the character of insult. "A person commits an offence if the person publicly and intentionally insults the national anthem in any way." [1049] The nature of the spectacle of insult is also precisely (though still vaguely) described: altering the lyrics of the national anthem or performing it "in a distorted or disrespectful way;" [1050] or otherwise publishing the anthem in an insulting way.[1051] Part 3 defines "insult (侮 辱), in relation to the national anthem, means to undermine the dignity of the national anthem as a symbol and sign of the People's Republic of China."[1052] Publication (發布) is also defined broadly to include any communication to the public in any form, or the distribution of any such communication.[1053]

[1046] Ibid., Part 2 §4 (stand solemnly, deport oneself with dignity, avoid disrespectful behavior).

[1047] Ibid., Part 3 §§6(1)-(2).

[1048] Ibid., Part 3 §6. Exculpation for offense is possible where a person can put forward a "reasonable excuse" the scope of which remains to be clarified.

[1049] Ibid., Part 3 §7(2)

[1050] Ibid., Part 3 §7(1).

[1051] Ibid., Part 3 §§7(3)-(4).

[1052] Ibid., Part 3 §7(8).

[1053] Ibid.

Provision is made for distinguishing the words and sounds of the Anthem from similar word groupings and sounds.[1054] But notice the tension and thus the tight control of music and lyrics--does one insult the national anthem by signing the lyrics officially required between 1978 and 1982? The Anthem, then, as a site of contestation, itself reminds the singer of the political affirmation built into its performance.

Part 4 concerns the promotion of the national anthem. Appropriate gestures--and the rituals of spectacle that reify the state--require education. This reflects a long developing position of the central authorities, and one that is meant to cure what the central authorities understood to be a primary cause of the disruptions of the protests in Hong Kong since June 2019 (and possibly back before the 2014 Umbrella Movement). [1055] It reinforces the drive toward the development of a national patriotic front and the elimination of foreign elements within Hong Kong's political culture. Spectacle, then, is seen as an important element of re-education in the service of the state and the protection of the integrity of its political-economic model.

More specifically, Part 4 directs that primary and secondary educations must incorporate the national anthem in their curriculum, including its singing, history and the etiquette regarding it.[1056] Such education is focused not just on ritual but on its signification: "on the history and spirit of the national anthem."[1057]It also requires all sound and television broadcasters to play the national anthem when requested by the Communication Authority. It distinguishes, as well between the National Anthem Ordinance for Hong Kong, and the National Anthem Law of the People's Republic of China, the supremacy of which in matters relating to the anthem is acknowledged.[1058]

[1054] Ibid., Part 3 §8.

[1055] Discussed essay Chapter 7, supra (patriotic education of the young).

[1056] National Anthem Ordinance, supra, Part 4 §9.

[1057] Ibid., Part 4 §9(1)(b)(i).

[1058] Ibid., Part 5§11(3)(National Anthem Law (《國歌法》) means the Law of the People's Republic of China on National Anthem, adopted at the 29th Meeting of the Standing Committee of the Twelfth National People's Congress on 1 September 2017.

Part 5 includes a number of supplementary provisions. provides the basis for treating the Hong Kong version of the National Anthem Law differently from the one otherwise applicable to the rest of the nation. It states that in case of inconsistencies between this ordinance and the Law of the People's Republic of China on National Anthem adopted by the NPC, this ordinance should be applied. Part 6 contains consequential amendments to other ordinances, for example adding passages regarding the use of national anthem to the Trade Marks Ordinance. In addition, the National Anthem Law includes three Schedules. Schedule 1 sets out the lyrics and score of the national anthem in a stave notation. Schedule 2 sets out the lyrics and score of the national anthem in a numbered musical notation. Schedule 3 sets out the occasions on which the national anthem must be played and sung under clause 5.

Taken as a whole, then the National Anthem Ordinance (國歌條例草案) is a comprehensive regulatory system for the observance of the primary gestures of sovereignty, order, and fidelity to the nation, and it follows, to the political-economic model under which it is organized. Its symbolic importance cannot be underestimated. It is passed within a context in which the Anthem itself has been a source of political challenge in Hong Kong especially after 2014 and the beginning of the last phase (in retrospect) of the internationalist movement in Hong Kong. "The anthem has been booed at football matches, where soccer fans have at times sang "Glory to Hong Kong", a song that has become a rallying cry for the democracy movement in the city. "[1059]

The anti-anthem protests appear to have arisen in the shadow of heightened feelings that emerged during the 2014 Umbrella Movement and the battle over the nature of representative government within the SAR. The anti-anthem

---

[1059] Twinnie Siu and Clare Jim, "Hong Kong passes China national anthem bill amid protests by democracy lawmakers," Reuters (3 June 2020); available [https://www.reuters.com/article/us-hongkong-protests-anthem/hong-kong-passes-china-national-anthem-bill-amid-protests-by-democracy-lawmakers-idUSKBN23B0BT].

protests appear to have arisen among heightened feelings that emerged during the 2014 Umbrella Movement and the battle over the nature of representative government within the SAR. It became visible during the 2015 World Cup Campaign. And ironically it appears to have been fueled by missteps among Mainland Chinese organizations.

> Mr Sutcliffe [Hong Kong Football Association Chief Executive] traces the surge in tension to June, when the Chinese Football Association (CFA) issued a promotional poster ahead of the qualifier against Hong Kong. The poster shows images of three players and warns: "This team has players with black skin, yellow skin and white skin. Best to be on guard against such a multi-layered team!" Unsurprisingly, some Hong Kong fans derided the poster as racist. Following the controversy, the booing began during a qualifier against Bhutan, and continued until last weekend's friendly with Myanmar.[1060]

The regulation is not unusual as to type,[1061] but its timing and its scope tends to emphasize the transformation of the understanding of Hong Kong within the organization of the Chinese State.

More importantly, the National Anthem Ordinance is a strong gesture directed to the international community. It serves as a spectacle for the consumption of domestic and international audiences for the performance of a ritual of separation--in this case of the detachment of Hong Kong from its international connections. It serves as another gesture reinforcing the line of

---

[1060] Juliana Liu, "Hong Kong-China: A Growing Football Rivalry or Just Politics?," *BBC News* (17 November 2015); available [] ("'We've been requesting that fans respect the anthem. That they behave, generally,' he says. 'But at the end of the day, it's very difficult when you have a crowd of 6,000 people, and there is an element in that crowd that wants to voice their opinion. It's very difficult to stop them.'").

[1061] Ng Kang-chung and Laurie Chen, "Explainer: how do countries around the world foster respect for their national anthem?," *South China Morning Post* (9 November 2017); available [https://www.scmp.com/news/hong-kong/politics/article/2118933/explainer-how-do-countries-around-world-foster-respect-their].

the central authorities that Hong Kong's character as an international city has fundamentally changed. That change now produces a quite different manifestation of Hong Kong's global position. Hong Kong has now begun decisively to develop away from an identity marked by the autonomy of its political and civil model (and guaranteed by international instruments), to one marked by its position on China's Silk Roads as a purveyor of economic and financial services within the greater Pearl River City complex (and guaranteed by the Chinese constitutional order). To keep the state and its Silk Road free of danger, that new positioning for Hong Kong then requires protection against the three evils of separatism, extremism, and terrorism. The external manifestation of that protection has been an object of the Shanghai Cooperation Organization and the security arm of the Belt and Road Initiative. [1062] The internal manifestation necessarily requires the cultivation of patriotism and its outward symbols, along with mechanisms for punishing those who would corrupt this system.[1063]

What does One Country, Two Systems mean in this context? It means principally that Hong Kong must be subject to national objectives, national priorities, and be faithful to core national principles that further the integrity of the state, and its political-economic model. Beneath that, local variation (substantial from the perspective of the Central Authorities--and thus the Two Systems part of the principle) is permitted to take local context into account, in this case including the common law traditions and organization of Hong Kong along with local culture. Sensitivity to this was already apparent in the 2018 version of the National Anthem Bill that included a chart showing the differences between the Mainland and the SAR versions of the Ordinance.[1064]

[1062] Sam Dupont, "China's war on the "Three Evil Forces," Foreign Policy (25 July 2007); available [https://foreignpolicy.com/2007/07/25/chinas-war-on-the-three-evil-forces/] (terrorism, ethnic separatism, and religious extremism).

[1063] See discussion essays Chapters 7, 13, supra.

[1064] Legislative Council Panel on Constitutional Affairs, Local Legislation to Implement the National Anthem Law, LC Paper No. CB(2)1063/17-18(03) (For discussion 23 March 2018); available [https://www.legco.gov.hk/yr17-18/english/panels/ca/papers/ca20180323cb2-1063-3-e.pdf], Annex 2 Outline of the Proposed Content of the National Anthem Bill of the Hong Kong Special

But events after June 2019 produced a retreat of sort from sensitivity to the practices of Hong Kong. The current version of the Ordinance appears to be closer to the national model with less leeway for regional variation. That, too, is a strong gesture, by the central authorities now convinced that autonomy and sensitivity to local variation must be more carefully managed through the imposition of national rituals of patriotism.

It is not surprising, then that these transformations continue to meet local resistance. That resistance crystallizes the old and now receding conceptualization of Hong Kong as an international city; the protestors use brilliantly the language of a conceptualization of Hong Kong, and the internationalist foundations of its law, based on the primacy of civil and political rights. For those sympathetic to the protesters and their aims, the National Anthem Ordinance is seen as an encroachment by Beijing on Hong Kong's autonomously protected personal rights, especially individual freedom of speech.[1065]

> "It is a restriction on personal liberties, freedom of expression," Au Nok-hin, who served as a legislator from 2018 to 2019, tells TIME. Past moves by Chinese authorities perceived to be quashing freedoms have sparked huge demonstrations in Hong Kong. Thousands of protesters turned out on Sunday to march against a national security law, which China's top lawmaking body announced last week it plans to implement for Hong Kong. Maya Wang, a China senior researcher at the rights group Human Rights Watch says the national anthem bill would be a "grim development" for Hong Kong. "Looking at this law and the upcoming national security legislation, there is an unmistakable trend towards the end of Hong

---

Administrative Region "Our legislative principle is to maintain the purpose and intent of the National Anthem Law to fully reflect its spirit and to preserve the dignity of the national anthem, so that our citizens would respect the national anthem, whilst taking into account our common law system and the actual circumstances in Hong Kong." ¶5 2018 Legislative Bill, supra).

[1065] The Basic Law of the Hong Kong Special Administrative Region of the People's Republic of China; available [https://www.basiclaw.gov.hk/pda/en/basiclawtext/chapter_3.html], Art. 27.

Kong as a place where people can speak without fear," she says. "It is a step towards greater and more comprehensive restrictions on freedom of expression that tracks with the trend overall in the rest of mainland China."[1066]

For some, the cancellation of the vigil and the passage of the National Anthem Bill are closely inter-related. "Thousands of people have defied a police ban in Hong Kong to mourn the victims of the Tiananmen Square massacre, after the city's legislature passed a law criminalising the mockery of China's national anthem."[1067] And local resistance is not always suppressed, even after a year of sometimes quite violent street action. "Thousands flooded Hong Kong's Victoria Park on Thursday night for the annual candlelight vigil to mark the anniversary of the 1989 Tiananmen Square crackdown, defying a ban on the mass gathering imposed by the police for the first time on health protection grounds."[1068]

Here one is brought closer to the spectrum of spectacle, and of the ritualized gestures that make for spectacle, in Hong Kong. Social spaces for symbolic expressions[1069]--the anthems of protests--are now matched by the formalized ritual of the overarching architecture of an imagined community now made

---

[1066] "Hong Kong's National Anthem Bill Is Sparking Renewed Protests. Here's What to Know," *Time* (27 May 2020); available [https://time.com/5842352/hong-kong-national-anthem-bill-protests/].

[1067] Verna Yu, "Hong Kong protesters hold banned Tiananmen vigil as anthem law is passed," The Guardian (4 June 2020); available [https://www.theguardian.com/world/2020/jun/04/hong-kong-tiananmen-vigil-ban-china-national-anthem-bill-protest].

[1068] "Tiananmen vigil in Hong Kong draws thousands despite coronavirus-related ban," South China Morning Post (5 June 2020); available [https://www.scmp.com/news/hong-kong/politics/article/3087623/tiananmen-vigil-hong-kong-draws-thousands-despite] ("Police, who had warned they had thousands of riot officers ready and would enforce anti-coronavirus rules limiting groups to a maximum of eight people each, stood back as the crowds poured into the park in Causeway Bay and took up a couple of soccer pitches").

[1069] Alberto Abruzzese, Alberto "La piazza come spazio sociale e simbolico," Laura Barbiani (ed.) *La Piazza Storica Italiana: Analisi di un sistema complesso*, pp. 77-119. Venezia : Marsilio, 1992).

real by the ritual expression of its superior reality in the rituals of anthem.[1070] That supra ritual then expresses not just control but the manifestation of the social order which it has its performers affirm.[1071] But each of these rituals is itself a site for contestation. The rituals of the observance of the June 4th Incident in Hong Kong signals societal and political fracture within Hong Kong; the lyrics and music of the National Anthem itself is a contested site, the memory of which exposes the larger historical fractures of the nation as it moves from one historical era to the next.[1072]

These two spectacles of remembrance,[1073] one of the source of difference, and the other of the nature of unity, seek both to unite and separate in accordance with the thrust of the memory. Thus, though it "is an implicit rule that participants in any social order must presuppose a shared memory,"[1074] the juxtaposition of the shared memory of the June 4th Incident in Hong Kong and the allegiance ritual of the national anthem suggest that the thrust of unity necessarily also draws boundaries. Both spectacles and their ritual expressions, "are modern totems--signs by which nations distinguish themselves from one another or reaffirm their 'identity' boundaries."[1075] The link between language and gestures,[1076] and between gesture and meaning is clear as the abstractions that shape both are ritualized and concretely manifested.

[1070] Benedict Anderson, "Imagined Communities: Reflections on the Origin and Spread of Nationalism" (London: verso, 1983).

[1071] Karen A. Cerulo, "Sociopolitical Control and the Structure of National Symbols: An Empirical Analysis of National Anthems," Social Forces 68(1):76-99 (1989)

[1072] Tim F. Liao, Gehui Zhang, and Libon Zhang, "Social Foundations of National Anthems: Theorizing for a Better Understanding of the Changing, supra.

[1073] Paul Connerton, *How Societies Remember* (Cambridge, 1989).

[1074] Ibid., p. 3 (our images of the past commonly serve to legitimate a present [and sometimes a future] social order"; Ibid.) .

[1075] Karen A. Cerulo, "Sociopolitical Control and the Structure of National Symbols: An Empirical Analysis of National Anthems," supra, p. 78

[1076] Edward T. Hall, Silent Language (New York: Anchor Books, 1959) ("The link between language and gestures is much closer than between language and . . . other cultural systems" Ibid., p. viii).

The spectacle of the anthem may contribute to continued international reaction. That reaction is bound up in the potency of the Anthem as well as its symbolic signaling. Here the National Anthem Ordinance will likely be understood as an overt (if banal) continuation of efforts to construct a new identity for Hong Kong as a national rather than an international space.[1077] One of the most intriguing is the Inter-Parliamentary Alliance on China (IPAC) an informal multilateral effort beneath the formal layers of government but deeply embedded within it.[1078] But it is likely that unless it plays a collateral role in the de-coupling of the Chinese and American post global trade empires, or plays into the domestic politics of Europe, there is little that will be done other than, as the UK (and Taiwan) indicated, will be the taking in of refugees.

Formal passage of the National Anthem Ordinance (along with the national security law) will further strain relations with the US. Donald Trump has threatened to revoke economic and trading privileges Hong Kong enjoys on the basis that its wide-ranging autonomy has been undermined by Beijing. This speaks to another level of spectacle and gesture, to its cultural politics in the international sphere.[1079] Mike Pompeo, the US secretary of state, on Wednesday met four former student leaders of the 1989 Beijing protests and asked how the US could "help China move towards democracy", according to Wang Dan, a Tiananmen activist. Mr Wang has previously been barred from entering Hong Kong.[1080] But absent the protection of the spectacle of affirmance, it is hard to imagine that the Americans will have much to offer beyond the rituals of contestation at the international level.

And that brings the global order back full circle to a post-global age whose characteristics sometimes mimic that of a time

---

[1077] Caroline Brooke, "Changing Identities: The Russian and Soviet National Anthems," *Slavonica* 13(1):27-38 (2013).

[1078] Discussed in essay Chapter 29, infra.

[1079] Michael Herzfeld, "The cultural politics of gesture: Reflections on the embodiment of ethnographic practice," Ethnography 10(2):131-152 (2009).

[1080] Nicolle Lu and Tom Mitchell, "Hong Kong defies ban to mark Tiananmen Square crackdown," *Financial Times* (4 June 2020); available [https://www.ft.com/content/223449ca-15e9-45ba-9287-9ff8729e4faf].

when global integration was viewed with a certain amount of terror. In the meantime, Western academics will continue to interpret the Sino-British Joint Declaration, perhaps in the hope that if they study it hard enough, the parties will be convinced that it is something worth considering going forward. China will invest substantially more effort into singing its way to unity [1081] --an effort that is likely to be far more effective than the high level discourses of those great doctors of international law interpreting a document made effectively inscrutable by the necessities of politics.

––––––––

National Anthem Bill Contents[1082]

Clause   Page
Part 1 Preliminary
1. Short title   C13
2. Interpretation C13
Part 2
Playing and Singing of National Anthem
3. Standard for playing and singing   C15
4. Etiquette for playing and singing   C15
5. Occasions on which national anthem must be played and Sung C15
Part 3
Protection of National Anthem
6. Offence of misuse of national anthem C19
7. Offence of insulting behaviour C21
8. Music, words or score to be regarded as national anthem, or its lyrics or its score C23
Part 4
Promotion of National Anthem
9. Inclusion in primary and secondary education C27

––––––––––––––

[1081] Stanley Waterman, "National Anthems and National Symbolism: Singing the Nation," in Brunn S., Kehrein R. (eds) *Handbook of the Changing World Language Map* (Dordrecht: Springer, 2020); pp. 2603-2618.
[1082]   Original   available   [https://www.legco.gov.hk/yr18-19/english/bills/b201901111.pdf].

A BILL
To
Provide for the playing and singing of the national anthem, for the protection of the national anthem, and for the promotion of the national anthem, in Hong Kong; and for incidental matters.

Preamble
WHEREAS—

(1) the national anthem of the People's Republic of China is a symbol and sign of the People's Republic of China;

(2)   all individuals and organizations should respect the national anthem, preserve the dignity of the national anthem, and play and sing the national anthem on appropriate occasions; and

(3) an Ordinance is to be enacted to preserve the dignity of the national anthem, to regulate the playing and singing, the broadcast and the use of the national anthem, to enhance citizen awareness of the People's Republic of China, and to promote patriotism:

NOW, THEREFORE, it is enacted by the Legislative Council as follows—

1. Short title

Part 1 Preliminary

This Ordinance may be cited as the National Anthem Ordinance.

2.   Interpretation

(1) In this Ordinance—***national anthem*** (國 歌) means "March of the Volunteers" (a translation of《義勇軍進行曲》), the national anthem of the People's Republic of China under the Constitution of the People's Republic of China; ***national flag*** (國 旗) has the same meaning as in the National Flag and National Emblem Ordinance (116 of 1997).

(2)   In this Ordinance, a reference to the lyrics, and the score, of the national anthem is a reference to—
(a) the lyrics, and the score, set out in the stave notation of the national anthem in Schedule 1; or
(b) the lyrics, and the score, set out in the numbered musical notation of the national anthem in Schedule 2.

(3) In this Ordinance, except in section 5, a reference to playing and singing the national anthem includes—
(a)singing the national anthem;
(b) playing the national anthem on musical instruments; and
(c) playing a recording of the national anthem.

Part 2
Playing and Singing of National Anthem

3. Standard for playing and singing
The national anthem must be played and sung in a way that is   in keeping with its dignity.

4. Etiquette for playing and singing
(1) This section applies in relation to an occasion on which the national anthem is played and sung.
(2) While the national anthem is being played and sung, the etiquette to be followed by the persons who take part in or attend the occasion is—
(a) to stand solemnly and deport themselves with dignity; and
(b) to not behave in a way disrespectful to the national anthem.

5. Occasions on which national anthem must be played and sung

(1)   On each occasion set out in Schedule 3, the national anthem must be played and sung.

(2) The Chief Executive in Council may, by notice published in the Gazette, amend Schedule 3.

(3) In this section, a reference to the national anthem being played and sung is a reference to the national anthem being played on musical instruments in accordance with the standard score, or an official recording of the national anthem being played, for the singing of the national anthem.

(4) In this section—
official recording (官方錄音), in relation to the national anthem, means a recording of the national anthem provided for the purposes of this section on a website of the
Government;
standard score (標準曲譜), in relation to the national anthem, means a score of the national anthem provided for the purposes of this section on a website of the Government.

Part 3
Protection of National Anthem

6. Offence of misuse of national anthem

(1) The national anthem, or the lyrics or score of the national anthem, must not be used—
(a) in a trade mark or commercial advertisement;
(b) at a private funeral event; or
(c) on an occasion, at a place, or for a purpose, prescribed under subsection (5).

2) The national anthem must not be used as background music in a public place.

(3) A person commits an offence if the person, without reasonable excuse, uses the national anthem, or the lyrics or score of the national anthem, in contravention of subsection (1) or (2).

(4) A person who commits an offence under subsection (3) is liable on conviction—
(a) for a contravention of subsection (1)(a)—to a fine at level 5; or
(b) otherwise—to a fine at level 2.

(5)   The Chief Executive in Council may, by notice published in the Gazette, prescribe an occasion, place or purpose, for the purposes of subsection (1)(c).

(6) In this section—
public place (公眾場所) means a place to which the public or a section of the public may or are permitted to have access from time to time, whether by payment or otherwise.

7. Offence of insulting behaviour

(1) A person commits an offence if, with intent to insult the national anthem, the person publicly and intentionally—
(a) alters the lyrics or score of the national anthem; or
(b) plays and sings the national anthem in a distorted or disrespectful way.

(2) A person commits an offence if the person publicly and intentionally insults the national anthem in any way.

(3) A person commits an offence if, with intent to insult the national anthem, the person intentionally publishes—
(a)   altered lyrics or an altered score of the national anthem; or
(b) the national anthem played and sung in a distorted   or disrespectful way.

(4) A person commits an offence if, with intent to insult the national anthem, the person intentionally publishes the insulting in any way of the national anthem.

(5) Except as provided under subsection (3) or (4), a person does not commit an offence under this section by publishing—
(a) altered lyrics or an altered score of the national anthem;
(b) the national anthem played and sung in a distorted   or disrespectful way; or
(c)   the insulting in any way of the national anthem.

(6)   A person who commits an offence under this section is liable on conviction to a fine at level 5 and to imprisonment for 3 years.

(7) Proceedings may only be commenced for an offence under this section before whichever is the earlier of the following—

(a) the end of the period of 1 year after the date on which the offence is discovered by, or comes to the notice of, the Commissioner of Police;
(b) the end of the period of 2 years after the date on which the offence is committed.

(8) In this section—
insult (侮 辱), in relation to the national anthem, means to undermine the dignity of the national anthem as a symbol and sign of the People's Republic of China;
publish (發布) includes—
(a) to communicate to the public in any form, including speaking, writing, printing, displaying notices, broadcasting, screening and playing of tapes or other recorded material; and
(b) to distribute, disseminate or make available to the public.

8. Music, words or score to be regarded as national anthem, or its lyrics or its score
For the purposes of this Part—
(a) a piece of music (whether or not including words intended to be sung or spoken with the music) is to   be regarded as the national anthem if the piece of music so closely resembles the national anthem as to lead to the reasonable belief that the piece of music is the national anthem or a part of the national anthem;
(b) words (whether or not in writing) are to be regarded as the lyrics of the national anthem if the words so closely resemble the lyrics of the national anthem as to lead to the reasonable belief that the words are the lyrics of the national anthem or a part of the lyrics; and
(c)   a score is to be regarded as the score of the national anthem if the score so closely resembles the score of the national anthem as to lead to the reasonable belief that the score is the score of the national anthem or a part of the score of the national anthem.

Part 4
Promotion of National Anthem

9. Inclusion in primary and secondary education
(1)   The Secretary for Education must give directions for the inclusion of the national anthem   in   primary   education   and in secondary education—
(a) to enable the students to learn to sing the national anthem; and
(b) to educate the students—
(i)   on the history and spirit of the national anthem; and
(ii)   on the etiquette for playing and singing the national anthem.

(2)   In this section—
primary education (小學教育) has the meaning given by section 3(1) of the Education Ordinance (Cap. 279);
secondary education (中學教育) has the meaning given by section 3(1) of the Education Ordinance (Cap. 279).

10.   Inclusion in sound broadcasting and domestic television programme services

(1)   This section applies if, under the terms and conditions of   a broadcasting licence, the licensee may be required by a determination or direction of the Communications Authority to broadcast announcements in the public interest, or to include material in the public interest, in the licensed service.

(2) By a determination or direction that has been made in relation to the broadcasting licence, the licensee may be required to broadcast the national anthem by an announcement in the public interest, or material in the public interest, in the licensed service.

(3) The Communications Authority must make a determination or direction in relation to the broadcasting licence, requiring the licensee to broadcast the national anthem by an announcement in the public interest, or material in the public interest, in the licensed service on each date that is or may be stipulated under subsection

(4) The Chief Executive may stipulate a date for the purposes of subsection (3).

(5) A stipulation under subsection (4)—
(a) must be published in the Gazette as soon as practicable after it is made; and
(b) is not subsidiary legislation.

(6)   In this section—**broadcasting licence** (廣播牌照) means—
(a) a licence granted under section 13C(2) of the Telecommunications Ordinance (Cap. 106), or such a licence renewed under section 13E(2) of that Ordinance; or
(b) a licence granted under sections 8(1) and 10(1) of the Broadcasting Ordinance (Cap. 562), or such a licence extended or renewed under section 11(1) of that Ordinance; **Communications Authority** (通訊事務管理局) means the Communications Authority established by section 3 of the Communications Authority Ordinance (Cap. 616).

Part 5 Supplementary Provisions

11. Application of laws of Hong Kong

(1) Offences in relation to the national anthem in Hong Kong are investigated, and persons are prosecuted, according to the laws of Hong Kong.

(2) If there are inconsistencies between this Ordinance and the National Anthem Law, this Ordinance is to be interpreted and applied as a special application or adaptation of the National Anthem Law.

(3) In this section—**National Anthem Law** (《國歌法》) means the Law of the People's Republic of China on National Anthem, adopted at the 29th Meeting of the Standing Committee of the Twelfth National People's Congress on 1 September 2017.

Part 6 Consequential Amendments

Division 1—Enactments Amended
12. Enactments amended

The enactments specified in Divisions 2 and 3 are amended as set out in those Divisions.

Division 2—Amendments to Trade Marks Ordinance (Cap. 559)
13. Section 11 amended (absolute grounds for refusal of registration)

(1)   After section 11(6)(a)— **Add** "(ab) the national anthem;".

(2) Section 11(9), Chinese text, definition of 國旗 and 國徽—

Repeal the full stop Substitute a semicolon.

(3) Section 11(9)—**Add in alphabetical order** "*national anthem* (國歌) means the national anthem and its lyrics and score within the meaning of the National Anthem Ordinance (of 2019) as extended by section 8 of that Ordinance;". Clause 14

Division 3—Amendment to Legislation Publication Ordinance (Cap. 614)
14. Section 4 amended (contents of database)

After section 4(1)(a)(v)—**Add** C35 "(vi) the National Anthem Ordinance (of 2019);".

Schedule 1
Stave Notation of National Anthem * * *

Schedule 2
Numbered Musical Notation of National Anthem * * *

Schedule 3
Occasions on which National Anthem must be Played and Sung

1. Oath-taking Ceremony—
(a) for taking the Oath of the Chief Executive under section 16A of the Oaths and Declarations Ordinance (Cap. 11);
(b)   for taking the Oath of the Principal Officials under section 16B of that Ordinance;
(c)   for taking the Judicial Oath under section 17 of that Ordinance;
(d) for taking the Oath of Fidelity and the Executive Council Oath under section 18 of that Ordinance; or
(e) for   taking the Legislative Council Oath under section 19 of that Ordinance

2. A national flag raising ceremony, including—
(a)   Flag Raising Ceremony held by the Government at Golden Bauhinia Square;
(b) Flag Raising Ceremony held by the Government to celebrate the Anniversary of the Founding of the People's Republic of China; and
(c) Flag Raising Ceremony held by the Government to celebrate the Anniversary of the Establishment of the   Hong Kong Special Administrative Region of the People's Republic of China

3. National Day Reception held by the Government to celebrate the Anniversary of the Founding of the People's Republic of China

4. Reception held by the Government to celebrate the Anniversary of the Establishment of the Hong Kong Special Administrative Region of the People's Republic of China

5. Ceremony held by the Government to commemorate the victory day of Chinese people's war of resistance against Japanese aggression

6. Ceremony held by the Government to commemorate those who died in the defence of Hong Kong

7. Ceremony held by the Government on Nanjing Massacre National Memorial Day

8. A major sporting event held by the Government

9. Ceremonial Opening of the Legal Year

Explanatory Memorandum

The objects of this Bill are to provide—
(a)   for the playing and singing of the national anthem;
(b)   for the protection of the national anthem;
(c)   for the promotion of the national anthem; and
(d)   for incidental matters.

2. The preamble sets out certain information to provide a context in which to understand the Bill. The Law of the People's Republic of China on National Anthem is listed in Annex III to the Basic Law. The Bill is to implement the Law of the People's Republic of China on National Anthem in Hong Kong.

Part 1—Preliminary (Clauses 1 and 2)
3. Clause 1 sets out the short title.

4. Clause 2 contains the definitions of **national anthem** and **national flag**. It also explains the meaning of a reference to the lyrics, and the score, of the national anthem, and a reference to
playing and singing the national anthem.

Part 2—Playing and Singing of National Anthem (Clauses 3 to 5)
5. Clause 3 provides for the standard for playing and singing the national anthem.

6. Clause 4 provides for the etiquette to be followed by the persons who take part in or attend an occasion while the national anthem is being played and sung.

7. Clause 5 provides for the playing and singing of the national anthem on each occasion set out in Schedule 3.

Part 3—Protection of National Anthem (Clauses 6 to 8)
8. Clause 6 prohibits misuse of the national anthem or its lyrics or score. A contravention of the prohibition is an offence.

9. Clause 7 prohibits a person from publicly and intentionally altering the lyrics or score of the national anthem, and from so playing and singing the national anthem in a distorted or disrespectful way, with intent to insult the national anthem. This clause also prohibits a person

from publicly and intentionally insulting the national anthem in any way. It further prohibits a person from intentionally publishing the altered lyrics or score, intentionally publishing the national anthem played and sung in a distorted or disrespectful way, or intentionally publishing the insulting in any way of the national anthem, with intent to insult the national anthem. Clause 7(8) contains the definitions of *insult* and *publish* for the purposes of the prohibitions. A contravention of any of the prohibitions is an offence.

10.   Clause 8 provides that a piece of music, words or a score is to be regarded as the national anthem or its lyrics or score for the purposes of Part 3 if the piece of music, words or score so closely resembles the national anthem or its lyrics or score as to lead to the reasonable belief that the piece of music, words or score is the national anthem or its lyrics or score, or part of the national anthem or its lyrics or score.

Part 4—Promotion of National Anthem (Clauses 9 and 10)
11.   Clause 9 requires the Secretary for Education to give directions for the inclusion of the national anthem in primary education and in secondary education.

12.   Clause 10 applies if, under the terms and conditions of a sound broadcasting licence or domestic television licence, the licensee may be required by a determination or direction of the Communications Authority to broadcast announcements in the public interest, or to include material in the public interest, in the licensed service. By a determination or direction that has been made in relation to the licence, the licensee may be required to broadcast the national anthem by an announcement or material in the public interest in the licensed service. Moreover, the Communications Authority must make a determination or direction in relation to the licence, requiring the licensee to broadcast the national anthem by an announcement or material in the public interest in the licensed service on each date that is or may be stipulated by the Chief Executive.

Part 5—Supplementary Provisions (Clause 11)
13.   Clause 11 provides that offences in relation to the national anthem in Hong Kong are investigated, and persons are prosecuted, according to the laws of Hong Kong. This clause also provides that if there are inconsistencies between the Ordinance and the Law of the People's Republic of China on National Anthem, the Ordinance is to be interpreted and applied as a special application or adaption of that Law.

Part 6—Consequential Amendments

14.   Clauses 13 and 14 contain consequential amendments.

Schedules

15.   Schedule 1 sets out the lyrics and score of the national anthem in a stave notation.

16.   Schedule 2 sets out the lyrics and score of the national anthem in a numbered musical notation.

17.   Schedule 3 sets out the occasions on which the national anthem must be played and sung under clause 5.

✳ ✳ ✳

Chapter 29

Friday, 5 June 2020
Creating the Inter-Parliamentary Alliance on China; Signifying the June 4th incident (六四事件) and the Democratic International: The International Response to the HK National Security Law

These essays have been chronicling the measures taken by Chinese central authorities to re-frame the basis on which Hong Kong's status, going forward to full absorption, perhaps before the official end of the term of the Sino-British Joint Declaration in 2047.[1083] Ironically, it now appears that the measures undertaken by all sides in the contest between the Chinese central authorities, Hong Kong protesters, and the international community has had the singular consequence of detaching the state of the political model for Hong Kong from the Sino-British Joint Declaration.[1084]

One can now more clearly observe the elaboration of measures, at least from the Chinese side, that seem to be moving the "One Country, Two Systems" principle, from one grounded on international law guarantees, to one grounded on national constitutional principles and protections.[1085] To that end the Sino-British Joint Declaration no longer has any meaning for Chinese officials. [1086] At the same time one can note the profound change

---

[1083] Joint Declaration of the Government of the United Kingdom of Great Britain and Northern Ireland and the Government of the People's Republic of China on the Question of Hong Kong (19 December 1984); available [https://www.cmab.gov.hk/en/issues/jd2.htm].

[1084] Discussed in essay, Chapter 25, supra.

[1085] Discussed in its most recent manifestation in essay Chapter 27, supra.

[1086] "The Commissioner's Office urges some British politicians to change course and avoid going further down the wrong path," Statement of the Office of the Commissioner of the Ministry of Foreign Affairs of the People's Republic of China in the Hong Kong Special Administrative Region (4 June 2020); available [http://www.fmcoprc.gov.hk/eng/gsxw/t1785715.htm]. This is not the first time the central authorities have taken this position. See, "China says Sino-British Joint Declaration on Hong Kong no longer has meaning," *Reuters* (30 June 2017);

on the side of the Hong Kong protesters. They are no longer content, as they were before July 2019, to contest one off legislation that might appear to encroach on their freedoms. Now they increasingly see their political-economic model under To Systems principles as protected against encroachment even by the state under superior principles of international law and its guarantees of civil and political rights.[1087] For them, Hong Kong's political way of life is inherent in their own political culture and thus protected by international law and norms beyond the technical guarantees of the Sino-British Joint Declaration.[1088]

Hong Kong's internationalism, of course, has caused a substantial engagement with the foreign by central and local authorities. These essays have suggested that all of these measures taken by Chinese central authorities will produce not just reaction in Hong Kong, but also among those members of the international community who continue to hold a different view of the Sino-British Joint Declaration and its continuing international character, at least through 2047.[1089] That engagement by Chinese officials appears to have had two thrusts. The first is to distill ad detach Hong Kong from the mainstreams of foreign law, politics, culture, societal expectations and connections. The second is to more deeply embed Hong Kong within its national context, free of foreign influence.[1090] This effort, to some extent, situates the situation in Hong Kong within larger conversations in China about the role and effect of foreign influence on its own development.[1091]

---

available   [https://www.reuters.com/article/us-hongkong-anniversary-china/china-says-sino-british-joint-declaration-on-hong-kong-no-longer-has-meaning-idUSKBN19L1J1] ("It was not immediately clear if Foreign Ministry spokesman Lu Kang was attacking just the idea of continued British involvement in Hong Kong, which marks the 20th anniversary of Chinese rule on Saturday, or the principles in the document.")-.

[1087] See discussion essay Chapter 17, supra.

[1088] Discussed in essays Chapters 17-18, supra.

[1089] Discussed in essays Chapters 10-11; 14-15, supra.

[1090] Discussed in essays Chapters 7-8, 13, 16, supra.

[1091] This is nicely described in Han Liu, "Regime-Centered and Court-Centered Understandings: The Reception of American Constitutional Law in Contemporary China," *The American Journal of Comparative Law* 68(1):95-150 (2020) (describing the golden age of projection of the ideologies of American judicial review into China and its reception by academic and administrative elites

Despite increasingly more pointed protests and challenges by the Chinese central authorities, the international community has also elaborated its position to be more in line with that of the Hong Kong protesters, as popular manifestations in Hong Kong have changed in scope and character since June 2019. [1092] That alignment, however, appears to have been reactive. [1093] There is little to suggest that the international community is driving the normative thrust of events despite the best efforts of Chinese officials to paint a different picture. But that reaction can be potent (at least within the international community within which China seeks to assume a leading role), at least potentially, in response to emerging Chinese measures against the protesters.

To some extent, it is the United States rather than the United Kingdom that appears to have assumed the mantel of mouthpiece for traditional internationalism applied to the situation in Hong Kong. As was recently reported:

> So far, the U.S. has led the backlash against the Chinese central government's decision to bypass Hong Kong's legislature and institute a national security law in the region. When Beijing announced the measure on May 21, U.S. officials declared their opposition almost immediately. They called it a "death knell" for Hong Kong's freedoms, introduced a bipartisan bill to sanction Chinese authorities who enforce the law, and released statements condemning it as a "violation" of the Sino-British Joint Declaration. Trump then promised to yank the city's trade privileges.[1094]

---

before it was substantially transformed and diminished from the start of the leadership of Xi Jinping)). See also essay Chapter 16, *supra.*

[1092] Discussed in essays Chapters 10-11; 14-15, supra.

[1093] Discussed in essay chapter 23, supra.

[1094] Naomi Xu Elegant, "Why the U.S. acts as an enforcer of the Hong Kong deal between Britain and Beijing," *Fortune* (4 June 2020); available [https://fortune.com/2020/06/04/us-enforce-hong-kong-handover-uk-china/]

That is another irony, especially given the position of the Trump Administration on internationalism generally and multilateralism specifically.[1095] But again, mirroring the context in which Chinese officials act, for American officials the situation in Hong Kong is deeply contextualized within the now quite fluid realignment of relations between the United States and the People's Republic. To those ends, Hong Kong appears to be a convenient piece to be played in a much more significant game.[1096]

One of the most interesting responses of the international community under the leadership of important figures in the United States, has been informal, but potentially no less powerful for its character. Lawmakers from several countries announced on Friday the formation of a new coalition formed to counter the "challenge" presented by China's ascendancy on the world stage.[1097] The Inter-Parliamentary Alliance on China (IPAC) [對華政策跨國議會聯盟对华政策跨国议会联盟对中政策に関する列国議会連盟] is comprised of 18 politicians, including U.S. Senators Marco Rubio and Robert Menendez. Other members represent Australia, Canada, Germany, Japan, Norway, Sweden, the U.K. and the European Parliament.[1098]

The group's stated mission is to increase collaboration between "like-minded legislators" to craft a "strategic approach" on issues related to China.[1099] One of its core principles is quite

---

[1095] Michele Kelemen, "Secretary Of State Pompeo Blasts Past U.S. Multilateralism, Defends 'America First'," NPR (4 December 2018); available [https://www.npr.org/2018/12/04/673397981/secretary-of-state-pompeo-blasts-past-u-s-multilateralism-defends-america-first].

[1096] Ibid. ("Washington sees Hong Kong and the city's special trade status as a means by which it can retaliate against Beijing for its treatment of the city and for other, separate grievances.").

[1097] Marco Rubio, in a video posted on Twitter announcing the launch of the group; Inter-Parliamentary Alliance on China, "Today we Launch #IPAC" (4 June 2020); available [https://twitter.com/ipacglobal/status/1268678597868388358].

[1098] Amy Gunia, "Lawmakers Form Global Coalition to Tackle the China 'Challenge'," *Time* (5 June 2020); available [https://time.com/5848808/inter-parliamentary-alliance-china/].

[1099] Inter-Parliamentary Alliance on China, "What We Do" (no date last accessed 15 March 2021); available [https://ipac.global/].

relevant: "A free, open, and rules-based international order that supports human dignity is created and maintained through intention. The persistence of such an order requires like-minded countries to participate actively in its governance and enforcement." [1100] This is a core responsibility of democratic states.[1101] Here one can better understand the most potent of the consequences of the protests in Hong Kong, at least for the liberal democratic order--the detachment of Hong Kong's political model from Chinese operational sovereignty, and its embedding within an international baseline governance order.[1102]

IPAC members have developed a five point strategy that is meant to coordinate action by the liberal democratic state camp "and to help craft a proactive and strategic approach on issues related to the People's Republic of China." [1103] These include (1) safeguarding the international rules based order; [1104] (2) protecting human rights;[1105] (3) promoting far trade practices;[1106] (4) strengthening security; [1107] and (5) protecting national integrity.[1108] In a sense, the situation in Hong Kong constitutes a peripheral point of conflict within the much broader parameters of the five point strategy. Nonetheless, Hong Kong is deeply embedded within them as the point of contact for clashes between the two systems.

[1100] Ibid. "Statement."

[1101] Ibid.

[1102] Amy Gunia, "Lawmakers Form Global Coalition to Tackle the China 'Challenge'," ("The organization describes its goals as safeguarding the international rules-based order, upholding human rights, promoting fair trade, strengthening security and promoting national integrity.")

[1103] Inter-Parliamentary Alliance on China, "What We Do," supra.

[1104] Ibid. ("The People's Republic of China must be held to the standards of the international legal order, which itself must be protected from distortion").

[1105] Ibid. ("Relations between states and the PRC must give due prominence to universal human rights").

[1106] Ibid. ("The PRC must be held to the standards of the rules based order, especially those as set out by the World Trade Organization").

[1107] Ibid. ("Democracies must develop complementary security strategies to address challenges presented by the PRC").

[1108] Ibid. ("The PRC must not be permitted to compromise the sovereignty or institutions of any developed or emerging markets through lending, investment, or by any other means").

Indeed, by September 2020 IPAC posted a summary of its initial Hong Kong campaign.[1109] The campaign calls for the liberal democratic camp to develop and implement a principled and coordinated response to what is termed China's "clear breach of its treaty obligations to the citizens of Hong Kong, [which] will severely undermine the rights of 7 million Hong Kong citizens, and [which] poses a grave challenge to the international community."[1110] That principled and coordinated response to Chinese measures that ultimately were expressed in the passage of the National Security law,[1111] were divided into three parts. First, the campaign focused on the development of policy designed to reduce strategic dependency on China. "This should form part of a broader effort to review and recalibrate relations with the People's Republic of China, at both a national and international level."[1112] Second, the campaign looked to coordinate efforts to offer sanctuary to Hong Kong's protesters, which "would offer a path for Hong Kong citizens seeking an escape route as a last resort."[1113] The last would directly invoke the mechanisms of UN centered internationalism by demanding that the UN "Secretary General to designate a UN Special Envoy to monitor and to report on Hong Kong."[1114] Ultimately, the object of the IPAC coalition is to coordinate a disciplinary response to Chinese measures, one deeply entwined within the web of international (or at least liberal democratic) consensus.[1115]

The object of IPAC, then, appears to be to create a "Democratic International." More specifically, IPAC is based on the belief that China represents a global challenge which must be countered by the principles of traditional Western liberal democracy. This was expressed in a video widely circulated on Twitter (it seems that Twitter has become the most important

---

[1109] See IPAC, "Campaign: Hong Kong" (posted 8 September 2020); available [https://ipac.global/campaign-hong-kong/].
[1110] Ibid.
[1111] Discussed in essays Chapters 24-25 , supra.
[1112] Ibid.
[1113] Ibid.
[1114] Ibid.
[1115] Ibid. ("It is crucial that the People's Republic of China is held accountable for its international treaty obligations to the people of Hong Kong.").

means of political communication in this decade) by Marco Rubio, and legislators from a number of other states, who served as the initial constituting group around which IPAC was organized make this clear.[1116] That democratic internationalism is nicely described in the five strategies of IPAC as well as in its Hong Kong campaign. And it nicely aligns with Marco Rubio's direction of the Congressional Executive Commission on China on which he served as co-chair.[1117] These objectives, then, are to be applied not just to the situation in Hong Kong but also elsewhere to establish a baseline for defining global relations with China. Related to that objective is another: But also in disciplining political elements within the liberal democratic order who stray from these core organizing principles.

The power of the establishment of IPAC, and what it suggests about the potential rise of a new "Democratic International," requires a powerful public signification. To that end, it comes as no surprise that the announcement of the establishment of IPAC should coincide with the anniversary of the June 4th 1989 Incident at Tiananmen Square. That felicitous timing is also amplified by the simultaneous blockage of the traditional commemoration of that anniversary in Hong Kong.[1118] Indeed, both Chinese and Western liberal democratic actors have sought to amplify their actions against each other and within Hong Kong around this anniversary and for very good reason. But each draws different lessons, and each seeks the alignment of the anniversary with the legitimization of the two diverging poles of rationalizing Hong Kong's status--the one centered around its national character, and the other around its international status.

[1116] Marco Rubio and others, "Today we Launch #IPA" (4 June 2020), video posted on Twitter announcing the launch of IPAC); available [https://twitter.com/ipacglobal/status/1268678597868388358].

[1117] "The Congressional-Executive Commission on China was created by Congress in October 2000 with the legislative mandate to monitor human rights and the development of the rule of law in China, and to submit an annual report to the President and the Congress." Congressional-Executive Commission on China, "About"; available [https://www.cecc.gov/about]. See also discussion essay at Chapter 15, supra.

[1118] Discussed in essay Chapter 27, supra.

The anniversaries of events which in retrospect are constructed as significant--that is whose meaning acquires political and cultural importance for collectives--tend to serve as important objects, signs, which become critical elements of collective meaning making. That meaning making has both active and passive aspects. *Its passive aspects* are historical--in the sense that the event becomes a past object whose meaning produces principles, taboos, and ways of thinking about the world--socio-political lessons--which can then be taken by those who must measure the risks of their behavior or choices against the "lessons" of the event now encased in governance meaning. In this aspect it serves as a regulatory device--the meaning of the event provides the measure against which current actions can be assessed. Anniversaries reinforce the legitimacy and continued power of collective meaning making through the rituals of memory--these are pageants for the reaffirmation and reinforcement of meaning making through which a society constitutes itself. They make the assessment and disciplinary aspects (the meaning) of the commemorated event self-evident.

Just as important, anniversaries have increasingly important *positive or active aspects*. It is in this aspect that the anniversary (and the lessons of the underlying event commemorated) is invoked to extend meaning--to leverage its lessons for application to another event. Additionally, anniversaries can be used to align new meaning making with the past event, and in that way to seek to legitimate it. This extension by analogy or invocation has played a powerful role in social or political movements. Mass society tends to prefer the development of collective meaning through the construction of analogy and the exercise of aligning current triggering events (that can be exploited for these ends) to past events which have been invested with cultural-political significance.

It is in this sense that an anniversary provides a means of signifying a current event. Here the anniversary brings the event forward as a meaning-object (a bundle of meaning) that can serve to contribute (and shape) not just the interpretation of current events--but also to legitimate reactions and responses to them. It is important here to distinguish between the *anniversary* as an amplifying object, and the underlying *event* that is commemorated. The underlying event provides meaning and legitimacy. The invocation on the anniversary provides the necessary alignment between the past event (and its "lessons" teaching, directions, commends, etc.) and current action.

The anniversary of 1989 Tiananmen Protests, the June 4th incident (六四事件) has become a powerful anniversary both within and outside of China. The underlying event involved the eventual suppression of the '89 Democracy Movement involved in popular manifestations demanding political change and occupying Tiananmen Square in central Beijing. The popular manifestations had started in mid-April 1989 and ended on June 4 when the government declared martial law and sent the military to occupy central parts of Beijing. The event acquired greater symbolic importance because during the course of events on 4th June 1989 military units ordered to clear out Tiananmen Square fired into the crowd trying to block the military's advance causing substantial death and injury to the protestors.

The lessons drawn from the events by Chinese officials was very different from that drawn by officials elsewhere. For Chinese officials, the incident reinforced a wariness of more open and robust popular manifestation and of the danger of the forms of liberal democratic expression for the integrity of its political-economic model. It is a reminder of the need to protect that system from reactionary elements who use the cover of popular manifestation to seek revolution. For liberal democrats it was interpreted in almost the opposite way, as the suppression of democratic expression and the thwarting of the will of the people through disproportionate use of force.

Tiananmen (the June 4th Incident) remains highly sensitive in China, where its commemoration is not encouraged. But it is also highly sensitive elsewhere where its commemoration is encouraged, especially in liberal democratic Western states, and Hong Kong. And, indeed, the anniversary of the June 4th Incident has been used increasingly as a marker of the transformation of Hong Kong.

From the Chinese side, the anniversary is the time to reinforce, by action, measures which tend to reinforce the core lessons and meaning of the event. This is the time to reaffirm the paramount importance of the stability and integrity of the state, of sovereignty and the suspicion that instability is at base a manifestation of foreign interference or the corruption of foreign ideas, of the reaffirmation of the political-economic system and particularly the leading role of the Chinese Communist Party. The anniversary would be the time to reaffirm the supremacy of responsibility for the advancement of economic, social, and cultural rights under the guidance of the vanguard, and to reinforce the lesson that civil and political rights may be best manifested through the established institutionalized collective in the service of economic, social and cultural objectives. It is no surprise, then, that the period around the June 4th Incident would be the time that Chinese authorities would move forward the National Security Law for China, then block commemoration of the June 4th Incident within its national borders (as something bordering on declarations of disloyalty to the state and its governance order), and then push through the National Anthem Law for Hong Kong.[1119]

From the side of the Hong Kong democrats, and leading elements of liberal democratic states, the anniversary of the June 4th incident is the time to reaffirm the lessons of that event as well. But those lessons are very different--the inevitable progression toward the rejection of the Marxist-Leninist political-economic model, the illegitimacy of violent suppression of popular manifestations of political will, and the reaffirmation of the supremacy of civil and political rights within any governance order. The anniversary, for liberal democrats, is also the moment to reaffirm their conviction of the illegitimacy of vanguard governance (at least when institutionalized within a Leninist organization), the primacy of individual over collective rights, and the supremacy of human rights discourse in the ordering of states and societal orders.

[1119] See essay in Chapter 28, supra.

Lastly, it is a time, for certain elements of this liberal democratic collective, to advance a positive aspect of the anniversary--the ideal of the supremacy of international law and norms, and of international collective constraints on national organization and manifestations of political power. It is no surprise, then, that this would be the time to establish the Inter-Parliamentary Alliance on China (IPAC) as an informal international organization of leading political figures acting informally but always able to marshal national political authority at the appropriate moments. It is the time when states can (whatever their motivation or objectives) impose sanctions on Chinese officials under cover of the de-legitimating lesson commemorated in the West around the June 4th Incident.

And lastly, it is the perfect moment for the Congressional-Executive Commission on China (created by the U.S. Congress in 2000 "with the legislative mandate to monitor human rights and the development of the rule of law in China, and to submit an annual report to the President and the Congress")[1120] to reinforce its mission. The establishment of IPAC was certainly an important element of that strategy. But it was not the only action taken. In addition to statements which appear on its website,[1121] and this year more pointedly through the introduction of a bipartisan resolution on the thirty-first anniversary of the June 4th Incident drives home the point.[1122] In a statement delivered with the introduction of the resolution, CECC Commissioner Vicky Hartzler (R-MO) declared: "Hong Kong represents a brave bastion of individual freedom, democracy, and free market capitalism in the face of China's constant authoritarian threat. I applaud their courage in their advocacy for the freedom of expression, a chilling

---

[1120] HR 4444 (106th Congress 2000), §§ 301-309, as part of the China Trade Bill of that year; available [https://www.cecc.gov/about/legislative-mandate].

[1121] See Congressional-Executive Commission on China, "Tiananmen at 31: Commissioners Introduce Bipartisan Resolution and Condemn Imposition of National Security Law in Hong Kong" (4 June 2020); available [https://www.cecc.gov/media-center/press-releases/tiananmen-at-31-commissioners-introduce-bipartisan-commemorative].

[1122] The text of the House Resolution may be accessed here [https://www.cecc.gov/sites/chinacommission.house.gov/files/documents/S MITNJ_203_xml%20%28002%29.pdf].

reality 31 years after China's brutal crackdown of the protests in Tiananmen Square."[1123]

And, thus, of course, the anniversary powerfully amplifies the message consistently delivered by Marco Rubio, of one of the CECC co-chairs, and a past candidate for the presidency of the United States, in forming the Inter-Parliamentary Alliance on China (IPAC) and directing its work.[1124] IPAC will be as powerful a force for the disciplining of liberal democratic principles as it presents a challenge to Chinese authorities. These disciplinary actions have already been much in evidence in the United States. In November 2019, the United States had enacted the Hong Kong Human Rights and Democracy Act,[1125] This measure was meant to augment the policy originally embedded in the United States-Hong Kong Policy Act of 1992.[1126] An additional measure is also

---

[1123] Congressional-Executive Commission on China, "Tiananmen at 31, *supra* ("The aggressive actions taken by communist Beijing over the last year against Hong Kong and its people, shows the world exactly what China's agenda is – suppression of peaceful demonstrations, degradation of democratic institutions, and a lack of regard over Hong Kong's autonomy. I applaud all Members signing onto this resolution, solidifying America's unity to Hong Kong and their cause for freedom""").

[1124] Congressional-Executive Commission on China, "Tiananmen at 31, *supra* (quoting Marco Rubio at the time of the introduction of the House Resolution on the anniversary of the June 4th incident "As the Chinese government and Communist Party continues to systematically repress its citizens as well as Uyghurs, Tibetans, and actively undermines Hong Kong's autonomy, the United States remains committed to honoring the memories of those who perished and keeping their legacy alive.")

[1125] Pub. L. 116-76, 113 Stat. 1161; 22 U.S.C. ¶¶5725-5726 (Hong Kong Human Rights and Democracy Act of 2019); available [https://www.congress.gov/bill/116th-congress/house-bill/3289] ("This bill addresses Hong Kong's status under U.S. law and imposes sanctions on those responsible for human rights violations in Hong Kong. (Hong Kong is part of China but has a largely separate legal and economic system."). For an excellent discussion, see, Jason Buhi, "America's New Covenant with Hong Kong: The Hong Kong Human Rights and Democracy Act of 2019," *Texas International Law Journal* 55(2): 269-295 (2020).

[1126] Robert Delaney and Owen Churchill, "Donald Trump signs Hong Kong Human Rights and Democracy Act into law, brushing off China's warnings," South China Morning Post (28 November 2019); available [https://www.scmp.com/news/china/diplomacy/article/3039673/donald-trump-signs-hong-kong-human-rights-and-democracy-act] ("The law will, among other mandates, allow Washington to suspend Hong Kong's special

working its way through Congress, one that will add potentially significant bite to U.S. countermeasures against China (and reduce the favorable trade position of Hong Kong). The Hong Kong Autonomy Act, [1127] was introduced as another American countermeasure against Chinese passage of the Hong Kong National Security Law. "The bill is a response to moves by Beijing to impose a new national security law over Hong Kong, a move that critics fear will effectively ban all opposition activity in the city.... As well as punitive measures against individuals, the Hong Kong Autonomy Act requires sanctions against any foreign financial institution that knowingly conduct "significant transactions" – as defined by the US Treasury – with the designated individuals."[1128]

Thus emerges the length and extent of the internationalist counterthrust against China's efforts to transform the One Country-Two Systems principle more to its liking and better aligned with its political-economic model and its governing ideology. The counterthrusts do the same thing in reverse--under the leadership of the United States, they impose costs on states that undermine core internationalist values through programs of targeted sanctions and move forward the liberal democratic camp's redevelopment of a multilateral network of like-minded political figures to ensure the dominance of its vision in international circles. The Hong Kong Human Rights and Democracy Act was emblematic. As Jason Buhi noted: " the HKHRDA's narrow focus carries with it a clear diplomatic message that the U.S. remains willing to address Hong Kong issues as Hong Kong issues should the PRC maintain the status quo. Should mainland authorities attempt to exert more direct control of the city, however, the HKHRDA may quickly find

---

trading status based on an annual certification by the US State Department about whether the city retains a sufficient degree of autonomy under the "one country, two systems" framework").

[1127] Pub. 116-149 (116th Congress, July 2020).

[1128] Owen Churchill and Robert Delaney, "US Senate passes bill that could punish China for Hong Kong national security law," South China Morning Post (26 June 2020); available [https://www.scmp.com/news/world/united-states-canada/article/3090631/us-senate-passes-bill-would-punish-china-hong-kong].

itself a secondary consideration as U.S. policy toward Hong Kong gets swept into broader Sino-American foreign policy disputes."[1129]

Together these acts suggest now that the internationalist position on Hong Kong remains strong enough to generate legislation, and solidarity among developed states. But are the measures developed strong enough to have effect? Certainly if one measures the effects by its power to change China's course of action, then the answer is likely no. On the other hand, if one measures the effects by its ability to discipline the liberal democratic camp to advance its normative agenda, then the answer might be a qualified yes. More importantly it suggests the continued authority of the United States to take the lead. That perhaps is the greatest value of these measures. But then, in a very real sense, that is perhaps the greatest value of the National Security Law for the Chinese. In the end, the issue is about leadership. And what is now more clearly emerging through the imposition of measures and countermeasures is that both the United States and China are willing to ensure their respective leadership roles within their respective camps, and in the process continue to guide the development of their respective political-economic models.

* * *

[1129] Buhi, "America's New Covenant with Hong Kong," supra., p. 293.

Chapter 30

Wednesday 1 July 2020

Fundamental Principles (Fu Yan 符言): On the Ideological Thrust of the Draft "Law of the People's Republic of China on the Maintenance of National Security" 《中华人民共和国香港特别行政区维护国家安全法（草案）》

> Regions governed by the principles of stability, savior-faire, scrupulosity, and serenity enjoy prosperity without exception. Be skillful in diplomacy but cause uneasiness. Remain humble, mindful, calm, and good willed on the watch for conquest and demolishment.[1130]

Many of the critical responses by central and local authorities since the start of the June 2019 protests evidence the strategic insights of Guiguzi (鬼谷子), the ancient collection of texts on rhetoric and statecraft compiled from the time of the Warring States period and faithful to 道教 (Dàojiào).[1131] That connection with ancient understandings of the way, the path toward success, is very much in evidence at this moment. Having waited patiently for the greater part of a year (and after what, from its perspectives have been provocations and warning shots dating back to at least 2014 in current form), the vanguard has now acted decisively an in an act the character of which is unmistakable. It is imbued with the counsel of Guiguzi's Fundamental Principles (Fu Yan 符言). "The master of people (ren

---

[1130] Guiguzi（鬼谷子）, *Guiguzi: China's First Treatise on Rhetoric; A Critical Translation and Commentary* (Hui Wu (trans.); Carbondale: Southern Illinois University Press, 2016 (before 220 A.D.)); Book II.12.1, p. 483((Fundamental Principles (Fu Yan 符言)).

[1131] Guiguzi also serves as a useful framing of strategic and rhetorical choices in other important respects considered in the essays, supra, at Chapter 3 (Mend-Break (Di Xi 抵巇)), Chapters 8 (Assessing (Quan 權)), Chapter 12 (Resist-Reconcile (忤合 Wuhe)), Chapter 20 ((Open-Shut (Bai He 稗閤)), and now in this Chapter 30 (Fundamental Principles (Fu Yan 符言)).

zhu 人主) cannot be thorough enough. Without thoroughness, all officials become unruly. When a family dysfunctions, its exterior and interior connections are broken. It does not know if it is open. When the open-shut is in a chaotic condition, it is impossible to see the basics."[1132]

Since the end of May 2020, when the National People's Congress approved the drafting and enactment of a National Security Law for Hong Kong, there has been much anticipation of its content. [1133] That action alone decisively realized the internalization of Hong Kong's political future within the Chinese domestic legal and constitutional order. It served as well as the performance of that sovereign expression--the act of asserting sovereignty, not just over the physical space that is Hong Kong, but over its political system without interference from or attachment to the international order from out of which that sovereignty was recognized. That performance undertaken on the stage of the National People's Congress was a very necessary final step in the formal expression of Chinese authority and independence. It served as the declaration of national power and simultaneously a rejection of Western forms of internationalism that had been the basis of much of the global conversation around globalization since the elimination of the Soviet imperial system in the late 1980s that had so captured the imagination of Western intellectual and political elites.[1134]

In the drafting and enactment of the National Security Law the central authorities put the capstone on a long developing strategy to bring Hong Kong "home"--the unruly province is made to conform to its principal responsibilities to the center. Now

---

[1132] Guiguzi (鬼谷子), *Guiguzi: China's First Treatise on Rhetoric; A Critical Translation and Commentary,* supra, Book II.12.7.

[1133] Yen Nee Lee, "China approves controversial national security bill for Hong Kong," *CNBC* (28 May 220); available [https://www.cnbc.com/2020/05/28/china-approves-proposal-to-impose-national-security-law-in-hong-kong.html] ("The NPC voted 2,878 to 1 in favor of the bill, which will pave the way for its Standing Committee — a smaller decision-making body — to proceed to working out details of the legislation to be implemented in Hong Kong. Six abstained from the vote").

[1134] Francis Fukuyama, *The End of History and the Last Man* (NY: Fee Press, 1992)

detached from a reliance on forces that gather beyond the borders of the state, the people are again reminded that they must inward, not outward, in the ordering of their affairs and in the construction of the political structures within which provincial affairs may be ordered to achieve a centrally managed prosperity and stability. That is the essence of *Fu Yan* 符言 realized through the imposition of the National Security Law. It is the summation strategy--the culmination act of the rhetorical strategies invoked during the course of the year.[1135] It serves as the signification of the transformation of One Country-Two Systems through law--aligning its name with its reality.[1136]

In the process of that alignment, or repairing the dysfunctions within this unruly special administrative region, Hong Kong is now witnessing the penultimate step in that process of being folded back into the sovereign order of the nation. The process of its production was spectacular.[1137] The description of what was to become the National Security Law was announced on 20 June through a detailed description of what is anticipated to be the text of the Hong Kong National Security Law circulated through the Xinhua news organ.[1138]. It is likely close to final and

---

[1135] Guiguzi (鬼谷子), *Guiguzi: China's First Treatise on Rhetoric; A Critical Translation and Commentary*, supra, Book II.12.8 ("Remain attentively quiet and watch the world beyond reach to gain insight. All evil makes its move in the dark").

[1136] In their commentaries to this part of Guiguzi, Hui Wu and C. Jan Swearingen note the intimate connection of this rhetorical approach with Western semiotics and the even earlier Augustinian tradition of naming. Guiguzi (鬼谷子), *Guiguzi: China's First Treatise on Rhetoric; A Critical Translation and Commentary*, supra, n. 179.

[1137] On the value and use of spectacle and gesture in the decisive moves by the central authorities to transform the base operating rules for Hong Kong autonomy as practiced and as a legal artifact, see discussion essay Chapter 28, supra.

[1138] "法制工作委员会负责人向十三届全国人大常委会第十九次会议作关于《中华人民共和国香港特别行政区维护国家安全法（草案）》的说明 2020 年 06 月 20 日 [The person in charge of the Legal Affairs Commission gave an explanation on the "Law of the Hong Kong Special Administrative Region of the People's Republic of China on Maintaining National Security (Draft)" to the 19th meeting of the 13th National People's Congress Standing Committee, June 20, 2020]; available [http://npc.people.cn/n1/2020/0620/c14576-31753969.html].

appears ready for enactment. "The details of the law's 66 articles were kept secret until after it was passed. . . . The law came into effect at 23:00 local time on 30 June, an hour before the 23rd anniversary of the city's handover to China from British rule."[1139] Again, the importance of spectacle to drive home the point--Hong Kong no longer expresses its autonomy through the superior principle of Two Systems; rather China expresses its responsibility to its patriotic peoples through autonomy granted under the superior One Country principle. As for the rest--they are expected to comply with law or be punished now in accordance with law.

The gesture of secrecy ought not to be dismissed for the power of its symbolism. "Only a handful of people had seen the full text of the law before it was enacted, a source of considerable controversy in Hong Kong. They did not include the territory's Chief Executive, Carrie Lam."[1140] The signification could not be lost on all of the factions of Hong Kong (as well as on foreign elements deeply invested in the debate about the character and status of Hong Kong). That secrecy also had psychological and strategic effect. The local factions were caught unprepared to meet these developments. "The lack of extensive consultation of even Hong Kong's top officials and legal chiefs is stoking concerns among lawyers in the city, who fear China will undermine the rule of law by trampling on the British-style judiciary that is independent from government as a deliberate separation of powers."[1141] At the same time they had nothing concrete against which to organize manifestations of resistance--and especially manifestations of resistance that might be used to mobilize the global community invested in an internationalist character for

---

[1139] "Hong Kong security law: What is it and is it worrying?," *BBC News* (30 June 2020); available [https://www.bbc.com/news/world-asia-china-52765838].
[1140] Ibid.
[1141] Natasha Khan, "Hong Kong Lawyers Warn China's Security Law Will Erode Legal Autonomy," *The Wall Street Journal* (26 June 2020); available [https://www.wsj.com/articles/hong-kong-lawyers-warn-chinas-security-law-will-erode-legal-autonomy-11593172506?] ("'The national security law is already exerting its impact even before it is enacted,' said Johannes Chan, the former dean of the University of Hong Kong's law school. 'It's clear that the law will have a severe impact on freedom of expression, if not personal security, on the people of Hong Kong.'" Ibid.).

Hong Kong. One recalls here the application of *Guiguzi's* Resist-Reconcile (忤 合 Wuhe) approaches [1142] --by a directed and strategic inclusion-exclusion strategy that effectively reconciles the patriotic element and resists the protesters in its constitution of the new measures.

All of this, of course in the service of Fundamental Principles (Fu Yan 符言) and the decisive end of family disharmony. There is an added layer of relevant significs here. Recall that 符 (fú) can signify the tally used by officials as credentials in ancient China (bingfu 兵符). It is the symbolic expression of authority (yinfu 音符; as in a musical note and thus the connection with the National Anthem Law). But also connotes the figures drawn by Daoist priests to expel evil and bring good fortune (Hiale yi zhangfu 画了一張符). It can signify an inconsistency with facts (bùfu 不符). Here the National Security law assumes the objectified incarnation of a symbol or a charm--it accords with the expression of One Country Two Systems developed by the central authorities. It overcomes the ideological inconsistency (bùfu 不符) of the current situation in Hong Kong through the symbolic power of the new credential of authority (bingfu 兵符) in the form of the National Security Law itself. And it does this through language (Yan 言)): "言有尽而意无穷" [Words and meanings are endless].[1143]

As enacted on 30 June 2020, the Law of the People's Republic of China on Safeguarding National Security in the Hong Kong Special Administrative Region"[1144] serves as the key marker of the end of a long road of progress that was initiated by

---

[1142] Discussed in essay Chapter 12, supra.

[1143] For a simplified explanation of the expression, see 言有尽而意无穷 Baidu; available [https://baike.baidu.com/item/言有尽而意无穷/6687317].

[1144] 《中華人民共和國香港特別行政區維護國家安全法》 [Law of the People's Republic of China on Safeguarding National Security in the Hong Kong Special Administrative Region] L.N. 136 of 2020 B2345; available [https://www.gld.gov.hk/egazette/pdf/20202444e/es220202444136.pdf]. English translation at [https://www.gld.gov.hk/egazette/pdf/20202448e/egn2020244872.pdf]

the vast demonstrations of early June 2019. The exuberance of those early weeks, and its hope for the preservation and perhaps expansion of the singular development of Hong Kong's democratic political model were dashed. Now that defeat has been comprehensively enacted into law--first by the (not to be overlooked) National Anthem Law, [1145] and now critically important, by the National Security Law.

Thus fresh, immediate and unmarred by the accretions of commentary, the text of the description of the Draft National Security Law appears ripe for consideration, at least in the version circulated through Xinhua News Agency. There is one core point that is worth emphasizing, especially because it will tend to be ignored either as self-evident (it is not) or an illegitimate (it is also not). It proceeds from the assertion at the core of the measure:

> The Central People's Government has an overarching responsibility for national security affairs relating to the Hong Kong Special Administrative Region. It is the duty of the Hong Kong Special Administrative Region under the Constitution to safeguard national security and the Region shall perform the duty accordingly.

This puts right the relationship between One Country and Two Systems principles in accordance with the fundamental ordering principles of the Chinese political-economic model. It upends the calculus of development and challenges the presumptions of the core principles of liberal democratic internationalism (at least as applied outside the liberal democratic metropolis). This is the ultimate exercise of Fu Yan 符言 in the service of the central authorities.

Much analysis will likely focus on the details of the National Security Law for signs of the extent to which Western liberal democratic notions of civil and political rights will be transformed (eroded) to better align with the CPC's primary focus on economic, social, and cultural rights, with an emphasis on

---

[1145] See discussion essay Chapter 28, supra.

security and the development of productive forces. [1146] That analysis, however, misses a fundamental point of the legislation. The National Security Law is essential to the protection of the integrity of the core responsibility of the Communist Party of China (CPC), as a vanguard party charged with the task of moving all of the nation toward the goal of the establishment of a communist society in China. Hong Kong may be permitted to deviate from a uniform march toward that core objective--to strive for that perfection at its own pace and consist with its own stage of development--but that different pace does not change the direction of the political development of Hong Kong. Sooner or later, Hong Kong must advance toward the establishment of a communist society, and must do so in any case, under the leadership of the CPC. The rest is merely a matter of local context, of timing, and of the pragmatic realities of balancing an unalterable core political goal with the necessity of every era of historical development.

The perfection of Chinese Marxist-Leninism is a central element of the political work of the Chinese Communist Party. The European/Western (Soviet and allied) approached (1) Marxism as a normative systems of values and (2) Leninism as the system of principles of political organization of vanguard leadership of the nation as (a) permanently fixed and (b) immutable. As a consequence, the fundamental work of a vanguard (Communist) Party was to perfect the individual (the ideal worker, the ideal member of the masses into whom the correct values could be inculcated and naturalized. This represents a variant of the approach of Western liberal democratic political norms that is grounded as well on notions of progress through the elimination of "false consciousness" through substantial societal disciplinary mechanisms. Western liberal democracy and Western Marxist-Leninism views its ideology the way it embraced its religion--as perfect when received, and thus, as reducing politics to an interpretive exercise.

That, of course, is both the genius of that system (whether expressed as liberal democracy or as Marxist-Leninism): the

---

[1146] See discussion in articles cited at notes 10 and 12, supra.

system (and its values) is received as perfect--the manifestation (implementation) of that perfection is not. As a result society is organized to maximize the effects of an iterative process through which the individual is disciplined and perfected through a constant measurement, an eternal assessment, against the standards of perfection to be realized by the perfect internalization of the ideological system received. Religion has been the most successful in developing the language of this process--but modern states have not been less effective--the United States through the legalization of its political and normative systems, and the Soviet Union through its (far more imperfectly realized) system of Communist bureaucratization. In any case, where the ideology is perfect and immutably, it is left for organs of societal control to develop mechanism's for the interpretation of perfection and its application to individuals and institutions subject to the perfection of the normative principles on which the collective order (economic, political, cultural, ethnic, religious, etc.). Here the failure to adhere strictly to the immutable perfection of the ideology is fatal to the integrity of the system. That is something Soviet Communism experienced, and it accounts, at times, for the turbulence of Western style cultural revolutions, as groups seek to seize control of the mechanisms of interpretation of the fundamental ideology.

Chinese Marxist-Leninism views this as effectively rightist error. Rather than center the perfection of the masses, Chinese Marxist-Leninism has evolved into an iterative dialogue between ideological development and national historical context. It is within that iterative process--ideological development pushes forward the (progressive) project of moving the collective toward the establishment of a communist which then moves society to new eras of development (under the leadership of the vanguard)--that it is possible to speak about the perfection of the individual and mass organizations as expressions of this process. As a consequence, the core ideology of the political-economic system is understood, at least in part, as a work in progress, the content of which will be heavily dependent of the stage of historical development and the context in which it is to be manifested. The core remains unchanged--the ultimate obligation to establish a communist society through the leadership of a vanguard

(Communist) party whose own legitimacy is dependent on delivering concrete progress toward that goal and ensuring a forward (always forward) movement of society through the historical stages of development through which it is necessary (whatever they may bring) to the ultimate end. Failure, of course, is fatal to the legitimacy of the vanguard, and threatens the integrity of the fundamental ideology on which the system is predicated. A

As a result, and certainly in a more or less ideologically stable way since the 1990s, the CPC has driven political reform forward (as the vectors of direction are understood within the perspective of their founding organizational premises) through the perfection of the expression of its ideological line "to suit the times", and then focused on the discipline of the masses to align their behavior with what suits the times (from an ideological perspective). Perfection of ideology, expressed in the perfection of the cage of regulation through which it is expressed, *is a necessary predicate* to the (consequential) perfection of the masses, mass organizations, and the discipline of error committed by either. As a consequence, one can perfect the individual (and the collectives into which individuals are embedded) only through and after one perfects the core ideology and its expression in policy to suit the historical era, and always with the understanding that such perfection is merely a step toward the ultimate perfection of the establishment of a communist society within China.

But there is nothing in the iterative process that suggests that progress must be undertaken uniformly. Put differently, there is nothing that suggests that this forward moving iterative process must occur in the same form and in lock step throughout the country and among all of its people and institutions. Indeed, the reverse has always been true. Beyond the need for *strict uniformity* within the ranks of the Chinese Communist Party, the essence of the CPC's political work is grounded on the notion that the various parts of the Chinese collective must be brought forward toward the ultimate goal with an eye toward their context and historical development. It follows that there is no inconsistency in modulating the actual application of core ideology to suit the place and times and the local context, balanced against pragmatic needs of the state in its global relations.

That difference, in effect, provides the *ideological basis for One Country Two Systems*, and simultaneously its rejection of any attempt to reconstitute it as a *Two Systems One Country* principle. For the West, of course, that meant the imposition of a political settlement that was (like most of the West's ideology, simply because that is the way people who adhere to that ideology naturally approach the meaning of things) permanent. For the CPC, however, it meant only a recognition that Hong Kong was in a different stage of development, that this stage of development could be tolerated because of its pragmatic benefits (at least for a time, e.g. through 2047), but that the underlying core ideological objectives could not be threatened. That is, that whatever differences were tolerated, Hong Kong, like the rest of China, must be managed toward the realization of the ultimate goal that supports the legitimacy of the current political model (at the risk of repetition but one worth making in a world populated by euphemism--the establishment of a communist society throughout China).

Simply put, this appears to be the only legitimate way for understanding things from out of the premises on which the legitimacy of the current Chinese political-normative system is built. It is self-evident, and thus inconceivable to accept principled alternatives, that this framework both permits and limits and ultimately directs the relation of the Hong Kong special waivers to the governance of the rest of China as all parts move toward yet another new era of historical development. As a consequence, the objections of the West are viewed as mere political interference by the Chinese, the objections of local Hong Kong people as proof of the need for stronger measures to naturalize the governing ideology. And for the West, the intentions of the Chinese national authorities are viewed as a fundamental breach of promises and an attack on universal core values.

Thus understood, the National Security Law, like the law respecting the national anthem and national symbols, becomes easier to understand. Note here I am not suggesting acceptance, merely that an understanding from the internal perspective of the ideology from which they are legitimated is necessary for appropriate analysis, and then political judgement based on the politics of those with the power to make and drive political decision making. The contents of the National Security Law as described through the announcement in Xinhua on 20 June 2020, make that approach quite clear.[1147]

Much analysis will focus on the details of the National Security Law for signs of the extent to which Western liberal democratic notions of civil and political rights will be transformed (eroded) to better align with the CPC's primary focus on economic, social, and cultural rights, with an emphasis on security and the development of productive forces. That analysis, however, misses a fundamental point of the legislation. The National Security Law is essential to the protection of the integrity of the core responsibility of the CPC, as a vanguard party charged with the task of moving all of the nation toward the goal of the establishment of a communist society in China. Hong Kong may be permitted to deviate from a uniform march toward that core objective--to strive for that perfection at its own pace and consist with its own stage of development--but that different pace does not change the direction of the political development of Hong Kong. Sooner or later, Hong Kong must advance toward the establishment of a communist society, and must do so in any case, under the leadership of the CPC. The rest is merely a matter of local context, of timing, and of the pragmatic realities of balancing an unalterable core political goal with the necessity of every era of historical development. It is not for nothing, then, that those who might continue to defend a broader autonomy now express concern.[1148]

[1147] "法制工作委员会负责人向十三届全国人大常委会第十九次会议作关于, supra.

[1148] "'From these initial details, this new law presents unprecedented legal questions that we will have to confront in coming years,' Simon Young, a barrister and professor at the University of Hong Kong's law school, told Reuters." Yew Tian and Greg Troode, "Beijing to have sweeping powers over Hong Kong security law, stoking concerns," *Reuters* (20 June 2020); available

At the same time, there is much value in studying the details of the description of the draft. The emphasis on the perfection of the legal and constitutional system are a clear signal of the overall importance of the notion of *iterative perfectibility* at the heart of Chinese New Era Marxist-Leninism. The embedding of "Two Systems" within the overall constraints of Chinese Marxist-Leninism, is meant to drive home the point both as to the impermanence of the waivers and its character, as well as the unavoidable need to accept the constraints of a vanguard party people's democratic dictatorship framework within which such deviations will be permitted. The key here is the impermanence of the character of the Two Systems waivers--the latitude permitted today (with respect to civil and political rights) is unlikely to survive long as Hong Kong is managed into its own new era of development. The expectation is, of course, that such civil and political rights exceptions will wither as the political culture of Hong Kong becomes better aligned with that of the rest of China. The National Security Law is an instrument in that (long term) process.

As for much of the text of the National Security Law there is a symmetry that is meant to reinforce the contingency of Hong Kong's special status as entirely dependent on the Central authorities, and as well, on conformity to the core principles of the Chinese political-economic model. Thus, for example. the Hong Kong government is given authority to set up its national security committee, headed by the HK Chief Executive along with three secretaries and the head of local security. However the committee itself is to be advised by officials appointed by and serving as the means of oversight, by the central authorities in Beijing. Likewise, much of the implementation of the national security law is to be undertaken by local officials and their security apprentice (police, and the like). These would include the creation of a new unit dedicated to national security cases. The exact details of each of the described offenses will also be described with greater specificity. Hong Kong authorities will have jurisdiction over this

---

[https://www.reuters.com/article/uk-hongkong-protests-security/beijing-to-have-sweeping-powers-over-hong-kong-security-law-idUSKBN23R0FC].

entire apparatus, except in those circumstances, still to be specified, in which the central authorities choose to take over the investigation.

In addition, though local police will rely on their traditional authority, and local judges will be designated to hear cases, the central authorities will establish a National Security Agency office in Hong Kong with broad authority to supervise and advise local officials (presumably including the judiciary, though that is not clear) on strategy, collect information, and to some extent manage investigation. Lastly, the National Security Law will preserve the essence of Hong Kong's rule of law superstructure (presumption of innocence, and conformity to the international human rights conventions). However, where local law (or its interpretation) is inconsistent with the national security law, the national security law prevails, with ultimate authority over such matters (including the interpretation of the HK National Security Law) will be vested in the Standing Committee of the National People's Congress.

The provision that is most likely to raise eyebrows is the one that provides the strongest evidence of the ideological premises driving the National Security law: the "four types of crimes including the crime of secession, subversion of state power, terrorism, collusion with foreign or foreign forces endangering national security," They are all ambiguous, in the Chinese style, though there is some constraint by alignment with the CPC Line and the scope of its initiatives. The key term, though, the collusion with foreign forces, suggests not just the need to pull Hong Kong away from its role as an international city, but also the view that in the face of the unalterable incompatibility of national and foreign models of politics and political norms, any foreign interaction might potentially be understood as polluting. Certainly at its broadest, it opens all foreign engagement to scrutiny. At its narrowest, the statute provides a basis for accountability for the political work of individuals aligned with foreigners. But it more likely to be read proactively as a means of furthering the vanguard party's Basic Line than be read narrowly as a constraint on its projection into Hong Kong. More troubling for the current situation in Hong Kong is its effects on the relationships between Hong Kong people and international civil society already well integrated into Hong Kong's political life.

Ironically, this provision is unfortunate to the extent it is read as evidencing Chinese conceptions of foreign interactions. If that is the case, it might provide liberal democratic and other states with evidence that Chinese projections of soft power is itself driven by this premise and that therefore ought to be carefully scrutinized. It may certainly add weight to the allegations made by some Western states of Chinese collusion within their territory. The effect, then, may be to accelerate the trend toward decoupling that Chinese officials suggest is not in anyone's interest. Here China may itself be driving that conversation, and its effects in the West may not produce positive results for Chinese strategic objectives, especially those tied to the Belt and Road Initiative. But that remains to be seen.

Whatever the specifics of the National Security Law, it is already having the intended effect. By 26 June 2020, the Wall Street Journal reported the reactions of Hong Kong's elite lawyers: "Some supporters of the opposition movement have scrubbed their social-media accounts, while teachers and election candidates are facing greater scrutiny by officials of their public comments. 'The national security law is already exerting its impact even before it is enacted,' said Johannes Chan, the former dean of the University of Hong Kong's law school. 'It's clear that the law will have a severe impact on freedom of expression, if not personal security, on the people of Hong Kong.'" [1149] Lawyers raised a number of additional concerns—from the reservation to the Hong Kong Executive (with guidance from Beijing) to appoint judges under the National Security Law, to the transfer of ultimate interpretive authority to the National People's Congress. [1150]

In any case, the National Security Law appears to suggest: to be in accord with the time, it is necessary to beware of misconstruing the situation. It suggests a marriage brought about

---

[1149] Natasha Khan, "Hong Kong Lawyers Warn China's Security Law Will Erode Legal Autonomy," supra.
[1150] Ibid.

by forces beyond one's control. The National Security Law for Hong Kong suggests, at least for the people of Hong Kong, that to be in accord with the times it is necessary to reconcile oneself to a situation in which one is not in control of the circumstances of one's life.[1151] It marks the beginning of a new cycle for Hong Kong. The cycle initiated by the protests of 9 June 2019 appear to have come to a close with the passage of this Act. It is now only left to adjust to the new order. It is a triumph for the ideological progress of the central authorities and a vindication of their power expressed through the extension of order from the center outward throughout the most fragile of the core regions of the state--the special autonomous regions. For the international community it suggests the new field of ideological engagement, and the character of its stakes. For the rest of the world, it suggests the new field of play as the character of emerging imperial orders becomes far more clearly visible.

The irony, of course, is that future generations will wonder to what extent that march of what now appears inevitable was accelerated by the protest themselves. Certainly the protest movement sharpened the contours of the conflict. And for that they served a purpose that will outlive the current state of relations among the major players and their ideologies. It significantly changed the way in which the Chinese diaspora may well be reconstitute, and possibly used (eventually) to project ideas into China, as well as to receive them from the center. Though the story that is Hong Kong has yet to be finished, it is clear now that this chapter has come to its end. This is an end very different from the one that the immense crowds flooding the streets of Hong Kong on 9 June 2019 envisioned. But as one looks to the future--from either side of the now much greater gulf that separates One Country from Two Systems partisans, it may be useful to consider two things.

The first is this: "We the Chinese nation have the spirit to fight the enemy to the last drop of our blood, the determination

---

[1151] *I Ching* (Rudolf Ritsema and Stephen Karcher (trans) (New York: Barnes & Noble, 1995), Hexagram 54 (Converting Maidenhood--kuei mei)

to recover our lost territory by our own efforts, and the ability to stand on our own feet in the family of nations."[1152]

And the second:

"言有尽而意无穷" [Words and meanings are endless].[1153]

✳ ✳ ✳

[1152] Mao Zedong, "On Tactics Against Japanese Imperialism" (27 December 1935); in Quotations From Chairman Mao (The Little Red Book) (NY: Award Books, 1971), p.116.
[1153] See text at note 14.

Chapter 31—After-Word

Tuesday 28 July 2020
The Clean Up Begins in Earnest: The End of the 2014-2020 Protest Movement and the Emergence of New Era Hong Kong

The clean-up in the wake the fundamental re-ordering of the Hong Kong political system framework has now begun. Any continuing belief in the narrow application of the new rules, any hope that the move by the central authorities were essentially cosmetic, is now assuming a definite character as fantasy. The central authorities meant what they said when they assured the people of Hong Kong that the rules would be benign. But those assurances were made from the perspective and world view of the core of leadership of the central authorities. For Chinese patriots the new rules will have little effect on daily life, though perhaps one might be challenged to sharpen sensitivity in their performance of patriotism under the guidance of the vanguard.[1154] For everyone else, though, conditions will change, and change sharply. For patriots, there is the performance of allegiance specified in the National Anthem Law.[1155]

Who is the "everyone else"? Again the central authorities have been clear: people who are not patriots--separatists, subversives, terrorists, and those who collude with foreign actors. For them the re-imagined political model of Hong Kong's superstructure offers the non-negotiable compulsion to obey the rules or face punishment. "These two things, democracy for the people and dictatorship for the reactionaries, when combined, constitute the people's democratic dictatorship."[1156] For those who reject the embrace of the patriotic front, there is the

---

[1154] Discussed essay in Chapter 25, supra.

[1155] National Anthem Bill, Ordinance No. 2 of 2020; available [https://www.legco.gov.hk/yr18-19/english/bills/b201901111.pdf] (hereafter National Anthem Ordinance). See discussion essay Chapter 28, supra.

[1156] Mao Zedong, "On the People's Democratic Dictatorship" (30 June 1949); available [https://www.marxists.org/reference/archive/mao/selected-works/volume-4/mswv4_65.htm].

compulsion of the National Security Law. [1157] And what better gesture to inaugurate the New Era for Hong Kong under Two Systems Within One Country principles than the punishment of those who are held responsible for the chaos and the storm that threatened the political order of the nation and the stability and prosperity of its people in the eyes of the central authorities. The lack of patriotism inherent in their actions, a position taken by the central authorities almost from the start of the protests in Jun 2019, [1158] must be rectified--and as a gesture with great signification for the future of the nation, rectified publicly and in ways that have global impact.

The meaning and consequences of this division will fall quite spectacularly on the protesters generally and more specifically on their leaders. The case of Benny Tai Yiu-ting (戴耀廷) provides the template moving forward. Professor Tai is a Hong Kong legal scholar and democracy activist, Associate Professor of Law at the University of Hong Kong and associated with Occupy Central movement, He will become, along with other leaders, the face of the fate of the protest movement and its ambitions for themselves, their foreign allies, and their vision (now discredited within official circles) for Hong Kong.

By the middle of July 2020, Benny Tai's then recent essay was circulating widely among a wide circle of adherents and opponents. He posited a ten step process that would inevitably end in China facing international pushback for its choices in the way in which it governs the SAR. [1159] That essay, and quite

---

1157 《中華人民共和國香港特別行政區維護國家安全法》 [Law of the People's Republic of China on Safeguarding National Security in the Hong Kong Special Administrative Region] L.N. 136 of 2020 B2345; available [https://www.gld.gov.hk/egazette/pdf/20202444e/es220202444136.pdf]. English translation at [https://www.gld.gov.hk/egazette/pdf/20202448e/egn2020244872.pdf]
1157 See discussion essay Chapter 28, supra. See also discussion essays Chapters 25, 27, and 30.
1158 See discussion essay Chapter 3, supra.
1159 戴耀廷真攬炒十步　這是香港宿命 – 戴耀廷 [Benny Tai, Frying Hong Kong in Ten steps; this is the fate of Hong Kong]). The original link, of course, has been removed.　The text may be accessed　(original Chinese and a crude English

provocatively given the times, sought to predict the trajectory of events from now until Hong Kong is effectively transformed, and with it the international order (for which Hong Kong served as a sort of nodal point--the proverbial canary in the mine). His object was declared boldly enough: to resist by pulling his Chinese adversaries down the cliff with him to see who survived and in what form.[1160] He speculated about a ten-part path of resistance for Hong Kong in the shadow of its new legal order. The tenth step proved to be the most provocative:

> By the tenth step, we had taken the CCP and jumped off the cliff together. What will happen after that, I can't write it anymore, because it has exceeded the boundary of Hong Kong. How the international community deals with the CCP, and how much the sanctions have shocked the CCP and Chinese society, is unpredictable now. The world beyond ten steps may be a new beginning for Hong Kong and China. I remember a sentence in the famous song "Do you hear the people sing": "Is there a world you long to see? Then join in the fight, that will give you the right to be free!" You want to see a new one The world? bring it on! Join this struggle and fight for your freedom![1161]

At roughly the same time It should be noted that the Chinese Central Authorities have accused Professor Tai of "illegally manipulating" the city's polling system, challenging the new

---

translation) at [https://lcbackerblog.blogspot.com/2020/07/the-situation-in-hong-kong-post-script.html].

[1160] Ibid. ("港人由威脅攬炒轉化為真攬炒，其實是悲哀的，必是因現實處境已看不到其他出路，與其被當權者逼到崖邊跪地求饒，不如主動反撲，把他也拉下崖，看哪一個在跌出懸崖後仍能死裏逃生。").

[1161] Ibid. ("到第十步，我們已攬着中共一起跳出懸崖，之後會發生甚麼事，我已寫不下去了，因已超出香港界線。國際社會怎樣對付中共，制裁對中共及中國社會的震撼有多大，是現在所不能預見的。十步以外的世界或許是香港和中國的新開始。我記起抗爭名曲《Do you hear the people sing》中一句：「Is there a world you long to see ? Then join in the fight, that will give you the right to be free !」你想見到一個新的世界嗎？來吧！加入這抗爭，去為你的自由去爭戰吧！").

national security law and acting as a political agent for foreign forces.[1162]

> Turning its ire on Tai, a legal academic and co-leader of the Occupy movement in 2014, the office suggested the primary he helped organise flowed from the anti-government protests sparked by the now-withdrawn extradition bill last June, describing him as "one of the culprits" behind the social unrest. "Benny Tai was a key organiser of the 'unlawful' Occupy Central movement and an advocate of 'Hong Kong independence' and the scorched-earth mentality," the statement read, accusing him of serving as "a political agent of foreign forces".[1163]

It seems, then, that even by the end of July 2020, Benny Tai's timeline had gotten out of joint. Much of it will likely be wishful thinking--especially those parts of the timeline that assume that the democrats will continue to be permitted to anticipate in politics in the shadow of the National Security and National Anthem Laws. That is unlikely, even at this early stage in their implementation. Much more apparent-- step eight and the detention of pan democrats;[1164] and step ten, the imposition of sanctions from abroad

---

[1162] Kimmy Chung, "Hong Kong elections: Beijing accuses Occupy protest leader Benny Tai of breaking national security law through primary poll," South China Morning Post (14 July 2020); available [https://sg.news.yahoo.com/hong-kong-elections-beijing-issues-122538202.html] ("Beijing has issued its strongest condemnation yet of a controversial election primary held by Hong Kong's opposition parties, singling out organiser and long-time activist Benny Tai Yiu-ting, whom it accused of "illegally manipulating" the city's polling system, challenging the new national security law and acting as a political agent for foreign forces.")

[1163] Ibid.

[1164] Pan democrat is the name given to a political alignment of groups with broadly shared values and approaches to the democratization of Hong Kong. Recall that in the 2019 November elections, " saw pan-democrats take nearly 90 percent of 342 seats with 71 percent of eligible voters supporting resistance to the authorities' increasingly heavy-handed approach." Zoe Leung, "The Future of Pan-Democrats in Hong Kong," MSN (July 10, 2020); available [https://www.msn.com/en-us/news/world/the-future-of-pan-democrats-in-hong-kong/ar-BB16A8uX].See, Raymond Kwun Sun Lau, "he political predicament of the pan-democrats in Hong Kong under Chinese rule: Being

By the end of July the pressure on the leaders of the protest movement became more visible. Chief among them was the effects on Benny Tai. This from the *South China Morning Post* lifts the curtain on that performance:

> The University of Hong Kong's governing council sacked legal scholar Benny Tai Yiu-ting on Tuesday over his criminal convictions for the Occupy protest movement he co-founded in 2014. Tai, an associate professor of law and outspoken opposition activist, learned his fate on Tuesday night after the HKU council reversed a recommendation by the university's senate earlier this month that there were not enough grounds to dismiss him although his actions amounted to misconduct. Responding to his dismissal, Tai said on Tuesday that academic institutions in Hong Kong "cannot protect their members from internal and outside interferences", adding that the university council's decision "marked the end of academic freedom in Hong Kong".[1165]

Professor Tai has remained committed to his principles even as it became clear that the Central Authorities were changing the fundamental premises within which they would interpret their "deal" on Hong Kong. He has been a key voice in the social movements in Hong Kong for a long time and continues to seek to engage in politics and other work in the SAR. He appears to be no friend of the current administration.

But several things ought to be remembered. as one considers this action and what is to come:

---

victims or beneficiaries?," *Asian Education and Development Studies* 8(4):498-510 (2019); Stephan Ortman, "Political Development in Hong Kong: The Failure of Democratization," *Asian International Studies Review* 17(2:199-219 (2017.
[1165] Chan Ho-him, "University of Hong Kong governing council sacks legal scholar Benny Tai over convictions for Occupy protests," *South China Morning Post* (28 July 2020); available [https://www.scmp.com/news/hong-kong/politics/article/3095043/university-hong-kong-governing-council-sacks-legal-scholar].

1. The Central Authorities have been quite transparent about their offense, and their intentions, ever since the 2014 Occupy Movement and the Umbrella Movement.[1166]

2. The Central Authorities are patient.[1167] They bank their objectives and move swiftly when the opportunity presents itself. That presentation of opportunity is based on a balancing of costs and benefits within the much larger objectives of the Central Authorities within which Hong Kong plays an important but by no means central role.

3. The protests that started in June 2019 appeared to convince the central authorities that the vanguard of threatening conduct was located within the educational system, one more closely tied to educational elite internationalism and its narratives, than to the emerging national narrative on the role, purpose and content of education and its involvement in social life.

4. That realization occurred at about the time that the Central Authorities sought to (and quite publicly) to reform education and its delivery in the Mainland. That reform provided a template far too appealing to confine to the areas of China outside of its SARs.

5. The evolution of Marxist Leninist sovereignty--Chinese sovereign internationalism--developed to the point where it could serve as a basis for decision making, only within the last several years. The Belt and Road Initiative provided a conceptual and pragmatic basis for building an internationalism autonomous of the global internationalism the principles of which had guided the initial agreement on the transfer of Hong Kong back to China in the 1980s.

[1166] On the Umbrella Movement, see, e.g., Stephan Ortman, "The Umbrella Movement and Hong Kong's Protracted Democratization Process," *Asian Affairs* 46(1): 32-50 (2015).

[1167] Chris Lau and Sum Lok-Kei, "Four of nine Occupy leaders jailed for up to 16 months over roles in Hong Kong's 2014 umbrella movement," *South China Morning Post* (24 April 2019); available [https://www.scmp.com/news/hong-kong/law-and-crime/article/3007414/occupy-sentence-hong-kong-lawmaker-tanya-chan-be] .

6. China had by 2019 refined both its law making and constitutional conceptions to the point where necessary action could be well justified within its own conceptual universe, And indeed, that development required something splashy to make the point. Hong Kong appeared increasingly to serve hat purpose as its social turmoil provided the context necessary to restore order--both physically and conceptually along the lines of New Era Marxist Leninism. This was an opportunity too good to pass up.

7. China's refined legalization of social credit systems[1168] also produced the ability to better take stock of who in Hong Kong would be subject to the rewards for good behavior and those who would be punished--and by punished one increasingly understood that to mean to be subject to social disabilities designed to induce conforming behavior. The development of social credit along with the emergence of a powerful framework under the Belt and Road Initiative were crucial elements to China's moves in 2020 to reassert authority over Hong Kong on its own terms.

8. The last and key element pushing forward Chinese thinking was the now fully developed New Era ideology. It was not for nothing that the key elite journals in Beijing had been stressing key features of the New Era Marxist Leninism, centered on the Communist Party as the leadership vanguard, and the state as the nexus of collective national efforts to attain the eventual goal of establishing a communist society in all of China. Hong Kong increasingly was viewed from this perspective as an aberration going in the *wrong direction*. It was aberrational as well because it could no longer be treated as something distinct from the rest of the development of the Pearl River delta. Physical and conceptual aberration produced a contradiction that violence

---

[1168] See Larry Catá Backer, "Next Generation Law: Data-Driven Governance and Accountability Based Regulatory Systems in the West, and Social Credit Regimes in China," *Law &: Southern California Interdisciplinary Law Journal* 28(1):123-172 (2018); available [https://gould.usc.edu/why/students/orgs/ilj/assets/docs/28-1-Backer.pdf].

in Hong Kong only confirmed. China only had to wait for the opportunity to resolve the contradiction.

9. And then the opportunity arose because of a perception (not unreasonable) that those who might effectively exact too high a price for any action to change the conditions of the China-Hong Kong arrangement were in no position to counter Chinese action *effectively*. That calculation was actually based on at least two key factors. First, the West had been in a process of critically rejecting its own foundations in endless and self-destructive critiques that effectively served Chinese interests by increasing a sense of delegitimization of post 1945 globalization. Second, the COVID pandemic distracted the West, especially the United States, already weakened because of the stubborn determination by its elites to destroy themselves in their civil war for control of the instruments and concepts of power there.

On this basis the rest is (at least conceptually) straightforward. It was only a matter of time before Hong Kong's educational system would be rectified, and the key aberrational elements disciplined.[1169] That discipline builds on what had already been started in the delayed rectification of the leadership of the 2014 Umbrella Movement.[1170]

This is, indeed, the guiding spirit of the Central Authorities: "dismissal as an act that punished "evil" and upheld justice."[1171] For those keeping score, one will be able to determine

---

[1169] Ng Kang-chung, "Hong Kong protests: Baptist University refuses to renew contract of lecturer convicted over role in demonstrations," *South China Morning Post* (27 July 2020); available [https://www.scmp.com/news/hong-kong/politics/article/3094908/hong-kong-protests-baptist-university-refuses-renew] (opposition lawmaker Shiu Ka-chun).

[1170] Chris Lau and Sum Lok-Kei, "Four of nine Occupy leaders jailed for up to 16 months over roles in Hong Kong's 2014 umbrella movement," supra ("Two founders of the city's biggest civil disobedience movement, academics Benny Tai Yiu-ting, 54, and Dr Chan Kin-man, 60, were given the longest jail terms, at 16 months, while legislator Shiu Ka-chun, 49, and League of Social Democrats vice-chairman Raphael Wong Ho-ming, 30, received eight months each. Because of poor health and his years of contribution to society, Reverend Chu Yiu-ming, 75, the third founder, had a 16-month sentence suspended for two years.")

[1171] Chan Ho-him, "University of Hong Kong governing council sacks legal scholar Benny Tai over convictions for Occupy protests," supra.

the spectrum of faculty accommodation by the extent of rectification of institutions and individuals during the next six months. The more interesting question will be to see the extent to which the Central Authorities translate (with Hong Kong characteristics) the emerging national approach to education.[1172]

There is nothing left to tell. If there was any doubt about the fundamental character of the change, and of the extent of the victory of the central authorities in their contest with the local representatives of global internationalist elites in Hong Kong, those doubts are dissipating quickly. What looked like a possibility in June 2019, by June 2020 had been squashed. By July 2020 the evidence of the squashing has only begun to be recognized. That suppression will likely go on for some time. There is still much for the central authorities to do if they are to make good on their ambitions to bring Hong Kong back decisively onto the nationalist camp and ensure that whatever their scope of autonomy, it remains firmly within boundaries set by and compatible with, the objectives of the vanguard and its leadership.

And the price to be paid? That appears to be a price worth paying by the central authorities. None of it can come as a surprise, especially that of the Americans. They have done what they have threatened and what appears to be at the core of their internationalist wheelhouse--targeted sanctions and impediments to efficient projection of Chinese economic power into the United States. Beyond that--nothing. This is something it appears the central authorities can live with. And it is a calculus that is hard to argue with--especially as China's Belt & Road

---

[1172] See, e.g., Larry Catá Backer, "Measures for the Appointment and Management of Foreign Teachers (Draft for Solicitation of Comments) [外籍教师聘任和管理办法（征求意见稿）]," Law at the End of the Day (25 July 2020); available [https://lcbpsusenate.blogspot.com/2020/07/measures-for-appointment-and-management.html] (foreign faculty); Larry Catá Backer, "An All-Around Cultivation of Socialist Morality--中共中央 国务院印发 [Issued by the Central Committee of the Chinese Communist Party]: 《新时代公民道德建设实施纲要》 [The Outline of the Implementation of the Construction of the Moral Citizen in the New Era]," Law at the End of the Day (3 November 2019); available [https://lcbackerblog.blogspot.com/2019/11/an-all-around-cultivation-of-socialist.html] (here university staff)

Initiative begins to develop enough to insulate China from the worst effects of these efforts. As Benny Tai suggested, perhaps oblivious to its self-referential element: "prepare for an unstable future" [準備應對不穩定未來].1173

And a short postscript on the campaign to "punish evil and uphold justice"):

(1) It was reported on 29 July 2020 that "Hong Kong's new police unit enforcing the national security law arrested four student members of a pro-independence group on Wednesday after it announced its mission to build the city into a republic. The arrests of the suspects, aged 16 to 21, in Yuen Long, Sha Tin and Tuen Mun marked the first such crackdown on anti-government activists not at the scene of street protests."1174

(2) On 30 July it was reported that four individuals ranging in age from 16 to 21 were arrested for inciting secession from a Facebook post of their since disbanded group.1175 "Randy Shek, a member of the bar council of the Bar Association, said on Thursday the absence of a definition for a seditious act in the legislation imposed on Hong Kong a month ago left enforcement of the law ripe for misuse. . . . Pleading for the law to be used only as a last resort, Professor Fu Hualing, law dean of the University of Hong Kong, said: "Arresting teenagers for setting up a Facebook group does not help with protecting China's national security. Nor can it generate confidence in the law."1176

1173戴耀廷真攬炒十步　這是香港宿命 - 戴耀廷 [Benny Tai, Frying Hong Kong in Ten steps; this is the fate of Hong Kong]), supra.

1174 Danny Mok and Emily Tsang, "Four members of Hong Kong pro-independence group arrested by police officers from national security unit," South China Morning Post (29 July 2020); available [https://www.scmp.com/news/hong-kong/law-and-crime/article/3095240/least-three-core-members-hong-kong-pro-independence].

1175 Gary Cheung and Clifford Lo, "National security law: lawyers challenge arrests of former Studentlocalism members for Facebook post supporting independence," *South China Morning Post* (30 July 2020); available [https://www.scmp.com/news/hong-kong/politics/article/3095382/national-security-law-lawyers-challenge-arrests-former].

1176 Ibid.

(3) On July 31, 2020, it was reported that a group of troublemakers were being sought for arrest.[1177] "Police in Hong Kong are seeking the arrest of six pro-democracy activists living in exile in Western countries, including the UK, media reports say. . . . The UK and Australia are among countries that have suspended their extradition treaties with Hong Kong in recent weeks. Germany did so on Friday - one of those reported to be on the new "wanted list" has received asylum there. *Who are the 'wanted'?* Chinese state TV network CCTV said six people were wanted on suspicion of inciting secession or colluding with foreign forces - both crimes can be punished with up to life in prison under the new security law."[1178] Ray Wong, one of the individuals on the wanted list stated that the "list of "wanted" exiles had been drawn up to "intimidate" pro-democracy activists who are trying to drum up international support for their cause."[1179]

And Benny Tai? On 6 January 2021 it was reported that Benny Tai, along with over fifty other people, was arrested "in an unprecedented crackdown over an unofficial election primary organised by pro-democracy parties last year. It was the largest mass arrest since the introduction of the national security law (NSL) in June."[1180]

The international community, led to some extent by the United States, will continue to ramp up the techniques that they have unveiled since the start of the protests in 2019 (sanctions loss of special preferences in relations, migration). [1181] The

---

[1177] "Hong Kong 'seeking arrest' of fleeing activists," BBC News (31 July 2020); available [https://www.bbc.com/news/world-asia-china-53616583].

[1178] Ibid.

[1179] Ibid.

[1180] Helen Davidson, "Hong Kong arrests: who are the pro-democracy activists being targeted?," *The Guardian* (6 January 2021); available [] ("The group, accused of subversion and facing penalties of up to life in prison, included legislators and candidates, campaigners, pollsters, students and lawyers, ranging from young people to political veterans.")

[1181] Donald J. Trump, "The President's Executive Order on Hong Kong Normalization" (14 July 2020; available

political and academic elites in the United States appear to be coalescing around a policy response to the actions of the Chinese central authorities with respect to the situation in Hong Kong as it has developed since June 2019 and adopted it as the standard response going forward in Hong Kong's "New Era." That approach is made up of a combination of (1) *gesture* for internal consumption by those members of the American population that matter (that is that influence mass opinion and drive decision making by critical actors in the academic, economic, societal and religious spheres); (2) quite *targeted sanctions* action against certain actors within the national organs of China and the local organs of Hong Kong that will sting but which are incapable of exacting enough reaction to actually affect policy; (3) and some measure of protection for local champions of international (and American) values through programs of targeted *asylum*. Mr. Trump's 14 July 2020 Executive order will likely serve as the template for Western responses to Chinese action for the near future.[1182] It promises substantial focus on global narrative, a limited and contextually appropriate set of irritating measures against specific individuals in China, and a very limited protection of locals.

Ironically, it is the deployment of this toolkit of techniques as it has developed since June 2019 that appears to have convinced the Chinese central authorities that they could bear the international costs of a much more aggressive and quickened approach to the political incorporation of Hong Kong. As it has been for the Chinese central authorities, By now, of course, the territory of the SAR is less important than is the idea of the territory of the SAR as a nodal point in the boundary making

---

[https://trumpwhitehouse.archives.gov/presidential-actions/presidents-executive-order-hong-kong-normalization/].

[1182] In his analysis of the Hong Kong Huan Rights and Democracy Act, Jason Buhi, for example, identifies five tools at the center of the U.S. response. These include the crafting of annual reports by the Secretary of State, easing visa denials for people exercising political rights compatible with the norms of the United States, requiting ministerial reporting on compliance with export law restrictions, adding protections for renditions of US citizens to China, and direction for targeted sanctions. Buhi, "America's New Covenant with Hong Kong," supra, pp. 282-292.

between the American and Chinese post global imperial orders. For the protesters, or at least a number of them, it offers, through the practice of asylum, a foreign perch from where they can continue to try to develop and project their ideas and objectives back into Hong Kong. This is an old model now refashioned for a modern age.

The rest is to be expected on both sides as they work diligently to refine their ideologies in the shadow of the other and then seek to market their respective approaches to the rest of the world.[1183] Each has become the threatening foreign element who define what is unacceptable in their own home societies and how the danger to the homeland is constituted.

> Both Mr. Xi and Mr. O'Brien see in the other the incarnation of threat in the form of what the Chinese call the "black hand" of foreign interference. And both would be right. New Era Chinese Communist internationalism is grounded on the need to expand the space within which its own way of seeing the world and operating within it may be used to develop collective activity (and to protect the integrity of that activity from others). The Belt and Road Initiative cannot help but serve these ends (in part) if it is to remain true to the essence of Leninism. But the same is true of literal democratic internationalism, the power of which, of course, produced both the victory of the allies in 1945, and the reconstruction of the world and its orders thereafter. Robust mechanisms for leading by example, for controlling narrative, and for insisting that friends, allies, and business relations adhere to the core premises of either system would be then viewed by the other as aggressive acts--as the projection of power over the very

---

[1183] Larry Catá Backer, "Brief Thoughts on 习近平 中国共产党领导是中国特色社会主义最本质的特征 [Xi Jinping, The Leadership of the Communist Party of China is the most essential feature of socialism with Chinese characteristics], Read Against US National Security Advisor Robert C. O'Brien "The Chinese Communist Party's Ideology and Global Ambitions," Law at the End of the Day (17 July 2020); available [https://lcbackerblog.blogspot.com/2020/07/brief-thoughts-on-xi-jinping-leadership.html].

fabric of "reality" at the expense of the other. In that context, both Mr. Xi and Mr. O'Brien are honest enough to come as close as possible to admitting that convergence is not possible, and indeed, that the more vigorous expression of each requires both de-coupling, and an aggressive effort to extend the "jurisdiction" of narrative.[1184]

Hong Kong, again, serves as a nodal point, but this time in the differentiation of the two great post global imperial projects. There are no surprises. And it is important to remember that this is a starting, not an ending, point, in the US response. The object is the situation in Hong Kong, of course. However, there are far larger stakes involved as well in the reordering and control of global economic and political ordering. Both China and the US have given notice to expect substantially more.

One comes here, then, to the function of this last essay as epilogue in the story of Hong Kong related in these essay. It is useful to recall the nature of epilogue. Its etymology--from the Greek and Latin *epilogos*--commonly signify not a conclusion, but the recognition of that conclusion though the addition (*epi*) of words (logos) that conform the point from which a new beginning is recognized. An epilogue is an after-word, the point of turning to look to what now happens after the end of events that separate the historical from the contemporary. The story of Hong Kong's era of internationalized political liberalization is done. It is merely a matter now to recognize the great gap that separates the conclusion of the story from what comes after. Here, like local and central authority officials in the wake of the passage of the National Anthem and National Security Laws for Hong Kong, one engages in clean-up to make way for and adjust to changed circumstances going forward.

The central authorities, themselves, provided the after-word with which these essays ends. That after-word was incarnated as a new "Election Law" for Hong Kong in the form of a set of deep reforms of the Hong Kong Basic Law with respect to

---

[1184] Ibid., ¶5.

its electoral system and in the construction of its legislative body.[1185]

> Beijing has amended Hong Kong's Basic Law, or constitution, to almost halve the proportion of directly elected representatives in the city's legislature, which already had limited powers, and require all candidates to be vetted for political loyalty. The changes will also strengthen China's control over the "election committee" that chooses Hong Kong's chief executive, expanding its size and abolishing seats that had been held by directly-elected district councillors.[1186]

The new election law, signed by President Xi and enacted by the 27th Session of the Standing Committee of the 13th National People's Congress[1187] adds the final element to the construction of Hong Kong along national lines. It gives the move toward centering a Hong Kong patriotic front model[1188] some political teeth; this is especially notable in the form of the obligations of candidate vetting committees to conduct candidate checks for compliance with the National Security Law. "Chinese and Hong Kong officials have described the law changes as necessary to ensure the principle of "patriots governing Hong Kong" in the

---

[1185] What is referenced here as the new Election Law is actually changes to two Annexes of the Hong Kong Basic Law. See, Annex I to the Basic Law of the Hong Kong Special Administrative Region: Method for the Selection of the Chief Executive of the Hong Kong Special Administrative Region (March 2021); available [http://www.xinhuanet.com/english/2021-03/30/c_139846522.htm]; Annex II to the Basic Law of the Hong Kong Special Administrative Region: Method for the Formation of the Legislative Council of the Hong Kong Special Administrative Region and Its Voting Procedures (March 2021); available [http://www.xinhuanet.com/english/download/2021-3-30/AnnexII.pdf].

[1186] Emma Graham-Harrison, "Beijing cuts Hong Kong's directly elected seats in radical overhaul: Measures are passed to increase Beijing's control of city, including vetting of election candidates," *The Guardian* (30 March 2021); available [https://www.theguardian.com/world/2021/mar/30/hong-kong-china-brings-in-voting-system-changes?CMP=Share_iOSApp_Other].

[1187] "China's top legislature adopts amended annexes to HKSAR Basic Law," *Xinhua* (30 March 2021); available [http://www.xinhuanet.com/english/2021-03/30/c_139846350.htm].

[1188] Discussed in essay, Chapter 25, supra.

wake of months-long and often violent anti-government protests in 2019 and the introduction last year of a new, wide-reaching national security law, banning secession, subversion and collusion with foreign forces."[1189]

It is an after-word, though, in the sense that it merely formalizes changes that were already much in evidence during the clean-up period that started with the enactment of the national Security Law.[1190] Here at last one comes face to face with the realities of what has been accomplished in the long arc of action and counter action that has produced the trinity of law that amounts to the legal memorialization of the changes that now define the "new era" Hong Kong. Hong Kong is now as defined by its National Anthem Law, it National Security Law, and the modifications to its election rules in its Basic Law, as it is by any other national or international measure. It is a city of patriots where patriotism marks the dividing line between full participation in the community and the threat of rectification. This "new era" is now impossible to avoid, and for liberal democratic forces looking in from afar, it is now also difficult to avoid.[1191]

[1189] James Griffiths, "Beijing passes new 'patriot' election law for Hong Kong that restricts opposition," CNN (30 March 2021); available [https://www.cnn.com/2021/03/30/asia/china-hong-kong-elections-intl-hnk/index.html].

[1190] Emma Graham-Harrison, "Beijing cuts Hong Kong's directly elected seats in radical overhaul: Measures are passed to increase Beijing's control of city, including vetting of election candidates," supra ("The city's most prominent opposition voices have mostly been jailed, fled into exile or are facing trial, and pro-democracy lawmakers resigned from the legislature in a bloc last year after several of their members were disqualified for being "unpatriotic")

[1191] "EXPLAINER: What's behind Hong Kong election law changes," AP (11 March 2021); available [https://apnews.com/article/beijing-democracy-hong-kong-elections-china-1785423948048076727f64ba378ddaaf]; 白信 客座评论：后疫情时代的 "东升西降"[Bai Xu, "Guest Commentary: "The East Rises and the West Falls" in the Post-Epidemic Era], *Deutsche Welle* (11 March 2021); available [https://www.dw.com/zh/客座评论后疫情时代的东升西/a-56842380] (相形之下，本届 "两会" 政协主席汪洋在大会开幕式上主张关于促进针对香港青年爱国主义教育的主张，只能算作重复 1989 年天安门运动之后北京政权所采取的爱国主义教育政策。[In contrast, Wang Yang, chairman of the CPPCC National Committee of the "Two Sessions", advocated at the opening ceremony of the conference to promote patriotic education for Hong Kong youth, which can only

These essays, then, end in a very different place than where they began. The road from the exuberance of the protesters on 9 June 2019 to the uncertainty and adjustment to life under what appears to be a vigorously enforced National Security Law in July 2020 could not have been predicted. The arc of development, however, is profound. What the future holds is even harder to guess. But what is clear is that by June 2020 Hong Kong was set on a very definite path profoundly different from that which it thought it was making for itself in the heady days of June 2019, when, for a short time, the idea that successfully challenging the Chinese central authorities appeared plausible with the backing of a committed international community.

Hong Kong is no longer an international city in its pre-2019 sense. The One Country Two Systems central contradiction of 1997-2019 has been resolved as far as the central authorities are concerned and we now embark on Hong Kong's New Era. Hong Kong now is a Chinese city with substantial international connections, and some autonomy in matters that do not threaten its stability (political) or prosperity (economic) as managed by the central authorities. It is a city with a history that will be preserved, and a future that appears to be taking it in a direction quite different from that envisioned by many in Hong Kong in 2019. The international community continues to preserve the older vision of Hong Kong, one in which its territorial sovereignty was vested in China but its political sovereignty was internationalized and protected by the international community. And the local people who risked so much in this cause, who shared a vision of autonomy now supplanted by one with the national authorities at the center, they are now scattered to the winds or living quietly.

———

Post Script 25 March 2021:

———

be counted as a repetition of the patriotic education policy adopted by the Beijing regime after the Tiananmen Movement in 1989.]).

Recent news reports from Hong Kong suggest yet another diplomatic skirmish between old and new Empires over a site of imperial conflict--Hong Kong. At the end of March Reuters reported that China sought to declare invalid (in accordance to the laws of China as applied in this context and in furtherance of Chinese interests) a form of passport issued by the UK to its overseas citizens (recognized as the UK determined in accordance with its own laws and in furtherance of its own sovereign interests).

> The Hong Kong government on Thursday confirmed a Reuters report that it had told 14 countries to stop accepting a British travel document that many of its young people use to apply for working holiday visas in Europe, North America and parts of Asia. In a move seen by some envoys as a diplomatic affront, the government informed the foreign consulates in a letter that it no longer considered the British National Overseas (BNO) passport a valid travel document as of Jan. 31.[1192] "

The response from the United Kingdom was not unexpected, and in line with a traditional approach to the protection of the sovereign prerogative of states. "'The UK will continue to issue British Nationals (Overseas) passports which remain valid travel documents.'"[1193] The stakes are high, of course. As several million Hong Kong residents are eligible for such passports and

---

[1192] Greg Troode and Anne Marie Roantree, "Exclusive: Hong Kong tells foreign governments to stop accepting special British passport," *Reuters* (25 March 2021) ("The letter, seen by Reuters and confirmed by the Hong Kong government after the story was published, demanded that its Hong Kong passport should be used instead").
[1193] Ibid.

effectively a ticket out of Hong Kong as it enters its new era.[1194] The practice of "passportization" is not without controversy.[1195]

Beyond the usual petty games that are the stuff of entertaining the masses by feeding the propaganda organs of empire, there is an important ideological element to the move that may be worth considering at some leisure. To some extent, it is possible to frame these decisions from the lens of Mao Zedong's germinal and still profoundly influential insights developed in his "On the People's Democratic Dictatorship" (30 June 1949) in commemoration of the 28th anniversary of the CPC. Two insights are readily apparent. The first is the notion of the value of people as critical elements in revolutionary struggle. Controlling people (especially those who might be turned to counterrevolutionary purposes) is essential to the success of the work of a vanguard.

> Revolutionary dictatorship and counter-revolutionary dictatorship are by nature opposites, but the former was learned from the latter. Such learning is very important. If the revolutionary people do not master this method of ruling over the counter-revolutionary classes, they will not be able to maintain their state power, domestic and foreign reaction will overthrow that power and restore its own rule over China, and disaster will befall the revolutionary people.[1196]

Second, the work of the vanguard is critically hampered where it is unable to rectify counter revolutionary thinking. To those ends it is important not merely to ensure that foreign vanguards not have access to local potentially threatening popular elements, it is

---

[1194] Shawna Kwan, "U.K. Grants Five Passports a Minute to Hongkongers as China Tightens Grip," *Bloomberg* (4 December 2020); available [https://www.bloomberg.com/news/articles/2020-12-04/u-k-grants-hongkongers-five-passports-a-minute-as-exodus-looms].

[1195] Kristopher Natoli, "Weaponizing Nationality: An Analysis of Russia's Passport Policy in Georgia," *Bostin University International Law Journal* 28:389-417 (2019).

[1196] Mao Zedong, "On the People's Democratic Dictatorship" (30 June 1949) Selected Works Vol. 4, reprinted in Marxists.org; available [https://www.marxists.org/reference/archive/mao/selected-works/volume-4/mswv4_65.htm].

also important to maintain substantial control of the element oneself.

That, of course, is the essence of building a strong people's democratic dictatorship--what may be understood to be a work in progress in Hong Kong.

> You are not benevolent!" Quite so. We definitely do not apply a policy of benevolence to the reactionaries and towards the reactionary activities of the reactionary classes. Our policy of benevolence is applied only within the ranks of the people, not beyond them to the reactionaries or to the reactionary activities of reactionary classes. . . Here, the method we employ is democratic, the method of persuasion, not of compulsion. When anyone among the people breaks the law, he too should be punished, imprisoned or even sentenced to death; but this is a matter of a few individual cases, and it differs in principle from the dictatorship exercised over the reactionaries as a class.[1197]

And thus its essence--democracy for the people (defined by reference to their patriotic loyalty expressed through the practices and behaviors indicated by the vanguard, for example through the National emblems and Anthem laws). For the rest of the population there is only to obey and to rectify false belief and action--or be punished (for example through operation of the National Security Law).

There can be no middle way in this principle, nor in the underlying political-economic model from which it derives its legitimacy. And efforts of foreign states to project their power through their power of citizenship and residence will be viewed necessarily as a gross interference in the establishment of a proper peoples' democratic dictatorship in Hong Kong. From the perspective of the Chinese vanguard this must be both necessary and good; the result inevitable. From the perspective of the liberal democratic states, the opposite is true; it evidences a gross

---

[1197] Ibid.

violation of the rules of international comity and an interference with national authority to determine the character and availability of access to its own polity. This contradiction will not be easy to resolve. The contradiction is made harder to confront where the discursive needs of internal and external communicators--of performance of principle for inside and outside objectives--are themselves incapable (for the moment) of rationalization.

✳ ✳ ✳

Index

[References are to pages]

✳ ✳ ✳

Hong Kong Between "One Country" and "Two Systems"

About the Book*: Hong Kong Between "One Country" and "Two Systems"* examines the battle of ideas that started with the June 2019 anti-extradition law protests and ended with the enactment of the National Security and National Anthem Laws a year later. At the center of these battles was the "One Country, Two Systems" principle. By June 2020, the meaning of that principle was highly contested, with Chinese authorities taking decisive steps to implement their own understanding of the principle and its normative foundations , and the international community taking countermeasures. All of this occurred well before the 2047 end of the 1985 Sino-British Joint Declaration (中英联合声明) that had been the blueprint for the return of Hong Kong to China. Between these events, global actors battled for control of the narrative and of the meaning of the governing principles that were meant to frame the scope and character of Hong Kong's autonomy within China. The book critically examines the conflict of words between Hong Kong protesters, the Chinese central and local authorities, and important elements of the international community. This decisive discursive contest paralleled the fighting for control of the streets and that pitted protesters and the international community that supported them against the central authorities of China and Hong Kong local authorities. In the end the Chinese central authorities largely prevailed in the discursive realm as well as on the streets. Their victory was aided, in part by the COVID-19 pandemic of 2020. But their triumph also produced the seeds of a new and potentially stronger international constitutional discourse that may reduce the magnitude and scope of that success. These essays were written as the events unfolded. Together the essays analytically chronicle the discursive battles that were fought, won and lost, between June 2019 and June 2020. *Without an underlying political or polemical agenda, the essays retain the freshness of the moment, reflecting the uncertainties of the time as events unfolded. What was won on the streets of Hong Kong from June to December 2019, the public and physical manifestation of a principled internationalist and liberal democratic narrative of self-determination, and of civil and political rights, was lost by June 2020 within a cage of authoritative legality legitimated through the resurgence of the normative authority of the state and the application of a strong and coherent expression of the principled narrative of its Marxist-Leninist constitutional order. Ironically enough, both political ideologies emerged stronger and more coherent from the conflict, each now better prepared for the next.*

Little Sir Press (State College, Pennsylvania, USA)
ISBN: 978-1-949943-03-0 (ebk) ; 978-1-949943-05-4
(paperback)

www.ingramcontent.com/pod-product-compliance
Lightning Source LLC
Chambersburg PA
CBHW052117270326
41930CB00012B/2657